WILLIAM WELLS AND THE STRUGGLE FOR THE OLD NORTHWEST

WILLIAM WELLS
AND THE STRUGGLE FOR
THE OLD NORTHWEST

William Heath

University of Oklahoma Press : Norman

Also by William Heath
The Walking Man
The Children Bob Moses Led
Blacksnake's Path: The True Adventures of William Wells
Devil Dancer

Library of Congress Cataloging-in-Publication Data

Heath, William, 1942–
  William Wells and the struggle for the Old Northwest / by William Heath.
     pages cm
  Includes bibliographical references and index.
  ISBN 978-0-8061-5119-9 (hardcover : alk. paper) 1. Wells, William,
1770–1812. 2. Miami Indians—Biography. 3. Northwest, Old—
History—1775–1865. 4. Indian agents—United States—Biography.
5. Soldiers—United States—Biography. 6. Indians of North America—
Wars—1750–1815. 7. Miami Indians—Wars. I. Title.
  E99.M48W454 2015
  976.9′03092—dc23
  [B]
                                    2014026613

The paper in this book meets the guidelines for permanence and durability
of the Committee on Production Guidelines for Book Longevity of the
Council on Library Resources, Inc. ∞

1 2 3 4 5 6 7 8 9 10

For my dear friends Frank and Holly Bergon

CONTENTS

ILLUSTRATIONS

FIGURES

MAPS

PREFACE

O! I have ta'en
Too little care of this! Take physick, pomp;
Expose thyself to feel what wretches feel,
That thou might shake the superflux to them,
And show the heavens more just.

Shakespeare, *King Lear*

The French novelist Stendhal stated that he had witnessed the significant events of his time; we can say even more of William Wells, who participated in events at the epicenter of the history of his time, distinguishing himself as a Miami warrior and then as an American scout and agent. His story epitomizes the clash of cultures in the Old Northwest, showing how the Indians lived, fought for their homeland, and dealt with defeat. Since he was always the man in the middle, moving between two worlds, this book also depicts the lives of the Anglo-American pioneers, paying attention to *both* Indian and white perspectives. Wells is worthy of comparison with such famous frontiersmen as Daniel Boone, Davy Crockett, and Kit Carson. His multilingual skills made him a valuable interpreter. Yet he remains a largely unknown figure. He lacked a publicist like Daniel Boone's John Filson and, unlike Crockett, did not fill that role himself. Furthermore, because he achieved renown in two worlds in mortal conflict with each other, his was a tale of twisted allegiances; thus if he is a hero, he is a very ambiguous one. What follows is an accurate account of his remarkable exploits that demonstrates in detail the role he played and helps us to understand the events and issues that mattered on the expanding American frontier.

Wells was a man of action, not reflection. As is frequently the case in human affairs, however, he was often acted on by forces beyond his control. To tell his story, I therefore need to tell a larger one. Decisions made by President Thomas Jefferson, for example, shaped American Indian policy, triggering William Henry Harrison's land-grabbing treaties, arousing Tecumseh's angry response, and placing Wells at Fort Dearborn on the day of his death. To explain how and why these events happened, I have written not only a biography of an unsung American hero but also a study of relations between whites and Indians at the time. Because Wells was raised as an Indian, I have re-created the culture of the Miamis and their allies. Wells was deeply torn by his dual identity. His conflicted feelings and contradictory actions dramatize the clash of values on the American frontier. Did his ultimate loyalty lie with the Miamis, the United States, or himself and his desire to get ahead? Perhaps more than anyone else of his stature, Wells embodied the struggle for control of the Old Northwest.

Meaningful research begins with Paul A. Hutton's groundbreaking essay "William Wells: Frontier Scout and Indian Agent" (1978). Until now, the only book-length history to discuss in detail the life of Wells is Harry Lewis Carter's *The Life and Times of Little Turtle* (1987). Although mentioned in many studies of the frontier, Wells is often dismissed by what one scholar termed "the side-road assassination technique," whereby "relatively minor characters with whom the historian does not sympathize are taken into a short paragraph where they are made to look wicked or ridiculous or very very small for a couple of sentences, almost in a couple of words; and done away with. There is no argument, no balancing of good and bad, no fuss. . . . Falsehood is not required, for a partial truth will do."[1] Although Wells has often been unfairly condemned, his career was complex and many of his actions are not easily judged. What is needed is a detailed retelling and a balanced assessment of his life based on the historical record.

I first became aware of Wells when Bil Gilbert, in his fine book on Tecumseh, noted that, "of the many who lived both as a red and white, Wells was one of the few who rose to positions of prominence among both peoples." Distinguished frontier historian Richard White aptly added that Wells was "a figure as thoroughly a product of the

middle ground as any person in the *pays d'en haut* [the upper country of French Canada]. . . . He was a servant of empire but had deep
loyalties to the people whose interests the country he served sought
to subvert." Milo Quaife's observation that "the true history" of the
life of this "famous frontier scout . . . surpasses fiction" deepened my
interest and stimulated me to write a novel, *Blacksnake's Path: The True
Adventures of William Wells*.[2]

My agent, Michele Rubin, who knew I had put ten years of research
into *Blacksnake's Path*, suggested that I next write a documented
study, updating my research and reconfiguring my interpretations.
This is not the place for a lengthy discussion of the relative merits
of historical fiction versus works of history. If both are done well,
they should complement each other. In general, the stylistic bar is
set higher for literary fiction and the novelist's imagination has more
room to improvise. On the other hand, the historian can only present what his or her sources will support, making for a different set
of challenges. The success of both forms depends, in part, on readers
hearing authentic voices: in fiction of created characters, in history of
the people of the time. Both require writers who can evoke the past.[3]

One reason I first decided to write a novel about Wells was the
lack of specific information on the seven years he spent in captivity.
As I worked to solve that problem in the present book, I discovered
two essays written by Wells, which I used and supplemented with
citations from other captivity narratives that bear on his experience.
Thus in *Blacksnake's Path* I created scenes that dramatize his life as a
Miami, while in *William Wells* I orchestrated quotes and commentary
that illustrate how what happened to him could be illuminated by the
accounts of other captives in the Old Northwest.

After the prologue recounting how Wells went to Fort Dearborn
at the start of the War of 1812 in a doomed effort to arrange a peaceful evacuation, *William Wells and the Struggle for the Old Northwest*
proceeds chronologically. During the eighteenth and early nineteenth centuries, the Wells family was in the vanguard of pioneers;
their moves—from northern Virginia, to western Pennsylvania, to
Kentucky—recapitulate the story of the advancing frontier. In 1784,
when he was thirteen, Wells was captured by the Eel River Miamis,
brought to Snake-fish Town, and adopted by the chief of the village.

Chapter 2, "Becoming Miami," draws upon numerous captivity narratives to present a fresh analysis of the experience. Billy Wells became Blacksnake and walked the warpath with the Miamis, even serving as a decoy to ambush flatboats during the bloody skirmishes of the 1780s, which one contemporary estimated cost the lives of fifteen hundred Kentuckians. Having proved himself a man, he married and had a son.[4]

To punish the hostile "banditti" who had been raiding the frontier, Washington sent General Josiah Harmar to attack Kekionga (Fort Wayne), but his troops were badly beaten by Little Turtle's warriors. I learned during my research that Harmar's Defeat and many other significant battles have rarely been studied closely. To rectify this, I provide a well-documented analysis of all the major conflicts of the period. The most important was St. Clair's Defeat in 1791, when Little Turtle's confederacy of warriors killed more than half of an American force of twelve hundred. Wells led a group of Miami snipers during the fight. This little-known battle was three times as costly to the Americans as Custer's Last Stand.

The following year, Wells switched sides for complex reasons I discuss in the text. Realizing his exceptional ability, General Rufus Putnam asked Wells to help conduct a treaty, which was an anomaly for the time in that it recognized the right of the Indians to sell or *refuse to sell* their lands. Putnam then hired Wells to spy on Indian councils held along the Maumee River in 1792 and 1793. Wells, now married to Little Turtle's daughter Sweet Breeze, was the only American at these heated deliberations. When he brought the news that peace negotiations had failed, General Anthony Wayne was so impressed by his knowledge of the Indians that he made him his head spy (scout). Wells gathered a group of experienced woodsmen who captured Indians for information and protected Wayne's army on its advance into northern Ohio. At the battle of Fallen Timbers, he gave Wayne key advice about when to attack.[5]

In 1795, when Wells served as interpreter at the Treaty of Greenville, he stood both literally and figuratively on the middle ground between his American commander Wayne and his Miami father-in-law Little Turtle and had to argue *both* sides of their debate. For much of the rest of his life, Wells served as the Indian agent for the Miamis at Fort Wayne. He took delegations of chiefs to confer with Washington, Adams, and Jefferson. He also helped implement Jefferson's civilization program, which proved to be more appealing in theory than in practice. To explain the origins of Jefferson's failed Indian policy, I examine the president's character, philosophy, and actions. Although Bernard Sheehan and Anthony Wallace have written good books on his policy, neither details how it was implemented in the Old Northwest.

During his years as Indian agent, Wells was frequently at the center of controversy. The secretaries of war he served under acknowledged his expertise but doubted his loyalties. He resisted the assistance of the Quakers because he thought he and Little Turtle could run the civilization program better (and profit on the side). Sometimes he regretted the treaties he helped Governor William Henry Harrison impose and encouraged the Indians to protest against them. Not surprisingly, because Wells became "the best-hated man" in Indiana Territory, he was fired in 1809. He spent the remainder of his life trying to get his old job back. When a religious revival led by the Shawnee Prophet was combined with Tecumseh's militant movement, Wells forecast the coming storm, attracting the animosity of both brothers. In the last months of his life, he worked to keep the Miamis out of Tecumseh's confederacy.

His effort to rescue the beleaguered garrison at Fort Dearborn, and his consequent martyrdom, brought a heroic end to his career. Wells Avenue in downtown Chicago was named in his honor, as were Wells Street and Spy Run in Fort Wayne and a county in Indiana. In sum, he was an extraordinary man with many flaws, a figure in the midst of everything that mattered on the frontier. Throughout his life he was torn by conflicting values, seeing the dilemmas of his day from frequently incompatible perspectives and embodying the tragic multicultural struggle for the Old Northwest.

The Founding Fathers did not want their treatment of American Indians to be at the center of the national narrative. They had triumphed during the Revolution over a major military power (albeit with crucial French aid), and it was an article of faith that the new Republic was destined for greatness. Consequently, the first presidents and many other Americans downplayed, and even covered up, what was happening beyond the Appalachians. Washington and Jefferson, if not Adams, understood the importance of the West. They formulated policies intended to put the best face on the brutal realities of that region. Historians of the period, with some notable exceptions, have followed their example, paying scant attention to American Indian culture, the wars for the Old Northwest (not to mention the South), or the pacification, expropriation, and removal programs that followed. Not one biography of Washington gives an adequate account of what was termed Indian Affairs or of the several thousand settlers and Indians killed. The equivalent would be a biographer of Lyndon Johnson mentioning the Vietnam War in passing. The analogy is appropriate, and the ratio of Anglo-American casualties comparable, when we recall that the population of the United States in the 1790s was 5 million.[6]

General histories are equally at fault. In Gordon Wood's *Empire of Liberty: A History of the Early Republic, 1789–1815* (2009), a highly praised 778-page overview, the Indian campaigns in the Northwest from 1789 to 1795 are covered in three pages. Wood is the foremost American historian of this period, and I have learned much from his books. Yet in *Empire of Liberty*, as soon as he ventures across the mountains, his discussion becomes less reliable. To choose one example, he notes that at the start of the War of 1812 General William Hull ordered the evacuation of Fort Dearborn, "which eventually took place on August 15."[7] What he fails to mention is that the Indians then ambushed more than ninety people and killed sixty, including Wells, whose name does not even appear in the book. Little Turtle, who played a major role in Washington's war for the Old Northwest and the uneasy peace that followed, is cited only once. One of my intentions is to demonstrate why such omissions are regrettable.

Although presidential biographers and other scholars have been reluctant to accept the central importance of Indian relations in our early nation, a group of dedicated historians have done impressive work on American Indians and the Old Northwest. In the nineteenth century Lyman Draper compiled 480 volumes of invaluable primary and secondary material for the Wisconsin Historical Society; his work was ably continued by Milo Quaife. The best contemporary overview of the period is Richard White's *The Middle Ground: Indians, Empires, and Republics in the Great Lakes Region, 1650–1815* (1991). Other essential authors are James Axtell, Colin Calloway, Andrew Cayton, Gregory Dowd, R. David Edmunds, Bil Gilbert, Reginald Horsman, Ann Keating, James Merrell, Larry Nelson, Elizabeth Perkins, Daniel Richter, Wiley Sword, Alan Taylor, and Anthony Wallace, among others.

My study of Wells is based on the deceptively simple dictum of Leopold von Ranke that the essential task of the historian is "to show what actually happened." Of course this goal is forever elusive. The past cannot be recaptured. Nevertheless, some works of history are more eloquent, accurate, and reliable than others. Furthermore, the task of historians is not only to present the facts but also to interpret them, to give shape and meaning to human events. To write vividly and validly about the past, I have told much of the story of William Wells through direct quotes from a multitude of primary sources. I agree with Conor Cruise O'Brien that a reliance on paraphrase can too easily serve a historian's preconceptions, smooth over significant complications, and smother the actual voices of the period.[8] At the same time, direct quotation brings another set of problems. Microfilm and manuscript sources can be difficult to decipher; spelling, grammar, usage, punctuation, and capitalization present a small chaos. "Potawatomi," for example, is spelled at least a dozen different ways. Purists should be forewarned that on these issues I compromise. While I don't change word order or verb tense, I do sometimes correct spelling, capitalization, and punctuation so that the reader does not get bogged down. My goal is to retain the flavor of the period and remind readers that we are exploring the past, a time when people talked and thought differently. Furthermore, many primary sources have already been "corrected" in various ways by previous editors. Most of my quotes are short and often several appear in a single paragraph, concluding with an endnote that cites my sources in sequence. To keep a long book from being longer, I usually confine my agreements and disagreements with other scholars to the notes. For the most part, I let the narrative speak for itself and strive to set the record straight. Nevertheless, I owe a huge debt to previous scholarship and cite secondary sources where they are especially relevant.

William Wells and the Struggle for the Old Northwest is written not only for scholars but also for general readers with a genuine curiosity about the Old Northwest. I hope that they find it both pleasurable and informative. My aim for this work of history dates back to the Greeks—to delight and instruct.

During the course of my research, I visited some thirty-three archives and read more than five hundred books and three hundred articles. Thanks to the invaluable assistance of Hood College's research librarian Aimee Gil, I am now able to access most of these sources, as well as many more, through my computer. I am especially grateful to Frank Bergon and Peter Dorsey for their detailed comments on my book, as well as Holly Bergon, Andrew Cayton, Larry Nelson, Michele Rubin, and Richard White for their support and advice. I want to acknowledge my sister Alice and her husband Lloyd Baker for fostering my interest in Ohio history. I also wish to thank Charles Rankin, Alessandra Jacobi Tamulevich, Tom Krause, Steven Baker, and Anna María Rodríguez at the University of Oklahoma Press; copy editor Gary Von Euer; and the two scholars who approved my manuscript and made many helpful suggestions, Ann Durkin Keating and Robert M. Owens. As always, my greatest debt is to my wife, Roser Caminals-Heath, whose love is my guiding star.

WILLIAM WELLS AND THE STRUGGLE FOR THE OLD NORTHWEST

PROLOGUE

In the spring of 1812 William Wells was serving as subagent and interpreter for the Miamis at Fort Wayne. Perhaps more than anyone on the frontier, he understood both the Indian and white perspectives, though like most men of his time he was seeking personal advancement. Few people, either Indian or white, trusted him. Many Miamis felt he favored the Little Turtle faction over other groups. William Henry Harrison had his doubts about Wells, but given the present crisis, he informed Secretary of War William Eustis that his services were essential: "Hated & feared as he is by a great majority of the surrounding Indians, he is nevertheless able from his influence over a few chiefs of great ability to effect more than any other person particularly with regard to the *now* all important point of obtaining information."[1] A week after this letter, Little Turtle died and thus Wells's usefulness greatly diminished. His years as a man at the center of the action would soon end—at a time when renewed hostilities swept the frontier and war with Britain was imminent.

PRESIDENT MADISON'S WAR

West of the Appalachians, the War of 1812 began on 7 November 1811 at the Battle of Tippecanoe—and it would end at the Battle of New Orleans in January 1815, after the peace treaty was signed. Harrison, governor of Indiana Territory, had marched nine hundred men up to Tippecanoe to provoke the Shawnee Prophet in the absence of his brother Tecumseh. Harrison claimed a triumph over a force at least twice the size of his actual foe. In fact, the Americans left forty-eight men on the field, and twenty more would die later of their wounds. Indian losses were about half that number. Nonetheless, it had been a victory of sorts for the Americans, and the warriors involved hungered for revenge. The battle had been a serious setback, but Tecumseh and the Prophet were determined to rebuild their pan-Indian confederacy.[2]

The warriors who had fought against Harrison were convinced that they had held their own against the Americans and that, with more men and ammunition, the victory would have been theirs. Once weather permitted, they began raiding targets of opportunity on the Illinois frontier. In February 1812 Governor Ninian Edwards wrote to Eustis, "The Winnebagoes, Kickapoos & Potawatomies composed the principal strength of the Prophet's army and are certainly greatly irritated by their losses." From Fort Dearborn (Chicago) the interpreter Jean Lalime warned that the Potawatomis "are full of the fire of revenge. The war has begun and it will not end until we make some fatal blow on them."[3]

Two settlers, Liberty White and Jean Baptiste Cardin, were murdered in early April at a farm on the Chicago River; the former met a particularly gruesome death. Nathan Heald, commander at Fort Dearborn, declared that White's body was "the most horrible object I ever beheld in my life." Unsure who had perpetrated the atrocity, Heald ordered all Indians to keep their distance from the small fur-trading post at Chicago. By the spring of 1812 settlers west of the Wabash were in grave danger. Edwards told Eustis that the only way to stop the raiding parties was to destroy the Indian villages. The secretary of war, described by one military historian as "a piddling incompetent," was at a loss about how to respond.[4]

As Indian attacks shook the frontier, Congress was moving closer to declaring war against Great Britain. Grievances had been festering in the United States since the Revolution: the British had long refused to abandon their fur-trading posts in the West and continued to use force to remind the Americans who ruled the waves. At seaports in the East, searches and seizures, impressments, blockades, and maritime rights were bones of contention. During Madison's first term, discontent reached the boiling point. Yet at a time when diplomacy was essential, the Senate rejected Madison's choice for secretary of state; when sound finances were needed, the national bank's charter was not renewed; and when military strength was crucial, all the Americans could muster were a paper army and a mosquito fleet of flimsy gunboats. Not surprisingly, the British shunned the United States's carrots and mocked its sticks. Napoleon's big battalions were the only thing they feared.[5]

Although the United States was unready, Henry Clay asserted that "the militia of Kentucky are alone competent" to conquer Montreal and Upper Canada. By stacking the right committees and twisting a sufficiency of congressional arms, the War Hawks prevailed. Thus a reluctant Congress voted to declare a war the country was ill-prepared to fight. "Many nations have gone to war in pure gayety of heart," Henry Adams drolly wrote, "but perhaps the United States was the first to force themselves into a war they dreaded, in the hope that the war itself might create the spirit they lacked." On 18 June 1812 President Madison signed the declaration without warning the western forts that they were in jeopardy.[6]

Ironically, as Congress pushed for a military solution, the British Parliament was moving to repeal the Orders in Council that had offended the Americans. Fate then intervened in the person of a lunatic, who on 11 May shot Prime Minister Spencer Perceval, author of the harsh legislation. The scramble to form a new government meant that it wasn't until 16 June that Lord Castelreagh announced that the Orders in Council would be suspended. Congress was unaware of these conciliatory developments, while American garrisons in the West were left to the tender mercies of the hostile Indians. Back in March, Governor William Hull of Michigan Territory had warned that, left unsupported, "Detroit, Michilmacinack, and Chicago, must fall."[7]

Lt. Porter Hanks, commander at Mackinac, first learned that war had been declared when on 17 July 1812 Capt. Charles Roberts surrounded his fort with seven hundred warriors and demanded its surrender. Hanks capitulated without firing a shot. Governor Harrison realized the seriousness of the situation: "The loss of Michilamacinack will be probably followed by the capture of Fort Dearborn and the suspension of offensive measures by Governor Hull's army will I fear give great strength to the British party among the Indians."[8]

Hull had assumed command of two thousand army regulars and Ohio militia in early June. He marched them up to Detroit, crossed into Canada, moved toward the British fortress at Malden, and then stopped in his tracks. A short, corpulent man more fond of the bottle than of battle, Hull, like many American commanders of that period, apparently was selected on the basis of age, weight, and military ineptitude. As he dillydallied, the situation deteriorated: his supply lines were exposed, he lost a boat containing valuable documents, suffered setbacks in skirmishes with Tecumseh's warriors, and abandoned his plan to attack Malden. When Mackinac fell, Hull ordered a withdrawal. "I shall immediately send an express to Fort Dearborn with orders to evacuate that post and retreat to this place or Fort Wayne," he wrote to Eustis, "provided it can be effected with a greater prospect of safety than to remain. . . . Captain Heald is a judicious officer, and I shall confide much in his discretion." Curiously, the letter Hull then sent to Heald implied that Mackinac had not surrendered to the British, and it did not give the commander the choice to defend or surrender Fort Dearborn at "his discretion."[9]

THE DECISION TO EVACUATE FORT DEARBORN

Hull's order arrived at Fort Wayne by 3 August. The fort's commander, Capt. James Rhea, consulted with Benjamin Stickney, the newly appointed Indian agent, and with William Wells, the controversial figure fired from that position in 1809. Both Rhea and Stickney were out of their depth; the former was an alcoholic, and the latter was inexperienced. Wells knew that Mackinac had surrendered and that Hull's promise of "Friendly Indians" at Fort Dearborn was wishful thinking. If the garrison tried to evacuate via Lake Michigan and sail to Fort St. Joseph, they could fall prey to the British navy. The only hope would be to escort them back to Fort Wayne, and the best man to lead such an expedition was Wells himself, who conveyed his forebodings and his plan in a letter, the last he would ever write, to Harrison: "The British and Indians took the post of Mackanac . . . without firing a Gun—I fear the Post of Chicago has met the same fate before this time—Captain Heald is ordered to retreat through the woods to this place or Detroit, immediately—I expect this order will not reach him in time to enable him to do so—I am endeavouring to raise Some Putawatamies & Miamis to cover his retreat, should the enemy suffer him to commence it." Wells had personal reasons for wanting to rescue the garrison. His niece Rebekah, daughter of his older brother Sam, was married to the fort's commander, Nathan Heald. Winamac (Catfish), a Potawatomi, was sent on to Fort Dearborn with Hull's message. Wells was delayed several days before he could recruit thirty Miami warriors. They were willing to escort the garrison back to Fort Wayne but not to fight the hostile Indians gathered at Fort Dearborn.[10]

Because Fort Wayne might soon be in danger, the women and children were to be sent to Piqua, in Ohio. Wells's daughters—Anne, Rebecca, and Mary—would go, but his wife Polly was expecting and would stay at the fort with William Wayne, who was fifteen, and their two-year-old son Sammy to await Wells's return.[11] Perhaps Wells cast one wistful look back at his family as he and the Miami escort rode off. Their route, through a mixture of forest, swamp, and tallgrass prairie, passed through several Potawatomi villages along the Elkhart River. On his way to Fort Dearborn with Hull's message, Winamac had let the Indians know of the evacuation. Word spread to the Potawatomis on the St. Joseph and Kankakee as well, and many headed to Chicago, hoping to receive a share of the fort's supplies.

When Wells arrived, either on the evening of the 12th or the morning of the 13th, hundreds of Potawatomis, Kickapoos, and Winnebagos, most painted for battle, were gathered outside the fort. Wells realized that the situation was desperate. Due to his ties with Little Turtle, he was on friendly terms with Five Medals and other older Potawatomi peace chiefs, but many of the younger men viewed him as a traitor to his adoptive people.

Located near the present Michigan Avenue Bridge, Fort Dearborn was protected on three sides by a bend in the Chicago River. Constructed in 1803 by Capt. John Whistler, grandfather of the famous American portrait painter, the fortification was defended by a double row of twelve-foot-high oak palisades topped by iron crow's-feet. Two-tiered log barracks lined each wall, and from projecting block-houses on the southeast and northwest corners, three cannon com-manded the inner and outer walls and the surrounding country. On the north side an underground passage and sally port, providing an alternative water supply or escape route, led from the bastion to the river. The garrison had a deep well, a brick powder magazine, and a substantial stand of small arms. Matthew Irwin, factor at Chicago, asserted that Fort Dearborn "was remarkably well calculated to hold out against Indians. . . . It contained a sufficiency of men to protect it and was situated on an eminence, overlooking in every direction, a level Country."[12]

The U.S. Indian agency and factor's storehouses stood west of the fort, and a vegetable garden spread out to the south. A community of fur traders occupied a cluster of nearby cabins; a few farmers sold produce to the garrison. Across the river was the home of John Kinzie, the local silversmith and leading fur trader, whom Wells had known since 1790. Kinzie, who came to Chicago in 1804, quickly became a center of controversy. Captain Whistler had complained about his conduct to Eustis. Doctor John Cooper considered him "a man of ungovernable temper," and the doctor's successor Isaac Van Voorhis reported that Kinzie and his son-in-law Lt. Linai Helm were plotting to start an Indian war. In sum, Fort Dearborn was a den of intrigue. Not only was the fort surrounded by hostile Indians, but the men inside, thanks largely to Kinzie's machinations, were divided into factions that undermined Heald's command.[13]

Captain Heald had received Hull's order to evacuate the post from Winamac on 9 August, yet he waited for Wells to arrive before decid-ing what to do. His orders left him no choice, but did Wells urge him to defend the fort in spite of them? James Corbin, a soldier at Fort Dearborn, recalled that the officers consulted "on what course should be pursued, whether we should leave the fort or not." Another source relates that "Capt. Wells urged Major Heald not to leave the Fort, as he did not like the way the Indians acted." Darius Heald, the command-er's son, heard a different version from his parents: "Wells thought there would be difficulty, yet thought they might effect their escape, & strongly advised the attempt, saying the longer they remained the more Indians there would be ready to intercept them. . . . There was . . . no opposition to evacuation by any of the officers." Major Heald's account makes no mention of a debate, merely stating that "the neighboring Indians got the information as early as I did, and came in from all quarters in order to receive the goods in the factory store. . . . Capt. Wells . . . arrived with about 30 Miamis, for the purpose of escorting us in, by the request of General Hull." Eight years afterward, John Kinzie said that he and Wells had advised against evacuating the fort, which was well supplied with arms.[14] Whatever advice Wells gave at this time, Heald decided to obey Hull's orders, and Wells was then asked to meet with the Indians to arrange a peaceful evacuation.

Wells and Heald met with two of the most militant Potawatomi war chiefs, Blackbird (Siggenauk) and Mad Sturgeon (Nuscotomeg), as well as peace chiefs Black Partridge (Mucktypoke) and He Who Sits Quietly (Topinbee), who arrived at the last minute. Exactly what was promised at this meeting is in dispute. Did Wells and Heald agree to turn over not only the fort's supplies but also its arms and ammunition? John Kinzie recalled: "They [the Potawatomis] professed friendship & gave assurances that they would conduct the troops safely thro but it was always observed that they all came in hostile array. . . . Heald showed the Indians the Arms, Ammunition goods etc. which were to be given to them for their safe conduct." Although the terms for a peaceful evacuation were agreed upon, Wells left the council skeptical of the warriors' intentions: "Wells . . . told Heald that he would be attacked, that the Indians with whom he had mingled, did not say so, but he judged it from their appearances and actions."[15]

Approximately seven hundred Indians, most of them warriors, had gathered around the fort by the early evening, intensifying Wells's premonitions. Did the fort have sufficient arms, ammunition, and provisions to withstand a siege? Lieutenant Helm asserted that these were in abundance, whereas Darius Heald stated: "They had but few provisions and but little ammunition." Captain Heald was convinced that his orders left him no choice but to leave. Wells, and possibly Kinzie, then argued that "the ammunition & liquor ought to be destroyed as the latter would only inflame them & and the former would undoubtedly be used in acts of hostility." Heald agreed, though he had already shown the fort's munitions to the Indians and did not want to break his word. Kinzie did not want to destroy the considerable supply of liquor, fearing that his business would be ruined, but he went along in the hope that the government might reimburse him later.[16]

The men tried to keep their destruction of the arms, ammunition, and liquor a secret. Kinzie ventured down to the sally port to dump the powder into the river, but was apprehended by two Indians who asked him about the strange sounds they had been hearing from inside the fort. Kinzie told them that "we had been opening barrels of pork & flour & were preparing to march next day—this satisfied them for the present but I perceived they were on the alert & it would be unsafe to attempt throwing the powder in the River, so it was thrown in the well." Not only did the noise of smashing kegs of powder and barrels of liquor and breaking muskets alarm the Indians, but also the smell of the whiskey poured down the well must have wafted over the walls. By morning the deed had been done, leaving the Indians in a vengeful mood.[17]

Supplies were distributed the following day to almost eight hundred Indians. Once they realized that they were not going to receive any powder, angry warriors demanded an explanation. When Wells stated that there was none left to give, they asked why he had destroyed it. His blood up, Wells cavalierly replied that he "had dreamed that the water-gods wanted it." A chief with his face blackened for war cautioned that he and his men "had painted their faces so as to fast and . . . dreamed that it would not be well for the Americans to leave" if they had deceived them. Not a man to back down, Wells retorted that "he sometimes painted too and had been dreaming too, that the Great Spirit told him he must leave . . . the next day." One Potawatomi recalled his father's account: "They were dissatisfied because the whiskey, fire-arms, and ammunition were destroyed." Clearly the distribution of the fort's supplies had backfired. "If they had fulfilled their word to the Indians," Black Hawk later asserted, "I think they would have gone safe."[18]

That evening Wells's worst fears were confirmed. Black Partridge reported to Wells, Heald, and the interpreter William Griffith that the Potawatomi peace chiefs were unable to restrain the warriors, who were determined to attack the convoy after it left the safety of the fort. The chief reported that he had heard "leaden birds [musket balls and bullets] singing in his ears." Black Partridge felt such shame at his failed efforts that he handed Heald a medal he had received from Harrison for signing the Fort Wayne Treaty of 1809. Kinzie, in retrospect, summarized the grim situation: "Capt. Wells received information the night before we marched that we should be attacked but we had then given everything away and could not retract."[19]

None of the known sources mentions if anyone in the garrison slept that night. What we do know is that before Wells mounted his favorite thoroughbred and led the evacuation of approximately ninety-five people from Fort Dearborn the morning of 15 August 1812, he had painted his face, in the fashion of a Miami warrior, for battle. This indicated, Gen. Thomas Hunt recalled, "that he understood the purposes of the Indians and was ready for them." Even his most inveterate enemy, John Johnston, had to admit that the audacious act was characteristic of him: "He was a brave and reckless man and had the greatest contempt of death—Wells of his own accord, blackened his face."[20] On this, the last day of his life, he was determined to act bravely and to die, if die he must, in a blaze of glory.

CHAPTER ONE

LIFE AND DEATH ON BEARGRASS CREEK

Samuel Wells, the great-grandfather of William, moved to Stafford County, Virginia, around 1700. Before his death in 1716, he and his wife, Eleanor Carty Wells, had five children. Charles, his eldest son, married Mary Elizabeth Edwards in 1733 and their eldest son, Samuel, born 6 September 1734, was William's father, who married Ann Farrow. They lived on 220 acres just west of the Potomac Path (U.S. 95) on the south side of Quantico Creek a mile from Dumfries. A signature site in the area was that of slaves pushing hogsheads of tobacco along the rolling roads that converged on Dumfries and led to Quantico Creek, where the casks were conveyed to ships. At the height of its economic power in 1763, the exports and imports at Dumfries rivaled the tonnage at Philadelphia and New York.[1]

William's father, Samuel, was a customer at Daniel Payne's popular emporium. In addition to powder, shot, and farming tools, he ordered "1 mans best Sadle . . . Irish Soape . . . 1 best Razor & Case . . . 1 pack cards, 1 Mans fine hatt . . . 1 wine Glass." For Ann he bought a silk handkerchief, worsted hose, and Irish linen. A contentious person, he appeared in court as a plaintiff, defendant, and witness. When he sold his land in 1767 and moved west, he was seven years in arrears on his land taxes. Tobacco is a labor-intensive, soil-depleting crop, and the overuse and erosion of the land silted up the Quantico, which became useless for shipping. Within decades Dumfries became a ghost town, its celebrated brick buildings in ruins.[2]

At the end of the French and Indian War in 1763, King George III issued the royal proclamation that forbade settlements on the west side of the Appalachian watershed and reserved that area for Indians in order to protect the tribes from land-hungry colonists and to preserve the British fur trade. Speculators such as George Washington and the Virginia-based Ohio Land Company could no longer purchase land directly from Indian nations. To proclaim is one thing, however, and to enforce another. Since the British left only a small garrison at Fort Pitt, settlers began to cross the mountains and stake their claims because they saw the area as "a realm beyond law." Washington expressed his views to his land agent William Crawford in 1767: "I can never look upon that proclamation in any other light (but this I say between ourselves) than a temporary expedient to quiet the minds of the Indians. It must fall, of course, in a few years, especially when those Indians consent to our occupying the lands."[3]

THE WELLS FAMILY HEADS WEST

The Treaty of Fort Stanwix of 1768 opened the floodgates to western migration. In the seventeenth century the Iroquois, armed with Dutch and British muskets, had overrun the Ohio Valley, exterminating smaller tribes such as the Eries and driving other nations further west. They, in turn, armed with French muskets, forced the Iroquois back to their homeland in New York. Yet by "Right of Ancient Conquest" the Iroquois sold the Kentucky hunting ground of the Shawnees, who had no say in the treaty, thus beginning a thirty-year war by the Indians in defense of the Ohio River boundary. Samuel Wells seized the opportunity, crossing the Appalachians to settle by Jacobs Creek, a tributary of the Youghiogheny, in present Everson, Pennsylvania. The southwestern portion of the state was also claimed by Virginia in a dispute that lasted until 1780. On a trip to inspect Ohio Valley land with Crawford in the fall of 1770, Washington stayed two nights at Jacobs Creek with John Stephenson, a local leader.[4]

William Wells was born nearby in 1770. The exact date is not known. He would live his first nine years in one of the most hotly contested parts of the country. When the Reverend David McClure visited the area in 1771, he found the Lord's work greatly neglected. The settlers "made the Sabbath a day of recreation, drinking & profanity." He preached at John Stephenson's and noted: "Christmas & New Year holly days, are a season of wild mirth & disorder here." After visiting the home of William Crawford, McClure wrote in Latin: "Holy things are not much observed in his house. He has a virtuous wife, but, alas, he at this time lives in fornication; the scandalous woman, according to what they say, he keeps not far off from his house." Passing through Jacobs Creek two years later, Nicholas Cresswell met Crawford at his mistress's house: "The woman is common to him, his brother, half brother, and his own Son, and is his wife's sister's daughter at the same time. A set of vile brutes."[5]

Samuel Wells and his elder sons took part in the whiskey-drinking, festive, and licentious life that was typical of the Appalachian frontier. Proof can be found in surviving court records: "Upon the information of Joseph Beeler Gent., that a certain Samuel Wells and Johanna Farrow doth at this time and hath for some time past beat wounded and evilly treated Ann the wife of the aforesaid Samuel." Ironically, the signer of this order was William Crawford. Joanna was Samuel's niece and his relationship with her may have been similar to that of Crawford and his mistress. If Samuel beat Ann, chances are Billy Wells often felt the sting of his wrath too. On 28 March 1780 the court "ordered that Saml Wells be summoned to appear before the next Court to answer the Petition of Ann Wells his wife & . . . that he be at peace toward sd Ann and all other good subjects of the Commonwealth." By that time, however, Samuel Wells, his long-suffering wife, and their seven children had left for Kentucky.[6]

During the years that the Wells family lived on Jacobs Creek, hostilities with the Indians were a constant threat. John Murray, earl of Dunmore and governor of Virginia, understood that the frontiersmen were in no mood to obey legal authority: "They do not conceive that Government has any right to forbid their taking possession of a Vast tract of Country, either uninhabited, or which Serves only as a Shelter for a few Scattered Tribes of Indians." Given these attitudes, Dunmore knew that conflict with the Indians, who were more than a few scattered tribes, was inevitable. What was called Lord Dunmore's War began in April 1774 with some wanton killings along the Ohio, including the murder of relatives of the Mingo war leader Logan, who exacted a bloody revenge. In June, Dunmore ordered a two-pronged attack: General Andrew Lewis led the Virginia militia toward the

Shawnee villages while Dunmore headed a second force from the Pittsburgh area. Samuel Wells marched with Dunmore in Capt. John Stephenson's company, which encountered sporadic opposition; on one occasion "Saml. Wells . . . came nigh getting a shot at an Indian," but he saw no actual combat. The crucial battle took place at Point Pleasant on 10 October 1774 when Cornstalk led several hundred Shawnees on a dawn attack against the Virginians and a fierce, day-long, tree-to-tree fight ensued. Above the fray, Cornstalk exhorted his men to "Be strong! Be strong!" Militarily the battle was a draw, but its long-term consequence, after Cornstalk signed a peace treaty, was the Indians' loss of Kentucky.[7]

In 1775 Samuel formed a ten-man company that canoed down the Ohio to Limestone (Maysville), and then followed a buffalo trace (Ky. Route 68) to present Mays Lick. The men explored the area before choosing a spot by a creek that emptied into the North Fork of the Licking. They built cabins near an old Indian war road before they left. In July 1776 Samuel Wells and his eldest son Sam conducted further explorations. One night Sam heard the voices of Indians on a nearby warpath headed toward Blue Licks, the site of a bloody ambush in 1782.[8]

During the Revolution, Samuel served in the Thirteenth Virginia and was stationed at Fort Pitt. He probably went with Gen. Edward Hand and five hundred mounted men, including Capt. John Stephenson and Col. William Crawford, on an ill-fated expedition derisively known as "the Squaw Campaign," which came upon two small Delaware camps and killed one man, two women, and a boy. Visceral fears bred virulent hatred. Gen. Thomas Gage wrote in 1767 that "all the People of the Frontiers, from Pennsylvania to Virginia inclusive, openly avow, that they will never find a Man guilty of Murther, for killing an Indian." Government policy, however bungled, was not genocidal; but a widely condoned practice among frontiersmen was to kill peaceful Indians to provoke a war of extermination. White Eyes and Cornstalk, Delaware and Shawnee chiefs who wanted peace, were murdered at this time. Many settlers had lost loved ones in Indian raids and everybody wanted tribal lands.[9]

After he returned from his Revolutionary service, Samuel Wells decided to take his family to Kentucky. We can only speculate about the reasons: Pennsylvania was about to win its dispute with Virginia and thus his land title might not be valid; he owned slaves, and Pennsylvania opposed slavery; the local courts had him under scrutiny for the abuse of his wife Ann; the rapid increase of settlers in the area was driving off the game; and finally, no doubt he was hearing praise for the boundless opportunities to be found in Kentucky, the sum of all hopes for land-hungry pioneers. "What a Buzzel is amongst People about Kentucky," one man wrote at the time, "to hear people speak of it one Would think that it was a new found Paradise." Samuel purchased a flatboat in the spring of 1779 and drifted with his family down the Ohio toward an area that would soon prove to be risky enough on its own: a place known as "the Falls."[10]

FLATBOATING DOWN THE OHIO

Samuel and his brother Hayden and their families accompanied William Pope, who testified in 1826 that "he came to Louisville about 22 May 1779 with his family" from Virginia. George Washington's grandmother was a Pope—George was born on Pope's Creek, in Fauquier County—and Pope's wife Penelope was related to Samuel Wells. William Pope traveled to Kentucky with his brother's and sister's families and some single men, including William Oldham and Bland Ballard. A large group made the dangerous trip safer.

Constructing flatboats often required professional help. Usually they were about forty feet long, with a cabin in the back that included a fireplace with a stick-and-clay chimney. A large steering blade pivoted from a sturdy forked stick in the stern, and there were sweeps on the sides. In addition to pioneer families, the boats carried slaves brought from Virginia, as well as a few horses, cows, chickens, and hogs, to say nothing of supplies and prized possessions. Living conditions on board were cramped, dirty, and malodorous. Yet in those days flatboats were an essential means of heading west. "The lowly raft," Dale Van Every wrote, "had become an ark sweeping a whole people into possession of an empire."[11]

At Pittsburgh the muddy Monongahela joined the clear waters of the Allegheny to form the Ohio, which meant "the beautiful river," a wide stream whose serpentine course extended for a thousand miles westward before it added its considerable strength to the mighty Mississippi. The river was an essential route settlers took to colonize Kentucky and the Old Northwest. In March 1779 the Ohio had overflowed. This was not unusual in early spring because of heavy rains and melting snow. The extensive bottomlands were inundated, making the river a mile wide in several places, but by early May it had receded within its banks and was running smoothly at a few miles an hour. Billy's older brother Sam was in the advance boat, keeping a lookout in the water and on shore for potential trouble. Submerged trees called sawyers or planters as well as driftwood could damage the bottom of the boat. The islands might have treacherous shoals, sandbars, whirlpools, and eddies, while sudden bends and changes in the current could run a boat aground or leave it stalled in stagnant backwater. To warn the other flatboats about approaching dangers, Sam blew on a conch shell.[12]

Travelers were impressed by the natural beauty of the Ohio, the abundance of wildlife, and the bounteous land. For the first five hundred miles the river—when it wasn't flooded—remained from four hundred to six hundred yards wide; near the Falls (Louisville) it widened to over seven hundred yards. In general, hills close to one bank meant extensive bottomlands on the other, a pattern that alternated over the entire trip. The high hills and tall trees cast long shadows across the water, and the boats moved from sunshine to shade and back again. The frequent sharp bends gave the impression of floating on a series of lovely lakes. Because few pristine forests remain east of the Mississippi, it is now difficult for us to imagine the prodigious size of the trees—many thirty feet in circumference and over one hundred feet tall. Among the papaws and willows lining the banks were huge sycamores with gnarled trunks, peeling white bark, and a hollow core large enough to conceal Indian warriors. The well-watered bottoms were replete with beech trees, as well as maple, plum, cherry, locust, and elm festooned with vines and creepers. On nearby hills stood towering poplar, walnut, chestnut, oak, and hickory trees. In May the pungent odor of wildflowers and grape blossoms permeated the air. A savvy frontiersman could see in these rich bottomlands and forested hills a fortune in cut timber and cleared farmland.[13]

As the Ohio rolled to the southwest, it gathered power and volume from large streams entering from north and south. From the Big Sandy to the mouth of the Kentucky, both on the southern side, travelers entered a hunter's paradise. Fifteen years earlier, George Croghan had written: "The country hereabouts abounds with buffalo, bears, deer, and all sorts of wild game, in such plenty, that we killed out of our boats as much as we wanted."[14] The same bounty existed in 1779. Flocks of ducks, geese, turkeys, partridge, and quail were omnipresent; the waters teemed with catfish weighing up to one hundred pounds, as well as schools of pike, buffalo, sturgeon, perch, and carp, whose backs rippled the surface and slapped the bottom of the boat. Although Shawnee attacks between the Scioto and Big Miami Rivers soon became commonplace, in 1779 flatboats were rare and the Wells flotilla passed that area unscathed.

During the voyage the families had ample time to make new friends and renew old acquaintances. Billy and John Pope were the same age. William Oldham and William Pope were fellow veterans of the Revolution. "Oldham was much attracted to Penelope, the young daughter of his friend, and announced his intention of coming back to claim her for his bride,"[15] which he did in 1783 when he was thirty and she was fourteen—a common age for a woman to marry in those days. As we shall see, on 4 November 1791, Billy Wells, then the Miami warrior Blacksnake, and Lieutenant Colonel Oldham, commander of the Kentucky militia, would have a fateful encounter. The end of the trip was signaled by the rumbling of the Falls, a mile-long set of rapids where the river dropped twenty-four feet. Above the rapids, on the Kentucky shore, the boat landed at the mouth of Beargrass Creek, near the newly formed town of Louisville.

GEORGE ROGERS CLARK

George Rogers Clark was the preeminent figure on the Kentucky frontier. His actions had a major influence on events in the Old Northwest and helped shape the life of William Wells. After stopping at the Falls in May 1778 with a force of 150 men, Clark had captured Kaskaskia, Cahokia, and Vincennes from the British. His conquests in

Illinois Territory were short-lived, as Henry Hamilton led a combined force of British regulars, French-Canadian volunteers, and assorted Indian warriors to retake Vincennes. In the winter of 1779 Clark's situation was dire; his only options seemed to be to retreat or wait helplessly for his impending doom. Clark, however, took pride in defying expectations: "I saw the only probability of our maintaining the Country was to take advantage of his [Hamilton's] present weakness, perhaps we might be fortunate: I considered the Inclemency of the season, the badness of the Roads &c—as an advantage to us, as they would be more off their Guard on all Quarters."[16]

Clark resolved to take Vincennes with fewer than two hundred men, on the perilous assumption that Hamilton would not anticipate he would be "so mad as to attempt to march 80 Leagues through a Drowned Country in the Depth of Winter." Convinced that "nothing but the Most daring conduct would Insure suckness," he set an example for his men. On the final days of their arduous march, when they faced the chest-high inundated Wabash, he blackened his face with gunpowder, "gave the war whoop and marched into the water." The French settlement welcomed the Americans, and Hamilton, taken by surprise, surrendered the fort. Clark's victory left the British wary that he might take Detroit.[17] He did not "conquer" the Northwest Territory, but his capture of Vincennes, and his subsequent destruction of Shawnee villages in Ohio in 1780 and 1782, kept the British and their Indian allies from launching offensive operations and thus helped to protect the Wells family and other Kentucky settlers during the Revolution.

Following his recapture of Vincennes, Clark met with various tribes in the area, including the Miamis. "I had been always convinced . . . our Genl Conduct with the Indians was rong," he wrote later. "Inviting them to treaties was . . . imputed by them to fear and giving them great presents confirmed it." What worked was not "soft speeches" but tough talk. The Indians had to understand that "we are always able to crush them at pleasure." He told them: "I am a man and a Warrior and not a councilor. . . . I carry in my Right hand war and Peace in my left."[18] If they wanted to fight, he would fight; if they wanted peace, he would dictate his terms. Clark was certain that this was the way the Indians liked to do business, although it violated their customs and ignored the important distinctions between war and peace chiefs. His unfortunate assumptions would shape American Indian diplomacy for decades.

Although French inhabitants had welcomed the Americans upon their arrival, before long the cultures clashed and American credit collapsed, leaving economic chaos in its wake. Picture the dilemma of the typical man living in Vincennes. Following the French and Indian war he had pledged his loyalty to the British; then during the Revolution, as control of the town repeatedly changed hands, he vowed to support the latest victor. In 1780 Augustin Mottin de la Balme appeared with a French mercenary force, giving him a fleeting hope for a renewal of French rule; finally in 1783 the Revolutionary War ended, leaving the typical settler unsure of his loyalties and resentful of the sudden influx of rowdy American settlers.

Louisville was destined to become an important trading center because of its location at the Falls of the Ohio, yet in 1779 the site was not a desirable place to settle. Although it was situated on a high plain rarely in danger of flooding, numerous small ponds and nearby swamps bred mosquitoes and spread disease. Most settlers preferred the rich land on Beargrass Creek, where tall trees, plentiful springs, and a network of beaver dams sustained the soil. The Wells family claimed tomahawk rights, cleared the forest, and erected a cabin for themselves as well as a smaller one for their slave family of Jacob, Cate, and their three girls.[19]

Shortly after their arrival, Sam Wells volunteered for a raid led by Col. John Bowman against the Shawnee villages. A force of 296 men crossed the Ohio, and by the evening of 29 May they were a few miles from Chillicothe on the Little Miami. Bowman divided his force, sending Benjamin Logan's men to one side and William Harrod's to the other for a three-pronged attack at dawn. The result was unsynchronized: some men charged into the village and others took a more cautious approach. Women and children fled while the warriors defended a fortified council house, where Chief Black Fish was mortally wounded. Fifteen Kentuckians, shielded by an oak log near the council house, received heavy fire that killed seven. Bowman refused to come to the rescue. Warned that Simon Girty and one hundred Mingos were fast approaching, he ordered a retreat, leaving ten dead men behind. That did not deter the men from auctioning off their captured plunder, which included 163 horses and a wealth of silver ornaments. Although Bowman claimed victory, one veteran stated that, "the campaign was well nigh a total failure." The Kentuckians had not triumphed, but they had put the Shawnee villages on the defensive.[20]

Clark had counted on Bowman's men to enable him "to Reduce the Garrison of Detroit." For the rest of the Revolutionary War the capture of that town would remain his "Principle Design." On 4 October 1779, Col. David Rogers, bringing military supplies from New Orleans, was ambushed near the Little Miami. Rogers and over forty of his men were killed and five captured. This defeat, the first of many along the Ohio River, meant that Clark would have to postpone his plans to take Detroit for another year.[21]

BEARGRASS STATIONS

"There are but two lawyers here," John Todd wrote from Kentucky to William Preston, "and they can't agree."[22] His remark foreshadowed the litigious history of early Kentucky, where disputed land claims made a palimpsest of every boundary map, and a host of court cases dragged on into the nineteenth century. As a veteran of Lord Dunmore's War and the Revolution, and as someone who had explored Kentucky and built a cabin on the North Fork of the Licking, Samuel Wells had several claims. Whether they were valid in the Louisville area was the question, since John Floyd owned the land where Wells had settled.

On 8 November 1779 Floyd arrived in Louisville and found the Wells family and about ten others squatting on Beargrass Creek. His first impulse was to drive them off, but since his slave Bob cut his foot and winter was coming on, he needed help constructing his station. Thus the Wells family became dependent on Floyd, whom Clark termed "the most capable man in the country." He was six feet tall and his straight black hair, flashing black eyes, high cheekbones, and dark complexion were an inheritance from his Indian grandmother. During the Revolution he had sailed on the privateer *Phoenix* to prey upon British shipping. Captured and taken to England, Floyd escaped to Paris, where Marie Antoinette, impressed by his charms,

The Ohio Valley Frontier, 1776–1788. Map by Bill Nelson. Copyright © 2015 University of Oklahoma Press.

gave him a set of silver buckles. Ben Franklin provided his passage home. William Preston, the surveyor of Fincastle County, sent Floyd several times to select good land in Kentucky.[23]

Floyd and his wife, Jane, with the help of the Wells family, built their station on the Middle Fork of Beargrass Creek. The rectangular fortification, with cabins on each side, was protected by palisades and had a nearby spring. On 14 November William Fleming and other land commissioners arrived to settle titles in the Louisville vicinity. Virginia had granted four hundred acres of "waste and ungranted lands situated on western waters" to settlers who had made improvements prior to 24 June 1776. The Land Act of 1779 extended a "settlement right" to anyone who had raised a crop of corn before 1 January 1778, and a preemption of one thousand acres for an additional fee. Because of his military service, Samuel Wells secured at least four hundred acres, but his family would remain at Floyd's Station through the winter.[24]

Snow began falling in late November and remained on the ground until March. All over Kentucky people endured what in retrospect was called "the Hard Winter." Rivers and streams turned to ice, killing the fish; wild turkeys fell frozen from their roosts; deer and buffalo died by the thousands; livestock perished. "Go through the cane and see cattle laying with their heads to their side, as if they were asleep; just literally froze to death . . . a heap! a heap! of them died." Trees frozen to the sap would split open with a loud crack and crash to the ground. Because it was too cold to reload their rifles, hunters knew they only had one shot at their target. As the last "Johnny cake" was rationed out, flour became "as dear as gold dust." The buffalo meat was so poor it had to be "boiled with pounded corn to thicken it." When John Floyd tried to write to his friends in Virginia for aid, the ink froze in his pen. In late February he reported "the severest winter that was ever known. . . . We have but ten families with us yet."[25]

The Wells family and their slaves suffered along with everyone else at Floyd's Station. In his travels around Kentucky, land commissioner Fleming was appalled by the unwholesome living conditions. In Harrodsburg, for example, "the whole dirt and filth of the Fort, putrefied Flesh, dead dogs, horse, cow, hog excrements and human odour all wash into the spring . . . and makes the most nauseous potation of the water imaginable and will certainly . . . render the inhabitants to this place sickly." In March, following the Hard Winter, Fleming stated that sickness had killed settlers at the Falls in large numbers. The extreme cold and the lack of solid food made the young especially vulnerable. After Jane Pope Helm lost all three of her children, she and her husband Thomas determined to move elsewhere. Another victim of the spreading sickness—referred to as "the ague" or "the bloody flux" and accompanied by "a bilious remitting fever" and "black vomit"—may well have been Anne Wells, Billy's mother, who died at this time. If so, George Hartt, the lone doctor in Louisville, submitted her to treatments that exacerbated her illness:

quicksilver-laced laxatives, doses of calomel, blistering plasters, and frequent bleedings. Most patients passed away within two weeks.[26]

"All they had to do was keep the Indians from killing them," recalled Kentucky pioneer James Wade, "though they were sometimes hard pressed to do this." As soon as spring arrived, the Wells family and other settlers were anxious to leave the fetid conditions of the stations and start clearing their own lands. The warm weather also brought waves of Indian raiding parties, armed by the British, looking for targets of opportunity. The capture of the notorious "hair buyer" Henry Hamilton did not thwart this strategy; if anything, the conflict escalated: "It would be endless and difficult to enumerate to Your lordship," British general Frederick Haldimand wrote to Lord Germain, "the Parties that are continually Employed upon the back Settlements."[27]

Nevertheless, in the spring of 1780 optimism at first prevailed. Louisville was incorporated, with John Floyd and William Pope among its nine trustees. Col. George Slaughter brought 150 state troops to the fort and 300 flatboats arrived with settlers, who filled six new stations on the Beargrass. Everyone assumed there was safety in numbers, which led to an overconfidence that cost lives. "In this state of things it is no matter of surprise that soldiers were shot near the fort, or that in the settlements of Beargrass lives were lost, prisoners taken and horses stolen, with frequent impunity." Though the myth of the frontier celebrates the stalwart pioneer in his isolated cabin, the reality was different: "The almost incredible number of distressed and defenseless families settled through our woods for the sake of subsistence instead of adding to our strength are in fact so many allurements, and most become a daily sacrifice to the savage brutality of our inhuman enemies." On 31 May 1780, John Floyd wrote from his station: "Hardly one week pass[es] without someone being scalped between this and the Falls and I have almost got too cowardly to travel about the woods without company."[28]

Realizing the vulnerability of the Kentucky outposts, Maj. Arent de Peyster, the British commandant at Detroit, lavished presents on his Indian allies and urged them to invade the settlements. Capt. Henry Bird left Detroit with 150 soldiers and some 700 warriors gathered by Alexander McKee. Their objective was the newly erected Fort Nelson in Louisville; if it fell, all Kentucky would be at their mercy. The men brought two cannons that could shatter log palisades. On 9 June 1780 Bird's force reached the Ohio. Rather than attack Louisville and the Beargrass stations, McKee's warriors insisted on targeting two exposed outposts on the South Fork of the Licking River. Twelve days later they surrounded Ruddle's Station. When the Americans "saw the Six Pounder moving across the field, they immediately surrendered." Isaac Ruddle stipulated that all prisoners should be taken to Detroit, although Bird "forewarn'd them that the Savages would adopt some of their children." McKee recalled that "the violence of the Lake Indians in seizing the Prisoners, contrary to agreement, threw everything into confusion." Two days later Martin's Station "surrendered without firing a gun. The same Promises were made & broke in the same manner, not one pound of meat & near 300 Prisoners."[29]

Although few captives were killed, Bird had been shocked by how they were treated. When a rumor spread that Clark was "daily expected" in Louisville, he decided to retreat.[30] The attacks demonstrated that exposed outposts were defenseless against cannon. The preference of the Indians for easy plunder over strategic advantage, however, meant that the Wells family and other settlers on the Beargrass were relatively safe for another year.

When Clark returned to Louisville he called for an attack on the Shawnee villages, this time bringing a cannon captured at Vincennes. Samuel and Sam Wells were among the more than four hundred militia from the Falls commanded by John Floyd and William Linn. In August an army of about one thousand Kentuckians crossed the Ohio and headed up the valley of the Little Miami toward Chillicothe, which was deserted. Proceeding to Piqua on the Mad River, Clark attacked the village. The fighting, "with a savage fierceness on both sides," continued for two hours until the warriors retreated back into the town, some taking refuge in a fort built by the British. Clark brought up the brass six-pounder, whose "balls shivered the stockade wherever they struck." The warriors shot back until the cannon fire, "playing too brisky on their works," forced a retreat. The Americans lost at least twenty-two killed, the Shawnee a similar number.[31]

Billy Wells no doubt heard his brother Sam and other men boast about their exploits. They had only captured forty horses, but they had burned the main Shawnee towns and destroyed "eight hundred acres of fine corn & great quantities of beans, peas, potatoes," thus making it much harder for the Indians to counterattack in force. Clark's reputation soared because he had retaliated for the taking of Ruddle's and Martin's stations. One man assured Virginia governor Patrick Henry that Clark's "name alone would be worth Half a regiment of men."[32]

THE LONG RUN MASSACRE

The most exposed outpost in the Louisville area, known as Jefferson County, was Painted Stone Station on the north bank of Clear Creek above present Shelbyville, which was run by Daniel Boone's brother Squire. In the spring of 1780 he had taken a dozen families and several single men to his 1,400-acre preemption located twenty-one miles east of Linn's Station, the last on the Beargrass. A wagon road marked by "mile trees" connected the two stations. In the spring of 1781 Sam Wells, following a dispute with John Floyd, was expelled. Since it was too dangerous to settle on their land near Painted Stone, the Wells family moved to Linn's Station.[33]

In a plea for help to Governor Thomas Jefferson, Floyd summarized the plight of the Beargrass stations in April 1781:

> We are all obliged to live in Forts in this Country, and notwithstanding all the Caution that we use, forty seven of the Inhabitants have been killed & taken by the Savages, besides a number wounded since Jany. . . . Whole families are destroyed, without regard to Age or Sex. . . . Not a week passes & some weeks scarcely a day without some of our distressed inhabitants feeling the fatal effects of the infernal rage and fury of those Execrable Hell Hounds. Our garrisons are dispersed over an Extensive Country, and a large proportion of the Inhabitants, are helpless Widows & Orphans.

Only General Clark's indomitable spirit and military skills, as well as the fact that the settlers were unable to leave, had sufficed to "keep this Country from being left entirely desolate."[34]

No death that spring was more deeply felt than that of William Linn, whose station served as a refuge for many of the widows and orphans mentioned in Floyd's letter. His sons, William and Asahel, were friends of Billy Wells. On the morning of 5 March 1781, Linn had left ahead of a group going to Louisville. When shots were heard in the woods, a party that included Sam Wells investigated, finding Linn's horse. The next day they discovered his mutilated body. The torn-up ground indicated that he had fought bravely to the last.[35]

The situation at Painted Stone rapidly became untenable, as persistent Indian raids picked off the settlers. In April three young men out clearing ground for the spring crop were fired on: one was killed, one captured, and one escaped. Squire Boone, still in his shirttail, and a dozen other men grabbed their guns and set out in pursuit. They, in turn, were ambushed by a war party led by Simon Girty. Two were killed and Boone was shot twice: "So badly wounded was he," Boone's son Moses recalled, "none thought he would recover—his arm was badly shattered, & when it healed, that arm was an inch and a half shorter than the other." Girty delighted that "he had made Squire Boone's white shirt fly." Squire was at least as tough as his more famous brother. He had, by his own reckoning, "Rec'd Eight Bullet Holes through him and . . . been in seventeen engagements with the Indians." In spite of his disabling injuries, he wanted to stay and make a stand, but a majority of the settlers at Painted Stone "were determined to leave."[36]

In December Jefferson had authorized Clark to raise two thousand men to capture Detroit, but few were willing to enlist. In early August he left Pittsburgh with 250 raw recruits and started down the Ohio. When Col. Archibald Lochry failed to meet him at Wheeling with one hundred men from Pennsylvania, Clark left a message that he would "move on slowly" so that they could join forces in a few days. Aware of Clark's intentions, the British in Detroit sent one hundred rangers under Capt. Andrew Thompson and three hundred Indians with Alexander McKee to thwart his plans. Ten miles below the mouth of the Big Miami, Joseph Brant, leading ninety Mingos and ten whites, ambushed Lochry on the morning of 24 August 1781. Thirty-six were killed and sixty-four captured. After Lochry surrendered, he was tomahawked by an enraged warrior.[37]

Clark was in Louisville when he received word of Lochry's defeat. On 7 September he told his Council of Officers that he wanted to march up the Wabash, destroy the Miami villages, and, if possible, push on to Detroit. "I am ready to lead you on any Action that has the most distant prospect of Advantage," he asserted, "however daring it may appear to be." But the board stated that "under our present Circumstances, it is impossible to carry on an Expedition." A discouraged Clark dispersed his army. Two of the soldiers sent to Linn's Station were Sam Wells's old friends from Jacobs Creek: Sam Murphy and Valentine Crawford's son William.[38]

McKee strived in vain to keep his Indian force together. Instead they broke off "in small parties, some going home, others going after Horses . . . so that we were Reduced to a small Number, not able to attack the falls." McKee and Brant still had two hundred warriors who "agreed to cross the country and attack some of their small forts and infest the Roads,"[39] thus posing a serious threat to Painted Stone and the Beargrass settlements.

At this time, two couples wished to be married at Linn's Station. Bland Ballard headed for Brashear's Station, at the mouth of Floyd's Fork, to bring the only Baptist minister in the area, John Whitaker. Spotting signs of an Indian war party, Ballard immediately went to warn Painted Stone, where plans were already under way to evacuate. Two men had been killed in a nearby cornfield a few days before. When twenty-four light horsemen under Lt. Thomas Ravenscraft arrived as an escort, everyone prepared to leave the next morning, 13 September 1781. Because there weren't enough packhorses, the families of Squire Boone and the widow Hinton would have to wait for a later escort. Ten-year-old Isaiah Boone, however, got permission to go. Sporting a "three-cornered cocked hat, gold fringe & a cockade, sent him by his brother in Kaskasia, & nicely beaded shot pouch, & a small gun given him by his father," the boy mounted a packhorse and rode off with the main party. In case of attack, the women and children were to dismount and take cover while the men protected them.[40]

After a few miles, Sgt. James Welch of the militia became ill; a dozen men remained behind to care for him. By midday the main caravan of settlers, packhorses, and cattle was strung out along the narrow wagon road near the ford at Long Run when they were attacked by a Miami war party. Hearing the cries of the wounded and realizing they were outnumbered, Ballard and others cut off the packs so that the women and children could mount the horses and make a dash for it, with the men running from tree to tree and firing to protect them. An elderly black woman pulled up her petticoats and shouted as she began to run, "Every man for himself and God for us all."[41] The safety of Linn's Station was eight to nine miles away.

Young Isaiah Boone, who had dismounted, was knocked down by the swollen waters of Long Run, soaking both him and his gun. As he scrambled out he spotted an Indian behind a tree on the opposite bank. George Yount saw Isaiah raise his gun and asked what he was doing.

> "I'm pointing at an Indian that has been trying to kill me."
> "Why didn't you shoot him?"
> "My gun is wet and won't go."
> "Where is he?"
> "There he is," said Boone pointing to the clay bank & at that moment the Indian peeped up his head & Yount shot him through the neck & killed him—& he rolled into the water."

Yount then told the boy to get away. As Isaiah ran, he dropped his gun and shot pouch. He managed to mount a packhorse behind a woman and her child, and, to make it run faster, he smacked it repeatedly with his three-cornered hat, and lost that, too, before he reached Linn's Station.[42]

The men who had stayed behind with Lieutenant Welch first suspected an ambush when they saw a frightened horse on the road. Proceeding with caution, they surprised two Indians and rescued their three captives. Rachel Van Cleve, baby sister in her arms and brother by her side, told them her mother, two of her siblings, and at least six other people were dead.[43]

Billy Wells saw the survivors of the attack straggle into the station. Floyd assembled twenty-seven men, including Samuel and Sam Wells, and they rode off before sunrise to recover the wounded and bury the dead. A few hours after their ambush, the Miami war party had been joined by more than one hundred Indians led by McKee and Brant. McKee decided to "take Possession of the Ground they had drove the enemy from and to wait their coming to bury their dead." The Indians were slashing open packs and collecting plunder scattered along the wagon road when the Kentuckians rode into view. The dispersed warriors were able to rush forward and attack from several sides, giving Floyd's men time to fire only one volley before trying to escape. Several were killed on the spot, including Samuel Wells. Floyd was fleeing on his favorite horse "Shawnee" when a low branch hit his head and knocked him off his mount. Sam Wells saw his predicament and "two or three times wheeled his horse & presented his gun & kept the Indians at bay—finally he dashed forward, & gave his horse up to Col. Floyd, who was so fatigued, that after jumping upon the horse, balanced on his breast several rods before he got finally righted & asaddle." Sam then ran alongside Floyd all the way back to Linn's Station.[44]

"I have this minute returned from a little Excursion against the Enemy," Floyd wrote to Clark, "& my party 27 in number are all dispersed & cut to pieces except 9 who came off the field with Capt. Asturgus mortally wounded and one other slightly wounded, I don't know yet who are killed. . . . I cant write guess at the rest."[45]

Two days later some three hundred men from the Beargrass stations returned to the scene of the fighting. They faced the grim task of gathering the bodies, many bloated and mutilated beyond recognition. At least twenty-five settlers had been killed in the two battles. The dead were buried in a sinkhole at the site and their names carved in a nearby tree trunk. At Painted Stone, Squire Boone had assumed the worst when some panic-stricken cattle, one with a horn shot off, returned to his station. He and his son Moses had primed their guns for a fight to the death. Because McKee's warriors had already left the area, they were rescued unharmed.[46]

The defeat had one positive aspect, celebrated at the time and in later accounts: "the magnanimous gallantry of young Wells" in saving Floyd, who in gratitude gave Sam a gift of land. The two men put aside their former enmity and became good friends. Billy must have been impressed that his brother Sam was such a hero of those dark days that women vied for his attention. On 30 December 1781 he and Mary Spears were united by "the first marriage bond ever written in Jefferson County."[47]

WAR IN KENTUCKY CONTINUES

Like many other children in Kentucky, eleven-year-old Billy Wells was now an orphan. Within two years the precarious life on Beargrass Creek had cost him his mother and father. Indian raids bringing death and desolation and the hardships of the frontier must have toughened him beyond his years. William Pope, a prominent figure in Jefferson County, became his guardian. The Pope family had a cabin at Sullivan's Station and one in Louisville. Samuel Wells's will suggested that he was relatively prosperous. He owned five slaves: "Negro fellow Jacob . . . Wench Cate . . . gal Sarah . . . gal Cis . . . gal Nan," valued at 222 pounds. He also had thirteen head of cattle, twenty-seven sows and shoats, two ewes, and a lamb. Farming implements included axes, saws, chains, hoes, sickles, and plows. His hunting rifle was lost at Floyd's Defeat, but he did own three steel traps. Signs of genteel living were few: one chest, a table, two dishes, a teakettle and teapot, and two decks of cards.[48]

Sullivan's Station was on a bluff overlooking the South Fork of the Beargrass two miles east of Louisville near the present Bardstown Road. William Pope, an important if unpopular man in Jefferson County, was appointed as a lieutenant colonel in April 1781. James Sullivan told Clark: "the Generality of the people is much averse to serving under him." A few years later John May wrote, "I found that Col. Pope had conducted himself so very imprudently & had given himself up so entirely to Drink that he had nearly ruined himself."[49] He was, in short, probably not a figure Billy looked up to or admired. Deprived of one father, he had not found another. What Pope did believe in was education, hiring William Johnson at one hundred pounds a year to teach his son John as well as Billy Wells. John Pope, for one, was a serious scholar, especially after he caught his arm in a cornstalk mill and it had to be amputated below the shoulder. No longer able to be a woodsman, he came to prefer the life of the mind.

Billy and the other boys at the Beargrass stations had responsibilities. In the mornings they would take their dogs and chase the deer and wild turkeys from the cornfields; as the crop ripened they had to scare away crows, squirrels, and hogs. In spite of their efforts, at night the raccoons would feast in the fruit trees. They also had to keep a sharp ear out for the bells of cows browsing in the woods, and an even sharper eye for Indians lurking around the settlements to steal horses, take prisoners, or lift the scalps of the unwary. These dangers haunted their nightmares. The boys gathered berries and nuts, caught crawfish along the creek, and fished in the nearby ponds. Billy was old enough now to dress like the men in leather breeches and a baggy shirt. He no doubt owned a gun and knew how to hunt, skin, and gut the game he shot, then cut and pack it to bring back to the station.[50]

Although the British had surrendered at Yorktown on 16 October 1781, combat in the West intensified in 1782. In April Col. David Williamson and one hundred men from Pennsylvania massacred men, women, and children in cold blood at Gnadenhütten, a Delaware village of Moravian converts on the Tuscarawas: "in all ninety-three, tomahawked, scalped & burned, except one boy, who after being scalped made his escape." In June, when Gen. George Washington's friend Col. William Crawford led another Pennsylvania force in a failed effort to destroy Wyandot and Delaware villages near Upper Sandusky, he paid a terrible price for Williamson's atrocity: "The unfortunate Colonel in particular was burned and tortured in every manner they could invent," William Irving wrote to Washington. In retribution for the slaughter of the innocents at Gnadenhütten, the warriors made Kentucky their prime target.[51]

On 16 August 1782 several hundred laid siege to Bryan's Station, a few miles north of Lexington. The Indians destroyed the crops, killed the livestock, stole the horses, and withdrew. They were pursued by a mounted force of 182 men under Col. John Todd, which reached Blue Licks on 19 August 1782. Suspecting an ambush, Daniel Boone advised caution, but hotter heads prevailed. Maj. Hugh McGary accused anyone who wouldn't follow him of being a dastardly coward and charged across the river. The Kentuckians advanced, came under a withering fire from several sides, and in five minutes were routed. It was, in one survivor's words, a "Direfull Catastrophy." The cream of central Kentucky lay dead on the field, including Todd, Col. Stephan Trigg, two majors, and eight captains. Daniel Boone, who lost his son Israel in the battle, wrote to Governor Benjamin Harrison: "We can scarcely Behold a spot of Earth but what reminds us of the fall of some fellow adventurer, Massacred by Savage hands . . . if something is not speedily done we [no] doubt will wholly be depopulated."[52]

To avenge Blue Licks, Clark's army of about one thousand men burned several Shawnee villages and destroyed thousands of bushels of corn. Ten Indians were killed as well as four Americans. "We got a few scalps and prisoners," Clark reported. As a result of this attack, Shawnee warriors were reduced to isolated raids as they spent the winter struggling to feed their families.[53]

The Indians had concentrated their attacks on central Kentucky in 1782, yet Jefferson County and Sullivan's Station were not spared. In July a slave couple belonging to William Pope was captured. The woman was killed "because she didn't follow them willingly." On Christmas morning Billy Wells's schoolteacher William Johnston was riding with a few friends when they were ambushed. One man was killed instantly. When Johnston attempted to flee, his horse was shot. He raised his gun but it didn't go off and he was captured. On 7 July 1783 the Weas at Ouiatanon returned him in a peace overture. Johnston reported that his "Usage among the Savages had been kinder, than I by any Means could have expected," and resumed his teaching. Billy Wells and the other boys must have tried to break the tedium of rote learning by asking him to tell enthralling tales of life among the Indians on the Wabash.[54]

In early April, John Floyd donned a scarlet coat bought in Paris and headed toward the salt works at Bullitt's Lick. He was accompanied by his brother Charles, Sam Wells, and others. At a branch of Brooks Run, they were ambushed. One man fell dead and Floyd was mortally wounded. Sam brought the sad news to the Beargrass. "The best beloved man in Kentucky" and "the main Stay & Support" of Jefferson County was dead. He was buried on the knoll behind his station. Years later, his wife was buried beside him, wrapped in his scarlet cloak.[55]

After Floyd's tragic death, Indian attacks decreased. On 3 September 1783 the Peace of Paris ended the American Revolution. Without consulting their Indian allies, the British ceded the territory above the Ohio and promised to evacuate Detroit and other forts in the Old Northwest. Feeling secure, the people of Louisville turned their attention to more mundane things. The Popes moved to the Pond Settlement southeast of town. Sam fulfilled his father's dream and established Wells Station on the wagon road about four miles due west of Painted Stone. A few years later Squire Boone purchased the station and Sam moved near Louisville.[56]

In the summer of 1783, Daniel Brodhead opened a retail store in Louisville. Women bartered the linsey from their looms for calico, straw bonnets, and cotton handkerchiefs. Men traded their pork and corn for hunting rifles, steel traps, feed, seed, and farm implements. For those who hankered after the finer things, there were silks and satins, fashionable furniture, pewter and chinaware, trinkets and horn combs, Madeira, and a good cigar. Sugar, coffee, and tea from the Caribbean were shipped upriver from New Orleans. Woodsmen could exchange their peltry at John Sanders's "keep" (a covered flat-boat moored nearby) and receive certificates of deposit to use as currency. One home in Louisville had glass windows, prompting a boy to run to his mother and cry, "O, Ma! I just saw a house with specs on!"[57]

By the spring of 1784, the town consisted of fifty or sixty scattered houses, mostly log, a few frame. One tavern boasted a billiard table. The civic-minded spoke of paved streets, brick houses, and a dancing school. On Sundays young ladies under parasols promenaded along the shoreline and were courted by swains in silk stockings. The dominant note, however, was more vulgar. "In truth I see very little doing but card playing, drinking, and other vices among the common people," one visitor wrote, "and am sorry too many of the better sort are engaged in the same manner."[58] While Billy Wells and the other boys played marbles and mumblety-peg, the men engaged in the rough and tumble of wrestling matches, horse races, shooting contests, cock fights, wolf baiting, and gander pulls. The latter, a test of a man's insensate heart and sure grip, involved galloping past a live gander—neck greased, webbed feet tied to a low-hanging branch—and, in one swift motion, yanking off its head.

In the spring of 1784, Billy Wells, Will and Asahel Linn (William Pope was also their guardian), and Walt Brashears, who had recently arrived with his family from Maryland, went camping at Robert's Pond. A series of sinkholes in this area were known as the Fishpools, which were connected by an underground stream where eyeless fish were caught. Another set of large ponds drained into Pond Creek. It was a wonderful place to hunt and fish, with beaver dams and plenty of geese, swans, and ducks. A light snow had fallen during the night and the boys had tracked and shot a bear cub and were determined to carry their prize home. As they were preparing their triumphal load, they were suddenly seized by a small war party of Delawares and Miamis. In broken English the Indians demanded to know where they came from. Under the threat of brandished tomahawks, the boys insisted that their home was in Louisville, thus concealing the existence of the nearby Pond Settlement. Thirteen-year-old Billy Wells and his three friends were then bound and taken into the forest.[59]

CHAPTER TWO

BECOMING MIAMI

We will never know exactly what happened on that snowy day in March 1784 when Billy Wells and his three friends were taken prisoner by the Indians. Narratives from the period describe people in similar situations, however, and two secondhand accounts provide a few details. Many Indians spoke enough broken English to say "How de do" and make their intentions clear; and a raised tomahawk was eloquent. "I could not move," a captive recalled, "and by the time I looked around . . . one Indian was right up to me and held out his hand and I took hold of it. I have no language to tell you how I felt." Walt Brashears tried to run, as did William Linn, even though a dead bear cub was strapped to his back, but both were quickly caught. The Indians patted William on the back and gave him the Delaware name of "Little Fat Bear," while the more nimble Brashears was called "Buck Elk." Billy Wells was named "Apekonit," or Wild Carrot, possibly because of his reddish hair. Other captives were valued for that reason. Frances Slocum's "fine growth of chestnut brown hair" was "admired . . . almost to the point of worship" by the Miamis. Ben Allen was captured by two Shawnee warriors: they "took off my hat. Saw my red hair, and patted me on the head . . . and said, 'Indian.'"[1]

The Indians apparently had come upon the boys by accident and demanded that they direct them to their homes. The Pond Settlement, where Wells and the two Linns lived with their guardian William Pope, was isolated and exposed, so they bravely refused to reveal its location and insisted that they were from Louisville. "You lie!" they were told, and no doubt they were threatened, but they stuck with their story. Since the essential tactic of the small war party was a swift attack and a hasty retreat, the boys were promptly taken across the Ohio. Once on the Indian shore, they faced an arduous 150-mile trek to the Delaware villages on the White River.[2]

The four boys probably handed over any clothes the Indians desired. Charles Johnston, for example, reported that one of his captors "repeated the word, 'Swap-swap'—and demanded that I should give him my shirt for his, a greasy, filthy garment, that had not been washed during the whole winter." Captives were often stripped of hats, coats, shirts, pants, and shoes. What they usually received in return were a pair of moccasins, a breech clout, and sometimes a blanket. Oliver Spencer said that after he had run about four miles in his bare feet, "my master . . . supplied me with a pair of moccasins and seemed much pleased when in return for them I gave him my pocket handkerchief," but when Oliver presented his hat to another of his captors, it was "dashed on the ground" and later burned. Still, his effort to join in the spirit of the "swap" made sense, since Indian culture valued reciprocity and the exchange of gifts. Many a captive found that moccasins were superior to shoes for the hard traveling that lay ahead. John Tanner, age nine, was made to run four days without shoes until his bare swollen feet were lacerated with splinters and thorns; then he was given moccasins, "which afforded me some relief." James Axtell, a scholar of the captivity experience, argued that this "first transaction" of replacing shoes with moccasins was literally and figuratively a crucial first step in transforming captives into "White Indians."[3]

Prior to his captivity John Tanner was frequently flogged by his father and he often thought to himself, "I wish I could go and live among the Indians." Billy Wells and the other boys probably talked about Indians by day and had troubled dreams about them at night. The boys knew that they most likely faced one of two fates: adoption or annihilation. How they conducted themselves could determine whether they lived or died. Those from ten to fifteen were prime candidates for adoption (Billy was thirteen), and a show of spunk and fortitude might impress their captors. Thus they determined to be on their best behavior and endure hardships without complaint. They may not have known that sometimes a grieving family demanded a blood sacrifice, regardless of the qualities of the captives.[4]

Buffalo tugs were used as cords; the boys were bound around the waist and possibly the neck. Their hands weren't tied behind their backs, since that impeded the speed of their retreat, which was of the essence during the first few days. The country of southern Indiana across from Louisville was hilly and forested. There was no easy, direct route to the Delaware villages. Chestnut Tree Place—present Anderson, Indiana—was a likely destination. They proceeded in single file, leaving as little trail as possible, with an Indian in front and one behind each boy. The last Indian held a switch to whip any laggards and make sure no sign was left behind. If a search party tried to rescue the boys, they may have assumed their captors were Shawnees on the Mad River in Ohio and thus headed in the wrong direction.

The first day the boys were compelled to make haste. They may not have eaten until the evening, but we know what they had for dinner: the bear cub that the boys had killed. Charles Johnston described a similar preparation: "We regaled ourselves upon the flesh of the cubs, which to me was excellent eating, although the manner of dressing was not such as to improve its quality or to suite a delicate taste. Their entrails were taken out, and after the hair was thoroughly singed from their carcasses, heads, and feet, they were roasted whole." Indians were used to feasting and fasting. The prisoners weren't and they worried where the next meal was coming from. Nor were the boys accustomed to eating wild game without salt or bread, yet as Sancho Panza said, "Que no hay mejor salsa que el hambre" (there is no better sauce than hunger). Sometimes, when bread was available, it was unsavory. Alexander Henry was offered a loaf cut with the bloody knife of a Chippewa warrior who had just murdered his fellow Englishman. Another captive had trouble stomaching a dish of "deer guts, dried with the dung, and boiled all together." On the other hand, Ben Allen thought his first supper of fat buffalo meat boiled with cornmeal was "elegant." Charles Johnston won favor with his captors by preparing a "delicious dish" of chocolate-flavored dumplings, noting that "all savages are particularly fond of sweet things."[5]

As far as we know, the small war party that captured the four boys had not killed anyone or stolen any horses. Often large war parties broke into smaller groups to raid the settlements and reunited later.

Thus many captives witnessed the Indians preparing the scalps of their victims. The inside was scraped clean, tied and stretched on a hoop of twig, dried by the campfire, and painted red. Mary Jemison reported: "those scalps I knew at the time must have been taken from our family by the color of the hair. My mother's hair was red." Jonathan Alder saw an Indian holding the scalp of his brother in his hand, "frequently giving it a shake to shake off the blood," while a fellow captive recognized the scalps of her husband and child: "How do you suppose we felt?"[6] Billy Wells had not been harmed, but Indians had killed his father three years earlier and the father of the Linn boys. Regardless of the situation, the threat of death was ever-present and each captivity experience was traumatic.

After dinner, Indians enjoyed a good smoke. If they thought there was a danger of pursuit, they camped in a sinkhole so that their fire was not visible at night. Oliver Spencer provided a vivid description of how his captor, White Loon, cut some tobacco, tossed a small offering into the fire, mixed the rest with dried sumac leaves, packed his pipe, and lit it: "[He] smoked a few whiffs, then handed the pipe to his companion, who also smoking a few minutes returned it; the Indians thus alternately puffing until the tobacco was consumed, frequently filling their mouths with smoke and forcing it through their nostrils, closing their brief use of the pipe with a peculiar suck of the breath and a slight grinding of the teeth."

Indians talked little while they smoked, making laconic observations as the others grunted approval. They were not always taciturn, however; in camp they enjoyed jokes, pranks, and games of chance. Johnson's captors played a card game called "Nosey," where "the winner has the right to a number of fillips, at the nose of the loser." Once he fell asleep and awoke to find an Indian contently smoking his pipe while sitting on him as if he were a footstool. The boys would not have been allowed to talk among themselves. The sooner they learned some Indian words, the better. If an Indian spoke English, the boys were told, as George Girty said to John Brickell, "You are a prisoner, and we will take you to our town and make an Indian of you; and you will not be killed if you go peaceably."[7]

At night Billy's hands were tied behind his back and his feet were bound. A cord went around the waist, fastened to an Indian sleeping on each side, and an additional cord, sometimes with a bell attached

(Thomas Ridout stated that he "could not stir without it ringing"), was placed around the neck and fastened to a nearby stake or tree. If a captive complained, he would learn that Indians knew how to say "Damn you soul" or "Damned son of a bitch" and other cuss words unavailable in their own language. The boys might be given a blanket; everyone slept with feet to the fire. Often prisoners were so exhausted that they had no trouble sleeping. Others were tormented all night, like Mary Jemison, by "gloomy forebodings" of their impending fate. If it rained, the cords could tighten and cause excruciating pain. Oliver Spencer said he "suffered from the violent straining of my arms behind my back," and Ridout awoke to find his hands so black and swollen he could not move his fingers for several hours. A few prisoners freed themselves; on occasion, they killed their captors in the process. Spencer managed to escape. When the Indians were about to find him, however, he ran up and told them he had only been picking raspberries. Although one Indian wanted to kill him, another saved his life.[8]

Chestnut Tree Place was at least a week of hard traveling away. As they moved north, out of the hills and into a flat land of forests interspersed with swamps and prairie, the Indians slowed down to hunt. Deer, bear, elk, and buffalo were the preferred game, as well as wild turkeys, ducks, and other waterfowl. Jonathan Alder said that once they were not in danger of pursuit, they "feasted sumptuously. . . . The Indians seemed more cheerful. . . . They told jokes, laughed, and talked." He and his fellow captives were "no more tied with the rope at night and could lie down and rise up at our leisure, but the Indians still kept a little watch over us." How each boy fared depended on the person who had first taken him and now owned him. A boy to be adopted was usually treated kindly and received an equal share of food; however, some captors were cruel. On occasion Indians feasted while their prisoners starved. A few captives were regularly beaten, others killed. If the Indians obtained alcohol, the dangers escalated. Usually one or two remained sober to guard the prisoners, while the others enjoyed a drunken frolic. In these circumstances, individuals intended for adoption might be murdered. "The Indian I was with had whisky," John Brickell recorded. "He and the two warriors got drunk, when one of the warriors fell on me and beat me. I thought he would kill me. The night was very dark, and I ran out into the woods and lay under the side of a log." Upon his return to camp, Brickell said that he was "much pitied on account of my bruises."⁹

Near Chestnut Tree Place they made preparations for their arrival. Stripped of any remaining clothing, the boys wore breech clouts and were painted various colors. "Those whom they smut with black, without any other colour, are not considered of any value, and are by this mark generally devoted to death." Candidates for adoption usually received a scalp lock: "My hair was cut off, and my head shaved, with the exception of a spot on the crown, of about twice the diameter of a crown-piece. My face was painted with three or four different colors; some parts of it red and others black. A shirt was provided for me, painted with vermillion, mixed with grease. A large collar of wampum was put round my neck, and another suspended from my breast." If there were no razor, the prisoner's hair was pulled out. This was done by dipping the fingers in dry ashes and yanking a tuft out at a time by the roots. The ears were pierced and hung with ornaments. They were given deer-hoof rattles and taught to chant and dance. Fresh scalps were fastened to a long pole, and the warriors gave a shout of triumph for each one.¹⁰

Female relatives, dressed in their finest, came to greet the successful warriors. Captives might be attacked on the outskirts of the village by angry women grieving for lost family members. Billy Wells knew what came next: the running of the gauntlet, a standard practice among woodland Indians. The villagers formed two parallel lines from the outskirts of their town to the council house. Usually they were armed with tomahawks and knives as well as sticks and stones. Prisoners painted black could be killed on the spot, while youngsters intended for adoption might receive few if any blows. Much depended on whether the village was in mourning.¹¹

The boys may have heard in Kentucky what James Smith was told by an Indian: "I must run between these ranks, and that they would flog me all the way, as I ran, and if I ran quick, it would be so much better, as they would quit when I got to the end of the ranks." Charles Stuart observed that although the Indians were heavily armed, "they did not strike with the Axes, and only Used the Heads and Handles of their Tomahawk, But used the Blades of the Cutlasses tho' not with so much Severity as To Kill." Although intended for adoption, nine-year-old John Brickell reported: "I had no chance, for they fell to beating me so that I was knocked down, and every thing that could get at me beat me, until I was bruised from head to foot." Fortunately, a Delaware chief then rescued him.[12]

One secondhand account stated that Billy Wells and the other boys "won the favor of their new masters, by the patience with which they suffered captivity and fatigue, and the cheerful interest they appeared to take in the occurrences of the march." Forced to run the gauntlet, they at first "submitted bravely" to the abuse and beating, but "the Linn blood became heated" and the boys retaliated. Asahel struck one of his attackers with a sudden left-handed punch and knocked him down. The warriors, delighted with his spunk, "applauded it with loud shouts and laughter." A donnybrook ensued: "Kentucky against the field—the heroic lads fought against odds, but displayed such prowess that they soon cleared the ring, and were rescued from . . . their captors, who were particularly amused by the efficiency and odd effect of the left-handed blows of the younger Linn." This version may contain a grain of truth. The gauntlet was not only a means for the Indians to vent anger at enemies but also a test of the mettle of their captives. Margaret Paulee reported: "I saw two boys named Moffit, who were brought in and forced to run the gauntlet. They were started and one turned upon the first blow and returned it, which pleased the Indians so that he escaped the balance and was adopted."[13]

William and Asahel Linn and Walt Brashears stayed with the Delawares; because Billy Wells had been captured by a Miami, he was taken to Snake-fish Town (Kenapecomaqua) on the northwest bank of the Eel River about six miles from its merger with the Wabash (Logansport). There he may have faced another gauntlet. A more serious concern was a society that practiced ritual cannibalism. They had "the power to procure prisoners and none [had] the power to release them after being once surrendered." In 1764 Thomas Morris was taken prisoner at the Miami stronghold of Kekionga (Fort Wayne) and claimed by this society. At that moment, young chief Pacanne rode up and put his hand on Morris's neck: "I thought he was going to strangle me out of pity: but he untied me, Saying . . . 'I give this man his life. If you want meat (for they sometimes eat their prisoners) go to Detroit. . . . What business have you with this man's flesh, who is come to speak to us?'" Morris was offered a pipe to smoke and received the ministrations of "two very handsome young Indian women . . . who seemed to compassionate me extremely. . . . Happy Don Quijote, attended to by princesses!" Fortunately Billy was adopted by the village chief, the Porcupine (Kaweahatta), and thus protected from the dreaded society.[14]

All of the nations north of the Ohio adopted captives. Years later Wells wrote: "When an Indian loses one of his friends by death, he believes that if the place is not supplied by adoption, more of his friends will die." The relatives of the dead person decided if they wanted to adopt or sacrifice the prisoner. Sometimes a captive received the dead person's name and was expected to display the same attributes. Among the Miamis it was often true that "the one who was adopted did not take the place of the one who died—he or she merely freed the spirit to walk the spirit path." In the council house the man who held Billy, possibly the chief's brother the Soldier, would have given an account of his capture. The procedure Wells faced next has been best described by James Smith:

> The old chief holding me by the hand, made a long speech very loud, and when he had done he handed me over to three young squaws, who led me by the hand down the river bank into the river until the water was up to our middle. The squaws then made signs to me to plunge myself into the water, but I did not understand them; I thought that the result of the council was that I should be drowned, and that these young ladies were to be the executioners. They all three laid violent hold of me, and I for some time opposed them with all my might, which occasioned loud laughter by the multitude that were on the bank of the river. At length one of the squaws made out to speak a little English (for I believe they began to be afraid of me) and said, *no hurt you*; on this I gave myself up to their ladyships, who were as good as their word; for though they plunged me under water, and washed and rubbed me severely, yet I could not say they hurt me much.

Delaware women took Francis Slocum and "sang Indian songs all the while they were washing the little girl." John M'Cullough suspected foul play, until he was told "me no killim, me washim." Jonathan Alder was bathed by his Indian mother, who "stripped me stark naked and commenced rubbing me with soap, some of the finest British soap that could be bought. She talked the entire time that she washed me." Another captive was told the purpose of the ritual: "Go down white man, come up red man."[15]

Billy was dressed as a Miami, with earrings, a nose bob, silver bracelets on his arms, and Miami moccasins, decorated with the tribe's distinctive diamond design, as well as leggings, breech clout, and shirt. Alexander Henry was unhappy with his freshly shaved head and new attire until he noticed that "the ladies of the family, and of the village in general, appeared to think my person improved, and now condescended to call me handsome, even among Indians."[16]

Although Billy Wells understood few Miami words, the Porcupine probably addressed him on the duties and privileges of being a Miami. James Smith was told: "My son, you are now flesh of our flesh, and bone of our bone . . . you are adopted into a great family, and . . . are now one of us by an old strong law and custom." The chief assured him he had "nothing to fear," that they would "love, support, and defend" him as they did themselves because he was now "one of our people." At the time Smith didn't realize the importance of "this fine speech," but from then on "we all shared one fate." After John M'Cullough listened to an oration from a chief, he was handed over to "an Indian . . . sitting on the hearth smoking his pipe; he took me between the legs, (he could talk very good English,) and asked me several questions, telling me I was his brother." His Indian family, after "they set up a lamentable cry, for some time . . . shook me by the hand, in token they considered me to stand in the same relationship to them as the one in whose stead I was placed." For a captive to achieve an Indian identity could be exhilarating. "What a transition! passing from immediate danger and apparent certain death to a renovated life!"[17]

THE WHITE INDIANS OF AMERICA

Being captured, taken to Snake-fish Town, and adopted was only the first stage of the process by which Billy Wells became a Miami. In the years ahead he would learn to speak, think, and act like a Miami; he would acquire a new set of skills in order to conduct himself properly in his village, during the hunt, and on the warpath. He would become what the settlers called a "White Indian" or "Squaw Man" or "Renegade." He would "go native." Since the first Spanish explorers, thousands of Europeans had been captured by Indians; many adapted to and accepted their tribal lives and refused repatriation. "It is a remarkable fact," John Hunter stated, "that white people generally when brought up among the Indians, become unalterably attached to their customs, and seldom afterwards abandon them." The reason, he later added, was that "the Indian mode of life [contained] something peculiarly fascinating." These White Indians refuted European assertions that "civilization" was superior to "savagery."[18]

J. Hector St. John Crevecoeur noted that "many an anxious parent" went in quest of their captured children only to find them "so perfectly Indianized that many knew them no longer" and "absolutely refused to follow them." Captives said that among the Indians they enjoyed "the most perfect freedom, the ease of living, the absence of those cares and corroding solicitudes which so often prevail.... There must be in their social bond something singularly captivating, and far superior to any thing to be boasted of among us; for thousands of Europeans are Indians, and we have no examples of even one of those Aborigines having from choice become European!" A child of the Enlightenment as well as a Romantic, Crevecoeur exaggerated— some Indians did adopt white values, such as the Moravian converts on the Ohio frontier—but his puzzlement was justified. Why did many whites stay with the Indians, while few Indians, when given an option, accepted white culture? As Benjamin Franklin observed, if an Indian child brought up among the whites "goes to see his relations and makes one Indian Ramble with them, there is no persuading him ever to return." The willingness of whites to become Indian and the refusal of Indians to become white was deeply upsetting to Americans and a cause of animosity. Did the settlers hate the Indians more for not accepting white culture or for clinging to their own? Rather than saying, "I see your superiority and I'd like to join with you but I can't," the Indians, like Herman Melville's character Bartleby, simply said, "I prefer not to." And so did a significant number of their captives. When Frances Slocum was offered the chance to leave her

Miami family and live with her white relatives, she replied, "I have always lived with the Indians. They have used me very kindly. . . . Why should I go, and be like a fish out of water? . . . I cannot. I am an old tree. . . . I am happy here. I shall die here and lie in that graveyard, and they will raise a pole at my grave with the white flag on it, and the Great Spirit will know where to find me. . . . I cannot go. I have done."[19]

Gary Ebersole pointed out: "Captivity represents an ultimate boundary situation where human existence, identity, and ultimate meaning are called into question as the captive's world is turned topsy-turvy and his freedom and autonomy are stripped from him." When a captive was adopted, however, the process flip-flopped again: a new identity was forged and new freedom and autonomy were discovered. Even if an adopted captive, like Wells, was not expected to replace a dead Miami, what Indians referred to as a "requickening" or "resuscitation" could still take place and a new, reborn person emerged from the process. For better or worse, I might add, since I do not wish to idealize the experience of adopted captives, but rather to stress that they became different persons than they would have been had they not been captured. Frequently these transformations were not complete or irreversible. Colin G. Calloway noted that "confusion, not conversion" was typical of the renegades, such as Wells, who inhabited the middle ground between two worlds.[20] Wells would eventually return to white society while drawing upon his Indian skills to survive and, for a time, thrive in it. How he lived in both cultures is the larger subject of this book, but first we must complete our investigation of how Billy learned to become a Miami.

MIAMI CULTURE AND CUSTOMS

Captives who wrote sympathetically about the Indians stressed their gratitude for the care they received. "They are much kinder than their neighbors and to strangers than the whites are," Wells stated. His remarks were echoed by many others. John Brickell found that, "They treated me very kindly and in every way as one of themselves"; John Hunter, that "the whole tribe treated me with regard and tenderness.

. . . They took every opportunity, and used every means which kindness and benevolence could suggest, to engage my affections and esteem." While Indians could be ruthless in selecting fit candidates for adoption, once a person was adopted every effort was made to care for and cure their disabilities. Oliver Spencer reached his village with feet so swollen he couldn't walk. His Indian mother, "her pity . . . excited," boiled "a strong decoction of red oak and wild cherry bark and dewberry root" and patiently nursed him back to health; when John M'Cullough contracted pleurisy, for three weeks his Indian mother and an aunt "paid great attention to me . . . with regard to my drink and diet" until he was better.[21]

Margaret Paulee saw a warrior kill her one-year-old girl; yet at the Shawnee village he was "particularly desirous to atone for his barbarity by various acts of kindness." She gave birth to a boy several months later: "The squaws seemed very much delighted with my child, carrying it through the town, showing it with great joy, seeming to think it a great beauty." After her release, Margaret acknowledged that the Indians had demonstrated "an attachment toward me as ardent and affectionate as any I have ever known among my own friends and kindred."[22]

Although the Indians rarely used corporal punishment on adopted children, there were exceptions. Alder "received many a severe whipping" from his Indian sister Sally. Once she gave him a "merciless whipping" and called him a "dirty, lazy dog" for not skinning coons fast enough. Years later, after Alder returned to the white world, Sally came to visit and he told her his true feelings: "Sally, I would think a great deal more of you than I do if you had not abused me unreasonably when I was a boy and living with you. I respect you very much, but I can never love you as I do Mary and Hannah [his other Indian sisters], they always treated me so kind." When M'Cullough was caught stealing watermelons, a sadistic Indian punished him with the sharp-toothed bill of "a kind of fish . . . called a gar" wrapped in a rag and struck him, leaving "four scores, or scrapes, with it, from the point of the hip down to the heel—the mark of which I will carry to my grave." During his long life with the Indians, Tanner was treated badly on numerous occasions. He was "beaten almost every day" as a boy, was tomahawked from behind for falling asleep on a hunt, and, after he married, was beaten by his mother-in-law. Once an Indian stabbed his dog and tried to kill him. Eventually, Tanner was shot and "severely and dangerously wounded" by another Indian.[23] In sum, kind treatment was the norm for most adopted captives, yet the threat of cruel punishment was not uncommon.

"Such is Indian life," Alder recalled. "It is either feast or famine." At first "their food didn't agree with" him and he became "lean and haggard," but later he learned to relish it: "Dried pumpkins boiled with fat deer meat are about as good eating as a hungry person could wish." Ridout was served venison seasoned with dry herbs and fried in bear's oil on a pewter plate, along with green tea sweetened with maple sugar in a cup and saucer. Truman Stone used to tell his grand-children that "the best meal of victuals I ever ate was cooked by Mary Jemison." Frances Slocum served her relatives "breast of wild tur-key stewed with onions, quite a delicate dish." Smith remembered with particular fondness "potatoes peeled and dipped in raccoon's fat [that] taste nearly like our sweet potatoes [and] homony, made of green corn, dried, and beans mixed together." Thus Billy developed a taste for Miami food, which was more varied than the diet of most settlers. During periods of famine, he also learned how to fast and scavenge. In those grim times, as Thomas Morris remarked, "What an Indian can eat is scarcely credible."[24]

Young male captives assisted the women before they joined the Indian boys their age in their preparations for manhood. "The women cultivate corn, beans, potatoes, pumpkins and other common vegetables," Wells wrote, having briefly shared their labors. Tanner was made to "cut wood, bring home game, bring water, and perform other services not commonly required of the boys of my age," while Spencer stated, "I had now to make fires, carry water both for cooking and drinking, wash the homony when boiled in ashes, and assist the old woman in getting wood." Brickell recalled that "the squaws . . . plant and tend the corn; they gather and house it, assisted by young boys not yet able to hunt." Alder said he "soon learned to skin and stretch a coon or other skin as quickly and as neatly as any boy or squaw in the village," adding that "the Indian squaws . . . cut and carry all the wood, bring all the water, skin all the game . . . skin and stretch all the furs, plant the corn and beans, and cultivate and gather the crops . . . boys until they are twelve . . . are classed as squaws."[25]

Visitors to villages, who saw women working and men relaxing, assumed that an Indian woman's life was sheer drudgery, which may not have been the case: "Our labor was not severe," Mary Jemison insisted. The tasks of Indian women were "probably not harder than that of white women . . . and their cares are certainly not half as numerous, nor as great."[26] Since much of their labor was performed together in the fields and the village, women had opportunities to talk, laugh, sing, and share stories.

During his period of probation, Wells acquired the Miami language. When first captured, Alder was lonesome and depressed, because there was "no living soul that I could talk with or understand," but he learned "very fast, for the boys and girls took a great interest in my welfare and would try to amuse me and learn me to talk." Before long he "could understand a good deal of all three languages spoken in the village" and "began to enjoy myself to a large extent." Spencer could speak Shawnee in six months because "a greater part of all that I heard [was] accompanied, as their conversations and speeches were, with the most significant gestures." Learning a language is more than memorizing a certain number of words and rules. Fluency brings a new way of looking at, thinking about, and acting in the world. For Billy Wells a new language meant having another life.[27]

C. C. Trowbridge's 1820 account of Miami traditions suggests that Billy's powers of comprehension would have been tested daily at dawn by the Porcupine:

Every morning the father of the family rises about daylight and awakes his children by striking . . . the bench upon which they sleep & calling out to them to listen to him. He then addresses them in a kind of lecture, setting forth the good & the evil of the world and endeavouring to convince them of the necessity of adhering to the one & of avoiding the other. He draws parallels between the conduct of the good & their consequent happiness and respectability and contrasts these with the many striking instances of bad character they see.

Wells lived in what anthropologists term a "shame culture." He was judged by how well he achieved Miami standards of good behavior; when he failed to do so he was scolded and expected to feel ashamed. John Hunter was taught that he should "Never steal, except it be from an enemy, whom it is just that we should injure in every possible way." Thus, it was admirable to kill an enemy but abominable to murder a member of the tribe. Billy's education was reinforced by the fact that what being Miami meant was clearly understood. All the tribal members were on the same cultural page, at least for a time. Hunter was taught to excel at hunting, be "brave and cunning in war," defend the tribe's lands, protect the women and children, "obey and venerate the old people, particularly your parents," and not fear death. He should "propitiate the Bad Spirit, that he may do you no harm;—love and adore the Good Spirit, who made us all, who supplies our hunting grounds, and keeps us alive."[28]

Looking back on his captivity, John Brickell insisted: "The Delawares are the best people to train up children I ever was with. . . . Their leisure hours are, in great measure, spent in training up their children to observe what they believe to be right. They often point out bad examples to them and say, 'See that bad man; he is despised by every body . . . if you do as he does every body will despise you.'" If a man acted in a cowardly manner, they would point "the finger of scorn" at him and call him "Squaw!" On the other hand, "They often point to good examples as worthy of imitation. . . . Honesty, bravery and hospitality are cardinal virtues with them."[29]

James Smith demonstrated how shame culture encouraged a captive to become a good Indian. Captured at eighteen, he was expected to become a man quickly. When he got lost in the woods while hunting, his captors took his gun. When they saw him reading, they hid his books. Shortly afterward he complained that the load he was told to carry was too heavy. "They made a halt and only laughed at me, and took part of my load and added it to a young squaw's, who had as much before as I carried. This kind of reproof had a greater tendency to excite me to exert my self in carrying without complaining, than if they had whipped me for laziness." While his Indian father, Tontileago, was away, Smith offered a Wyandot visitor a shoulder of roasted venison, without maple sugar and bear's oil to season it. Tontileago was offended and told Smith that he had "behaved like a Dutchman. Do you not know that when strangers come to our camp, we ought to always give them the best that we have." Smith's apology was accepted because he "was but young." Tontileago told him that he "must learn to behave like a warrior, and do great things, and never be found in any such little actions." Next some women urged him to help them hoe corn; "the old men hearing of what I had done, chid me, and said that I was adopted in place of a great man, and must not hoe corn like a squaw." Smith added, "They never had occasion to reprove me for any thing like this again." Later, when he became lost during a snowstorm, he preserved himself by seeking shelter in a hollow tree. On his return to camp he was told: "Your conduct on this occasion hath pleased us much: you have given us evidence of your fortitude, skill and resolution: we hope you will always go on to do great actions, as it is only great actions that can make a great man." Smith replied that he "always wished to do great actions" and "never would do any thing to dishonor" them. The Indians approved of his behavior and promised to buy him "a new gun." Smith concluded: "By being bewildered . . . I lost repute, and was reduced to the bow and arrow; and by lying out two nights here, I regained my credit." After they returned his books and gave him a new gun, he said that for the first time his "heart felt warm towards the Indians."[30]

In a similar way, Billy aspired to become Miami, as for several years his life fell into a regular pattern. "The . . . children, both male and female," he wrote, "are early inured to hardships by their being compelled to fast and bathe their bodies every day in cold water." Even in winter weather, after the Porcupine's morning exhortation to excel, Billy immersed himself in the river. Before fasting, his face was blackened. As he got older the length of his fasts would increase to several days at a time, in preparation for his Vision Quest. At about age eighteen, his education was complete. He was now "old enough to be a man."[31]

Snake-fish Town was "situated on a very delightful spot of ground" on the northwest bank of the Eel River. The village center was "on an even, scrubby oak barren" at the mouth of Mud Creek, but it extended for a mile or so on each side, including a few hundred acres of corn fields. Bogs that were "almost impassable, and impervious thickets of plum, hazel, and black jack" served as a natural protection, as did willow and dwarf poplar trees, shrubs, brambles, and "a very coarse, but luxuriant grass" that provided feed for the horses. In the late 1780s the town had about four hundred residents.[32]

Billy did not lack playmates. The games of the boys enhanced stamina and honed their skills. Hunter recalled that "dancing, running races, wrestling, jumping, swimming, playing with the hoop, throwing the tomahawk, fighting sham battles, and holding councils, made up the most of our amusements." Wells stated that many captives found that "running, playing, and amusing themselves" was "much more pleasing . . . than the confinement of schools." Footraces were popular. Some captives could beat their Indian rivals at short distances, but rarely over the long haul. Alder asserted that "but three Indians . . . could outrace me." John Leeth won both short and longer races, including an intertribal four-hundred-yard event. He outsprinted his swiftest rival in the final stretch to "the great joy" of the Delaware chief who was his adoptive father, but "to the chagrin of the others." Envy was a touchy issue for captives in these highly competitive games. "I was careful not to exceed many of them in shooting," Daniel Boone said, "for no people are more envious than they in this sport. I could observe, in their countenances and gestures, the greatest expressions of joy when they exceeded me; and, when the reverse happened, of envy." Leg wrestling was a favorite of the Miami boys: "Seldom if ever would a boy take defeat smiling. They looked serious, sullen, or angry." Chief Clarence Godfroy described an archery contest in which every boy on two teams was given ten or twelve arrows, and then one contestant on each side would shoot his arrows into the sky as fast and high as he could: "Whenever an Indian's arrow hit the ground he had to stop shooting. If a brave shot nine arrows into the air before any of them hit the ground, nine would be his score." Another two-team contest involved rolling a hoop made of wild grapevine that the boys would try to hit with their arrows. Boys and girls also took pride in being good swimmers. Sometimes villages competed in lacrosse. As Thomas Wildcat Alford said, "All the games we played were calculated to develop strength, skill, and resourcefulness."[33]

The villagers watched the boys at play and evaluated their performances. Parents expressed pride in the accomplishments of their children. "The old men often [took] it upon themselves to advise the young." At night they would tell instructive and amusing "tales of fiction" as well as true stories of past exploits. Alder recalled "the pleasure of cracking nuts around the fires of the wigwams during the long winter evenings while the elder Indians were relating their wonderful adventures, either in war or hunting." He and the other boys "listened to these stories as [if they were from] some ancient oracle relating the history of his tribe and other marvelous stories that had been handed down from generation to generation." Smith remembered fondly the sage advice of Tecaughretanego, who was, in his estimation, "no common person, but was among the Indians, as Socrates in the ancient Heathen world." Hunter praised the "inspiring narrative" of Tshot-che-nou; Henry benefited from the wisdom of Wawatam; and Spencer was in awe of Cooch-coo-cheeh, "a sort of priestess."[34]

"Those story-tellers were masters of the art," Alford recalled. "They could tell offhand a story that would contain suspense, mystery, and surprise, with never a change of countenance to betray the fact that it was fiction." Many of Chief Godfroy's stories have been preserved. Several are humorous, such as "Why a Woman Wiggles When She Walks," which explained how the Great Spirit, while creating woman, became distracted by a dog wagging its tail. A grimmer example was a war story, recorded by Trowbridge, a gruesome account of mutual slaughter during a seventeenth-century battle between the Senecas and the Miamis.[35]

To become a skilled hunter and warrior, Wells had to learn woodcraft and survival skills. The Porcupine would have taught him to reward friends, seek revenge on enemies, revere his elders, and read the signs of the natural world:

> The knowledge of warfare, of history, and of nature, to know the habits of wild creatures, to know about trees, wild plants and fruits, to be able to judge of weather, to foretell what the seasons would be, whether a cold winter or a dry summer—there were signs one might learn to read all these things by—all these . . . constituted a well-rounded education for the average young Indian man.
>
> All these . . . called for a good memory, keen observation, and close application. . . . Endurance and self-control were taught so rigidly that those qualities had become a part of Indian character.[36]

Billy's education would have sharpened his senses. "Every sound of the forest had a meaning. . . . The track of beasts, the flight of birds, the changing colors of the woods, sky, and water were full of significance." John Hunter concluded, "Of all the traits which distinguish the Indian character . . . a nice discrimination is perhaps the most remarkable." The Miamis predicted a mild or harsh winter by whether the shuck was tight or loose on an ear of corn. Billy learned to hear the rain moving through the forest long before it arrived. A bent blade of grass, a turned leaf, a displaced pebble told a story. Moss on tree trunks and the positions of the moon and stars guided him through the woods. He could flake an arrowhead and start a fire by rubbing sticks. He knew how to track both animals and men: "The print of a foot," Little Turtle said, enabled the Miamis "to distinguish not only between men, women, and children, but even tribes." After this intensive training, whenever Wells stepped into the forest his senses were at full alert. "Indians learn to be close observers," Chief Godfroy said. "His life oftentimes depends on what he has seen and can remember."[37] Probably within a year of arriving at Snake-fish Town, Billy was dreaming in Miami, his mind focused not on returning to Kentucky but rather on pleasing his adoptive parents and earning praise. Like young Jonathan Alder, one day he must have admitted to himself, "I was getting to be an Indian in the true sense of the word."[38]

THE RECIPROCITIES OF THE HUNT

"The Indians live in villages from April to November," Wells wrote, "during which time the women cultivate corn, beans, potatoes, pumpkins, and other common vegetables. . . . The remainder of the year is spent in hunting." If he wished to become a man of distinction, Billy had to become a skilled hunter. In the eighteenth century the Miamis conducted buffalo hunts on the vast tallgrass prairies of central Indiana and Illinois, during rutting season in July and in the fall when the buffalo were fat. The entire village, including "old men and young boys," surrounded a herd and set fire to the grass on all sides. Thus entrapped, a great number could be killed, as many as two hundred in a single day. The women skinned them and prepared the meat, which was distributed by the chiefs "with great equity and justice."[39] The Weas, thirty-five miles southwest of Snake-fish Town at Ouiatanon (Lafayette), continued to pursue the rapidly diminishing herds in the latter part of the eighteenth century. Billy may have gone on a few buffalo hunts, but most of his winters were spent in small camps along the Mississinewa or Salamonie Rivers, where beaver, deer, elk and, above all, black bears were the game of choice.

Hunting was not a sport and pastime for the Miamis but rather a way of life and a system of belief. They had a profound respect for the game they hunted; if they behaved properly before, during, and after the hunt, they would propitiate the spirits of the game, and the animals would *willingly* offer themselves to be killed. If they did not, the animals would stay away. Although little is known about Miami hunting rituals, the information we have about Algonquian culture suggests that C. C. Trowbridge's assertion that there were "no ceremonies preceding the departure of a hunting party" and "no feasts connected with hunting" was misinformed. As prehistoric hunters in Spain painted the cave walls of Altamira with images of the large game animals they sought, using sympathetic magic to lure them to be killed, so, Calvin Martin has argued, "dreaming, divination, singing, drumming, sweating, and other forms of hunting magic" were basic to the success of the hunt among the Algonquians. "It was the preliminary spirit hunt . . . which really mattered; by the time the hunter got around to actually bagging the animal it was as good as dead," since in "the 'hunt dream,' performed the night or several nights before the physical hunt, a man's soul-spirit reveals the whereabouts of certain game." Each animal had its own Manitou, or spirit, which would respond favorably if the appropriate rituals were observed. Certain hunters had a particular affinity for the Manitou of a given animal, and they decided how, when, and where to hunt it. These men drew upon their spiritual powers and a pragmatic knowledge based on years of experience in stalking game.[40]

The success of the hunt depended on the weather. A very mild winter in 1786–87 was bad for the hunt, while the following winter, with snow six feet deep in the Miami country, was worse. In the late 1780s, when Billy was learning to hunt, times of famine were common. The fur trade also pressured Indians to slaughter animals for their peltry. During this period, deer and raccoon skins replaced beaver furs as the preferred commodity of the traders.[41]

Billy first hunted small animals—squirrels, raccoons, muskrats, otters, woodchucks, porcupines, and possum—as well as a variety of game birds—wild turkeys, pigeons, quail, ducks, geese, and other waterfowl. Once he had demonstrated his prowess with a bow and arrow, he was given a gun and joined the men. Ring hunts, in which a circular area was set on fire, were used to kill white-tailed deer in great numbers. Smith described the process: the hunters waited until rain was expected before setting fire to a large area of prairie, which, as it spread inward, drove the deer out of the tall grass, enabling them to kill about ten each. Another popular form was a candle hunt. A canoe was camouflaged with bark and bushes, and a small boy stood in the bow holding a lighted torch, which mesmerized deer along the bank of the stream so that they could be shot. "Deer came to the river to eat a kind of water grass, to get which they frequently immerse their whole head and horns," Brickell added. "They seem to be blinded by the light at night, and will suffer a canoe to float close to them. I . . . on one occasion killed twelve fine deer in one night." Savvy hunters knew the habits and habitat of the deer, and shot them at dawn and dusk when they left their hiding places to feed at the edges of the forest. Although Kekionga and Ouiatanon were the two closest trading posts, Wells and other hunters sometimes went down the Wabash to sell their deerskins at Vincennes.[42]

The Miamis were relatively late in entering the beaver trade. Traditionally the Indians admired beavers for their sagacity, industry, and sense of community: "They consult among themselves about what things they must do to maintain their Cottages, their Banks and their Lakes, and about everything that concerns the Preservation of their Commonwealth." Hunter stated, "Formerly, the Indians almost venerated the beaver, on account of the high rational faculties it revealed, in damming creeks, and building houses for its own accommodation, and particularly in educating its young, and avoiding dangers." Although the beaver trade undercut belief in the "Noble Beaver," Billy probably hunted them in the traditional manner.[43]

Beavers were easily killed on land, but in water they were elusive. Sometimes Indians would tap their dams to drain their ponds. Traps baited with bark or succulent shoots of saplings were also effective. In winter, when the ponds froze over, the hunters were able to attack their lodges. Smith described how they would "break a hole in the house," the beavers would then "make their escape into the water;

but as they cannot live long under water, they are obliged to go to some of those broken places to breathe, and the Indians commonly put in their hands, catch them by the hind leg, hawl them on the ice, and tomahawk them." If the hunter took hold of a front leg instead, Alexander Henry added, he could receive "severe wounds from their teeth." To avoid the risk of injury, some Indians grabbed the beaver by the back of the neck. Tanner said that he had "killed as many as one hundred in the course of a month." The tail of the beaver was a prized delicacy; care was taken "to hinder the dogs from touching the bones," and disposing of them in the water was forbidden so as not to "exasperate the spirits of the beavers" and "render the next hunting season unsuccessful."[44]

The black bear was held in the highest esteem by the woodland Indians and treated with an elaborate ceremonialism. Formal rituals were performed before the hunt, during the kill, and at the feast afterwards. Bears were honored for their intellect and strong medicine; they could stand erect like a man and resembled men in other ways: a skinned bear "is downright startling in its similarity to a stout, short-legged human body." Tales were told of women who had married bears, lived with them, and had children, as well as of a time when bears could speak with and even conspired against the Indians. Hunters with a special power over bears fasted before a hunt to induce visions, spoke with respect of the bear (often called "Grandfather" or "the Old Man of the Woods" or "the Master of the Forest" in order not to give offense), directed the hunt, and distributed the meat at the feast. If the hunt was conducted correctly, the hunters would find the bear "well minded" and willing to die; if not, an "evil-minded" bear might attack with fatal consequences. Hunters who were protected by good magic or medicine drove the bears from their winter dens and killed them at close quarters with a knife or tomahawk.[45]

Although captivity narratives contain vivid accounts of bear hunts, none involve the Miamis. However, the fact that two of the Miami moons were named February the Bear and March the Bear Cub, as well as the behavior of Wells after he left the Indians, strongly suggests that he and the Miamis held complex beliefs about and placed great importance on bears and bear hunting.

Indians preferred to hunt for hibernating bears in the late winter and early spring. James Smith's hunting party spotted scratches on a trunk and a hole about forty feet up that could hold a bear. A tall sapling was felled and placed against the tree; it was Smith's job "to climb up and drive out the bear," but he was unable to do so. Finally, a more experienced hunter managed to ignite some dry wood and shove it in the hole, which forced the bear down the tree, so that he could be killed with one well-aimed arrow. If climbing trees to fire bears out of their holes wasn't dangerous enough, Billy faced the more harrowing task of smoking them out of their caves along the Wabash and Mississinewa. The Miami boy selected "would get a tomahawk and a fire-brand and crawl into the holes to hunt the bears. When a brave found a bear he would hit him several times on the end of the nose as this was a very tender spot. The bear did not like . . . [that] so he would run out of the cave." The warriors outside would then kill the bear. Chief Godfroy added, "Miami Indians were very fond of bear meat."[46]

Alexander Henry's narrative best captures bear ceremonialism. While with the Chippewas he observed a pine tree with bear claw marks, broken branches, and a large hollow high up the trunk. The next morning he returned with a hunting party, who spent two days chopping the huge tree down. When Henry advanced toward the hole, "a bear of extraordinary size" emerged, which he was able to shoot "to the great satisfaction of our party." He then witnessed a classic conciliatory speech. His Indian mother took the bear's head in her hands and begged its forgiveness, calling her "grandmother" and placing the blame on "an English-man." Had a Chippewa killed the bear, the speech to propitiate its spirit would have pledged that they loved and respected the bear and had killed her in the proper manner and from necessity. The bear was then skinned, cut up, and carried back to the feast. "As soon as we reached the lodge, the bear's head was adorned with all the trinkets in the possession of the family, such as silver arm-bands and wrist-bands, and belts of wampum; and then laid upon a scaffold, set up for its reception, within the lodge. Near the nose, was placed a large quantity of tobacco." The next day Henry's trusted friend and brother Wawatam "blew tobacco-smoke into the nostrils of the bear, telling me to do the same, and thus appease the anger of the bear, on account of my having killed her." Wawatam gave a speech at the feast deploring "the necessity under which men laboured, thus to destroy their *friends*. He represented, however, that the misfortune was unavoidable, since without doing so, they could by no means subsist." Afterward, everyone "ate heartily," and "the head itself, after remaining three days on the scaffold, was put into the kettle."[47] The Miamis probably observed similar bear-hunting rituals: hunters fasted before the hunt, spoke conciliatory words to the dead bear, and held a ceremonial feast, especially if it was the first bear of the season or the initial kill for a young hunter.

The best evidence that Wells incorporated Miami hunting practices was provided by John Heckewelder, a Moravian missionary. On a trip down the Ohio in the fall of 1792, he and Wells often hunted together, shooting deer, buffalo, and bears. The Delaware custom was that "if a hunter shoots down a deer when another person is present, or even accidentally comes by before the skin is taken off, he presents it to him, saying, 'Friend, skin your deer.'" Wells said exactly that to him on such an occasion. When Heckewelder asked the reason, Wells replied that "it was the custom among the Indians on the Wabash." More telling was an episode when Wells shot a large bear that then "cried piteously." Wells went up and scolded the bear, swatting him with his ramrod for emphasis. Heckewelder inquired what he had said:

> I have ... upbraided him for acting the part of a coward; I told him that he knew the fortune of war, that one or the other of us must have fallen; that it was his fate to be conquered, and he ought to die like a man, like a hero, and not like an old woman; that if the case had been reversed, and I had fallen into the power of *my enemy*, I would not have disgraced my nation as he did, but would have died with firmness and courage, as becomes a true warrior.[48]

Wells talked to the bear sincerely, expecting him to understand; he assumed that bears shared the same high standards of bravery and correct conduct as the Miamis and that a state of war existed between bears and Indians—they were enemies. After he had returned to white society, Wells's mind, at least when he went hunting, was still Miami, and years later he would die "as becomes a true warrior."

VISION QUEST

In early March, when frosty nights were followed by warm, sunshiny days and the branches began to bud, the Miamis knew it was "sugar weather" and would leave their hunting camps and settle near a grove of maple trees. The bark of white beech or elm trees was stripped by the women and made into "vessels . . . that would hold about two gallons each." Then the maple was tapped by driving a tomahawk into the trunk to make a notch, where a long chip of wood was inserted as a spout. The sugar water that dripped out of the tree was gathered in bark vessels and conveyed to brass kettles of various sizes to begin the boiling process. When the water acquired the consistency of syrup, some of it was saved as molasses. As the boiling continued, the syrup became thicker and drier; it was then stirred until it formed a granular sugar of great sweetness. Both the black and white maple were tapped, as well as some walnut trees. "While the women collected the sap, boiled it, and completed the sugar," Henry wrote, "the men were not less busy in cutting wood, making fires, and in hunting and fishing." The sap only ran by day, and the trees bled best when the sun came out and melted a thin film of ice that had formed in the chill of the night. "The way that we commonly used our sugar while encamped," Smith reported, "was by putting it in bear's fat until the fat was almost as sweet as the sugar itself, and in this we dipped our roasted venison." Since periods of famine were more frequent than times of feasting during the long hunting season, the taste of maple sugar was a luscious interlude in the spring that must have brought tears to the eyes of many a Miami.[49]

During his teenage years when Billy Wells was learning to be a Miami hunter, he continued the spiritual discipline of blackening his face and fasting. At some point in the late 1780s, the Porcupine and his wife told him "that his education is complete and that he is old enough to be a man." He was taken to a small hut a few miles from Snake-fish Town and received the following speech from his father:

"My son, it has pleased all the great spirits that dwell above the skies and those that dwell on the earth that you should live to see this day: they have all seen your conduct since I first blacked your face: they know whether you have at all times strictly adhered to the advice I have given you; and I hope they will reward you accordingly. You must remain here until myself or some friend shall come for you."

Billy then fasted, without food or drink, for several days. When his final fast was over, his father returned for him, accompanied by friends and neighbors he had invited to a celebratory feast. Billy was "taken home and bathed in cold water, his head shaved all over except a small part on the top." He was served his meal "in a separate vessel for that purpose." After the feast, he was handed a mirror and bag of vermillion paint. Then he was presented to the company and told he was a man and "ever afterwards considered as such by the people of the village." We don't know for certain whether Billy's Vision Quest included a new name. One tradition maintained that when he became a man the Miamis no longer called him Wild Carrot (Apekonit) but "Blacksnake," suggesting young William Wells had displayed that serpent's honored attributes of keen sight, sagacity, skilled hunting, quickness, and elusiveness.[50]

CHAPTER THREE

WARPATHS

While William Wells was becoming Blacksnake, events beyond his ken or control were shaping his destiny as well as that of the Miamis. Although the Revolution officially ended with the Peace of Paris in 1783, Indian raids across the Ohio continued, as the capture of Wells in the spring of 1784 illustrates. In fact, the terms made the Indians of the Northwest more determined than ever to defend their homeland. "The treaty does not contain a single stipulation for the Indians," Gen. Philip Schuyler gloated to the Iroquois; "they are not even so much as mentioned. . . . We are now Masters of this island, and can dispose of the Lands as we think proper or most convenient to ourselves."[1] The British had abandoned their Indian allies, who, a year after Cornwallis surrendered in October 1781, were victorious at Blue Licks and Upper Sandusky. The United States now laid claim to all Indian land east of the Mississippi. Thus the Peace of Paris sowed the seeds for the bloodiest Indian war in American history.

AMERICAN TREATIES BY "RIGHT OF CONQUEST"

Benjamin Franklin played a key role in obtaining a treaty favorable to the United States and detrimental to the Indians. As he told his fellow commissioner John Jay, "We should insist on the Mississippi as our Western boundary." Franklin's opening gambit to British negotiator Richard Oswald was audacious. It held out the hope for a "sweet reconciliation" with the Americans that might keep them as a partner in the British Empire. But England, Franklin insisted, had been a cruel aggressor that had caused untold suffering by "its scalping and burning parties," and it needed to do something "voluntary" to demonstrate "good will."[2]

Lord Shelburne's administration was more concerned about the fate of the Loyalists than that of the Indians. Whenever they brought up the one issue, however, Franklin was sure to raise the other, delivering a diatribe on how the Loyalists had instigated Indian atrocities. To put the English on the defensive, on 12 March 1782, Franklin had published a hoax: a letter claiming the Americans had intercepted packs containing 950 scalps, including "29 little Infants' Scalps . . . ript out of their Mothers' Bellies," sent by the Senecas to Frederick Haldimand, governor of Quebec. Thus while the Americans avoided the issue of Indian ownership of the land west of the Alleghenies, Franklin exaggerated warrior atrocities to avoid pointed questions in turn about American ones, especially Gnadenhütten, which the English negotiators did not mention.[3]

Shelburne, while in the opposition, had denounced Britain's allies as "bloodthirsty savages." In defense of the treaty he blandly stated: "the Indian nations were not abandoned to their enemies; they were remitted to the care of neighbors . . . who were certainly the best qualified for softening and humanizing their hearts." Whether spoken with cynicism or naiveté, the divergence of Shelburne's words from reality is troubling. In the final negotiations, conducted by John Adams and John Jay while Franklin was bedridden with gout, the main debate was over the extent of American fisheries. Indian rights to their own land were never seriously discussed. Britain accepted the American demand for a Mississippi border, not to betray their Indian allies but rather to counter the power plays of Spain and France.[4]

George Washington had strong opinions about how the confederation government should implement the Peace of Paris. The best way to tie the frontier to the rest of the country, he argued, was to settle the area with veterans of the Revolution, who "would always be ready and willing (in case of hostility) to combat the Savages, and check their incursions." Since the Indians had been Britain's allies, the United States should "consider them as a deluded People" and allow them to remain within designated boundaries. In acquiring land from the Indians, Washington cautioned, "care should be taken neither to yield nor to grasp at too much." Treaties with the Indians would enable the government to control settlement of the Northwest, preventing land jobbers and "a parcel of Banditti" from "skimming and disposing of the Cream of the Country." In theory, this policy would be peaceful and progressive: "the gradual extension of our Settlements will as certainly cause the Savage as the Wolf to retire; both being beasts of prey tho' they differ in shape. In a word there is nothing to be obtained by an Indian War but the Soil they live on and this can be had by purchase at less expense, and without . . . bloodshed."[5] Washington's arguments were often repeated. Once treaties were signed and settlers arrived, hunting ground would shrink, the Indians would then sell their remaining lands cheaply and move toward the setting sun. It all seemed quite reasonable; but as Goya once warned, "The dream of reason breeds monsters."

When Detroit commander Major De Peyster informed the Wabash Indians of the terms of the treaty, they used "expressions not proper to be committed to paper." By "endeavoring to assist you," a Wea orator complained, "it seems we have wrought our own ruin." Mohawk chief Joseph Brant sneered, "England had Sold the Indians to Congress"; Little Turkey of the Cherokees added, "The peacemakers and our Enemies have talked away our Lands at a Rum Drinking." One warrior lamented: "The disgrace is almost killing us. . . . We are ashamed to Death for we don't consider ourselves conquered and our Warriors spirits are still strong & firm." The Americans even rubbed salt in the wounds: "Your Fathers the English have made Peace with us for themselves," Major Wall told the Shawnees, "but forgot you their Children, who fought with them, and neglected you like Bastards."[6]

Frederick Haldimand was grief-stricken and ashamed when he received a copy of the preliminary treaty in April 1783. Soon he was confronted by angry Indians telling him that "they never could believe that our King could pretend to cede to the Americans what was not his to give. . . . They were the faithful Allies of the King of England, but not his subjects. . . . They would defend their own Just Rights or perish in the attempt to the last man." Haldimand feared a repetition of Pontiac's Revolt, the Indian uprising that had provided a bloody coda to the French and Indian War. "These people," Haldimand assured Lord North in London, "have as enlightened Ideas of the nature & Obligations of Treaties as the most Civilized Nations have, and know that no infringement of the Treaty of 1768 . . . can be binding upon them without their Express Concurrence & Consent."[7]

Under pressure from Indians, fur traders, agents of the Indian Department, and his own conscience, Haldimand devised a policy to counter the harshest terms of the Peace of Paris. Britain would keep the frontier posts, support Indian rights to the land north of the Ohio, and encourage a confederacy in their own defense. The British cited the American refusal to reimburse the Loyalists for their losses or pay their prewar debts as justification for retaining the posts. The new policy was presented to thirty-five Indian nations gathered at Sandusky in the late summer of 1783. Joseph Brant called for a permanent confederation and asked what specific military support England was prepared to give the Indians, if it came to war with the Americans. The British reply was evasive. Yet the Indians knew that they had to make the best of a bad situation—even wavering British backing was better than none.[8]

At the Treaty of Fort Stanwix, 22 October 1784, the American commissioners bluntly told the Six Nations: "The King of Great Britain ceded to the United States *the whole,* by the right of conquest they might *claim the whole.* . . . You are a subdued people." In spite of eloquent arguments to the contrary, the Americans imposed their terms, which defined the boundaries of Iroquoia in upstate New York and compelled the Iroquois to cede their claims to the vast area north of the Ohio. Thus the Six Nations were effectively cut off from their Indian allies in the West, who now would have to sign treaties dictated by the Americans.[9]

The long, tangled history of the Iroquois and their western allies involved microbes, muskets, and beaver skins. As early as 1639 the Dutch, and later the English, armed the five Iroquois nations, giving them military superiority over their rivals in the fur trade. The best beaver furs were found in colder regions to the north, home of the Hurons, who were rapidly dying off from viruses carried inadvertently by Jesuit missionaries and French traders. Catastrophic deaths from disease soon spread to the Iroquois, who engaged in a series of mourning-wars to replenish their people. Iroquois warriors overran neighboring tribes—the Petuns, Neutrals, and Eries, for example—and forced the Miamis and other nations to flee further west. Armed by the French, these Indians, by the end of the seventeenth century, had driven the Iroquois back to upstate New York. Those who remained in the Ohio Valley, mainly Senecas, were known as the Mingos. By the early eighteenth century, the Miamis, Eel River Miamis, Weas, and Piankashaws had returned to their villages near the Wabash. For a time the Delawares and Shawnees were also dominated by the Six Nations, who had added the Tuscaroras to their confederacy, until they moved to Ohio and asserted their independence. Remnants of the Hurons and Petuns on the Sandusky became the Wyandots. The Ottawas, Potawatomis, and Chippewas, known as the Three Fires, also lived in what would soon be named the Northwest Territory.[10]

Although the Iroquois no longer occupied the Northwest, during most of the eighteenth century they still claimed it. The British supervisor of Indian affairs, Sir William Johnson, knew that the Six Nations did not even control the Mingos on the Ohio. In 1761 he made an agreement in Detroit that had the effect, according to one witness, of casting "off ye Onandago Yoke (of ye Six Nations) from ye Delawares, Shawanas, Wyandots, Picks or Twwtwees [Miamis], & others to ye Westward which makes those Nations a Separate Power Independent of the Six Nations." Lt. Gov. Cadwallader Colden warned Johnson that the best solution would be "to Treat with the distant Western Indians separately." Nevertheless, at Johnson Hall in July 1765 and then at the Treaty of Fort Stanwix of 1768, Johnson asserted that the Iroquois alone had the right to sell the land south of the Ohio, much of it Shawnee hunting ground. Lord Dunmore's War of 1774 was the result, as was the settling of Kentucky, which triggered ongoing raids and counterraids across the Ohio. Thus the Indian nations of the Old Northwest had good reason to distrust, if not detest, the Iroquois for ceding their lands and stigmatizing them as subject tribes metaphorically reduced to wearing petticoats. When the Iroquois capitulated once more at the Treaty of Fort Stanwix of 1784, those nations felt betrayed.[11]

The American commissioners next traveled down the Ohio to Fort McIntosh at the mouth of Beaver Creek. On 21 January 1785 they signed a treaty with "the sachems and warriors of the Wyandot, Delaware, Chippewa, and Ottawa nations." When the Indians asserted that they still owned the lands north of the Ohio, the commissioners "answered them in a high tone," telling them that "you being conquered, your lands must be at our disposal . . . to *give* not to receive." Erkurius Beatty recorded that the chiefs "spoke a great deal of Nonsense & our Commissioners spoke very pointed, which brought them to the Conclusion, that we were sole proprietors of the Country, & they obliged to come upon such terms as we pleased." The Americans, Delaware chief Buckongahelas reported, "said the Great Spirit was on their Side by which they had gotten . . . all the Country." Since they were "as strong as a hickory tree that is not to be overpowered," their plan was to survey and settle the land promptly. The chiefs who signed represented those villages most exposed to American frontiersmen, not the majority of their nations or Brant's confederated warriors, who reacted to news of the treaty with "disgust."[12]

Capt. John Doughty at Fort McIntosh cogently stated how counterproductive an American policy that dictated its terms by right of conquest would prove to be: "This treaty and the one at Fort Stanwix . . . have had the effect to unite the Indians and induce them to make a common cause of what they suppose their present grievances." Furthermore, the British were telling the Indians that they had not ceded their lands outright, but merely put them "under the protection of the United States" and that "our claim in consequence of that cession ought not to deprive them of their lands without purchase." As a result, the westward Indians would oppose American settlers with a formidable confederacy. When he learned of the treaty, British Indian agent Alexander McKee wrote that the "refractory Tribes will never tamely submit to be deprived of A Country, on which they think their existence depends."[13]

Although each peace treaty made war more likely, Congress assumed that Indian nations would acquiesce to yielding their land. What preoccupied the government was the problem of squatters and speculators. In the spring of 1785 Col. Josiah Harmar reported that the "country will soon be inhabited by a banditti whose actions are a disgrace to human nature." From Wheeling to the Great Miami "there is scarcely one bottom on the river but has one or more families." Gen. Richard Butler at Fort Finney was alarmed by the "boats passing daily to the falls [Louisville] with goods and families, and by the numbers which pass seem as if the old states would depopulate, and the inhabitants be transported to the new." Furthermore, "these people consider themselves out of the trammels of law, and have too great a propensity to remain in that lawless situation." Washington warned that speculators, "in defiance of the proclamation of Congress . . . roam over the Country on the Indian side of the Ohio, mark out Lands, Survey, and even settle them. This gives great discontent to the Indians, and will unless measures are taken in time to prevent it, inevitably produce a war with the western Tribes."[14]

Since the Ohio Valley lands were a crucial source of revenue for the insolvent nation, as well as the area where soldiers of the Revolution would live, it was essential to bring squatters and speculators under control. In 1784, 1785, and 1787, Congress passed ordinances to regulate land sales and to organize settlement. The government wanted to avoid the chaotic situation in Kentucky, where overlapping land claims created a lawyer's paradise. The territory would be blocked off into rectangular lines that ignored natural boundaries such as rivers and lakes, let alone Indian villages and hunting grounds. Then the Americans would survey the lands *before* they were sold to ensure clear title. Settlement, Washington said, should consist of a "compact and progressive Seating," which the Northwest Ordinance of 1787 defined as by specific townships, each with a section set aside to support education.[15]

The ideal was the classic New England town, complete with village green. As Rufus Putnam put it, "the western country should in their manners, morals, religion, and policy, take the eastern states for their modle." He and the Ohio Company followed this plan at Marietta in April 1788, the first settlement in Ohio. The site of numerous Indian mounds, soon the town had mulberry trees along its broad streets and public squares, and impressed early visitors by the industry of its inhabitants. Yet squatters were still rampant in the territory, and land hunger and Indian-hating were the dominant passions of the day. Before they "civilized" the Indians, the United States had first to civilize the lawless frontiersmen, bringing them under federal authority and making them "useful citizens." Thus the initial government of the territory would not be in the settlers' hands; instead Congress would appoint a governor, secretary, and three judges. At five thousand free settlers they could achieve self-government; at sixty thousand they could petition for statehood. The Federalists wanted orderly settlements in the Northwest where citizens practiced civic virtue, placing allegiance to the nation above selfish interests. The basic flaw in this enlightened scheme was that the United States itself did not have "clear title" to the land north of the Ohio. From the Indian perspective, all Americans were lawless squatters.[16]

Unless the Shawnees and Miamis signed peace treaties, war was inevitable. In October 1785 the U.S. Army constructed Fort Finney at the mouth of the Great Miami and called for a council. At Kekionga (Fort Wayne), American envoys received a "cool, and astonishingly indifferent, or rather irresolute and dubious" reception. They were "grossly insulted" by Miami warriors and their horses were stolen. Their conclusion: "This nation is somewhat hostile, and illy disposed." Because of British influence, "they will not easily be induced to receive the protection and friendship" of the United States. At the Shawnee towns, British agent Matthew Elliott told the Indians that they "had better fight like men than give up their lands and starve like dogs." When the reluctant Shawnees arrived on 14 January 1786, they did so in style. Moluntha and his warriors, followed by a head woman with the women and children, sang as they processed to the council house and took their seats—men at the west door, women and children the east. Informal talks were held until more Indians arrived; but most of the time the Shawnees played lacrosse by day and danced in the council house at night.[17]

Despite these elaborate Indian festivities designed to foster the goodwill necessary for negotiations, Richard Butler adhered to the pattern of previous treaties. The Shawnees were told that the British "had ceded the whole of the country on this side of the lakes to the Americans." As a result, the Indians "were now left to the mercy of the United States" and "ought to be thankful if allowed to occupy any part of the country." Kekewepelethy, or Great Hawk (also known as Captain Johnny), eloquently protested the "hard" American terms:

"The Great Spirit gave us this country, we do not understand measuring out the lands, it is all ours. . . . Brothers, you seem to grow proud, because you have thrown down the King of England." Then he placed on the table a belt of wampum that symbolized the Ohio River boundary. Butler took offense at this and accused the chief of using "improper language" and "the greatest falsehoods." He told him that he would "not alter" the terms, which were "liberal" and "just." If the Shawnees refused to sign, then the full power of the United States would be deployed "to distress your obstinate nation" and bring about "the destruction of your women and children." George Rogers Clark then took his cane, pushed the belt onto the floor, "and set his foot on it," causing the Indians to march out, "very sullen." Later Moluntha said that Kekewepelethy had been "misunderstood" and acknowledged that the Americans owned the country. He only hoped that they would "take pity on our women and children." After the treaty was signed, Butler recorded in his journal that "the Indians . . . continued drinking all" the next day. The treaty, he claimed, had been "transacted with great care, and gave the Indians perfect satisfaction."[18]

The reality was different. Iroquois warriors denounced the Treaty of Fort Stanwix and threatened the chiefs who signed it. Delaware chief Captain Pipe and the Half King of the Wyandots were compelled to renounce the Treaty of Fort McIntosh. On 29 April 1786 the "principal chiefs of the Shawnee," including Moluntha, sent a message to the British stating that the Americans "have deceived us, by telling us the King of Great Britain had ceded the whole country to them, and we were not sensible of the error we have committed till our friend [Matthew] Elliot explained it to us." The chiefs urged the British to give them aid and advice, since "we have been cheated by the Americans who are striving to work our destruction."[19]

In sum, the U.S. government had made a bad situation worse. By treating the Indians as conquered people and dictating terms, they had enraged them and brought the new country to the brink of a major war it was not prepared to fight. Colonel Harmar commanded only a few hundred ill-trained and poorly equipped troops in the Northwest. The lands north of the Ohio that were supposed to reward Revolutionary soldiers, provide homesteads for yeoman farmers, and fund the new nation would have to be paid for in blood.

KENTUCKY INVADES MIAMI COUNTRY

William Wells, now named Blacksnake, was unaware of the imposed treaties that compelled the warriors of Snake-fish Town to raid Kentucky and return with scalps, horses, and prisoners. Since no French or British traders resided in the village, the historical record is scanty. What we do know is that a series of bloody events near Vincennes caused the Wabash Indians in the summer of 1786 to display their military force.

After the Revolution, American settlers spread "like a plague of locusts in the territories of the Ohio River." About sixty arrived at Vincennes, some of them yeoman farmers but others backcountry desperados. In June 1785 John Filson visited the town of about three hundred houses and noted the friendliness of the neighboring tribes as well as the French inhabitants. He also saw that the Americans were converting their corn into whiskey and selling it to the Indians. In the fall when Filson returned, he found "a Considerable alteration in the disposition of the people"—a prohibition on selling "the noxious Juices had kindled a Spirit of Jealousy and aspersion between the French and Americans here." Even the court had been corrupted. As a result, "a hovering Cloud pregnant with innumerable evil was obvious over Post Vincent."[20]

Father Pierre Gibault shared Filson's dire assessment. Although Jean Marie Phillippe Le Gras and the other magistrates did what they could "to maintain good order," barbarism ruled, might was right, and theft and plunder prevailed. "Debauchery and dissoluteness are what pass here for genteel entertainment," Gibault observed. Without a military commander and a garrison, as well as a strong government and a solid prison, civilized society was impossible. "I could name a large number of people murdered in all the villages in these parts, French, English, and Spanish, without any consequences. . . . Within the last month I can count ten." He, too, put major blame on the liquor trade, lamenting that the Indians only sold their meat and peltry for "l'eau de vie," which unscrupulous traders were happy to supply.[21]

In the spring of 1786, a Piankashaw war party attacked a boat on the Wabash, killed one man, and wounded two others. The Americans sent to bring back the wounded men attacked some Indians from Vincennes who had recently traded their furs for whiskey. The Americans got the worst of the fight: three were killed and several wounded. One Indian was shot twice in the thigh. News of this skirmish spread "terror" to the French in Vincennes, while the Americans "immediately raised a Stockade . . . to defend themselves." Le Gras consoled the local chiefs, who "forgave the fault of the Americans in appearance though not from the heart."[22]

The most notorious American was Daniel Sullivan, whom Le Gras termed "a very dangerous man and pernicious to the public peace." His men built a blockhouse at Sullivan's Station on Little River near Vincennes and plowed their fields under armed guard. The truce that Le Gras negotiated was short-lived. A Miami war party killed several Americans at Bellefontaine, near Cahokia. In late May Indians shot one man outside Vincennes and burned another, leaving "the remainder of the body hung up in a tree." On 1 June 1786, John Filson wrote a petition to Congress requesting a land office, a regular government, and a strong garrison. The next day his canoe was ambushed and two of his men were "cruelly massacred." Filson fled, pursued by a "bloodthirsty savage" with a raised tomahawk in "his terrible right hand, to lodge me into the land of silence." English trader William Park concluded that "the Indians here are in a wavering situation they are mostly all gone to war." An American returning from Kekionga reported that twenty-six Miami war parties were in Kentucky; some Eel River Indians were seen returning from a raid on a station near Louisville with two scalps and a prisoner.[23]

On 21 June 1786, Indians shot at farmers in their fields, scalping one wounded man, William Donnally, before they fled. Sullivan's men sought retaliation. A friendly Indian under the protection of the French was shot and then scalped by Donnally's wife and "dragged . . . like a pig at the tail of a horse" through the town. The shocked French magistrates sent armed men to guard the local Indians and ordered the Americans to leave the village "Bagg and Baggage Immediately." Sullivan defied the mandate and scorned the French for defending the Indians.[24]

In mid-July Le Gras was warned that 450 warriors were approaching. Maj. Francis Bosseron met them with flags of peace and brought the chiefs into Vincennes for a talk. They carried "twelve *nattes*," or sacred war bundles, indicating several villages had sent warriors, each of whom was "anxious to avenge himself on the Americans." Le Gras gave the chiefs gifts and lighted a peace pipe, but made it clear that the French would fight to protect the Americans. The chiefs were "quite surprised," since "they had always counted upon the help of their brothers, the French," who "alone never deceive us." An Eel River war chief, probably the Soldier, told Le Gras that the Wabash Indians "for the last few moons" had been receiving war belts urging them "to destroy all the men wearing hats who occupy this island and who seem to be leagued against us to drive us away from the lands which the Master of Life has given to us." He and his warriors had resolved that "if we have to die, let it be bravely."[25]

The next morning the Indians opened fire on Sullivan's blockhouse. Again Le Gras negotiated with the chiefs, who argued that the French were also "insulted every day by the Americans" and "ought to help the Indians instead of stopping them." Le Gras reproached the Indians for their "lack of gratitude" and vowed that his men would protect the town. The chiefs agreed to lift their siege; but before they left their young men ransacked some American houses, stole horses, and slaughtered livestock. The Soldier warned that if his warriors had to return "at roasting ear time" in the fall "they would be able to make themselves doors in order to come in without asking anybody."[26]

During the negotiations, Le Gras learned that Kentucky vigilantes led by John Hardin and James Patten had attacked a friendly Miami and Piankashaw hunting camp near Saline Creek, killing six and wounding seven, all of them related to chiefs Pacanne and Montour. Hardin, however, was killed and his men "unanimously resolved to return" home. Le Gras could not understand why the Americans had killed their own allies and "cut and hacked them to pieces, a thing most unnatural, barbaric and repulsive." Fortunately, the Soldier's men did not learn of this atrocity, "which would have enraged them," until they reached their Wabash villages.[27]

If Wells was too young to accompany the Soldier to Vincennes, he would have heard warriors' accounts upon their return. As Americans and Indians exchanged murders and sought vengeance, pressure must have mounted for Wells and other boys his age to prepare for the warpath. Until Blacksnake proved his bravery and brought home a scalp, no respected girl of Snake-fish Town would wish to marry him.

As the Wabash Indians intensified their raids across the Ohio, Col. Levi Todd informed Governor Patrick Henry of Virginia that the Kentuckians wanted to "retaliate at pleasure." Since Secretary of War Knox knew the army was ill-prepared, he ordered Harmar to avoid deploying federal troops. Henry, therefore, authorized the Kentucky counties to call up their militias under the commond of George Rogers Clark. His plan was to lead a force directly against Snake-fish Town and Kekionga, while Benjamin Logan's men would attack the Shawnee villages at the headwaters of the Mad River.[28]

In mid-September twelve hundred men assembled in Louisville. Valuing their stomachs over strategic surprise, they insisted on marching first to Vincennes, where their provisions would be brought by boat. As they neared the town, Clark sent Daniel Sullivan ahead with twenty men, who captured a dozen "loitering" Indians. After being "examined & dismissed," they spread word of the American invasion. Because of low water on the Wabash, the boats arrived two weeks late with spoiled meat. Dissension had been prevalent from the start and now large numbers of men deserted. His force shrinking daily, Clark was still determined to proceed up the Wabash, destroying villages as he went. After two or three days of marching on half rations, the Lincoln County militia shouted "Who's for home?" and departed. The few hundred remaining troops "concluded that all had better return" and they, too, left for Kentucky in "vile disorder." Clark had been denied his long-sought victory over the Wabash Indians. The mass desertion of his men, however, may have averted a major defeat. A day's march up the Wabash, at Pine Creek near present Williamsport, hundreds of warriors, including the Soldier's Eel River men, had prepared an ambush for Clark's undisciplined militia.[29]

While Clark's debacle was taking place, on October 6 Benjamin Logan's seven hundred men arrived at Wakatomica. Since Moluntha had made peace, the Shawnees had not believed a deserter's early warning. As the militia rode into view, the chief hoisted the U.S. flag above the council house and welcomed them, wearing a white robe and a tri-corner hat and holding the treaty in his hand. The Kentuckians, who had not come to parley, took Moluntha prisoner. When

Hugh McGary demanded to know if he had been at Blue Licks, Moluntha indicated that he had. McGary then grabbed a small "squaw hatchet," shouted "I'll show you squaw play," and buried it in the chief's forehead. In spite of Logan's orders not to harm the prisoners, a defiant McGary vowed he would chop down any man who challenged his right to kill Indians.[30]

Col. Thomas Kennedy led a charge against a village on the opposite bank of the Mad River. As he rode down some fleeing women, he slashed left and right, cleaving the skull of one and slicing off the fingers of another, at which point "the squaws all fell to their knees and begged for their lives." One warrior was shot in the leg but managed to hide in the tall grass. While Captain Irwin was ordering his men to pursue the fugitive, "the Indian raised up and shot the Captain dead on the spot." William Lytle recalled: "We dispatched all the warriors that we overtook, and sent the women and children prisoners to the rear." At least ten Indians died in the initial skirmishing and twenty-eight were captured. Over the next several days, Logan's men reduced seven towns to ashes and destroyed fifteen thousand bushels of corn.[31]

At Mackachack, a Delaware who was courting a Shawnee was captured, confined to a cabin, and forced to stand on a stool with a rope around his neck and one arm tied to a wall. The next day, Simon Kenton stated, "a particular friend of mine" tomahawked him. When the fatal blow was struck, the young victim made an effort to maintain his dignity by holding his head high while adjusting and smoothing his breech clout "as well and carefully as he could."[32]

"I am sorry that this disgraceful affair should have happened," Harmar wrote to Knox, "as Melanthy had always been represented as a friend to the United States." Ebenezer Denny noted: "Colonel Logan destroyed all their towns, killed and scalped eleven Indians. . . . Molunthy . . . was tomahawked after he had delivered himself up. Logan found none but old men, women and children in the towns; they made no resistance; the men were literally murdered."[33]

Fearing that without British arms the Indian cause was doomed, Brant had sailed earlier to London. On 4 January 1786 he had asked Secretary of State Lord Sydney whether "his majesty's faithful Allies" would be supplied if war broke out with the Americans and received

vague generalities for an answer. Sydney had instructed Canadian
governor Sir Guy Carleton, Lord Dorchester, to avoid "open and
avowed Assistance, should Hostilities commence." Yet it would not
be "consistent with justice or good Policy to abandon" the Indians
to the tender mercies of the Americans. Dorchester wrote that the
Indians must "clearly understand" that Canada was "a small part of
the King's Dominions" without the power to declare a war that might
"involve half the globe with all the Seas in Blood." The Indians must
be assured of "our friendship . . . good wishes and . . . best endeav-
ours" to procure "a solid peace with the thirteen states." By the end
of the year, Dorchester had hardened his position: if the Americans
tried to take the posts "war must be repelled by war."[34]

Brant returned from England convinced that the British would
never fight on the side of the Indians. His goal was to keep the confederacy united in order to reach a just accommodation with the Americans. At a council held at the mouth of the Detroit River, he urged the
Indians to "be unanimous," obey "the Great Spirit," and confront the
Americans with courage and resolution. The fifteen "United Indian
Nations," including the Miamis and the Eel River tribe, drafted a
speech to their "Brothers" in Congress. The "mischief and confusion"
since the Revolution were due to American insistence on having their
own way, selecting council sites without consultation, assuming the
Indians were a conquered people, and negotiating with the nations
separately. To correct these wrongs, the confederation called for a
general treaty in the spring of 1787. Until then, the Americans would
have to keep their people "from crossing the Ohio." Otherwise, "fresh
ruptures" would result in "the unnecessary effusion of blood."[35]

Meanwhile, Clark tried to take charge at Vincennes. He comman-
deered supplies, ordered the local citizens to help rebuild Fort Patrick
Henry, and called for a council with the Wabash Indians, which they
refused. When three Spanish traders arrived in the town to barter
with the Indians, he arrested them and confiscated their trade goods.
This aroused the ire of James Wilkinson, a secret spy for Spain in Lexington. In December 1786 a Richmond, Virginia, paper published a
letter from "a gentleman in Kentucky" that accused Clark of "raising
a regiment of his own men" to serve his treasonous purposes. "Clark
is eternally drunk, and yet full of design. . . . A strike is meditated

against St. Louis and Natchez." Although Clark *would* become a drunkard and plot a filibuster expedition, Wilkinson's accusations were false at the time. Yet the damage had been done. The charges were sent to Congress, which ordered Harmar to garrison Vincennes and establish American authority there. By the spring of 1787, the chaotic situation that Filson and Gibault deplored the previous year had become worse.[36]

The Shawnees did not deliver the confederation's message to Congress until 17 July 1787. That same day Harmar's troops marched into Vincennes. Three days before that, Congress had passed the Northwest Ordinance, which belatedly stipulated that "the utmost good faith shall always be observed towards the Indians; their lands and property shall never be taken from them without their consent." But it also called for a territorial government and a survey of the land north of the Ohio. Thus the country that the Indians had wanted to establish as their homeland in a definitive general treaty with the United States was already in the process of being sold and settled. The slim chance for peace was now lost. The Wabash Indians, allied with the Shawnees, vowed to escalate hostilities in the hope that their terror tactics might stop the settlers from coming and force the government to reconsider its position. Among those who took the warpath was a young man from Snake-fish Town known as Blacksnake.[37]

THE MIAMIS RAID KENTUCKY

About the time he turned eighteen in 1788, Wells made the momentous decision to go on the warpath. He had been brought up to be a warrior and so his status in the village depended on bravery in battle. As a hunter he had acquired the skills of cunning, courage, and marksmanship. Until a young man had joined a war party, however, he could not paint himself with vermillion or hold up a scalp and sing of his valorous deeds. More important, he would not be considered "in all respects a man" and could not marry well. "It is not . . . extraordinary that they should love war," John Hunter wrote, "since . . . their happiness, their standing in society, and their sexual relations, make it necessary that they should excel, or at least strive to" on the field of battle. No wonder that a white captive like Wells, in a world where avoiding shame and winning praise were essential, sought distinction as a warrior.[38]

The Ohio Valley frontier was replete with stories of white captives who became warriors, sometimes raiding their own families. John Ward, for example, fought for the Shawnees at Point Pleasant, where his father died, and against his brothers. In his last skirmish he was mortally wounded, and his brother James heard him "groaning and calling for help in the Shawnee language." Timothy Dorman attacked his former neighbors and scalped the daughter of a man he once worked for. Stephen Ruddell grew up with Tecumseh and fought at Fallen Timbers. Colin Calloway concluded that "white warriors were a recurrent phenomenon" who "threatened Euro-American assumptions of racial superiority" and became objects of dread: "because it was feared they had become 'more Indian than the Indians,' renegades became the terror of successive frontiers." Thus Wells was doing what many others had done before him. He was also crossing a cultural line that might make his return to the white world impossible.[39]

White captives were not coerced to take the warpath. At eighteen, Wells may have been told that he was free to return to Kentucky. Jonathan Alder had seen among the Shawnees "our favorite hunting ground taken from us, our crops destroyed, towns burned, women and children sent off in the dead of winter, perhaps to starve," and as a result he despised the whites. "I . . . felt sorely on these occasions and acted as they do—revengeful and hateful to the race." He went on his first horse-stealing trip to Kentucky when he was sixteen: "To me, nothing seemed wrong so far as the whites were concerned. We had suffered so much at their hands that all seemed to be fair."[40] Snake-fish Town had not been attacked, yet Wells would have heard a litany of atrocity stories about the Big Knives, including Hugh McGary's murder of Moluntha and Daniel Sullivan's provocations in Vincennes. He must have seen scalps brought in and prisoners burnt. At this point in his life he knew which side he was on.

Traditionally, the woodland Indians engaged in two kinds of wars. National wars against other nations were approved by war chiefs and village elders, who planned a campaign and requested a commitment from many warriors. In contrast, small war parties usually originated in a simpler way. "When an Indian wishes to go to war," Wells wrote, "he informs one or two of his most intimate friends of his intention, and asks them if they will go with him. The party is then made up by their informing as many as they wish. Their intentions are kept a secret from all the others. . . . The party always leaves the villages in the night secretly."[41] Probably Blacksnake first went on the warpath in this way. Yet intensified hostilities between the Wabash Indians and the Americans may have blurred the old distinctions. In the late 1780s the Indians were waging, in effect, a national war by means of small war parties. The council house must have been the site of eloquent debates until it was decided to launch relentless and merciless attacks on Kentucky settlements and flatboats coming down the Ohio River.

Even small war parties had to observe elaborate rituals in order to foster each warrior's purity and power. The leader fasted to induce a guiding vision. Blacksnake and the other young men also fasted and visited the sweat house, where they drank bitterroot tea. Sexual contact with women was strictly forbidden during the campaign. Each man prepared his weapons and packed parched corn and jerked meat in his blanket roll for his rations, as well as strips of deerskin and sinews to mend moccasins. Of greatest importance was the sacred war pack, or *natte*, which contained the totem of the tribe. Wells wrote that "the war budget" held "something belonging to each of the party, and representing some animal, as for example a snake's skin, a buffalo's tail, a wolf's head, a mink's skin, or the feathers of some extraordinary bird." His contribution was probably the skin of a blacksnake. Thomas Morris noted, "They carry their God in a bag, which is hung in the front of their encampment, and is visited by none but the priest." In the evenings on the march, Hamilton recorded, "they sung to their budget God in uncouth but melancholy strains." The *natte* contained powerful magic, which, if properly respected, would ensure the success of the war party. For the Miamis and other woodland Indians, this meant they would triumph over the enemy and return home safely.[42]

The leader's reputation depended on bringing his men back unharmed, especially any teenage boys seeing their first action.

The wise old Tecaughretanego summed up the essential strategy to James Smith: "the art of war consists in ambushing and surprising our enemies, and in preventing them from ambushing and surprising us." At a time when their numbers were diminishing, Indians felt acutely the loss of a single man. To prevent this from happening, it was imperative that all warriors observe the proper rituals. The person selected to carry the sacred pack on his back always "marches in front, and leads the party to the enemy." When the warriors camped for the night, "No one is allowed to lay his pack on a log, nor is any one suffered to talk about home or about women while the party is going towards the enemy." The hearts of four-legged animals were "carefully preserved" and then "cut up into small pieces and burnt." Meat was roasted on specially prepared sticks and eaten almost raw, since "the more blood they eat, the more heroic and vicious they will be in battle." Stepping over the fire was forbidden, "every one must go round it and always in the same direction with the sun." The fire was laid out from west to east. The old men, "those who are respected," camped on the south side and the young men, "those who respect," on the north. The young men were expected "to cook the food for the old men . . . furnish them wood . . . mend their moccasins & leggings . . . bring them water, and minister to their every want." Wells probably assisted his maternal uncle and learned the rules of war from him. No guard was posted at night, but weapons were kept handy and a warrior would nudge the man next to him if he sensed danger.[43]

The important thing to note is that these taboos demanded individual discipline. Since each warrior knew that he would be shunned if he failed to conduct himself properly, no corporal punishment was required to maintain order. James Smith, one of the few men at the time to study the Indian art of war, stated that it was "a capital mistake" to assume that the Indians were "undisciplined savages" who did as they pleased in a fight. "They are the best disciplined troops in the known world. . . . As they are a sharp, active kind of people, and war is their principal study . . . they have arrived at considerable perfection." Indian warriors were usually under "good command," promptly obeyed orders, and could "act in concert" on an extensive field of battle. Richard Butler noted: "the young fellows . . . have grown up through the course of war, and trained like young hounds to the blood." No wonder Col. Henry Bouquet, the victor at Bushy Run, called the Algonquians "the best Warriors in the Woods."[44]

In the evenings around the campfire, the leader of the war party would discuss his plans and "deliver speeches to the men, in order to animate and encourage them" but also to remind them of the dangers they faced. Hamilton overheard a Miami chief say, "Young men! We are now going to war . . . let us bear in mind that some of us must fall, and the rest return in mourning. . . . We must die, when it is the willing of . . . the master of life. . . . Our method of making war is by surprise . . . let us act our part as men." At a similar gathering the warriors responded, "Ho, Ho! It is well. We are ready to die: you have only to speak." When one aged warrior was asked why he still wanted to fight, he said, "I am too lame to run away, War is my vocation, I had rather after my death have my flesh torn off the bones by wild beasts, than that it should lye to rot idly in the ground." This was the warrior ethos that Blacksnake shared.[45]

On 7 July 1790, Harry Innes in Danville wrote to Secretary of War Henry Knox about the "depredatory war and plundering" Indians had conducted in Kentucky since the fall of 1783. After admitting that it was "difficult and almost impossible to discriminate what tribes are the offenders," Innes estimated that in the past seven years "fifteen hundred souls have been killed and taken in the district, and . . . upwards of twenty thousand horses have been taken and carried off" as well as other property. One historian has concluded that the Indians killed 3,600 people in Kentucky between 1775 and 1795. Another calculated that there was "in the late 1780s a death by violence rate on the order of 450 per year." Even though the Revolution was over, when Blacksnake went on the warpath Kentucky remained "a dark and bloody ground."[46]

Despite Indian hostilities, people kept coming in increasing numbers. In 1787 alone, Innes counted at least nine thousand new settlers. By 1795 more than 200,000 had arrived, most following the Wilderness Road but a significant minority the Ohio.[47] Those who moved to growing towns like Lexington might lose their horses but were in little danger of losing their lives. On the other hand, families who ignored the warnings and left their neighbors behind to blaze tomahawk rights (stake a claim) and build cabins out in the forest were asking for trouble and often got it. Numerous outlying cabins were attacked. Some pioneers put up a stout defense, but many left no record behind except the lingering stench of charred timbers and decomposing flesh. In time even the smells faded and underbrush covered the ruins of what once had been a farm.

Indians observed no "civilized" rules of war. Noncombatants were fair game. In fact, war parties preferred to prey upon the most vulnerable—women, children, unarmed farmers in their fields. Frontiersmen reciprocated when they attacked Indian villages. "Algonquians in practice recognized no such cultural area as a battlefield," Richard White noted; "they killed their enemies when and where they found them unless they were ritually protected." Catching the unwary by surprise was their favorite strategy. "They always thought it honorable to deceive and injure those with whom they went to war," Jacob Burnet recalled, "by any means in their power." Although the "Indians were always worse in the spring and fall" and were particularly "troublesome at corn planting time," Kentuckians in exposed areas were never safe. Many lived in dread. Who knew when a lethal attack might come? Despair, madness, even suicide were common. Sarah Graham could recall "14 persons, that I knew their faces, [who] committed suicide." Daniel Blake Smith has argued that while Kentucky seemed to promise a golden land of "opportunity and abundance, it often delivered something else . . . a strong dose of fear."[48]

Because Kentucky survivors rarely knew what tribe let alone which individuals had attacked them, it is impossible to state exactly when and where Wells went on the warpath. What we do know is that the Wabash Indians were actively at war against Kentucky settlers in 1788, as shown by a sampling of reports from the period. In the spring Maj. John Hamtramck at Vincennes informed Harmar that "scalps are dayly brought in supposed to come from Kentucky" and in the fall he learned that "every day 5 & 6 scalps were brought in [to Kekionga] by those Indians [the Miamis], that a number of our prisoners were burnt." A few weeks later, Hamtramck had this report confirmed: "two Shawnees . . . told me . . . that every day there were scalps and prisoners brought at Miami and many of the prisoners burn." In the following spring a Wea chief was heard to boast, "We have killed white men, we have stold their horses, we are now going to steal their cows, and after that we will go and get their women to milk them."[49]

Wabash war parties often crossed the Ohio on makeshift rafts near the mouth of the Kentucky and followed that river to Elkhorn Creek, whose branches near Lexington were the site of many exposed cabins. The warriors marched in Indian file, each man stepping in the footsteps of the one before, and maintained a strict silence in enemy territory. Often the first signs of a nearby cabin were the sound of axes chopping trees, a rooster crowing, or the smell of wood smoke. An experienced warrior would then scout ahead. The men would strip for action and apply war paint. "An Indian when he attacks his enemy is generally nearly naked," Wells wrote, "and his body is painted with different colours, commonly red." Each man retrieved his personal emblem from the sacred pack and tied it to "that part of his body directed by his ancestors." Face paint was designed to "strike their enemies with terror, and indicate by external signs the fury which rages within." Blanket rolls and other baggage were cached and guarded by one or two of the boys. "Their custom is to drag themselves along the ground on all fours like cats and approach within pistol shot." When the family came out of the cabin for the morning milking or other daily chores, on a given signal the warriors opened fire and, howling like wolves, rushed in with raised tomahawks for the kill. The cardinal principle of Indian warfare was to "approach like a fox, fight like a bear, and disappear like a bird." In minutes the deadly work was over and the warriors had faded back into the forest, leaving behind a scene of devastation.[50]

The intention was to terrorize the settlers into abandoning their homesteads and fleeing back east. Thousands did leave, and thousands more died, but nothing could stop the rising tide of immigration. In response the Indians fought with even greater fury. The war whoop alone was appalling. On hunting expeditions, Tanner had seen it drop a buffalo in its tracks and cause a bear to fall from a tree. In a sudden Indian attack near Cincinnati a man named Fergus Clemante fell dead, but his body showed no signs of "any shot or hurt & those who laid him out believed he lost his life by fright." Even more terrifying was the prospect of being scalped. Some survived the ordeal. James Chenoweth recounted how an Indian had scalped his mother: "with 'the very dullest and jaggedest knife that she ever felt,' he cut the skin around her head just below the hair line. He then took his knife between his teeth. With both hands wrapped in her hair and with his foot on her back, he tore off the entire scalp." A tall tale of the time went: "I'll tell you, that scalping was the worst one I've ever had. Yes sir, it was the worst by far!"[51]

Warriors felt compelled not only to kill, but also overkill, the settlers. Mangled bodies sent a message: "You will die horribly here, go away." In addition to scalping, most murders involved further mutilations. Blacksnake may not only have taken scalps but also committed more gruesome acts. To cite a few examples: Ebenezer Denny wrote in the fall of 1788 that the Indians had killed a soldier near Louisville and "not content with scalping him, cut him in four quarters and hung them up in the bushes." Moses Boone recalled finding a body that was "shockingly mutilated—one leg & one arm cut off & each hung up on saplings—as was some articles of clothing. The remainder of the body laid there, head much mangled. . . . The body was gathered together & buried." Given the traumatic nature of these assaults, we can comprehend why a woman, who escaped from her cabin after witnessing the slaughter of her husband and children, "went back that night and laid in her husband's bosom all in a gore of blood."[52]

Ironically, Indian atrocities united whites in what Peter Silver termed "a magnetic rhetoric of suffering" that fixed attention on "the sight of attacks and not their causes." A shared sense of victimization brought settlers of different ethnic backgrounds together in a frontier consensus that their problems would be solved only by the "utter extirpation" of "the savages." Thus the legitimate grievances of the Indians were brushed aside in favor of "one sight—a mutilated corpse" that seemed to settle all arguments.[53]

Blacksnake probably was left behind to guard the baggage on his first excursion before he engaged in stealing horses. Young Jonathan Alder joined a party that stole horses on a Saturday evening, knowing that the whites would sleep in on Sunday, and then they made a dash for the Ohio. Because speed was of the essence to outrun the pursuit, they kept on existing roads, often old buffalo traces. At the river, they put their supplies in a canoe, swam across with the horses, and returned home in triumph to tell their story. William Lytle recalled the following dialogue after his party confronted Indian horse thieves on the opposite bank of the Ohio:

> "Go home, you're too late."
> "You thieving rascals, aren't you ashamed of yourselves?"
> "Not at all," was the cool reply. "All we get in rent for our Kentucky land are a few horses now and then."

This speaker might possibly have been Wells, another captive, or an Indian who knew English.[54]

One of the few battles of this period, Grants Defeat, took place on 20 August 1789 after a war party had "tomahawked and scalped some of Colonel Johnson's negroes, at or near the Great Crossings of the Elkhorn, and stole some of Capt. Lyman Buford's horses" and retired to Eagle Creek in southern Indiana. Twenty-six Kentuckians followed the Indians to their camp and opened fire on about forty warriors. A few were killed on each side, including the brothers Samuel and Moses Grant, before the outmaneuvered Kentuckians made a break for the river and were rescued by a fortuitous flatboat. The location of the camp suggests that Miami warriors, possibly including Blacksnake, were involved in the battle.[55]

Wells must have repressed his doubts about fighting against the Kentuckians. A deeply conflicted person could not have succeeded as a Miami warrior, although some white captives on the warpath did have a sudden change of heart. Little Turtle told the story of a captive who accompanied a war party to Kentucky. As they crept toward an isolated cabin, he "jumped to his feet and went with all his speed, shouting at the top of his voice, 'Indians! Indians!'" A more tragic tale was that of "a young man of wild and savage appearance" who, in the summer of 1787, appeared outside a cabin and managed with his broken English to explain that he had been captured as a boy and that he as well as his Indian father and brother were on "a war expedition to Kentucky." The neighbors suspected treachery and demanded that he show them where the supplies and canoe were hidden. With great reluctance, he took them to the camp, where they killed his father but his brother escaped. The young man was then compelled to lead them to a canoe concealed by the Ohio River. There, they shot his brother dead. The deserter, having paid a terrible price for his divided loyalties, "never regained his tranquility of mind."[56]

ATTACKING FLATBOATS ON THE OHIO

Provocative information about the activities of young Wells as a Miami warrior was provided by a person who hated him and wished to slander his reputation. On 6 November 1810 John Johnson, then Indian agent at Fort Wayne, wrote to Secretary of War William Eustis: "This evil disposed man was taken prisoner by the Indians at 15 years old, some time after we find him on the Ohio River under the pretense of being a white man lost in the woods, inveigling boats to shore and murdering and plundering the defenseless emigrants descending that river."[57] Johnson's charges, however ill-intentioned, might contain a grain of truth. No primary source mentions a russet-haired boy from Snake-fish Town luring flatboats to shore in the late 1780s, but there are several accounts of white captives being used for exactly that purpose.

The number of boats coming down the Ohio was remarkable. From 1 June 1787 to 15 June 1788, Josiah Harmar at Marietta informed Secretary of War Knox that he had counted 354 flatboats carrying 9,516 people, 315 wagons, 4,195 horses, 686 cattle, 845 sheep, and 33 hogs. What we don't know is how many of these people reached their destinations safely. On 26 May 1788 Maj. John Wyllys wrote to Harmar that "a considerable party . . . has placed itself near the mouth of the Great Miami for the purpose of hindering boats in which they have succeeded in several instances." Some were picked off when adverse winds drove them near shore; others had landed to take on supplies; a few had been boarded "in the midst of the stream" by Indians using captured flatboats. In July 1788 Arthur St. Clair informed Knox that "the Western tribes have been successful in their depredations on the Ohio River . . . by these excursions they gratify at once their passion for avarice and revenge and their desire for spirituous liquors."

In 1790 Major Hamtramck sang the same song: "The Indians of the Miami continue their depredations on the Ohio." Three years later a Spaniard in St. Louis reported that "the savages kill all the Americans they find on the Belle Riviere."[58]

When the Indians succeeded in taking a flatboat, few of their victims lived to tell the tale. The usual practice was to drop the dead in the water, sometimes take captives, then plunder the boat and set it adrift. When a company of men went out to bury victims from a previous attack along the Ohio, Benjamin Allen recalled that "a keel boat came down with every person in it dead. They stopped the boat at Limestone. Found an Indians fingers in it, that had been chopped off" as he tried to board. How many boats met a similar fate and how many emigrants died? Traveling down the Ohio in 1792, John Heckewelder noted that the mouth of the Scioto River was a favorite spot for the Shawnees to wait in ambush: "many Kentucky boats passing here have been attacked and seized by these warriors. . . . It is said that in the past 2 years two hundred and fifty people have either lost their lives at this place or been taken captive."[59] From the late 1780s to the early 1790s, at the height of the hostilities, hundreds more must have perished further down the Ohio where the Wabash Indians, including Blacksnake and the Eel River warriors, raided Kentucky and waylaid flatboats.

Charles Johnson wrote a vivid account of white captives used as decoys. On 20 March 1790 John May, his clerk Charles Johnson, Jacob Skyles, William Flinn, his "traveling companion" Dolly Fleming, and her sister Peggy saw smoke rising by the Ohio. Then two white men appeared "on the same side of the river where the fire was. They called to us, and implored us to receive them on board the boat, declaring that they had been taken prisoners by the Indians some weeks before" but had managed to escape. They spoke so eloquently of their sufferings "our feelings were excited towards them, and we discussed the question of going on shore." May, Johnson, and Skyles were opposed; "Flinn, and the two females, accustomed . . . like most of the first settlers on the frontier, to think lightly of danger of Indians, urged us to land." Finally compassion trumped caution. In consequence, a war party rushed out of the woods. May told the men to use every effort to regain the current, but it was too late. Fifty

Indians, "rending the air with the horrible war-whoop, poured their whole fire into our boat. Resistance was hopeless—to get from the shore impossible." When May waved his nightcap as a sign of surrender, he was shot. Dolly Fleming was also killed. The rest were taken prisoner by Captain Snake, a Shawnee war chief.[60]

After the Indians had plundered the boat, stripped their captives of "the greater part of" their clothes, and built a fire, the two white decoys arrived. "The name of one was Divine, the other Thomas. . . . They solemnly declared, that they had been compelled by the Indians to act the part which had brought us into their hands . . . and expressed great concern, that they had been the unwilling instruments of our captivity." In reality, one was lying. A black captive told Johnson that Divine, but not Thomas, had been an active participant in the ruse. The following day, when a canoe with six men appeared, "Divine, ingenious in wicked stratagems, seemed to be perfectly gratified to aid the savages" in decoying the boat near shore, where all six were shot, scalped, and "thrown into the river." In the early afternoon, three more boats appeared. This time the Indians, with Johnson and other captives rowing, pursued them in May's boat without success. The warriors had to content themselves with the "rich booty" found in the two abandoned flatboats, including twenty-eight horses. The chiefs distributed the plunder "in a manner that seemed perfectly satisfactory to all." The next day, having gathered "a booty . . . of sufficient value," the Indians returned to their villages, where the captives met differing fates: Johnson was ransomed; Skyles was cruelly tormented but eventually escaped; Peggy Fleming may have been raped by her Cherokee captors before she was rescued; Flinn was "burnt at the stake, and devoured by the savages, at the Miami towns [Kekionga]."[61]

Sometimes white supplicants at the river's edge really were escaped captives. Jim Downing, for example, killed his elderly captor with an axe, jumped on a horse, and "reached the Ohio at the mouth of Scioto," where he found the first food he'd had in three days: "a wild turkey's nest with eleven blood-shot eggs—ate them all raw . . . tasted delicious." When he saw two boats coming down the river, he "begged them to take him on board," saying that he "had run away from the Indians." The passengers "were fearful of him," but one man ventured closer in a canoe and told him to "ride out into the river as far as he could, & if any Indian was any where seen, he would shoot [him] for treachery." Downing was rescued and taken to Maysville (formerly Limestone); he then led Simon Kenton and his men to the Indian camp, "but all had gone several days." What they did find was the old Indian that Downing had killed. His body was wrapped in two blankets with "a paint bag on his breast; & by his side a butcher knife; looking glass, comb, scissors, awl & patch leather, laid by his right hand, & a pipe-tomahawk at his feet." Downing, who became a Baptist, said he "always regretted killing the old chief."[62]

Although the most notorious location for attacks on flatboats was the mouth of the Scioto, numerous lethal incidents occurred further down the Ohio, especially in 1788. In the spring of that year Thomas Ridout and four other men on a voyage to Louisville spotted in the bushes the wreckage of a flatboat. Then "a boat . . . full of people" approached them, "whom we soon, to our surprise and terror, dis-covered to be Indians almost naked, painted and ornamented as when at war. . . . About twenty leaped into our boat like so many furies, yelling and screaming horribly, brandishing their knives and tomahawks, struggling with each other for a prisoner." Ten men and a black woman were captured by the war party, who divided the booty from the boats and prepared to return to their villages, but not before they killed two of the prisoners. A white man named George Nash, captured as a boy and "now a chief among the Shawanese," assured Ridout that he would not be harmed because he was owned by "a good man" who would ransom him in Detroit.[63]

Ridout was brought to a village on the White River. There he saw the results of other recent assaults on flatboats: "several rich suits of clothes were brought to this village belonging to some French gen-tlemen." These had belonged to three French scientists and a "Mr. Pierce of Maryland" who had been slain on 28 March 1788. Among captives brought to the village, Ridout saw Col. Joseph Mitchell and his son. His flatboat had been lured to shore by a white flag of friend-ship, waved by Shawnee Jim, who brought his men on board and said, "You! Your flour, whiskey, boat and all are mine." After a brief struggle, the two were taken captive. Colonel Mitchell was beaten later by Shawnee Jim and his son was burned at the stake to avenge the dead. Ridout "saw the young man run out of the house naked, his ears having been cut off and his face painted black, the Indians following with the war-whoop and song." Ridout could see smoke from their fire in the woods and heard "the groans of the poor sufferer, and then his shrieks . . . under new tortures." That night the Indians beat their wigwams with sticks to drive away young Mitchell's spirit. For weeks afterward, Ridout feared that he would suffer the same fate, but fortunately he was ransomed.[64]

The use of decoys continued into the early 1790s. When Thomas Marshall descended the Ohio with a large family, he was hailed from the northern shore by James Girty, who said his brother Simon had sent him "to warn all boats of the danger of permitting themselves to be decoyed ashore." James said Simon regretted the injuries he had "inflicted on his countrymen" and wanted to make amends. "White men would appear on the bank," James warned, "and children would be heard to supplicate for mercy.—But . . . do you keep the middle of the river, and steel your heart against every mournful application which you may receive." Marshall's boat was not molested and no more was heard of Simon Girty's remorse.[65]

One of the last accounts of decoys on the Ohio can be found in a narrative about Capt. William Hubbell. In March 1791, his flatboat of nine men, three women, and eight children heard "a voice, at some distance below them, in a plaintive tone, [that] repeatedly solicited them to come on shore, as there were some white persons who wished to obtain a passage in their boat." Sensing "an Indian artifice," Hubbell kept to midstream, and "the voice of entreaty was soon changed into the language of indignation and insult." They were then fired on by Indians in three canoes. The flatboat escaped, but three of the white men died and four were badly wounded. After the skirmish, "a little son of Mr. Plascut" calmly asked Hubbell if he would remove a musket ball from his forehead. The almost-spent bullet had lodged just under his skin. "That's not all, captain," the boy said, raising his arm to show where he had been shot in the elbow. When his distraught mother asked why he had not spoken sooner, the boy replied that he was following the captain's orders "to be silent during the fight." Six boats that came down the river shortly afterward suffered a worse fate: several were taken and the occupants killed.[66]

Another set of targets on the Ohio appeared in the fall of 1788 and the spring of 1789 when Columbia, Cincinnati, North Bend, and South Bend were founded on the northern shore between the Big and Little Miami Rivers. Since many settlers were killed, the area was known as "the Miami slaughter-house," although the Shawnees were also active there. One of the first to fall, in September 1788, was Kentucky historian John Filson, whose surveying party "tangled with a roving band of Miamis." Blacksnake and other warriors from Snake-fish Town may have been in the area, yet no one knows who killed Filson, later memorialized by W. H. Venable:

> *Deep in the wild and solemn woods,*
> *Unknown to white man's track,*
> *John Filson went one autumn day,*
> *But never more came back.*[67]

Let this stanza serve as an epitaph for the hundreds of people, most nameless, who died in this bloody undeclared war in the Ohio Valley. The Indians were fighting desperately to retain their villages and hunting grounds; but they were confronted by an unstoppable influx of settlers determined to get land and build homesteads in spite of any danger.

BLACKSNAKE FINDS A WIFE

After the warriors completed their raids, Wells reported, "each person returns his war bag to the commander of the party, who gives the budget to the man who has taken the first prisoner or scalp and he is entitled to the honor of leading the party home in triumph." As they neared Snake-fish Town, the victorious warriors shouted the scalp-halloo repeatedly to indicate how many they had slain.

When the war party failed, the men retired secretly to their wigwams. If any of their fighters had died, the leader entered the village with "some broken bows and arrows" in his hands as the warriors cried out, "We are dead!" The women would "utter terrible howls" until the dead were identified, "then . . . only the relatives . . .

redouble[d] their outcries." It was "not uncommon" for a returning war party "to dispatch an express with news of their defeat and the death of young warriors." When the people then gathered to mourn their friends and relatives, they were overwhelmed with "surprise and joy" to see them alive. This false report caused no anger, since the deception was "considered innocent."[68]

Upon their return from a victory, the warriors processed through the village doing the stooped, shuffling, and stamping steps of the Buffalo dance. At the council house, the medicine man suspended the sacred war pack from a pole, where two women tended to it and sang to thank the Great Spirit for the victorious return. The singers mentioned "each warrior by name in the course of the song," and as a man was identified he stood up and gave the women a gift. Later the council house would be the site for feasting, singing, and dancing until dawn. "Those of the party who injured the enemy the most," Wells wrote, "serve out the feast to the people." Finally each young warrior gave a gift to an older warrior, retrieved his own totem from the sacred pack, and stored it in a special place until the call went out for the next war party.[69]

The scalps were hung in the council house and the warriors related how each had been obtained. Since they fought in sight of each other, and status depended on what they had done, accuracy was expected. A warrior who exaggerated was mocked. Having taken a scalp and achieved deeds of valor, Blacksnake could participate in the Discovery Dance, where each warrior in turn danced around the fire with the skin of a crow in his hand, struck a painted post with the skin, and recounted his brave acts in "a kind of half-singing to recitative." The Dog Dance was also performed by the warriors. The hearts and livers of slain dogs were fastened in strips to a tall pole. "The braves begin to dance by declaring their exploits in loud, almost deafening yells. They come to the pole, two at a time, and try to bite off a piece of the raw liver or heart and swallow it." Anyone who got out of step "must leave the dance."[70]

Prisoners brought back to Snake-fish Town who were not adopted faced a terrible fate. If a grieving relative demanded revenge, they would be painted black, severely beaten as they ran the gauntlet, and then burned at the stake. A few were singled out for extreme torment.

No need to dwell on the gory details here, but what was perhaps most troubling in the eyes of settlers was the way women and children were often the most active participants. Mothers took pleasure in seeing their young sons inflict pain and bathe themselves in the victim's blood. Wells probably witnessed such activities and saw prisoners die by fire.[71]

After he had been on the warpath Wells married, probably in 1789 or 1790. "Not infrequently when one distinguishes himself" by good conduct during a campaign "he is rewarded with the hand of some pretty girl," the daughter of an elder warrior. Wells wrote about three kinds of marriage among the Miamis: a consensual agreement just between the man and woman; another where the man must first win the approval of her parents; and a third option, "considered the most honorable," when the young man's parents select the appropriate partner and arrange the marriage through an elaborate system of gift-giving between the two families. Wells does not specify which, if any, of these scenarios applied to him.[72]

Narratives from the period suggest that the initiative may not have been taken by Blacksnake. "It is a common thing for a young woman, if in love, to make suit to a young man," Smith noted. She might be aided by the women of the village: "The squaws are generally very immodest in their words and actions, and will often put the young men to the blush." When Spencer killed a wildcat, his Indian mother placed "her forefingers together (by which sign the Indians represent marriage) and then pointing to Sotonegoo [an orphan girl she had adopted], told me. . . . I should have her for a wife." Smith was warned that Chippewa women sometimes caught a young boy in the woods and stripped him "to see whether he was coming on to be a man or not." Margaret Paulee noted that young women "do the principle part of the courting, the men being for the most part modest even to bashfulness." Alder concurred: "A squaw . . . will make her business known to you and if it is acceptable, when bedtime comes she goes to bed with you. . . . No person can object as they belong to themselves and can do as they please."[73]

Several captives recalled that courting couples used "the language of the eyes" to make their feelings clear. Alexander Henry noted how the women "condescended to beguile, with gentle looks, the hearts of passing strangers" and "heightened the color of their cheeks, and really animated their beauty, by a liberal use of vermillion." One touching courtship ritual was recounted by a Mr. Biggs. A Miami woman, seeing his hair was "very long and thick, and much tangled and matted," with first a coarse and then a fine comb, "combed out my hair very tenderly . . . and loused my head nearly one hour. She went to a trunk and got a ribbon, and greased my hair very nicely." He then slept with her for the next three nights. "She was a very handsome girl, about eighteen years of age, and beautiful full figure, and handsomely featured and very white for a squaw." Women also took the initiative at frolic dances in the evenings. Dressed in their finest, and covered with broaches that jingled when they moved, the women danced in a circle around the men. "In this dance a young woman is permitted to select the brave she wishes to dance with, by simply taking her place behind him. When she extends her hand, if it is bare . . . it is an indication that he will be acceptable to her as a lover or perhaps a husband."[74]

Although he lived with the Indians for many years, John Tanner was reluctant to marry, since he still thought he would return to white society. One day a woman asked him to smoke with her: "I took her pipe and smoked a little, though I had not been in the habit of smoking before. She remained some time, and talked with me, and I began to be pleased with her." Even though they slept together, he did not marry her until his Indian mother told him that his conduct would "put this young woman to shame, who is in all respect better than you are." Tanner then "sat down by the side of Mis-kaw-bun-o-kwa, and thus we became man and wife."

A common courtship custom of the Great Lakes Indians was first recorded by Cadillac: A young man carrying a torch enters a girl's tent at night, and if she signals to him "he tells her his love." Trowbridge found the same custom among the Miamis in the late eighteenth century:

> Generally, when a young man becomes fond of a girl . . . he goes secretly to the lodge of her parents, in the night, and entering softly with a small piece of bark by way of a torch light, he gives her a slight shake. She awakes and looks up at him, and upon her answer at that eventful moment depends

the result of his attempt. If she is fond of the young man and disposed to marry him she sends him away, with a smile, half-consenting at the same time to stay. Another visit after this finishes the courtship and the female makes room for her lover at her side.

"If she . . . blows out his light," Jonathan Carver stated, "he needs no further confirmation that his company is not disagreeable." Although the man took the initiative by entering the wigwam, the woman made the decision whether or not to accept his overtures. "I consider this practice as precisely similar to bundling in New England," Alexander Henry wrote, adding that "children born out of wedlock are very rare among the Indians."[75]

If Blacksnake entered the wigwam of the woman of his choice and received a favorable response, and his purpose was honorable, he would have waited until his lover's father woke up before he departed, "leaving behind him his blanket or something else as a proof that he did not come with a design to sport with the girl, but with serious intention to marry her." He would then shoot a deer or some other large game animal, and leave it at the door of her lodge. Young men and women were permitted a degree of promiscuity— that was their private affair—but marriage was public and demanded the proper rituals. For one thing, Miamis could only marry outside of their respective clan. Although Wells's wife might have been a Wea and her Indian name is unknown, probably she was a Kilatika, or Eel River Miami, called "Nancy" in English. Since Blacksnake was the adopted son of a village chief, his bride would have been from a respectable family, and reciprocal gift-giving would have sealed the alliance.[76]

"When a choice is made," Wells wrote, "the relations of the young man collect what presents they think sufficient for the occasion, go to the parents of the intended bride, made their wishes known, leave the articles . . . and return without waiting for an answer." Trowbridge added that the groom's father stated that "they have come to bring them fire, water & moccasins," an allusion to the expectation that Blacksnake would care for his wife's parents in their old age. The young woman's relations then consulted, Wells stated, "and, if they agree to the match, they collect suitable presents, dress the girl in her best clothes, and take her" to her intended. In the procession to the lodge, the father walked in front, followed by the girl wearing "all the finery they can muster," with the mother in the rear. Once everyone was seated, the father of the bride thanked the groom and his parents for selecting his daughter and for giving his family appropriate presents, thus granting approval to the match. The groom gave a horse or other valuable present to his bride, who presented it to her eldest brother on behalf of her husband. During the next hunting season, the brother would provide the couple with choice meat, which the wife in turn gave to her mother-in-law for a final festivity that concluded the gift-gifting and the honeymoon.[77]

Since descent among the Miamis was matrilineal, a couple usually lived temporarily with the wife's parents and helped provide for them during "a year of bride-service." After a designated date or the birth of the first child they could live where they wished. Most likely Wells's marriage followed these formalities, but it might have been of a more casual nature. A Delaware informant told John Heckewelder that the courtship process could be very simple. When a man saw an "industrious Squaw," he went to her, placed "two forefingers close aside each other, make two look like one—look Squaw in the face." If she smiled that constituted a *yes* and he took her to his wigwam. "Squaw love to eat meat!" the man added, "no husband, no meat! Squaw do everything to please husband! He do the same to please Squaw! Live happy!"[78] We don't know how happy Wells was with his Indian wife—much of their marriage would have involved each fulfilling clearly defined sex roles; thus Blacksnake spent most of his time with men and she with women—but we do know that they had a son, born about 1790.

Although promiscuity prevailed among the young, marriage was serious and adultery severely punished. Most couples were monogamous, at least for a time, yet divorce was easy—a partner could simply leave, although the man might have to contend with a wife's angry brothers. Conjugal sex was also restricted. Men avoided any sexual activity before, during, and after going on the warpath. Women were also taboo during their periods, pregnancies, and initial nursing. Since women nursed their children for several years, men were tempted to find other mates. "Polygamy is permitted among the

Indians," Wells wrote. "A man may have as many wives as he pleases, and young men are instructed by their parents to get as many as they can, but by no means involve themselves or friends in any quarrels with their neighbors."[79] Before long Blacksnake would marry another Indian woman—Sweet Breeze, daughter of Miami war chief Little Turtle. His second marriage took place after Snake-fish Town had been destroyed and "Nancy" and his son taken prisoner. Over the next two years Blacksnake would intensify his activities as a Miami warrior, fighting at the side of his father-in-law.

CHAPTER FOUR

LITTLE TURTLE TRIUMPHANT

"I shall now point out ye disposition of the Indians," a trader who returned from the Shawnee towns in northwest Ohio reported in 1786. "The warrior chiefs in conversation, both drunk & sober, say their old counselors & Kings have given up the land to the Big Knife; but we the chiefs of the warriors have not given our consent—& if the surveyors come to survey the land, or if any of the white people come to sit down on it, we will then put our old men & chiefs behind us & fight for our land while we have a man." The ham-fisted policy of the Confederated Congress, by imposing a series of treaties that claimed Indian lands by right of conquest, had aided the process by which peace chiefs were supplanted by war chiefs, leading to an intensification of hostilities. The Indians were convinced that because the Americans had not negotiated in good faith or given appropriate presents, they had lied to them and wanted "their land for nothing." As a result, the trader warned, the warriors were determined to fight and would defend their country "with as severe attacks as ever have been made by Indian nations."[1]

HENRY KNOX AND AMERICAN INDIAN POLICY

After Benjamin Logan's raid in 1786, Blue Jacket's Shawnees left the Mad River and moved near the Miami stronghold of Kekionga, where Little Turtle was war chief, as did the militant faction of the

Delawares led by Buckongahelas. Those three nations alone could muster over 1,000 warriors, with reinforcements down the Wabash: 400 Weas and Kickapoos at Ouiatanon as well as Blacksnake (Wells) and 150 others at Snake-fish Town.[2] Several thousand Potawatomis, Ottawas, and Chippewas were a week's march away.

Joseph Brant's confederacy had told Congress, "they will be at peace with the Thirteen Fires, if they keep on their own side of the River Ohio, & don't settle or survey their side of it." Harmar was informed that officially the British discouraged the Indians from going to war, but Alexander McKee and other agents encouraged them, "I am sure they do some things under the rose that is not right. In short . . . if Congress is determined to sell the lands & have them surveyed, war must be the end of it at last, & the people of Kentucky & the frontiers of this country must evermore be a prey to the Indians," who would show no mercy: "They don't mean to keep many prisoners now, but kill all before them." Harmar was cautioned that if the United States assumed force would settle matters, Indian warriors comprised "a good army in the woods."[3]

When Harmar and his men arrived in Vincennes on 17 July 1787, he quickly learned that the problems there didn't concern only Indians. The French-speaking habitants greeted his troops as "real Americans" or "Bostonians" to differentiate them from the Kentucky "Big Knives." Barthelemi Tardiveau, who knew the local situation, informed Harmar that the frontiersmen tended to "mistake the idea of licentiouness for that of liberty" and adhered to "the maxim that 'no injury done to an Indian is punishable.'" This meant: "No treaty of peace, likely to be lasting, can be made with the Indians except you are invested with powers energetick enough to keep the whites under subjection." Unless Harmar could establish "order, peace, justice," and the rule of law, the result would be "jumbled elections, mob-made magistrates, pick'd juries, and partial laws." The Indians, too, must believe in the authority of the United States because "if they discover your weakness, they will harass you incessantly." Without two thousand troops and posts up the Wabash, his small garrison could "answer nothing."[4]

With Miami chief Pacanne as his guide, Harmar inspected the French towns of Kaskaskia and Cahokia. In September he held a conference with 120 Wea and Piankishaw Indians, asserting that if they did not live "in peace and friendship" and "persisted in being hostile that a body of troops would march to their towns and sweep them off the face of the earth." Harmar then distributed presents of "no great amount" and declared that the Indians "were highly satisfied with the treatment they received." The next month Maj. John Hamtramck was left in charge of the Vincennes garrison. A Catholic who spoke French, he had a good rapport with the habitants but lacked power to enforce order on the frontier. In May 1788 he reported that eighty of those "highly satisfied" Weas that Harmar had dealt with the previous September were "out at war on the Ohio," and scalps from Kentucky were "dayly" brought to their villages. Seeking vengeance, on 18 August 1788, Patrick Brown and his sixty men killed nine members of Pacanne's peaceful band of Miamis and arrogantly refused to return the horses his men had stolen. Miami warriors promptly raided Kentucky in retaliation.[5]

There were, in effect, two "foreign policies" on the frontier. The United States wished to sign peace treaties with friendly Indian nations and, under the guidelines of the Northwest Ordinance of 1787, to purchase their lands. Indians who refused to cooperate would be considered hostile and face military reprisals. Frontiersmen, on the other hand, *deliberately* killed peaceful chiefs and their people to stop the government from differentiating between good and bad Indians. They favored a policy that exterminated them or caused them to retreat into the wilderness.

Hamtramck continued to report frequent Indian raids, and again the Kentuckians brought out their militia. Maj. John Hardin and 220 men marched toward the Wea towns on the Wabash. On 9 August 1789 they came upon a Shawnee hunting party of twenty-two people and killed "three men, a boy, three squaws, & a child & took two children prisoner." A few days later Daniel Sullivan and a Michael Duff from Kaskaskia were seen walking the streets of Vincennes "with two scalps fastened on a stick." Hamtramck wrote to Harmar: "It is very mortifying to me to see the authority of the United States so much sneered at and not having sufficient power to chastise the aggressors." Harmar could only hope that General St. Clair's appointment as governor would "add to the dignity and consequence of Congress."[6]

Arthur St. Clair was fifty-two when he arrived in Marietta in July 1788. Born in Edinburgh, Scotland, he fought under Wolfe at Quebec. After the war he settled in America and married Phoebe Bayard of Boston, whose dowry enabled the purchase of an estate in western Pennsylvania, where he rose to prominence while his wife descended into insanity. During the Revolution, he was court-martialed but exonerated for the loss of Fort Ticonderoga. He redeemed himself at Trenton and Princeton, winning the trust of General Washington. A haughty and self-important man, he lacked the common touch for democratic politics; the Pennsylvania electorate rebuffed his run for governor by ten to one. The Confederated Congress, however, elected him president and then governor of the Northwest Territory.

At Marietta he urged the settlers: "cultivate a good understanding with the natives, without much familiarity; treat them on all occasion with kindness, and the strictest regard to justice," but beware of falling into their "customs and habits" as so many frontiersmen did; rather, "induce them to adopt yours." St. Clair was skeptical about the possibility of peace with the Indians. The rapid spread of the settlements, and the "unequivocal" way the United States had let them know "our pretension to the country," he told Knox, had created consequences that were "so dreadful to them . . . there is little probability of there ever being any cordiality between us." St. Clair was convinced that "a war with the Western tribes, at least . . . [seemed] inevitable." He outlined a plan for a synchronized invasion by hundreds of U.S. regulars and thousands of militia against three Indian towns. His principal target: "The Shawnese, Delawares, and Miamis . . . the hostile tribes who live at the Miami Village—Kikayuga [Kekionga] is the name."[7]

Henry Knox was directly responsible for Indian affairs during this period. He had dropped out of Boston Latin when he was twelve to support his abandoned mother, clerked in a bookstore, and eventually owned one. During the Revolution, after the cannon and mortars he brought from Fort Ticonderoga and Crown Point helped break the siege of Boston, he was given command of the continental artillery. It was Knox who arranged Washington's crossing of the Delaware; later he fought at Princeton, Brandywine, Germantown, Monmouth, and Yorktown. In March 1785 the Confederated Congress named him secretary at war in charge of an inadequate army and an as yet nonexistent navy as well as supervisor of at least 75,000 Indians that lived between the Appalachians and the Mississippi. An amiable, ambitious man with an imposing three-hundred-pound presence, he was George Washington's most trusted New England adviser. "Go to General Knox," Hamilton advised a desperate office seeker. "They say Washington talks to him as a man does with his wife." Shays's Rebellion convinced Knox that the Articles of Confederation needed to be replaced and the nation's military strengthened. If the United States had an adequate army, Knox lamented, those troops could have been "ordered immediately to Springfield" and the crisis averted. "Our political machine," he concluded, "composed of thirteen independent sovereignties, have been perpetually operating against each other and against the federal head ever since the peace."[8]

Because many Federalists shared Knox's views, a Constitutional Convention met at Philadelphia in 1787. George Washington became the first president of the United States on 30 April 1789. Knox went from being secretary *at* war to secretary *of* war and retained his responsibilities for Indian affairs. Throughout his tenure from 1785 to 1794, he was acutely concerned with the world's perception of the new nation. Like other founding fathers, Knox believed that the character of individuals as well as countries should be scrutinized and judged. Without proper behavior, honor and dignity could be lost. He once told Mrs. Mercy Warren he could picture "two or three hundred million of our posterity with their eyes fixed on our conduct, ready to applaud our wisdom or execrate our folly." If the government was not effective, "our posterity will hold our memories responsible." Knox knew the "Black Legend" that had spread in the wake of the brutal Spanish conquest of the Aztecs and Incas. "It is a melancholy reflection," he wrote in 1794, "that our modes of population have been more destructive of the Indian natives than the conduct of the conquerors of Mexico and Peru. . . . A future historian may mark the causes of this destruction of the human race in sable colors."[9]

Knox repeatedly urged the United States to pursue an enlightened policy toward the Indians, one that would treat them with beneficence and justice and not stain the national character. In time, he believed that the Indians would accept "the blessing of civilization," leave the "barbarous ages" behind, and participate in American society's "present degree of perfection." Yet this policy was laced with contradictory statements, false information, and inept actions that would result not in peaceful accommodation but in a major effort to "extirpate" most of the Indians in the Northwest. Knox favored conducting peace treaties with the Indians as though they were "foreign nations." Any who remained on the warpath were considered "banditti." Sometimes he identified the culprits as a band of a hundred or more Shawnees and renegade Cherokees who preyed on flatboats on the Ohio River. When the Shawnees and warriors of other nations congregated near Kekionga, the issue became more complex than punishing a few "wicked and blood thirsty" banditti, yet that inappropriate term remained in use and confounded adequate preparations for either peace or war.[10]

If war were to be waged, to maintain the national honor it had to be a "just war." The difficulty Knox faced was that the frontiersmen were not innocent victims of Indian aggression. They, too, had committed atrocities. Knox noted "the present confused state of injuries between the said Indians and the frontier people south of the Ohio. . . . The injuries and murders have been so reciprocal, that it would be a point of critical investigation to know on which side they have been the greater." The question was, then, how "a nation solicitous of establishing its character" ought to conduct itself. One option would be "raising an army, and extirpating the refractory tribes entirely." Due consideration suggested "that both policy and justice" called for "treating with the Wabash Indians: for it would not be just in the present confused state of injuries, to make war on those tribes without having previously invited them to a treaty, in order amicably to adjust all differences." Neither Knox nor the United States, however, would admit or adjust the most serious Indian "differences." Nonetheless, if any nations refused to sign, no matter how unfair the terms, that would make a war upon them "just."[11]

THE MIAMIS AT KEKIONGA

In October 1787, Congress "empowered" St. Clair "to hold a general treaty" with the Indian tribes north of the Ohio "so that peace and harmony may continue." The fundamental problem that all previous treaties were flawed was ignored: they "may be examined but must not be departed from, unless a change of boundary beneficial to the United States can be obtained." St. Clair should "not Neglect any opportunity . . . [for] extinguishing the Indian rights to the Westward as far as the River Mississippi." In addition, he should identify "the real headmen and Warriors of the several Tribes" and use "every means in your power . . . [to] attach [them] to the United States." Finally, St. Clair must make "every exertion" to break up "all Confederations and Combinations among the tribes, and to conciliate the white people inhabiting the frontiers towards them." If Congress would not admit that previous treaties had been imposed unfairly and that dictated cessions of Indian land were invalid, then no "just and liberal" treaty was possible. By scheming to bribe chiefs, break up the confederacy, and "purchase" lands the Indians did not want to sell, American peace efforts could only result in causing a war the new country could ill afford and was unprepared to fight.[12]

In the spring of 1788 messengers were dispatched to the Indian villages with St. Clair's request to attend a general treaty at the falls of the Muskingum (Zanesville, Ohio). By midsummer, deep disagreements emerged among the leaders of the confederacy. Those closest to the American settlements, especially the Wyandots, Delawares, and Mingos, only wanted previous treaties adjusted. Those from farther away—the Miamis, Delawares, and Shawnees at Kekionga, as well as the Wabash villages—insisted on the Ohio River boundary. Brant argued for a compromise that would allow settlements east of the Muskingum, where Marietta had recently been established. At Roche de Bout on the Maumee, McKee told the Indians "not to go, that altho' Gov. St. Clair should promise them peace, that the Kentuck people would brake it immediately." The Wyandots tried to soften the adamant stance of the Miamis, presenting them with a belt of white wampum. Little Turtle refused it, and when they placed it on his shoulder "he turned himself on one side and let it fall to the ground."[13]

Meanwhile, St. Clair unwisely sent a small company up the Muskingum to erect a council house. A roving band of Chippewa warriors killed three of the men and stole their supplies. St. Clair took this as a deliberate provocation on the part of Brant's confederacy, thus escalating this minor incident into a major obstacle to peace. "The

The Old Northwest Frontier, 1788–1812. Map by Bill Nelson. Copyright © 2015
University of Oklahoma Press.

flag of the United States has been fired upon," he declared. Any further meetings would be conducted under the guns of Fort Harmar,
next to Marietta. To keep negotiations alive, Brant sent St. Clair a
message: "From the misconduct of a few individuals . . . you have
extinguished the council fire. . . . It is our wish to live in peace . . . we
propose to give the United States all the lands laying on the east side
of the Muskingum." When Brant learned that St. Clair had dismissed
his conciliatory offer as "altogether inadmissible," he concluded that

"nothing could be done with the United States that they [his Indian allies] would be satisfied with."[14]

By alienating Brant's Mohawks and other moderates, St. Clair had driven more warriors, probably including Blacksnake, into Little Turtle's militant camp. Instead of a grand gathering of nations, he was met by a motley crew who were hardly representative. John Heckewelder later stated that he did not recognize "the name of even one Great Chief." The most prominent was Captain Pipe of the Delawares. No Shawnees or Miamis attended, nor did the Wabash tribes. In addition to Cornplanter's Senecas and other Iroquois, several hundred Delawares, as well as some Wyandots, Ottawas, Potawatomis, Chippewas, and Sauks were present.[15]

Congress had expected that St. Clair would avoid "a language of superiority and command" but rather meet with them "more on a footing of equality." Instead St. Clair's conduct followed that of previous negotiators. He refused to "make the least deviation from" earlier treaties, claiming that the terms were "most generous" and the "fixed" boundaries were "unalterable," reiterating the old right of conquest argument Congress thought it had replaced with a "policy of purchase," and telling the chiefs they must accept the American terms. The United States wanted "to be at peace with all the Indians," but "if you will have war you may have war." The two treaties signed at Fort Harmar in January 1789, instead of establishing a lasting peace, made armed conflict with the Indians inevitable. The coerced chiefs gathered their presents and agreed to "renew and confirm" the boundaries imposed at Fort Stanwix in 1784 and Fort McIntosh in 1785, thus completing, as Denny noted, "the last act of the farce."[16]

In December 1788, St. Clair had confided to John Jay that "No treaty, I believe, will secure the lower frontier at present." If possession of Ohio lands was the object, then Congress "must prepare to chastise the Western nations as early in the summer as possible." St. Clair praised his own accomplishments at Fort Harmar, noting that the "Negociation was both tedious and troublesome . . . but . . . I am persuaded their general Confederacy is entirely broken: indeed it would not be very difficult, if Circumstances required it to set them at deadly variance." St. Clair *had* succeeded in dividing the Wyandots and Iroquois. By undercutting Brant, however, he had strengthened the militant warriors at Kekionga. On 15 June 1789 Knox told Washington: "the United States have not formed any treaties with the Wabash Indians," who had been exchanging reciprocal atrocities with the Kentuckians for years. Given this confused situation, no "just" war could be declared without first inviting the hostile nations to settle matters peacefully at a treaty. Knox insisted that the Treaty of Fort Harmar exemplified the government's "policy of purchase," yet for the Indians the issue was not fair payment but rather the right *not* to sell their lands at all.[17]

Since the Indians saw the Treaty of Fort Harmar as unjust, Blacksnake along with many other warriors continued to attack boats on the Ohio and to raid into Kentucky. Hamtramck sent repeated messages up the Wabash, warning the Indians to "cease their depredations" or "be severely chastised." St. Clair cautioned Washington not to expect "that the Kentucky people will or can, submit patiently to the cruelties and depredations of those savages; they are in the habit of retaliation, perhaps without attending precisely to the nations from which the injuries are received." Washington replied that it is "highly necessary that I should, as soon as possible, possess full information whether the Wabash and Illinois Indians are most inclined for war or peace. . . . I would have it observed forcibly that a war with the Wabash Indians ought to be avoided by all means consistent with the security of the frontier inhabitants, the security of the troops, and the national dignity." In December, Knox sharpened the government's position to St. Clair: "The President of the United States is extremely desirous of a general treaty with the Wabash Indians. . . . If the Indians should refuse to attend the invitation to a treaty the United States would be exonerated, from all imputations of injustice in taking proper measures for compelling the Indians to a peace, or to extirpate them."[18]

In early January 1790, a skeptical St. Clair agreed to send one final message to the Wabash Indians, urging them to attend a peace treaty at Vincennes: "The Miamis, and the renegade Shawnees, Delawares, and Cherokees, that lay near them, I fear are irreclaimable by gentle means. The experiment, however, is worth making."[19] The last hope of a peaceful resolution was in the hands of Antoine Gamelin, whose destination was the Miami stronghold of Kekionga, where the warriors of Little Turtle, Blue Jacket, and Buckongahelas had concentrated.

Henry Hay's journal provides a rare glimpse of what life was like at Kekionga during the winter prior to Gamelin's arrival in April 1790. Situated where the St. Joseph from the northeast and the St. Mary's from the southeast form the Maumee, which flowed east to Lake Erie, the place was of great strategic importance. The French and British had built forts there to control the Wabash portage between the Great Lakes and the Ohio-Mississippi valleys. British and French fur traders lived in log houses north of the Maumee, near Le Gris's Miami village. Pacanne's smaller village was across the St. Joseph a mile or so to the northwest. The Shawnees established Chillicothe and Piqua along the Maumee, while Delaware towns were up the St. Joseph and on the St. Mary's. Three days after Hay's arrival on 18 December, Little Turtle's war party of some fifteen men returned from a raid. One American captive was tomahawked by a warrior to avenge "his own relations killed lately." Hay saw who was in charge of the town when Le Gris ordered some French boys to unload a boat and bring the warriors across the river, where "he Billetted them like Soldiers so many in each House. . . . This he ordered in a very polite manner, but quite like a general or a commandant." Later the warrior showed Hay the dead American's heart: "It was . . . like a piece of dryed venison, with a small stick run from one end of it to the other & fastened behind the fellows bundle that killed him, with also his Scalp."[20]

Kekionga was a multicultural community, where French and English traders mixed easily with the Indians and respected their customs. Six times during the four months of Hay's visit, Le Gris and Little Turtle returned from their nearby hunting camp, bringing him turkey and venison in exchange for a hearty breakfast, a glass of tea, a taste of Madeira, and an occasional bottle of rum. In February when the Shawnee brought in a young prisoner named McMullen, Hay and two other traders went to Chillicothe to learn his fate. Although he had been "painted as black as Divils" and made to shake a deer's hoof rattle while he sang "*Oh Kentuck*," the village chief Black Beard ordered that he not be harmed. Instead the Indians shook hands with him, "a good sign" that he would be "adopted by one of the Roy'l Family." Sometimes traders were able to intervene and save lives.

Hay's journal provided no support for the American contention that those at Kekionga were pro-British and encouraged war.[21]

Although he denounced the business of him and his fellows as "a Rascally Scrambling Trade," Hay enjoyed the rich festive dimension of their lives. Drinking, dancing, singing, and feasting filled many an evening. Not only Christmas, New Year's, and Mardi Gras, but also saints' days and the queen's birthday were celebrated. Every Sunday "the Ringing of three cow bells" summoned people to prayers at the home of Mr. Barthelmi; Louis Payet led the service while Hay and John Kinzie, the local silversmith, played flute and fiddle. Sunday evenings they feasted on roast turkey, venison, or veal, washed down with Port or Madeira. One time Hay made "Tangrie for the Ladies, and Grogg for the Gentlemen," all "dressed in their best bibs & Tuckers," some sporting cockade hats adorned with ostrich feathers. Hay and Mrs. Adamher walked a minuet, followed by some *Dance Ronby*, featuring a bawdy chorus sung by Mrs. Rangard. Hay was often "infernally drunk" and the next day had swollen feet and a sore head. Once an intoxicated James Abbott "gave me his daughter Betsy [age twelve] over the bottle."[22]

Le Gris and Little Turtle arrived to celebrate New Year's Eve. Hay reported that at three in the morning, an Indian woman "came to shake hands with me when in bed." The next day, as Hay made the rounds kissing "all the Ladies young and Old," he found that Le Gris was "rather drunk." Jean Baptist Richerville (*Peshewa*, or Wildcat), acting chief of Pacanne's village, was a shy young man whose mother was the real force in the family. After her first husband returned to Canada, Marie Louise married Charles Beaubien and now ran her own "Trading Place" on the Eel River. Hay and several other men, including Richerville, decided to form a society called the Friars of St. Andrew. In the evenings they serenaded the ladies; for Mardi Gras they dined at the chief's home; after flood waters had inundated the town, they "gave the ladys a row upon & down the River," while Kinzie played his fiddle and Hay the flute.[23]

In January an illuminating episode took place that involved both Snake-fish Town and Kekionga. Rumors spread that French trader Antoine Lasselle had been taken prisoner by the Weas. Le Gris decided to send Little Turtle "with a belt . . . to inquire into this matter." Then Lasselle wrote that everything was "perfectly quiet." Thus Little Turtle's mission was not needed. A week later Lasselle arrived, accompanied by Blue Jacket. In the meantime, Snake-fish Town, between Kekionga and Ouiatanon, had received conflicting rumors and reports. The Soldier and the Porcupine asked Jacques Godfory, a French trader in their town, to inform Le Gris that the untrue accusations were from Le Lache [the Coward], who was "a great Rascall." Lasselle had brought a second letter from the two chiefs, reiterating that Le Lache was a "bad Indian" and that Le Gris should not "harken to the Doggs of the Village" or "believe those bad Birds" who create "very bad things & disturbances." Hay concluded that Lasselle had been purposely confused with the guilty party, "one Fouché," to harm him. Finally the Porcupine and his brother told Le Gris and Richerville "not to believe any false reports" from unreliable men but only to "harken" to "people of character and chiefs who may be depended upon—for they cannot tell a Lye."[24]

This exchange implies several things: French traders from Kekionga were often in Snake-fish Town; the Soldier and Porcupine shared authority in the village; and relations between the two chiefs and Le Gris were touchy, yet both sides kept in communication to prevent disruptive forces from undermining their confederation. Furthermore, by 1790, Wells (Blacksnake) probably had been to Kekionga, met Little Turtle, and may have already gone to war with him.

In late March two Shawnee war parties returned with prisoners who said that if the Wabash Indians refused to sign a peace treaty at Vincennes, the Americans "meant to fight them." A week later Hay left Kekionga—a distinctive place on the eve of its destruction.

HARMAR'S DEFEAT

On his mission up the Wabash, Antoine Gamelin was given the run-around. The Piankashaws at Vermillion had to consult the Miamis; the Kickapoos had to ask the Weas, who "could terminate nothing without the consent of our elder brethren, the Miamis." Nobody was pleased with St. Clair's message, which dared them to accept or reject his peace offer "as you please"—his tone was so "menacing" that Gamelin removed that statement. The chiefs chided him for not bringing rum "to put the old people in good humor" and powder and ball for their hunters: he "should know that a bearer of speeches should never be with empty hands." At Snake-fish Town both Porcupine and the Soldier were absent. In Kekionga on 23 April 1790, Gamelin explained the Fort Harmar treaty, "which displeased them." Blue Jacket said that the Big Knives had often deceived them and now they plotted "to take away, by degrees, their lands." Le Gris stated that the "young men" who signed that treaty were "not chiefs" and were "without authority." He insisted on sending the speeches to "all our neighbors, and to the Lake Indians. . . . [The Miamis could not] give a definitive answer without consulting with the commandant at Detroit," who represented "their father" the British.[25]

On 1 May 1790, St. Clair wrote to Washington that the failure of Gamelin's mission was "nearly tantamount to a declaration" of war. "The United States must prepare effectually to chastise them," he told Knox, who was still preoccupied by "the said banditti Shawanese and Cherokees, and some of the Wabash Indians." On 7 June he ordered Harmar to assemble three hundred militia and one hundred federal troops, "mounted on horseback for the sake of rapidity," to eliminate them. Harmar and St. Clair did not share Knox's notions about a banditti of two hundred bad men; their sights were set on Kekionga. In July the two men met at Fort Washington to plan an expedition of fifteen hundred militia and four hundred federal troops to "the Maumee towns [Kekionga]," while Hamtramck would lead five hundred men up the Wabash against the Piankashaws at Vermillion, the Weas at Ouiatanon, and Blacksnake's village Snake-fish Town. Knox approved the plan and ordered St. Clair as "a point . . . of delicacy" to inform the British "at a proper time" that Detroit was not a target. The purpose of the expedition was "to exhibit to the Wabash Indians our power to punish them for their positive depredations, for their conniving at the depredations of others, and for their refusing to treat with the United States when invited thereto. This power will be demonstrated by a sudden stroke, by which their towns and crops may be destroyed."[26]

The Washington administration faced obvious difficulties in conducting an effective Indian policy west of the Appalachians. A month could elapse between Harmar sending a letter to Knox and receiving his response. Even so, troubling questions remain: How did a policy of securing peace with the Indians turn into an invasion of their country? How did Knox's fear of "banditti" on the Ohio become an attack on Little Turtle's confederacy? How much was Washington involved in deciding on a war that would last five years and cost many lives? Apparently when St. Clair and Harmar shifted the campaign to Kekionga, Knox accepted their decision, naively assuming that "a sudden stroke" would meet little resistance. Even though the four hundred mounted men ordered to "extirpate" two hundred banditti had become two thousand men, mostly infantry, Knox thought that their march of 160 miles into uncharted Indian country would be "so rapid and decisive as to astonish . . . [the] enemy." If Knox was confused, so was Washington. A month after St. Clair and Harmar had planned their militant strategy, he asked Knox, "What steps shall be taken to restrain . . . Hostilities? Whether the orders given, and measures adopted, are adequate to the Peace on the Western Frontiers?" In his message to Congress in December, Washington conflated "certain banditti" with the nations near the Wabash as the focus of the expedition, justifying the war not only because of "depredations" on the frontier but also because of the plight of people "carried into a deplorable captivity."[27] Thus, ironically enough, both the "depredations" of Blacksnake and the "captivity" of Wells helped justify the war.

Senator William Maclay of Pennsylvania was suspicious when Washington appointed one of his Revolutionary officers to be secretary of war during a time of peace. "Give Knox his army," Maclay warned in April 1790, "and he will soon have a war . . . in less than six months with the Southern Indians."[28] After Congress doubled the army to twelve hundred, Maclay's prediction came true—in terms of time but not of opponent. In October Harmar's men reached Kekionga.

St. Clair revealed his true sentiments when he told Harmar that it might be "improper to restrain" the "savage ferocity" of the militia, since the Indians "should be made to smart for their treachery." Lt. Ebenezer Denny feared the worst when the Kentuckians arrived at Fort Washington in mid-September: "They appear to be raw and unused to the gun or the woods"; many were "old, infirm men and young boys" who wanted "to see the country without rendering any service whatever." Veteran frontiersmen, preferring to kill Indians on their own terms, had sent substitutes. Harmar was "much disheartened" by the quality of the militia and could only hope that they would "stick to the text, and not leave me in the lurch." When colonels James Trotter and John Hardin began "disputing for the command," Harmar divided the militia into three battalions under majors Hall, McMullen, and Ray that would be led by Trotter, while Hardin was made overall commander of the militia, "subject to the orders of General Harmar." Knox had doubts about Harmar, advising him of rumors that he was "too adpt to indulge . . . to excess in a convivial glass."[29] Federal troops also left much to be desired—recent immigrants in need of clothes and a ration of whiskey or New England farm boys with limited prospects. These raw recruits had no idea what it meant to fight skilled warriors defending their homelands.

By the time Harmar's army left Fort Washington on 30 September, the total force was 1,453, of whom 320 were regulars. Most of the troops were infantry facing a two-week trek through the wilderness to Kekionga. Major Fontaine led a small battalion of dragoons, mostly Kentuckians; Major Ferguson's artillery consisted of three cannons, one of them a six-pounder. The men who looked after the cattle, packhorses, and baggage proved to be less than competent. Every morning, patrols went out looking for stray or stolen horses. From Cincinnati the army followed Clark's 1782 trace to Old Chillicothe, which it reached on 6 October.[30]

An ominous sign was found on 10 October near the ruins of Piqua on the Big Miami. The Indians had "killed a cub bear, the skin of which they cut up in small pieces, and placed them on stumps, in order to let us know that we were discovered, and to give us a hint that our scalps were in danger." The army passed by Lorimier's Store and Chillicothe, destroyed during Benjamin Logan's 1786 campaign. This was the farthest Kentucky raids had previously ventured. Now Harmar and his men had to rely on their guide Daniel Williams.

On 13 September, Thomas Irwin recalled, "8 or 10 mounted men went out in Search of Some horses that had Been Lost over Night Started a Smart young Indian with a Bow and arrow They took him prisoner Brought him to Camp there was 2 of the troops Could Speak the Indian tounge very well he and they Spoke freely together he Stated the Indians at first intended to make a Stand at the Towns give that up and intended to move their families and Burn their Towns." He was "a half breed about twenty years of age, and . . . a most sullden dog." The Shawnee prisoner said "that the Indians at the Maumee Village were in great consternation and confusion—and the prospects were they might be easily defeated if found in that Situation." At the St. Mary's, Harmar called a council of his officers. "It was determined that a detachment under command of Gen. Hardin should proceed, by forced marches, to the villages on the Maumee. In order to interrupt them in their flight, and secure their goods and peltries if possible." Hardin's six hundred volunteers set out the next morning, but that evening a thunderstorm with lots of lightning "perplexed the guides." The army halted at midnight, "not knowing where they were or whether they had been going forwards or backwards."[31]

St. Clair informed Detroit of Harmar's campaign *before* the army left Cincinnati, giving British agents time to warn the Indians. On 6 October their spies sent back an inflated report that 2,500 men were on the march. Little Turtle and other chiefs dispatched runners to ask the villages near the Great Lakes to come to the defense of Kekionga. One trader wrote, "they are collecting from all quarters and are determined to make an attempt to cut them [the Americans] off." Even though warriors responded with "spirit and alacrity," it was apparent that most reinforcements would arrive too late. Therefore, the chiefs decided to evacuate and set fire to Kekionga. Francis Slocum recalled that "the women and children were all made to run north." Le Gris informed the traders that their log houses, which might "shelter . . . their enemies," would be reduced to ashes. The Miamis helped them "to retire with the bulk of their goods," but all their powder and ball was confiscated, livestock were killed for food, and a thousand bushels of corn were burned. Little Turtle's plan was to catch Harmar's army by surprise.[32]

On the afternoon of 15 October, Hardin's detachment marched into the smoldering ruins of Kekionga. "The Indians, not many in number, suffered them to cross the river, supposing no doubt that the whole army was there." Two mounted men in the fields west of the St. Joseph were fired upon before they dashed away; "their horses came into camp that night with bloody saddles." Two other Indians hiding by the bank of the river were shot at, and the body of one "was found in the Brush that Day." The militiamen immediately "ran from town to town in pursuit of plunder, contrary to orders." Many of the hiding places where the Indians had stashed supplies were uncovered as this "rabble" ransacked the nearby Shawnee and Delaware villages.[33]

Harmar's army reached Kekionga on the 17th at one o'clock. The town was "beautifully situated" at the bend where the St. Joseph met the Maumee, a "fine transparent stream" some seventy yards wide. The traders and Indians had retreated "in the utmost consternation, leaving behind them vast quantities of corn and vegetables." The troops camped near the old fort and the charred logs of the traders' houses. Major Ferguson noted that "Indian dogs & Cows came into our Camp this day which induced us to believe the families were not far off." An "old French captive" said that "the Indians were scattered in the woods, and were not able by any means to fight" the Americans since "they had not got any assistance from other tribes." Signs indicated that many Indians had fled northwest toward the Potawatomi villages on the Elkhart.[34]

On the morning of 18 October, Harmar sent Colonel Trotter and three hundred men, mostly militia, with provisions for three days "to reconnoiter the country & endeavor to make some discoveries of the enemy." The rest of the army moved to Chillicothe, a Shawnee village on the Maumee. The troops spent several days "searching in the hazel thickets for hidden treasure." Digging up "six brass kettles buried in the earth, containing thirty-two silver dollars," added to the frenzy. Trotter's men crossed the St. Joseph and followed the trail of the evacuation. At a nearby prairie an Indian on horseback was pursued, killed, and scalped by some mounted Kentuckians. Then a second Indian was spotted. The officers, leaving the militia stranded in the middle of a field, joined in the chase until he was brought down. A man named Johnson stepped forward to shoot the wounded man, but his pistol misfired, and "the Indian raised his rifle, and shot him." Johnson was escorted back to camp, lingering "speechless till near sundown" before he died. Trotter proceeded cautiously for a few miles, seeing "considerable sign" but no Indians. Then a "much frightened" horseman reported to Captain Armstrong

that he had been chased by "fifty mounted Indians." Fearing a larger
force nearby, Trotter was unnerved by the news. When Harmar fired
a cannon at sunset to call in looters, he took that as a signal to return
to camp.[35]

Harmar greeted Trotter with harsh words. Colonel Hardin, "anxious for the character of his countrymen," was granted permission to
command the same detachment and complete the final two days of
the mission. That evening, Captain McLure of the militia and a wagon
master named M'Clary killed an Indian, cut off his head, and hung it
on a pole outside Harmar's marquee, "as a sort of trophy." McLure
boasted that he deserved the same bounty paid for killing a wolf.
The young captured Shawnee identified the dead man as a Delaware
chief: "Capt. Punk! Great man!" In his journal Harmar merely wrote:
"Two Indians killed & scalped this day by the cavalry, & one killed
at night by Capt. McLure. A great number of horses lost last night."[36]

On the morning of the 19th Denny noted that Hardin's detachment
left "with great reluctance." Many of them "dropped out of the ranks
and returned to camp," leaving Hardin with a force of about 150 militia and 30 regulars. They forded the St. Joseph and headed northwest
along a well-worn trace (near present U.S. 33). Several miles away
from Kekionga, two Indian dogs emerged from the woods. Fearing
an ambush, Hardin ordered a halt and deployed companies to scout
the area, finding only a recently abandoned Indian camp. Hardin then
resumed his march, but neglected to inform Captain Faulkner, whose
company, on the far side of a small bushy hill, was left behind. Major
Fontaine's mounted men scouted ahead. They reported "a great deal
of fresh sign," which suggested that the Indians "appeared to be
retreating as fast as possible." The troops were "keen to pursue" and
had advanced a few miles, before Hardin, realizing that Faulkner's
company was missing, sent part of Fontaine's cavalry to get them. At
about this time two Indians on foot were spotted; they threw down
their packs and escaped into the heavy underbrush. Then a shot was
heard in the distance, thought to be a warning signal. Convinced that
the Indians were on the run, Hardin hurried his men forward. A low
wooded hill on the left and a watery marsh of tall grass on the right
narrowed the trail as it neared the Eel River. A vanguard on horseback led the way, followed by the rest of the troops in single file. A

campfire was spotted ahead; scattered trinkets sparkled along the trace, apparently dropped by the fleeing Indians. At this point, Hardin called a halt.[37]

Hardin and his men had wandered into the home territory of Little Turtle, whose village was only a few miles away on the Eel River. The Miami war chief had first come to prominence in 1780. On a mission to liberate Detroit from the British, Col. Auguste Mottin de la Balme and some sixty adventurers had taken possession of "a well-stocked warehouse" at Kekionga. His next objective was Tacumwah's trading post on the Eel River near Little Turtle's town. Tacumwah (The Other Side) was the sister of Pacanne, mother of Jean Baptiste Richerville, and wife of Charles Beaubien, whose store had been pillaged. On 5 November the Frenchman's dreams of conquest ended on the banks of the Eel River. Little Turtle's Miami warriors attacked at dawn, killing La Balme and most of his men.[38] Since that celebrated exploit, Little Turtle had been the war chief of Le Gris's village, leading numerous war parties on raids into Kentucky.

Little Turtle had been watching the Americans closely. Harmar made a major mistake when he divided his force and sent out detachments. The two Indians on horseback whom Trotter's men killed were trying to lure the troops toward the woods where Little Turtle's warriors waited in ambush. Instead they were cut off by militiamen on their fast Kentucky horses. Now Hardin's dwindling force had been decoyed down a narrow path that left them strung out between warriors positioned behind trees on the hill and others hidden in the marsh.

The first volley came from the hillside: "Ten men in the advance guard were shot down, one rose & escaped." Nicholas Tomlinson, a scout, was "literally shot to pieces." When the troops sought shelter in the marsh, they were met by a volley from that quarter. "Many of the militia threw away their arms without firing a shot, ran through the federal troops, and threw them into disorder." Hardin tried to get his men to stop. Captain Armstrong and his thirty regulars, along with a dozen militiamen, stood their ground as Little Turtle's fighters gave a war whoop and raced forward with raised tomahawks. Others charged on horseback. The battle was over in minutes. "They fought and died hard," Armstrong recalled of his men, of which only a handful survived. He saved himself by hiding in the muddy waters of the marsh. Captain Faulkner's company, still trying to catch up with Hardin, met two men on horseback, "each with a wounded man behind him. . . . They called out, 'For God's sake retreat! You will all be killed! There is Indians enough to eat you all up!'" Faulkner's men "formed a line across the trace and took trees." They were joined by Hardin and a few other officers, but most militia continued their "helter-skelter" flight. The pursuing Indians "came within 80 or 90 yards and halted" out of gunshot range. The rear guard waited for stragglers until dusk and then returned to the camp.[39]

"I never Could Learn how many was Killed in that Scrape," Thomas Irwin recalled. McKee was told that "three hundred men [were] killed on the spot, the Indians lost only one man." Since about one hundred Americans were engaged, and most of them ran, that number is impossible and even Armstrong's estimate of one hundred dead is too high. Over twenty of his regulars died; no one knows exactly how many militiamen were killed—forty were missing. John Bradford provided a more accurate figure: "Fifty-two men were killed in a very few minutes." Some of the militia were probably shot down as they fled, bringing the total to at least sixty. None of the American participants noted which Indian nation they were fighting. An unreliable British account claimed that Hardin was attacked by "a Party of Shawanese and Potowatomies." Although many historians are vague about this battle, they usually credit Little Turtle and his warriors. Wells, perhaps our best source on the Indians involved, wrote that "Colonel Hardin . . . met three hundred Miamies on the head of Eel River, commanded by the celebrated Miami Chief, Little Turtle, an action took place, the whites were defeated, and the Indians had one man killed and two wounded." While Wells overstated the number engaged and perhaps underestimated Miami losses, Little Turtle's warriors were victorious. Hardin was so distraught about "the shameful conduct of his men" that "he shed tears of sorrow." Harmar wrote in his journal that Hardin's command "was worsted this day . . . owing to the shameful cowardly conduct of the militia who threw away their arms and would not fight. The loss is considerable."[40]

The militiamen who survived the ambush were "panic struck" and in no condition for combat. Many had dropped their muskets as they fled. When Hardin suggested a return to the field of battle to bury the dead, Harmar replied that "the men's spirits appeared to be very low . . . the sight of the mangled bodies would make them much more so." On 20 October the men were ordered "to burn and destroy every house and wigwam" left standing in the nearby towns, including 20,000 bushels of corn.[41] Ironically, Americans usually raided villages during harvest season, destroying vast fields of corn, yet they claimed ownership of Indian land because the "savages" were not farmers but mere hunters and gatherers.

On the 21st, Harmar's army withdrew, marching six or seven miles to the southeast. That evening Daniel Williams, a former captive and now a trusted scout, reported that "about one hundred and twenty Indians" had returned to Kekionga. Seeking "to retrieve the credit of the militia," Hardin told Harmar that the clear moonlit night provided "a good opportunity to steal a march on the Indians" and catch them by surprise. Harmar reluctantly agreed to send back under the command of Major Wyllys "all the federal troops that could be spared" and "one hundred of the best militia." Hardin thought that number too few. After a discussion among the officers, a force of sixty regulars, three hundred militia infantry, and forty cavalry "were ordered to be ready to march at midnight." Due to delays among the militia, the men did not arrive near Kekionga until sunrise. Major Wyllys called a halt and deployed his troops. Major Hall's battalion was to circle to the left, crossing the St. Mary's and moving toward the west bank of the St. Joseph. When the shooting started, they could attack from the rear. Major McMullen's battalion would stay on the right flank, upriver from where the main force, consisting of the sixty regulars, Major Fontaine's forty cavalry, and some one hundred militia under Hardin, would cross the Maumee at the ford.[42]

The Indians, returning to their various villages, were not forewarned of the American attack. Had Hall, "who had gained his ground undiscovered . . . not wantonly disobeyed orders, by firing on a single Indian, the surprise must have been complete." On the right wing, McMullen's men "fell in with a small party of Indians . . . and disobeyed the orders . . . in pursuing them," thus leaving the main force at the Maumee ford unsupported. To slow Hardin's advance, Little Turtle rushed his snipers down to the orchard near the traders' town while he gathered his forces. David Morris recalled that "as soon as Gen. Hardin entered the river, the Indians opened a brisk fire upon him, from all along the bank where they had concealed themselves." Seeing the militia hesitate, Fontaine charged across the ford and into the village, but most of the cavalry did not follow his example. As he and a few of his men came around a hazel thicket, they encountered a group of Indians, who may have been decoys, at a campfire. Fontaine fired his pistol and drew his sword before he was "pierced with several balls, but continued on his horse for some time," clinging to his saddle with the last of his strength before he fell. Although several of his men were wounded, they managed to retrieve his body and retreat.[43]

Major Wyllys then arrived with his regulars, who crossed the Maumee and marched toward the village. There they were met with a ferocious attack by Little Turtle's Miami warriors, who had been hiding in the hazel thicket and a nearby cornfield, and Blue Jacket's Shawnees, rapidly arriving from their towns to the east. The Indians fired their weapons and then rushed forward for an intense combat of tomahawk against bayonet. Jonathan Heart recalled "many instances in which, while the Indians was giving the fatal Blow with his tomahawk, he fell by the Bayonet," and vice versa. Wyllys was one of the first to fall; a warrior retrieved his "very large, cocked hat . . . and wore it through the subsequent part of the battle." The remnants of Wyllys's men ran toward the St. Joseph with the Indians in hot pursuit. Hardin had directed his men to cross to the west bank of the river "in order to obtain an opportunity of treeing . . . leaving Wyllys to his fate." Hardin's men were joined by Hall's battalion "returning from the pursuit of scattering Indians." This combined militia force engaged the Indians already attacking them as well as those who had overwhelmed Wyllys. At the St. Joseph a fierce fight took place with only a "narrow creek . . . between the two parties; a smart fire commenced and was kept up. The Indians attempted to force their way across but were repulsed." Soon the stream ran dark with blood from the slain on both sides. As the lethal contest raged on, Delaware and Ottawa warriors joined the fray, and the outnumbered militia suffered heavy losses. Hardin gave the word to retreat, saying, "Let every man do the best he can to escape." Not long afterward, McMullen's men were sighted returning from a running tree-to-tree skirmish with a few Shawnees. Assuming that they were the vanguard of Harmar's full force, the Indians withdrew, leaving the defeated Americans briefly in possession of a battlefield that had cost them dearly.[44]

After Fontaine was killed, a few of his men rode back to tell Harmar that the troops were in a hard fight and needed reinforcements. Harmar refused to commit all his men, "saying that he would not risk his whole army to save Hardin's detachment." In truth, Harmar's force was too distant and demoralized to be of much assistance. His regulars had been decimated and the militia was in disarray. Only thirty men went and soon met Hardin's militia in full retreat.[45]

I have discussed Harmar's Defeat at some length because it is an important and often misunderstood battle that has rarely been studied in detail. Military historian Leroy Eid aptly described the events on the 22nd as "a series of disorganized engagements." The battle consisted of separate actions at the ford of the Maumee, in the area of Le Gris's village, and on the banks of the St. Joseph, as well as several local skirmishes. One participant noted that "each party endeavored to out flank the other & keeping in constant motion the Indians had but little chance of fighting from under cover excepting running & treeing as it is called. The combatants were scattered for several miles & in some places the one party was overpowered by the numbers and the other party beaten at a short distance. It was a hard fought battle but the Indians kept the ground." Although the militia displayed courage at times, they had also failed to support the regulars, who in the two engagements lost seventy-five out of ninety men with three wounded. The militia in both battles lost a total of 108 men with 28 wounded. The fact that only three of their wounded survived shows how exposed the regulars had been. Captain Armstrong later testified that two key factors in the defeat were: "the un-officerlike conduct of Colonel Hardin . . . and the cowardly behavior of the militia." He vowed never to "willingly fight for the one, or be commanded by the other." Nonetheless, Harmar claimed that he had won the day. "If that was a victory," one veteran recalled, "I never wish to see a defeat."[46]

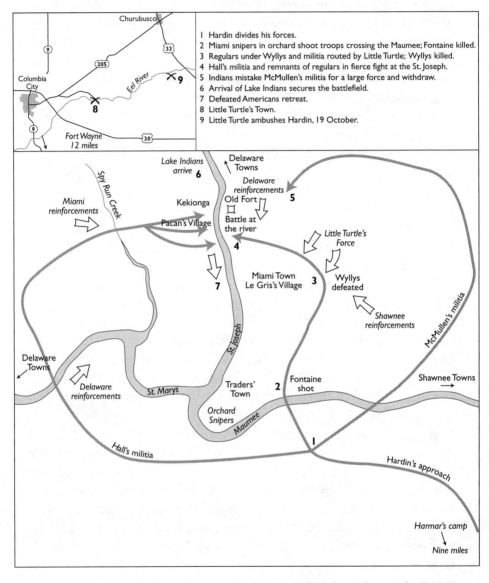

Churubusco

9

205

33

Eel River

X 9

Columbia
City

9

X
8

Fort Wayne
12 miles

30

1 Hardin divides his forces.
2 Miami snipers in orchard shoot troops crossing the Maumee; Fontaine killed.
3 Regulars under Wyllys and militia routed by Little Turtle; Wyllys killed.
4 Hall's militia and remnants of regulars in fierce fight at the St. Joseph.
5 Indians mistake McMullen's militia for a large force and withdraw.
6 Arrival of Lake Indians secures the battlefield.
7 Defeated Americans retreat.
8 Little Turtle's Town.
9 Little Turtle ambushes Hardin, 19 October.

Lake Indians
arrive 6

Delaware
Towns

Delaware
reinforcements 5

Miami
reinforcements

Spy Run Creek

Kekionga

Pacan's Village

Old Fort

Battle at
the river
4

Little Turtle's
Force

Miami Town
Le Gris's Village 3

Wyllys
defeated

7

Shawnee
reinforcements

McMullen's militia

Delaware
Towns

Delaware
reinforcements

St. Marys

St. Joseph

Traders'
Town

Orchard
Snipers

Maumee

Fontaine
shot 2

Shawnee Towns

Hall's militia

1

Hardin's approach

Harmar's camp

Nine miles

Harmar's Defeat, 19 and 22 October 1790. Map by Bill Nelson. Copyright © 2015
University of Oklahoma Press.

Like many an unsuccessful general before and after him, Harmar tried to put the best face on a debacle. In his diary the evening of the 22nd he wrote:

> Fine weather. The detachment under Major Wyllys & Col. Hardin, performed wonders, although they were terribly cut up. Almost the whole of the federal troops were cut up, with the loss of Major Wyllys, Major Fontaine, & Lt. Frothingham—which is indeed a heavy blow. The consolation is, that the men sold themselves very dear. The militia behaved themselves charmingly. It is supposed that no less than 100 warriors of the savages were killed upon the ground. The action was fought yesterday morning near the *old fort* & up the river St. Joseph. The savages never received such a stroke before in any battle that they have had.

St. Clair also accentuated the positive in his letter of 29 October to Knox: "I have the pleasure to inform you of the entire success of General Harmar at the Indian towns . . . of which he has destroyed five in number, and a very great quantity of corn and other vegetable provisions. It is supposed that about two hundred of the Indians likewise have fallen." Washington was not deceived: 183 American dead told the sad story. He had predicted that the expedition would meet with "a disgraceful termination under the conduct of B. Gen. Harmar. I expected *little* from the moment I heard he was a *drunkard.*" On 24 January 1791, Washington told Congress: "There is reason to fear the defeat of the army on the frontiers will be severely felt, as there is no doubt but the Indians will, in their turn, flushed with victory, invade the settlements."[47]

Indian losses, although heavy in their view, were far fewer than American claims. Wells wrote that on the 22nd they had fifteen killed and twenty-five wounded. While those may be lower than the actual numbers, the total casualties did not exceed fifty. Yet many historians have accepted St. Clair's inflated figure, asserting that the Indians and Americans each lost two hundred men, thus turning Little Turtle's triumph into a bloody stalemate. Furthermore, although many of their best men were slain, the militia did not behave "charmingly" as Harmar claimed—most of the regulars blamed their "dastardly behavior" for the defeat. Blue Jacket reported that the Indians, augmented by seven hundred Ottawa warriors, planned to attack Harmar's army during its retreat "but the Ottawas, through the superstition of their conjurors, were persuaded that if another action took place, they would lose great numbers, withdrew themselves in the night, without consulting the other nations." The bad omen that drove the Ottawas away and saved Harmar from a worse defeat was a lunar eclipse that began at 12:40 A.M., 23 October, and lasted 51 minutes.[48]

Harmar's problems with the militia continued during the retreat. At Old Chillicothe, he stated that Trotter and McMullen should be hanged for their "un-soldier-like conduct." For their part, the militia blamed the expedition's failure on their commander. A court of inquiry exonerated Harmar, finding that his conduct merited "high approbation." This verdict was a whitewash. Harmar was not the drunk Washington feared he was—"Give the Devil his due," Major Doughty said, "that was a damned falsehood"—but his persistence in sending small detachments into Little Turtle's home country was a recipe for disaster.[49]

WELLS VISITS KENTUCKY

Did William Wells participate in Harmar's Defeat? An 1820 essay on the battle cited "Captain Wells who was with the Indians at the time." Indiana historian Jacob Dunn said he "served with distinction" and won "admiration for his dash and courage." Wells wrote with authority about how Little Turtle ambushed Hardin, and he provided credible information on the fight for Kekionga, stating that Little Turtle was in command of three hundred Miamis and supported by "a body of five hundred Indians" led by their own chiefs: "The Shawnees . . . by . . . *Blue Jacket*, the Delawares by *Buckingeheles*, and the Ottoways and Chippeways by *Agashewah*," whose warriors arrived at the end of the conflict and, due to the eclipse, left the next morning. When Quaker missionary Gerald Hopkins visited Fort Wayne in 1804, Wells showed him the battlefield, pointing out the skulls of soldiers on the banks of the St. Joseph and the tree where Little Turtle's nephew had been killed. Thus Wells probably fought for the Miamis; furthermore, at about this time he won the respect of Little Turtle.[50]

Hamtramck left Vincennes with 330 men and reached the Vermillion on 10 October, where his troops burned the deserted Piankashaw village. His instructions were to proceed up the Wabash to Ouiatanon and Snake-fish Town and destroy them too. The Kentucky militia balked at the prospect of attacking the Wea stronghold and deserted in droves. Hamtramck, who had "calculated very much to receive a sever drubbing" because his force was "very small," gladly withdrew. His math was correct: six hundred warriors were waiting in ambush at Big Pine Creek. "Altho' I have not had the fortune of seeing an enemy," he wrote to Harmar, "I hope I have diverted the Indians on the Wabash from giving assistance to the Indians of the Miamie."[51]

Hamtramck's abortive campaign may have kept Wabash warriors away from the defense of Kekionga. Yet even if Wells had been part of the planned ambush, he would still have had more than a week to join Little Turtle's forces. Since he would lead a group of sharpshooters at St. Clair's Defeat the following year, he may have been among the warriors, including Little Turtle's nephew and Chief Richerville, who picked off the troops as they crossed the Maumee. He may also have been involved in the interrogation of the five prisoners taken, two of whom were killed. He might have fired on his own brother, Sam Wells, who served in the Kentucky militia and was entrusted by Harmar to bring news of the battle back to Fort Washington.[52]

Ever since Wells's capture in 1784, his brothers had continued to look for him. Carty, a trader along the Wabash, urged Hamtramck to help "get him from the Indians." As a full-fledged Miami, Blacksnake was free to go where he wished. When he was at Vincennes in late 1788, Hamtramck learned his identity. Carty made a trip to Snake-fish Town in January 1789 and asked Wells to return to "his home & kindred." Because Carty had married and did not live with the family when Wells was a boy, Blacksnake did not recognize him. He "thought this white ambassador was trying to deceive him for some purpose or other, & would not return with him." He did have "some recollection of his early life—the pond where he was taken—his cabin home & surroundings, & thought he might recognize his elder brother Samuel." Darius Heald stated that Sam then went to Snake-fish Town and Blacksnake agreed to visit his relatives in Kentucky. In Heald's version, "he readily recognized the pond & surroundings;

the home cabin & spring. Then he became fully satisfied that Samuel Wells was his brother—staid with him a few days, & then returned to the Indian people & remained with them for some time."[53]

Thus prior to Harmar's Defeat, Wells had already made contact with his family in Kentucky and considered the possibility of returning. We can only speculate about why he chose to stay with the Miamis. He was twenty at the time, a married man with a baby boy, and a respected warrior. As discussed in chapter 2, "Becoming Miami," there were many understandable reasons why certain captives adapted readily to Indian life and why a young man like Wells would take the warpath against his own people. His situation was probably similar to that of a white prisoner named Nicholas Deanhoat whom Col. Thomas Proctor met at Venango in the spring of 1791: "He was dressed in the Indian garb, and what I was grieved to see, his ears were cut around and each hung with a considerable weight of lead, designed to stretch them to a proper length." When Proctor offered him money and clothing to return home, "he declined it, saying that he could not live so agreeable with the white people as with the Indians." Blacksnake probably was angered at the American attack on Kekionga and elated by Little Turtle's triumph, yet he also knew that the warriors were outnumbered and retaliation was imminent. What he did not know, but must have feared, was that Snake-fish Town would soon be a target.

After Harmar's Defeat, Little Turtle and Blue Jacket went to Detroit to ask Maj. John Smith for aid. Their people needed food and clothing for the winter and military supplies to resist the next American invasion. McKee in particular did all that he could to provide for their needs, yet the British equivocated and talked of peace. As weak as the American lines of communication were, those of the British were far worse—many months could elapse before London responded to messages from Detroit. Meanwhile the Kentuckians wanted revenge for Harmar's "Late Unfortunate Defeat." On 20 November 1790, colonels Levi Todd and Robert Johnson wrote to Harmar: "The importance of a blow immediately after the stroke given by you, and in a different quarter, must evidently prove fruitful in good consequences. . . . the general sentiment favors a volunteer expedition . . . against the Weas Towns." Gen. James Wilkinson urged Harmar to recommend him to lead the militia, vowing that his "main object" would be to destroy Ouiatanon and the nearby villages, along with "all the provision and *living creatures* to be found in & about them." Harmar approved the expedition, suggested that Wilkinson command it, and assented to his genocidal plans: "Any reduction in their numbers becomes an inseparable deduction from their power to do mischief."[54]

St. Clair was deluded about the exploits of Harmar's men, claiming that "the Indians fled before them wherever they appeared" and recommending that Knox build a fort at Kekionga. In Hamtramck's more sensible view, burning houses and destroying corn did not constitute much of a victory, since the Indians could rebuild their wigwams "with as much facility as a bird does his nest." He suggested a mounted force in the spring designed to "surprise them in their towns." That would be better than signing a treaty, which the Kentuckians would "certainly be the first to break" so that they could launch "private expeditions against the Indians and kill them whenever they meet them." As usual, Knox was concerned about the nation's image: seeking land cessions at this time would have a "voracious aspect" and "an absurd appearance." He told Washington that "another and more efficient expedition" was needed "to punish a banditti of robbers and murderers, who have refused to listen to the voice of peace and humanity." These "obnoxious tribes . . . ought to be made to feel the inconveniences of their conduct." In January 1791 the president asked Congress to increase federal and militia troops to three thousand each.[55]

Although Indians rarely went to war in the winter, they wanted to keep the initiative and maintain the Ohio River boundary. On 2 January 1791 a band of twenty-five Wyandots and Delawares surprised a new town at Big Bottom on the Muskingum above Marietta, killing eleven American men, one woman, and two children, and capturing three others. "Our situation is truly critical," Rufus Putnam wrote to Washington. "We are in the utmost danger of being swallowed up. . . . Unless Government . . . send a body of troops for our protection, we are a ruined people." Eight days later, some two hundred Wyandot and Shawnee warriors, led by Blue Jacket, laid siege to Dunlap's Station on the Big Miami, about seventeen miles from Cincinnati. For twenty-five hours Lt. Jacob Kingsbury's beleaguered garrison of "thirty-five men, old and young, sick and well" withstood heavy gunfire and flaming arrows, which fortunately failed to ignite. Abner Hunt, a surveyor, was tortured to death within sight of the station, but Kingsbury refused to surrender. On the second day, reinforcements arrived. Before the warriors fled they "killed all the stock, destroyed the grain & burnt all the out buildings." The survivors abandoned the settlement.[56]

Shawnee, Mingo, and Cherokee warriors intensified their attacks along the Ohio. On 22 March 1791 Capt. David Strong was in charge of fifty-three men, twenty-seven in a large boat and the remainder walking along the Kentucky shore, when the Indians opened fire and killed twenty-three. Next they shot a Captain Hughes and used his pirogue to go after others. Shortly afterward, as described in the previous chapter, they tried to overtake Capt. William Hubbell. When his group escaped, they waylaid Jacob Greathouse and a flatboat of emigrants, murdering "10 Americans, & 20 women & children." Because Greathouse's brother Daniel had been involved in the murders of Chief Logan's relatives, he and his wife were tortured to death. On 24 April one war party brought back "papers & letters" informing the Indians that Harmar had resigned and Governor St. Clair was now in charge of the American forces. The Shawnee then sent a warning to the neighboring nations that "the Americans would make a second attack on them" and called "for all the warriors to assemble & to take courage & not to be surprised in their villages."[57]

JAMES WILKINSON ATTACKS SNAKE-FISH TOWN

To keep the onus on the Indians before commencing offensive operations, Knox sent Col. Thomas Proctor to make a final peace proposal to "the Miami and Wabash Indians." The speeches from Knox and St. Clair, however, contained both a treaty request and "threatening sentences." If the Indians refused American terms, which St. Clair would "dictate" to them at Fort Washington, they would face "a decisive stroke of a superior army" that would result in the "absolute destruction of you, your women, and your children." American ambassadors tried to ensure the Iroquois' neutrality and even urged the Senecas "to make strong war" against the hostile Indians. At a "great encampment" on the Maumee, Brant and McKee suggested that the Indians accept the Muskingum as a compromise boundary provided the Americans renounced "the Idea of taking possession of the country as conquered Land."[58]

Knox chose Brig. Gen. Charles Scott to command the expedition against Ouiatanon. A veteran of the Revolution and senior military officer in Kentucky, Scott had ample reason to hate Indians: they had killed two of his sons. Denny remarked that this "temporary expedition, entirely of militia" was "for the purpose of amusing the Indians" until St. Clair's army was ready for a fall campaign. Knox told Scott that his mission was "to inflict that degree of punishment which justice may require . . . demonstrating to them that they are within our reach, and lying at our mercy." He was to select 750 "choice men" and attack "the Wea, or Ouiatanon towns of Indians . . . sparing all who may cease to resist, and capturing as many as possible, particularly women and children." Scott's attack would be followed by others, if necessary. These opportunities "to combat the Indians according to your own modes of warfare," Knox added, "would be highly gratifying to the hardy and brave yeomanry of Kentucky."[59]

Since April the Weas had known that the Americans were coming. They ended their winter hunt six weeks early to arrange a common defense with the Piankashaws and Kickapoos. In late May five hundred men gathered on the Wabash at Ouiatanon, but when scouts mistakenly reported that the Americans were headed for Kekionga, the warriors left to help defend the villages there. On 2 June 1791, four miles from Ouiatanon, Scott ordered Hardin and sixty mounted militia to attack two small camps in the prairie, whose defenders were easily overwhelmed. When Scott's force reached "the eminence which overlooks the villages," they found "the enemy in great confusion, endeavoring to make their escape over the river in canoes." Wilkinson, Scott's second in command, rushed forward with his men and "by a well directed fire from their rifles, destroyed all the savages with which the five canoes were crowded." Hardin's men attacked a nearby Kickapoo village, killing six and taking fifty-two prisoners.[60]

The next morning Wilkinson led 360 men to Kethtipeanunk (Tippecanoe), which he thought was Snake-fish Town. A few Indians fired on them, wounding three. Among the seventy houses were homes of French traders, containing "books, letters, and other documents" as well as "a variety of household goods, peltry, and other articles." There was even "a tavern, with cellars, bar, public, and private rooms." Wilkinson burned the town and left. In all, Scott reported, "without the loss of a single man by the enemy, and five only wounded," his men had "killed thirty-two, chiefly warriors of size and figure, and taken fifty eight prisoners," while not committing any "act of inhumanity." After releasing the old and infirm, he returned with forty-one women and children, who would be held hostage at Fort Washington.[61]

Most historians have accepted Scott's version. Yet his account of killing some thirty "warriors of size and figure" without losing a single man looks suspect. One veteran of the campaign recalled: "We killed several of the men who were obstinate, and would not surrender—some of the women in attempting to save themselves by crossing the river, were shot by some of our worthless fellows. . . . There were not more than 20 men in the village when we arrived." McKee learned that Scott's militia "killed eight" at the two camps. Hardin was able to capture women and children because they thought the gunfire indicated the return of a war party. "They did not realize their mistake, till they came to a Rising ground close to the village when they were all made Prisoners." A young boy ran to warn Tippecanoe, where only three old men stayed behind to defend the town. As for not one "act of inhumanity," a prominent Wea chief was killed and "literally skinned." David Zeisberger recorded that the Kentuckians "destroyed a Wea town . . . killed twelve men, among them an old chief, whom they treated barbarously and worse than the Indians." In fact, old men, women, and children were in the five canoes Wilkinson's men fired on, few warriors were engaged, and the death toll was lower than thirty-two. Scott lost none of his men, but on his return three drowned in the White River.[62]

Joseph Brant was meeting on the Maumee rapids with "all the Principal Chiefs of the Western Tribes and was in a fair way, to bring [them] to peace," when a runner reported that an American army from Kentucky was headed for Kekionga: "immediately the war hatchet was handed about to the Chiefs and Warriors of different tribes." Brant went to seek military support from the British. McKee reported that 1,057 warriors had rushed off to join their Miami allies. Word that the militia had burned the villages at Ouiatanon and "massacred . . . old men, and carried off . . . women & children," only strengthened the Indians' resolve to fight. Scott's message to the "Red People living on the . . . Wabash" exacerbated matters. He told them that if they came to Fort Washington on 1 July and were resolved for peace, the prisoners would be released; but if the hostilities continued their warriors would be "slaughtered," their villages "ransacked & destroyed," their women and children "carried into captivity," and the survivors driven to the other side of the Great Lakes. When a few Wea chiefs went to Fort Washington, they were told that their families would not be freed until a larger peace was established.[63]

Once St. Clair and Knox realized that it was the Wea village of Tippecanoe that had been burned to the ground in Scott's expedition, they ordered Wilkinson to lead five hundred militia and destroy Snake-fish Town. A small man of charming manners who craved wealth and power, Wilkinson knew that the best way to stand tall in the eyes of Kentuckians was to kill Indians. He had long argued that a strike force of mounted men was the best way to catch the enemy off guard. During the Revolution, he had apprenticed his ambition to Benedict Arnold and served under St. Clair at Ticonderoga, Trenton, and Princeton. But Wilkinson always knew where his true loyalties lay: he was a fervent patriot and partisan of the glorious cause of himself. A conspirator by nature, he rose in the ranks by betraying friends and enemies alike. By twenty-one he was a brigadier general. His marriage to Ann, of the Philadelphia Biddles, added a dollop of class and a fat dowry to his rising fortunes. His appointment as clothier-general enabled him to line his pockets, not to outfit the army. When word of his dubious bookkeeping reached General Washington, he resigned before he could be dismissed.[64]

In 1784 Wilkinson moved to Lexington and began to upstage and backstab his rivals. He knew, one of them wrote, "that the way to men's hearts was *down their throats*. He lived freely, and entertained liberally" and his followers "loved him dearly, because they loved his beef, his pudding, and his wine. They served to propagate his opinions, to blazon his fame, to promote his popularity." Soon he became the most prominent man in the district. To finance his grandiose designs and vast enterprises, Wilkinson contrived an audacious scheme. Since 1783, Spain had controlled the lower Mississippi and denied Kentucky farmers the lucrative markets of New Orleans. A gratuity of a pair of thoroughbreds to the proper authority in Natchez smoothed his way downriver to a meeting with Esteban Rodríguez Miró, the Spanish governor who was susceptible to tall tales and low deals. In return for opening the Mississippi to trade, Wilkinson promised that he could "alienate the Western Americans from the United States, destroy the insidious designs of Great Britain and throw [Kentucky] into the arms of Spain." When Rodríguez asked why he was willing to betray his country, Wilkinson replied that in the Revolution he had fought for the "happiness" of the United States, and now he was "at liberty . . . to seek my own." Wilkinson returned to Lexington in an ornate carriage drawn by four prancing horses with two liveried slaves as outriders. New Orleans, he announced, was now open to trade—but only in his boats. He was now "Agent 13," a spy in the pay of Spain, and on his way to becoming "the most consummate artist in treason that the nation ever produced."[65]

Everything worked out as planned, for a while. Profits rose for Kentucky tobacco farmers, by the spring of 1788 Wilkinson's cargo boats lined the docks in New Orleans, and the coin of the realm jingled in his money pouch. But Kentucky did not secede, as promised. Washington's constitutional government garnered support and Wilkinson lost his monopoly when the Treaty of San Lorenzo opened the Mississippi. His countermove was to promise that if certain "notables" were bribed, Kentucky would align with Spain. He supplied a list of twenty-two likely candidates and requested a slush fund of thirty thousand dollars. Rodríguez knew that Wilkinson might be plotting "to enrich himself at our expense," yet he paid him handsomely because he provided valuable information about American intentions. Nevertheless, Wilkinson's debts soared. To restore his honor and stave off his creditors, Wilkinson decided to revive his military career. Kentuckians called him "General," and what were redskins to a man who had fought the redcoats! Wasn't a name in arms the best way to become the Washington of the West?[66]

On 1 August 1791, Wilkinson's force of five hundred mounted Kentuckians left Fort Washington and followed Harmar's route toward Kekionga. This was all part of his "original plan" to "feint . . . boldly at the Miami villages" before veering west toward Snake-fish Town. His guides advised him to stay on old Indian trails that avoided difficult bogs. Instead he plunged ahead, skirting ponds, fording rivers, and slogging through "a thick swampy country." On the 6th a scouting party came upon four warriors, killing one, while the others fled to the north. In the late afternoon of the next day the militia crossed the Wabash a few miles from Snake-fish Town. Wilkinson ran forward to examine the town, but because of "a continued thicket of brambles, black-jacks, weeds, and shrubs" he could not get "a satisfactory view." The Kentuckians could see "several children playing on the tops of the houses" and hear "the hilarity and merriment that seemed to crown the festivity of the villagers, for it was the season of the green corn dance."[67]

Snake-fish Town was "scattered along the Eel River for three miles, on an uneven, scrubby oak barren, intersected alternately by bogs almost impassable, and impervious thickets of plum-hazel and black-jacks." When word came that "the enemy had taken the alarm and were flying," Wilkinson "instantly ordered a general charge." The mounted militiamen splashed across the shallow river into the heart of the town, meeting only minimal resistance from a few old men. "Six warriors, in the hurry of the charge, and two squaws and a child were killed; thirty-four prisoners were taken, and an unfortunate captive released." Two militiamen were killed and one wounded. Through sheer happenstance the Porcupine, "with all the prisoners and a number of families, was out digging a root which they substitute in the place of the potato"; the Soldier and sixty warriors were scouting for an attack from another direction; and the rest of the men had "rode up the river to a French store [probably Tacumwah's near Little Turtle's town] to purchase ammunition." Therefore Blacksnake was not present to defend his family.[68]

The next morning Wilkinson "cut up the corn, scarcely in the milk, burnt the cabins, mounted my young warriors, squaws and children in the best manner in my power, and leaving two infirm squaws and a child, with a short talk." Then he marched toward the villages down the Wabash. After slogging "through bog after bog, to the saddle-skirts in mud and water," Wilkinson's militia once more burned the cornfields of Tippecanoe, Ouiatanon, and the Kickapoo town. By this point "murmurings and discontent among the men" indicated it was time to go home to Kentucky. Upon his return he boasted that he had "destroyed the headquarters of the Wea Nation," thus confusing Ouiatanon with Snake-fish Town by assuming that the Porcupine, because his "numerous British credentials" were found in the village, was "the King" of the Weas. Among the prisoners Wilkinson brought to Fort Washington were not only the Porcupine's "sons and sisters" but also Blacksnake's wife and young son.[69]

ST. CLAIR'S ARMY

The St. Clair campaign was a study in ineptitude, from the president down to the raw recruits. Since it reflected no credit on his admin-istration or the new nation, Washington's biographers have given this costly fiasco minimal coverage. Washington's failures were in the quality of his appointments and his inadequate oversight of their operations. Secretary of War Knox approved a plan that was doomed from the start, selected the wrong method to recruit the troops, the wrong people to supply them, and the wrong general to lead them. The catastrophic result was St. Clair's Defeat, which is ignored by Knox's most recent biographer.[70]

Following Harmar's Defeat of 1790, Washington felt "obliged to strike these bad people, in order to make them sensible of their madness," and urged Seneca chief Cornplanter to make a peace mis-sion to the Miamis to "prevent them from being swept off the face of the earth." The American peace initiatives, richer in threats than inducements, went nowhere. Meanwhile, Knox prepared for a major expedition. Although he had previously explained to St. Clair that "establishing a strong fortification" at Kekionga was neither feasible nor affordable, he now made the goal of the campaign a post there that "would curb and overawe not only the Wabash Indians, but the Ottawas and Chippewas, and all others who might be wavering." To ensure superiority "to all opposition, and to prevent the trouble and expense" of further operations, a force of three thousand troops would be needed. In March 1791 Congress called for 2,000 six-month levies and made St. Clair commander. The actual number of recruits was 1,674 and militia 418, which, added to the regulars, gave St. Clair a force of over 3,000—at least on paper.[71]

Inflated reports of what Harmar, Scott, and Wilkinson had accomplished gave the Americans an unrealistic sense of the difficulties they faced. Knox believed he could "overawe" the Miamis and their allies in four months, and then establish and maintain a garrison at Kekionga, even though it would have been 160 miles from Fort Washington and surrounded by hostile Indians. St. Clair later admitted that he had "very sanguine expectations" for his campaign, assuming that his troops would be disciplined, supplies would arrive on time, and the enemy warriors would be "inferior, in point of number, to ours." He "thought the proposed force equal to the design" of "taking post at the Miami villages, and restoring peace and harmony between the savages and the United States," since the Indians would not assemble in sufficient numbers to fight, but rather either "desert their towns . . . or sue for peace."[72]

The levies recruited in the spring had to trudge across the mountains and come by boat down the Ohio to Cincinnati, reaching Fort Washington in late summer. John Symmes observed that they "appeared to be totally debilitated and rendered incapable of this service, either from their youth (mere boys) or by their excessive intemperance and abandoned habits. These men . . . from the prisons, wheelbarrows and brothels of the nation . . . will never answer our purpose for fighting Indians." Others called them "miserable beings picked from the dunghills of the United States," "the offscourings of large towns and cities, enervated by illness, debaucheries and every species of vice . . . moreover, badly clothed, badly paid and badly fed," and "the worst and most dissatisfied troops I ever served with." In addition, the militia was composed "chiefly of substitutes, and totally ungovernable, and regardless of military duty, or subordination." St. Clair was shocked: "The troops were totally ignorant of field-duty; and drunkenness . . . prevailed in a most extraordinary degree . . . a great part of which had never been in the woods in their lives, and many never fired a gun." Despite lethal punishments, desertions continued, and many had "rotten legs" or were "wheelbarrow men" unfit for duty. They resembled the "pitiful rascals" Falstaff recruited for Prince Hal: "Tut, tut! Good enough to toss, food for powder, food for powder. They'll fill a pit as well as better; tush man, mortal men, mortal men."[73]

Knox chose two cronies to supply the St. Clair expedition. William Duer, the contractor, was a New York entrepreneur with his eye on the main chance who resigned from the Treasury Department to speculate in federal securities. The nation's first inside trader, he helped cause the financial panic in 1792 and spent the last years of his life in prison. Before his downfall, Duer and "Lady Kitty" were prominent in Federalist high society. At his wedding Washington presented the bride Catherine, a daughter of William Alexander, Lord Stirling. Knox had hired his friend so that he could pay his many creditors. Samuel Hodgdon, the quartermaster general of the United States, served under Knox in the artillery during the Revolution. Although he engaged in various risky enterprises, his failing was incompetence rather than corruption. Army officers considered him "totally unfit for such a business."[74]

Although time was of the essence, the supplies that arrived at Fort Washington were tardy and defective. St. Clair blamed this on "the gross and various mismanagements and neglects of the quarter master's and contractor's departments." Duer was preoccupied by his own shady dealings, while Hodgdon was often penny-wise and pound-foolish in his efforts to economize, sending army surplus from the Revolution. Most of the supplies were shipped from the east when they could have been prepared more efficiently in Pittsburgh. St. Clair at Fort Washington had to act as quartermaster until Hodgdon arrived on 10 September. "The delays attending the movements of our army were ruinous to the last degree," Symmes later wrote. "From June to September the army seemed motionless."[75]

The condition of the supplies met with sharp condemnation. The clothing for the levies was "infamous" and "inferior"—shirts were too tight, hats and coats were "extremely bad," and shoes popped their seams. Camp kettles and canteens were scarce, as were axes and entrenching tools. Many of the guns were "unfit for use." Two forges arrived without an anvil. Much of the ammunition had to be "fixed," a tedious process of packing powder into musket cartridges and filling artillery shells. The powder was "of very inferior quality." Cartridge boxes and powder kegs fell apart. Lacking cartridge paper, the troops rarely practiced marksmanship. The carriages for the cannon had to be rebuilt and the guns remounted, and four-pound shot arrived for three-pound cannon. Packsaddles from Philadelphia were "large enough for elephants." St. Clair diligently made up for many of these deficiencies, turning Fort Washington into "a large manufactory on the inside."[76]

Horses and tents presented more serious problems. When the horses arrived at Fort Washington, they were already in bad shape: "Hardships and inattention during a long and tedious water-passage had unfitted them for the arduous service to which they were devoted." St. Clair's men did not march until October, a fatal delay: "after the first frost falls the food in the woods is gone and horses must starve in a wilderness." Accounts of the campaign noted, "ye horses are enfeebled & die daily . . . ye badness of ye roads, rendered still worse by ye heavy rains, had worn ye horses down." Since they supplied the army, the more packhorses that died the less viable the campaign became. The tents were new, but they let rain through like "a sieve." The men were "wet, cold & uncomfortable," diarrhea and dysentery "with a long list of other complaints" spread, and their powder was "damaged by exposure to air and moisture." Capt. Samuel Newman wrote: "Tent leaked as usual, & ye Contractor got his Benediction."[77]

When General Harmar saw that most of the men were "collected from the streets and prisons of the cities," and their officers were "totally unacquainted" with fighting Indians, he "predicted a defeat." He was astonished that St. Clair "should think of hazarding, with such people, and under such circumstances, his reputation and life, and the lives of so many others" against "an enemy brought up from infancy to war." Nevertheless, he urged his friend Lieutenant Denny to "go on the campaign; some will escape, and you may be among the number."[78]

If the troops were inadequate, supplies were defective, and it was already autumn, why didn't St. Clair call off the campaign? He later argued that he had no choice: "the orders to proceed with the expedition were express and positive . . . no discretionary power to lay

it aside was vested in me." Knox disagreed: "he [St. Clair] was constituted the sole and competent judge . . . and invested with plenary
powers for that purpose." Knox repeatedly urged St. Clair to make
haste: the president "enjoins you, by every principle that is sacred,
to stimulate your operations in the highest degree, and to move as
rapidly as the lateness of the season, and the nature of the case will
possibly admit." Given Washington's mandate, the "vast expenses,"
the high public expectations, and the presence of the troops, St. Clair
pushed ahead. Perhaps his most fatal flaws were overconfidence in
his abilities and a profound underestimation of his foe. He marched
into the wilderness without "a single person . . . who had ever been
through it" and without knowing the force of the enemy because
"it was impossible to obtain intelligence. Spies cannot be sent into a
camp of savages: no reward that could be given would induce any
person to attempt it. . . . No such person . . . was to be found." Marching blind into enemy territory, St. Clair followed "a compass-course,
conjectural indeed" and refused to admit how closely his movements
were being observed. Not "a single Indian had been seen," he later
said, "except a few straggling hunters." That was an astonishing
claim, since in the forty-five days prior to his defeat, Indians were
sighted about fifteen times, at least three soldiers were killed, several
captured, and over a hundred horses stolen. Unlike their unsuspecting commander, the disgruntled soldiers knew that Indians lurking
in the woods were watching them.[79]

St. Clair should have postponed the expedition until the spring;
instead his army spent the last weeks of September constructing Fort
Hamilton, twenty-five miles north of Cincinnati. The plan was to cut
a road to Kekionga, building two forts along the way to protect the
supply lines. For this purpose the troops had eighty soft-bladed axes
whereas one thousand sharp ones were needed. St. Clair prided himself on the "ease and celerity" with which his order of march could
become a battle line. In his absence, Gen. Richard Butler issued an
alternative plan, which St. Clair then overturned: "From that moment
his coolness and distance increased," St. Clair recalled, "and he seldom came near me." Tension between the generals intensified while
the army was constructing Fort Jefferson. The first frost appeared on
13 October, killing forage for the horses. Butler suggested that with "a

thousand picked men of the army, he would go forward to the Miami villages, and take post there, while I might finish the fort with the remainder." St. Clair "laughed in his face" and "with great gravity" the next morning rejected the proposal. Butler, for his part, felt that he had been "treated with contempt."[80]

On 10 October Col. William Oldham, who had shared a flatboat with Billy Wells in 1779, arrived with 320 Kentucky militia, including Sam Wells. Although most were substitutes, "old, and by no means woodsmen," the militia was excused from fatigue duty in order to serve as scouts and flankers. Soon they began to desert, as did many levies whose six-month service was over. When food supplies were delayed, more militia left, "& ye remainder swear they will not stay if they are to be reduced in their rations." On 23 October, the day Fort Jefferson was completed, two servants were executed for stealing horses in order to "go off to ye Indians" and a levie for shooting "his comrade." Nevertheless, desertions continued: "Much dissatisfaction among the militia and levies; the latter claim their discharges." Yet St. Clair felt "compelled to move on," Sargent wrote, "as the only chance of continuing our little army." His plan was to march the poor levies "so far into the enemy's country that they may be afraid to return."[81]

On 27 October Piamingo and nineteen other Chickasaws joined the army as scouts, but then departed on a ten-day excursion that left St. Clair's troops exposed to an ambush. On 31 October, after a week of stormy weather, Oldham reported that sixty militiamen had run off, intending to plunder the packhorses from Fort Jefferson. The rest were on the verge of mutiny. Without consulting General Butler or his other officers, St. Clair ordered Hamtramck's First Regiment to pursue the fleeing militia "about twenty-five miles below Fort Jefferson, or until he met the second convoy [from Fort Washington], and then return and join the Army." Winthrop Sargent regretted the loss of "300 effective men . . . the best in the service," and William Darke added: "we are deprived of one fourth of the army in the heart of the savage dominions." Thus St. Clair, like Harmar before him, had divided his diminished forces—not to engage the Miamis but to "overawe" his remaining militia.[82]

On the evening of 31 October, 100 head of cattle and 212 pack-horses loaded with enough flour for ten days arrived. St. Clair was "so exceedingly afflicted with the Gout" that a litter was "made to carry him like a corpse between two horses." The army remained encamped on 1 November, perhaps because St. Clair was too ill to travel, or, as Sargent imagined, because the general needed time "to make up dispatches for the war office." The next day the army resumed an old Indian trail they had followed since Fort Jefferson, where 120 of the ill and infirm had been left behind to man the garrison. After the departure of the First Regiment, St. Clair's forces amounted to 1,453 men, many in no condition for combat. The army was accompanied by more than one hundred "women and retainers," including packhorse men, artificers, drivers, drovers, servants, prostitutes, washerwomen, mistresses, wives, and children. "Thank God I have now my Compliment of Women," Captain Newman wrote, "ye fair sex which accompany my regiment." He gave a few names: Mary Hastings, "a damned Bitch"; Mrs. Gordon, who smuggled canteens of rum to his men; and Mrs. Brady, with her infant, who was allowed "to follow ye Camp during decent conduct."[83]

On 3 November St. Clair's tatterdemalion troops marched six miles, seeing "fresh signs of the savages" on the way, and prepared to camp by a small creek; but the land was low and liable to flooding. Lieutenant Denny scouted ahead two miles and found "pleasant dry ground, on bank of a creek about twenty yards wide," assumed to be the St. Mary's but really a branch of the Wabash, which was "fordable" at the time. The army reached the ground in the early evening; "the men much fatigued prevented the General from having some works of defense immediately erected." Breastworks would have to wait for the morning. Due to his confusion about the rivers, St. Clair thought he was a day's march from Kekionga, almost fifty miles away. The elevated land by the Wabash was "barely sufficient to encamp the army," which was deployed in a rectangle consisting of two parallel sides of four hundred yards each and seventy yards apart. Three levie battalions protected by "four pieces of artillery" comprised a long line facing northwest on ground that descended "gradually in front" to the Wabash. Two levie battalions, Lt. Col. William Darke's Second Regiment, and another battery formed a similar line facing southeast. Capt. William Faulkner's riflemen supported by a company of horse made up the shorter northern flank, while

Capt. Jonathan Snowden's cavalry beside Buck Run defended the south. Camp followers, support staff, horses, livestock, wagons, and supplies were concentrated in the middle, as were the marquis of St. Clair and his principal officers. To prevent further desertions, the militia was stationed a quarter mile over the river in an open plain to the northwest that had been the site of "an immense number of old and new Indian camps." Colonel Oldham, seeing fresh prints of horses in the mud, predicted a morning attack. In addition, six sentinel outposts of at least thirty-five men each guarded the perimeter. Bushy marshland and a dark forest of almost leafless trees surrounded the Americans. A light snow had fallen, leaving patches of white beneath the black trunks. The weary men, many coughing and chilled to the bone, huddled around stick fires in front of their tents before they went to sleep.[84]

ST. CLAIR'S DEFEAT

Matthew Bunn, a levie from Massachusetts, was captured near Fort Jefferson by Delaware warriors. At Kekionga "an old grey headed chief" shook hands and warned him to stop crying or he would be killed. Then "they brought a white man to examine me, which he did very closely, concerning the army, and what situation they were in." His interrogator might possibly have been Blacksnake, now married to Little Turtle's daughter Sweet Breeze. What is significant is that the Indians were collecting precise intelligence about St. Clair's army while he remained in ignorance of theirs. Bunn recalled that "the savages were gathered together in this town for a general rendezvous, and remained here, in number fifteen hundred, or thereabouts, for one week, and then they all marched to meet Gen. St. Clair's army."[85]

Wells related that "a considerable altercation arose amongst the Indians" over who should lead their combined force of eleven hundred men. Little Turtle, Buckongehelas, and Blue Jacket were obvious candidates. Buckongehelas threw his support to Little Turtle, "saying that he was the youngest and most active man," who had proved his ability to improvise on the spot against Harmar's army. Little Turtle then made a bold decision: to attack St. Clair's army before it could reach Kekionga. The chief "reviewed his men and gave them orders" on "an extensive plain" near the Maumee. He divided them into bands of twenty, with four men to hunt each day. Thus "his warriors were well supplied with provisions" as they advanced. Simon Girty reported that the troops "were never in greater Heart to meet their Enemy, nor more sure of success, they are determined to drive them to the Ohio."[86]

The nations marched in widely separated columns, communicating via runners. For days "the wood re-echoed their songs of War." When spies informed them of the proximity of St. Clair's forces, Little Turtle and the other chiefs "concluded to encamp, it was too late, they said, to begin the 'play.' They would defer the sport till next morning." In the battle, Wells said, "each nation was commanded by its own Chief," who were "all governed by *Little Turtle*, who made the arrangements . . . and commenced the action under his immediate command." Indian armies often attacked at dawn in a half-moon formation, moving rapidly on each flank to encircle the enemy. They rarely if ever choose to fight a large and heavily armed force camped on high ground—hence Little Turtle's plan was especially daring. The Miamis, Shawnees, and Delawares would surprise the militia while the Wyandots, Mingos, and Cherokees attacked the American front line by the Wabash and the Ottawas, Potawatomis, and Chippewas came from the rear.[87]

Capt. Jacob Slough, a levie in Maj. Thomas Butler's 1st Battalion, was pitching his tent when Capt. Edward Butler noted that "if a party was sent out" they might catch "some of the rascals" stealing horses. Two dozen sergeants from Col. George Gibson's regiment volunteered to follow Slough. They proceeded a mile up an Indian trail before dividing into two parties, "forty yards apart on each side of the path." In a short time, a few Indians appeared, were fired on, and fled. Fifteen minutes later "a large party of Indians" glided through the forest on the left and then "another party, nearly the same number, passed to the right." George Adams, an experienced woodsman, said, "it would be prudent for us to return." Around midnight, Slough informed Colonel Oldham "that the camp would be attacked in the morning." He then warned General Butler and offered to contact St. Clair, but Butler replied that he should get some rest. Whether because of his animosity toward St. Clair, or because he discounted the danger, Butler did not convey Slough's information to his gout-ridden commander.

Robert Branshaw, a Kentucky ranger posted in advance of the militia camp, said, "It was in the gray of the morning . . . [and] I was standing near one of the guard-fires, conversing with a comrade, when suddenly I saw some twenty or thirty painted savages dodging around among the trees in front of us, as if with the view of taking us by surprise." Branshaw raised his rifle and fired. "The smoke had not cleared away from my piece, when a terrific volley was poured in upon us, accompanied with appalling yells as it might be from a thousand throats, and at the same time I saw the Indians springing out from their covers in every direction and rushing down upon us in overwhelming numbers." When Branshaw turned to flee, he saw that his comrade was already dead. "As we fell back upon the militia close behind us, they in the wildest alarm discharged their pieces at the approaching savages, and then turned and fled for their lives through the little hollow back to the main camp."[88]

The troops had paraded under arms at "ten minutes before day-light" but were dismissed to collect the packhorses. Before dawn Sargent had visited Oldham, and he returned to headquarters when the attack began. "The firing of the enemy was preceded for about five minutes by the Indian yell, the first I ever heard; not terrible . . . but more resembling an infinitude of horse-bells." Others said it was like the clamoring of cowbells or the howling of wolves. Except for "a very faint and feeble fire from their small guards," the panic-stricken militia quickly collapsed into "the most ignominious flight . . . dashing 'helter-skelter' into our camp" and throwing several battalions, "not then quite formed, into some confusion." After rushing past the first line they collided with the second, where most stopped. Slough "saw colonel Oldham in the rear of the flying militia, calling them cowardly rascals, and ordering them to stop; the last time I saw him he was with major Ferguson with the artillery." Ferguson fired his cannon at "the Indians who were pursuing the flying militia . . . which put them in great confusion, but they were soon rallied by their leader on horseback, dressed in a red coat." Probably that was Blue Jacket, who displayed conspicuous bravery throughout the conflict.

Many of the militia, who had thrown away their weapons, clustered in the center of the camp, too frightened to fight.[89]

As drums beat the call to arms, the soldiers fixed bayonets, formed battle lines, and commenced firing. Maj. Thomas Butler's battalion, which had been thrown into the greatest disorder by the routed militia, never completely recovered. "It was but a few minutes," Denny recalled, "until the men were engaged in every quarter. The enemy from the front filed off to the right and left, and completely surrounded the camp. . . . They advanced from one tree, log, or stump to another, under cover of the smoke of our fire." Van Cleve recalled that "the smoke was settled about three feet from the ground." Protected by a tree trunk, he fired at any warrior who showed his head. The army was "crowded together on a few acres . . . and . . . surrounded by half their number of Indians, whose every shot could not fail of killing or wounding three or four of our men: while our platoons, in returning their fire, three times in four, saw not an Indian, they being hid behind trees, but still our men fired on mechanically at they knew not what." Many of the six-month levies had been "brought into the field, without time for instruction and never having fired even a blank cartridge." On the other hand, John Clark's battalion and a company of William Faulkner's riflemen fought hard and "lost but few men."[90]

Little Turtle placed Blacksnake in charge of a squad of sharpshooters who concentrated on taking out Capt. Mahon Ford's artillery. Sargent "was astonished to see the amazing effect of the enemy's fire," particularly against "the artillery of the front line." St. Clair, noting that "every man of them is a perfect marksman," said that "the great weight" of the Indians' attack "was directed against the center of each [line], where the artillery was placed, and from which the men were repeatedly driven with great slaughter." Because the cannons occupied elevated ground, while the Indians crouched behind fallen logs and bushes in the ravine in front of them, most of their ordnance sailed ineffectually over the warriors' heads. Cannonballs were later "found lodged in the bodies and limbs of trees thirty feet above the ground." In their initial pursuit of the militia, the Indians had gained possession of the four cannon on the first line, but they were soon driven back by regulars with fixed bayonets. Over the next two hours the artillery remained at the center of contention, "round which a Hundred of their bravest Men fell," including all but one officer and Colonel Oldham. Van Cleve recalled seeing "our men & officers laying scalped around the pieces of Artillery." Years later, Wells recounted that, "he killed and scalped that day until he could not raise his arms to his head."[91]

The adrenalin rush of combat briefly cured St. Clair's debilitating gout. Although three of his horses were shot before he could mount, he found that his "pains were forgotten" and he "could walk with a degree of ease and alertness." To shore up his defenses, he ordered Col. William Darke to "charge . . . with a part of the second line" and turn one flank of the warriors. "This was executed with great spirit. The Indians instantly gave way, and were driven back three or four hundred yards; but, for the want of a sufficient number of riflemen to pursue this advantage, they soon returned, and the troops were obliged to give back in their turn." Darke's charge left a gap in the American lines, which the Indians exploited, rushing forward into the middle of the camp to kill the unwary. St. Clair ordered additional charges with similar results. "The battalions in the rear charged several times and forced the savages from their shelter," but after yielding ground "they always turned . . . and fired upon them back; indeed they seemed not to fear anything we could do. They could skip out of reach of the bayonet and return, as they pleased." This suggests that Little Turtle had instructed his men on how to respond to bayonet charges. By withdrawing, they could lure the soldiers out into the open, encircle them, and counterattack with devastating effect. Van Cleve, who was part of a small force that pursued the enemy into "a small valley filled with logs," noticed "an Indian throwing his blanket up & down at the side of a tree," probably as a strategic signal to his fellow warriors.[92]

After two hours, a lull in the fighting occurred as St. Clair shored up his lines and the Indians regrouped. The Second Regiment made a desperate charge but "was cut up, two officers only being left alive." The warriors, vowing to "conquer or die," counterattacked and drove them back. "Many of the Indians threw away their guns, leaped in among the Americans, and did the butchery with the tomahawks." They "pursued their pursuers with great slaughter into the Camp. . . . The ground was covered with the dead and the dying whose groans mixed with the shouts of the combatants, all was stained with blood." Branshaw recalled the gruesome climax of the battle as "a wild horrid dream, in which whites and savages, friends and foes, were all mixed together in mad confusion, crossing and recrossing each other, and melting away in smoke, fire and blood, amid groans, shouts, yells, shrieks, the clashing of steel and cracking of fire arms, all blended into one loud, continuous roar." Once the Indians had killed the officers, many of the men "despaired of success, gave up the fight, and . . . crowded in toward the center of the field, and no exertions could put them in any order even for defense." The camp followers were utterly vulnerable. A few women took firebrands and tried to drive out "the skulking militia and fugitives of other corps from under wagons and hiding places." Others "were running to and fro, wringing their hands and shrieking out their terrors; some were standing speechless, statues of horror, with hands clasped and eyes fixed upon the not very distant scene of strife; some were kneeling and calling on Heaven for protection; some were sobbing and groaning in each others arms; and several had swooned from fright and lay upon the ground as if dead."[93]

After being shot off his horse, Gen. Richard Butler "continued to walk . . . along the line, with his coat off and his arm in a sling, encouraging the men, and retired only after receiving a second wound in the side." Brought to the center of the camp, he was attended to by the army surgeon. Denny found him propped against a pile of knapsacks. A Virginia cadet nearby was suddenly hit in the knee cap "by a spent ball, and cried so loudly with pain and alarm, that . . . Butler actually shook his wounded side with laughter." Denny assumed that the general would recover, but Sargent was sure that "from the nature of his wound [he] must have expired within a few minutes of the troops quitting the field." Butler ordered his younger brother Edward to leave him to his fate and save their wounded brother Thomas. Shortly afterward, warriors killed General Butler and ate his heart; his scalp was sent "to Joseph Brant with a severe Sarcasm" for not taking part in the battle.[94]

As the American lines collapsed, the Indians subjected the soldiers to a deadly crossfire. After two hours of fighting, the men were "depressed in spirits by the loss of their officers, and huddled together in crowded parties in various parts of the encampment where every shot from the enemy took its effect." Denny recalled: "the distress too of the wounded made the scene such as scarcely can be conceived; a few minutes longer, and a retreat would have been impracticable." St. Clair ordered "another charge . . . as if with the design to turn their right flank, but, in fact, to gain the road." Gathering "the greatest part of the troops and such of our wounded as could possibly hobble along with us," the men, "pressing like a drove of bullocks," charged from the rear line, catching the warriors by surprise, and then veered south toward the road. St. Clair admitted that the retreat was "a very precipitate one; it was, in fact, a flight . . . the greatest part of the men threw away their arms and accouterments, even after the pursuit, which continued about four miles, had ceased." "The conduct of the army after quitting the ground was in a most supreme degree disgraceful," Sargent said. The officers lost even "a shadow of command." One survivor related, "the whole army ran together like a mob at a fair."[95]

St. Clair was mounted on a weary packhorse "that could not be pricked out of a walk." To his credit, he did stop to organize a rear guard led by Maj. John Clark. They performed heroically but could not protect the dispersed and demoralized remnants of the retreating army. "Such a panic had seized the men," Denny said, "that I believe it would not have been possible to have brought any of them to engage again." Indeed, as Sargent observed, the Indians "had it in their power to have cut us off, almost to a man." One account credits Little Turtle for stopping the slaughter. Another factor was hunger for booty. A British witness wrote that "it is probable the plunder of the Camp saved the whole of Gen. St. Clair's Army from destruction."[96]

Tales were told of hairbreadth escapes from the pursuing warriors and of the fate of those less fortunate. Richard Allison, the army's senior surgeon, mounted his waiter behind him while four men clung to his "powerful and spirited horse." A woman grabbed the tail of Denny's horse; "she was rewarded for her confidence in his generosity" when he brought her to Fort Jefferson. Van Cleve lugged a boy for two miles until he became exhausted, yet they both "got in safe." William Kennan carried a friend on his back with warriors gaining on them. To avoid his own "certain death," he freed himself by cutting his friend's fingers and saw "him tomahawked before he had gone thirty yards." Catherine Miller, known as "Red-headed Nance," had a "narrow escape on that dreaded day." She was tall, with flowing red hair, and was running from the battle with her infant in her arms. To save her own life, she left the child to its fate. Fortunately the infant was adopted by a Wyandot family at Sandusky.[97]

Absent from the battle was the First Regiment, who had proceeded beyond Fort Jefferson without catching the sixty militia deserters. On the morning of 4 November, they "heard a noise like cannon," and Hamtramck "gallantly ordered" his men to fix bayonets and march forward. After six miles, one sardonic solder recalled, they "break-fasted!" When Hamtramck was informed of the defeat, he returned to Fort Jefferson, a haven for the most seriously wounded. The shattered army arrived in Cincinnati on 8 November and encamped on Deer Creek. The officers abandoned their men for drier quarters and the result was "very great disorder" as drunken soldiers rampaged through the town. St. Clair took to his bed, "from which it was not expected I should ever arise, for eight days food of any kind never entered my lips."[98]

The victorious Indians returned "to divide the plunder and regale themselves with whiskey. . . . The Warriors, painted red and black, dressed themselves in the Officers' Cloathes, and some in those of the soldiers, putting on their heads the fierce cocked hat, they looked like an American Army in Masquerade." After "plundering and stripping the dead, securing everything that they could individually appropri-ate to themselves, and after being gorged with feasting, principally on slaughtered bullocks, they began to drink and carouse." In February Capt. Robert Buntin returned to the site and saw that "those unfor-tunate men who fell into the enemy's hand, with life, were used with the greatest torture—having their limbs torn off; and the women have been treated with the utmost indecent cruelty, having stakes as thick as a person's arm, drove through their bodies." One survivor recalled that "the freshly scalped heads were reeking with smoke, and in the heavy morning frost looked like so many pumpkins in a cornfield in December." "Such a horrid scene," Daniel Bradley believed, "was never acted before in this country. Braddock's Defeat & Harmar's expedition is not to be compared to this."[99]

How many Americans died in St. Clair's Defeat? Early estimates ranged as high as twelve hundred. Wells said that the Indians killed

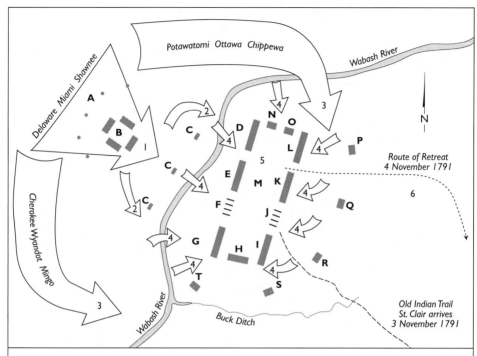

St. Clair's Defeat, 4 November 1791	Sequence of Battle
A Kentucky militia sentries	1 Little Turtle's Miami, Shawnee, and Delaware warriors first attack the Kentucky militia camp, causing panic. The Kentuckians retreat to the main camp, hotly pursued by the Indians.
B Kentucky militia camp	
C Small army outposts	
D Maj. Thomas Patterson's New Jersey Battalion	
E Maj. John Clark's Pennsylvania Battalion	
F Capt. Mahlon Ford's Artillery Company	2 Little Turtle's warriors begin to assault the main camp.
G Maj. Thomas Butler's Pennsylvania Battalion	
H Capt. Jonathan Snowden's Dragoon Company	3 The Potawatomis, Ottawas, and Chippewas on the left bank, and the Mingos, Wyandots, and Cherokees on the right, rapidly encircle the American camp.
I Capt. Nicholas Hannah's Virginia Battalion	
J Capt. James Bradford's Artillery Company	
K Maj. Henry Gaither's Maryland Battalion	
L Maj. Jonathan Heart's Second Infantry Regiment	4 The surrounded American army is attacked on all sides, taking heavy losses.
M St. Clair's tent, camp followers, wagon masters, cattle, etc.	
N Capt. William Faulkner's Pennsylvania Militia Rifle Company	5 St. Clair orders a series of unsuccessful bayonet charges to drive back the Indians.
O Capt. Alexander Truman's Dragoon Company	
P Ens. David Cobb, Jr.'s outpost	6 After suffering devastating losses, the Americans break through the Indian lines and retreat.
Q Capt. Nicholas Hannah's outpost	
R Ens. Edward Turner's outpost	
S Capt. Samuel Newman's outpost	
T Ens. Hugh Purdy's outpost	

St. Clair's Defeat, 4 November 1791. Map by Bill Nelson. Copyright © 2015 University of Oklahoma Press.

nine hundred. "Sinclaire's Defeat," a sad song of the time, stated "we left nine hundred men," adding "such a dreadful carnage may I never see again." Sargent recorded that 623 officers and men were killed and 253 wounded, as well as 24 "artificers and packhorse men" and 30 women. Denny lists 630 officers and men killed, 283 wounded, without including the men and women who accompanied the army. Several officers and soldiers died within days of their wounds, and the exact number of camp followers who perished is unknown. Probably 650 troops and more than 50 civilians died. In sum, the army's total casualties were over one thousand and the number of American dead on the battleground above seven hundred—more than Braddock's Defeat or any battle of the American Revolution. It was the biggest victory the Indians ever won against the U.S. Army, which lost roughly one-third of all the nation's troops in one day. St. Clair called it "as unfortunate an action as almost any that has been fought."[100]

While the American death toll was very high, Indian losses were remarkably low. Wells said that "only about thirty Indians were killed in the battle, and about twenty died afterwards of their wounds." Sargent recorded thirty Indian deaths while John Norton estimated twenty to twenty-five. Given the magnitude of the victory, one contested question remained: who was responsible—Little Turtle or Blue Jacket? For years to come, both men would claim the honor. Most historians have credited Little Turtle as the chief who planned the successful strategy. John Sugden, however, has derided what he called "the Little Turtle myth," pointing out that some primary sources named Blue Jacket as the leader and citing John Johnston's assertion: "There never was . . . a Commander-in-Chief in any battle fought by the Indians of the N.W. They have no organization of any kind." An Indian commander *did* have to achieve a consensus among "an intertribal council of war leaders," yet James Smith correctly wrote that it was "a capital mistake" to assume that Indians lacked organization and discipline. "They are under good command, and punctual in obeying orders: they can act in concert, and when their officers lay a plan and give orders, they will cheerfully unite in putting all their directions into immediate execution." Although American incompetence contributed to the defeat, the key factor was the competence of Indian leadership. The warriors did "act in concert." The method of marching to battle, the synchronized war whoop before the firing started, the initial attack on the militia whose flight disrupted the regular troops, the half-moon formation and encircling movements, the focus on shooting the officers and taking out the artillery, the withdrawal and counterattacks against the bayonet charges—all suggest a shared strategy.[101]

To bolster his case for Blue Jacket, Sugden asserted that Wells was "dishonest, vocal, and self-seeking" as well as "volatile but unreliable." There may be some validity to these inflated charges, yet Little Turtle's intelligence, eloquence, courage, and military prowess were not invented by Wells, but acknowledged by his contemporaries, as were Blue Jacket's abilities; he and his Shawnee warriors played at least as prominent a part in the actual battle as Little Turtle and his smaller force of Miamis. Oliver Spencer struck the proper balance, recalling that Blue Jacket was "considered one of the most brave and accomplished of the Indian chiefs, second only to Little Turtle and Buck-on-ge-he-la, having signalized himself on many occasions, particularly in the defeats of Colonel Hardin and General St. Clair."[102]

The Indians were elated by their success. John Brickell recalled: "We then found ourselves a rich people." His Delaware father's "share of the spoils" from St. Clair's army included "two fine horses, four tents, one of which was a noble *markee*, which made us a fine house. . . . He had . . . axes, guns, and every thing necessary to make an Indian rich. There was much joy amongst them." The British hoped that the American defeat would lead to negotiations: "They would probably listen to any Reasonable Terms of accommodation, if they saw a prospect of its being establish'd on solid Grounds." McKee shared this hope: "I most sincerely wish, that the Americans, now convinced of the difficulty of subduing a Brave & warlike race of People, may listen to the Voice of Equity and Reason and establish a firm & lasting Peace on the Principles of natural Justice & Humanity."[103] Little Turtle also favored negotiations, even though the Americans would never accept the Ohio River as a boundary. Rather, they would raise larger armies and try to take the land by force. In spite of his two great victories over the United States, Little Turtle knew that the Indians could not continue to win against such a numerous and determined people—and so did William Wells.

CHAPTER FIVE

WILLIAM WELLS,
AMERICAN SPY

On 13 July 1792 the interpreter that Rufus Putnam had requested from Kentucky stood before him at Fort Washington. About five feet, eight inches tall, with a freckled face, he was "a young man of respectable family by the name of Wells." He related that "on his way to school in Kentucky 8 years ago, he was captured by the Eel River & afterwards adopted into the family of the chief of that nation, where he became a good hunter and a useful man among them." Putnam was impressed: "He appears a young man of good natural abilities and of an agreeable disposition; I propose to employ him as an interpreter and have encouraged him to hope that if he is found capable and faithful he will be continued in that business." Wells acknowledged his participation in St. Clair's Defeat and gave "good, thorough, & reliable accounts of all that happened there, & has made known where the Indians' cannon were buried." His father Kaweahatta (the Porcupine) having "given him freedom to go where he pleased, even to visit his brothers in Kentucky, he went first to Post-Vincent, where he found an opportunity to visit his brothers in the vicinity of Louisville." Hamtramck in Vincennes had already "recommended him to quit the Indians," and when Putnam was informed of his language skills, "he sent for him, & took him into the service of the United States."[1]

SWITCHING SIDES

Why did William Wells switch sides? No doubt he was motivated by the opportunity to free his own family, whose members were among the fifty-six prisoners held at Fort Washington. John Heckewelder observed that when he was reunited with "his adopted relatives, his mother and sisters . . . they . . . shed many tears."[2] Apparently Wells didn't tell Putnam that he had two Indian wives and a child, and that his father-in-law was Little Turtle. That would have raised too many questions about his ultimate loyalties. Once his Snake-fish Town family was released, he would rejoin Sweet Breeze and Little Turtle at Kekionga. His brother Sam must have told him repeatedly that his knowledge of the Indians was of great value to the Americans. St. Clair had lamented that it was impossible to find a single person capable of spying on the Indians and scouting for his ill-fated army. Wells was that man. Putnam saw his talents, hired him as an interpreter for a dollar a day, and suggested he might find permanent government employment. Patriotic feelings in the Ohio Valley were precarious. Individualistic frontiersmen pursued their own interests. James Wilkinson's treachery was an extreme case, yet his suggestion to the Spanish that prominent Kentuckians could be bribed to betray their country was no figment of his imagination. Escaped captives' returning to their families, or former captives' rejoining the Indians, were regular occurrences. For Wells to leave the Indians and work for the government was not unusual. What was exceptional was his particular set of skills. He knew the Wabash and Maumee valleys from Vincennes to Lake Erie; he spoke several Indian languages; and he understood the points of view of the Miamis and of their allies.

In January and February 1798, Count C. V. Volney conducted several interviews with Wells and Little Turtle while they were in Philadelphia. He asked Wells "whether there were many whites who adopted the savage life from choice, and why they preferred it to what we call civilized life." In his detailed answer Wells provided insight into his own motivations, both for staying with and leaving the Miamis. When he was a boy among the Indians, Wells found "running and playing . . . more agreeable . . . than the restraints of school." Although "well treated" by his Miami parents, he "could never forget the scenes and pleasures [he] had already tasted" back in Kentucky. He admitted that the influence white men could achieve among the Indians "flatters their vanity" and that "the licentious life . . . with the squaws indulges the prevailing passion of their headstrong youth." The problem was that "a great warrior must do nothing but hunt and fight." He could not establish a farm, bring up children in safety, and own private property: "Were Little Turtle to return home and die tomorrow, all his presents, clothes, hats, trinkets, would be distributed . . . and nothing go to his wife or children." Unable to accumulate wealth for his family, or, as he aged, to hunt and fight, a man would come to "regret [his] rambles when too late."[3]

In spite of Little Turtle's triumphs, Wells knew that the Indian world was in grave jeopardy. American armies would invade until the warriors were defeated, and then the settlers would get the land. By switching sides, Wells was both committing an act of betrayal and making a rational choice founded in self-interest. Already the area between the Big and Little Miami Rivers had four towns and over two thousand settlers. Cincinnati had more than two hundred houses, protected by Fort Washington. An adjacent stockade held the fifty-six prisoners. Heckewelder was not impressed with the local citizenry, noting "frequent quarrels" between the military and the town, cutthroat competition among the local merchants, pervasive drinking and gambling, and a plentitude of idlers: "from what respectable persons say, they are a bunch of Sodomites."[4]

It became obvious how depraved some of these frontiersmen were following the funeral of the Wea chief Jean Krouch, who had come from Vincennes to visit his captive relatives. Putnam ordered that he receive "all military honors" and burial in the local churchyard, yet that night "malicious persons dug up the body . . . dragged it down the road, & stood it upright. They also tore down the flag and flagpole, & threw them into a mudhole." In the morning the body was reburied and the flag replaced, but the next night "the flag . . . was torn down & mutilated, but the body was left alone. Once again a flag was raised, & a guard posted, and nothing further happened."[5] Such events reminded Wells how intensely frontiersmen hated Indians and that he, a former "white savage," would have many American enemies.

What had brought Putnam to Cincinnati and drawn Wells into his service was the result of government policies following the devastating defeat of 4 November. After Lt. Ebenezer Denny brought the news to the president, Washington was infuriated:

> It's all over—St. Clair's defeated—routed;—the officers nearly all killed, the men by wholesale. . . . You have your instructions, I said, from the Secretary of War. I had a strict eye to them and will add but one word—*beware of surprise*! I repeat it—BEWARE OF SURPRISE!! You know how the Indians fight us. . . . And yet!! To suffer that army to be cut to pieces, hacked, butchered, tomahawked, by a surprise—the very thing I guarded him against!! O God, O God, he is worse than a murderer!

That Washington, who prided himself in mastering his hot temper, gave vent to his rage rings true. When he addressed Congress, however, he employed bland language to mitigate the disaster: "Although the national loss is considerable according to the scale of the event, yet it may be repaired without great difficulty, excepting as to the brave men who have fallen on the occasion, and who are a subject of public as well as private regret." He also advised Knox to "prepare and publish . . . a statement of those circumstances" that led to the defeat.[6]

To sustain the national image of moral rectitude, Knox presented a slanted version of events. While in the past he had admitted that the Kentuckians were as responsible for hostilities as the Indians, now he asserted that Indian "aggressions were entirely unprovoked" and that the Americans had always worked to establish "a liberal peace." Any problems related to the treaties of Forts Stanwix and McIntosh were solely due to "certain turbulent and malignant characters [who had] excited uneasiness and complaints." The treaties at Fort Harmar had established a *"principle of purchase,"* which the tribes had not questioned—disputes about boundaries had nothing to do with the hostilities. Blame should be placed on "the unprovoked aggressions of the Miami and Wabash Indians upon Kentucky and other parts of the frontiers, together with their associates, a banditti, formed of Shawanese and outcast Cherokees." Knox claimed that the present war was merely a "remnant of the late general war" and a product of "incurable habits of enmity against the frontier inhabitants" by some "refractory Indians."[7]

Benjamin Hawkins, well versed in Indian affairs, was perturbed by Knox's obfuscation of American policy and sent a rebuttal to Washington. During the Revolution, he noted, we "acknowledged the Indians as brothers [who were] possessors of the soil on which they lived." But after the war "they were treated as tenants at will [and] we seized their lands" by right of conquest. "This doctrine," Hawkins insisted, "was the source of their hostility." We have made only "feeble efforts to purchase peace" and, if we contemplated invading their country, "we may bid adieu to peace; their attachment to their native soil is such that they will part with it but with their lives." It would be "better for us to be passive for the present," rather than send an expedition that might escalate the conflict into a war with Great Britain.[8]

In defense of federal Indian policy, Washington wrote out a point-by-point refutation. He suggested that the Indians preferred war. Therefore, it was idle to speculate about peace efforts, since "we are involved in actual War! Is it just? or, is it unjust?" That was the question. Remaining passive and on the defensive was "not only impracticable against *such an enemy,* but the expense attending it would be ruinous both to our finances and frontier settlements." The solutions were pragmatic and military. He ordered Knox to send an offer of peace to the hostile tribes while strengthening the army by recruiting better men, well trained and equipped, for longer enlistments, and under a new commander—Anthony Wayne.[9]

St. Clair's Defeat received a muted reception in the eastern states. European events and local interest stories dominated the newspapers, not the failure of the country's Indian policy in the West. This "oblivion," Andrew Cayton argued, was part of a deliberate effort by the leaders of "the new republic in the winter of 1792" to underplay events that reflected badly on our national character. For a country that had defeated Great Britain to be humiliated by "savages" in the forests of Ohio did not fit with the glorious destiny that America had envisioned for itself. A few voices challenged our self-imposed amnesia. "Do we not commit the same offense against reason and justice in attempting to take their hunting grounds from them without their consent, that Great Britain committed against the American colonies in attempting to tax them without their consent? . . . Is there any honor to be acquired by killing Indians?" How could a nation conceived in liberty waste so many lives and so much treasure to deprive the Indians of their homeland? Rather than answer these troubling questions, St. Clair's Defeat was seen as a source "of shame, not pride, [an event] to be explained away rather than celebrated or mourned." In the West, moral qualms were not a problem. Hugh Henry Brackenridge urged: "Instead of warding off blows, give one. . . . [we have been] watching beasts of prey, who come against our folds instead of penetrating the forests where they haunt, and exterminating the race."[10]

On 3 April 1792, Knox ordered Capt. Alexander Trueman to "repair to the Miami Villages" with a peace offer that contained assertions that could only offend the Indians. On behalf of the president, Knox said "that the War which exists is founded in error, and mistake on your part," and he indicated that the United States considered all past treaties as binding. Isaac Freeman and John Hardin carried similar messages from Wilkinson, suggesting a treaty but including threats. Wayne sent two Indians with another peace offer, while an American spy, William May, pretended to desert in order to learn the fate of the previous messengers.[11]

Putnam, a veteran officer of the Revolution and a founder of Marietta, was selected as the American ambassador. Knox's instructions were that he should, *in the strongest and most explicit terms,* renounce . . . all claims to any Indian land which shall not have been ceded by fair treaties, made with the Indian Nations." The United States maintained, however, that the treaties at Fort Harmar were "fair," while the Indians considered them imposed and unjust. Brant saw the true situation: if the Americans wanted peace, "relinquishing the Idea of having the Muskingum Treaty [Fort Harmar] fulfilled, is in my opinion the principle object that prevents accommodation." But on this key issue, the Americans would not budge; they refused to give up any land they had gained by previous flawed treaties. Knox did take one step in a better direction: Putnam was instructed to assure the Indians that "they have the right to sell, and the right to refuse to sell, and that the United States will guarantee them their said just rights." Putnam would be accompanied by John Heckewelder, the former Moravian missionary, and he should "keep General Wayne constantly informed of your progress."[12]

As soon as Putnam reached Fort Washington on 2 July, Mr. Francis Vigo arrived from Vincennes with the grim news that Trueman, Hardin, and Freeman had "fallen a Sacrefise." Also, on 25 June, a war party of Chippewas and Shawnees attacked soldiers mowing hay outside Fort Jefferson, killing four and capturing fifteen, eleven of whom were later murdered. Since that was the day Putnam planned to hold a meeting there with the Indians, Heckewelder concluded that "this expedition was directed against us . . . their purpose was to answer us with a tomahawk in our heads." The deaths of the messengers and the attack on Fort Jefferson convinced Putnam that a council on the Maumee would be suicidal. Instead he proposed to Knox that he visit Vincennes to conclude a preliminary treaty that Hamtramck, probably with the aid of Wells, had made with several Wabash chiefs in March.[13]

Before Putnam departed for Vincennes, Wells helped him compose a message to "Kaweahatta, the great Chief on the Eel River," requesting him to be at Vincennes on 20 September "to establish a lasting peace." The Porcupine, Wells assured Putnam, was "a very Sensible man . . . the best Speaker among all the Indian nations [and] the Greatest Chief" in terms of influence along the Wabash. "Wells thinks he is disposed to peace," Putnam told Knox, even though he had not signed the preliminary treaty with Hamtramck, who "was no more than a war Captain." For that reason the Porcupine had sent his brother the Soldier, also a war captain. Due to Wells's advice, Putnam dressed as a civilian since "if we mean to make a peace with them we ought to accommodate our selves to their Ideas of propriety."[14]

On 20 August, the boats stopped at Louisville, where Wells visited with Sam, his wife Mary, and their four children. Louisville now had 150 wooden houses, plus one of brick and one of limestone, and occupied the "fine high plateau" by the river. Men in silk stockings and women sporting parasols were common—as were eye gougings at the local taverns. Several thousand settlers, many with slaves, lived on the branches of the Beargrass. A fog from the river conducive to fever kept the town from growing more rapidly. As the journey continued down the Ohio, Wells demonstrated his prowess as a hunter. It was on this trip that Heckewelder related how Wells scolded a whining bear "in the Wabash language" for not dying "like . . . a true warrior." He shot a buck and, according to "the custom among the Indians on the Wabash," he gave it to Heckewelder. He even killed a few buffalo: "Wells shot a fat cow, & a calf weighing 134 lbs., the meat of which was found to be very juicy." At the mouth of the Wabash, Putnam hosted a feast—of "buffalo, bear, deer & pork, a turkey, 2 ducks, a pike, & turtle soups, besides various vegetables." Wells, neither an officer nor a gentleman, was not invited.[15]

On 12 September they reached Vincennes. When the Indians on the bank saw the captives, they "fired off their guns for joy and afterwards sang songs of rejoicing in their own peculiar melodies." Putnam released the captives as an "unconditional act of generosity." Vincennes had prospered for years, but lately the fur trade had decreased and the Indians had departed, leading to heightened tensions between the habitants and the Americans. Indians from seven Wabash and Illinois nations were present when the treaty opened on 24 September. Heckewelder was bedridden with a "bilious fever," so Wells gave advice on proper procedure. "Let us Smoke a Pipe of Friendship," Putnam said as Wells lighted the pipes. Putnam shook hands with the chiefs, "beginning with those who live in the East, and ending with those who live in the West, according to custom." He told them that he would "always speak to You from my Heart, not from my Lips only," and that he had come to remove the "dark Cloud" hanging over them and to bury the tomahawk. An Eel River chief replied, "My Older Brother! All Your Brothers have heard You and rejoice at what You have said . . . we will consult among ourselves, and will return You an Answer tomorrow." From the start Putnam established a tone of equality and friendship, avoiding the military threats that had marred previous American treaties.[16]

John Baptist Du Coigne of the Kaskaskia spoke for all the nations. "The French, English & Spaniards never took any lands from us." Since "you are many and so are we," to avoid quarrels "we desire you to remain on the other side of the river Ohio," sending only your "Traders among us." A disruptive note was sounded when an Eel River chief, possibly the Soldier, bluntly referred to Wilkinson's raid,

"My bed has been disturbed," and presented two strings of black wampum. But thanks to the "good things" Putnam had said now "all darkness is removed. The sky is clear and I can speak with cheerfulness." He insisted on the Ohio River boundary: "We think it best for you to live Yonder, with your faces towards us, and we to live here with our faces towards you. When we want to see you we can go thither; & when you want to come & see us you can come hither." These sentiments were approved by all the chiefs, including a Wea named the Kickapoo Woman.[17]

The following morning, Putnam responded. To ensure that "there be no mistake made," he asked for clarification: were all American settlements north of the Ohio to be abandoned? He wanted to know "how much land You have given to the French at this place" and whether they, too, were expected to leave. Du Coigne replied for the chiefs: "It is not our intention that any persons settled on this side of the Ohio, should move away.—Our request is that no other settlement shall be made." They would not sell land that held the graves of their ancestors. All the Indians asked was that the United States show pity for their women and children, give clothing to those who "are running naked," and "send something every spring to make them glad." Then a young chief added, "Our throats are dry. A dram would not hurt us, and after that we will retire to eat." Putnam, treaty in hand, said: "Let us now drink a Dram."[18]

On 27 September the peace was accepted. Putnam continued to display tact and diplomacy: "The White People commit to writing what they transact, that the paper may speak when they are dead. Your custom is to record by Belts. We shall do it both ways." He told them that they were "now under the protection of the United States"; then Wells and the other interpreters read the treaty. The Fourth Article was crucial:

> The United States Solemnly guarantee to the Wabash and Illinois Nations or Tribes of Indians all the lands to which they have a just claim, and no part shall ever be taken from them but by a fair purchase and to their satisfaction. That the lands originally belong to the Indians, it is theirs and theirs only, that they have the right to Sell and a right to refuse to Sell and that the United States will protect them in their Said just rights—

In conclusion, Putnam and then the chiefs "who had received belts" fired eight cannon shots and received "4 large oxen, bread & brandy for a feast."[19]

The next day Putnam caught a fever and was "so ill for several days that we doubted his recovery." As the sickness spread, several people died. The nations, "rejoicing in the peace, held a dance in the town hall: "all vied with one another to look as shocking and hideous as possible." Heckewelder said that the ceremony "presented such a sight as I am unable to describe. But it was all conducted properly, after their own fashion." Then a large amount of goods were distributed to 686 Indians, with special gifts for the chiefs.[20]

After Putnam's fever broke, he summoned Wells on 7 October and made him a challenging offer. Putnam wanted him to deliver a speech requesting the hostile Indians to send some of their "Wise Men" to Marietta, where he would conduct a treaty. If Wells failed, he was to report to Fort Harmar as soon as possible so that Putnam would know whether they would "treat of peace with the United States or not." As pay, Wells would receive three hundred dollars, "and if he Succeeded So far as to induce the Chiefs of the hostile tribes to Send a deputation to Muskingum" the amount would be increased to five hundred dollars. Wells knew that Trueman, Freeman, and Hardin had been killed on similar missions. But Putnam's proposal was a test of his bravery and loyalty and the money was hard to resist, so he accepted. Riding a horse Putnam gave him, he left that day. No longer an interpreter, Wells was an American spy.[21]

COUNCIL AT THE GRAND GLAIZE

In December an anxious Putnam wrote to Knox: "I conceive it necessary for me to waite Some time longer for Mr. Wells and the Indian Chief who went with him for if they are not murdered they certainly will be here as Soon as possible whether they Succeed in persuading the Dellawares &c &c to accompany them or not." The next day he informed Wayne that he had not heard from the Indians. "Nor have I ever had much expectation that they would harken to the invitation . . . nothing but a Sevear whiping will bring these proud Savages to a

Sence of their intrest." He concluded: "Mr. Wm Wells who I Sent with
some Eel Creek Chiefs to the hostile tribes with a Speech . . . I fear has
Sheared the fate of poor Truman or other wise he would have ben at
Muskingtum before I left it the only hope I have is that he may have
made his escape back to Post Vincent. . . . But whether he be dead or
alive, confident I am that the tribes to whom he was Sent have not
listened to the voice of peace."[22] If Putnam thought that the mission
was doomed, why had he sent Wells to face almost certain death?

During the period when the American peace messengers were
murdered, Washington and Knox had also been recruiting "friendly"
Indians to contact their hostile brothers on the Maumee. Echoing
Washington's words, Knox told the Seneca chief Cornplanter that the
Americans could "easily replace" their losses from St. Clair's Defeat
and "in the long run" they were certain to conquer; "if much evil
befall the bad Indians, they will have brought it on themselves." Any
"good Indians" had better be on the winning side. In March a delegation of forty-eight Seneca headmen came to Philadelphia, where
Washington assured them that the United States "require no lands
but those obtained by treaties, which we consider fairly made, and
particularly confirmed by the treaty of Muskingum [Fort Harmar] in
the year of 1789." As long as the Americans insisted on this position,
even though their previous treaties were not "fairly made," peace
was unlikely. The Senecas were entertained, given $1,500 worth of
presents, and a similar amount in annuities for promoting the American peace offer at a grand council on the Maumee.[23]

The centerpiece of American peace policy in 1792 was the recruitment of Joseph Brant, who had helped establish the Indian confederacy. Knox sent a flattering letter to Brant, assuring him that "the
President . . . considers your mind more enlightened" than other
Indian leaders' and asked him to meet with Washington. Brant
replied that first he needed to have his trip approved by "the Western
nations." He then told McKee, "My taking this jaunt to the American
seat of Government, will enable me to form an idea of their intentions." The time had come to make a deal with the United States: "If
their demands are such as we cannot comply with, then the best of a
bad bargain must be made." When Brant arrived in Philadelphia on
20 June, he reiterated his conviction that the Americans had to abandon the treaty of Fort Harmar as a valid basis for peace and accept a

compromise boundary at the Muskingum. Knox listened but did not hear. Instead, assuming that Brant could be bribed, he offered extensive land and a lifelong pension, which Brant refused. Although he had agreed to carry the American proposal, Brand told British minister George Hammond that it was "far from meeting his approbation personally."[24]

Knox assured Wayne "that considerable dependence may be placed on Captain Brant—He is well acquainted with the subject, and if his faithfulness in the cause he has undertaken be equal to his intelligence he will probably effect a treaty." Brant was delayed by illness at Niagara, where he wrote frankly to Knox that his peace policy was likely to fail: "There are now great numbers of Indians collected . . . determined upon a new boundary line. In short, they are all sensible, that what has hitherto been done, which I fully explained to you, was unfair; and . . . peace will not be easily established, without relinquishing part of your claim."[25]

Hendrick Aupaumut, a Mohican from New Stockbridge, whose people had "a long tradition of friendly contact with the Miami, Shawnee, and Delaware," was sent by Knox in May with instructions to tell the hostile Indians that General Putnam would be at Fort Jefferson "to conclude a truce." Aupaumut believed "that if the Western Nations could be rightly informed of the desires of the United States, they would comply for peace." Although Brant warned him that he was on a fool's errand and that "it would be advisable to let the British send this message," Aupaumut proceeded to "the grand council fire" at the rapids of the Maumee, known as Roche de Bout, where McKee had his store. He presented Captain Pipe a four-foot belt of wampum featuring fifteen rows and fifteen squares, since Kentucky and Vermont had recently become states. In his talk Aupaumut softened the American terms and emphasized a promise by the United States to redress Indian grievances against the settlers and to remove their advance forts. On 27 July Aupaumut arrived at the Glaize, where the council would ultimately meet, and repeated the American peace offer; but McKee warned: "Do not mind what he says, for he is sent by the Big knives. If you do believe him, then you will be a miserable people."[26]

Following St. Clair's Defeat, the Miamis, Shawnees, and Delawares at Kekionga had moved to the Glaize, the confluence of the

Auglaize and Maumee (Defiance, Ohio). The site was on an ancient warpath stretching from Lake Erie to the Ohio and points south. Captain Johnny's Shawnee town was already there. Blue Jacket and Snake established villages down the Maumee on the north shore. Little Turtle's Miamis settled on the west bank of Bean Creek, which entered the Maumee from the north. Eight miles to the south on the Auglaize stood Big Cat's main Delaware town. Scattered among these villages were renegade Cherokees, refugee Conoys and Nanticokes from the Chesapeake Bay, and families of Mohawks, Cayugas, and Senecas. One isolated cabin was occupied by Cooch-coo-cheeh, an Iroquois wise woman whose advice the men sought before they went to war. French and English traders from Kekionga had built stores and houses on high ground at the mouth of the Auglaize. Cornfields spread for miles along both rivers.[27]

In the late summer of 1792 the some two thousand people living within ten miles of the Glaize were joined by more than one thousand other Indians who had come for the grand council. Before the meetings began, Aupaumut had time to learn the disposition of the tribes. The Shawnees, he was told, "are very high for war . . . the Miamies likewise," but among the Delawares he found discontent. Their "Head Heroe" Buckongahelas accused the Wyandots, Iroquois, and British of giving his people the tomahawk and laying "the foundation of our ruin." Now the Delawares were "the front door" where danger entered while other nations lived in safety. He no longer wanted to hear "the advice of Simon Girty, the White man, nor of any of my nation who resides at the Forks [the Glaize]." The Delaware peace faction, however, were unwilling to break openly with the Shawnees. The situation was complicated by reports that Wayne's army was preparing for an invasion of Indian country. When Brant's son Isaac arrived on 17 September, he said he was present when Washington "did take up dust, and did declare that he would not restore so much dust to the Indians, but he is willing to have peace." Aupaumut witnessed "the war party" of various tribes "dispute with the party for peace . . . almost every day."[28]

At the council in early October, the Senecas' speaker Red Jacket presented the American position: Since the Indians sided with Britain in the Revolution and lost, all the nations must seek "as good a peace as we could get for ourselves." Even though "the Great Spirit above was so kind as to assist you to throw the Americans twice on their backs," now that the United States offered peace the Indians must not be "too proud spirited and reject it, lest the Great Spirit should be angry with you." Buckongahelas replied that "we who are one color . . . have one heart and one head. If any Nation strike us, we must all feel it." The Seven Nations of Canada warned that "the Americans want to take our Country from us." The various tribes should act "as one nation, and if [the Americans] do not agree to what we shall determine on: Let us all strike them at once." The Senecas received their strongest rebuke from Red Pole, speaker for the Shawnees. "You are still talking to the Americans," he said. He "threw down at the Seneca's feet the strings on which he had spoke" and demanded that they admit their collusion with the enemy and turn over "all the speeches" they had received in Philadelphia.[29]

"You have talked to us a little too roughly," Red Jacket responded. "You have thrown us on our backs." The Iroquois had told the Americans that the Indians were upset about losing their lands. Washington wanted to discuss this issue, yet Red Jacket admitted: "He did not say he would give up the Lands, but that he would satisfy the Indians for them. . . . If the Forts he had made in the Country gave uneasiness he would remove them."[30]

The climax of the council came on 7 October when Red Pole delivered an impassioned speech indicting American actions and intentions. He told the Five Nations (Iroquois) that while they had been talking to Washington, the Americans had sent two armies to destroy the Indians in the West. From captured documents the warriors knew that the Americans intended to build forts at Kekionga, the Glaize, and the mouth of the Maumee, and then take Detroit from the British and drive "all the Indians entirely out of the Country" or reduce them to working like beasts in their fields. A durable peace could only be based on the Ohio River boundary line. "You have told us that Washington says he will make us a compensation, if the Lands were not purchased of the right owners. We do not want compensation; we want a restitution of our lands which He holds under false pretenses." The messengers had been killed because they had followed paths made bloody by the armies of Harmar and St. Clair.

If the Americans wanted peace, and destroyed their forts north of the Ohio, they would "meet them next spring at Lower Sandusky (Freemont, Ohio), where all the parties who formerly settled the Boundary Line, must be present." When they realized that most of the Indians accepted the Shawnee position, Red Jacket and the Five Nations relented: "We now join with you & will put our heads together, and endeavor to get all our Lands back . . . and we will meet you in the Spring."[31]

Wells left Vincennes the same day that Red Pole convinced the Indian nations to agree on the Ohio River boundary and to meet with the Americans. Although Putnam assumed he had been murdered, Wells had traveled in safety thanks to the protection of two powerful chiefs: the Porcupine and Little Turtle. Traveling up the Wabash he saw how the major Indian villages—Terre Haute, Ouiatanon, Tippe-canoe, Snake-fish Town, and Kekionga—had been destroyed. Not all the Miamis followed Little Turtle to the Glaize; one faction, including Wells's first wife and son, settled on the Mississenewa, and others moved to the St. Joseph. Wells preferred living with Sweet Breeze; he had worked hard to free his Eel River family only to abandon them. By the time he reached the Glaize the assembly was over, and Little Turtle had taken two hundred men on the warpath. The Shawnees, who had more warriors and received more aid than the other Old Northwest Indian nations from the British agents (several were mar-ried to Shawnee women), had dominated the meetings. Although Red Pole and not Blue Jacket was their speaker, the Five Nations had protested that "the Head warriors" of the Shawnees sat in front at the council house, instead of "your Sachems [who] are the proper manag-ers of publick affairs."[32]

Wells's arrival was noted by McKee: "A Messenger from some of the Posts on the Ohio or Post Vincent found means by way of the Wabash to get to the Miamis and delivered a message on the Subject of Peace." Wells had presented "in Council, some letters addressed to [Captain] Pipe and Talebaxuche [the Grand Glaize King]" and "endeavored to prevail upon some of the Chiefs to accompany him to Fort Jefferson." The Indians rejected the offer as "foolish" and uninformed. They had already decided that "the Council fire is to be lighted at the Foot of the Rapids at Lower Sandusky."[33]

At the Glaize Wells met twelve-year-old Oliver Spencer, who had been captured near Cincinnati the week before Wells first arrived at Fort Washington. He asked the boy about his "family, their residence and rank." Spencer had been adopted by Cooch-coo-cheeh, whose daughter was married to George Ironside, a British trader Wells knew. He also recognized John Kinzie, George Sharp, and others who had moved their stores from Kekionga. Spencer described Wells as "a prisoner at large among the Indians," indicating that he had been told not to return via "the bloody path" to either Fort Washington or Marietta, which was why Putnam had not heard from him. After informing the chiefs of the liberal terms of the treaty signed in Vincennes, Wells retired to Little Turtle's village to spend the winter with Sweet Breeze.[34]

During this time Wells must have reflected on the choices he had made in the past year. Putnam's treaty was a step in the right direction, since it established a valuable precedent that the Indians had a right to sell or *not* sell their land. What he did not know was that nine of the chiefs who went east to meet Washington died of illness on the way and that the Senate would later reject the treaty because it did not permit government preemption of Indian lands. Perhaps he shared Brant's belief that a compromise might work—if the Americans would abandon their outposts and limit settlement to the Marietta and Cincinnati area. He probably felt vindicated in switching sides since at Vincennes he had helped the Indians establish terms for a just peace.[35]

A few days after the grand council, Indian spies reported that, "either an expedition against some of their towns was contemplated by the Americans or that provisions were on their way to supply the outposts under a strong convoy." At dawn on 6 November 1792, Little Turtle's warriors ambushed troops escorting a convoy of packhorses to Fort St. Clair. "The attack was sudden," John Adair reported, "and the enemy came on with a degree of courage that bespoke them warriors." The soldiers engaged them in hand-to-hand combat and forced a retreat, but the Indians counterattacked and launched flanking movements. Having received no assistance from the nearby fort, Adair's men sought its safety after suffering six killed, five wounded, and four missing. Two warriors died. Little Turtle's main target was a hundred packhorses; his warriors killed a few and stole the rest. His strategy was to cut off the advanced American posts, depriving them of food and supplies. He repeatedly urged this tactic over the next two years, but the confederacy was now controlled by Blue Jacket's Shawnees.[36]

Wells returned to Vincennes in early February and reported that the Indians wanted the Americans to abandon their settlements north of the Ohio. His news of Spencer led to the boy's being ransomed and returned to his family. Hamtramck wondered why the Indians insisted on having "the American commissioners and the English face to face" at the forthcoming treaty. Wells answered that it was "to ascertain the true story" of the boundary line established after the Revolution at the Peace of Paris and subsequent treaties. Hamtramck then hired Wells as an interpreter in Vincennes. On 25 May Wayne asked Hamtramck to procure "an Embassy to go to Sandusky in order to attend the treaty" originally scheduled for the spring but then postponed, and to return by way of Fort Jefferson carrying a white flag. "This embassy's name is William Wells," Hamtramck told Wayne. "I have made no Bargain with him, but only promised that he should have a liberal Reward." His mission "was a dangerous one, for he was suspected by many of the chiefs to be a spy and frequently in danger of losing his life." If the hostile Indians discovered that Wells was spying for the Americans, not even Little Turtle could save him.[37]

THE FAILED PEACE NEGOTIATIONS OF 1793

The Five Nations were entrusted to deliver the decision of the grand council to the Americans. At a Buffalo Creek conference in November 1792 attended by General Israel Chapin and British officers, Red Jacket failed to state clearly their terms. He asserted that "the Confederacy were satisfied, and promised to abide by our advice" to hold a treaty with the Americans. The Indian nations would meet "at the Rapids of the Miami, next spring." They were the rightful owners of land on the east side of the Ohio that they might be willing to sell for land on the west side. Red Jacket did not specify that the confederacy would only meet if the Americans abandoned their advanced posts and agreed that *all* the land north of the Ohio belonged to the Indians; and he gave the false impression that the Indians would accept a cash compensation.[38]

When Cornplanter met with Wayne at Pittsburgh in December, he also softened the grand council's ultimatum, suggesting that the spring meeting was to learn "the terms on which he [Washington] would make peace," not to establish a fixed boundary. Only the Shawnees were adamant that "the river Ohio shall be the line." The Iroquois had broken their pledge to the confederacy in order to situate themselves as mediators between the Ohio Valley Indians and the Americans. Knox agreed that the United States would hold a treaty. He deliberately made no mention of preconditions, assuming that once they were face-to-face with American commissioners the chiefs would compromise. His strategy was to present the government's motives in the best possible light. "The sentiments of the great mass of the Citizens of the United States are adverse in the extreme to an Indian War," he explained to Wayne. Furthermore, "the opinion and pity of the world is easily excited in favor of the oppressed . . . Indians." Thus it was "advisable to embrace every expedient which may honorably terminate the conflict," since continued hostilities would make "the extirpation and destruction of the Indian tribes . . . inevitable." He assured Wayne, "if after every measure peace cannot be obtained but at the price of a sacrifice of national character, it is presumed the Citizens at large will unite as one Man in prosecuting the War with the highest degree of Vigor." While Knox was laying the groundwork for a just war, Wayne thought the treaty was a farce. His idea was to send his army, "about Twenty five Hundred Commissioners," armed with the "power to *dictate* terms to those haughty savages—or to exterminate them at our pleasure."[39]

John Graves Simcoe had assumed his duties as governor of Upper Canada in 1792. The linchpin of British policy in the Northwest Territory was to support the Indian confederacy in order to maintain a buffer state between Canada and the United States. For Simcoe the goal was to slow American expansion, not to insist on the Ohio River boundary. He refused an American offer to supply provisions, fearing they might use the movement of goods as a cover for strengthening

their advance posts. Brant told him "the Indians would feel themselves less independent, if they were victualled by the United States."
Simcoe predicted that the Americans would "not offer any thing like
equitable conditions, & tho' the Indians should give up all the Country to the Westward of the Ohio that is *under settlement* still the avarice of Mr. Washington will insist upon the full Execution of Treaties
which the Indians reject, as fraudulent & inadmissible." Peace was
not the government's goal: "I am inclined to believe that the Commissioners do not expect it; that General Wayne does not expect it;
and that the mission of the Commissioners is in general contemplated
by the People of the United States, as necessary to adjust the ceremonial of the destruction and pre-determined extirpation of the Indian
Americans."[40]

The Indians of the Old Northwest were angry when they learned
that the Five Nations had not mandated their preconditions: "the
Ohio for a Boundary Line, and the Removal of the Forts, established
in our Country." They postponed the council until the confederacy
could consult at Roche de Bout before they met with the American
commissioners at Lower Sandusky, "that We may be well prepared
and all of one mind to speak to them."[41]

Congress authorized "a sum not exceeding one-hundred thousand
dollars" for the negotiations. Knox told the commissioners that the
treaty of Fort Harmar should be the basis of the peace, since it "is
regarded as having been formed on solid grounds—the principles
being that of a fair purchase and sale." He wanted clear boundaries
confirmed as well as the sole right of the United States to preempt
and purchase Indian land. Tribes with just claims not present at Fort
Harmar would be entitled to "a liberal compensation." The commissioners were given leeway to relinquish "lands westward of the Great
Miami, and north of the Ohio, from the intersection thereof by the
Great Miami [roughly the Indiana-Ohio border]"—with the exception of a tract given to George Rogers Clark's soldiers—and any of the
military posts outside the treaty boundaries. They should deal with
separate nations, not with the confederacy; "sets of silver ornaments"
were provided for "influential chiefs" as well as "twenty thousand
dollars in species" for "gratuities." The negotiations had to end by
1 August, and "whatever shall be the result of the treaty, you will
inform Major General Wayne . . . as expeditiously as possible."[42]

Knox gave contradictory instructions to Wayne. His troops, stationed near Cincinnati since May, should refrain from any hostile actions during the negotiations. Should peace not be obtained, however, Wayne was to have his men "prepared for vigorous offensive operations and in perfect readiness to move forward from the Ohio by the twentieth of July or at furthest by the first of August." He was to ensure that his force was "superior to the highest force of the Enemy so that as little as possible be left to accident." The army's objective was to establish "a strong post . . . at the Miami Village with a large Garrison of at least one thousand efficient Troops" as well as "subordinate posts" on the road to Kekionga and down the Maumee to Lake Erie. Washington added a warning, in Knox's euphemistic phrase, about "a possibility of being compelled to engage in a disagreeable situation," that is, don't repeat St. Clair's blunder and suffer a disastrous ambush. Wayne argued that the advance posts needed support. The Indians "will procrastinate the treaty," he predicted, "to deprive us of the benefit of the forage for our Cavalry—which they dread more than any other kind of troops, & *with just cause.*"[43]

In July "a Mr. Wells" sent a message to Wayne that Indians would council at Roche de Bout before they met with the Americans at Lower Sandusky "when the grass is three inches high." During the summer, Wayne's supply convoys to Fort Jefferson alarmed the Indians. When Knox cautioned that "any forward movement in force would occasion the destruction of the Commissioners and imputations upon our good faith," Wayne protested: "It does not require a Miscrosopick eye, to see thro' this insidious policy. . . . Mr. Simcoe only means to amuse & trifle with our Commissioners until everything is in perfect readiness . . . to dictate the boundary line—'or to let slip the dogs of war.'" Wayne was angry that his *"preparatory arrangements . . .* [had caused] unnecessary alarms & apprehensions" and that his *"word of honor"* to keep the truce had been doubted. It was naïve not to see that war was imminent.[44]

When Benjamin Lincoln of Massachusetts, Beverley Randolph of Virginia, and Timothy Pickering of Pennsylvania arrived at Niagara, they stayed with Simcoe at Navy Hall. The governor described them as distinguished by "that low Cunning . . . which is held for Wisdom by People who like the Subjects of the United States, naturally self-opinionated, have a very trifling share of education." Simcoe planned to smother the commissioners with kindness. McKee and John Butler were to avoid being seen "in the light of *Mediators* between the contending parties" but rather to secretly advise the Indians of their "real interests." Since they would be "narrowly watched" and if negotiations failed the United States would blame "the obstinacy of the . . . Indians [and] the interposition of British Agents" rather than "the injustice of the Federal Government," they should adopt "some ceremonious system" based on "kindliness & urbanity" that would place their conduct beyond reproach.[45]

Joseph Brant arrived at Roche de Bout on 22 May. He knew that the United States would never accept the Ohio River boundary, yet he thought they might agree to a Muskingum-Cuyahoga line. When the Shawnee accused him of undermining the confederacy, Brant complained that "bad birds" were spreading evil reports about him. The "Shawanoes, Delawares and Miamis, held Private Councils many nights, to which none of the Six Nations [Iroquois] were invited." In a show of unity Brant joined a delegation to the commissioners at Niagara.[46]

On 7 July 1793, Brant asked if the commissioners were "properly authorized to run and establish a new boundary line between the lands of the United States, and of the Indian nations." The following day they responded: "We answer explicitly that we have that authority. Where this line should run, will be the great subject of discussion at the treaty between you and us; and we sincerely hope and expect, that it may then be fixed to the satisfaction of both parties. Doubtless some concessions must be made on both sides." Brant replied: "We think, from your speech, that there is a prospect of our coming together." His optimism was shared by Aupaumut, who reported to the Quakers that "a desire for peace was gaining ground amongst" the Indians.[47]

When Wells reached Roche de Bout on 10 July, "there were about 1400 Indians assembled & Continued to arrive daily. Ten days later they amounted to twenty four hundred; *Eighteen hundred* of whom were *warriors*." Wells saw this as a sign "that the nations were assembled for war" because when Indians attend peace treaties "they are careful in bringing their women and children on, in order to obtain more presents." The sentiment for peace was undercut on 15 July when Creek warriors "accompanied by a British officer [George Welbank]" arrived, announced that they were at war with the Americans, and boasted that they and the Cherokees had "destroyed several villages & all the frontier inhabitants" in their vicinity. They presented a twist of red tobacco and asked the council for a declaration of war so that the American army would be forced to fight on two fronts.[48]

Because he was "adopted and consider'd as one of them," Wells was probably present on 23 July when Brant was harshly criticized for his conduct at Niagara. Buckongahelas even broke protocol, interrupted Brant's account, and demanded why he had spoken instead of a Shawnee chief, who would have insisted on the Ohio River boundary. "I have no other view but the interest of the Indians," Brant said. An Ottawa chief came to his defense, stating that "no part of the Commissioner's Speech appears unreasonable . . . we therefore think a Meeting ought to be held." As debates continued, often the Shawnees, Wyandots, Miamis, and Delawares gathered separately to consult, while Brant met with the Chippewas, Ottawas, and Potawatomis. Finally, the Shawnees decided to confront the commissioners. The Wyandot chief Carry-one-about "formed the Message & Lieut. Selby put down the Words in Writing."[49]

The commissioners moved to Matthew Elliott's house at the mouth of the Detroit River on 21 July. There on 30 July, Carry-one-about told them that the previous deputies "did not fully explain our meaning." He demanded the immediate "removal of all your people from our side of the river" and asked, were the commissioners "fully authorized by the United States [to] firmly fix the Ohio River as the boundary between your people and ours?" The commissioners explained at length how various treaties and subsequent settlement made that "impossible." Most significantly, they said that previous American negotiators had "put an erroneous construction" on the Treaty of Paris—since the king "had not purchased the country of you, of course he could not give it away." Hence past American claims to Indian land by right of conquest were fallacious. "We now concede this great point." They acknowledged that "the property, or right of soil, of the great country above described, to be in the Indian nations, so long as they desire to occupy the same." In spite of this crucial admission, the commissioners insisted that no settlements could be withdrawn and that the United States could preempt Indian land, should they wish to sell, "to the exclusion of all other white people whatever."[50]

"The countenances of the Indians were so sedate, solid, and determined," Jacob Lindley observed, "that notwithstanding the propositions held out appeared to be liberal . . . yet such was their jealousy and want of faith in our government, that I was afraid they would not take [them]." The next day, Carry-one-about, with Simon Girty translating, told the commissioners that all the treaties from Fort Stanwix in 1784 on "were not complete. There were but a few chiefs who treated with you. You have not bought our lands; they belong to us. You tried to draw some of us off. . . . We are sorry we cannot come to an agreement; the line has been fixed long ago." Apparently the negotiations had ended, but Matthew Elliott informed Captain Johnny that "the last part of the speech was wrong." After a brief consultation Girty told the commissioners: "Brothers, Instead of going home, we wish you to remain here for an answer from us."[51]

The chiefs returned to Roche de Bout and for ten days debated how to respond. Brant supported Indian unity while arguing against an insistence on the Ohio: "We declare our sentiments from the bottom of our hearts that the Boundary of the Muskingum if adopted in General Council, is for the interest of us all and far preferable to an uncertain War." Afterward, he claimed that chiefs of the Shawnees, Wyandots, Delawares, and Seven Nations of Canada told him that "we mean to adopt your opinion respecting the Boundary line." That night, however, "Col. McKee had a private Meeting with the aforementioned chiefs" and convinced them to maintain the Ohio boundary. Brant's version may have been self-serving, and, as Reginald Horsman sardonically remarked, "records of midnight councils on the Maumee create few space problems in any library," yet Wells's neglected account provided corroboration: "several of the principle head Chiefs—particular the Shanowas & Delawares used to meet in private Council at McKees [who] . . . always promised, that the King their father would protect them & offered them every thing they wanted in case they went to war such as arms ammunition & provision [but only if they] . . . make the Ohio the boundary Line." On three occasions the majority of the council "determined for peace & to send for the Commissioners—but Col. McKee always made them rescind next day—by his promises over night."[52]

The commissioners anxiously examined reports on the disposition of the Indians. On 8 August a letter from Aupaumut gave them hope: "all the nations were for peace, except the Shawnese, Wyandots, Miamis and Delawares; that these had at length yielded to the opinion of the other nations; and that peace would probably be made." A dozen Munsees and Chippewas confirmed Aupaumut's account, but an Ottawa contradicted it: "the Shawanese and others are strong for war." Horatio Jones, an interpreter, said that "the four nations . . . remained obstinate," but that Brant and the Farmer's Brother "had twice addressed them, urging them to agree to a peace; were going to speak to them a third time." Jones added that among even the Shawnees, Wyandots, Delawares, and Miamis, "near one half were disposed for peace."[53]

A Quaker delegation staying at Elliott's farm indirectly witnessed the treaty process. They saw Chippewas from Mackinac on their way to the council "dressed, and painted with black, red, green, and blue; having turbans round their heads, with pikes and prongs of skins, feathers, hair, sticks, &c. projecting eighteen inches out from the sides of their heads." Blue Jacket came to dinner "dressed in scarlet, with gold tassels, and a laced hat" but was "very reserved" about discussing the possibility of peace. When the northern Indians returned in a warlike mood from the council, many were drunk. In the middle of the night one Munsee near the tents of the Quakers shouted, "I am called a Devil. A Devil I am, & as a Devil I will behave; & I neither fear the Big Knives, nor the English." He beat his fist against a tree, waved a scalping knife in the air, and declared, "I am a man—I am a warrior." A Wyandot expressed succinctly the situation: "if 'mericans love peace, give us our lands—stay that side 'hio—shake hands—call brothers;—but if 'mericans come take our country, where deer plenty, turkeys, wild cows—good land—then war—always war."[54]

On 16 August 1793, two young Wyandots, who "looked wild and afraid," handed General Lincoln a message from the Indians. Previous treaties with the United States, it asserted, were invalid, since the chiefs "through fear, were obliged to sign any paper that was laid before them." These "few chiefs of two or three nations only [were] in no manner authorized to make any grant or cession whatever" without permission of "the general confederacy." American compensation for Indian land was flatly rejected: "Money, to us, is of no value." A better solution would be to "divide . . . this large sum of money, which you have offered to us," among white settlers to induce them to move. If the Americans wanted peace, the solution was obvious: "Restore to us our country, and we shall be enemies no longer." In return for admitting that previous treaties had been based on false assumptions, the commissioners had expected that "we should, for such a favor, surrender to you our country." But the United States had no right of preemption:

> We consider ourselves free to make any bargain or cession of lands, whenever and to whomsoever we please . . . our only demand is the peaceable possession of a small part of our once great country. Look back, and review the lands from whence we have been driven to this spot. We can retreat no farther, because the country behind hardly affords food for its present inhabitants; and we have therefore resolved to leave our bones in this small space to which we are now confined.[55]

General Lincoln announced that "since it was not possible to make the river Ohio the boundary" the negotiations had ended. The commissioners viewed the message "as a very contemptible speech" and promptly sent word to Knox and Wayne that "the Indians have refused to make peace." Lincoln added: "they had received just such an answer as he could have wished." Jacob Lindley wondered "what his meaning was," but Lincoln's journal made his thinking clear. "Be fruitful and multiply and replenish the earth, and *subdue it*," he wrote, was "the original plan of the benevolent Deity." If the Indians refused to become "tillers of the ground," they had "no reason to complain, if other nations" cultivated their land and fully peopled it, since "the savages" were destined to "become extinct." The only commissioner to express remorse was Pickering in a letter to his friend Aupaumut. Even Heckewelder found the speech "both Impertinent & Insolent" and was certain it was of British origin. Although McKee and Lieutenant Selby were involved in its composition, the sentiments had been expressed numerous times by various chiefs. What offended the Americans was the speech's eloquent accuracy.[56]

Nevertheless, speaking the blunt truth is not always the best policy. The Indian hard line made continued conflict inevitable. Brant wrote to the British that the Shawnees, Delawares, and Miamis had been "too much under the guidance and influence of some white people." He called a conference in the fall and proposed the Muskingum boundary, but it was too late. McKee, for his part, told Simcoe that "the malevolent, disappointed & all ill disposed" would blame him for the failure of negotiations. Captain Johnny spoke for the confederacy to the British: "Father, the fault is not ours as we required nothing of them but our just right & peace with the United States. . . . We expect now to be forced again to defend ourselves & our country. . . . We need . . . your protection & friendship." Simcoe was troubled by "the baneful consequences should Hostilities recommence on the Frontiers," but he still felt obligated to arm the Indians while trying to avoid direct British involvement that might lead to war with the United States.[57]

Did the Americans honestly intend to make a just treaty with the Indians and should the chiefs have agreed to negotiations? For Wayne, only force of arms could settle the issue. Thomas Jefferson wrote that the proposed treaty was "to prove to all our citizens that peace was unattainable on terms which any one of them would admit." Knox and Washington had offered an olive branch to give Wayne time to sharpen American swords. At least publicly, they had hoped an agreement might be reached. The commissioners had some leeway, and the Indians might have convinced the Americans, in Washington's words, "to recede from the present boundary" drawn at Fort Harmar and possibly to abandon Fort Jefferson, their most advanced post. That would have infuriated Wayne, while establishing a fragile peace. British agent John Butler, who was present, later remarked of the failed treaty: "I thought that the most favorable Opportunity that Perhaps would Ever Occur for them [the Indians] to make an Advantageous Peace and Save the greatest Part of their Country."[58]

Darius Heald gave two accounts of an "agreement" Wells made with Little Turtle before leaving to inform General Wayne that the peace negotiations had failed. In the earlier version, Wells told Little Turtle that if they were "engaged in war . . . that they would not kill each other, but spare the others life & also do what they could to promote peace between the whites & Indians." The second version added more detail: the meeting was in the morning under a big tree on a bank of the Maumee, and Wells pointed to the heavens and said, "'Till the sun goes up in the middle of the sky we are friends. After that you can kill me if you want to.' Still they always remained friends, and agreed that if in war . . . if one recognized the other while fighting, he would never aim to hit him." Later retellings often emphasized the idea that since the whites and Indians were at war, the two, if they met in battle, had vowed to kill each other, thus supporting the conventional wisdom that incompatible cultures were in a fight to the death. Heald's accounts were probably based on an actual event, but we will never know for certain what was said. Since Wells had helped Putnam achieve what he considered a successful treaty at Vincennes, the two men probably discussed the failed negotiations as well as the danger of facing each other in combat. In the coming year, while Little Turtle prepared his men for war, he also suggested that the Indians of the Old Northwest should consider making peace with the Americans.[59]

CHAPTER SIX

SCOUTING FOR MAD
ANTHONY WAYNE

On 11 September 1793, after a four-day trek through the wilderness, an exhausted William Wells arrived at Fort Jefferson from the Indian council on the Maumee. He reported to Hamtramck that "all the nations were for peace, but that the Shawnees and Delawares under the influence of McKee prevented it." As a spy for the Americans, Wells had demonstrated "very convincing proof of his attachment to his country." Hamtramck told Wayne:

> Permit me, Sir, to recommend him to your Excellency to be one of the best of men who can be employed in the army. There is not an inch of ground in this country, but he is well acquainted with. He knows every trail, knows where the Indians could be found if they did not choose to show themselves and I have not the least doubt but he would serve, tho he has other expectations and pressed very much by his friends to return to them. I think, Sir, that he might be brought to us by procuring him an officer's commission, and continuance in the Indian department. I know well his influence with the Wabash Indians.

WAYNE'S AMERICAN LEGION

At Fort Hamilton, Wilkinson was also impressed. Based on information he received from Wells, he suggested that Wayne strike "the implacable Tribes" at the Glaize and "destroy their corn, captivate

179

their wives & children, and break up" their settlements. Wayne, how-ever, must be on constant alert: "Wells is of opinion the Enemy will make it a point to strike at your Convoys, and . . . you will find it a difficult matter to protect them, they can attack your scouts, when & where it may best suit, & in any force they may find necessary." What Wells recommended was "a rapid movement" to the site of St. Clair's Defeat, building a fort there for an invasion of Indian country.[1]

"I anxiously wait the arrival of Mr. Wells," Wayne wrote to Wilkin-son the same day, "as also a Mr. [Nicholas] Rosencrantz with a Sen-eca Chief named Big Tree. . . . They were at the private councils of the hostile Indians, at the same time with Wells, by a comparative view of the intelligence they may give, we may be enabled to point out a proper direction to our movements and operations." In mid-September, Wayne examined Wells "very minutely" for three days and took his written testimony, which he believed to be "authentic." He was "very well informed & most certainly in the confidence of the Indians, from his prowess in war, he has often accompanied them in their desultory parties & took a conspicuous part against us on the fatal 4th of November 1791." Wayne hired him on the spot to serve as a scout. "I have made it in his interest—to be & continue faithful to the United States, for this campaign at least."[2]

Wells stated that McKee had promised that "the King their father would protect them . . . [and] furnished the whole of the Indians with arms ammunition scalping knives & tomahawks as soon as the treaty was over." The Indians were "determined . . . in making a General War & destroy the whole of the frontier inhabitants." North of the Ohio they had 1,520 warriors, but that number could exceed 2,000 if Wayne moved as slowly as St. Clair's army had. Wells recommended that "the nearest & best route" for the army would be to occupy the site of St. Clair's Defeat and then to follow the Auglaize to its con-fluence with the Maumee. To counter Wayne's advance, the Indians would ambush his convoys and look for an opportunity to attack the army. Should Wayne's Legion reach Roche de Bout, Wells was "decid-edly of Opinion, that not only the Militia about Detroit but also the British troops wou'd advance to Oppose us." Rosencrantz confirmed the machinations of McKee. After the commissioners left empty-handed, he had "ordered three beaves to be killed in order to make a war feast" and "the Hatchet was passed & generally accepted." Only Brant and the Six Nations refused to sign. Wells's report was the more precise and useful of the two; it explained why the treaty failed and directed Wayne toward the Maumee villages where the Indians had gathered. Neither Little Turtle nor the Miamis had played a large role in the rejection of the treaty or the insistence on continuing the war— McKee's influence over the Shawnees had been decisive.[3]

At forty-eight, Wayne was a veteran of the Revolution. His baptism of fire came on 8 June 1776, at the end of the ill-fated Quebec campaign, when he protected the American retreat at Three Rivers and was then left in command of Fort Ticonderoga. He joined the Continental Army as a brigadier-general, and at Brandywine his Pennsylvania Line held Chadd's Ford during the American withdrawal. On the night of 20–21 September 1777, Wayne suffered heavy losses when his position at Paoli was overrun by a superior British force. His men avenged their defeat two weeks later at Germantown via a vicious bayonet charge that routed part of Howe's troops: one British officer stated that "never before had we retreated from the Americans." For the rest of the war, Wayne inscribed his signature with the cold steel of the bayonet, demonstrating that the bold use of that weapon could turn the tide of a battle. At Monmouth Court House, he led a bayonet charge that forced Cornwallis's crack troops to withdraw. His most celebrated feat was the storming of Stony Point, a British stronghold on a granite crag in the Hudson highlands that commanded the river. Making deadly use of bayonets, Wayne's men ascended the heights at midnight and captured the fort. Although wounded, Wayne refused to quit the field, thus assuring his fame as the "Hero of Stony Point." The next year he helped thwart Benedict Arnold's scheme to betray West Point to the British.[4]

Sent to Virginia, Wayne combined decisive aggressiveness with tactical prudence. At Green Spring Plantation near Jamestown on 6 July 1781, in an attempt to trap Lafayette's army, Cornwallis's infantry, hidden in the woods, made a sudden massed advance. Outnumbered seven to one, Wayne audaciously ordered a bayonet charge, causing this superior force to recoil at the unexpected onslaught. Before the British could regroup, Wayne pulled back to protect Lafayette's retreat. Two months later he was shot in the thigh by a skittish

American sentry. It was his fifth and worst wound of the war, absenting him from the siege of Yorktown but not from the surrender of Cornwallis. The following year, Wayne served under Gen. Nathaniel Greene in Georgia. His first taste of Indian warfare came when his camp outside Savannah was attacked at night by three hundred Muskogee Creeks allied with the British. Wayne's men met tomahawks with bayonets, killing some twenty of the warriors, including their chief. When the British evacuated Savannah, Wayne's men marched in (later he would occupy Charlestown). A grateful Georgia legislature awarded him a rice plantation of 830 acres on the Setilla River.[5]

Wayne was a hard taskmaster, drilling his men relentlessly and repeatedly lashing anyone derelict in his duty. He gained the epithet "Mad" when he ordered that his spy Jemy the Rover receive twenty-nine lashes for disorderly conduct. "Then Anthony is *mad*, stark mad," Jemy said, calling him "Mad Anthony Wayne!" The name did not imply insanity, but rather a hot-tempered rash action. Although he had a swashbuckling streak and could be irascible and acerbic, Wayne was often meticulous and methodical. A stickler for detail, he was called "Dandy Andy" because of his fastidious appearance and eye for sartorial splendor. The theater of war was a metaphor he took literally: combat provided a stage where a man established character and earned esteem. Momentous events required proper attire. A soldier should take pride in his uniform and perform with aplomb. Cocksure and vain, Wayne basked in adulation and played favorites. William Eaton, who later won fame at Tripoli, said that Wayne was "industrious, indefatigable, determined and persevering. . . . When in danger he is in his element; and never shows to so good advantage as when leading a charge."[6]

After eight years of military glory, Wayne did not thrive in civilian life. His rice plantation in Georgia ran him into debt, threatening his family estate of Waynesborough. His relations with his wife Polly, never strong, became strained as her health failed. Wayne was a known womanizer whose favorite from 1781 on was Mary Vining, a Delaware beauty to whom he finally became engaged shortly before his death. Was Wayne the best man to lead the newly formed American Legion? He had served with distinction, yet Washington did not brush over his flaws: "More active and enterprising than Judicious and cautious. . . . No economist it is feared. Open to flattery; vain; easily imposed upon; and liable to be drawn into scrapes. Too indulgent . . . of his Officers and men. Whether sober, or a little addicted to the bottle, I know not." Jefferson dismissed him as "brave but nothing else." Yet everyone agreed that Wayne would take the fight to the Indians. Wayne accepted the job on condition that he should have plenary powers to conduct the war and be answerable only to Knox and the president. It was one of Washington's wisest decisions. Although Wayne's talents were "purely military," British minister George Hammond warned London that "General Wayne is unquestionably the most active, vigilant, and enterprising officer in the American service."[7]

Congress had authorized an American Legion of five thousand men in the wake of St. Clair's defeat. The four Sub-Legions of 1,280 soldiers included a company of artillery, four of riflemen, eight of infantry armed with muskets, and a troop of mounted dragoons. Soldiers were distinguished by the colors of their uniforms, and sorrels, grays, chestnuts, and bays differentiated the dragoon units. Recruitment languished and the Legion never achieved full strength. Given the fate of the unfortunates who marched and died with Generals Harmar and St. Clair, a man would have to be desperate, a damned fool, or suicidal to enlist for three years at low wages to fight the Indians. Some officers selected men of high quality, but most recruits were cut from the same tattered cloth as those of previous campaigns: "So worn, so wasted, so despised a crew, / As e'en the Indians might with pity view," lamented one poetic officer. Training began in earnest at Legionville, twenty miles from Pittsburgh, in the summer of 1792. Wayne relied on stern measures to stop desertions. Some were shot, a few branded, and many flogged—repeat offenders joined the "Damnation Club." By the time the Legion moved to Hobson's Choice near Cincinnati in May 1793, the men were shaping up. If the riflemen would place trust in their marksmanship, "the Infantry in heavy buck shot & the bayonet, the Dragoons in the sword, & the Legion in their Un[i]ted prowess," victory was assured. By autumn the recruits had completed their apprenticeship in what Wayne had termed "this dreadful trade of DEATH."[8]

A few days after his arrival at Fort Washington, Wells witnessed military punishments. Although Wayne would have preferred to "lead Gentlemen to their duty by a silver thread," he was convinced that without strict discipline his recruits would remain "no better than so many Contemptible Rabble." On the morning of 19 September 1793, James Irwin walked the gauntlet, his forehead was branded with a D for desertion, his head shaved, and he was "Drum'd out of the Legion with a Rope about his Neck." Five men received one hundred lashes each for respectively being drunk on guard duty, sleeping at his post, attempting to desert, striking a sergeant, and "going to the Village of Cincinnati without Liberty." Wayne's battle orders specified "the fatal consequences that will attend them should they give way or fall back" before the enemy. If the riflemen retreated, they would be cut down by the cavalry; if the cavalry refused to charge, they would be shot by the infantry; and if the infantry failed to advance, they would receive a deadly fire from the artillery. Wayne expected his men to take fighting Indians personally. He spoke of haughty savages whose insolent actions were an affront and a challenge to each man's honor. "The Legion must be made superior to insult" and the Indians humbled or obliterated.[9]

Wayne's plan to march in September was delayed "by a Malady called the *Influenza* which has pervaded the whole line." The Legion left Hobson's Choice on 7 October and by mid-month were encamped on the site of what would become Fort Greeneville later that year. Wayne's orders of march were calculated to prevent ambush; however, on some days the line of marching men extended for five miles and made them vulnerable. When some soldiers escorting packhorses near Fort St. Clair were left without an officer, they "fell on the stores, knocked several of the heads of whiskey kegs in . . . stole a considerable quantity of flour and salt. . . . The greater part of the command was intoxicated and in such a situation that ten Indians would have massicreed the detachment." A week later Cornet William Blue and twenty of his dragoons were grazing horses in a prairie near Fort St. Clair when he spotted a few Indians. Blue ordered a charge, but only three men obeyed him; after a short pursuit, four Indians opened fire from behind a log. "Blue turned his horse expecting his other men to be nigh, but found they had all deserted him and gone to camp."

Two sergeants were killed; Blue and a private escaped. Private Daniel Davis, who led the retreat, was promptly put on trial. His grave was dug while the court deliberated. He was sentenced to be shot, and the troops assembled to witness the execution. After a stern warning that his orders would henceforth be carried out, Wayne pardoned Davis. Two days later Wayne kept his word: Edmond O'Brien was shot for falling asleep on duty.[10]

On 17 October near Fort St. Clair, Lt. John Lowry and Ens. Samuel Boyd with ninety men, escorting a convoy of packhorses, were attacked at sunrise by Wyandots and Ottawas led by Little Otter. The warriors "rushed on with savage fury and yells which panic struck the whole party (excepting the two officers and about 15 or 20 men . . .) and they all fled." When Lowry fell even his loyal men "lost heart and began to give way." Lowry, Boyd, and thirteen soldiers were killed and eleven men captured; twenty-six wagons were plundered and sixty-two horses stolen. Although Wayne claimed that the men put up "an obstinate resistance against superior numbers," other sources stated that fewer than fifty warriors were involved. Both attacks suggest that in spite of Wayne's rigorous training, his troops were still unprepared for Indian warfare.[11]

On 6 October Wayne made James Flinn "Captain of Spies & Guides" with authority to raise forty men to serve for six months. Two weeks later he selected Wells for another assignment:

Sir, Confiding in your bravery and knowledge & abilities, I hereby promise you in behalf of the United States of America the same pay & emoluments as that of a Captain in the Legion, for the term of one year from and after the 14th day of Sept. 1793 or until discharged, in consideration of which you are faithfully to obey & execute such orders & instructions as you may from time to time receive from me, as far as practicable & to the best of your powers knowledge & abilities.

Clearly Wayne held Wells's skills in high regard and wanted him to serve as his personal spy, or scout, separate from Flinn's command.[12]

In late October, Gen. Charles Scott and nine hundred mounted Kentucky militia arrived, including Maj. Sam Wells and famed frontiersman Simon Kenton. Wayne ordered Kenton to join Maj. William

McMahon and eighty-four federal troops to scout for hostile Indians near the Auglaize. Wells may have accompanied this expedition, which discovered several Indian trails and signs of considerable activity. McMahon was eager to attack the nearest village, but Kenton was too experienced to risk lives needlessly. An advance against an enemy of unknown force would be "imprudent," he advised, leading them back to camp.[13]

Based on past experiences, Wayne distrusted the militia. He told Knox that he would never "commit the honor & dignity" of the Legion to a major battle with Indian warriors while the Kentucky militia "were stealing a march very wide from the Army—in order to burn a few Wigwams & to capture a few women & Children . . . leaving the Legion to contend with the combined force of the Savages." By the time Kenton and McMahon returned, it was too late in the season for offensive operations. On 2 November Wayne ordered Scott's militia "to strike at the Hunting Camps of the hostile Indians, and . . . a settlement of Delawares, situated on the head waters of the White River." They were to march the next morning, taking "such a direction as your guide W. Wells (brother of Maj. Wells . . .) will point out until you fall in with the hunting camps & town . . . which you will make every exertion to break up and destroy, by killing or capturing the hostile Savages." They were to report at Fort Washington before returning to Kentucky "covered with Laurels." In truth, Wayne was sending the militia on a "desultory expedition" which might reward them with a few scalps. Once the Kentuckians learned they weren't headed directly home, half of them deserted. The remaining 488 marched on 4 November, following St. Clair's road to the west. On the second day they "got into a flat swampy Country," and in the evening a heavy rain turned to snow. They veered to the south, crossing swamps and streams before reaching "a large Creek supposd White River." Wells's scouts fired on two Indians and recovered a horse, skins, and blankets. Over the next two days they came upon a few deserted Indian camps. "Our firing at the game served to put the Indians on their guard," Garrett Burns recalled, "and they kept out of our way. . . . We discovered, afterward, that, instead of our pursuing Indians, they were following us; for every night they had endeavored, as we were told subsequently, to steal our horses. . . . In this way we scoured the whole country and finally returned without accomplishing anything."[14]

John McDonald, the first biographer of Wells, stated that during this diversionary exercise "on the bank of the river St. Mary, he discovered a family of Indians coming up the river in a canoe. . . . The moment the canoe struck the shore, Wells heard the cocks of his comrades' rifles cry, 'nick, nick,' as they prepared to shoot the Indians; but who should be in the canoe but his Indian father and mother, with their children!" Wells ordered his men to hold their fire, telling them "that that family had fed him when he was hungry, clothed him when he was naked, and kindly nursed him when sick." The Kentuckians then "went to the canoe, and shook hands with the trembling Indians in the most friendly manner." Although this sentimental conclusion is doubtful, Wells may have come upon his Eel River family, who did winter in that area, and warned them "to keep out of the reach of danger." Since the Porcupine died not long afterward, this was the last time Wells would have seen him alive.[15]

The militia gone, Wayne felt relieved. "Let the Legion be completed & I wish no *further or other force*." He sent the dragoons to Kentucky to graze their horses and constructed a large fort: "an oblong square about six hundred yards long & three broad. Inclosed with picketts fifty yards without the hutts all round. Two hundred and fifty yards without the pickets . . . [were] nine block houses—three in front, three in rear, and one on each flank, where our guards are kept." With a combined defense of palisades, bastions, blockhouses, and redoubts, the fifty-acre encampment was a town in itself (six blocks of Greenville, Ohio, fit within its walls) and was "the largest fort in the Northwest Territory." Wayne vowed that he would "render this camp unassailable against the combined force of the Savages & call it *Greeneville*."[16]

On 14 November Wayne sent Captain Flinn and his spies to gather "intelligence & scalps." Wells went on a similar mission, returning in early December with two prisoners, who said that, "the Indians are in considerable force & the chiefs now in council at Auglaize. 1000 warriors assembled to oppose the Legion." Since deserters informed the Indians that Wayne had suspended his offensive until the spring, "all the warriors were called in." Wells and one of his captives indicated where some of St. Clair's cannon were concealed: "2 were under a large log . . . securely hid, and the two six pounders were thrown in a creek." Wayne decided to visit the battleground, bury the dead, and recover the cannon. In January 1792 Wilkinson had led an expedition, finding seventy-eight bodies at the snow-covered site. His men "had not a sufficiency of spades &c. to do justice to the undertaking, and left great numbers unburied."[17]

Wayne arrived on Christmas Day. Information from Wells, the prisoner, and American spy William May enabled the men to find "4 pieces of cannon." Maj. Henry Burbeck built Fort Recovery on the battleground: "a rectangular picket fortification with four corner blockhouses positioned like bastions" with portholes for artillery. The skeletal remains of over four hundred slain were scraped together in a huge pile—"on every skul bone you might see the mark of the skulping knife"—and buried in "a large Grave in the center of the Garrison." Edward Butler recognized a fractured thigh bone of his brother Richard. Capt. Alexander Gibson was placed in charge of Fort Recovery, defended by the cannon that Wells's warriors had captured at St. Clair's Defeat, which he had now helped recover for the Legion. As the year ended, one officer recorded that "Capt. Wells of the spy company still continues to fetch in Indian Prisoners, taken by him & his brave Lieut. & soldiers." The information provided by these and subsequent captives he brought in would prove to be crucial.[18]

WELLS'S SPIES AND THE SIEGE OF FORT RECOVERY

Wells formed a company of spies composed of experienced woodsmen with knowledge of the Indians. A few had been captives, others were seasoned frontier fighters. The courageous deeds of Wells and his men during the months leading up to the battle of Fallen Timbers would become legendary. "This little band of spies," James McBride stated, "performed more real service during the campaign than any other corps of equal numbers." The most remarkable was Robert McClellan, a packhorse master stationed at Fort Hamilton. McClellan, "one of the most athletic and active men on foot, that has appeared on this globe," reputedly could leap over a horse, a team of oxen, and once, on the parade ground at Fort Greeneville, a covered wagon eight-and-a-half feet high. Unless he used a pole this prodigious vault would be too tall a tale, but clearly he was exceptionally agile. Washington Irving described his later adventures as a fur trader on the Missouri in *Astoria*. "McClellan was a remarkable man," Irving wrote; during the Wayne campaign "he had distinguished himself by his fiery spirit and reckless daring, and marvelous stories were told of his exploits." Other notable early recruits were Paschal Hickman, Dodson Tharp, William May, Tabor Washburn, and David Thomson.[19]

Wells and McClellan captured three Delaware women in late December and sent one to her people with an offer of peace. In early January George White Eyes, two other warriors, and Robert Wilson, who served as interpreter, arrived at Fort Greeneville bearing a flag: "Great Warriors, We are sent to you by the Chiefs of the Delaware Shawanese & Miami Nations in consequence of a Message received from a Mr. Wells, by one of the prisoners that he took from us . . . some time since VIZ 'that you would listen to peace, provided the Little Turtle, and the Porcupine wou'd come to your Camp in the course of twelve days.'" The Indians asked Wayne to hold a council and promised that they would "call in all their warriors." The message appeared to be authentic since it was endorsed by Buckongahelas, Blue Jacket, Little Turtle, and other chiefs.[20]

"It will now be necessary that you give convincing & unequivocal proofs of your sincere wish & desire for peace," Wayne responded, telling the chiefs and warriors to deliver all their "American or White Prisoners" to Fort Recovery within thirty days and to "restrain all & every of your Warriors" from committing any depredations. If these conditions were met, they should come to Fort Greeneville with a white flag "on or before the 14th of February." Wayne told Capt. Alexander Gibson at Fort Recovery to expect Indians carrying a white flag, but he warned him that "most scrupulous precaution & pointed vigilance are necessary to combat the art and treachery of the insidious enemy." Wayne questioned whether the Indians truly wanted peace or were merely trying to "gain time in order to secure their provisions & to remove their women & children from pending destruction." He regretted the loss of "the present Golden Opportunity" to strike the villages near the Glaize when the swamps and rivers were frozen. Because of the temporary truce, offensive operations would have to be postponed until the summer.[21]

In early January, Wells's "expert woodsmen," seeking "the best route . . . to Grand Glaize," came upon a hostile camp. In the ensuing fight three soldiers and five Indians were killed. Two weeks later, Wells accompanied Capt. William Eaton's men back to the same area, where they "broke up a Hunting Camp returning safe to this place loaded with fur & other spoils." After each mission, Wells and his spies shuttled between Forts Greeneville and Recovery carrying letters from the two commanders. Wayne's aide-de-camp William Henry Harrison recalled that Wayne asked Wells "to go to Sandusky and take a prisoner, for the purpose of obtaining information." He replied that "he could take a prisoner, but not from Sandusky." Wayne asked why. "Because . . . there are only Wyandots there." "Well . . . will not Wyandots do?" "For the best of reasons . . . Wyandots will not be taken alive." In the next months Wells brought in Delaware, Shawnee, Potawatomi, and Miami prisoners, but not one Wyandot.[22]

On 23 January a Seneca chief called both Big Tree and Stiff Knee fatally stabbed himself at three in the afternoon in the middle of the parade ground. He had been a "dear friend—the friend of my Heart"—of Gen. Richard Butler, killed at St. Clair's Defeat, and had vowed to "sacrifice three of the Hostile Indians" in memory of his friend. When the Delaware peace delegation arrived, Big Tree was visibly disturbed. He had only killed one Delaware warrior and needed two more to fulfill his vow. He began drinking and that evening had a heated quarrel with the three messengers. After they left he became despondent, fearing that a peace treaty would curtail his revenge; finally he took his own life in a fit of despair. He was "buried with the honors of war," John Buell recorded, with Wayne and his officers present. Afterward the men had a glass of wine in the general's newly completed house. Wayne sent Nicholas Rosencrantz to Cornplanter's Town with "the necessary presents and a speech of Condolence," adding that "it may not be amiss to suggest, that his insanity or Melancholy was probably occasioned" by the appearance of the dubious peace delegation.[23]

On 22 February, a week after the truce had expired, Wayne's Legion spilled its own blood. At eight in the morning shots rang out and two lieutenants fell mortally wounded. Both John Bradshaw and Nathaniel Huston were "promising young officers." During a drunken quarrel, Bradshaw had shouted at his former friend, "Damn you, I don't keep tavern, leave my house." Huston had taken offense and "urged on by some of the officers . . . sent a challenge." John Buell noted that "this is the fifteenth duel which has been fought within one year and all by young officers," killing one and wounding several. The two were buried side by side. Drums beat at both funerals, but Wayne "would not suffer any firing over their graves." He did not prosecute the seconds who encouraged the duel or prevent future challenges. Like other officers of the Revolution, Wayne saw dueling as a sign of high spirits and a manly defense of honor.[24]

Five months later, Cornet William Blue challenged George Dunn in a dispute over "a very trifling business" about a horse. Dunn was shot in the body and shortly before he died he told his opponent: "You are a passionate young man, Mr. Blue, look on me and let it be a warning for you to govern your passion in future and I forgive you and wish you may prosper hereafter." Unfortunately, Dunn's noble words did not change Blue's behavior nor end the needlessly tragic practice of dueling.[25]

Wayne admitted in March that there was "something rather Misterious, in the present Conduct of the savages." Although no prisoners had been returned, neither had the Indians "committed any Murder or depredations" for over a month. He thought there was still "a possibility that they are inclined for peace," but he was "determined to establish a strong post on the banks of *Au Glaize*." He had sent Maj. William McMahon with Wells and "a small detachment to reconnoiter" the area. Wells captured a Delaware "Warrior & his Squaw." The man informed McMahon "thro' the Interpreter Mr. Wells" that in February the Indians held a council to discuss how to respond to Wayne's peace offer. The chiefs had agreed to "a surrender of the prisoners" and would send a delegation with a flag before long. The second night after their capture, however, the two Indians escaped. Since they had been treated "with kindness and attention," Wayne suspected that "the story of a *flag* &c was altogether a fiction."[26]

Venturing into hostile Indian country to take prisoners was perilous work, requiring cunning as well as courage. Day after day Wells and his spies put their lives at risk. Under at least the threat of torture, the captives usually provided valid information. John McDonald, a scout for Capt. Ephraim Kibby at that time, wrote a detailed account of how Wells made his most celebrated capture. Wells and his men "were confidential and privileged gentlemen in camp, who were only called upon to do duty upon very particular and interesting occasions. They were permitted a *carte blanche* among the horses of the dragoons, and when upon duty went well mounted." Wayne gave Wells "orders to bring into camp an Indian as a prisoner, in order that he could inter-rogate him as to the future intentions of the enemy." Near "the French stores" (Fort Loramie, Ohio) "they found three Indians camped on a high, open piece of ground, clear of brush, or any underwood." They crawled forward on hands and knees, using a fallen log as cover, and "determined to kill two of the enemy, and make the third prisoner." Wells and another spy took aim and shot two of the Indians while McClellan pursued the third, who jumped from a high bank into a stream, "the bottom of which was a soft mud." McClellan "sprang upon him, as he was wallowing in the mire." After a brief struggle he surrendered. "He was very sulky, and refused to speak either Indian or English." When the men "washed the mud and paint from the prisoner . . . he turned out to be a white man, but still refused to speak, or give any account of himself." Wells understood his feelings and persuaded him to talk. His name was Christopher Miller; he had been captured by the Shawnees at Blue Licks in 1782.[27]

At Fort Greeneville, Miller was questioned thoroughly. "He is a perfect savage," Wayne wrote, "but speaks English tolerably well." Miller said that "the Delawares Miamis & Shawanoes had assembled at Grand Glazie on or about the 9th of February in order to bring in the Prisoners & to agree upon the terms of peace." Simon Girty and Capt. Matthew Elliott, however, delivered a message from Colonel McKee at Detroit that urged them "not to make peace with the Americans upon any terms whatsoever" and promised to supply them if they would "Continue the War." In consequence, the Indians determined to prepare for "another General Battle . . . & in the interim to way lay the path or road in order to cut off the convoys of stores & provisions" for the American outposts. Miller said eight hundred warriors were near the Grand Glaize, identified "a very good straight road" that led toward their villages, and helped locate another of St. Clair's cannon and a howitzer. He then went home and returned with his brother Nicholas, who had previously escaped from the Shawnees, and they became two of Wells's best scouts.[28]

On 17 April 1794, Wayne sent a convoy of supplies to Fort Recovery escorted by "a Mr. Wells & a few spies with the Chickasaw Indians" who were "going in quest of prisoners scalps & information." Wayne assured Captain Gibson that Wells was "perfectly acquainted with that business" and "he may be able to give you some interesting information by which you may have it in your power to make a push at some party of savages." Gibson sent Wells's spies, along with Ens. Samuel Dold and four privates, toward the Auglaize. At a small Indian village, Wells encountered "8 or 10 savages whom he fired on & wounded some of them." Wells told Gibson that "it was on a very disadvantageous spot of Ground where the skirmish took place, otherwise he would have been able to Give a better account of the party, as his men all behaved well." A week later, Gibson requested Wayne's permission to take "a tour in company with Mr. Wells, towards the Auglaize with a small party, I think we might make some interesting discoveries in that quarter." The result was a mid-May skirmish in which Major McMahon's dragoons, guided by Wells, returned with one scalp.[29]

The British had sent out their own "young men to bring us a prisoner that we might know what the big knives were doing." The Shawnees, Delawares, and Miamis at the Glaize complained to McKee that "this Wells has now four times done us mischief." William Sullivan, a captured deserter, told McKee "that Wells and May two Spies, with 16 others dress and paint themselves like Indians and were out on a scout when he deserted." They were "paid 40 Dollars for every Indian Scalp, besides a Dollar each pr. day, and one thousand Dollars are offered for the scalp of Simon Girty." Wayne's intention, Sullivan said, was to "fortify at the Glaize, and proceed from thence as far as he could towards Detroit." Many of the men in the Legion were "determined not to reenlist . . . the duty is extremely hard and the men are punished severely for slight offenses."[30]

Lord Dorchester in February had given the Indians inspiring words: "I shall not be surprised if we are at war with them [the United States] in the course of the present year; and if we are, a line must be drawn by the warriors." Convinced war was "inevitable" and that John Jay's peace "Embassy will be fruitless," in April Governor Simcoe began building Fort Miamis near Roche de Bout, defended by two hundred men of Maj. William Campbell's Twenty-Fourth Regiment. Seeing the fort as a sign of support, the Indians sent out war parties. On 13 May a convoy was attacked eight miles north of Fort Hamilton "by 40 Indians who killed Eight Infantry and one Dragoon—they were charged and retreated, But have taken about 40 horses." One Indian was killed. Two weeks later, Lt. David Strong's convoy was attacked near Fort St. Clair and lost "Horses loaded with Two Hundred new bags" of provisions.[31]

Wells in late May brought Wayne "recent intelligence [that] the Enemy are collected or Collecting in force at Roche de Bout, where a large body of British troops are also Assembled under the Command of Governor Simcoe." Sent by Wayne to warn Captain Gibson "of an intended Operation against the Legion," Wells then scouted the flanks of the force gathered at Roche de Bout to prevent a surprise attack on Fort Recovery. By mid-June Wells was back at Fort Hamilton, where he received a letter from his brother Sam that gave "favorable accounts" of the recruitment of the Kentucky militia. He then accompanied some Choctaws and Chickasaws to Fort Greeneville, where Wayne told them that they would "now have an Opportunity to punish" their hereditary Indian enemies at Grand Glaize. The Choctaws and Chickasaws, along with Wells's scouts and a few soldiers, went ahead to spy on the enemy. On 22 June two captured Shawnees stated that "if they [the British] would help them it would probably be war, but if they would not, it would be peace, that the Indians would no longer be set on like dogs, by themselves, unless the British would help them fight." Meanwhile, McKee sent Blue Jacket to gather "the Chippewas & Northern Indians" for an attack on the Legion.[32]

Wayne told Gibson that the Choctaw and Chickasaw scouts could be identified by "a bunch of Yellow ribbon tied to their top knot or hair." He urged General Scott to make haste with the Kentucky militia: "every hours delay is an injury to us & an Advantage to the enemy." Wayne said he had "sent out . . . select parties composed of the most superb woodsmen & Indians, one towards the Old Miami Villages & the other towards Grand Glaize, & the third consisting of Forty five Choctaw & ten of our best & most confidential spies in a direction between Grand Glaize and Roche de Bout in order to reconnoiter & take prisoners." Wells and his men were with this last party. On 27 June near Girty's Town (St. Mary's, Ohio) they fought with a large number of hostile Indians. A Miami told the British that "Wells had killed 5 more of his Nation" before he withdrew, with "the loss of One Choctaw." On 28 June Wells reported to Wayne: "the Enemy . . . [was] in great force & advancing." Fort Recovery was in grave danger and "must be relieved which may lead to a General Action." Wayne sent a convoy of three hundred packhorses escorted by ninety riflemen and fifty dragoons commanded by Major McMahon.[33]

Reinforced by hundreds of Ottawas and Chippewas from the North, a thousand Indian warriors, "with a number of French and other white men in the British interest," had left the Grand Glaize on 19 June to attack Wayne's legion. The warriors moved slowly, camping in the early afternoon to allow the hunters to bring in meat. The main force consisted of Wyandots, Mingos, Shawnees, Ottawas, Chippewas, and Miamis; some three hundred Delawares and Potawatomis followed behind. Because of their delayed arrival, it was rumored that Buckongahelas's men were still drinking rum back on the Auglaize and were "not being hearty in the war." When the hunters spotted "a party *of the enemy dress'd like Indians,*" a skirmish ensued in which at least one Chickasaw was killed. The following day several hundred warriors fought with Wells and his Choctaw auxiliaries thirty miles from Fort Greeneville. An Ottawa scout returned from Fort Recovery and reported that "there was a number of Americans encamped . . . beside the Garrison," with a large convoy of packhorses grazing nearby. The Bear Chief of the Ottawas, supported by the Chippewas, insisted on attacking. The other chiefs reluctantly gave their consent, and on the night of 29 June a force of 1,159 warriors advanced for a morning ambush.[34]

Before dawn a Chickasaw scout named Jemy Underwood arrived at Fort Recovery and tried to warn Captain Gibson that "there were a great many bad Indians nigh the Fort." He had seen "a great many Tracks & heard much firing." Without an interpreter, Gibson could not understand Jemy, laughed in his face "and did not believe him." About the same time, seven men let the cattle out of the pens to graze, returning to the fort without incident. While the officers ate breakfast, some soldiers and packhorse men prepared to take the convoy back to Fort Greeneville. Once they left the clearing and entered the woods, they were fired on "by a few Indians." Major McMahon "rushed out of the fort with his cavalry and charged into the woods," where a thousand warriors were waiting for him. By the Wabash, "he received a heavy fire from the Savages which Killed or Wounded about one half of the Cavalry." McMahon was among the first to fall. The Indian gunfire "increased to a prodigious weight" and centered on Capt. Asa Hartshorne's men protecting McMahon's flank. The captain was shot in the thigh; two men tried to carry him to safety. Hartshorne gave them his watch and said, "Save yourselves, boys, I'm a dead man." He was "tomahawked before his men were out of sight." To rescue the others, Gibson ordered Lt. Samuel Drake and Ensign Dold and their men to advance. At the edge of the woods, they collided with the retreating escorts and pursuing Indians. Taking a stand "on the brow of a hill, two hundred yards distant from the fort," the soldiers put up a brisk fire that delayed the warriors "for a few Minutes, which gave Opportunity for many to Escape." Outnumbered and attacked on several sides, however, they were compelled to return to the fort. Meanwhile, the remnants of McMahon's cavalry "retreated & halted near the Block House on the lower side, when they were again fired on." They "sprung off of [their horses] and got into the fort as best they could."[35]

"By this Time the Savages had Effectually surrounded the Garrison & fired from every Direction, & advanced as far as They could find Stumps & Trees to cover Them, some got within 60 or 70 Yards." The Indians had ambushed the convoy, captured hundreds of horses, and killed some twenty Americans with only three dead on their side, but at this point the tide of the battle turned. The Ottawas and Chippewas "were so foolishly animated" that they "assailed the fort with great fury . . . carrying axes and hatchets for the purpose of cutting down the pickets; but they were met with such a galling fire from the fort that it checked their progress" and they were forced to withdraw. For the rest of the day the two sides exchanged gunfire. "The balls were heard continually striking against the pickets and logs of the blockhouses, and whizzing over the heads of those in the garrison." Captain Gibson "caused many shells Cannister Shot & some Six pound balls to be thrown amongst them, all of which seemed to take little effect." The Americans saw at least one British officer with the Indians, who was "judged to be a person of distinction, from a three-cornered hat and plume and gay apparel which he wore." The British had planned "to turn the cannon taken at St. Clair's Defeat against the fort." Warriors were seen flipping over logs in a vain quest to find them. But because of the information Wells and his captives had provided, those guns now defended Fort Recovery.[36]

When night fell, dark and foggy, the Indians sought by torchlight to retrieve their casualties. Jonathan Alder, then with the Shawnees, described how he and three others under a constant fire from the fort rescued an injured man, "shot in the bowels," whose wound "had turned green around the bullet hole." The man "groaned wonderfully" as they ran off and placed him on a litter, only to die shortly afterward. Alder recalled thinking at the time: "we are four live men risking our lives for one dead one." Some of the Indians used long poles with hooks on the end to drag their men "out of gunshot range. . . . They were seen up the creek putting the bodies on horses and bearing them off." The Indians faked a retreat the next day, trying without success to lure the garrison into an ambush. On the morning of 1 July, after a brief exchange of gunfire, the Indians withdrew. Gibson sent a patrol out to determine "whether the Savages had Gone Off, or was waiting for an advantage." By noon Gibson concluded that the warriors had retreated, leaving a few of their dead on the field of battle.[37]

"I must observe with grief," a British officer at the battle wrote, "that the Indians had never it in their power to do more—and have done so little." Yet he had some good news: "Wells, May and the Chickasaw Chief were killed in this attack." McKee passed the report on to Lt. Col. Richard England at Detroit: "The Mountain Leader, the Chickasaw Chief, was killed two days before the attack and Wells and May, as I am informed, were both killed on the 30th, with two more

Chickasaws." McKee wrote Governor Simcoe that "Wells was killed in the engagement." From Detroit, word of the death of the dreaded William Wells was forwarded to Montreal: "the Indians . . . had taken and killed 325 horses and thirty head of Oxen, and about fifty men including the Mountain Leader . . . Wells & May two Spies." In late July McKee finally learned from an American prisoner that "Wells, May, and Millar (3 Spies) were not in the action, for that 2 days before, they returned to Fort Grenville."[38]

Wayne reported the American losses at Fort Recovery as "twenty one Officers & Soldiers killed & twenty nine wounded during the Action. . . . The Dragoons suffered most—out of Fifty . . . twenty One were either killed or wounded." No mention was made of the pack-horse men, but McKee asserted that all, "except 7 or 8, were killed." The bodies of seventeen soldiers were buried and "the dead Horses dragged out into the woods." Three soldiers had been captured; two reached Detroit. Gibson wrote that eight dead Indians left on the battlefield were scalped, noting that the warriors "had dragged off nine of their dead from behind the stumps, these were killed out of the block houses." A British officer present said the Indians lost three men in the initial ambush and seventeen in the foolhardy storming of the fort, and they had suffered an equal number of casualties. Although McKee and others repeated these figures, probably the losses were higher. A Potawatomi told Wells that he saw "the bodies of Shawanees & Potawatomies, 10 Chippewas—two Wyandots & about 16 Tawas [Ottawas]." Gibson's men found several dead Indians in the woods. "The Indians have told me repeatedly that they had between forty and fifty killed," Wells wrote, "and upwards of one hundred wounded, a number of whom died. This was the severest blow I ever knew the Indians to receive from the whites."[39]

Wayne immediately sent Wells to study the battlefield. By 4 July he reported back. "Mr. Wells . . . has reconnoitered the ground Occupied by the savages in the attack, as well as the encampment & trails both of their Advance & retreat." The Indians had marched in seventeen columns and "not less than from fifteen to seventeen hundred Warriors [were] in the Action," twice as many as in St. Clair's Defeat. Wells "was an authority & well acquainted with the Numbers in that action," and he had stated that "every appearance & circumstance" suggested that the Indians' losses had been "much greater" in the attack on Fort Recovery. When the Chickasaw scouting parties returned to Fort Greeneville, they reported that they saw "a considerable number of armed white men in their rear" with blackened faces, who "encouraged the savages to persevere in the assault." Three were British officers, "who were dressed in scarlet & appeared to be men of great distinction." A Potawatomi warrior Wells captured said that "the Chippewas & Tawas [were] much disgusted & angry with the Shawanees, who they suspected of having fired upon their rear whilst attacking the Fort" in order to avenge their women who had been raped by Lake Indians on their way to the battle. These mutual jealousies and recriminations had led to "bad conduct during the action." The Lake Indians departed, leaving the Shawnees, Delawares, and Miamis "very uneasy for their situation."[40]

Wells played a major role during the events leading up to and following the attack on Fort Recovery. The information he and his captives provided was essential in recovering St. Clair's cannon. He and his scouts had given the first warning of the enemy's advance and had tracked the retreat of the Indians, learning the best routes from Fort Recovery to their villages. Hamtramck later wrote that Wells "took a number of prisoners from whom the Commanding General got important information, one in particular, gave us the information of fifteen hundred Indians that were a coming, and this intelligence was of the first consequence to the army," enabling Wayne to forward "a large quantity of provisions that was absolutely necessary for our campaign and it arrived at the most advanced post we had, and the very next day the Indians . . . attacked Fort Recovery."[41] Without those supplies, the fort could not have held out against a siege. Wells and his spies would go on even more dangerous missions once the Legion began its march toward the hostile Indians gathered at the Grand Glaize (Defiance, Ohio).

WAYNE'S LEGION MARCHES

On 18 July Captain Gibson sent Wells on another scouting mission to the Auglaize. Three days later he returned with a Potawatomi prisoner who stated that 1,454 warriors had attacked Fort Recovery, albeit several hundred arrived late. Eight Eel River Indians, including "the

Soldier," had been involved. He had gone to Philadelphia to present Putnam's treaty, but the Senate rejected it and several chiefs died during the journey. Therefore, he had returned to the warpath. Little Turtle had traveled to Detroit in late July and asked Lt. Col. Richard England for "twenty men and two pieces of cannon to go to attack Fort Recovery." Without British military aid the warriors would have to abandon "their plan . . . to stop the progress of the American army." Although Little Turtle was "the most decent, modest, sensible Indian I ever conversed with," England could only "talk him over" on the issue of direct assistance and dismiss him "seemingly contented." If the British were using the Indians as pawns, Little Turtle realized that the time had come to negotiate. For that sensible advice, he was accused in council of cowardice. The chief vowed that he and his Miamis would fight on, but Blue Jacket was now in command.[42]

Wayne's Legion of 2,000 men and 720 Kentucky volunteers under Generals Charles Scott and Robert Todd left Fort Greeneville on 28 July. Brig. Gen. Thomas Barbee's eight hundred militia stayed behind "to bring up the heavy ordnance and public Stores." It was a "severely warm" day and Wayne pushed the men so hard the lines became strung out. The rapid advance over rough ground killed packhorses and "Greatly fatigued the Troops," causing "general discontent and apprehension among the officers of the Legion. . . . Even Indian Wells complains of the manner in which we march and says if we do not alter it we shall be most undoubtedly whipped." The terrain was worse on the third day: "We proceeded with usial Velocity Through Thickets almost impervious, thro Marassies, Defiles & beds of Netles more then waist high & miles in length." In the evening, they reached Beaver Creek and began constructing a one-hundred-yard bridge across a swamp that was impassable for their wagons.[43]

While work on the bridge progressed, Wells and his spies guided a group called the pioneers who cleared a road toward the St. Marys. Captain Kibby from Columbia led another scouting party of sixty-five men and Maj. William Price commanded an advance guard of Kentuckians. All these men spread out into the surrounding forests to prevent an ambush. In the evening each encampment was protected by breastworks and sentinels. Because his scouts were superior to St. Clair's, making his army difficult to surprise, the Delawares called

Wayne "Blacksnake," a serpent famed for its cunning. Since that was Wells's Miami name, it may have actually referred to Wayne's personal scout. Despite these precautions, three thousand men crossing a wilderness of wetlands and forests inevitably fell out of formation and became vulnerable to attack. Had Blue Jacket's warriors circled around the Legion and attacked Barbee's militia escorting a supply convoy, they might have won a significant victory that left the army isolated and exposed. One of Wayne's harshest critics even asserted that sometimes the Legion's columns became so "broken deranged & intangled . . . as to have afforded the whole Army an easy prey to 500 Indian warriors." Blue Jacket, however, had decided to wait and give battle near the British fort on the Maumee.[44]

On 1 August the army forded more swampy creeks before coming upon "a large beautiful prairie well cloathed with grass and interspersed with delightful clumps of trees." The vast open space gave Wayne a chance to view the entire Legion and volunteers. Near an abandoned Indian village at the St. Marys, Wayne's men erected Fort Adams, a small two-blockhouse structure. Intense heat, high humidity, and pestering mosquitoes rendered the task tedious. Yet the work went on, contrary to the advice of Wells who said that he had "seen the waters of the St. Mary's so high that they were more than knee deep where the Fort stands." Wayne had retired for a nap when he "escaped, by about six inches, being mashed to Death by the Body of a tree" that fell on his tent. He received "a severe stroke on his left leg & ankle—his pulse was gone—but by the application of a few volatile drops he was soon restored to good spirits and comfort." He was saved by "an old stump . . . which prevented the body of the tree from crushing me to atoms." Wayne was left "much bruised & inwardly injured," as indicated later by "frequent discharges of blood & by an almost total loss of appetite."[45]

Historians have speculated whether Wayne's near-fatal accident was deliberate. "Well it might have been," Richard Knopf wrote. "Wayne had enough enemies, Wilkinson, his second in command among them," who witnessed the event. On the other hand, Alan Gaff concluded that "it is ludicrous to presume that anyone would choose to kill Wayne by felling a tree on him in the middle of the legion camp as he took an afternoon nap." The tree did not fall by natural causes but by soldiers building the fort. Wilkinson, as we have seen, thrived on treachery. After Wayne learned of his duplicity, he concluded that the event was "probably premeditated." At that time Robert Newman, a deputy quartermaster serving as a surveyor, disappeared. Wells discovered "the trace of a horse & a few men on foot bending toward the enemy's settlements." He concluded that Newman "must either be lost or fallen in the hands of the Indians." Fearing the latter, one soldier wrote, "It is hoped he will not give accurate information of our strength"—which is exactly what he did. A prisoner Wells captured ten days later stated that Newman had told the Indians to attack Wayne's army when it was marching and "how to distinguish the officers from the soldiers." Further information confirmed that Newman "came in Voluntarily to give . . . notice of the Advance of the Army."[46]

Newman was a cat's-paw in a larger conspiracy with Wilkinson at its center. In July 1793, Hamtramck noted that "Generals Wayne and Wilkinson . . . after being for some time very great, have declared war." Wilkinson privately called Wayne "an despotic, vain glorious ignorant general" and connived to destroy his career; publicly, he often criticized his actions. Wayne sometimes heeded his advice, yet Wilkinson was convinced that "the C. and C. . . . will hear *no mans Opinion*." During the advance, Wilkinson barraged Wayne daily with his concerns about inadequate scouting and faulty "security against surprise." As the army neared the Grand Glaize, Wells proposed "that a light or mounted Party should be pushed forward to strike them during their confusion" at the approach of the Legion. In support of "Wells' project," Wilkinson argued that "a sudden blow at this moment pushed with vigour, would exasperate their panic and disperse the Enemy . . . many of their wives and children might fall into our hands and an important disunion might be accomplished." Wayne rejected the plan in order to keep his force intact. Wilkinson was positioning himself should Wayne be defeated. Furthermore, Newman later said, he had conspired with the contractors to delay supplies, and that the plot not only involved getting Wilkinson "the Command of the Army" but also had "a much Greater object in View, the Union of Canady, and the Country Northwest of the Allegany Mountains and to form a Separate empire distinct from the United

States," which would "produce amity & unity between Kentucky and Canady." Since Newman was a notorious liar, his account of this larger conspiracy remains dubious.[47]

Wayne persistently railed against the shortcomings of his contractors Robert Elliott & Eli Williams, accusing them of placing their private interests ahead of public service. In letter after letter he denounced "the Neglect and imbecility of the Contractors." They faced the daunting logistical problem of transporting food and supplies via packhorses deep into a wilderness where hostile Indians waited in ambush. Wilkinson's go-between was Robert Elliott's brother, whose influence was unclear. Nonetheless, tardy supplies did delay Wayne's advance, giving the Indians more time to gather their forces. Evidence about whether the contractors practiced deliberate sabotage is not conclusive, but that Wilkinson was conspiring is beyond doubt—he was still in the pay of Spain and had offered his services to Britain. Although Wayne suspected that a faction was trying to undermine his campaign, he did not learn of Wilkinson's treasonous actions until January 1795. His deceit did not prevent President John Adams, after Wayne's death in 1796, from appointing him the commander in chief of the U.S. Army.[48]

Wells reconnoitered the most "direct path to Au Glazie" and reported "favorably both as to Water and ground—consequently that will now be our route." Lt. James Underhill, placed in charge of Fort Adams, garrisoned by forty invalids, "expressed . . . despair" over his exposed position and wished "the Indians would immediately come and tomahawk himself and his detachment, to prevent him for cutting his own throat." On 4 August the Legion, augmented by Barbee's eight hundred Kentucky volunteers, resumed their march, crossing through "intolerable thick woods & . . . almost impassable defiles" as well as "low flat country, which has the appearance of being wet and swampy at any other season, but is at present totally destitute of water—the land fertile and well timbered." On 5 August "Wells declared the distance to be further than he expected." The next day he reported "that he had been in the vicinity of the nearest town . . . and was satisfied the enemy had not received any previous intelligence of our movements." He proposed that a group of mounted men be sent forward to strike the village. Wilkinson backed the plan and finally

Wayne agreed to send Major Price with 150 volunteers and Kibby's 65 men. They advanced to the Auglaize, found an old town "long evacuated"—although they did see some Indians on horseback—and returned at sundown.[49]

As the Legion reached the Auglaize and marched toward Big Cat's Delaware town, Wells discovered that "the savages were abandoning their possessions, and were not in force to resist us." Wayne considered attacking the main villages at the confluence with the Maumee but "at about 11 o'clock at night the order was countermanded." Wilkinson concluded that "the Old Man . . . cannot consent to divide the smallest portion of reputation with any officer. . . . To be first every where . . . he deems absolutely essential to the glory of the Commander in Chief."[50]

When the Legion viewed the evacuated villages at the Grand Glaize on 8 August, they were amazed. "A most beautiful situation," Nathaniel Hart wrote, "large fields of corn, both sides of the river." A Kentucky volunteer elaborated: "we found plenty of corn, beans, cucumbers, potatoes, and all kinds of vegetables." Lt. John Bowyer added: "This place far excels in beauty any in the western country, and believed equaled by none in the Atlantic States." Wayne ordered a gill of whiskey for each of his men and congratulated "the Federal Army upon taking possession of the Grand Emporium of the hostile Indians of the West. The extensive and highly cultivated fields & gardens on the margin of these beautiful rivers, shew us that they were the work of many hands, and afford a pleasing prospect of boundless supplies of grain as the troops progress toward the lakes." This scene of agricultural abundance, however, did not compel the Americans to acknowledge that the Indians weren't so "savage" after all.[51]

On 9 August Wayne ordered the construction of a garrison "elegantly Situated" on "the point formed by the junction" of the Maumee and Auglaize "commanding a handsome View up & down the Rivers." Capt. John Cooke wrote: "The Fort as it stands is in my opinion so near the banks of both rivers, that in the course of three years at most the banks with a part of the Fort must inevitably wash away." Major Burbeck, the chief engineer, placed blockhouses at each corner, with cannon ports on the three sides facing outward, and walled in the fort with twelve-foot-high pickets. Later a ditch eight feet deep, complete with a drawbridge, and an earthen "parapet" would be added for protection against artillery. Wayne named it Fort Defiance and challenged "the English, Indians, and all the devils in hell to take it."[52]

On 10 August Capt. Edward Miller recorded in his journal: "Wells and McClelland, two of our principal spies, went out in company of 4 men to endeavor to find out the situation of the Indians and to bring in a prisoner if possible." This was Wells's final act of derring-do as captain of Wayne's spies, inspiring a dozen accounts by participants in the campaign. The most fulsome, by John McDonald, asserted that the boldness and bravery exhibited by Wells and his men in "this action of real life" was worthy of the "sublime muse" Homer summoned to depict "his invincible hero" Diomede. Wells, McClellan, Hickman, May, and the Miller brothers dressed and painted as Indians had proceeded down the Maumee toward Roche de Bout. After scouting an Indian encampment, they hid beside a path until dusk and captured an elderly Shawnee and his wife, "loaded with roasting corn & beans from a nearby field." On their return, they passed a Delaware camp with "a noble marquee" and a smaller tent beside it. Wells and his men made an audacious, if not foolhardy decision to enter the camp as Indians. In case of trouble, their guns would be primed. "They had come off unscathed in so many desperate conflicts," McDonald wrote, "that their souls were callous to danger. As they had no rivals in the army, they aimed to outdo their former exploits." Previous captives had been taken because they realized too late that Wells and his men were not Indians. That Wells could ride into a Delaware camp and strike up a conversation epitomized his courage, verbal skills, and fluid sense of identity. He believed that he still was, or could at will become, a Miami.[53]

The Shawnee couple were guarded by Paschal Hickman and Nicholas Miller while the other four men rode to the camp, where a few warriors were "merrily amusing themselves" around a fire. "Wells, who could speak several languages, approached in the night, disguised in Indian dress, held a parley with them." Sitting on his horse, his gun resting on the pommel of his saddle, he "asked if they had any thing to eat," was told by several voices, "Yes, plenty," and was invited to stay the night. "The chief asked an old Squaw of the party to cook some hominy for the weary newly arrived warriors." Then more Indians stepped out of the marquee and asked where they were from. Wells "made a plausible reply" but must have sensed he was in grave danger. He and his men had entered the camp of Big Cat, whose adopted son John Brickell recalled that "Wayne's spies came right into our camp.... [They] boldly fired on the Indians." The shooting started when Wells overheard an Indian whisper a warning that these were "bad men" or "Washington's men." Two accounts state that Wells's gun snapped (other sources differ) when the spies fired once, wheeled their horses, and dashed away. The first Indian to fall was "the old Squaw who tumbled into the fire where she was engaged in her act of kindness & hospitality—much to Wells' regret." Before they reached the safety of the trees, however, a bullet shattered Wells's right wrist and McClellan was hit in the shoulder blade.[54]

In spite of their painful wounds, Wells and McClellan rode for miles "before they could rest or receive the aid of a surgeon." Their agony must have been excruciating. One man sped ahead to fetch the doctor while the others brought the prisoners. The group returned to Fort Defiance at noon on 12 August. The wounds of Wells and McClellan were serious enough that Wayne paroled them from further combat. As a result, "this was their last exploit" together as American spies. The Shawnee man Wells captured told Wayne of Newman's betrayal and stated that some seven hundred warriors were determined "to fight us at the rapids," with five hundred more Wyandots and Ottawas on the way. Two hundred British troops were at Fort Miamis, which was defended by cannon, and eight hundred regulars and militia in Detroit could support them. Wells was fit enough to relate that he "did not expect there were more than 7 or 8 Indians but found 14 or 15," asserting that "they killed three and thinks they wounded the fourth." McKee heard a less heroic story: "A scouting party of Americans carried off a man and a woman yesterday morning between this place and Roche de Bout and afterwards attacked a small party of Delaware in their camp, but were repulsed with the loss of a man whom they either hid or threw into the river. They killed a Delaware woman." Brickell, who was there, does not mention the woman's death. That a dead spy was tossed in the river is unlikely.[55]

On 13 August Wayne sent Christopher Miller and the Shawnee man Wells had captured with "a flag and a friendly talk" to the

Indians. Wilkinson doubted Miller's loyalty, arguing that "he will give information that we have no cannon with us and may expose us in other respects." Miller, for his part, said he "valued his neck more highly than the general. He was satisfied the Indians would not respect the message and would roast him alive." Wayne vowed that "if they roasted him he would roast a whole hecatomb of Indians to his manes." He invited "each & every of the hostile tribes of Indians to appoint deputies to meet me & my Army without delay—between this place & Roche de Bout, in order to settle the preliminaries of a lasting peace." But should this invitation be disregarded & my Flag Mr Miller be detained," he would order the immediate execution of the seven Indians he held captive. Although Wayne had planned to advance from Fort Defiance in the morning, the march was delayed because of his severe gout, giving him another day to recuperate and Wells's injured wrist more time to heal.[56]

THE BATTLE OF FALLEN TIMBERS

Christopher Miller met Wayne's army on 16 August with a message from George White Eyes, the Delaware who had proposed peace in January. Miller estimated that the warriors did "not exceed one thousand" and that they intended to fight. In contrast, their message was conciliatory: "Brothers, don't be in too great a hurry." The Indian nations needed time to consult. "Brothers, if you are sincere in your hearts you will set down where you are & not build forts in our village [Grand Glaize]—And in the Space of ten days you shall see us coming with the Flag before us." Wayne found the answer "evasive" and "entirely calculated to gain a few days time" to gather more warriors.[57]

Wilkinson again urged Wayne to make a night attack on the enemy, but Wayne refused. By noon on 18 August the Legion reached Roche de Bout, named for "a small island of creggy rocks of considerable height" in the middle of the Maumee. "The margins of this beautiful river exceed all description," one soldier wrote. The ruins of a few French trading houses occupied the southern bank. The main Indian camp was a short march away near Fort Miamis, and the troops assumed that "tomorrow will in all probability produce . . . victory or death." Wayne wanted a detachment of Kentuckians to discover "the nature of the intermediate ground, and the position of the enemy" before he attacked. Scott expressed "some fears" about bringing on a general engagement. In a fiery response, "the C. and C. told him with a heavy oath, that he did not understand him! That this should not be, by God!" Hamtramck, who had never seen Wayne so angry, swore that *"the Old man was mad!"*[58]

Since Wells was injured, scouting missions were entrusted to Capt. George Shrim, regarded by Wilkinson as "a poltroon and no woodsman." Major Price's 180 mounted volunteers advanced a few miles, to "a point where a large body of the enemy had been out in the morning and had formed a line as with design to receive our army." Shrim's band "were ambuscaded by a heavy party—all of whom were mounted," and William May was taken prisoner. If Wells had been present, this encounter might have been avoided. On the other hand, he might have shared the same fate as May, "long . . . associated with the turncoat William Wells as a key American spy." In 1792 Wilkinson had ordered May to desert to the British to spy on them. After living among the Indians, he escaped, bringing valuable information. The Indians wanted revenge. May told his captors that Wayne "intended to attack them the Next day,—unless the General should determine to build a Fort in which Case he would not advance until the day following." Accounts vary on how May was killed. One stated: "They took him to the British fort, and the day after their arrival tied him to a burr-oak at the edge of the clearing, made a mark on his breast, and riddled his body with bullets—Thus ended poor May." But for his shattered wrist, thus also might have ended William Wells.[59]

Major Price assured Wayne that the Indians "would fight him the next morning" at the same position near a large swath of fallen timber. Wayne decided not to advance. Instead he dispatched Price, Kibby, and Shrim on scouting expeditions and ordered his men to fortify his camp. The result was Fort Deposit, a combination of low earthworks topped by log breastworks with small corner bastions, where the troops were to leave their "provision stores and baggage" so that they could move lightly and quickly. Price discovered an ambush and told Wayne that "the Enemy had made a stand to receive him in front" at a distance of about five miles. Shawnee informants later confirmed this report: "they formed a line, one flank touching the River, the other extending into the woods. A part of the left was in the prairies, covered in the front by some ponds." McKee wrote that on the 19th "the Indians to the number of 1300 marched Early to the most advantageous Ground, but a Strong detachment of Cavalry only made their appearance and retired as Soon as the Indians shewed themselves."[60]

Wayne did not attack on the 19th as the Indians had expected. One reason for his delay may have been advice from Wells, who knew that warriors fasted before battle. If Wayne waited until the following day and did not attack early in the morning, many would return to their camps. "Wells knew when they would be cooking breakfast," one veteran recalled. Wells also warned Wayne not to let the Legion be outflanked on his left side as he advanced, suggesting that he send four of the army musicians "into the wood to make it appear that the left wing was trying to flank them—thus the Indians were made thin near the River, [as] planned by Wells."[61]

John Norton's account demonstrated the wisdom of this advice:

> The Americans not advancing, the second day another line was formed in most advantageous situation, the left flank being perfectly covered by a steep bank, and the River, which was there deep . . . the whole line extending through the woods. Both these days, the Warriors of the Confederate Bands suffered much from thirst and hunger, some of them having taken their stations fasting. The enemy also failed to advance this day. The succeeding day, many of the Warriors, to alleviate the sufferings of the former, did not hasten to take their stations, but remained in the encampment. The Wyandots alone, in a body, marched up to the ground that had been chosen the first day: they formed the right wing, consisting of something short of 150 men:—they were accompanied by thirty volunteers from the Detroit Militia. The left, consisting of the other Confederate Tribes, was not complete.[62]

Due to the Americans' good strategic decisions and better fortune, the Indian warriors were not at full strength as they spread out through the underbrush and fallen timber north of the Maumee while Wayne's Legion and the Kentucky volunteers advanced toward them on the morning of 20 August.

Wells's advice was a crucial factor in the conflict. Jonathan Alder recalled: "If an Indian expects to go into battle, he will eat nothing in the morning," on the valid belief that he had a better chance to recover from abdominal wounds. When the Legion did not attack the Indians for two days, "they thought this might be one of Wayne's stratagems to weaken our men" since he probably had learned of their fasting from a prisoner. Many warriors decided to "eat their breakfast before starting out to the battleground. . . . When the firing commenced . . . some were eating breakfast, some were yet cooking, and a large portion on the road." Only one-third of the warriors were in position to fight. Isaac Weld was told two years later that "the Indians now hungry from having fasted for three entire days, determined to rise from their ambush in order to take some refreshment." Wayne attacked when he did, the British believed, because "he had received information from his scouts, now equally cunning with those of the Indians, of their proceedings."[63]

An early-morning shower delayed Wayne's deployment two hours. Major Price scouted ahead with two companies of Kentucky militia, supported by Captain Cooke's advance guard of seventy-four men, and followed by the Legion marching in two columns led by Hamtramck on the left and Wilkinson on the right. Wayne was in the center with the dragoons, light infantry, and small artillery. Most of the Kentucky volunteers began in the rear and then fanned out to the far left. In total, Wayne commanded about 2,500 effective troops. Leading the way were Price's Kentucky scouts, who, when they neared the place of the previous day's ambush, "got water & stripped off all unnecessary clothing." Lt. William Sudduth selected two men to ride one hundred yards in advance "to guard us against surprise. . . . They moved on briskly & had not advanced more than one hundred yards until they fell into an ambuscade and were both shot down" by Indians concealed in the tall grass. Then a large body of Indians, whose guns made "a tremendous roar at a very short distance," attacked. When the Kentuckians fired at the advancing enemy, they "dropped in the weeds & bushes & commenced a heavy fire," compelling Price to "retreat to the main army."[64]

The Kentuckians fled "in utmost confusion through the front guard of the regulars" some four hundred yards behind them. Obeying

Wayne's order that soldiers running from the enemy should be shot, Captain Cooke told his men "to fire on them." The Kentuckians "turned off to the right" and continued their flight until they met "the main army which was briskly advancing to support us." Cooke's men faced the brunt of the Indian pursuit. The regulars on the right flank, in danger of being overrun, "got into confusion and began to fly." Cooke rallied these men and gave the Indians "three well-directed fires" before he too was "obliged" to retreat.[65]

The position of the Indians was in advance of where Price had encountered them the previous day. Their line extended from the river "near three Quarters of a mile Obliquely upward." The vast majority occupied the high ground among the fallen timber, with the Wyandots anchoring the right wing. The undermanned Ottawas to their left "suffered the American advanced guard to approach within pistol shot, when they rushed in upon them, firing and pursuing them through the plains, until they perceived the main body formed in order, and the Cavalry passing down on the other side, to cross in their rear, they then retreated towards their former station," which threw other warriors, breathless from running several miles from their camp toward the fighting, "into disorder." The retreat of Price's Kentuckians and the advance guard of regulars had disrupted Wayne's Legion, which was not yet in battle formation. A more concentrated force of Indians might have driven a wedge into the disorganized American lines, leaving them exposed to piecemeal assault. Instead some warriors took defensive positions in the fallen timber, while others aggressively sought to turn the American flanks.[66]

When he heard the first shots and saw his advance scouts and guards in full retreat, Wayne ordered the Legion to form two lines and prepare to charge. The early morning rain had dampened his drumheads, however, and his muffled signals did not reach Hamtramck on the left and Wilkinson on the right. One result was that Capt. Robert MisCampbell led a premature charge of his cavalry against Indians near the river. Seeing MisCampbell's danger, Wilkinson "ordered a rapid charge to support & save him if possible," but his riflemen were slowed by "the height and strength of the grass in the prairie." The infantry on the bluff made better progress and "the charge succeeded as directed, the enemy making little or no resistance, but fell back from ravine to ravine loading & firing at a considerable distance as we advanced." The enemy fled, yet "poor Miss Campble who had mix'd with them, was kill'd with several of his men."[67]

Seeing the enemy in his front, Wayne "gave orders for the second line to advance to support the first & directed Major General Scott to gain and turn the right flank of the savages. . . . At the same time . . . [Wayne] ordered the front line to advance & charge with trailed arms & rouse the Indians from their coverts at the point of the bayonet." William Henry Harrison, who displayed conspicuous valor that day, warned Wayne not to "get into the fight yourself and forget to give me the necessary field orders." Wilkinson and Hamtramck may not have actually received these orders, but in fact both of their commands began to move forward almost in unison, forcing the enemy to give ground. One veteran recalled that Wayne smacked the side of his horse with his hat, and cried out with "a voice as terrific as thunder—'Drive them—Drive them—Drive them to hell, until their legs stick out!'" Hamtramck's regulars and some Kentucky volunteers on the left encountered fierce resistance from Wyandot warriors and Detroit militia, who were positioned behind fallen trees and protected in front by an almost impenetrable thicket. Finally they were "out flanked and infiladed . . . until they retreated" with a loss of at least nine Wyandots, "three of whom were Chiefs—the volunteers from Detroit had five killed." On the right, Wilkinson's advance met with "resistance so feeble, that we began to apprehend a deception." Lt. Leonard Covington and his dragoons charged among the fallen trees and chopped down a few straggling warriors with their swords.[68]

Stephen Ruddle, who fought for the Shawnees, summed up the conflict: "we tried to out flank them and surround them, but to our astonishment the whites out flanked us and all of a sudden made a charge at us." One chief later told James Fenimore Cooper that "the red men could not fight the warriors with 'long knives and leather stockings'; meaning the dragoons with their sabers and boots." Outnumbered and outmaneuvered, the warriors "raised a shrill hallow . . . that ended the battle. In less than two minutes the firing ceased & the Indians retreated." Norton reported that "the warriors reluctantly left the ground." They fell back while supporting their friends with a sustained fire, "until they had got a sufficient distance when they all retired, carrying off their wounded." Wilkinson protested that Wayne "appeared tranquil—no attempt was made to profit by our victory. . . . Instead of letting loose 1700 men upon the disordered rear of the dismayed fugitives, we made a dead halt the moment the fire of the enemy ceased." When the Indians reached Fort Miamis, they demanded British aid, but the gates remained shut—an insult the warriors never forgot or forgave.[69]

Wayne ordered a gill of whiskey for each soldier and rode in triumph over the battleground, declaring that neither the British nor the Indians could withstand the cold steel of a bayonet charge. When he saw that a few of Capt. Mahlon Ford's artillery men had taken off their shirts, however, he was enraged: "I have fought under the hottest and coldest suns," he snapped, "and such a thing is never permitted; nor shall it be now. It is damned cowardly—that's all!" The sight of sweaty chests offended the fastidious general more than bloody ones. Wilkinson claimed that Wayne issued no orders "for collecting the public axes or the Baggage & Blankets, droped in the pursuit, or for collecting & burying the dead." Wounded regulars were "brought in and dressed." Some three hundred volunteers saw action and eleven died, including six of Price's scouts. Hamtramck's men on the left, fighting mainly against the Wyandots, suffered more than half of the casualties. In all, thirty-three Americans were killed that day, one hundred were wounded, and at least eleven died later. The Americans were convinced that Indian losses doubled their own, yet McKee said nineteen had died; Norton, "something between twenty and thirty." The Wyandots lost three prominent chiefs; Little Otter and Egushawa of the Ottawas were gravely wounded. Wells concluded: "The Indians were governed by British influence, and had no commander of their own; consequently they made little resistance. It is said they had twenty killed and fifteen wounded."[70]

Although Blue Jacket commanded, the way the battle was fought suggested British advice. From a European perspective, fallen timbers presented a formidable defensive position against a frontal assault. Yet the river and bottomlands on their left curtailed the ability of the warriors to maneuver in their traditional half moon formation, while the Kentucky militia closed off their right wing. The Indians were most effective when they could change their positions incrementally as they outflanked their adversary. At the battle of Fallen Timbers, however, a critical shortage of warriors and a constricting terrain put them on the defensive and hamstrung their offensive operations. They were unable to take advantage of their initial ambush and the retreat of Wayne's advance scouts and regulars. Although their losses were less than half those suffered at Fort Recovery, "this battle," as Wells wrote later, "was the finishing blow."[71]

In the afternoon, Wayne's army advanced to "within sight of the British Garrison" a mile away and camped "on a high Bank in a thick Brush." Antoine Lasselle, a French Canadian, was captured near the river "painted and dressed as a Savage" and "armed with a double barreled fusee." He was "known to Wells, our confidential Guide & partisan, who says He is a good man." Hamtramck interrogated him in French. Lasselle swore he had been compelled "to go into the Battle tho' he had not fired his gun—which from examination appeared to be true." He had been a trader at Kekionga for nineteen years before Harmar's invasion; since then he "lived chiefly at Bean Creek . . . at the Little Turtle's town." He said "the Indians were averse to fighting . . . but that Elliott & McKee had dragged them into it. He reports the force opposed to us to be between 8 and 900 Indians and 47 white men." This accurate information outraged Wayne, who had congratulated his troops on their "Brilliant Success . . . against the combined force of the hostile Indians, aided by the Militia of Detroit, and countenanced by the British Garrison." He wrote to Knox: "From every account the enemy amounted to two thousand combatants" who had been defeated with heavy losses by his less than nine hundred men. Wayne placed Lasselle in irons and ordered an inquiry whether he came "under the Character of a Spie." A British drummer who confirmed the inflated figure of "2000 Indians and the whole Detroit militia" was well treated, while Wayne called Lasselle a "damned villain" and threatened to cut off his head. He was later acquitted, not because Wells testified that he had ransomed "unfortunate Captives in the hands of the Indians," but rather because he placated Wayne by revising his math.[72]

On the evening after the battle, the Legion encamped near Fort Miamis "beat our Drums Blowed our trumpets & went to Bed." Wayne and the British commander of the garrison Maj. William

Campbell then exchanged gasconades that brought their two countries to the brink of war. On 21 August Campbell sent a flag and a
letter asking why the Legion had approached his fort. Wayne replied
that "the most full & Satisfactory . . . [answer] was announced to
you from the muzzles of my small arms, yesterday morning in the
action against a horde of Savages in the Vicinity of your post, which
terminated gloriously to the American Arms." Wayne came "within
pistol shot [of the fort] & found it to be a regular strong work." The
troops were "all full with expectation and anxiety of storming the
British garrison," an act that would have started a war. The next day
Wayne demanded to know why the British had built a "Fortification
in the Heart of the settlements of the Indian tribes now at War with
the United States." Campbell responded that he would not abandon
the fort without specific orders. Any troops coming within range of
his cannon should expect "the Consequences attending it." Although
"the match was *lighted*," the commander did not open fire.[73]

The Americans began "setting fire to & destroying every thing
within view of the Fort & even under the Muzzles of the Guns." Clark
reported: "Our foragers and volunteers destroyed and pillaged the
fields of corn and gardens of the savages and burnt large stacks of
hay." One volunteer said that "opposite our Camp was the noted
Col McKees Stores which we had the pleasure of seeing reduced to
Ashes together with all the Indian & French Houses up to Ft. Defiance." McKee depicted the atrocities: "The American Army have left
Evident marks of their boasted Humanity," by digging up graves and
"with unparalled barbarity" driving stakes through them. By instigating the war, McKee had displayed his own share of inhumanity,
yet the Americans did lay waste to the area, desecrate graves, and
commit deplorable acts: a wounded Charles Smith of the Detroit militia was "quartered alive."[74]

Although under orders not to start a war, Wayne may have wanted
to provoke the British into firing the first shot. Several American
deserters swore "that he proposed to attack . . . and was only dissuaded from it by his Officers." Campbell was confident that without
"Heavy Guns," Wayne could not have taken his garrison. Another
witness asserted: "If Wayne had been fool enough to have attempted
to storm this Fort he must have filled the ditch which surrounds it

with the dead bodies of half his army." Since the cannon did not fire, war between the British and Americans was averted and the Indians were left with a disheartening defeat.[75]

While musicians played the dead march and sixteen mortars fired grenades, the Legion buried its dead. That Wayne was now "inflated with his Imagenary prowess & the importance of his puny victory" infuriated Wilkinson: "we have destroyed prodijeous quantities of Corn, but we have in truth done nothing which might not have been better done by 1500 Mounted Volunteers in 30 days." He could only conclude that "fortune, the blind goddess" had enabled an incompetent general to claim a great victory: "Happy man, when folly and incapacity, is remedied by a concurrence of fortunate contingencies, equally improbable and unexpected!" Wilkinson would have to revise his schemes and plot anew.[76]

On August 23, the Legion withdrew to Fort Deposit and the next day returned along the Maumee to Fort Defiance, destroying Snake's Town and Girty's Town on the way. Many of the "wounded men with broken limbs" had been "thrown into wagons, among spades, axes, picks, etc." and the jolting and jostling of the rough roads left them "lying in extreme pain." A few died during the four-day trip. Impressed by Fort Miamis, Wayne wanted to strengthen Fort Defiance. For the next three weeks his men added earthworks, a deep ditch, and heavy timber to the walls and blockhouses, until Wayne could declare that the fort would "defy all the artillery of Canada." He was so pleased with it that "he told Major [Thomas] Hunt, the commandant, that 'If the British came to see him he would only have to turn up his breech to them.' 'What then?' says the Major. 'Why tell them to kiss your arse!' replied the old man."[77]

Wells cautioned Wayne that the route he proposed to Kekionga was "impracticable for carriages," but the general "laughs at this information." Wells learned that Little Turtle had argued against attacking Wayne without British support and "the morning of the action, told [Antoine Lasselle] they were beat, as he had but 900 men." The chief and his Miami warriors were by the river. On 13 September Wayne sent the Shawnee woman Wells had captured with a speech to the Indians now camped on Swan Creek near Lake Erie. After warning that the United States could crush them and "the British had neither the power nor the inclination to protect" them, Wayne added: "Open your minds freely to me, & let us try to agree upon such fair & equitable terms of peace, as shall be for the true interest & Happiness of both the white & red people & that you may in future plant your Corn & Hunt in peace & safety." If they wished to negotiate, they were to return all prisoners and send their "Sachems and Chief Warriors" to Fort Greeneville. This peace offer was laced with unrealistic promises, yet Wayne knew he had the upper hand. Before he marched from Fort Defiance, he told Major Hunt: "In case of a flag from the Indians . . . you will receive & treat them with kindness."[78]

Wayne and his Legion arrived at Kekionga on 17 September. "This had been a fortified place and very handsome," a volunteer wrote, "but at present it is grown up with Thorn, Crab and Plum Trees." Where the Miami villages once stood were five hundred acres of "fine meadows, all cleared fit for mowing, good land, well timbered," giving every appearance that it had been "one of the largest settlements made by the Indians in this country." Wells must have been torn by mixed emotions as he viewed the place where he had lived briefly with Sweet Breeze and helped Little Turtle triumph over General Harmar. Wayne built a fort, named by Hamtramck in his honor, on elevated ground on the south side of the Maumee with a "beautiful commanding situation near the Miamis Villages." The square fortification had a two-story blockhouse at each corner, barracks lining the thick log walls, and a ditch around it. A guardhouse was over the main gate and "a separate blockhouse was also raised in front of the fort." "I am now obliged to perform with the skeleton of the Legion," Wayne wrote to Knox, "as the body is daily wasting away . . . & unless effectual means are immediately adopted by both Houses for raising Troops to Garrison the Western posts—we have fought bled & conquered in vain."[79]

By mid-September, McClellan and Miller were scouting again, mainly for deserters from Wayne's army. On 11 October Tappon Lasselle arrived at Fort Wayne with three prisoners to ransom "in exchange for his brother . . . now at liberty." He reported that the Indians were meeting in council with Brant, Elliott, and Simcoe and that "all the nations except the Shawnee are for peace." Wayne gave Antoine a peace speech and he and his brother returned to Detroit.[80]

After their demoralizing defeat, 2,500 Indians gathered at Swan Creek and asked for British food and assistance. Isaac Williams noted their "Melancholy Situation" and lamented, "You all seem to be entirely Lost. . . . Surely we will be in the Greatest Distress Imaginable" unless efforts were taken "to plan our affairs." In mid-October, a Wyandot chief told Simcoe: "Father . . . your children have been now eleven years fighting; you always gave us reason to hope for your assistance. We are now low spirited by waiting so long, and we are nearly at the end of our expectations." The western nations "positively demanded assistance from the British . . . stating . . . their readiness to accompany the King's Troops in an immediate attack on the [American] Forts." Since the British response was equivocal, most of the tribes decided to seek peace. Antoine Lasselle in Detroit informed Little Turtle and Buckongahelas that Wayne had indicated that if the Indians made peace the Americans would withdraw "over the Ohio." On the other hand, he also said "he was informed by the American Officers that they only waited till Wells was cured of his wounds to send him in pursuit of the Indians through the Woods with a party of two hundred men," reinforced by eight hundred more in January, and that they were planning an invasion of Detroit in the spring. Thus as the Indians contemplated peace, the dreaded William Wells still loomed in their imaginations as a threat of renewed hostilities.[81]

CHAPTER SEVEN

INTERPRETING PEACE

Wayne later acknowledged that the Soldier (Shamakunesa) "first took us by the hand" at Greenville in September 1794 and asked for terms. He and Charley (Katunga) had assumed leadership of Snake-fish Town following the death of the Porcupine. Wells must have convinced the Eel River Miamis to come in; he no doubt translated their questions and Wayne's response. For the rest of his life, Wells would be the man in the middle, the interpreter, translating the words and worlds of Americans and Indians as they discussed repeatedly the profound difficulties of achieving a just and lasting peace.[1]

PREPARING FOR PEACE

The next nation to step forward was the Wyandot. Isaac Williams, Jr., a trusted *métis* (a person of Indian-white parentage) spokesman, delivered a message from Tarhe (the Crane), the headman who had consolidated his power following the death of three other principal chiefs at Fallen Timbers. On 4 November Wayne sent a speech to the Wyandots and "every other tribe and nation of Indians, whom it may concern." He warned them to avoid the "bad advice" of the British, "people [who] had neither the power or inclination to protect you," and proposed the Treaty of Fort Harmar as "a preliminary [for] a permanent . . . peace." Although that treaty was as badly flawed as its predecessors, Wayne and Knox insisted that it was a model of

219

honest diplomacy. Since the boundary specified at Fort Harmar did not extend to Wyandot villages on the Sandusky, both Tarhe and Williams indicated that they would accept the proposal.[2]

At a Brownstown council in mid-October, the British made a concerted effort to retain their Indian allies and protect Upper Canada. Governor Simcoe told them that he was "still of opinion, that the Ohio is your right and title." He dismissed Fallen Timbers as a "skirmish" in which "General Wayne . . . obtained some trifling advantage over a part of your People." They "should not listen to any terms of peace from the Americans but to propose a truce" until they could regroup and drive the settlers across the Ohio. Brant advised the Indians: "Amuse the Americans with a prospect of peace" and then "fall upon them early in the spring & when least expected." McKee then distributed "presents far beyond anything that they had before received." The Indians had been given bountiful supplies and empty British promises in the past, however, and the betrayal at Fort Miamis still rankled: "the Chiefs & Nations are much divided—some for peace & some for war." The British were convinced that "the Shawnees are determined to stand it out to the last," but Blue Jacket confided to Antoine Lasselle's brother that "his wishes, at present, were for peace."[3]

While the British were feeding and clothing all the Indians at Swan Creek, and preparing their warriors for a spring offensive, on 19 November John Jay's Treaty, which called for the surrender of Detroit in 1796, was signed in London. The advance of French armies in Europe had reversed British strategy. In February Lord Dorchester had told the Indians that war was imminent with the United States, yet in October he wrote to the Americans that Great Britain wanted a peaceful resolution to the Indian war and wished the status quo to be maintained until a treaty was signed. In the fall President Washington led more than ten thousand troops and crushed the Whiskey Rebellion in southwestern Pennsylvania. Wayne saw French influence behind the revolt. Even if Britain wanted peace, he worried that "the savages are playing a very artful game" by offering to negotiate with the Americans while plotting to continue the war.[4]

French victories in Europe as well as the debacle at Fallen Timbers stimulated Canadians to break with the British and make overtures to the Americans. The Lasselle family encouraged the Indians to visit Greenville and sign a treaty. Their motives were far from altruistic: "we will make a Partnership for Spiritous Liquors," Antoine wrote to his nephew Jacques, "money is to be made." His plan was to supply American forts. On 29 December 1794 Hamtramck reported that "a number of chiefs of the Chippeways, Ottawas, Socks, and Potawatamies arrived here [Fort Wayne] with the two Lassells"; chief Jean Baptiste Richerville and his Miamis would follow. In early January the delegation appeared at Greenville, where a large council house was being built. Wayne delivered a written speech, which Wells interpreted to the chiefs, citing the Treaty of Fort Harmar as the basis for "Establishing a permanent peace—which shall continue as long as the wood Grows & the water runs. . . . I . . . am rejoiced to find that the Great Spirit has opened your eyes to discover & your hearts to feel the happy dawn of approaching peace—which like your glorious sun defuses joy health & happiness to all Nations of this World." Was Wayne aware of the chasm between his lofty rhetoric and harsh reality? Whatever treaty the Indians signed, their prospects for living happily ever after were dim.[5]

Although the Miamis were eager to bury the tomahawk, Richerville said, "it is not Our Hatchet, it is the Hatchet of the White Hats [British] who put it in our hands; it is our most ardent wish to bury it in the very spot [Kekionga] where the fire of War was kindled, so that we may Kindle the fire of peace in its very place." Wayne insisted that the treaty be held at Greenville, which was more convenient and where the ground was not bloody from previous battles. Should the negotiations turn hostile, it was also a much safer location.[6]

Blue Jacket, "elegantly arrayed with a scarlet coat [with] two gold epaulets," arrived at Greenville on 8 February, representing the Shawnees, Delawares, and Miamis. He vowed never to listen to the British again because "our hearts & minds are changed—& we now consider ourselves your friends & Brothers." He exchanged prisoners and his red jacket for a blue American one. After the chiefs departed, Wayne, who admitted he was "as sick & tired of this kind of war as any man in America," exulted to Knox that "the infamous *Blue Jacket*" had been "suing for peace" and that "the whole of the late Hostile tribes have now come forward" and admitted that the

British had made them blind and deaf: "Hence it follows that the Legion, are excellent Oculists & Aurists, & that the bayonet is the most proper instrument, for removing the Film from the Eyes—& for opening the Ears of the Savages, that has ever yet been discovered— it has also an other powerful quality! it's *glitter* instantly dispeled the darkness, & let in the light." Wayne informed Timothy Pickering that he had signed preliminary articles with eight tribes representing "at least Four thousand fighting men—the greater portion of which were actually in the Action of the 20th of August last." This inflated figure was not only intended to impress the new secretary of war but also to verify Wayne's achievements in war and peace.[7]

Pickering, an American commissioner in 1793, would never forgive Simcoe for twice shaking his hand and wishing him success in making peace, "although he had taken secret measures to prevent it." He was certain that "the British and their agents [were] the sole causes and fomenters" of the Indian war; at a fall council with the Six Nations he refused to permit a "British Agent or Spy to be present at the Council fire of the United States." In April, Pickering sent Wayne instructions: the Indians would receive $25,000 in gifts and $10,000 in annuities, which was "intended to compensate for the loss of the Game." The "*general* boundary line" was to follow the one established at Fort Harmar, with the addition of military posts like Forts Defiance and Wayne that had been recently established: "but *all* these Cessions are not to be insisted on; for *peace* and not *increase* of *territory* has been the object of this expensive War."[8]

Although Pickering stated that the Fort Harmar treaty should be the basis of the Greenville agreement, previously he had acknowledged that the American right of conquest doctrine was "unfounded in itself and . . . unintelligible and mysterious to the Indians," and because this "unfortunate construction" had "probably been the main spring of the distressing war on our frontiers, it cannot be too explicitly renounced." Yet he wanted Wayne to preserve the boundaries that had been established by that same "unfortunate construction" at Fort Harmar. The utter contradiction in this logic failed to register with either Pickering or Wayne, who maintained that the United States was acting with honor and honesty.[9]

"The most important" rule to establish, Pickering told Wayne, was that the United States had the exclusive right to preempt Indian land.

Should the Indians offer to surrender more land, Pickering advised that good things come to those who wait: "When a peace shall once be established, and we also take possession of the posts now held by the British, we can obtain every thing we shall want with a tenth part of the trouble and difficulty which you would now have to encounter." Pickering urged Wayne to adopt a mild, friendly manner in order to "conciliate their confidence and esteem," as well as a "firmness which will command their respect." Finally, he predicted: "The Chiefs will meet you I expect with signs of humiliation," in which case "the *causes* of their humiliation . . . may be left unnoticed."[10]

Richerville and Blue Jacket had signed preliminary articles of peace, but Little Turtle and Le Gris had yet to visit Greenville. Nor had the Wabash nations, with the exception of the Eel River Miamis, come forward. In March Wayne ordered Wells to "proceed to Fort Knox taking the Yellow Beaver [a Potawatomi] under your protection" and to "return to this place with such Chiefs & warriors as may accompany you." Wayne assured the Indians: "Mr. Wells who is both your friend and my friend, will explain . . . [the preliminary treaty] fully & clearly to you. . . . Mr. Wells will shew you the way to Greene Ville where you shall receive a sincere welcome from Your friend & Brother." Wells may have stopped at Fort Wayne, where Le Gris arrived in late March. Hamtramck found him "a sensible old fellow, and no ways ignorant of the cause of the war, for which he blames the Americans, saying that they were too extravagant in their demands in their first treaties; that the country they claimed by virtue of the definitive treaty of 1783 was preposterous." Little Turtle continued to hold out, however, probably in the hope that the British might still direct their cannon against the American forts.[11]

The Indian council at Fort Knox began on 19 April. Wells translated as the Sun, a Potawatomi chief, asked the Americans not to build villages north of the Ohio or on the Wabash, but rather send "as many Traders as you please . . . to swap with us. . . . When we go away, I hope you will give us something to eat, & not a little Keg, but a big one." He added, "we are done fightin,—My Brother this is a firm peace, I will never break it, I told Magee [McKee], I dispised him." Capt. Thomas Pasteur assured all the Indian nations: "On the 15th of June next . . . a permanent peace [would be] established that will last to the end of time." It was not his decision where villages would be built, but he promised to "induce the traders" to measure fairly and not use "too small a Bottle." On 22 April Pasteur delivered "a speech from the great Genl. Wayne . . . [brought] by our brother Mr. Wells." Several Indians asked that "Mr. Wells . . . go to the great chief as soon as possible" and "beg him to move the treaty" to Kekionga. Pasteur argued that since the British have told "too many lies . . . on that Ground," Wayne preferred "a clean, undefiled spot." In the end the Indians agreed to go to Greenville.[12]

On his return Wells was robbed by eight Delawares near Louisville of his horse and possessions, "with many threats and abuses." Because Yellow Beaver intervened, "he was permitted to Escape with his life." Wells, now a peacemaker, was more hated than blessed.[13]

By late May Wells and Yellow Beaver were in Cincinnati, where Wilkinson introduced them to the Baptist preacher Morgan Rhys: "Met Capt. Wells (alias Indian Wells) a man who has been among the Indians for a number of years, being taken prisoner when a boy— He fought with them in the battle against St. Clair. And came afterwards, over to the Americans and received a Captaincy. There was a fine lusty Indian with him . . . a good specimen." In early June Wells headed for Greenville and Rhys followed, witnessing on the way a family reunion:

> I met some white prisoners going home with their Father, one had been out 15 years & could not talk a word of English. The other (which was older) had married & had his squaw with him. The scene was truly affecting. A parent embracing his lost sons richly adorned with Indian trinkets in their noses and ears & one of them not able to speak a word to him. He knew him only by a particular mole which he had on his back & when the son who was now 19 years of age, knew the person who examined him was his Father he fell on his knees before him & wept—could the Father refrain from tears? No. My son which was lost is found![14]

No doubt Wells had witnessed similar scenes, which were common on the frontier at this time, as many prisoners were returned on the eve of the treaty. What a man then known as "Indian Wells"—whose name summed up his dual identity—would have felt beggars the imagination. From his point of view, being redeemed from captivity was a mixed blessing.

THE TREATY OF GREENVILLE

Historian James Merrell pointed out that in Benjamin West's famous painting, *Penn's Treaty with the Indians* (1771), and in most other depictions of colonial conferences with the Indians such as Edward Hicks's *The Peaceable Kingdom*, "no one has noticed the interpreter's absence." Indeed, "the alchemy of interpretation, the very essence of the American encounter, has been all but forgotten." Yet interpreters, as cultural brokers between white and Indian worlds, were central to forest diplomacy. Without them, no communication would have been possible. Interpreters were not merely translators, but the linchpins of the peace process. Howard Chandler Christy's painting *The Treaty of Greeneville* (included in this book's illustrations), which has hung in the State Capitol Building of Ohio since 1945, is a welcome exception. At the center stands Wells, dressed in buckskin, with Little Turtle on his right holding out wampum and Wayne on his left scrutinizing a piece of paper. Wells talks as he gestures with both hands. It was he who could make a belt of white wampum and black marks on a paper speak to each other. His role at the Treaty of Greenville was all the more remarkable because Little Turtle was his father-in-law, and Wells had served his commander-in-chief Wayne as if he were a surrogate father.[15]

Long experience keeping their confederacy together had made the Iroquois adept at council negotiations. Their ritual procedures were followed when the United States met with Indian nations. Once weary emissaries arrived at the council ground, for example, an At the Woods' Edge Ceremony was performed. Speaking metaphorically, the host would "Brush the Briers from your legs . . . anoint the Bottom of your feet . . . wipe the Dust out of your Eyes and Throat . . . clear your Bodies from the Sweat and Dust, and . . . heartily bid you welcome." Additional rites of hospitality would clear the minds and soften the hearts of guests in preparation for negotiations. A ceremony of condolence was held in which the recently dead were "covered" by an expression of grief and giving proper gifts. Before a peace treaty could begin, the hatchet was ceremoniously withdrawn from the heads of the warriors and buried. Finally, when one side came to surrender, they gave formulaic speeches that diverted blame for hostilities and asked for mercy, begging the victors to take pity on their women and children.[16]

Indians could only trust an interpreter who understood their cer-emonies—hence the difficulty of finding a "fit & proper Persons to goe between."[17] Wells was fluent in Miami and conversant in Dela-ware, Shawnee, and Potawatomi. He understood Indian culture well enough to be a genuine mediator. His adoptive father, the Porcupine, had been a highly respected peace chief, and Little Turtle was a skilled war chief and forceful orator. Finally, Wells had been interpreter at Vincennes for a treaty the Indians considered fair.

Indian councils were genuine deliberations, calling for premedi-tated thought and a methodical process. The finest orators spoke, time was provided for a considered response, and an argument had to be reiterated before a rebuttal was given. In many ways this system was more "civilized" than any American practice. Indian diplomacy was not preserved in its purity, however; the firing of the fort's guns, the offering of toasts, the giving of European goods (including pres-ents and payoffs), and the keeping of written records were obvious innovations. The way speeches were delivered was a challenge for any interpreter. Public oratory called for heightened rhetoric, for-mulaic metaphors, symbolic constructs, rhythmic repetitions, kin-ship obligations, and subtle shadings of meanings. The tone of voice, emphatic gestures, facial expressions, and body language conveyed the appropriate gravitas. Only an interpreter immersed in Indian culture could comprehend these essential ingredients. Furthermore, the arcane mysteries of wampum had to be mastered. Hamtramck observed that "speaking to an Indian without it is like consulting a lawyer without a fee." Wampum reminded a speaker of what he intended to say and confirmed his words. If a dialogue was to take place, wampum had to be received and reciprocated in the proper manner. From the Indian perspective, they lost more land whenever a man at a table with a quill pen made marks on foolscap.[18]

An interpreter had to be someone that both sides knew and trusted to speak "their words and our words, and not his." As a former cap-tive and "white savage," Wells's loyalty was suspect; yet he had impressed Putnam, Hamtramck, and Wilkinson when they first met him; he had served Wayne as a personal scout, as a messenger of peace to the Wabash Indians, and now as his head interpreter. Despite his betrayal by switching sides, many, but not all, Indians trusted

Wells. This was a tribute to his abilities. A man of unquestioned courage and resourcefulness, his verbal skills and expertise in Indian customs and beliefs were beyond dispute. An interpreter could shape the debate. By softening harsh language he could tone down a note of discord. He might by subtle omissions of words and manipulations of protocol shift the direction of the discussion. Because of this potential power, he was closely watched. More Indians understood English than is generally acknowledged, and Wells was not the only person doing the translating. In addition, what Wells said might not be exactly written down. Often the person recording a treaty condensed, repressed, or rephrased the actual words spoken. We have a lengthy official transcript of the Treaty of Greenville, but only one primary source on a dispute among the Indians, and no description of Wells's role in behind-the-scenes discussions. What did he say privately to Wayne and Little Turtle? How much did his advice shape their intense debate, which commanded center stage in the council house? Wells was a man of divided loyalties, but he usually knew on which side his bread was buttered.[19]

When Little Turtle came to Fort Defiance on 1 June, Joseph Andrews, the surgeon's mate, was impressed: "His deportment is modest & manly—his visage is marked with penetration—he never gets intoxicated." The next day he breakfasted with the officers, toured the fort's gardens, and expressed pleasure at the improvements, "but soon after assumed a melancholy air & observed that the land was once his own property." He then led a Miami delegation to Greenville, bringing at least one wife with him and possibly Sweet Breeze, who had given birth to Anne (Ahpezzahquah) in 1793 and Rebecca (Pemesahquah) in 1795. Wells and his wife were often separated. To avoid the hazards of the Indian war, she had lived part of the time at the home of Sam Wells and part on Bean Creek with Little Turtle. If she was with her husband at Greenville, she probably lived in the Miami camp.[20]

Following the advice of Wells, Wayne observed Indian rules of hospitality and treaty protocol. Andrew Cayton has argued that civility was used at the treaty as a means of gaining legitimacy and Indian consent to American sovereignty. Since a large number of Delaware, Ottawa, Potawatomi, and Eel River Indians were present, Wayne kindled the council fire at Greenville on 16 June and said: "The Great

Spirit has favored us with a clear sky and a refreshing breeze for this happy occasion." Then he covered the fire up again. As other tribes arrived, Wayne repeated the ceremony: "Brothers, I take you by the hand, and welcome you to Greenville. The great council fire has already been kindled, and the calumet of peace has been smoked. . . . I will give you, my brothers, what will make your hearts glad." When drinking got out of hand, Wayne issued "orders against furnishing the Indians with Ardent Spirits." Only the commander in chief could "indulge the Indians with Spirituous Liquors in Moderation."[21]

The diary of Morgan Rhys provided a rare glimpse of Indian life at Greenville. He arrived on 18 June and visited their camps. "Many of ye copper colored brethren are in a state of nature, unless it be a little rag about their middle. Often have fantastic dresses, most have blankets to lye on, & wrap about them when they please." Rhys saw one man "take great pains" to paint himself properly, "looking at ye glass to admire his own performance," and observed "the dexterity of their boys in shooting with bows & arrows. One of them hit a penny piece 10 yards off the first stroke." The nights were filled with beating drums and dancing: "It surpasses my genius to describe it. I dare say it pleased them very much . . . now and then a woman intermixed with the circle of the men, which is generally the most numerous—the Indian males having more leisure to play & dance than the females." He noted that "a few of the squaws look well & have pleasing complexions" and admired their skill at making "neat Moccasins." He learned that two chiefs had died in a duel and that a Seneca had "stabbed himself" to death. In the Potawatomi camp he witnessed a dispute between two chiefs: "One was orating with all his might to the rest. . . . An old Chipeway chief got up & answered him with great vehemence. The other Indians nodding their assent and after their council manner saying yuh. . . . A person might suppose by their zeal & energy of action, that they were quarreling, but at the close of the speech . . . they shook hands as a token of friendship." The speakers *were* quarreling, but protocol allowed them to express strong emotions and remain friends. No doubt such scenes were common as the Indians hotly debated whether to accept Wayne's terms.[22]

On 23 June "the noted Little Turtle who was commander in chief at the defeat of St. Clair" arrived, accompanied by Le Gris and seventeen other Miamis. Wayne told them that he was still awaiting the Wyandots, Shawnees, and Five Nations. The next day some rockets for "the exhibition intended for the 4th of July" exploded, setting a house on fire. Had the blaze spread to the powder magazine, Rhys noted, "all would have been over with us!" Wayne called the Indians together to explain what had happened and why his armed men paraded in the morning and evening and on occasion fired their guns. To calm their fears, he gave the tribes permission to use the fort's outlying redoubts for their separate council houses. Time dragged in the Indian camps, and on 30 June Le Gris suggested to Wayne that "as it was a cool day, we would hope you would give us a little drink . . . a glass of wine." Potawatomi chief the Sun "looked rather sulky. He complained they had not enough to eat and drink, that he had often pain in his bowels." His people were "tired of eating beef." Le Gris suggested: "You have some things of which we have not yet had any: we would like some mutton and pork, occasionally." Wayne had no pork and the lamb was to comfort the sick, yet he gave "each nation . . . a sheep for their use, and some drink for them and their people . . . to make their hearts glad and dry their tears; at present we will have a glass of wine together. I wish to see all happy and contented."[23]

Greenville lacked the carnival atmosphere that greeted Indian delegations to the nation's capital in Philadelphia. Only seven men were authorized as traders, and Legion officers were ordered to keep a sharp eye out for "all suspicious Persons, and particularly upon People who may Attempt to come into this Cantonment, from any of the British Posts or Garrisons." The troops manned their stations before daybreak and after the drums beat evening retreat. "No Indian whomsoever" was permitted near "the Bastions, Block Houses . . . Laboratory, or Magazines." Wayne issued a special alert for the 4th of July ceremony, featuring fireworks and fifteen-gun salutes. The next day Reverend Rhys's sermon "The Altar of Peace" asked the United States to sacrifice "their love of conquest and enlargement of territory" by respecting each tribe's "indefeasible right of soil." Army chaplain David Jones remarked that these words were "not well suited to our Idea of the foundation of American Rights to the Soil." By the time the council began, over a thousand Indians were encamped around Greenville.[24]

Wayne uncovered the council fire and opened full negotiations on 15 July. The first order of business was the swearing in of Wells and the other interpreters. Wayne cautioned that if they broke their "sacred promise" to "faithfully interpret all the speeches made by me to you, and by you to me . . . the Great Spirit will punish them severely hereafter." The Indians addressed Wayne as "Elder Brother" at the start of every paragraph, paused at intervals for their words to be translated, and presented strings or belts of wampum. Wayne did the same, calling the Indians "Brothers" or "Younger Brothers." He lighted the sacred calumet of peace and presented it to the Soldier, who had first offered peace, then to the Wyandots, and so on around the circle. He then asserted that the Fort Harmar treaty should be the basis of a permanent peace, advising the Indians to take a few days "to resolve, coolly and attentively, these matters." Because his preliminary agreements were based on Fort Harmar, Wayne assumed the Indians would simply ratify it. Three days later, however, Little Turtle asserted that "that treaty was effected, altogether by the Six Nations, who seduced some of our young men to attend it," and admitted that he was "entirely ignorant of what was done at that treaty." A Chippewa chief also said he knew "nothing of the treaty." This was not what Wayne wanted to hear, but he promised in two days "to explain fully the treaty . . . of which so many plead ignorance."[25]

That evening Blue Jacket arrived and expressed his firm desire to make peace, but confessed that his "people have not come forward so soon as you would wish" and warned Wayne that he "must not . . . expect to see a great number." Wayne assured the Shawnee: "I am well convinced of the integrity of your heart." The next day Blue Jacket, with Christopher Miller translating, met Wayne in private. He said that McKee had accused him of acting on behalf "of some evil spirit" because his "imprudent conduct" had "deranged . . . all our plans for protecting the Indians." He had called Blue Jacket "the enemy of your people [for] seducing [them] into the snares the Americans have formed for their ruin." We don't know what Blue Jacket was promised, but throughout the peace treaty he supported Wayne.[26]

On 20 July Wayne explained in detail the treaties of Forts Harmar and McIntosh. He urged the Indians to "consult among yourselves [about the terms], and when we meet again, speak your thoughts freely." The next day Massas, a Chippewa speaking for the Three Fires and "the tribe of Little Turtle," vowed to "throw the hatchet into the middle of the great lake" to ensure the peace, but he complained that "we had not good interpreters" at Fort Harmar and received no compensation when the Delawares and Wyandots sold their land. A Wyandot chief made "so acrimonious" a reply to these accusations that Wayne blocked its interpretation. Once again Little Turtle was a dissenting voice: "I would be glad to know what lands have been ceded to you, as I am uninformed in this particular. I expect that the lands on the Wabash, and in this country, belong to me and my people."[27]

On 22 July Little Turtle informed Wayne that the boundary line of the treaty "cuts off from the Indians a large portion of country, which has been enjoyed by my forefathers time immemorial, without molestation or dispute. The prints of my ancestors' houses are everywhere to be seen in this portion." He asserted that "my forefather kindled the first fire at Detroit," and from there the line extended from the headwaters of the Scioto to its mouth, down the Ohio to the Wabash, and "from thence to Chicago on Lake Michigan." He also chided his brother Indians for not speaking with one voice and for being "rather unsettled and hasty" in their conduct. For him, a war chief, to emerge as the most forceful speaker at the council offended several peace chiefs, most notably Tarhe of the Wyandots, who performed the traditional ceremonial rituals of surrender and sided with Wayne on every key issue in dispute.

"Elder brother! I now take the tomhawk out of your head" in order to bury it deep, Tarhe said. "I now tell you that no one in particular can justly claim this ground—it belongs in common to us all." Next he performed the cleansing ceremony: wiping blood from the body, tears from the eyes, opening the ears, clearing the throat, and placing the heart "in its proper position." Finally the bones of slain warriors were buried. "We speak not from our lips, but from our hearts, when we are resolved upon good works. . . . We are all of one mind who are here assembled." Tarhe insisted that the treaty of Fort Harmar was "formed upon the fairest principles" and the Indians were only grateful that the Americans "pitied us, and let us hold part [of the land]. . . . Be strong, brothers, and fulfill your engagements." Tarhe's public capitulation helped to conceal Wayne's behind-the-scenes maneuvering. Some Indians later complained that they were "intimidated by the threats of the General saying he would drive them back into the Sea if they did not acquiesce in his demands."[28]

Little Turtle was a lone voice calling for a just treaty. Although Blue Jacket rarely spoke, he made a strategic move by sitting with his uncles the Wyandots and his grandfathers the Delawares. These, the two largest delegations, were determined to accept Wayne's treaty. Blue Jacket suggested that Wayne talk to the Wyandots first, which removed Wells from a position of influence except when Little Turtle spoke. On the 23rd several chiefs of the Three Fires passed large belts, smoked the great calumet, expressed thanks to the Great Spirit, blamed the British, and begged Wayne "to have pity on my helpless offspring." They buried the hatchet and expressed hopeful sentiments: "We will make a new world and leave nothing on it to discomfort our children." As to the boundary line, there was nothing to question. Pleased with this show of harmony, Wayne promised to dine with all "chiefs in person, and due rotation."[29]

Wayne knew Little Turtle was his main rival at the treaty and was determined to refute his arguments. On 24 July he promised the Three Fires compensation for their land. Turning to the Miamis, he pointed out that Little Turtle had claimed a country that embraced "all the lands on which all the nations now present live." Within Miami territory the French and British had posts; Wayne named Detroit, Vincennes, Ouiatanon, and Kekionga, among others. The "English and French both wore hats, and yet your forefathers sold them . . . at various times, portions of your lands." Why should the Miamis object to receiving compensation "for the lands you have ceded to them by former treaties"? Wayne pressed his advantage by using the right of conquest argument the United States had officially renounced. "All the country south of the great lakes has been given up to America," Wayne told the council. He cited the Treaty of Paris and, most importantly, Jay's Treaty, which mandated British withdrawal from Detroit in "ten moons." Wayne relied on ritual to close the deal: "we have nothing to do but bury the hatchet and draw a veil over past misfortunes. . . . I also dry the tears from your eyes and wipe the blood from your bodies with this soft white linen." Certain that he had silenced

Little Turtle, Wayne promised in two days to "show . . . the cessions you have made to the United States." Tarhe closed by thanking "this great chief" Wayne, "who has . . . caused us to agree in the good works which have been done."[30]

On 27 July Wayne read and explained the articles of the proposed treaty, which set aside a dozen "reservations" for U.S. forts and trading posts within Indian territory. As usual, Tarhe came to Wayne's defense, congratulating him for acting "with great equity and moderation in dividing the country as you have done; we are highly pleased with your humanity towards us." Little Turtle was not pleased. "This is business of the greatest consequence to us all," he reminded the council. "This occasion calls for your serious deliberation." The issues at stake presented "difficulties which require patience to remove, and consideration to adjust."[31]

Two days later, Tarhe, speaking for the Wyandots, Delawares, and Shawnees, accepted the treaty: "We shall never be happy or contented if you do not take us under your powerful wings." The United States was "the master of the lands," he said. "We leave the disposal of the country wholly in your breast." Speaking for the Potawatomis, Weas, and Kickapoos, Little Turtle offered a rebuttal. "You have told us to speak our minds freely," he told Wayne, "and we now do it. This line takes in the greater and best parts of your brother's hunting ground." Since the Miamis were "the proprietors of those lands," he wanted Wayne to run the boundary from Fort Recovery down the Great Miami rather than southwest to the mouth of the Kentucky. He denied that the Wabash Indians had sold land to the French and British; rather, they had allowed them to live among them as traders. They had first met the French at Detroit and then at Kekionga, "that glorious gate which your younger brothers had the happiness to own, and through which all the good words of our chiefs had to pass from the north to south, and from the east to the west." He suggested that the United States and the Miamis share the carrying place on the Little River, which connected Kekionga to the Wabash. As to a French fort in Chicago, "we have never heard of it."[32]

During the negotiations a letter from Pickering was on the way, urging Wayne not to push the lines beyond those drawn at Fort Harmar, which did not include Fort Recovery. Ironically, Little Turtle was asking for boundaries that Pickering would have approved, but Wayne responded by rejecting all of the chief's recommendations. A border along the Great Miami would be "very crooked" and might cause "unpleasant mistakes," while "You all know Fort Recovery, as well as the mouth of the Kentucky River." This was a specious argument; no clear boundary line existed between the two places. Since the Miamis would receive a thousand dollars a year, Wayne saw no point in sharing the profits from the Little River portage, which sometimes brought in a hundred dollars in a day. The Miamis who had lived at Kekionga "may now rekindle their fires at that favorite spot." Wayne did agree to Little Turtle's request that "some of their former traders" might live there too. Wayne had the articles of the treaty read again and asked the nations, one by one: "Do you approve of these articles . . . and are you prepared to sign them?" Ten answered in the affirmative. Although "Little Turtle seemed not hearty in the Business . . . he assented to it with rather Some apology." Wayne told them it would take "two or three days" for the treaty to be properly engrossed before it could be signed.[33]

On the afternoon of 2 August, a wife of Little Turtle died. Reverend Jones recorded that she was buried "with military musick & The Discharge of three Canons the Indians, who are the morners do not follower the Corps to the grave. She was carried by our Fatigue Men, & after I returned to the Morners who were all seated on Skins & blankets, I delivered a Short Sermon, which was well interpreted by mr. wells . . . I received Thanks from the Little Turtle." Both grief and discontent with the terms prompted Little Turtle not to sign the final copy on 3 August with the other chiefs. Despite Little Turtle's spirited debates with Wayne, Blue Jacket asserted that "cheerful unanimity" had marked the proceedings and asked that "two chiefs from each nation" be permitted to visit the president in Philadelphia. On 7 August gifts were distributed, with Wayne leaving each nation to decide the recipients. The chiefs received medals.

As a capstone to his support for Wayne, Tarhe made a final proposal: "I inform you all, brother Indians, that we do now, and will henceforth, acknowledge the Fifteen United States to be our father, and you will all for the future look upon them as such—you must call them brothers no more." An "impartial father, equally regards all his children; as well those who are ordinary, as those who are more hand-some." Wayne consented: "I now adopt you all, in the name of the President and Fifteen Great Fires of America, as their children, and you are so accordingly." Being father did not mean the same thing to Wayne and to the Indians. He assumed it reinforced his patriarchal authority to control them, while they believed that it increased his paternal responsibility to look after them. Having completed the ritu-als of surrender, they expected their American father to have pity on and care for all his children.[34]

On 10 August the great Delaware war chief Buckongahelas spoke to Wayne: "All who know me, know me to be a man and a warrior; and I now declare, that I will, for future, be as strong and steady a friend to the United States as I have heretofore been an active enemy." At the day of the signing, Wayne had pressured Little Turtle to sign as well, but the chief had answered that if "he was forced to do it he would, but that there was little use in putting his hand to a Treaty, which his heart could not approve of." Probably following private discussions with Wells, however, Little Turtle asked Wayne to meet with the Miamis, Eel River, and Kickapoos on 12 August. After a close study of the treaty articles, he now credited Wayne with "modera-tion and liberality." Little Turtle told Wayne that during their heated debates he had spoken his sincere thoughts about the treaty. Now "it was his determined resolution to adhere religiously to its stipula-tions." He was the last chief to sign the treaty and he would be the last to break it. Wayne would "daily experience . . . his sincere friend-ship," since he planned to reside at Fort Wayne. Finally he asked that "Mr. Wells might be placed there as a resident interpreter, as he pos-sessed their [the Miamis'] confidence as fully as he did that of their Father."[35]

MEETING PRESIDENT WASHINGTON

Following the Treaty of Greenville, Wells and his family moved to Fort Wayne and settled west of the St. Joseph on the site of old Kekionga. Little Turtle resided at Turtletown on the Eel River a dozen miles away. Most of the Miamis established villages on the Mississinewa near its confluence with the Wabash. The government built a house for Blue Jacket at Fort Wayne, but the majority of the Shawnees lived at Wapakoneta on the upper Auglaize. The Delawares returned to the White River. Back in Philadelphia, Wayne accepted accolades for his great victory, renewed his courtship of Mary Vining, and tried to counter the machinations of Wilkinson, who confided to Baron Hector de Carondelet of Spain that his ambition was "to keep down the military establishment, to disgrace my Commander, and to secure myself the commandant of the army." Wilkinson strived to convince James McHenry, the new secretary of war, that a court of inquiry was needed to judge Wayne's decisions. For his part, Wayne told McHenry that it did "not require any great degree of penetration to discover the real Object of the Malignant and groveling charges exhibited by that worse of all bad men, to whom I feel myself as much superior in every Virtue—as Heaven is to Hell."[36]

On 11 July 1796 the British evacuated Detroit, which was occupied by Colonel Hamtramck's American troops two days later. In August the tribes assembled at Forts Wayne, Defiance, Miamis, and Detroit for the first distribution of annuities, which had not arrived. They referred to Wayne as "General Wabang," or "General Tomorrow" because of the delay. After the Miamis received their annuities at Fort Wayne, Wells accompanied Little Turtle and the Soldier to Detroit to join other chiefs headed for Philadelphia, "to visit their Great & good Father General Washington at the seat of Government or Great Council fire—agreeably to their Unanimous request at the close of the late treaty."[37]

Since the Treaty of Paris in 1783, Detroit had been a major bone of contention between the United States and the British. As a center of Upper Canada's domination of the fur trade and the place where the Indians were armed and encouraged to wage frontier war, Americans viewed the town as a den of iniquity. The settlement was clustered along a few unpaved streets that ran parallel to the river; the one- and two-story houses had sloping roofs, dormer windows, stone chimneys, and front porches. The population was predominantly French fur trappers of the *pays d'en haut*, a motley crew who wore brilliantly hued shirts, blue cloth sashes, and red bandanas; the women wore short skirts over long petticoats and wide-brimmed straw hats to shade their faces. Hundreds of Indians thronged the streets by day, selling their peltry, bartering with passersby, and begging. Some "old squaws" offered their daughters "pro tempore, to the highest bidder." Although Hamtramck had restricted the sale of liquor, public drunkenness was common, and at dusk all Indians were banned from the town and its four gates swung shut.[38]

In late September the French philosopher Comte de Volney arrived in Detroit, asked Wayne for quarters, and then "abruptly" moved in with Hamtramck. Disillusioned with the French Revolution, he had come to the United States to study its soil and climate, not to plot against it, but Wayne kept "a watchful eye upon him." At Hamtramck's home, Volney met Wells and Little Turtle, an encounter that would lead to several interviews in Philadelphia.[39]

The chiefs traveling to Philadelphia would be led by John Heth of the 3rd Sub Legion, and accompanied by three interpreters: William Wells for the Miamis, Christopher Miller for the Shawnees, and Whitmore Knaggs for the Chippewas. At the last minute, Little Turtle and Blue Jacket had a dispute over who deserved the most credit for St. Clair's Defeat. They were rivals "for fame & power," Wayne wrote, and Little Turtle, who was "daily gaining ground with the Wabash Indians—refuses or declines to proceed in company with Blue Jacket." This show of pride was a costly error, since the Soldier, who was no orator, would now represent the Miamis. Wayne provided Wells with a strong recommendation to McHenry:

> To Mr. Wells we are much obliged for bringing about the late treaty, Mr. Wells has rendered very essential services to the United States from early in 1793 until this hour by carrying messages—taking prisoners, & gaining intelligence,— it was he who first brought me an account of the failure of the proposed treaty [of 1793]. . . . In the Campaign of 1794, I appointed him Captain of a small Corps of confidential Spies—a few days before the Action of the 20th August, he captured two Indians, from whom we received interesting information, but in attempting the same evening to take an other small camp of Delawares near Roche de Bout, he received a severe Wound from a Rifle ball . . . which continued to exfoliate, for upwards of Eighteen Months . . . which . . . in my opinion will entitle him to pension.

This compensation would be "economical . . . just & political," Wayne said; if the government did not reward such a person, they could not expect "to be served with fidelity in the future."[40]

After weeks of muddy roads, axle-breaking mountains, and shabby towns with flea-bitten taverns, in late November Wells and a delegation of Miami, Shawnee, Chippewa, and Potawatomi chiefs arrived in Philadelphia. This city of some 50,000 was the showcase of the nation, presenting a world unlike anything to be seen in the West. One purpose in bringing the chiefs to the capital was to awe them with the magnificence of American civilization. Three-story red brick houses lined wide streets laid out in a rectangular grid that began near the wharfs and warehouses along the Delaware. Thanks to Ben Franklin and other civic-minded men, these streets featured brick sidewalks, whale-oil lamps, and public water pumps. The High Street market, on three colonnaded blocks from Front to Fourth, was "the greatest boast of Philadelphians." Wednesday and Saturday mornings it was a cornucopia of the area's produce, from fruits and vegetables to fish, flesh, and fowl, as well as snapping turtles for soup, rabbits and raccoons for stew, and "Windward Island Rum sold by the hogshead."[41]

Wells and his Indian delegation noted Philadelphia's diverse population. The plain style of the Quakers had been superseded by an influx of newcomers: dispossessed Royalists and repudiated revolutionaries sought asylum from the Reign of Terror in Paris, as did ousted plantation owners from the bloody revolt in Saint Domingue (Haiti). Transatlantic ships unloaded Irish redemptioners, British indentured servants, Scotch adventurers, German farmers, and other European émigrés. Bright colors distinguished the aristocratic "better sort," whose ornate carriages clogged the cobblestone streets, while the hard-working "meaner sort" wore drab homespun and walked. Some men, known as "wet Quakers," powdered their hair and sported silver buckles on their shoes and linen ruffles at throat and wrists. "Quaker girls with their gray dresses, their uniform little bonnets, and their pale faces looked positively beautiful," yet many preferred the coquettish variety who "curl their locks, love ribbons, and cover their hats with silk and satin." Among the upper class, the customs and manners of England "generally prevailed"—although their European fashions were two years out of date.[42]

In public and among strangers, Indian visitors rarely displayed a lively interest in what they saw. One exception was at the docks, where the sight of the large ships "seldom fails to excite their admiration." They could "at once see the utility and advantage of large vessels over canoes." At the Delaware waterside they noticed numerous artisans at work, such as rope makers, riggers, caulkers, coopers, carpenters, sail makers, shipwrights, blacksmiths, and painters. Cargoes of the world's plenty were unloaded, stored in the large warehouses along Water Street, and conveyed by wagons across the country. African Americans comprised ten percent of the city's population. On Sundays, like everyone else in Philadelphia, they dressed in their finest for church and enjoyed an afternoon promenade. Race prejudice was "deeply rooted," however, and it was not unusual to see "white children strike colored children" or throw snowballs at "any colored man who passes." The Indians witnessed these and many other impressive and perplexing things in Philadelphia with an "affected apathy . . . yet, after having retired by themselves to an apartment for the night. . . . [They would] sit up for hours together, laughing and talking of what they had seen in the course of the day."[43]

Negotiations were held at the secretary of war's office. The Shawnee chief Red Pole told McHenry that "they wished to hear the President's advice, as soon as possible, having a great way to go to get to their nations." Blue Jacket boasted that he was a great warrior whose "name has been well known to your Nation." He offered to cast away a "testimonial" from Sir John Johnson, the British superintendent of Indian affairs, in exchange for another that verified he was "a good friend of the Americans." The Soldier, with Wells interpreting, spoke for "the whole of the Miamis, Eel River, Weas, Kickapoos and Piankeshaws and Kaskaskias tribes." He reiterated Little Turtle's argument at Greenville that the western boundary should be altered to preserve Miami hunting grounds. "His Nation has desired him to request that William Wells should live among them to reside on the Wabash. . . . They think he could be of great service in keeping them in good order and giving them good advice." Black Chief of the Chippewas and Asimethe for the Potawatomis expressed "the same wish and request respecting W. Wells."[44]

At 4 o'clock on 28 November they were invited to dinner at Washington's home. This was a social occasion, not an opportunity for

oratory, giving the chiefs a chance to share a meal with their great
Father. The presidential mansion on Fifth Street, a three-story building on loan from the debt-ridden financier Robert Morris, was surrounded by a brick wall that enclosed shade trees, a garden, slave
quarters, stables, and a carriage house. Washington regularly held
levees on Tuesday afternoon, but this was the first of four dinners he
would host for Indian delegations that week. He usually appeared
in formal attire: his powdered hair "gathered behind in a silk bag,"
wearing a black velvet coat and breeches with a pearl-colored vest,
yellow kid gloves, and a ceremonial steel sword in a white leather
scabbard. The president did not shake hands or engage in small talk
at dinner. Sometimes he absentmindedly drummed on the table with
his knife and fork, as if summoning the martial music of his glory
days gone by.[45]

Although Washington had aged rapidly in office and longed to
retire from public life, he was still a majestic figure. Over six feet in
height, his relatively small head and large body made him look even
taller. He had unusually large hands and feet, broad shoulders, a shallow chest, heavy hips, and a sagging stomach, yet he gestured and
moved with polished ease. John Adams attributed his remarkable
ascendancy to being a tall, handsome, elegant, graceful, and wealthy
Virginian, who had won admiration in combat, "possessed the gift
of silence," and "had great self-command . . . [of] his temper." Gouverneur Morris said the key to his character was a lifelong discipline
that restrained his very violent passions. Gilbert Stuart, celebrated for
his portraits of the president, agreed, noting that the sockets of Washington's eyes were the largest he had seen. "All his features . . . were
indicative of the strongest and most ungovernable passions, and had
he been born in the forests . . . he would have been the fiercest man
amongst the savage tribes."[46]

Washington knew how to govern the country because he had
already mastered the task of governing his own fiery temperament.
He saw himself as a dutiful, deserving son and his country as his
true father—thus he must be about his father's business, serving his
nation's interests and winning approval in the process. John Adams
said that "he was the best actor of presidency we have ever had."
He had crafted himself into a national icon, a symbol, a paragon for

all to admire. It was the *idea* of Washington that held the country together (Daniel Webster called him "the great political cement") by providing an inspiring image of public service and private integrity. "My countenance never yet betrayed my feelings," Washington said; what people noticed was his gravitas, prudence, and judgment. He knew that the future of the country was in the West, the great stage where the nation would display its character and act out its destiny. For Washington to maintain his image of civic virtue incarnate and the nation to believe in its moral superiority, it was essential to keep a discreet silence about what was happening west of the Appalachians to American Indians and south of the Mason Dixon line to African slaves.[47]

The Indian policy Washington and Knox had created and McHenry inherited was designed to put the best face on events in the West, ensuring that the brutal realities of frontier expansion did not stain the new nation's character. Now that the war was over, the next phase was to place the Indian nations under federal protection, confine them within enclaves, and encourage farming. Washington knew that only "a Chinese wall, or a line of troops, will restrain Land jobbers, and the encroachment of settlers upon the Indian territory," but he addressed the chiefs as if a permanent peace had been established. The strategy was to buy time for incremental expansion. This policy, more "honorable" than simply letting the frontiersmen have their way, was not merely cynical: Washington wanted at least some Indians to own land, adapt white ways, and assimilate. He did not anticipate the speed with which, in Joseph Ellis's words, "demography trumped diplomacy" as a tidal wave of pioneers flowed west, sweeping away Federalist Indian policy.[48]

On 29 November McHenry read the president's short speech in praise of the Treaty of Greenville to the assembled chiefs before they departed. Because Americans loved justice, "a wise part" of the treaty was that it prevented "designing Men" from cheating the Indians of their land, which could only be sold to the United States. To "ensure a fair distribution" of annuities each nation should inform their interpreter of the proper recipients. "Your lands are good," Washington said. "Upon these you may raise horses and large Flocks of Cattle, by the sale of which you may procure the conveniences and necessities of life in greater abundance, and with less trouble than you do at present." Once the Indians showed a genuine desire to farm, the government would provide assistance. If the chiefs had "any thing in particular to say" before they left, they should address it to McHenry. To preserve his dignity and remain aloof from the difficult details, Washington preferred to delegate Indian negotiations to his secretary of war.[49]

"Washington speaks very smooth, will tell you fair stories," Joseph Brant had warned Indians in the past, "and at the same time want to ruin us." The president's brief remarks on this occasion were intended to brush aside any difficulties. The Soldier told McHenry that Washington had not responded to their request to change the treaty boundary nor acknowledged Wells as their agent. Red Pole suggested that Little Turtle receive the same gifts as the other chiefs—a suit of clothes, a saddle, and a rifle. A week later McHenry gave the president's reply. Washington asserted that because the Senate had ratified the treaty, he could not alter the boundary. He did agree to provide gifts for Little Turtle and "signed, for each of the Chiefs now present, a testimonial of his affection." He said that he would "keep in mind the request made in favor of William Wells" to be their agent and "for persons to teach you husbandry." In the meantime, he had "no objections to Mr. Wells residing on the Wabash."[50]

In 1796 Washington's most favored Indian nation was his "Beloved Cherokees," who had demonstrated their ability to farm and become "civilized." The president told them that "the experiment made with you may determine the lot of many nations." He had appointed "one of our greatly beloved men," Col. Benjamin Hawkins, to advise them, "because he is esteemed for a good man; has a knowledge of Indian customs, and a particular love and friendship for all the Southern tribes." Wells had similar abilities when it came to the tribes of the Old Northwest. Washington hesitated to name him Indian agent to the Miamis, however, because he was young and not a trusted friend of the president, the Miami nation was too small to merit an agent, and at that time "the experiment" of civilizing the Indians focused on the Cherokees.[51]

In early December a serendipitous encounter took place in Philadelphia between Indians from north and south of the Ohio. Wells had brought his delegation to the museum of Charles Willson Peale on the first floor of Philosophical Hall, one of an impressive group of government buildings on Chester Street with Independence Hall as the centerpiece. Peale was a self-taught child of the Enlightenment. He was an accomplished painter, ardent naturalist, and insatiable curator for his museum, which he termed "a world in miniature" and "a Repository of Natural Curiosities." One visitor was reminded of the biblical ark, but could "hardly conceive that even Noah could have boasted a better collection." Peale intended the museum to be a source of "useful knowledge" and "rational entertainment" that would inform, refine, and uplift its visitors. It was based on the classifications of Linnaeus to demonstrate the innate hierarchical harmony of the natural world. In truth, the place was a mishmash, a precursor of both the Smithsonian and P. T. Barnum, for in addition to stuffed animals, birds, fish, reptiles, and rocks, it displayed oddities such as the four-inch shoe of a merchant's wife from Canton, the trigger finger of the notorious murderer Broilman, a two-headed pig, and a five-legged cow.[52]

A stuffed American buffalo met the chiefs as they entered the museum. Most of the animals they had hunted were on display, including a few live rattlesnakes. An Indian promptly snatched one from its container, cut out its heart, and ate it. "They have an idea," Rubens Peale explained, "that if the living heart of a rattlesnake is swallowed, that no harm will attend them thereafter." What interested them most were exotic creatures from other continents: a duck-billed platypus, a hammerhead shark, a cockatoo, an albatross, a hyena. Peace pipes from the Treaty of Greenville were on display, a gift of Wayne during his triumphal return to the city the previous winter. How quickly complex experiences were reduced to a few historical artifacts! A delegation of chiefs from the South was also touring the museum. For a moment there was a tense standoff and "the rival tribesmen eyed one another, silent, hand on knife." Then Wells, who knew the Chickasaw chief Mountain Leader from the Wayne campaign, and Red Pole, who had lived in the South, defused the situation. "A conversation soon ensued by means of the interpreters" and it was agreed to hold a peace council the next day in a room Peale provided.[53]

McHenry welcomed this unexpected development. Red Pole assured the secretary of war that it was "the general wish of all the western Indians that they should be at peace with one another," and Mey-a-neta, a Chickasaw chief, agreed. After the assembled chiefs vowed to end all hostilities between their nations, Red Pole thanked "the Great Spirit, the preserver of all Mankind for permitting us to meet here together this day." The Mountain Leader warned that "the Country is over-run" with white settlers [who] by their encroachments . . . do mischief." He told McHenry: "On our way here, we found the road crowded with people. . . . We cannot help feeling some nervous forebodings from such an unexampled migration." Despite the chief's premonition that his land was doomed, Peale credited the council's success to the benevolent influence of his museum, which was "calculated to inspire the most perfect harmony."[54]

Wells had a last opportunity to see Washington on 7 December when the president appeared before Congress. Two months earlier Washington's farsighted "Farewell Address" had been published in the newspapers. Neither Indians nor slaves were mentioned. The president's basic concern was the nation's loss of common purpose. Hamilton's economic policy had divided the country, instigating an opposition led by Jefferson. Fearing that the states were united in name only, Washington warned against "the baneful effects" of partisan politics and the "impostures of pretended patriotism" that kindled "the animosity of one part against another." For the nation to remain strong, it was "the duty of every Individual to obey the established government" and to pay taxes. The United States must avoid "the insidious wiles of foreign influence" and "steer clear of permanent Alliances" that did not serve its national interest.[55]

A master of magnificent entrances and magnanimous exits, Washington arrived in style at Congress Hall in his cream-colored carriage drawn by six bay horses. He stood for a moment on the steps, allowing the crowd to gaze, as if he were posing for posterity and wished to turn his aging flesh into ageless marble. The short speech he read from the podium to the legislature asserted that his government's policies were "calculated to insure a continuance of the friendship of the Indians, and to preserve peace along the extent of our interior frontier." Now all that remained was "to protect the rights secured by the Indians by Treaty; to draw them near to the civilized state; and inspire them with correct conceptions of the power, as well as justice of the Government." Following the classical example of Cincinnatus, a few months later he would relinquish his power and retire to his beloved Mount Vernon. At a meeting with McHenry on 9 December, Wells was advised to uphold the government's pacification program as an interpreter at Fort Wayne. In return for three hundred dollars, he signed a statement: "I promise for what has been received and for what I may receive to promote the interest of the United States with the northwestern Indians." McHenry gave Wells gifts for Little Turtle—"a Dress Coat, Rifle, Saddle, and Bridle"—along with a "lasting Testimonial" of the president's love and affection: "What he asks from you is fidelity to your promises given in the Treaty" by preventing "your young men from doing injury to the frontier Settlers or their property." The decision to appoint Wells as Indian agent to the Miami had been left to Washington's successor John Adams.[56]

On the return trip, Red Pole's baggage was stolen. When they reached Pittsburgh, the chief "complained of a pain in his breast and head . . . [which] notwithstanding every possible attention" paid to him by three doctors developed into pneumonia. When the great peace chief died "to the inexpressible grief of the other Indians," Maj. Isaac Craig, the commandant at Fort Pitt, had him buried "in the most respectable manner" in the old Trinity churchyard and placed a commemorative headstone on his grave. In February, when the ice on the Ohio melted, Wells and the Indian delegation returned to their homes.[57]

WELLS AND LITTLE TURTLE IN PHILADELPHIA

The Adams administration was preoccupied by events in Europe. In response to Jay's Treaty, which favored the British, the French began seizing American ships. Napoleon's brother, now on the throne of Spain, sent messengers to invite the Indians to move west of the Mississippi, because their old fathers the French and Spanish had united against the Americans and British. When the French Directory refused to see American envoy Charles Pinckney, Adams faced the prospect of war. In response, the president sent Pinckney and two additional envoys to France. McHenry reluctantly went along with the plan while asking Congress to strengthen the military. "Should the French set on foot any of their projects in our Western frontier," James Ross warned in April 1797, "the Indians must infallibly Attach themselves to their old Allies." A month later Wilkinson informed McHenry: "Little Turtle is exerting himself to carry all the Indians on our borders to the West of the Mississippi. I would endeavour to countervail him . . . as he is a chief of unrivalled power and influence." Little Turtle went to Detroit in July and was disappointed not "to see their *Fathers, the French*."[58]

Wilkinson was playing a double game. Baron de Carondelet, Spanish governor of Louisiana, sent Thomas Power to discover "the General's dispositions" and whether he might lead an "insurrection" in Kentucky that would make him "the Washington, of the Western States." Wilkinson knew that Adams suspected that he "had formed improper connections with Spain." To counter these accurate rumors, he presented himself as a devoted friend of the Indians and a man working diligently to maintain the peace. Thus he helped arrange for Wells and Little Turtle to visit Philadelphia. In December he traveled with them to Pittsburgh, giving the Miami chief letters of recommendation and his own "Appeal to President Adams."[59]

Little Turtle still wanted the president to change the western boundary of the Greenville treaty. After they first met in January, Adams wrote to Wilkinson: "I . . . have received and observed him with attention. He is certainly a remarkable man. . . . We shall endeavour to make him happy here, and contented after his return." Aware that the thin-skinned Adams was often vilified by his enemies, Wilkinson played upon his feelings: "I know that whispers and innuendoes, are circulated, in secret, to wound my character. . . . To you then, Sir, permit me to look up for protection, against their shafts and arrows, which may be leveled against the honour of an absent, injured, innocent man." Adams took the saccharine bait: "I esteem your talents, respect your services, and feel an attachment to your person," but cautioned Wilkinson to avoid any violent action "to silence the villainous clamors and rumors of your connections with Spain and France." Having used Wells and Little Turtle as his unsuspecting fronts and with this "extraordinary endorsement . . . in his file, Wilkinson became impregnable to Federalist attacks."[60]

Because Little Turtle arrived at Philadelphia in bad health, McHenry sent him to Doctor Benjamin Rush, whose relentless efforts to stop the yellow fever epidemic of 1793 had won him both praise and condemnation. He almost identified the germ-carrying mosquitoes when he stated that the disease was caused by "putrid vegetable exhalation" from decaying waste and stagnant water near the docks. Unfortunately, Rush's cure consisted of "heroic bloodletting" and purging of the body, which weakened his patients—with lethal consequences. "My house was a Lazaretto," he said, citing the few who survived; but his enemies countered, "He is a perfect Sangrado, and would order blood enough to be drawn to fill Mambrino's helmet." Rush inoculated Little Turtle against smallpox and deployed elaborate methods to treat his gout: his remedies included "bloodletting, purging, vomiting, and nitre," along with "a warm foot-bath." Then came "opium, wine, porter, brandy, thirty drops of ether" followed by a "diet of fish, eggs, white meat and broth." Remarkably, the chief recovered from the doctor's ministrations.[61]

Rush conversed with Wells and Little Turtle on several occasions. "Mr. Wells . . . informed me that the Miami tribe of Indians worshipped a good spirit, and that they offered sacrifices of a deer's heart when they went to Battle." He introduced his son James to the chief "who commanded in the defeat of General St. Clair." Little Turtle called the boy "Wapemongua" or "White Loon . . . the name of his sister's son whom he had adopted." Rush arranged for Wells and Little Turtle to meet Count Volney and other notable figures.[62]

Little Turtle addressed the president in person on 7 February 1798. His speech, translated by Wells, was an eloquent summary of Indian grievances. "I as well as my people have felt and experienced the inconveniences of war," he said. Even though he did not like parts of Wayne's treaty, he had signed it to end the bloodshed. Since the boundaries of the treaty "could not easily be altered," he offered land along the Ohio in return for good hunting ground west of the Great Miami. He protested that land had been purchased illegally near Post Vincennes and that no one had been punished for murdering Indians there. To improve the annuity system, he suggested that "the several nations" each make a list of those supplies "which would be most acceptable to them." He asked that Wells be appointed as agent to the Miami and given "a tract of land for his trouble." He also wanted a trading post at Fort Wayne, a man to teach the Indians how to farm, and "a person capable to teach our Children to read and write." Little Turtle was outraged that stills had been built on the reservations since "the numbers of our people are much diminishing and we consider one of the principal causes to be the quantity of liquor sold to them by traders and others." The president should use whatever means were in his "power to check this evil." The loss of land, the drinking problem, and the mortality rate were all connected: "We are too much disposed to sell our land and Whiskey is a great Tempter."[63]

As they waited for Adams's reply, Wells and Little Turtle explored Philadelphia and were interviewed ten times by Count Volney, the French savant and world traveler they had met in Detroit. A member of the Assembly in the early years of the Revolution, he had escaped from prison during the Reign of Terror, eluded the guillotine, and "set out . . . to discover whether liberty, which was banished from Europe, had really found a place of refuge" in America. After trips to Syria and Egypt, he had written about his life among the Bedouins. Volney had traveled to Vincennes with "the design of spending a few months among" the Indians. When he saw a drunken "savage [stab] his wife, in four places, with a knife, a few paces from me," however, he decided that "there was no Arabian hospitality among them: that all was anarchy and disorder." Volney decided that "les Sauvages" of America lived "in the state of wild animals" rather than Rousseau's noble version of them. Since these dark notions colored his interviews with Wells and Little Turtle, his account must be used with caution.[64]

Nevertheless, his chapter "On the Indians or Savages of North America" provides invaluable information about Wells, Little Turtle, and Miami life. Volney intended to study Indian languages: "The only person in America capable of giving me the aid I wanted was a man by the name of Wells, who . . . had acquired an accurate knowledge of many of their dialects." He was accompanied by Little Turtle, "who contributed most to the defeat of St. Clair, and well-informed officers have assured me, that had his plan of waylaying stragglers, and cutting off convoys, been followed, Wayne's army would probably have shared the same fate." Volney noted that the chief suffered from "both gout and rheumatism, for which the government had eagerly provided him medical aid." He interviewed the two men in January and February, taking notes after each visit. "I first conversed with them on the climate and soil of the Miamis." Wells told him that the country was part forest, part prairie, and colder than Vincennes, with fertile soil, fine corn, and abundant game. As a result, the people were "a stout, well-formed race." While Volney and Wells talked, Little Turtle, dressed in a blue suit, pantaloons, and a round hat, "walked about, plucking out the hairs from his chin, and even from his eyebrows." This led to a discussion of racial pigmentation. Volney noted that the chief's "skin was as soft and fair as a Parisian's," while "Mr. Wells, who had lived, in their fashion, fifteen years among them," had a complexion that "appeared to be that of soot, or of smoked ham." His face reminded Volney of peasants in southern France and Spain, while "Little Turtle bore a strong resemblance to" five Chinese Tartars recently brought to Philadelphia by the Dutch collector Van Braam.[65]

Volney spread out a map and explained how people from Asia had crossed the Bering Straits to the Western hemisphere. Little Turtle astutely asked why it couldn't have been the other way around, with the Indians settling Asia. If he resembled the Tartars, why couldn't *his* ancestors have fathered *them*? Volney admitted the possibility but added that the "*black coats*" (missionaries) would only see that notion as heresy. That was their problem, Little Turtle replied. "We know every tribe at first sight," the chief said. He could tell by a moccasin print the age, gender, and tribe, while whites were known by their turned-out toes. Although Wells often mentioned that the Miamis farmed, Volney persisted in seeing them as hunters and gatherers who either starved or "gorged to the throat," abandoned the deformed and elderly, and obeyed the law of "Wild Nature . . . 'Be strong or perish.'" He even asserted that they were militarily inferior to the Kentuckians even though Little Turtle's exploits were proof to the contrary. Volney was in the presence of a true "Noble Savage," whose "superior sagacity" he admitted; yet he perverted many things Little Turtle and Wells said to fit his preconceptions.[66]

When Volney asked Wells whether "there were many men who adopted the savage life from choice, and why they preferred it to what we call the civilized life," Wells answered at length, noting that while most grown men did not go native, many boys enjoyed the freedom of life in the woods, and some males indulged in a "licentious life" with the Indian women. Wells denied that he had been such a man: "though taken away at thirteen, and adopted and well-treated [he] could never forget the scenes and pleasures" of his Kentucky upbringing. Volney's rhetoric is suspect, yet Wells's motivations for leaving the Miamis can be inferred from this account. An adult male was expected to fight and hunt, while his wife, overloaded with work, aged quickly. Under relentless pressure from white settlers, the Indian world had lost stability. The threat of death was pervasive and suicide a common occurrence. They lived for the day and did not possess farms or property and thus could leave no legacy for their children. Little Turtle lived in a log house, wore good clothes, drank tea and coffee, owned a cow, "and his wife makes butter," but he was scorned for doing so. "His first cow was killed by night, and he was obliged to feign ignorance of the man who did it," so as not to arouse jealousy. Wells and the chief preferred a more secure life. They knew that the old ways could not last and wanted to help the Indians adapt to the white world while "bettering" themselves in the process.[67]

Little Turtle was contacted by some Quakers, honored among the Indians for their peacemaking efforts, who "invited him to remain among them, promising him that he should want for nothing." Volney asked the chief why he didn't accept their offer. Little Turtle gave the question "a considerable pause, agreeably to the Indian habits of deliberation," before responding. He had become accustomed to life in Philadelphia, his clothes were "warm and comfortable," and he liked how compact and "convenient" everything was. The market outside the window provided "every thing we want, without the trouble of hunting in the woods." Lacking English and the skills of a tradesman, however, he could not live by his work. "I say to myself, which of these things can I do? Not one. I can make a bow, catch fish, kill deer, and go to war, but none of these things are done here. . . . Were I to stay with the whites, I should be an idle piece of furniture. . . . I must go back." Wells added: "If he delayed returning home, he would lose his credit among his countrymen. . . . When he gets home he must at once resume the Indian dress and habits, and not speak too favorably of ours, lest he should wound their pride, which is extreme." When Volney noted that clever philosophers in France maintained that envy, spite, and other vindictive passions only thrived "in civilized society," Wells replied: "let them spend a few months among the Indians, and they will change their opinion."[68]

Wells said the Wabash Indians were "better off than they were a few generations ago." During periods of peace they could "raise some corn and potatoes . . . cabbages and turnips. Their captives have planted peach and apple trees, and taught them to breed poultry, pigs, and even cows," just as the Creeks and Choctaws did. Yet now they were in danger of being overrun by white settlers. Little Turtle observed that the faces in the crowded market showed a far greater variety than among the Indians: "Such a diversity puzzles me very much." Volney explained that Philadelphia "was visited by all nations of the globe, and these, by marrying together, could not fail of producing great varieties." Little Turtle found this increase in numbers "quite inconceivable." It was only a few generations "since the whites first set foot among us, yet already they swarm like flies: while we, who have been here nobody knows how long, are still as thin as deer." Because they farmed and needed only a small field to support a family, the whites multiplied rapidly, while the game the Indians hunted needed "a great deal of ground." Given such a situation, "No wonder the whites drive us every year . . . from the sea to the Mississippi. They spread like oil on a blanket; we melt like snow before the sun. If things do not greatly change, the red men will disappear very shortly." Volney put his own slant on the expert testimony of Wells and Little Turtle, closing the chapter with a harsh critique of Indian life.[69]

Wells took Little Turtle to Peale's Museum, where a portrait of Joseph Brant had been added alongside wax replicas of Blue Jacket and Red Pole. When the chief requested to have his portrait painted, McHenry made the wise choice of sending him on 14 February to Gilbert Stuart: "The Little Turtle . . . is an Indian Chief of great consequence. I am desirous of having an expressive likeness of him, at half length, taken by a painter of eminence . . . no time may be lost in beginning and finishing such picture as soon as possible." Stuart was a master at capturing character by focusing on his subject's facial features. "It is no use to steal Stuart's colors," Benjamin West said, "if you want to paint as he does you must steal his eyes. . . . He nails the face to the canvas." His studio was in a stone barn behind his house on Main Street in Germantown. Stuart had won fame and fortune for his portraits of Washington. Once, in an effort to get the great man to be less stiff and formal, he urged him to forget that he was "General Washington and that I am Stuart the painter" and was firmly told he should never forget "who General Washington is." Stuart worked in quick strokes because his hands shook and chattered constantly as he painted Little Turtle and an Irishman at the same time. Both were witty talkers; each session featured a lively repartee that tested Wells's talents as a translator. One day when Little Turtle did not respond to his jibes, the Irishman declared that he had finally bested him. "You are mistaken," Little Turtle replied. "I was actually thinking of asking this man [Stuart] to place us on one canvass where we could stand face to face and exchange insults forever."[70]

Benjamin Rush introduced Wells and Little Turtle to his old Revolutionary companion Thaddeus Kosciusko. The Polish patriot had led a failed insurrection against Russia in 1794 and spent two years in a St. Petersburg prison. His room on Third Street could only accommodate four people. His head and knee were bandaged and he walked with a limp. "Every step you take," Rush had told him, "will remind you of your patriotism and bravery." He and poet Julian Niemcewicz admired Little Turtle as a fellow fighter for freedom:

> He is an extremely sensible man. All his ideas are sound and correct, not at all perverted by misconceptions and wrong arguments. . . . The point on which he insists the most is to urge the American government to forbid the importation of spirituous liquors among the Indians. He feels this is their bane. He is equally aware of all the perfidy in the politics of the Whites who foment divisions among them, involve them in quarrels, brutalize them with drink, finally, use every means to keep them in ignorance and to exterminate them in turn. This discussion itself saddened him. "Do not speak to me," he said, "of your superiority if you do not want to furnish me the means by which my nation may attain the same advantages."

Little Turtle presented Kosciusko with a pipe tomahawk and received in return a *burka* (a loose-fitting, sleeveless cloak of sea otter skin) and a pair of spectacles he had admired. He tried them and cried with delight, "You have given me new eyes!" Finally, after stating that he had used them to defend his oppressed people, Kosciusko gave Little Turtle a set of pistols and entreated him to "shoot dead the first man who ever comes to subjugate you or . . . despoil . . . your country."[71]

Washington brought extensive frontier experience to the presidency. He had fought and negotiated with the Indians for many years and owned vast tracts of land in the Ohio Valley. President Adams, on the other hand, had little or no interest in Indian affairs; his mind was focused on domestic policy and what he termed "the open assaults of France and the secret plots of England." Not only was the short, corpulent Adams (dubbed "His Rotundity") Washington's physical opposite, but he also differed from him psychologically. Washington had mastered his volatile temper; Adams was at the mercy of his. Washington had unified the country with his dignity, prudence, modesty, "disinterestedness," and civic virtue. Adams's capricious actions had divided it. He could not control his own cabinet, let alone the country. Both Jefferson and Hamilton cited with approval Franklin's remark that Adams was "always an honest Man, often a wise man, but sometimes, and in some things, absolutely out of his senses," which in Hamilton's version became: "always honest, *sometimes* great, but *often* mad." No successor could have filled Washington's shoes, but under Adams, Gordon Wood noted, the country came apart: "By 1798 public passions and partisanship and indeed public hysteria had increased to the point where armed conflict among the states and the American people seemed likely."[72]

Opposition to the Federalists concentrated around Adams's vice president, Thomas Jefferson. His admiration for the French, even during the Terror and Napoleon's dictatorship, and detestation of the British, although they were essential to the U.S. economy, were extreme. While the three American envoys sought peace in Paris, Jefferson advised the French to "drag out the negotiations." A newspaper war featuring scandalmongering and character assassination fed fuel to the flames. In Philadelphia, partisans wearing tricolored cockades, waving the flag of the French Revolution, and singing the

"Marseillaise," often clashed with a pro-British faction sporting black cockades and singing "God Save the King," to which their rivals responded with "Long live the Guillotine." While Wells and Little Turtle were in Philadelphia, this virulence reached Congress. In mid-February Roger Griswold, a Connecticut Federalist, beat Matthew Lyon of Vermont with a cane. Lyon defended himself with fireplace tongs, and the two men ended up tussling on the chamber floor.[73]

The president's reply to Little Turtle was delivered by McHenry on 20 February. Adams said he had "seriously deliberated on" his proposals but refused to revise the boundary, making the dubious claim that such a change would require new commissioners and a new treaty. St. Clair would "investigate" the two murders in Vincennes, which meant that nothing would be done. Little Turtle's suggestion that each nation prepare a list "of goods wanted for the ensuing year" was accepted, but the government lacked the funds to build a trading post at Fort Wayne. Although Adams "lamented" the spread of whiskey in Indian country, he left the enforcement of its prohibition to "the thinking part of his red Children" with only minimal government assistance. McHenry promised to supply farming equipment to those Indians who "shew a real disposition . . . in cultivating their land." Adams rejected Little Turtle's offer to provide Wells with land, but since the Indians considered him to be the "proper person" for the office and "a good man," he appointed him as an agent at a salary of three hundred dollars a year.[74]

Little Turtle's mission to Philadelphia had resulted in empty promises and a flat rejection of boundary revision. Without government support, any efforts to encourage the Miamis to stop drinking and start farming would flounder. While Wells and Little Turtle waited for the weather to clear and for Stuart to finish his portrait, they enjoyed the city. On 22 February they were guests at the Washington Ball held in John Rickett's Circus on 12th Street. Wells and Little Turtle occupied a prominent box in the balcony. The chief was dressed "in an American uniform with enormous epaulets. He appeared very content with the entertainment." They may have dined at the Binghams' mansion, the most opulent and ostentatious in Philadelphia. Anne Bingham was the queen of Federalist society and an Indian chief was a curiosity. They probably drank at the City Tavern, listened to music at Oeller's Hotel, and attended the New Theater, where class warfare was on display when the "gallery gods" demanded that plebeians in the pit doff their caps to them or be pelted with apples and pears.[75]

A week after Wells and Little Turtle left Philadelphia, dispatches from the three envoys in France arrived, indicating that the American mission had failed. The Jeffersonians demanded a full disclosure. When the messages were published in early April, they revealed that French agents known as X, Y, and Z had insisted on a multimillion dollar "loan" to France as well as a "*douceur*," or sweetener of a quarter million for minister Talleyrand. "You must pay a great deal of money," the Americans were told, to which Charles Pinckney responded, "No! No! Not a sixpence!" News of how the Americans had rejected this dishonorable bribe caught the opposition by surprise. A suddenly united country called for war against France. Adams and the Federalists basked in a brief period of popularity before they, in turn, overreached themselves by imprisoning or deporting their critics with the Alien and Sedition Acts.[76]

Wells and Little Turtle had impressed everyone in Philadelphia. Their remarkable friendship, based on mutual trust and admiration, was so crucial that the government intended to foster it. McHenry betrayed his anxiety when he asked Wilkinson whether Little Turtle was "satisfied" with his meeting with President Adams. "Apparently he had it much at heart to procure an alteration in the boundary line. I flatter myself however that he has left this city well inclined to peace." The usually penurious government had spent far more than "a sixpence" to ensure the chief's comfort and happiness. Expenses for transporting Wells and Little Turtle amounted to $740, while Wilkinson had provided shirts, boots, saddles, and firearms. In Cincinnati he hosted an $85 dinner in their honor. Wells and the Indian delegation spent a month at a local inn at the cost of $174.62½. In his five years as an interpreter, spy, and now an Indian agent, Wells had earned over two thousand dollars. On his return to Fort Wayne, he stopped in Louisville to visit Sam, whose prediction had come true that his younger brother's knowledge of the Indians would be of great value to the United States.[77]

Little Turtle (Mishikinakwa). This lithograph by Ralph Dille of the great Miami war chief was probably based on Gilbert Stuart's portrait, which was lost when the British burned Washington, D.C., in 1814. Courtesy of National Anthropological Archives, Smithsonian Institution (BAE GN 00794).

William Wells. This painting by an unknown artist is the only known image of Wells, pictured here in his captain's uniform. Courtesy of the Chicago History Museum (ICHi-56110).

Arthur St. Clair. Drawing
by John Trumbull. Cour-
tesy of William L. Cle-
ments Library, University
of Michigan.

Anthony Wayne. Cour-
tesy of the Filson Historical Society, Louisville,
Kentucky (PR675.0273).

"The Treaty of Greenville." This painting by Howard Chandler Christy shows William Wells standing between and interpreting for Little Turtle and Anthony Wayne. Note that he is gesturing as well as speaking. Courtesy of the Garst Museum and the Darke County Historical Society, Greenville, Ohio.

William Henry Harrison. Painting by Rembrandt Peale. Courtesy of William Henry Harrison's Grouseland, Indiana Territorial Mansion, Vincennes, Indiana.

"Tecumthah." The LeDru-Lossing portrait of Tecumseh. Courtesy of the Indiana Historical Society, Indianapolis.

TENS-QUA-TA-WA

or THE ONE THAT OPENS THE DOOR

Shawnese Prophet

Brother of Tecumthé

Painted for Gov. Lewis Cass by J. O. Lewis at Detroit 1825.

Tens-Qua-Ta-Wa, or The One That Opens the Door, Shawnese Prophet. An 1824 portrait by James Otto Lewis (1799–1858). Courtesy of the Indiana Historical Society, Indianapolis (E89 .L67 1836).

CHAPTER EIGHT

CIVILIZING THE INDIANS

Jefferson's Indian policy shaped the last twelve years of Wells's life. Although he never ventured west of the Shenandoah Valley, the young Jefferson found Indians fascinating. Only a remnant of them remained in Virginia, but he claimed he had "seen thousands . . . and conversed much with them." He informed John Adams in 1811 that "the great Outacite, the warrior and orator of the Cherokee . . . was always a guest of my father on his journey to and from Williamsburg. I was in his camp when he made his great farewell oration to his people the evening of his departure for England . . . his sounding voice, distinct articulation, animated actions, and the solemn silence of his people at their several fires, filled me with awe and veneration, although I did not understand a word he uttered." Jefferson's greatest gift was putting pen to paper, not public speaking—a skill he admired in Indian orators. Like many ambitious Virginians, he speculated in western lands. Yet Jefferson once swore to James Madison: "I never had any interest Westward of the Alleghney; & I never will have any." Three motifs of Jefferson's Indian policy emerge from this brief look at his early years in Virginia: a strong interest in Indians, a hunger for western lands, and a propensity to let rhetoric replace reality.[1]

THE ORIGINS OF THOMAS JEFFERSON'S
INDIAN POLICY

The scholarship on Jefferson is extensive, impressive, and contentious. He can be seen as the patron saint of American liberals or conservatives, but his critics argue he had a dark side. Here I sketch facets of his sensibility that had a direct bearing on his Indian policy in the Old Northwest and in particular on William Wells, who as Indian agent to the Miamis was complicit in the process by which Jeffersonian philanthropy yielded tragic results. Jefferson was a prodigy of the Enlightenment, but it is important to remember that he was a lawyer by training, a politician by profession, and a romantic idealist by temperament. John Adams said he was selected to draft the Declaration of Independence because he had "a masterly Pen." Jefferson knew how to use the power of words. Sophistic logic-chopping on behalf of the cause *de jour* came easily to him. He believed that what he said and wrote outweighed what he did, that smooth words could calm, or at least disguise, troubled waters: "No republic is more real than that of letters," he told Daniel Webster. Above all, he was a man of declarations more than actions, who placed great confidence in verbal affirmations or denials—despite the evidence.[2]

What Henry Adams termed "the contradictions in Jefferson's character" have provoked copious scholarly analysis, but no one has surpassed the narrative sweep of his classic *History of the United States . . . 1801–1809*. Of all the founding fathers, he wrote, "Jefferson could be painted only touch by touch, with a fine pencil, and the perfection of the likeness depended upon the shifting and uncertain flicker of its semi-transparent shadows." Like many subsequent historians, Adams was struck by the divergence of Jefferson's theory and practice, how his benign precepts were belied by the malign effects of his policies. "He did not speak exactly what he felt," Charles Francis Adams wrote, "either to his friends or his enemies. As a result, he has left over a part of his life a vapor of duplicity." Although he was popularly seen as the embodiment of "pure benevolence," a man who ruled only "to make the people happy," John Adams confided to Benjamin Rush, "you and I know him to be an intriguer." Jefferson should not be judged exclusively by members of the Adams

family, who opposed his policies, but their remarks capture disturbing aspects of his personality.[3]

In his astute analysis, Joseph Ellis noted Jefferson's use of compart-
mentalization, a propensity to "play hide-and-seek within himself"
that enabled him "to articulate irreconcilable human urges at a sufficiently abstract level to mask their mutual exclusiveness. . . . The
Jeffersonian magic works because we permit it to function at a rari-
fied region where real-life choices do not have to be made." Jefferson
positioned himself above the fray his very words had inspired if not
instigated. "With what majesty do we there ride out the storms!" he
wrote of Monticello to Maria Cosway. "How sublime to look down
into the workhouse of nature, to see clouds, hail, snow, rain, thunder, all fabricated at our feet!" As he built and rebuilt his mansion
on top of a mountain, so Jefferson loved to contemplate the grand
scheme of things and construct castles in the air. He liked to declare
that his favorite notions were self-evident truths and essential rights
grounded in the laws of nature—and that the vast majority of "the
people" agreed with him. For Jefferson, as for many Americans, freedom implied an escape from authority: nobody, except my sovereign
self, can tell me what to do. Anthony Wallace noted, "he, the apos-
tle of liberty, had a deeply controlling temperament." Given these
assumptions and a paternalism nurtured by years of "living like an
Antediluvian patriarch" among his progeny both black and white
at Monticello, Jefferson was a dangerous person to assume the role
of "father" to his Indian "children." With the exception of slavery,
nowhere was the gap between Jefferson's noble principles and insidious practices wider than in his Indian policy.[4]

The best introduction to Jefferson's mind and paradoxical character is his only book, Notes on the State of Virginia (London, 1787), a
natural history of his home state that celebrated the American Indian
in order to repudiate French zoologist Georges-Louis Leclerc Comte
de Buffon, whose Histoire naturelle (1761) stated that the moist climate
of North America stunted the growth and development of people
and animals alike. Jefferson took umbrage at this challenge to his
continent and wrote a lengthy response.[5]

Buffon was convinced that American males ("whether aboriginal
or transplanted," Jefferson noted) were distinctly inferior to their

European counterparts: "The savage is feeble, and has small organs of generation. . . . he has no vivacity, no activity of mind . . . these savages . . . lack ardor for their females, and consequently have no love for their fellow man . . . they have . . . no commonwealth . . . their heart is dry, their society cold, and their rule harsh." Their wives, mere "beasts of burden," took "little care" of their few children. Because Nature had denied them "the power of love," they had been reduced to a state lower than animals.[6]

Buffon's critique of the lack of love among Americans, which appears more French than factual, was augmented by Abbé Raynal, who noted "that America has not yet produced . . . one man of genius in a single art or a single science." His hackles raised, Jefferson launched into an energetic rebuttal. When defending the American Indian, he said, "I can speak of him somewhat from my own knowledge, but more from the information of others better acquainted with him, and on whose truth and judgment I can rely." This commendable humility enabled him to present a cogent argument that the male was not "defective in ardor," but rather "affectionate to his children," had "strong and faithful" friendships, and lived in a coherent society. Indian women "produce and raise as many children as the white women" and their warriors were brave but preferred "the destruction of an enemy by stratagem," unlike whites who honored "force more than finesse." Since their society valued personal freedom, "eloquence in council, bravery and address in war" were essential. To prove the Indian genius for oratory, Jefferson cited a speech Chief Logan delivered to Lord Dunmore in 1774, destined to become a standard in school textbooks. This embroiled Jefferson in controversy because Logan mistakenly blamed Michael Cresap for the death of his relatives: Daniel Greathouse was the real culprit. To his credit, Jefferson conducted an investigation. Previously, Cresap and George Rogers Clark *had* shot some Indians in a canoe. Jefferson corrected the record for later editions, but omitted the fact that his friend Clark, a hero in the West, had committed murder.[7]

What moved Jefferson was Logan's lamentation that since his relatives were dead no one would mourn his passing. In part, Indians interested Jefferson because they were doomed. Although his civilization program promised long and productive lives, the undertone of his policy suggested that he considered American Indians a vanishing species. "Spiritous liquors, the small-pox, war, and an abridgement of territory, to a people who lived principally on the spontaneous productions of nature, had committed terrible havock among them." By not specifying where the alcohol, disease, and "abridgement of territory" came from, his remarks suggested that the demise of the Indians was inevitable and outside human agency. Jefferson was one of the first Americans to excavate an Indian burial mound, whose "skulls were so tender . . . they generally fell to pieces on being touched." He used his study of Indian languages to conjecture about their origins in this hemisphere and expressed regret that many languages were irretrievably lost because "we have suffered so many Indian tribes already to extinguish."[8]

Although the Indians had been shaped by their distinctive culture and environment, Jefferson concluded that if those changed they were fully capable of changing too. They had a "moral sense of right and wrong," which was essential to being fully human, and lived in societies that valued freedom. Thus they were worthy of sharing the continent with the white settlers—provided they became "civilized." The men would have to abandon hunting for farming, the women farming for "domestic" chores. The vast forests and prairies would cease to shape their lives. To hasten the civilization process, those lands should be sold.[9]

Jefferson's depiction of Indian culture was incomplete but sufficient to show how Buffon was, to say the least, misinformed. Ironically, when Jefferson turned his attention to American slaves, he relied on the same pseudoscience employed by the French naturalist. Because Jefferson observed his own slaves, he thought he was an expert on their attributes. "The moment a person forms a theory," he had written, "his imagination sees, in every object, only the traits which favor the theory"; and he said of Don Ulloa's negative depiction of South American Indians, "It is very unfair, from this sample, to judge the natural genius of a race of men." Yet these were exactly the mistakes Jefferson made: what he presented in the *Notes* was a racist screed that used anecdotal evidence to draw biased conclusions. He was convinced that blacks and whites could never assimilate: "Deep rooted prejudices entertained by the whites; ten thousand recollections, by the blacks, of the injuries they have sustained; new provocations; the real distinctions which nature has made; and many other circumstances, will divide us into parties, and produce convulsions which will probably never end but in the extermination of one or the other race." All these factors characterized white-Indian relations as well. Although many slaves spoke English, practiced Christianity, and farmed, and thus were much further along in the "civilizing" process, Jefferson nevertheless declared that African Americans were beyond the pale, while American Indians could become citizens.[10]

Jefferson's plan called for a gradual emancipation in which all former slaves were "to be removed beyond the reach of mixture." The Jefferson Memorial in Washington is graced with his stirring phrase, "Nothing is more certainly written in the book of fate than that these people are to be free." But the next two sentences in his *Autobiography* have been omitted: "Nor is it less certain that the two races, equally free, cannot live in the same government. Nature, habit, opinion has drawn indelible lines of distinction between them." "Civilized" Indians had a place in Jefferson's "Empire of Liberty," but freed African Americans should be banished.[11]

During the Revolution, Jefferson took a hard line on Indian aggression. In August 1776 he wrote that the best way "to reduce those wretches" was to push "the war into the heart of their country. . . . I would never cease pursuing them while one of them remained on this side of the Mississippi." In person, he employed a different strategy. The first chief from west of the Appalachians with whom Jefferson negotiated, in June 1781, was Jean Baptist Du Coigne of the Kaskaskia. Governor Jefferson was irate over British use of Indian warriors, although the Americans did the same on a smaller scale. He had treated General Henry Hamilton as a war criminal because he was sure that the notorious "hair buyer" had paid Indians a bounty on scalps. Jefferson assured Du Coigne that "We, like you, are Americans, born in the same land and having the same interests." He explained the Revolution by stating that the British had treated the colonists as slaves in order to enrich themselves; but the Americans "were now grown up and felt . . . strong . . . and were determined to be free. . . . For this reason they made war on us." He told the chief: "If the English have injured you, as they have injured the French and Spaniards, do like them and join us in the war. General Clarke will receive you and show you the way to their towns. . . . He is our great, good, and trusty warrior; and we have put everything under his care beyond the Alleghenies." The dwindling Kaskaskia chose not to fight. Characteristically, Jefferson wanted it both ways: please keep the peace, but if you want to seek revenge, George Rogers Clark will arm you and "show you the way."[12]

Following the Revolution, Jefferson helped author and inspire the Northwest Ordinances of 1784 and 1787. The latter prohibited slavery in the territory and stipulated that "the utmost good faith shall always be observed toward the Indians, their lands and property, shall never be taken from them without their consent." Yet those ordinances were based on the assumption that colonists would replace Indians north of the Ohio. In 1786 he told Benjamin Hawkins, the country's foremost Indian agent: "The two principles on which our conduct towards the Indians should be founded are justice and fear. After the injuries we have done them, they cannot love us, which leaves us no alternative but that of fear to keep them from attacking us. But justice is what we should never lose sight of, and in time it may recover their esteem." As we have seen, Americans insisted on the right of conquest at treaty negotiations in the 1780s, compelling the nations of the Northwest Territory to go on the warpath to protect their lands. Jefferson, stationed in Paris from 1784 to 1789, was in no position to oppose those developments.[13]

Prior to St. Clair's Defeat in 1791, Jefferson was confident that the army would give the warriors "a thorough drubbing" and then we should "change our tomahawk into a golden chain of friendship. The most economical as well as most humane conduct towards them is to bribe them into peace, and retain them in peace by eternal bribes." In June 1792 George Hammond expressed Britain's concern that the Americans intended "to exterminate the Indians and take their land," but Jefferson insisted that all the United States wanted was clear boundaries, since they had "no views even of purchasing any more lands of them for a long time." As subsequent history would soon prove, this was far from the case.[14]

The next year Jefferson met again with Chief Du Coigne, a member of the delegation that came from Vincennes to Philadelphia with

Putnam's treaty. Secretary of state at the time, Jefferson played a prominent role at the meeting. Du Coigne presented "a black pipe" for the chiefs who had died on the trip, praised Putnam, and offered a white pipe. He then presented another pipe, on behalf of the Wea chief Crooked-Legs, who was too infirm to come and wanted to let the Americans know: "The English have a sugar mouth, but Crooked-Legs would never listen to them." Now that the Revolution was over, the chief was plagued by "the Kentuckians [who] take my lands, eat my stock, steal my horses, kill my game, and abuse our persons . . . have pity on us. . . . Be firm, and take care of your children." The next day Du Coigne reiterated the essential point the delegation wanted to make: "Father,—We fear the Kentuckians. They are headstrong and do us great wrong. . . . We cannot live if things go so." Washington had promised to look after his red children yet provided no effective protection. When Jefferson became president in 1801, the problem of settlers intruding on Indian land and wreaking havoc had worsened exponentially, but his administration, with its aversion to standing armies, did next to nothing to enforce the boundary. Instead Jefferson proffered sweet words and a promise of a better tomorrow if only the Indians would sell their lands and become civilized. The tribesmen would learn to their regret that it wasn't just the British who had "a sugar mouth."[15]

THE ELECTION OF 1800

Federalists had good reason to fear a victory by Jefferson in the election of 1800. He threatened to undermine Hamilton's financial system, neglect internal development, dismantle the nation's defenses while aligning it with France, and so weaken the federal government that the country might regress into anarchy. The Federalists, however, were fatally divided. They did not consider themselves a political party but a cosmopolitan elite that practiced disinterested civic virtue. Furthermore, their most prominent leaders, Hamilton and Adams, hated each other. Hamilton even published a pamphlet designed to sabotage Adams's presidential campaign. To a degree, the election hinged on which of his fellow founding fathers

Hamilton disliked the most—Adams, Jefferson, or his longtime rival Aaron Burr.[16]

In the election of 1800, Jefferson and Burr each received 73 votes. Although Jefferson claimed that "the people" supported him, in truth he owed his victory to the power given the South by the three-fifths clause and to Burr's brilliant campaign in New York. In this lame duck Congress, Federalists outnumbered Republicans in the House; states would have one vote each; nine states were needed to achieve a majority. As Garry Wills explained, "They were to exercise their own judgment, not to seek 'the popular will.'" Because Burr was antislavery, less opposed to federal policy, and might help unify the country, many Federalists preferred him to their archenemy Jefferson, described by a partisan newspaper as a "cool, dark, designing theorist." The pivotal figure was James A. Bayard, Delaware's sole representative. "I considered Mr. Burr personally better qualified to fill the office of president than Mr. Jefferson," Bayard said. "The means existed of electing Burr, but they required his cooperation."[17]

Hamilton had anticipated the possibility of a tie and exerted himself to influence the outcome, warning that Burr was a dangerous demagogue whose lack of any political theory meant that only an appetite for power guided his actions. His was a "great Ambition unchecked by principle, or the love of Glory. . . . He thinks every thing possible to adventure and perseverance. And although I believe he will fail, I think it almost certain he will attempt usurpation." In other words, if you want an American Bonaparte, vote for Burr. Whether Burr merited this indictment has ever since been in dispute. "A gentleman," he maintained, "is free to do whatever he pleases so long as he does it in style . . . [and] no ill-will is intended." Burr did not need others to validate his high opinion of himself. By not cloaking his ambitions in the rhetoric of civic virtue, he was the polar opposite of both Hamilton and Jefferson. Why did he refuse to state that he would not accept the presidency? As a lawyer he abided by the letter of what the Constitution stipulated; since no love was lost between them, he enjoyed watching Jefferson squirm as the House deadlocked repeatedly; he believed he was the best man to be president: if the House agreed, he would accept their judgment. In the end Jefferson's surrogates gave Bayard "assurances" and the tie was broken, leaving bitter feelings on all sides.[18]

Jefferson's first inaugural address, 4 March 1801, was a polished performance. His most celebrated phrase seemed to call for an end of partisan strife: "But every difference of opinion is not a difference of principle. We have called by different names brethren of the same principle. We are all republicans—we are all federalists." People at the time, and historians since, have seen these words as "full of conciliation" and "magnanimity," an offer of an olive branch to the defeated Federalists. But was that what he meant? When the Federalists were in power he predicted: "A little patience, and we shall see the reign of witches pass over, their spells dissolve, and the people recovering their true sight, restore their government to its true principles." Jefferson believed that Federalism was a temporary delusion and that the people were republican at heart. Joseph Ellis is correct that "Jefferson did not really mean what Hamilton and all the other commentators thought they heard him say." He wanted not a truce but a capitulation. All must agree "that a republican form of government and a federal bond among the states were most preferable." His "mollifying words" were a subtle way of stating what Khrushchev told Nixon, "We will bury you." In one letter, he said as much: "I shall . . . by the establishment of republican principles . . . sink federalism into an abyss from which there shall be no resurrection."[19]

Although Jefferson promised that only Federalists "guilty of gross abuses of office" would be fired, he did the exact opposite. One study found that "purely political reasons constituted the backbone of his effort to break Federalists' power" and eliminate an entrenched "aristocracy from . . . the federal government." Jefferson dismissed a higher proportion of opponents (46%) than Jackson (41.3%), the president many assume initiated the spoils system. In effect, Jefferson's plan called for eradicating the incipient two-party system. By repealing the Judiciary Act of 1801, Congress eliminated Adams's sixteen "midnight" judges. "Jefferson could only get away with mass displacements by pretending no such thing could happen," Garry Wills stated, "finding a fig leaf for the new judges' removal was what mattered."[20]

Jefferson was determined to lower the national debt. Against the advice of Secretary of the Treasury Albert Gallatin, Congress did not recharter the Bank of the United States, with the result that "America suddenly went wild in creating new banks," which provided needed

cash for common people but undermined the nation's financial stability. The army was drastically reduced in favor of local militias.
The navy's frigates were put in dry dock, leaving the seaports, which
were badly in need of defenses, to the protection of gunboats. Jefferson's reliance on the militia to fend off foreign invasion was naive
at best, yet he had legitimate concerns about a standing army led by
a Federalist officer corps and with a man as ambitious as Hamilton
waiting in the wings. A lack of federal troops meant that the government could not prevent settler incursions on Indian land. Although
some Federalists were guilty of extravagance, Jefferson's financial
policies were often penny-wise and pound-foolish at a time when the
country faced external threats from England and France and needed
national development.[21]

I have emphasized the divergence between Jeffersonian principles
and practice because it foreshadows problems with his Indian policy. When Jefferson said, "we are all federalists—we are all republicans," what he really meant and expected was that most Federalists
would "convert" to republicanism, party discord would cease, and
national harmony prevail. Likewise, when he spoke to Indians about
brotherhood and becoming one people, he was not saying that all
Indians and Americans were equal, any more than all Federalists
and all Republicans were equal. Through his civilization program
he expected Indians to become like white people or face the consequences. To understand and evaluate this policy, it is necessary to test
Jefferson's idealistic rhetoric against his actions. How, for example,
did his plans, which Little Turtle was expected to accept and William
Wells to implement, actually impact the Miamis?

WELLS AND LITTLE TURTLE IN WASHINGTON

In May 1801, Wells wrote to Jefferson's personal secretary Meriwether Lewis that "Little Turtle . . . wishes to visit our father, the
President, this fall, when Congress meets: he wishes to take five other
Chiefs with him." The delegation included two prominent Potawatomis, Five Medals and Topinbee (He Who Sits Quietly), Little Turtle's
nephew the Toad, and a Wea chief. From Pittsburgh they traveled by

stagecoach to Philadelphia, where Little Turtle thanked the Quakers for sending two ploughs to Fort Wayne in 1799. The day after Christmas, the chiefs were met in Baltimore at the Fountain Inn by the Society of Friends Indian Committee and taken to the home of Elisha Tyson. The Quakers said they saw "all mankind as their brothers." To replace the wild game, "we have thought it best for our Red brethren to give some attention to the cultivation of the soil." Little Turtle invited the Indian Committee to attend a Great Council at Fort Wayne and requested that "any information intended for them should be conveyed . . . through their interpreter, William Wells." Five Medals added his approval: "we wish our brothers, the Quakers, to render us those services they have proposed," noting that "having a good interpreter [was] beginning at the right end of the business."[22]

The following day Evan Thomas, who had visited the Wyandots at Upper Sandusky, noted that due to "Canadian traders residing among them" the Indians were frequently drunk. Little Turtle admitted that "most of the evils existing among the Red people, have been caught from the white people; not only that liquor which destroys us daily, but many diseases that our forefathers were ignorant of, before they saw you." The situation was so desperate that "our young men say, 'We had better be at war with the white people.' This liquor . . . is more to be feared than the gun or the tomahawk; there are more of us dead since the treaty of Greenville, than we lost by the years of war before, and it is all owing to the introduction of this liquor among us." To illustrate, Little Turtle told a parable:

> Brothers, when our young men have been out hunting, and are returning home loaded with skins and furs, on their way, it happens that they come along where some whiskey is deposited, the White man who sells it, tells them to take a little drink; some of them will say, "No, I do not want it"; they go on until they come to another house, where they find more of the same kind of drink; it is there again offered, they refuse, and again the third time; but finally the fourth or fifth time, one accepts of it and takes a drink, and getting one, he wants another, and then a third, and fourth, till his senses have left him. After his reason comes back to him, when he gets up and finds where he is, and asks for his peltry, the answer is, "You have drank them." "Where is my gun?" "It is gone." "Where is my blanket?"

"It is gone." "Where is my shirt?" "You have sold it for whiskey." Now, brothers, figure to yourselves what a condition this man must be in; he has a family at home—a wife and children who stand in need of the profits of his hunting. What must *their* wants be, when he is even without a shirt!

The Indian Committee was so moved by Little Turtle's eloquence that they resolved to go to Washington with a copy of his words and demand that Congress take action.[23]

Without the unflagging efforts of George Washington, the city that bears his name would never have been built. Infected early with "Potomac fever," he foresaw that river conveying the produce of the West to the nation's capital, making it "the grand Emporium of North America." The city would be a unifying symbol whose marble monuments would embody the nation's noble aspirations. Pierre L'Enfant's original design envisioned a grand metropolis. Broad avenues, lined with stately brick townhouses, would radiate from the widely separated Capitol and Presidential Palace, cut diagonally across a grid of lettered or numbered streets, and pause at fifteen squares or circles, each representing a different State, which would feature heroic statuary, memorial columns, luxuriant gardens, and ornate fountains. Neoclassical architecture inspired by the Roman republic would be the norm. Goose Creek was renamed the Tiber, and Jenkins Hill, site of the Capitol building, became Capitaline Hill. L'Enfant's worst fears were realized when Washington fired him for his extravagance and Congress provided neither funding nor oversight, causing "the first great land-grabbing boondoggle in American history."[24]

When Wells and Little Turtle arrived in late December 1801, the inchoate city made "the separation of powers" a painful reality: the unfinished President's House was divided from the incomplete Capitol building by a muddy road hopefully known as Pennsylvania Avenue. "Around the capitol are seen seven or eight boarding houses, one tailor, one shoemaker, one printer, one washing woman, a grocery shop, a pamphlet and stationary shop, a small dry goods shop and an oyster house." The members of Congress slept two to a room, ate mess at a common table, and shot partridge from the steps of the Capitol. An early visitor noted: "The 'mighty city' is nothing more than distinct groups of houses, scattered over a vast surface, and has more the appearance of so many villages, than a city. . . . The capitol, the president's house, and the different bulky public offices, form each a town within themselves." When speculators realized that Washington would not become a thriving metropolis any time soon, many abandoned their schemes, leaving a row of buildings here, another there, some lacking upper floors and roofs. Amid the tangled undergrowth and scrub oak, impoverished squatters and overworked slaves huddled in flimsy shanties. "The people are poor," one observer wrote, "and live like fishes, eating each other." The most pathetic figure was an unemployed visionary: "Daily through the city stalks the picture of famine, L'Enfant and his dog."[25]

The imperial pretensions of the incipient national capital drew the scorn of foreign diplomats condemned to endure a residency in so dreary a backwater. The person least disturbed by this hodgepodge was Jefferson. "There sits the President," one wag wrote, "like a pelican in a wilderness." After tearing down and building up his beloved Monticello, he took in stride the brick kilns in the front yard of his new home, no main staircase to the second floor, and leaking roofs. Jefferson's austerity measures ensured that it would be many years before the nation's rudimentary capital became a metropolis.[26]

Wells and Little Turtle attended a New Year's Day reception at the president's house, modeled after the Duke of Leinster's Palladian home in Dublin. One guest noted that Jefferson was "tall in stature and rather spare in flesh. His dress and manners are very plain; he is grave, or rather sedate, but without any tincture of pomp, ostentation, or pride, and occasionally can smile, and both hear and relate humorous stories." Margaret Smith recalled that "he turned toward me a countenance beaming with an expression of benevolence and with a manner and voice almost femininely soft and gentle." Jefferson had pale, freckled skin, blue eyes, and rusty red hair tinged with gray. His long limbs and large wrists did not suggest grace or strength; rather he was an angular man, ill at ease, who stood stiffly, shambled when he walked, and slouched with one shoulder higher than the other when seated. He often wore threadbare clothes and tattered slippers, even on public occasions.[27]

That morning Baptists from Cheshire, Massachusetts, had presented Jefferson with a "Mammoth Cheese," a gigantic wheel weighing 1,235 pounds. From the milk of nine hundred Republican cows and "produced by the personal labor of *Freeborn Farmers*, with the voluntary and cheerful aid of their wives and daughters, without the assistance of a single slave," the cheese had been brought by Reverend John Leland to show his congregation's gratitude for Jefferson's democratic principles and advocacy of religious freedom. When Wells and Little Turtle arrived, Jefferson invited them to go "to the mammoth room [the East Room] and see the mammoth cheese"; there they were served cake and wine. The president was "highly diverted" by the gift, but Federalists satirized the cheese as being, like Jefferson, smooth on the outside but rotten at the core.[28]

In his first annual message to Congress back in December, Jefferson had painted a rosy picture of the "peace and friendship that generally prevails" among the Indians, some nations even experiencing "an increase of population." When he met with Little Turtle on 4 January, however, the Miami chief presented a list of grievances that demanded immediate attention. Little Turtle expressed the "confidence" of all the Indians in "our Interpreter" William Wells, then turned his attention to articles of the Treaty of Greenville that had not been fulfilled. Settlers in Vincennes were crossing "over the line," and the threat of violence was imminent: "Father we therefore request that the lines may be run" to clarify the boundary. Supplies promised as part of the annuities were deficient, and a trading post at Fort Wayne was needed, as were farming equipment and a blacksmith shop. Lamenting the damage that had been done by the sale of "Spiritous Liquors" among them, he said: "Father, Your children are not wanting in industry, but . . . the introduction of this fatal poison" has kept the Indians poor and unhappy. He asked for "a conversation" with Dearborn to discuss these issues.[29]

A tall, heavy man with a face as craggy as the rocky coast of his native Maine (then a district of Massachusetts), Henry Dearborn was "genial in manner and imposing in appearance." A veteran of battles from Breed's Hill to Yorktown, in 1779 he participated in Gen. John Sullivan's devastating campaign against the Iroquois towns. He had won Jefferson's favor by being a staunch Republican from Federalist New England. Although he doubted the reliability of local militias, Dearborn drastically cut the armed forces. Frugality was the order of the day, which meant that everything, including Indian policy, would be run on the cheap. Wells presented a letter from William Henry

Harrison, who recommended him "as a Sober, active and faithful public Servant. His knowledge of the Indian language, and manners, is much greater than that of any other person in this Country." Dearborn reappointed Wells as an assistant agent for Indian Affairs, with a salary at six hundred dollars a year, plus four food rations "in kind or in money." Dearborn supported Jefferson's civilization program: "There ought, no longer, any doubt remain, of the practicability of changing their habits and manners, from a savage to a civilized state. It will require time, and patient perseverance . . . to produce the *whole* effect, which is so pleasing in contemplation, to every good mind." Whether there would be time, patience, or resources to achieve such benevolent prospects remained very much in doubt.[30]

When Jefferson replied to Little Turtle and the other chiefs, he reiterated his standard speech that "the same great spirit" had made the Indians "one people" with the Americans, who "cherish their interests as our own" and desire to live in peace. "We shall with great pleasure see your people become disposed to cultivate the earth and raise herds of the useful animals, and to spin and weave, for their food & clothing. These resources are certain: they will never disappoint you, while those of hunting may fail, and expose your women & children to the miseries of hunger & cold." Dearborn responded to Little Turtle's specific issues. The president was "willing to make good to his red children all real deficiencies"; he would ask Harrison to draw a proper boundary at Vincennes, supply the Indians at Fort Wayne with "ploughs and hoes . . . and a Blacksmith," and construct "a convenient building" for the distribution of annuities.

"We are happy to find our expectations have been realized," Little Turtle concluded. "What you have said to us shall be collected in our hearts & taken home and there communicated to your Red Children." In the afternoon Little Turtle's speech to the Friends in Baltimore was presented to Congress, who in March authorized the president "to prevent or restrain" the liquor trade. Wells wrote a year later thanking the Friends for their efforts: "the suppression of liquors in that country is the best thing that has ever been done for the Indians, by the United States; that within a year, not one Indian had been killed; whilst there had never been a year before since the treaty of Greenville in which there were less than ten killed, and some years as many as thirty." This happy situation would not last long, as strong drink continued to decimate the tribesmen.[31]

Jefferson met with Indian chiefs in Washington not only to demonstrate his good intentions but also to awe them with the strength of the new nation and convince them further resistance would be useless. Wells, for his part, was serving two masters. He was the government's Indian agent and an ambassador for Little Turtle's faction of the Miamis. The chief was, by any standards, an exceptional human being, whose influence would be enhanced by his negotiations with the government. Jefferson was sufficiently impressed to hold a "private conversation. . . . with the little Turtle in the presence of capt. Wells," in which he asked him "the opinions of the Indians with respect to a supreme being, the worship of him, and a future state, he answered me frankly, but I carefully avoided the impropriety of either controverting or concurring in those opinions, or of saying one syllable on the comparative merits of any religious opinions." Little Turtle "really appears to be a man of extraordinary talent," Dearborn wrote, "capable of doing much good or harm according as he may be induced to act." For their trip, each chief would receive a new hat, two shirts, and twenty-five dollars in goods at Pittsburgh. Little Turtle's "inducement" would be a yearly sum of $150.[32]

THE VINCENNES TRACT AND JEFFERSON'S GRAND DESIGN

Six months before Jefferson gave a sunny account of Indian affairs in his inaugural address, William Henry Harrison, governor of Indiana Territory, had depicted the situation in a darker hue: The Indians "say their people have been killed—their lands settled on—their game wantonly destroyed—& their young men made drunk & cheated of their peltries. . . . Of the truth of these charges I am well convinced." Furthermore, "a great many of the Inhabitants of our Frontiers consider the murdering of Indians in the highest degree meritorious." Because the boundaries established by the Treaty of Greenville were not clearly defined, hunters on Indian lands had slaughtered deer, bear, and buffalo until the latter had become "extinct" in the area. The dispirited tribesmen, mainly Piankeshaws, Weas, and Eel River, gathered in Vincennes and behaved like "the greatest Scoundrels in the world." Drunken Indians roamed the streets, fought, and broke into houses, killing the hogs and cows of the citizens and destroying their fences. "But in all their frolicks they generally suffer most severely themselves they kill each other without mercy," targeting leaders until "there is scarcely a Chief to be found amongst them." Harrison could tell at a glance whether an Indian was from "a Neighboring or most distant Tribe. The latter is generally well Clothed healthy and vigorous the former half naked, filthy and enfeebled with Intoxication." He urged Jefferson to avoid "the reproach which will attach to the American Character by the extirpation of so many human beings."[33]

Harrison was to the manor born—in his case "Berkeley" on the James River, where his family was prominent in the Virginia gentry and national politics. After immersing himself in the classics at Hampden-Sidney College, Harrison studied medicine in Philadelphia; but when his father died he opted for a military career, arriving in Cincinnati to witness the survivors of St. Clair's Defeat straggle into town. As General Wayne's aide-de-camp, he befriended Wells, who taught him about Indians in exchange for English lessons. Their relationship was renewed when Harrison became governor. Wells as Indian agent was answerable both to Harrison in Vincennes and to Dearborn in Washington. In addition to quarterly reports, Wells was to provide "a correct statement of all expenses incurred" and keep a journal "relating to disputes, complaints, misfortunes, etc. including . . . the progress of civilization among the Indians, and . . . remarks . . . relating to the natural history of the country, the population and the particular manners of the inhabitants." Harrison knew that Wells possessed a rare set of useful skills, but he soon learned that his agent in Fort Wayne followed his own agenda.[34]

Harrison was accustomed to taking what he wanted. Since Judge John Symmes, one of the largest landowners in Ohio, did not find him suitable for his daughter, Harrison married Ann while her father was out of town. Although the young man could not "bleed, plead, preach [or] plow," Symmes admitted that "he has talents . . . he may become conspicuous." As a delegate to Congress, he supported a law that made land easier to purchase on the frontier. In May 1800 Adams selected Harrison as governor of Indiana Territory. Jefferson reappointed him because he shared the president's two mutually incompatible goals: civilizing the Indians and obtaining as much land as possible to encourage rapid settlement. Dearborn ordered Harrison to find "a fair construction of that part of the Treaty of Greenville, which relates to land at Vincennes."[35]

Harrison learned of a "ridiculous transaction" made by some Piankashaw chiefs, who in 1775 had ceded to the Wabash Company a large tract of land, since obtained by speculators as part of "an infamous fraud." Previously, the Indians *had* granted the French about ten thousand acres near Vincennes. Nevertheless, Harrison asserted that the fraudulent Wabash Company sale of some million acres to the Americans was valid: "Our claims to lands around this place are More extensive than is generally imagined." Dearborn also asked Harrison to obtain a valuable salt spring near the mouth of the Wabash, suggesting that "the Little Turtle and Mr. Wells may be employed on such a mission to advantage." As for the Vincennes Tract, Dearborn cautioned him to "ascertain how much they [the Piankashaws] will agree to have surveyed." He should bargain for "the best terms possible," since "it would be very desirable that the United States should acquire the exclusive right to this Tract."[36]

Dearborn understood that the Wabash Company sale was illegal, yet he urged Harrison to claim as much of it as he could get away with. Negotiations opened in Vincennes in September. Little Turtle refused to attend, citing "the jealousy with which the [other] chiefs viewed the footing on which he stood with the United States." Harrison's assertion that the Wabash Company grant had been validated by the Treaty of Greenville outraged the Indians. A Wea chief said: "We gave no lands to our fathers the French. . . . We only lent them land to live on." While a Piankashaw insisted: "I am sorry the salt spring has been given away—it is mine—I don't agree to it." The chiefs did not want to "provoke the Great Spirit" by selling more land. Fusee, a Wea, concluded: "You are the first I have heard claim this land given to the French, who told you so lied." Wells stated that "St. Clair [had] directed . . . [Putnam] to inform the Indians, that a surveyor's chain should not be stretched on the opposite side of White River, and that the few settlements on them should be withdrawn."

Harrison's first biographer simply wrote: "Under these circumstances it required the utmost exertions of the Governor to bring them to a better temper; and in this he, with the assistance of captain Wells, completely succeeded." By a combination of gift-giving and arm-twisting they obtained the extensive Vincennes Tract. Wells, who knew that the claim was false, won Harrison's approval by supporting his demands. In return, he gained an enhanced role for Little Turtle in the official treaty that would be signed the following June at Fort Wayne.[37]

Jefferson's Indian policy was profoundly influenced by the revolutions in France and Saint Domingue (Haiti). He was in Paris in 1789 when the Bastille fell. Convinced that a new spirit of liberty would now spread across Europe, he welcomed the overthrow of Louis XVI and downplayed the mounting violence. The Reign of Terror peaked after Jefferson returned home, but what offended him was not that the guillotine held grisly sway. Instead Jefferson castigated William Short for reporting the horrid facts: "The liberty of the whole earth was depending on the issue of the contest, and was ever a prize won with so little innocent blood? . . . Rather than it should have failed, I would have seen half of the earth desolated. Were there but an Adam and an Eve left in every country, and left free, it would be better than it now is."[38]

Most chilling is Jefferson's acceptance of "revolutionary violence" regardless of the cost. He had more in common with Saint-Just and Robespierre than we like to admit. When Jefferson wrote to Short, the revolution had already been irredeemably betrayed by wanton executions. Not until Robespierre and Saint-Just had had their own heads lopped off, did he express regret and acknowledge for the first time, as Conor Cruise O'Brien noted, "that any 'atrocities' had *ever* been perpetrated!" Before long, however, he had reverted to his old faith that France, even after Napoleon Bonaparte had co-opted the revolution, was our natural friend, while Great Britain remained our inveterate enemy.[39]

The revolution in France inspired a series of gory events in their Caribbean colony of Saint Domingue. What began as a power struggle among the whites became a successful slave rebellion that made an ex-slave named Toussaint-Louverture the self-appointed governor

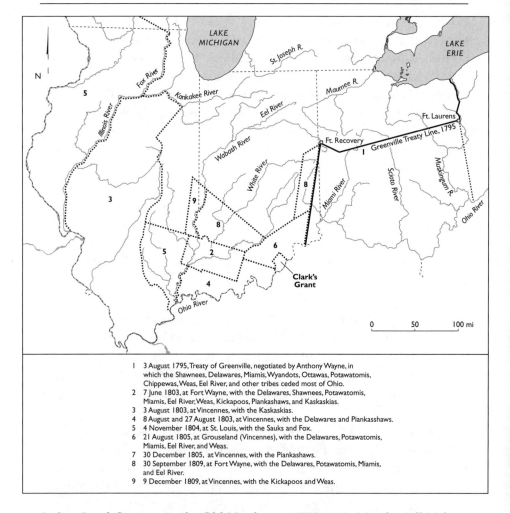

Indian Land Cessions in the Old Northwest, 1795–1809. Map by Bill Nelson.
Copyright © 2015 University of Oklahoma Press.

for life. The island was extremely valuable, producing two-thirds of
the world's sugar and one-half its coffee. Winning it back and restoring slavery was a major priority for Napoleon. In April 1801 he began
organizing an army of three thousand men to occupy Louisiana and
sent chargé d'affaires Louis Pichon to enquire whether the United
States would cooperate in the reconquest of Saint Domingue. Jefferson

gave full support: "in order that this concert may be complete and effective you must [first] make peace with England; then nothing can be easier than to furnish your army and fleet with everything, to reduce Toussaint to starvation." Thus in the summer of 1801, Jefferson plotted with France to return slavery to Saint Domingue. Once that had been accomplished, however, Napoleon would have taken Louisiana, fortified New Orleans, and rendered Jefferson's most celebrated accomplishment, the Louisiana Purchase of 1803, impossible. Once again Jefferson was pursuing incompatible policies.[40]

In the fall of 1801, Jefferson had second thoughts. Charles Pinckney in Paris wrote: "this Government intends sending out a large force to the island of Saint Domingo to replace things in their former situation. . . . You may also be assured that the occupation of Louisiana is with them a favorite object & that the cession has been absolutely made by Spain." Rufus King in London and Fulwar Skipwith in Paris warned that occupying Louisiana was a French priority. Plans were under way "of peupling that Colony," which would supply food, clothing, and timber for the other Caribbean islands, whose most "troublesome" men would be sent there. "One of the greatest armaments is preparing at Brest for the West Indies that has ever been known, an army of 30,000 men. . . . Genl. LeClerk . . . is to command the expedition."[41]

Leclerc's forces arrived in February 1802 and were at first successful, causing key black leaders to betray each other. Toussaint was arrested and sent to France, where he died in prison. When word reached the island in June that France had restored slavery in Guadeloupe, the tide of battle turned. "These men die with incredible fanaticism,—they laugh at death; it is the same with the women," Leclerc wrote. "This colony is lost. . . . What general could calculate on a mortality of four-fifths of his army?" In a few months Leclerc had lost 24,000 troops, far more from yellow fever than combat; in November he too succumbed. A ferocious war dragged on for another year, claiming some 350,000 rebel and 60,000 French lives by the time Haiti declared her independence on 1 January 1804.[42]

Jefferson was slow to recognize the danger Napoleon posed to mainland America and reluctant to take action. He applauded the French Revolution yet opposed the one in Saint Domingue and

wanted slavery restored. His racial phobias and Francophile sentiments blinded him for a time to Bonaparte's imperial designs. His
diplomatic response was an attempt to bluff the French with a threat
of force, yet the reality was that his reliance on local militias and his
positing of a military alliance with Great Britain lacked teeth. Napoleon knew a paper tiger when he saw one. As Henry Adams aptly
noted: "Had not . . . Toussaint's resistance intervened, ten thousand
French soldiers, trained in the school of Hoche and Moreau, and commanded by a future marshal of France, might have occupied New
Orleans and St. Louis before Jefferson could have collected a brigade
of militia at Nashville." The courage of Toussaint's troops and the
spread of yellow fever defeated Napoleon. "Damn sugar, damn coffee, damn colonies!" he finally exclaimed, abandoning both Saint
Domingue and his American empire. Thus in April 1803 Talleyrand
asked Livingston, "What would you give for the whole?" The result
was the Louisiana Purchase. Jefferson's triumph rode on the wings
of infectious mosquitoes and the arms of slaves seeking freedom.[43]

The purchase of Louisiana whetted the president's "appetite for
expansion . . . because expansion represented something close to an
end in itself for Jefferson." He rejected Montesquieu's doctrine "that
a republic can be preserved only in a small territory" and instead
"saw expansion as the indispensable concomitant of a stable, secure
and prosperous Empire of Liberty. Expansion was at the center of
Jefferson's reason of state." He exercised "royal" authority in foreign
affairs, Henry Adams noted, and his "overmastering passion was to
attain West Florida," which he insisted was a part of the Louisiana
Purchase, even though Spain, France, and expert opinion knew that it
was not. For years he tried threats and intimidation but failed to force
Spain to yield. His policy of bullying Spain was no more effective
than that of bluffing France. In sum, Jefferson's expansionist policies
called for acquiring as much land as possible as quickly as possible,
regardless of moral or legal obstacles.[44]

Jefferson was, literally, at home with duplicity. A person who could
decapitate a mountain to build a mansion with a sublime view of the
horizon was not averse to manipulating reality to fit his preconceptions. Monticello contained hidden stairways, dumbwaiters, disappearing beds, sliding double doors, circular rotating wall shelves,

secret pulleys, concealed wine cellars, and a writing machine that made a simultaneous copy. For years in that house he had carried on a clandestine affair with Sally Hemings, his dead wife's illegitimate half sister and his own slave. When in September 1801 James Callender—the scandalmonger he had secretly hired to smear his Federalist rivals—broke the story of "Sable Sally" in the *Richmond Recorder*, Jefferson kept above the fray. A few months later Callender was found dead in shallow water of the James River. In private Jefferson had raged against the "damned rascal" and expressed the wish that he be silenced. The president's friends threatened Callender in the press, sacked his office, and assaulted him on the streets of Richmond—but would they have gone so far as to kill him? A coroner's inquest ruled that the victim was drunk and drowned.[45]

In the winter of 1802–1803, when French occupation of Louisiana was expected, Jefferson explicitly outlined his duplicitous Indian policy in private letters to Dearborn, Hawkins, and Harrison. He informed Dearborn that it was imperative to acquire Indian land in the Southwest, especially along the Mississippi, to strengthen frontier defenses against Bonaparte's troops. Teaching the Indians to farm and establishing trading houses would compel them to sell more land, as would the presence of more Americans: "The Indians being once closed in between strong settled countries on the Mississippi & Atlantic, will, for want of game, be forced to agriculture, will find that small portions of land well improved, will be worth more to them than extensive forests unemployed, and will be continually parting with portions of them, for money to buy stock, utensils & necessities for their farms & families." They would be trapped in a kind of vise that would fix their fate. To Benjamin Hawkins, Jefferson sought to present this remorseless process in a more pleasing light: "While they are learning to do better on less land, our increasing numbers will be calling for more land, and thus a coincidence of interests will be produced between those who have lands to spare, and want other necessaries, and those who have such necessaries to spare, and want lands. This commerce, then, will be for the good of both, and those who are friends to both ought to encourage it." Hawkins, in other words, should support the program—or else. With twisted logic Jefferson compared the process to "the wisdom of the animal which amputates

& abandons to the hunter the parts for which he is pursued [that] should be theirs." Then he tried to soften the harsh metaphor: in the first instance the animal "sacrifices what is useful," but the Indian "what is not. In truth, the ultimate point of rest & happiness for them is to let our settlements and theirs meet and blend together, to inter-mix, and become one people." This was Jefferson's way of saying we are all Republicans, we are all Indians—only if the latter became the former could harmony prevail. He assured Hawkins that this policy was "consistent with pure morality," while it would "procure grati-fications to our citizens, from time to time, by new acquisitions of land."[46]

Jefferson's most disturbing letter was to Harrison, the man respon-sible for implementing his policy in the Northwest: "Our system is to live in perpetual peace with the Indians, to cultivate an affection-ate attachment from them, by everything just and liberal we can do for them within the bounds of reason." What was most reasonable, however, demanded a radical change in Indian society. The women should quit "the labor of the field" and learn to sow and weave while the men became farmers. Thus "they will perceive how useless to them are their extensive forests, and will be willing to pare them off from time to time in exchange for necessaries for their farms and fam-ilies." If this process was too slow, "we shall push our trading houses, and be glad to see the good and influential individuals among them run into debt, because we observe that when these debts go beyond what the individuals can pay, they become willing to lop them off by a cession of lands. . . . In this way our settlements will gradually circumscribe and approach the Indians, and they will in time either incorporate with us as citizens of the United States, or remove beyond the Mississippi." Should warriors be tempted to resist this inexorable process, "we presume that our strength and their weakness is now so visible that they must see we have only to shut our hand to crush them." Any tribe "fool-hardy enough to take up the hatchet" would be driven "across the Mississippi."[47]

There was nothing "gradual" about Jefferson's program. Harrison was told that time was of the essence and that he must take posses-sion of as much land as possible: "This crisis is pressing: whatever can now be obtained, must be obtained quickly. The occupation of

New Orleans, hourly expected, by the French, is already felt like a light breeze by the Indians. You know the sentiments they entertain of that nation; under the hope of their protection they will immediately stiffen against cessions of lands to us. We had better, therefore, do at once what can now be done." Jefferson outlined his strategy for negotiating with the weaker tribes: "The Kaskaskias being reduced to a few families, I presume we may purchase their whole country for what would place every individual of them at his ease, and be a small price to us." With the Potawatomis and Kickapoos, the United States should claim "all doubtful territory" and pressure the tribes "to *cede*, for a price, such of their own unquestioned territory as would give us a convenient northern boundary." In short, every nation had its price. "Of the means, however, of obtaining what we wish, you will be the best judge." At the end of his "unofficial and private" letter, Jefferson cautioned Harrison "how sacredly [its contents] must be kept within your own breast, and especially how improper" it would be to inform the Indians of the government's intentions. "For their interests and their tranquility it is best that they should see only the present [p]age of their history." Writing to Andrew Jackson, Jefferson encapsulated the purpose of his Indian policy: "In keeping agents among the Indians, two objects are principally in view: 1. The preservation of peace; 2. The obtaining of Indian lands." In other words, the mission of civilizing the Indians was essentially a method of keeping them peaceful until all their lands were gone. First titles would be extinguished, and then tribes would disappear.[48]

WILLIAM WELLS, LITTLE TURTLE, AND THE DELAWARE TREATIES

On 18 January 1803, six months before he knew of the Louisiana Purchase, Jefferson sent a secret message to Congress calling for "a Western Exploring Expedition." In order "to provide an extension of territory which the rapid increase of our numbers will call for, two measures" were necessary: The Indians should be encouraged to abandon hunting, and trading-houses would be established among them. "In leading them thus to agriculture, to manufactures, and civilization; in bringing together their and our settlements, and in preparing them ultimately to participate in the benefits of our government, I trust and believe we are acting for their greatest good." Two years later, Lewis and Clark made the expedition a reality. The western lands north of the 31st parallel, Jefferson realized, could be used for resettling tribesmen living east of the Mississippi. The land south of that line, however, was not reserved for yeoman farmers of the republic. Instead slave owners extended their kingdom, while an American protectorate was imposed on the people of Louisiana until they became "worthy" of citizenship.[49]

Jefferson defended the fraudulent sale of the Vincennes Tract, telling a Miami and Delaware delegation that the land had been "ceded and sold to white men" by their ancestors. He audaciously asserted that Harrison had only obtained "a little more than a third of our right." The Indians were not "satisfied with it," yet Jefferson insisted that they must submit. All he could promise was that "Mr. Wells, our agent," would provide them with a blacksmith and some farming equipment. Although the Louisiana Purchase meant that the government's need to gain Indian cessions was no longer urgent, nevertheless Jefferson maintained his land-grabbing policy, which Harrison promptly put into effect.[50]

Even though Wells had helped him in Vincennes, Harrison informed Dearborn in March: "Capt. Wells has certainly not exerted himself to pacify the Indians who have taken offense at the late Treaties." Rather he overstated how many Indians were "disaffected" by the agreement. "But when Wells speaks of the Miami Nation being of this or that opinion," Harrison wrote, "he must be understood as meaning no more than the Turtle and himself. Nine tenths of that Tribe who acknowledge Richardville and Peccan for their chiefs (but who are really governed by an artful fellow called the Owl and Long Beard . . .) utterly abhor both Wells and the Turtle." Harrison deliberately minimized Little Turtle's influence, but the majority of the Miamis did follow other leaders. Wells had incurred Harrison's ire by insisting that the Piankashaws and Kaskaskias could not sign away lands without permission of the Miamis. Harrison argued that in the past those weaker tribes had operated independently. Little Turtle's opposition to ceding the Vincennes Tract was easy to explain:

"Conscious of the superiority of his Talents over the rest of his race and colour he sighs for a more conspicuous theatre to display them." As for Wells, "a submissive deference to his talents, or a supposed coincidence of interests has caused the Agent of the United States to adopt the opinions and promote the views of the Turtle." In sum, "Capt. Wells's conduct in this affair certainly deserves severe animadversion." He had not foreseen the consequences of his disloyal actions and "some ridiculous *spice* of jealousy towards myself may have mingled itself with his motives." Wells must be told that his "zeal and fidelity" were mandatory if Harrison were to execute "the orders of the government."[51]

Harrison was not the first to question Wells's conduct. After a trip to Washington, the Shawnee chief Black Hoof complained to Dearborn that Wells "made many difficulties to our coming here" by failing to arrange the trip with Governor St. Clair; "we therefore inform you that we will not have any thing to do with . . . Mr. Wells in particular, we expect you will get a man who will pay more attention to his employment." A year later Dearborn warned Wells: "There appears to have been an unreasonable number of rations issued to the Indians at Fort Wayne in November last." These complaints would return every time Wells stretched his budget to feed an increasing number of starving Indians. After he had a warehouse and a blacksmith shop constructed, Wells had the first of many clashes with the new factor John Johnston, who challenged the Indian agent's authority over the blacksmith. Then a fire destroyed the buildings and Wells had to start over.[52]

When Harrison came to Fort Wayne in June to finalize the Vincennes agreement, supplies had not yet arrived and only Little Turtle and a few Potawatomis were present. The Owl had convinced most of the Miamis that "Little Turtle had sold to the United States the whole country, and that it would be claimed as it would be wanted." Harrison threatened to withhold the annuities of those tribes that didn't attend. The Shawnees who finally appeared "behaved with so much insolence, that the Governor was obliged to tell them that they were undutiful and rebellious children." The offended chiefs "left the council house in a body." Those tribes who remained spoke eloquently against the cession of the Vincennes Tract. To restore himself in the governor's favor, Wells played a crucial role: Harrison was "powerfully, though privately, aided by the Turtle, and boldly seconded in every proposition by the Potawatamies . . . [until] all opposition was finally silenced." Little Turtle and the other "Chiefs and Warriors" who signed, surrendered more than a million acres as well as the salt spring. Harrison used his control over annuities and a large contingent of Potawatomis demanding presents to compel consent. Wells and Little Turtle understood that Harrison was obtaining the Vincennes Tract for a ridiculously low price. Yet if the Indians could not defend those lands, or sell them now, they might end up with nothing. In the end, the chiefs made their marks, received enough presents to maintain their tribal positions, and went back to their villages feeling bitter and betrayed.[53]

Harrison returned to Vincennes to sign treaties with the Eel River, Kaskaskia, and other tribes. These Eel River Indians, whose headman was known as Charley, were remnants of Snake-fish Town. At the Treaty of Greenville, Wells had arranged for them to receive a separate annuity of five hundred dollars. After their village had been destroyed by Wilkinson in 1791, the tribe moved to the Mississinewa. Some returned to Eel River and established Old Town; others came to Vincennes and spent their annuities on liquor. The treaty with the Eel River Indians confirmed the agreement at Fort Wayne, while the Kaskaskia treaty ceded 7 to 8 million acres in Illinois, for which Chief Du Coigne and his dwindling band received less than two thousand acres, a five hundred dollar increase in annuities, plus one thousand dollars to pay a priest, build a church, and retire their debts. Harrison later confided to Dearborn: "The prospect of being enabled to live comfortably, was the great motive with him [Du Coigne], for selling his lands." Jefferson welcomed the extensive purchase in his third annual message to Congress: "The friendly tribe of Kaskaskia Indians with which we have never had a difference, reduced by the wars and wants of savage life . . . has transferred its country to the United States, reserving only for its members what is sufficient to maintain them in an agricultural way."[54]

While Harrison was negotiating in Vincennes, Wells led a few soldiers to see if a fort could be built at "Chicagou," a small fur-trading outpost that occupied a strategic location on Lake Michigan.

In January 1804 Dearborn increased his annual pay by $150, probably in gratitude for his and Little Turtle's assistance at the Fort Wayne treaty. He also granted Wells's request that the Potawatomi and Miami annuities should consist of money as well as goods, which often arrived late and damaged. The problem was that payment in cash opened the door to graft. The previous fall Harrison had received a report that several Indian agents were selling licenses to traders regardless of their qualifications. Wells admitted that "he gave licenses as usual to every body that asked for them," adding that Harrison "had not given him any orders to the contrary." Dearborn cautioned Wells the following spring: "You can have no doubts as to your authority as Agent with the Indians in that quarter, for prohibiting any white person from trading with the Indians without license within the Indian boundaries." Months later Five Medals received a letter from British agent Thomas McKee: "My Children, I am told that Wells has told you, that it was your interest to suffer no liquor to come into your country; you all well know that he is a bad man, you all well know the injustices he has done before you made peace with the long knives, by taking and killing your men women and children." Might this opportune proof of Wells's diligence in enforcing government policy be a forgery? Since he distributed cash to the Indians and collected license fees for traders, it is possible he abused his position to enrich himself. Whether he differed from other agents in this regard is difficult to determine. Strict honesty on the Indiana frontier at this time was rare, as each man brazenly strived to get ahead. Furthermore, Wells was operating within the ambience of Jefferson's duplicitous Indian policy and the ruthlessness of Harrison's greedy land deals.[55]

Harrison explained to Jefferson that his method of negotiating with the Indians was to avoid making an abrupt proposal, which "discomposes & agitates them extremely & is rarely Successful," but rather to allow "Sufficient time" to talk to the chiefs until they see "the advantages which they would derive from the Measure." He suggested that the "most desirable" tract the government should seek next was the land occupied by the Delaware between the White River and the Ohio. Since the Miamis had recognized the Delaware title but the Weas and Piankashaws "Contend Strenuously against it," he thought a general treaty council would be necessary. Dearborn ordered Harrison "to obtain the tract between the southern line of Vincennes territory and the Ohio." In two treaties in August of 1804, Harrison was able to get the Delawares and Piankashaws to comply. Article 4 stated that the Miamis had "explicitly acknowledged the title of the Delawares" at the Fort Wayne treaty of 1803, while in Article 5 the Piankashaws said they no longer objected to the sale. Prominent Delaware chiefs, including Buckongahelas, signed the agreement. Jefferson imposed his own interpretation of the purchase in his annual message to Congress: "the Delawares . . . desiring to extinguish in their people the spirit of hunting and to convert superfluous lands into the Means of improving what they retain, have ceded to us all the country between the Wabash and Ohio."[56]

Nothing shows the divided loyalties of Wells more than his impulse to protest American treaties he was hired to support. Two months after Harrison had purchased the Delaware tract, Wells sent a letter to James Wilkinson that included Little Turtle's opposition to the agreement. The chief stated that Harrison had purchased "our lands from Indians that has no right to sell them." Little Turtle urged Wilkinson to convince Jefferson not to approve the treaty, since the Miamis were greatly displeased with Harrison, who "has done us more harm than any man that ever came into our country." He had created new chiefs and given tribes titles to land they never owned in order to purchase them cheaply and "to make himself a great man at the expense of the Indians." Worst of all, "he has struck our existence at the root and I am afraid that his conduct will finally set us at war with each other." Wells added: "I am certain that the Indians would wish a war with the United States rather than sell the lands if they had any prospect of being supported by any foreign power." Little Turtle must have insisted on sending this brutally honest indictment of Harrison, but Wells should have realized that Wilkinson would pass it on to Dearborn.[57]

Dearborn continued to criticize Wells for "such profusions of provisions delivered to the Indians, it must not be continued to such an unreasonable amount." When he learned in December of Wells's letter to Wilkinson, he was outraged: "You ought to confine your official correspondence to this office & Governor Harrison," he scolded. If the Miamis had any claim to the lands that were sold, they should provide proofs, not issue "such threats of war as the Little Turtle has thought proper to make." He told Wells to assure the Miami chief that the government desired "to deal honestly and fairly" with the Indians. "But if they should have recourse to War for their purpose of securing a better title to their lands, or a happier situation for themselves and families, they will certainly be much disappointed."[58]

In the spring of 1805, three Delaware chiefs sent Billy Patterson, a *métis* who spoke English, to Wells with a message denying that they had sold "a large Tract of Land" to Harrison, who had told the chiefs he wished them "to become more civilized," giving them five hundred dollars to purchase farm equipment: "the Governor had been shutting up their eyes and stopping their Ears with his good words and got them to sign a Deed for their lands without their knowledge." The chiefs expressed "their confidence" in Wells to explain to the government that they had been deceived and were not "willing to sell the lands on the Ohio." Harrison blamed Wells: "I am convinced that this man will not rest until he has persuaded the Indians that their very existence depends upon rescinding the Treaty. . . . My knowledge of his character induces me to believe that he will go to any length and use any means to carry a favorite point and much mischief may ensue from his knowledge of the Indians, his cunning and his perseverance." Jefferson advised defusing the crisis through "Liberalities and patronage to chiefs of influence." If Little Turtle was trying to form "a great confederacy" to resist government policy, then "perhaps we . . . may have been defective in our kindnesses to him. A liberality towards him which would not be felt by us, might prevent great embarrassment & expense."[59]

Dearborn advised Harrison to assemble the Delawares, Miamis, and Potawatomis to explain the contested treaty and "satisfy the chiefs, generally, that the transaction was not only open and fair, but such as they have no right to object to." Those who had protested "ought to be severely reprimanded, and made to acknowledge . . . the impropriety of their conduct." If they refused, they would lose the president's confidence and would not be "admitted to any conference with him." Harrison sent Gen. John Gibson and Col. Francis Vigo to discover the cause of the discontent. They held a meeting at

Fort Wayne in June and advised the Indians not to "listen to any bad stories or any lying birds that may be flying about."[60]

When Gibson asked if the Delawares had been "defrauded and cheated" at the treaty, Tetepachsit responded: "We did not sell any lands to the United States last summer at Vincennes; the Goods we received there were a condolence present [for the recent death of Buckongahelas] and to pay for horses your people had stolen from us." Some young warriors told Gibson that "their chiefs . . . had sold the land and were afraid to own it . . . [and] that the Little Turtle and Wells had said the sum specified in the Treaty was a mere nothing and that they were cheated and imposed on." Wells then told the Delawares to "not be afraid to own that they had sold the Land." When Gibson asked if he recalled that two years ago Buckongahelas had confirmed that the Miamis recognized Delaware ownership, Wells said "he did not recollect it," but regretted the loss of the chief, who "was a great man . . . that . . . would be much missed by his nation." Although he now admitted its validity, in the past Wells had complained that "the Indians were very much imposed on at the late treaty at Vincennes." John Johnston stated that "there never would have been any noise about the Treaty had it not been occasioned by the Little Turtle and Wells." Gibson concluded that they had originated the protest and that Wells "seems more attached to the Indians than to the people of the United States."[61]

Harrison assured Dearborn that "the affair of the Delaware Treaty [would be] settled to the satisfaction of the President." If any Indians still opposed it, one man was responsible:

> A person situated as Mr. Wells is might have thwarted the measures of government for years without being detected but altho possessed of a good deal of cunning he has so entangled himself in the mazes of his own intrigues that he cannot move without making disclosures that are fatal to him. I could freely forgive him for the past if there was any security for his future good conduct but I believe that he is still doing his utmost to prevent a favorable issue to the proposed conference with the Indians.

Harrison wanted the treaty enforced to the letter: "If we recede one inch these people will be never satisfied until they have gained the ell." Little Turtle and other chiefs were angry with the Delawares "for selling the land without including them." Johnston told Vigo that Wells made "more money than any man in the Territory . . . that he cleared last year upwards of $6000." Since Wells could not have accumulated that sum "honestly," Harrison thought "that measures ought to be taken to control this vicious inclination or to remove him from office and from the Indian country." As Harrison scholar Robert Owens observed: "Wells, walking the tightrope between his adoptive people and his American employers, had slipped, and there was no net."[62]

Most of these accusations came from men with their own axes to grind. Several Miami chiefs were jealous of Little Turtle's power and prestige; Gibson had been directly involved in the original Delaware Treaty; and Johnston detested Wells and consistently criticized his conduct. Nonetheless, so much smoke probably indicated a real fire. Wells and Little Turtle knew that the Delaware Treaty was fraudulent and unfair, but they also wanted to renegotiate it in order to up the ante. When Wells told the Delawares that they had been paid too low a price for the land, he was speaking the truth so as to stiffen their resistance to the government's voracious policy. Johnston's estimate of Wells's wealth was no doubt exaggerated, but that he was using his position for personal gain was possible. At the same time, the trouble that he and Little Turtle caused was largely driven by their genuine concern for the deteriorating condition of the Indians. Although Wells's questionable conduct cannot be condoned, it can be understood.

In August 1805 the Wabash chiefs assembled on the lawn of Grouseland, Harrison's brick mansion at Vincennes. Moses Dawson stated that "all the difficulties were removed, which, by the maneuvers of the Little Turtle and the agent [Wells] . . . had agitated the Indians for about ten months previous." Little Turtle did get the Delaware chiefs to admit that the Miamis had only loaned them land on the White River that they had no right to sell. For a price, the Miamis then ceded additional land in southern Indiana. The United States recognized the Miamis, Eel River, and Weas "as joint owners of all the country on the Wabash . . . above the Vincennes Tract" and promised not to purchase "any part of the said country" without the consent of each tribe.

The Indian nations received increased annuities and four thousand dollars in gifts. The ceded tract contained "at least two million acres . . . of the finest land in the Western country," but Harrison lamented that he had to pay "as nearly as I can ascertain it about one cent per acre. This is much higher than I could have wished it to have been but it was impossible to make it less."[63]

Once again Wells had averted personal disaster by helping Harrison obtain a treaty. Somehow he gave Harrison a satisfactory explanation of his behavior, and the two men "agreed to a general amnesty and act of oblivion for the past" and a promise of "future good conduct . . . and mutual harmony." Little Turtle had gained a better price for the land and more say for himself and the Miamis in future cessions on the Wabash. In return, Harrison "promised the Turtle fifty dollars, per annum, in addition to his pension; and . . . directed Captain Wells to purchase a negro man for him in Kentucky, and draw on . . . [Dearborn] for the amount." It was a shady deal all around, which shamed every participant, but enabled Jefferson to boast to Congress that the treaty "completes our possession of the whole of both banks of the Ohio."[64]

THE QUAKER MISSION TO CIVILIZE THE MIAMIS

Nothing was more controversial about Wells's tenure as Indian agent than the question of whether he sabotaged the Quaker mission to civilize the Indians near Fort Wayne. At first, Wells encouraged the project, writing to the Friends in Baltimore in the summer of 1803 that the Miamis wanted to learn how to farm. Little Turtle urged the Quakers to visit Fort Wayne and see the condition of the Miamis for themselves. He thanked them for sending "implements of husbandry" but lamented that "the minds of our people are not so much inclined toward the cultivation of the earth as we could wish them." He did hope that "the Great Spirit will change the minds of our people, and tell them it is better to cultivate the earth than to drink whiskey." The Friends decided to send a delegation to Fort Wayne.[65]

On 30 March 1804, Gerald Hopkins, George Ellicott, Joel Wright, and Philip Dennis met with Wells, the factor John Johnston, and the fort commander Capt. John Whipple. They stayed with Johnston and spent their days with Wells, often dining at his home. One evening Little Turtle mentioned that *"he was but half well*, having been very sick last fall and expected to die." Wells stated that he had the gout, which was considered a gentleman's disease. "'Well,' said the Turtle, 'I always thought that I was a gentleman.'" Hopkins, who kept an account of the trip, provided a rare description of Sweet Breeze: "At the head of the table sat the interpreter's wife, who is a modest, well-looking Indian woman, and the daughter of a distinguished chief. She had prepared for us a large well roasted turkey, and also a wild turkey broiled, and for these she had provided a large supply of cran-berry sauce." She died within the year, probably from the epidemic that carried off Buckongahelas. The four children—Anne (Ahpezza-hquah), Rebecca (Pemesahquah), William Wayne (Wapemonggah), and Mary (Ahmahquauzahquah)—often stayed at their Uncle Sam's plantation and went to school in Louisville. Wells made sure that his own *métis* children would grow up "civilized."[66]

During walks around Fort Wayne, Wells showed the visitors skulls from Harmar's Defeat and explained how Little Turtle prepared his troops to fight St. Clair. During a meeting held at Wells's home, the Quakers urged the Indians "to alter their mode of living" before it was too late. If they learned to farm, to build wooden houses, and to weave their clothing, they would be comfortable, warm, and well fed. "Our beloved brother, Philip Dennis . . . [will] cultivate for you a field of corn [as well as other crops]. . . . He knows how to use the plough, the hoe, the axe, and other implements of husbandry." He also wanted to change gender roles: "Women are less than men. . . . It is the business of our women to be employed in our houses, to keep them clean, to sew, to knit, spin, and weave, to dress food for them-selves and families, to make clothes for the men and the rest of their families, to keep the clothes of their families clean, and to take care of the children." Whatever crops Dennis produced that year he would turn over to the Indians "as a token of our friendship.[67]

Little Turtle and the other chiefs decided that Dennis should not be located in one of the villages, "lest our younger brothers should be jealous of our taking him to ourselves." Wells led the Quakers to twenty-five cleared acres along the Wabash, the site of a former

Delaware town: "The land appears to be equal in quality to any we have seen." The farm was two miles west of present Andrews, Indiana. The nearest Miami settlements were at the forks of the Wabash and on the Mississinewa.[68]

Left on his own, Dennis was able to build a cabin and plant twenty acres of corn and one of turnips. By late August the corn "made an excellent appearance, having 2 and 3 ears on a stalk." Out of curiosity, many Indians appeared: "They would take a seat either on the fence, or in the trees, near the premises, and watch him with apparent interest in his daily engagement of ploughing and hoeing, but without offering to lend a helping hand." Only one family . . . were "industrious & attended to his directions." Some women "wished to work in preparing the ground and in tending the corn; from this he [Dennis] dissuaded them," telling them to go to Fort Wayne and learn to use the spinning wheel. The Indians "acknowledged that his corn was equal to any they had ever seen on the Wabash." Dennis gave his harvest to "neighboring chiefs for a winter supply" and returned to Baltimore, leaving "twenty-three hogs and pigs, seven of which were in good order to kill." In June, 874 Indians gathered for a council at Fort Wayne. Wells informed the Quakers: "the Delaware, Miami, & Eel River Indians have agreed to the request of the United States to send suitable men amongst them, to instruct them in building houses, making fences, etc., instead of giving them their yearly annuities in goods."[69]

The next year, Wells told the Quakers that he "would lose no time" in finding a person to farm the cleared ground left by Dennis. Sounding overly optimistic, Wells declared that "a spirit of industry existed among the Indians generally." The Delawares had employed men to split 23,000 rails for fences, and the Miamis and Eel River were expecting 40,000 more. Ten Miami families "had settled adjoining the place cultivated by Philip Dennis," with four men cutting rails for them and three more for the Eel River Indians. Twenty-five acres had already been cleared of a projected sixty. Wells predicted that "at least twenty-five families" would join the growing settlement. One Indian who worked for Dennis was building himself "a comfortable house, and cleared two acres more of ground." All the Indians needed, Wells insisted, were "good and suitable men to reside among them, and teach them how to work."[70]

Wells reported to the Friends in the fall of 1805 that elderly Eel River and Weas had moved to Dennis's farm and "would be followed by the younger branches of their tribes in the ensuing spring." The farm now had "at least four hundred hogs, and twenty cows, and the Indians at no village in this country live so comfortably as those at that place." At Fort Wayne, Wells hired Richard Palmer, a blacksmith, and David Stinchcomb, a carpenter, to mend tools and build houses, and John Conner and Peter Audrian to split rails. One hundred acres of land at Turtletown had been fenced in, and his people had "a large number of hogs and some cows." Wells predicted: "If this spirit of industry is kept alive for a few years, it will certainly have a powerful influence upon the minds of the Indians in many of the neighboring villages."[71]

In 1806 William Kirk, a Quaker, arrived with a letter from Dearborn ordering Wells to assist him in teaching the Indians to farm. Kirk accomplished little and Wells was preoccupied by financial matters. Dearborn had asked Captain Whipple and John Johnston to investigate whether "some incorrectnesses are mingled with Mr. Wells Agency Accounts, perhaps from his want of more accurate knowledge in Keeping Accounts." They reported "many improper charges" that required more investigation. Dearborn warned Wells that his "issue of provisions" to nearby Indians "ought to be very trifling. . . . Rigid economy and strict fidelity should govern every expenditure within your agency."[72]

Wells knew that Johnston had raised suspicions of his malfeasance. Dearborn's austerity, Wells's generosity with provisions, and sloppy bookkeeping were part of the problem—in addition to a desire to make money. Johnston was the polar opposite of Wells, and their simmering rivalry now boiled over. Of Huguenot and Scotch-Irish ancestry, Johnston came to America in 1786 at age eleven. As a young man he was a packhorse master during the Wayne campaign. In the fall of 1795 he was docked three months' pay for neglecting his duty and losing 55 of 185 horses. After a failed business venture in Kentucky, he went to Philadelphia, where he worked first as a scrivener in a law office and then in the War Department. Based on an embellished account of his business success, in 1802 Dearborn appointed him the factor at Fort Wayne. Johnston eloped with a sixteen-year-old Quaker, Rachel Robinson, who was expelled for marrying "out of meeting" and without parental consent. Strict piety marked her life. She bore four children at Fort Wayne, did not like living among Indians, and "would never let her children learn the Indian tongue, as she said . . . [they] were barbarians enough." Johnston was over six feet tall and maintained an upright, military posture. He was blond, with a large, ruddy face, wide mouth, and protruding chin. A tidy man, he prided himself on his good digestion. More narrow-minded than mean-spirited, above all he was patriotic. George Washington was "the gift of God to the American people," and Johnston's lifelong rule was "to go for our country, no matter who may govern it." Not surprisingly, he and Wells rarely saw eye to eye.[73]

The Indian factory at Fort Wayne during Johnston's tenure was an active place. Between 1802 and 1811, it was the most profitable trading post in the Old Northwest. As long as they could sell furs, tribal hunters were reluctant to become farmers. According to Jefferson's plan, the Indians did pile up debts at the store—$696 in 1804 and $2,041 by 1811—but they did not pay for them by selling their land. Johnston admitted to Dearborn in 1805 that his brother's "bad management" of their former business had created additional "bad debts . . . a considerable sum." Since then he had been "struggling to extricate myself from this embarrassment." Although Johnston was personally honest, the Indian factory faced serious problems. The long and circuitous method of delivery meant that "many of the articles were damaged and some embezzled." Finally, "every means that malice and disappointment could suggest was tried by the Traders to make the store unpopular." These were mainly French Canadians, who married Indian women, spoke their language, and conformed "to their customs and manners." Their "malice" peaked in October 1805, when an Indian burnt Johnston's house. Three years later a pirogue carrying a $3,881 shipment sank at Otter Creek. Wells was not the only man at Fort Wayne with money troubles.[74]

William Kirk was the catalyst for intensified conflict among Wells, Johnston, and Dearborn. Moravian missionaries on the White River found the Quaker to be "a very pleasant man," but the Delawares were not impressed: "This man tires his horse in vain," they said. "We do not need anyone to teach us how to work." When Kirk first visited Fort Wayne in 1806, Little Turtle told him of a plan for teaching

Indians to farm. Back in Baltimore, Kirk "prevailed on the Quakers to Lay this matter before the government as coming from himself." Dearborn approved and gave Kirk six thousand dollars. Wells had asked Dearborn if he and Little Turtle could come to Washington in the spring to present their project to "form a union of the scattered branches of the Miamis . . . [thus adding] greatly to their strength, respectability and welfare" while serving Little Turtle's civilization plan. Instead, Kirk returned in May 1807, having already spent half of his funds. A resentful Wells encouraged the chiefs to resist Kirk's assistance.[75]

When Kirk presented his "letter of appointment," Wells promised to "do all in his power to carry the views of government into effect," but added "the chiefs must be consulted first." After a lengthy deliberation they responded: "we believe the intentions of the Quakers are good, that they wish to do us good, but they have never helped us any." In the years since Dennis started his farm, the chiefs had not received any of the crops. "I never was more surprised in my life at any reply I ever heard," Kirk wrote. "It was so entirely different from the language they had always made to us before." Wells told Kirk he was surprised by the response, too, "but there was so much indifference about him that I could not help suspecting him for the cause." Charles Jouett, the Indian agent at Chicago, told Kirk that "Wells was able to do what he pleased with the Indians." The strategy of stalling and evasion continued when Wells informed Kirk that "the Five Medals had sent me word . . . that he did not want me." Then an old Indian told Kirk that he had heard Wells say that even though Congress "was paying them to work for the Indians . . . all the Quakers had done was done for themselves." This left Kirk with "no doubt on my mind that Wells had been the cause of all that had passed."[76]

Kirk was convinced that his mission would have succeeded had it not been for Wells, who "considers me as an obstacle in his way and if the money had been first in his hands . . . all would have went on smooth." He had no solid proof of deliberate interference, but "as his influence and intrigue with the Indians is superior to Truth . . . they will certainly say and do whatever he tells them." Wells wanted to thwart the civilization plan, "if it was not carried on by himself," because "the annuities has been a source of much profit and speculation to himself, and certainly will be as long as it is left in his hands." Little Turtle thanked Kirk for his "good intentions" and said he "must not blame him . . . [since] I had went forward without consulting the Indians," which Kirk admitted to be "true." Wells added that the Indians wanted assistance, but Kirk "had not done it right . . . that the Indians intended to go speak to the president themselves on the subject." When Kirk did go to Five Medals's town, the people seemed glad to see him and asked for assistance. Two white men whom Wells had hired to work at the village were "as much astonished as the Indians" at the runaround he had received. Kirk concluded that Wells might "materially injure me if I am to remain in the country," and he advised Dearborn not to let him come to Washington, but rather "some more disinterested interpreter . . . any other person than Wells, as many things . . . are a good deal confused."[77]

Kirk moved to Black Hoof's Shawnee village at Wapakoneta, where he was successful in teaching the Indians to farm but ran into financial difficulties when he "initiated a series of programs that rapidly outstripped his resources." Upon learning that Kirk had complained to Dearborn about him, Wells demanded an explanation. If he did not respond "immediately," Wells warned, "I shall consider what at present the report says to be true and govern myself according." Wells told Harrison: "I have done every thing in my power to carry the views of the President into execution among the Indians, under Mr. Kirke, but to no purpose." On the other hand, he boasted that he could implement Jefferson's program better "than any other person he could appoint" and urged Harrison to recommend him and assure the president "that any money that may be appropriated for this purpose, will not be misapplied." Meanwhile, having received Kirk's letter, the War Department cautioned Wells that he must avoid "a repetition of similar complaints . . . [or Dearborn would] adopt such measures as will place it out of your power to contravene the views of government" in the future.[78]

His position in jeopardy, Wells defended his actions to Dearborn, asserting that he had been "the only advocate in this country for civilizing the Indians and the only person that had made any attempt at it." He resented "such threts" that had been "throwed out at me" without the benefit of "an impartial Eye." Wells again asked to come to

Washington and explain himself. He told Dearborn how Kirk had stolen Little Turtle's civilization plan and spent "a Large Sum of money" before the Indians received "any benefit from it." Thus Kirk "was not capable to fill the appointment He had obtained by Intreague and Deception." Wells included a speech from Miami, Potawatomi, and Eel River chiefs to Jefferson. They acknowledged that in 1804, Dennis had raised a crop and given it to the Indians, but Kirk "had spent so much of the money you had given him for our use before he arrived among us, we thought it best for him not to take up residence among us." Johnston witnessed and nine chiefs signed the message.[79]

Before he received these letters in defense of Wells, Dearborn decided to deny his request to come to Washington, having already concluded who was to blame:

> Until you shall give satisfactory evidence of more useful zeal and honest candor, than your late conduct has evinced, no subterfuge will be admitted to extenuate the evident impropriety of your conduct in relation to the persons sent into that country for the express purpose of aiding the natives in the art of civilization. The circumstances attending this business render your intentions so self evident, as to require no other proof.... At all events, one or two things must be a fact, either that you possess no kind of useful influence with the chiefs in your agency or that you make improper use of what you possess. In either case you cannot be considered as well qualified for the place you hold.[80]

Wells must have realized that, regardless of any explanations he might offer, his days as an Indian agent were numbered. He had cooperated with Dennis and encouraged local Indians, with limited success, to participate in his experiment. After Dennis left, Wells hired men to split rails, build houses, and assist the Indians to become farmers. When Dennis was not replaced by competent persons, Wells and Little Turtle formulated their own civilization program, hoping to receive government money. The appearance of Kirk foiled their project, and Wells then helped to sabotage Kirk's mission. Whether Wells and Little Turtle, with government approval and support, could have carried on a more effective civilization program is an open question. Wells was already running a prosperous farm of his own, and Little Turtle was sincere in his desire to set a good example at his village, but the chief's privileged position was resented by other factions of the Miamis. Even though Kirk had some significant achievements among the Shawnees, his mismanagement of funds, especially in light of Dearborn's austerity measures, probably would have occurred even if he had carried out his original mission to the Miamis and Potawatomis.

Tribal jealousies, personal rivalries, and human greed undercut the Quaker attempt to teach the Miamis to farm. In this episode Wells appeared, for the most part, in an unfavorable light. Yet larger problems in the civilization program traced back to men with real power: Jefferson, for flaws in his original scheme; Dearborn, for his frugality and lack of oversight; and Harrison, for his insatiable hunger for Indian land. Harrison was singularly unsupportive of the program; his constituents did not want their Indian neighbors to learn to farm. They wanted tribal land. Bernard Sheehan concluded: "The civilizing plan was as well designed for the elimination of tribalism as the advance of the frontier was inimical to the life of the Indian. Ultimately, hating Indians could not be differentiated from hating Indianness. If the frontiersmen adopted the direct method of murdering Indians, humanitarians were only more circumspect in demanding cultural suicide of the tribes."[81] Because of Jefferson's austerity measures, troops were unavailable to keep frontiersmen from intruding on Indian lands, and civilization programs were never adequately funded. Harrison's treaties meant that Indian lands were constantly shrinking, disrupting the rhythms of tribal life and severing the taproot of their vitality. Dearborn, who like Jefferson never ventured west of the Appalachians, could only follow orders and pinch pennies.

As the primary sources repeatedly demonstrate, Indian alcoholism was a major impediment to the civilization program. At least as significant, but rarely discussed, was the importance of gender roles. Traditionally, it was the women who farmed, and they knew what they were doing: "They planted corn in hills three feet apart and with it placed beans. At the edge of the fields and between the hills they planted squash, pumpkins, and sunflowers." This combination of corn, beans, and squash, known as "the three sisters," was ecologically sound and diversified the food supply. The beans climbed up the corn stalks, leaving room on the ground for the squash, and the blend of crops helped replenish the soil. If farming was to succeed among the Indians, these skills needed to be incorporated; yet Dennis would not let Miami women assist him. Quakers working among the Senecas in western Pennsylvania for a few years combined the labors of women and men. It might have been possible to develop a system whereby the men did the plowing while the women tended to the hoeing and both sexes joined in the harvest. Quakers, as well as their fellow countrymen, had another set of gender expectations: women were keepers of the hearth, not tillers of the fields. Unfortunately, Americans were unable to accept, let alone incorporate, Indian cultural traditions.[82]

Jefferson's civilization plan was not a total failure, especially in the South. The Cherokees and Creeks made great strides. The evidence suggests that had the Indians been granted more time and protection, many within a generation or two would have passed Jefferson's civilization test. But his policies were unable to cope with the insatiable land hunger of the Americans, which the government encouraged by demanding cessions in treaty after treaty. By the end of 1807, Wells was still defending himself to Dearborn and pushing his own plan, which called for a concentration of the Wabash nations around his agency at Fort Wayne: "The Indians of this country are too much scattered for the United States to civilize them and I assure you that it is nothing but a waste of money to attempt any thing of the kind in their present state. It might as well be said that corn would grow in the woods without clearing the ground." To get back in the good graces of the government, Wells lent his support to Jefferson's land policy, implemented with vigor by Harrison, by arguing that the Indians should sell their hunting grounds, gather in villages, and commence farming. He saw a prominent role for himself in this process: "Men should be imployed in this business that was acquainted with the customs and manners of the Indians and who possessed influence among them. The Indians will not place confidence in a stranger . . . the plan I have mentioned . . . could be done with 3600 Dollars a year."[83]

Although Dearborn was unimpressed, he did not fire Wells, in spite of his suspicion that his agent at Fort Wayne had enriched himself at government expense. A larger danger was looming on the horizon, and, once again, the assistance of William Wells was crucial. A religious revival was sweeping through the nations of the Old Northwest, along with a new spirit of Indian militancy. The leaders were two brothers: the Shawnee Prophet and Tecumseh.

CHAPTER NINE

CONFRONTING TECUMSEH

In the first decade of the nineteenth century, new beliefs spread among the tribes of the Old Northwest, undermining Jefferson's civilization program and challenging the peace established at the Treaty of Greenville. At the same time that evangelical camp meetings were springing up in Kentucky, revivalist beliefs swept through Indian villages north of the Ohio. The most significant visionary was the Shawnee Prophet, whose brother Tecumseh led a militant pan-national movement determined to resist further cessions of tribal lands. Wells warned about the dangers of these developments, earning the animosity of both Shawnee leaders and their followers. He was already out of government favor for subverting Kirk's farming mission and protesting Harrison's land-grabbing treaties. Once more Wells was in the middle of the struggle between Indians and settlers. Since he saw multiple sides of issues and had conflicted feelings about them, he often acted in such contradictory ways that few trusted him. Did his ultimate loyalties lie with the United States, Little Turtle's faction of the Miamis, or only himself? In the last years of his life, Wells was the most-hated man in the territory.

THE VISIONS OF THE SHAWNEE PROPHET

On 15 June 1799, a Seneca in western Pennsylvania named Handsome Lake fell into a trance in which the Great Spirit told him that the Indians should put a stop to drinking, witchcraft, love magic, and other evil ways and return to the customs of their forefathers. During an apocalyptic vision two months later, he saw Jesus, George Washington, and The Punisher, who "delighted in devising sadistic torments to fit the crimes of his prisoners: the drunkard was forced to swallow molten metal . . . a promiscuous woman was made to fornicate with red-hot penes." To avoid such dire fates, sinners confessed to Handsome Lake, whose "Old Way" included a social gospel of domestic felicity and communal welfare. When he named "sundry old women & men of the Delaware nation" as witches who caused fatal illness, they were sentenced to death but pardoned. The Seneca orator Red Jacket was also under suspicion. Handsome Lake's teachings created a "true renaissance" among the Senecas but led to a rise of intertribal tension and disputes between his devout believers and their traditional leaders.[1]

Drunkenness, disease, and despair induced redemptive visions among the Delawares on the White River. Moravian missionaries nearby noted a drop in converts as alcoholism ran rampant: "No one who has not seen an Indian drunk can possibly have any conception of it. It is as if they had been changed into evil spirits." Epidemics took a terrible toll and the grief-stricken sought scapegoats: "The chiefs alleged that . . . two women, in the form of night owls . . . bewitched all the Indians, and brought them to a fatal malady." Unsuccessful hunting and smaller harvests resulted in "a general famine." The desperate villagers claimed that "the Brethren merely wanted to make the Indians tame, so that the white people might kill them as had been done at Gnadenhütten." When Buckongahelas told the missionaries, "Your teaching is only for white people," Brother Kluge did not help matters by asserting that the Delawares were living in "the slavery of sin and of Satan." In November 1803 an old woman named Beata was in the woods when a man appeared who claimed to be her grandfather. If the Indians wanted the deer to return, he said, they must "live again as you lived before the white people came into this land." Afterward, she was considered a seer who had swallowed "the good spirit" and spoke "the Word of God." In March 1805, "a man of enormous stature appeared unto her" and warned that if the Indians did not keep up tribal sacrifices "they would . . . perish." Beata "forbade all evil, drinking, fornication, stealing, murder, and the like." Since "she knew everything that the Indians do and think even though she does not see it," she could tell who "among them was bad and a master of poison." When Buckongahelas died in May 1805, the Delawares assumed that the death of so great a man must have been caused by witchcraft. Suspicion fell on Tetepachsit, an elderly chief who feared for his life.[2]

Tecumseh's town, on the White River near the Delaware villages, was aware of Beata's prophecies and Handsome Lake's religion. Like other woodland Indians, the Shawnee blamed witchcraft for the decimation wrought by disease. In November 1805 Tecumseh's younger brother Lalawéthika (Loud Mouth), who had apprenticed himself to Pegagashega (Change of Feathers) as a shaman, was in Black Hoof's town of Wapakoneta to help with "a great sickness." When Change of Feathers died, the burden of healing the Shawnees fell on Loud Mouth's less-than-capable shoulders. One evening he collapsed into a death-like coma. Revived, he reported that "he had a vision or revelation." Loud Mouth was an unlikely vehicle for prophesy. A fat, awkward child, he had accidentally poked out his right eye with an arrow. His contemporaries described him as "a talkative, blustering, noisey fellow, full of deceit," and "no warrior, but a low, cunning fellow." Often drunk, he beat his wife and boasted of a prowess he obviously lacked but that Tecumseh—a great hunter, fighter, and leader—had in abundance. Now transformed, Loud Mouth would be called Tenskwatawa (Open Door) or the Shawnee Prophet.[3]

In one vision the Prophet came to a forked road: those who turned right arrived at a beautiful land of fruit and flowers, but on the left "all *bad wicked* people" were damned to eternal torment and suffered Dantesque punishments for their crimes. Shamans must surrender their medicine bags or be killed. Everyone from age seven on must confess their sins to the Prophet. To "separate from these wicked . . . people," he and his followers planned to establish a village at Greenville and await an imminent "day of *Judgment*."[4]

The Prophet's teachings were both traditional and revolutionary. On one hand, he called for a return to an idealized past: the Indians were to live as they did "in olden days," dressing in skins; hunting with bow and arrow; keeping established sacrifices and ceremonies;

avoiding the white man's foods, tools, methods, and merchandise; bartering for their needs; and sharing with others. To ensure domestic tranquility, kind treatment should prevail among husbands, wives, and their children. Interracial marriages, especially with Americans, should be renounced. In practice, nothing furthered family harmony more than abstinence from alcohol. On the other hand, some aspects of the teachings were without precedent: those who allowed their campfires to go out or did not kill all their dogs should die. Most significant was a prohibition on medicine bags, an essential center of power in Shawnee belief. The Prophet also abolished the important women's council. While most European influences were banned, there were exceptions: warriors kept their horses and guns. Christian notions of sin, repentance, and salvation pervaded the Prophet's religion, which imposed new rituals. A change in leadership was mandated: elderly chiefs were pushed aside as the Prophet and his followers took control.[5]

When Tecumseh's band moved in with Roundhead's Wyandots, settlers in Champaign County warned Governor Edward Tiffin of Ohio that war belts were passing among the Shawnees on Stony Creek. Thomas Moore and three other men visited the village to inform the Indians that their behavior had alarmed their neighbors, who were "leaving their homes and flying from the settlements." Tecumseh vowed that his people "intended no harm ... [and] wished that true friendship might subsist." Upon leaving, the Indians "gave us their left hand in a very cool manner." One veteran frontiersman noted other signs of bad intentions. Tiffin sent Moore back with a message of concern about the Shawnees' "hostile appearances." The Prophet responded that their sole desire was "to worship the great God above us and put ourselves in a good place." Their people had been frightened by rumors that the settlers on Mad River were plotting to destroy them. The "foolish lies" of "bad people" were the cause of the trouble.[6]

In January the Moravians reported that the Shawnees "sacrificed day and night, at the direction of their teacher ... [who] assured them ... they would live 200 years more. ... The best of all these teachings is that they prohibit the drinking of whisky." Among the Delawares "the young people now rule." They "deposed their chiefs" and asked the Prophet to identify witches in their village, all of whom were suspected of pro-American sympathies. Tetepachsit was taken prisoner in mid-March and tortured to death. His own son "struck the old Chief on the head with the hatchet and threw him half-alive into the fire." Two former Moravian converts, Joshua and Caritas (Ann Charity), were tomahawked and burned, as was Billy Patterson, a *métis* chief who had visited Wells at Fort Wayne. When the Prophet's finger pointed at "their last remaining chief, old Hockingpomsga, . . . the friends of the Chief took their weapons . . . and threatened to kill anyone who should take part in this murder. This put a check on further slaughter." When the Delawares realized that the Prophet "had deceived them," they expelled him from their towns.[7]

Wells reported to Harrison that the Prophet had threatened to kill those who did not surrender "their Medicine or Magic Bag." He had "pronounced sentences of death upon all those whom he designated, and terrible to relate, three miserable wretches were instantly seized and committed alive to the Flames. One of them is Teteboxke, the head chief of the nation, a man of 80 years of age, and long the object of reverence and esteem." Harrison urged the Delawares to renounce their "dark, crooked and thorny" path, which could only lead to "endless woe and misery," and demand of "this pretended prophet" proofs of his divinity: "If he is really a prophet, ask of him to cause the sun to stand still—the moon to alter its course—the rivers to cease to flow—or the dead to rise from their graves. If he does these things, you may then believe that he has been sent from God." Should he prove to be a false prophet and "you pursue this abominable wickedness, [God's] vengeance will overtake and crush you."[8]

Harrison ought to have known that a total eclipse was expected. Frederick Fisher, a British trader, may have informed the Prophet, who proclaimed that on 16 June he would blacken the sun, a dreadful omen for the Shawnees. Many Indians gathered at Greenville to witness the miracle. At 11:32 A.M., the Prophet commanded the Great Spirit to do his bidding. The crowd watched in awe as the moon covered the face of the sun. "I have spoken the truth," the Prophet said, pointing to the sky. "See how darkness has shrouded the sun." As word of the Prophet's powers spread, pilgrims from the Great Lakes region headed to Greenville.[9]

In response to complaints from Black Hoof's Shawnees and Ohio settlers, Wells wrote the first of many letters to Dearborn warning that the Prophet's followers at Greenville "threatened to be trouble-some neighbors to the white people in that quarter—and . . . should be removed." Shakers near Lebanon, Ohio, were not alarmed but curious. Benjamin Youngs and two companions went to Greenville in March. Some Shawnees told them that the Prophet was "a very bad character . . . [who] deceived the people & enriched himself with their property, but said they 'The people have found him out, & will not believe him now.'" Receptive to signs of revelation, the Shak-ers rejected this negative assessment. At the center of the Prophet's village stood a 150-foot-long council house surrounded by some 60 wigwams. The prophet spoke in a "great house," and all believed in him because "he can dream to God."[10]

The Prophet had been ill. Youngs described him as "grave & sol-emn—his person of a common size, rather slender, & of no great appearance." He preached with his eyes closed and "sensibly spake by the power of God," complaining that "the *white people* . . . hated them because they would not be wicked any longer, & called the work of the good spirit . . . *foolishness & delusion.*" The Shakers, who had also suffered persecution, "felt as if we were among the tribes of the children of Israel. . . . Here we see the work of God . . . & this light shines in darkness & the darkness comprehends it not." The Prophet's people would not leave Greenville "until the *great spirit* bid them, and that the land all belonged to the *great spirit.*" Although "thousands" of Indians were expected that summer, Youngs noted that "they were scant for provisions." The few women in sight "were diligently employed about their fires & tent affairs," but if the village was already short of food, who would provide for the host of pilgrims expected in a few months? Upon their return, the Shakers sent "27 horses . . . loaded . . . with provisions" and exchanged further visits, but they were threatened at sword's point by a local militia officer "for showing charity to the poor Indians."[11]

On 31 March 1807, Wells informed Dearborn that "an unusual number of Indians have died at this agency" during the severe win-ter, but they appeared "to be in high spirits" because with their annui-ties ten men were hired to make improvements. To bring the Weas "near this place and form a union of all the scattered branches of the Miamis," Wells suggested purchasing land "as high up the Wabash as the High Lands [Terre Haute]." This ill-advised proposal sewed the seeds for Harrison's treaty of 1809, which enraged Tecumseh. Wells warned that the Lake Indians were headed to Greenville "for the double purpose of seeing the Shawney Prophet and . . . easy access to whiskey." Two hundred Potawatomi, Chippewa, and Ottawa men arrived at Fort Wayne in mid-April. Wells tried in vain to stop them. "It is evident now that the intentions of this Shawnee Prophet is to destroy the chiefs of his nation and become the first chief himself." His warriors had committed "depredations on the property of the white people in that quarter," murdered "two of the Shawanese on the Auglaize," and threatened Ottawa villages.[12]

Wells sent Anthony Shane, whose mother was Ottawa, to summon Tecumseh to hear a message from Jefferson. "Return to Fort Wayne and tell Capt. Wells that my fire is kindled on the spot appointed by the Great Spirit above," an angry Tecumseh replied. "If he has any thing to communicate to me he must come here . . . in 6 days." Unwilling to relent, Wells sent Shane back with a speech in Jefferson's name warning the Indians that their "large numbers" at Greenville had alarmed their white neighbors and urging them to leave "the land of the United States immediately." Tecumseh reacted with disdain: "The Great Spirit above has appointed this place for us to light our fires and here we shall remain. . . . The Great Spirit above knows no boundary, nor will his red people acknowledge any. . . . If his great Father had anything to say to him, he must send a man of note." He would exchange no more messages with Captain Wells. These sentiments were seconded by the Prophet: "Why does not the government send the greatest man they have to us—I can talk to him—I can bring darkness between him and me—nay more, I can bring the sun under my feet and what man can do this?"[13]

"I have done everything in my power to keep them from collecting in such large bodys at Greenville," Wells told Dearborn, "but have not been successful." Although the Lake Indians "have no bad design against the white people," such large numbers of warriors "will alarm our people and scare them from their homes." Denying the magnitude of a problem he did not wish to face, Dearborn shifted

the onus to Wells: "It is with regret that I perceive your authority and
influence are insufficient to prevent such disorderly conduct. . . . The
improper collection of Indians at Greenville ought not to have been
allowed; and if your own influence is inadequate, you must call on
Gov. Harrison for assistance." Many Indians were "religiously mad,"
Wells informed both Harrison and Dearborn. The Prophet "Defies the
united States to interrupt him and makes the Indians beleave that if
the government moves him from Greenville there will be an End to
the World." An additional two thousand pilgrims were expected in
August. "No time should be lost in sending this villain and his enso-
lent band" off U.S. land, a task that "can not be done with words."
From Ohio came a protest that "a numerous assemblage of Indians,
marching in bodies through our frontier settlements," was arousing a
suspicion of hostile intentions. The seventy-nine undersigned urged
Wells to use his "influences and exertions to have them removed as
speedily as possible." Dearborn blamed these troubles not on the
Prophet's inspiring visions but rather on the shortcomings of his
Indian agent. As skeptical of prophesy as the Shakers were credulous,
Wells was not only venting his animosity toward the Shawnee broth-
ers, who had insulted him, but also voicing the concerns of many
Indians and settlers on the Ohio frontier.[14]

THE BAD MAN AT FORT WAYNE

In May the scalped body of John Boyer was found near Lost Creek;
"two rattles and a bow and arrow [were left] lying across his back."
Many believed that the murder had been committed by Tecumseh's
band "to embroil the settlers with the Blackhoof party." On 24 June
1807, chiefs from both factions came to Springfield to resolve the
matter. The Champaign militia was on alert as the council gathered
"in the flat below Werders Tavern." Although the Indians had been
told to leave their weapons at Thomas Moore's gun shop, Tecumseh
appeared with "a splendid tomahawk," which he refused to surrender, vowing to leave if he could not "smoke in brotherly kinship that
calumet of peace." Col. William Ward, a haughty Virginian used to
having his orders obeyed, seized the pipe-tomahawk while the chief

"looked daggers" at him. A kindly old minister in the crowd then offered the chief "his pipe of clay with a stem about two inches and a half long." Tecumseh sneered at this puny gift as beneath his dignity and, with a flip of his wrist, tossed it in the bushes, leaving "the poor old preacher . . . perfectly astonished at this . . . insult to his friendly disposition." The chiefs exchanged accusations and the council ended with Ward demanding that the Indians deliver the culprit.[15]

Two days before this council, HMS *Leonard* fired upon the USS *Chesapeake* off Cape Henry near Norfolk, Virginia. Three Americans were killed and eighteen wounded before the ship struck her flag and allowed four of her crew to be impressed into British service. News of this aggressive act brought the countries to the brink of war and caused Jefferson to enact his ill-fated embargo. To defend Canada, the British realized that they needed the support of "His Majesty's Indian Allies." Many in the Northwest, including Wells and Harrison, assumed that their Indian problems were the fault of the British, who at that point had played no role in the Prophet's visions or Tecumseh's quest for pan-tribal unity. Now Sir James Craig, governor of Canada, called for a policy of public aid and secret encouragement. British Indian agents were told to "consult privately" with key chiefs, and in an "Artful and Clandestine manner [remind them of how] the Americans have obtained possession of their lands, and of their intention of ultimately possessing . . . the whole and driving the Indians out of the Country." Heading the list were the Prophet and Tecumseh, "who appears to be a very shrewd intelligent man." During the next year five thousand Indians came to Fort Malden for encouragement and supplies.[16]

In an impassioned message to the Indiana legislature in August, Harrison gave voice to the prevalent feeling of settlers on the frontier: "The blood rises to my cheek when I reflect on the humiliation, the disgraceful scene, of the crew of an American ship of war mustered on its own deck by a British lieutenant for the purpose of selecting innocent victims of their own tyranny! . . . At this moment . . . their agents are organizing a combination amongst the Indians within our limits, for the purposes of assassination and murder." Out of such sentiments the War Hawk faction in Congress emerged, favoring an invasion of Canada that would displace the Indians and extend

America's borders. Harrison assured Dearborn that while the Delawares and Wabash Indians were peaceful, the Shawnees and Lake Indians were "entirely devoted to the British." Wells also saw a conspiracy: "I believe the British is at the bottom of this business. The Indians is not hostile inclined as yet; I shall endeavor to keep them so until the Government can take some decisive steps." Speaking for the Great Spirit, the Prophet had asserted in the spring that "the Americans . . . are not my children. . . . They grew from the scum of the great water, when it was troubled by the Evil Spirit, and the froth was driven into the woods by a strong east wind. They are numerous, but I hate them. . . . They have taken your lands, which are not made for them." Frederick Fisher reported that in July, the Prophet had kicked a bowl of water and said that was how easily he could overthrow the Americans; then "he rose, discharged wind loudly, clapped his hand to his backside and exclaimed he cared no more for them than that."[17]

Harrison dispatched John Connor with a demand for the "immediate removal of the Imposter from our Territory" and informed Dearborn that Wells had threatened the Prophet "with the vengeance of the United States" if he stayed at Greenville. In early September Simon Kenton and four other frontiersmen went to investigate. They told acting Ohio governor Thomas Kirker that the concentration of warriors gave them "strong apprehensions something serious is brewing. . . . Should the number already assembled fall on this Settlement unprepared and unaided as it is . . . [it] must fall a sacrifice."[18]

Kirker sent Thomas Worthington and Duncan McArthur to Greenville. They arrived on 13 September and were met "in a friendly way." Some two hundred Indians crowded the council house to hear the Americans warn the chiefs that if they "let the British put the tomahawk into your hands," the United States will assemble thousands of soldiers who "will destroy you for your folly." Because the British in the past had "dealt treacherously" with them, Blue Jacket promised that the Shawnees desired "peace and harmony" and had no intention of fighting again. Any rumors to the contrary had malicious intent: "Brothers, the disturber of our peace appears to be seated at Fort Wayne [Wells] who I think is a bad man. I want you to take him away and place a good person in his stead."[19]

"Mr. Wells," the Americans told Blue Jacket, had been appointed by the president, who alone could fire him. To support his removal, they must present "well grounded charges against him by evidence that could be relied on." Wells had acted on complaints lodged against them by the Shawnees at Black Hoof's village. If they wished to make a case against Wells, they should talk to the governor in Chillicothe. The Prophet explained that he had moved to Greenville because "the Shawnees at Tawa Town would not listen to him, but prosecuted him" and divided the nation. Finally, he agreed to send some chiefs to meet with the governor. The delegation's interpreter Stephen Ruddel, who had grown up with Tecumseh, assured Kirker that "the Indians near Greenville had no hostile intentions towards the United States at present."[20]

"Vast crowds flocked to the courthouse," the Chillicothe *Fredonian* reported, "led thither by curiosity and the novelty of hearing an Indian address." Blue Jacket insisted on Shawnee neutrality: "We have laid down the tomahawk, never to take it up again." Tecumseh gave an oration on the unjust treatment of his people by the Americans: "he fearlessly denied the validity of these *pretended* treaties, and openly avowed his intention to resist the further extension of the white settlements," but firmly "disclaimed all intention of making war upon the United States." As had Blue Jacket at Greenville, Tecumseh saved his wrath for the agent at Fort Wayne: "Congress has a great many good men, let them take away Wells and put one of them there—we hate him. If *they* will not *remove* him, *we will!* When the Indians are coming to hear the Prophet, he sets doors to stop them. He asks them, 'Why do ye go to hear the Prophet? He is one possessed of a devil! I would as soon go to see a dog with the mange.' When we want to talk friendly with him, he will not listen to us—and from beginning to end his talk is blackguard—he treats us like dogs." Asked how he intended to "remove" Wells, Tecumseh said his people "would not adhere to him." Witnesses agreed that Tecumseh's demeanor and eloquence had carried the day. He was "one of the most dignified men I ever beheld," John McDonald recalled. "He dispelled as if by magic the apprehension of the whites." Satisfied that "the alarm has been without good foundation," Kirker disbanded the militia and conveyed Tecumseh's criticism of Wells to the president, while

Worthington invited the chiefs to a banquet at his estate, Adena. Jefferson told Dearborn that the Prophet was "a scoundrel who only needs his price." Years later he claimed that he saw "little danger" in his movement and decided to "let him go . . . unmolested."[21]

When he learned that the Shawnees at Greenville blamed him for any disturbances on the Ohio frontier, Wells wrote a letter that was printed in several local newspapers: "I have done every thing that could be done, to find out the intentions of the Indians and cannot discover any hostile appearances among any of the nations. . . . The commotions among the Indians, during the present season, was entirely occasioned by a religious fit [caused by] the Shawnees' imposter." Wells had advised people not to feed these pilgrims, but the Shakers "have from time to time, supplied . . . his insolent band, with provisions, which has enabled him to continue his residence at Greenville." The murder of John Boyer had been committed by Big Moon, "a half Wayndot and half Ottaway, that resides on Lake Erie, east of Sandusky." He had taken advantage of the gathering at Greenville "to revenge the death of one of his relations that he says was killed by the white people, two years ago." Thus Wells tried to calm fears and resolve the murder without hiding his opposition to the Prophet.[22]

In his biography of Tecumseh, John Sugden characterized Wells as a man "bound by neither responsibility nor truth. . . . His ceaseless tirades against the reformers interwove accurate information, astute observation, outright invention, and irresponsible alarmism. Tecumseh and his brother saw Wells as a serious problem, someone capable of undermining their relations with the whites by distortions and lies. They were not mistaken."[23] Wells was no paragon of virtue, but his warnings were neither unfounded nor mere invention. It was the "reformers" who presented both Indians and frontiersmen with "a serious problem." Wells knew personally the Delaware "witches" burned to death at the behest of the Prophet; he had fed hundreds of hungry pilgrims streaming into Fort Wayne; his letters to the government were based on complaints he received from Black Hoof and Ohio settlers. No love was lost between Wells and the Shawnee brothers, but regardless of what he said or did their followers at Greenville would inevitably have had to move behind the treaty line. Wells was premature in his concern about the British; and the Prophet's followers were not "mad" but, for better and worse, true believers. Yet as long as the Prophet fostered mutual aid and discouraged drinking, and Tecumseh organized a united resistance to land cessions, perhaps their notions made as much sense as Jefferson's duplicitous civilization program. While Tecumseh and the Prophet were trying to respond to a deteriorating tribal situation that defied viable solutions, Wells did his duty to warn the government about their disruption of both Indian society and the frontier settlers. Flawed as his actions may have been, Wells should not be made the scapegoat for the unfolding tragedy.

THE PROPHET, MAIN POCHE,
AND THE BRITISH THREAT

Wells knew that his job was in jeopardy. Responding to what he saw as a threat to the country and a challenge to his authority, he had urged the government to drive the Prophet and his followers away from Greenville. He sent his spies to "the different councils" but discovered "nothing of a serious nature as yet. . . . I shall keep watchful eyes on . . . the Indians and endeavor to penetrate their views." Once again he told Dearborn that "it would be a matter of the greatest importance to the United States and the Indians at this country could I have a personal interview with you." To secure his position, Wells wanted to meet face to face with the secretary of war, explain the problem the Prophet and Tecumseh presented, and convince him that "the first wish of my Heart [is] to promote the civilizing [of] the Indians."[24]

Wells informed Harrison that "two confidential Indians" had learned the Prophet promised his followers that "the great spirit will in a few years destroy every white man in America" and each of his warriors had "made himself a *war club*." Chiefs of several nations had met without telling Little Turtle and other loyal chiefs—evidence that the Indians were "forming an improper combination" with British support. In October Wells learned that warlike speeches circulated among the Indians at Malden. Even though the Indians at his agency would not "take up arms against the United States," the "Shawanese Imposter" was another story: "There can be no doubt but He is a british agent and no time should be lost on our part to destroy His influence among the Indians." The Prophet was no paid cat's paw, but in 1808 the British did hire Frederick Fisher both to spy on him and encourage friendly relations. "A large number of guns and a larger quantity of ammunition has been delivered to the Shawanees at the Prophet's hand by the British agent at Malden," Wells reported, possibly for an attack in the spring.[25]

In addition to warning the government about the Prophet, Wells praised his own role in preserving the peace and pushed for his farming program. His plan was to concentrate the Wabash tribes into "twelve Settlements" as part of a program headed by "Capt Hendricks the celabrated stock bridge Indian chief" and funded at "3600 Dollars a year." Johnston approved of Wells's response to the Prophet's challenge: "The Indians in our neighborhood are as friendly as I ever knew them," even though agents were passing war belts among the Lake Indians, "telling them they must soon wade to their ankles in blood against the Americans." Johnston also agreed that "the assemblage of vagabond Indians at Greenville . . . is likely to become a serious grievance . . . and in my humble opinion, if nothing else will do, force ought to be used."[26]

Harrison suspected the Lake Indians were playing "a double game." Informed of "a very unusual assemblage of Potawatomies in the vicinity of Fort Wayne," the governor directed Wells "to keep a watchful eye over them." Dearborn had other priorities: "I wish you could find sufficient leisure to visit Ft. Wayne for the purpose of ascertaining the real objects and views of Wells as well as the Indians at Greenville &c. I fear that Wells is too attentive to pecuniary considerations." The Potawatomis at Fort Wayne were headed by Main Poche, "the celebrated Bear Chief" of the tribe and "the greatest warrior in the west [who had] . . . more influence than any other Indian." Wells planned to win over the chief—"I shall take good care of him and if possible prevent his ever listening to the prophet again"— hoping that this project would earn Dearborn's "approbation."[27]

Main Poche was no ordinary Indian. To gain his favor Wells faced formidable obstacles. The Potawatomi chief from the Kankakee River was a *wabeno*, a dreaded sorcerer possessed of "great influence" over his people as well as other nations near Lake Michigan. He had been born with a maimed left hand that lacked fingers and a thumb; this deformity was seen as "a mark set on him by the Great Spirit" to distinguish him from other Indians and instill divine power. He was a fire handler as well as a shape-shifter who could change into a fireball or a beast of prey to destroy his enemies. He could not only cure illness, change the weather, or practice love medicine, but also conjure up evil magic to eliminate his rivals. Main Poche loved to fight his hereditary foes the Osage, boasting that he was invulnerable to rifle balls and invincible in battle. A large man of prodigious strength, as a badge of his ferocity he wore "a girdle . . . of human scalps . . . around his waist, and strings of bear claws and the bills of owls and hawks, round his ankles." When sober, he usually hid his hand, but "in liquor while rolling about naked it was always to be seen." At Greenville the Prophet urged him to curb his evil ways. Main Poche replied that the Great Spirit told him that if he ever stopped drinking or fighting he would become "a common man." He did not want to be seen as "inferior" to the Prophet and thus lose "his standing as a man of consequence among the Indian nations."[28]

During the winter, Fort Wayne was surrounded by hungry Potawatomis and other Lake Indians. "Their neglecting raising corn last season and attending to the call of the Shawnee Prophet," Wells reported to Dearborn, had left them "in a state of starvation. . . . I shall treat them well and keep them in good humor until I hear from you respecting them. The contrast between these Indians and the Indians at this agency is very striking." Wells wanted to give them "a moderate quantity of provisions . . . [as] the means of attaching them to the United States." Dearborn took a harder line: "If the Indians have been so inattentive to themselves and families, as not to have provided necessary provisions, they ought to suffer." Wells could give "some small supplies . . . to a few of the Aged," but was not authorized to give "considerable supplies" to the rest. Dearborn blamed the present crisis on the failure of Wells to support Kirk: "Wells has been very intent on making Money, and is at the same time very jealous of any interference with his Concerns with the Indians in his Agency."[29]

Wells informed Dearborn in March that "the Shawanese Prophet is about to move to the Wabash," where many Lake Indians planned to join him: "there is no doubt but He will put the tomahawks in their Hands and direct them to Strike the white people—and those Indians who will not Listen to him—I will leave nothing undone to defeat his plans—and preserve the peace." Wells mentioned "the Death of my son who was kild by accident a few days ago" and reiterated that "the Indians continue to hover round this place and are in great want of provision." We don't know the name of this teenage son by his first wife, from whom Wells had been separated since his marriage to Sweet Breeze (who died in 1805), but that spring his daughter Jane was born to an anonymous Miami mother on the Mississinewa. Wells had served the United States since July 1792 without a leave: "And having experienced great domestick calamity of late I have to request that you will allow me to spend the ensuing winter with my surviving children who are in Kentucky receiving their education."[30]

In spite of Dearborn's restrictions on provisions, Wells had been "more liberal with them then usual—all the Indians of this country . . . are in a perfect state of confusion, many of them appears to be wavering and undetermined" whether to align with the British or remain at peace. Since Main Poche had "unbounded influence" among the Lake Indians, Wells wanted to "secure his friendship" and make him "a counter poise to the prophet who is decidedly Hostile." Main Poche could be "a dangerous man as He was the pivot on which the minds of all the Western Indians turned." If antagonized he would be "a very troublesome Enemy—Consequently I spared no pains to secure his influence and attach him to the united states—I have succeeded, but I was obligest to be very liberal." Wells "gave him and his followers at defferent times nearly 800 Dollar[s]" worth of food and supplies, yet his "success" was dubious at best. Although Main Poche vowed his friendship, he intended to go on the warpath against the Osage. He remarked that Wells had "caught him like a wild horse at a salt lick and hobbled him: I can no longer range the woods as I please." All he and his war chiefs needed were bells at their necks so Wells would always know where they were. Jefferson should know that he would not fight for the British, but he said, "the Great Spirit has made me a warrior and I cannot sit Idle."[31]

Little Turtle and nine other chiefs went to the Mississinewa to prevent the Prophet from settling on the Wabash. Tecumseh told them that the move "had been sanctioned by the Great Spirit." He blamed the loss of Indian land on "the man at Vincennes the one at Fort Wayne and the one at Detroit," citing Wells, in particular, as someone who made himself great by cheating the Indians. Tecumseh claimed that Main Poche supported the Prophet and "had promised to meet him with all the western Indians on the Wabash." As for food, the Prophet said "He would Send 100 Horses to our settlements for provisions [and] that our frontiersmen . . . dared not refuse him—and if He only Looked at a white man, the man would give him any-thing he wanted." The loyal Potawatomi chief Five Medals pledged to combat the pro-British followers of the Prophet among his nation, warning that "the Western Indians appear to be disaffected to the United States. . . . Before these Indians will be quiet they must be put Down by force, or by Liberal treatment." Earth, an Eel River chief, told Wells that Tecumseh had denounced Jefferson's civilization pro-gram: "the President intended making women of the Indians—but when the Indians was all united they would be respected by the President as men."[32]

William Claus, head of Indian affairs for Upper Canada, closely monitored the Prophet's ascendency and sought to rally the Indi-ans to the British side. The Ottawa chief Little King told him that many of his people were angry over Governor William Hull's treaty at Detroit in November 1807 and "decidedly opposed to the Ameri-cans." Frederick Fisher arrived at Malden in May with a message from the Prophet "assuring . . . [Claus] of his friendship." Wells warned Dearborn that the Prophet "would most certainly commence a war against the white people if he could get the western Indians to join him." In September, his followers would concentrate at Tippecanoe. To ensure Main Poche's loyalty, and turn "a dangerous man" into "a useful man," Wells urged Jefferson to invite the chief "to visit the seat of government."[33]

In early June, John Connor brought a speech from Wells demand-ing that the Prophet return stolen horses. The agent's wry message noted that divine persons don't steal and that God punishes horse thieves. You "might as well cut the people's throats," Connor added, "as to take the means of subsistence from them at the moment they least could spare it." About forty horses had been stolen, Connor estimated, while twenty-two hogs and a cow had been slaughtered for food. "I found these Indians in a state of starvation, living on nothing but meat and roots." The Prophet was certain that Harrison in Vincennes "would assist him with provisions." The peaceful Fort Wayne Indians, who had diligently "raised plenty of corn," were destitute, Wells said, because hundreds of the Prophet's pilgrims "et up all they had as one Indian will not see another hungry, as long as he has anything to eat."[34]

The Prophet sent a conciliatory speech to Harrison in late June: "It never was my intention to lift up my hand against the Americans . . . [rather] to live in peace upon the land he [the Great Spirit] has given us. . . . The bad reports you have heard of me are all false and [I] beg you not to believe them. . . . We hope that you will assist our women and children with a little corn." Harrison admitted that he had received "a very bad report" from white settlers and neighboring Indian tribes alike, and warned the Prophet that any nations who "should lift up the Tomahawk" against the United States would be driven beyond the Great Lakes. If his people were for peace, however, "it is an inviolable rule with the 17 fires to permit every man to worship the great spirit in the manner he may think best." Harrison hoped during the Prophet's visit "to develop his character and intentions" so that he might be made into "a useful instrument in effecting a radical and salutary change in the manners and habits of the Indians."[35]

"I was told that you intended to hang me," the Prophet bluntly told Harrison in early August. "I also heard that you wanted to know . . . whether I was God or man . . . if I was the former, I should not steal horses. I heard this from Mr. Wells." His purposes were harmless, the Prophet insisted; his people simply wanted to "cultivate the ground." All they asked for was assistance: "If you give us a few articles, such as needles, flints, hoes, powder, etc. etc. we will take the animals that afford us meat with powder and ball." At Vincennes the Prophet "held services daily and preached vigorously to his proselytes." Harrison concluded that "the celebrated Shawnese Prophet . . . [was] possessed of considerable talents and the art of address with which he manages the Indians is really astonishing. . . . His denial of being under any . . . [British] influence was strong and apparently candid."[36]

Having seen the Prophet exhort his followers "to live in Peace and friendship with all mankind" and to avoid war, Harrison thought that the influence the Prophet had acquired would "prove rather advantageous . . . to the United States." He euphorically assured the legislature that there was "every prospect . . . of harmony and good understanding with our Indian neighbors." This was due to "that wise, humane, and beneficent policy which has been adopted by our government, and which forms so singular an exception to the treatment of savages by those who are called civilized." Like many a politician before and after him, Harrison celebrated American exceptionalism to conceal his own failure of leadership—his land-greedy treaties were actually the catalyst of the crisis.[37]

ESCORTING MAIN POCHE AND LITTLE TURTLE TO WASHINGTON

In September Wells received permission to escort Main Poche to Washington. Almost eight hundred Indians attended a council Wells held that month at Fort Wayne to distribute annuities: "I have got them to settle all their clashing interests." The chiefs renounced a war with the Osage and signed a petition to prohibit liquor sales. A delegation of "the commanding trumps of this country" departed in early November. On the trip Main Poche caused "much difficulty . . . owing to his thirst for strong drink." The delegation reached Washington in December, during the final months of Jefferson's divisive and contentious second term.[38]

In the fall of 1807, the president played prosecutor, judge, and jury, declaring his former vice president Aaron Burr guilty "beyond all question" of treason and approving General Wilkinson's imposition of martial law in New Orleans. Jefferson's intervention was discredited when Chief Justice John Marshall found that no act of treason had been committed and ordered Burr's release. After merchant ships had been seized by both France and England, Jefferson sought to maintain the rights of U.S. neutral maritime commerce without declaring war. His alternative was to try, "by fair experiment . . . the power of this great weapon, the embargo." Congress banned trade with other countries but strangled the American economy in the process. The once-popular president was ridiculed in the press. Smuggling and civil disobedience spread, which in turn caused the president to insist on stringent enforcement: To avoid combat with Napoleon's million-man army or England's superb navy, Jefferson waged war on the American people. Funds were provided to recruit soldiers, arm the militia, and build ships for the navy; by the summer of 1808, these resources were being used to enforce the embargo. Gunboats guarded the harbors and a small army deployed along the Canadian border. Gordon Wood concluded: "Perhaps never in history has a trading nation of America's size engaged in such an act of self-immolation with so little reward."[39]

Jefferson's admirable quest for measures short of warfare resulted in a deplorable failure to see the realistic consequences of his policies. He made little effort to explain to the people why such a heavy sacrifice was necessary. Thanks to the conflict in Europe, American maritime commerce had grown enormously. At least one-third of its sailors were Englishmen—for Britannia to rule the waves she had to man her vessels. Instead of seeking a viable solution, however, "Jefferson . . . converted . . . neutral rights into a great moral drama" that equated compromise with abject submission and a loss of national honor. Although alternative strategies existed, the issue was framed as one of "war, Embargo, or nothing." While some, like Harrison, supported this position, much of the country, and especially New England, loathed the embargo. A last resort to stricter enforcement trampled on constitutional protections against unreasonable searches and seizures as well as guarantees of due process and trial by jury. Thus the president committed the same despotic abuses for which he had castigated George III.[40]

Washington was still an incoherent place; the White House and Capitol remained unfinished; and the only business was politics. Tourists encountered a cultural backwater: "Neither park, nor mall, neither churches, theaters, nor colleges, could I discover so lately as the summer of 1806," Charles Janson wrote, while "tippling shops, and houses of rendezvous for sailors and their doxies" were plentiful.

At sixty-five, Jefferson had aged considerably: his hair was gray, his body slightly stooped, his voice a mere whisper. He complained to his closest friends of "a drudgery to which I am no longer equal" and welcomed retirement: "Never did a prisoner, released from his chains, feel such relief as I shall on shaking off the shackles of power." He refused to pass any measures that his successor would be obliged to implement. Josiah Quincy noted: "Fear of responsibility and love of popularity are now master-passions. . . . The policy is to keep things as they are, and wait for European events."[41]

Following the Lewis and Clark expedition, Indian delegations from the West became a common sight in Washington. Charles Janson observed a procession of Osage "ornamented with a variety of foxes' tails and feathers, bones, ivory trinkets . . . curiously carved shells, and pieces of hard polished wood," and with faces painted red and black. After performing tribal dances in exchange for rum, one chief "was found lifeless in bed . . . and his death was imputed to excess drinking and his great exertions the preceding evening." To these delegations Jefferson repeated his homily that all men were brothers and governmental intentions purely beneficent.[42]

Jefferson's speech to visiting chiefs had ossified into a set of formulaic phrases. Promises of prosperity—"A little labor in the earth will produce more food than the best hunts you can now make, and the women will spin and weave more clothing than the men can procure by hunting"—were backed by veiled threats: "My Children, we are strong, we are numerous as the Stars in the Heavens, and we are all gunmen, yet we live in peace and friendship with all Nations." But woe to any "nation rejecting our friendship . . . it shall never be in their power to strike us a second time." The more his mantra became disconnected from actual events west of the Appalachians, the more Jefferson insisted on his good intentions: "We never meant to control your free will; we never will do it." Consistently he urged the Indians to "leave off hunting for your living," but never did he order white settlers to "leave off hunting" on Indian lands.[43]

The chiefs delivered their speeches to Dearborn, and Jefferson responded on 21 December. He contrasted the "just and friendly conduct" of the United States to that of the British, "who are now endeavoring to engage you to join them in the war against us, should a war take place," while the American program of "temperance, peace and agriculture . . . will prepare you to possess property, to wish to live under regular laws, to join us in our government, to mix with us in society, and your blood and ours united will spread again over this great island." Smooth as these words sounded, Wells knew that the lure of "private property" and "regular laws" could only deprive the Indians of their lands.[44]

To Little Turtle, Jefferson spoke with affection—"My son: It is always a pleasure that I receive you here and take you by the hand"— but on the land question he offered evasions: "I have . . . always believed it an act of friendship to our red brethren whenever they wished to sell a portion of their lands, to be ready to buy whether we wanted them or not, because the price enables them to improve the lands they retain, and turning their country from hunting to agriculture, the same exertions will support them more plentifully." The phrase "whether we wanted them or not" must have grated in Wells's throat. When had the United States ever *not* wanted more land? When Little Turtle protested that the Detroit treaty with the Ottawas and Wyandots had taken Miami territory, Jefferson simply referred the problem back to Hull. Since the Potawatomis received gifts at the Grouseland treaty of 1805, he implied that Wabash lands did "not belong to the Miamis alone," thus undercutting Little Turtle's hand at future negotiations.

Of all the chiefs the president encountered, perhaps Main Poche was the most intimidating. Picture a huge Potawatomi clad in the skins of wild animals, wearing a belt of human scalps, and a fearsome scowl on his painted face. The soldier on guard must have quivered. Main Poche insisted on fighting the Osage if he wished. To his credit, Jefferson argued that war with the Osage was of national concern, since warriors "must cross the Mississippi which is always covered with our boats, our people and property. . . . Our interests require that the Mississippi shall be a river of peace." Main Poche remained adamant. All he wanted were "tokens" from the president that would signify he was a man of distinction.[45]

Capt. Hendrick Aupaumut, the Stockbridge Indian diplomat Wells preferred for his own program, had brought some Mohicans and Munsees to live on the White River and helped the Delawares become farmers. Jefferson predicted a bright future for "civilized" Indians:

> Nothing is so easy as to learn to cultivate the earth; all your women under-stand it, and to make it easier, we are always ready to teach you how to make ploughs, hoes, and necessary utensils. If the men will take the labor of the earth from the women they will learn to spin and weave and to clothe their families. In this way you will also raise many children, you will double your numbers every twenty years. . . . When once you have property, you will want laws and magistrates to protect your property and persons, and to punish those among you who commit crimes. You will find that our laws are good for this purpose; you will wish to live under them, you will unite yourselves with us, join in our great councils and form one people with us, and we shall all be Americans; you will mix with us in marriage, your blood will run in our veins, and will spread with us over this great island.

As pleasing as this prospect may have seemed to Jefferson, in the short term its sole purpose was to divide and conquer the last resistance. What the Indians needed to adopt American ways—sufficient land and time—was not available in his grand design. The president's promise of a doubling of their population in twenty years would prove to be a mockery of the reality.[46]

Jefferson issued a "Deposition," confirming that the Miamis had granted permission to the Delawares, Mohicans, and Munsees to settle on the White River but not to sell any land without Miami consent. Wells met privately with Dearborn the next day to discuss their differences. Like everyone else in Washington, the secretary of war was preoccupied by accounts of Napoleon's battles and British blockades. Events west of the Appalachians were of secondary importance and no cause for serious alarm. Wells tried to explain his response to the threat posed by the Shawnee Prophet and Tecumseh, and to justify his extra expenditures in order to feed the host of pilgrims passing through Fort Wayne. Dearborn thought Wells was playing a double game, questioned his loyalty, and blamed him for the failure of Kirk's mission to Fort Wayne. But he also felt that the Quaker's success at Black Hoof's Village had cost too much money. Therefore he wrote out a message for Wells to deliver to Kirk: "This is to advise you that on the receipt of this letter you will be considered as no longer in public employment."[47]

Although his rival had fallen, Wells knew that his own position might follow. The parsimonious Dearborn had repeatedly scolded him for his mismanagement of funds. On the day before Christmas, the secretary of war was not in his office, so Wells left a request for further instructions. Should he grant Main Poche's demand for five horses and other "presents"? Wells requested permission "to go and see my children in Kentucky and stay one month with them this winter." He included two invoices totaling $303 for his participation in past treaties and added, "I am conscious that no person has rendered the government more services than I have done." Although these bills were probably valid, under the circumstances Dearborn was certain to regard them, and Wells singing his own praises, with suspicion.[48]

On their return trip, the chiefs were invited to dine at George Ellicott's house on the Patapsco River. The small mill town that bore his family name was nestled in a hollow surrounded by seven hills. Main Poche refused to attend. In Washington he had sneered at "every civility tendered him," preferring to remain "shut up with his wife, in his apartments." Little Turtle "told him he was too large a man to give so poor a display of Indian politeness." Black Bird, a great hunter, came to dinner with the hide of a huge grizzly bear, "claws and teeth attached," slung over his shoulder, his cheeks slashed with vermillion, "a small coronet of eagle's feathers" in his hair, and a tobacco pouch, tomahawk, and scalping knife hanging from his embroidered belt. His wife's hat was laden with ribbons, feathers, and tinsel ornaments; her moccasins were embroidered with moose hair and porcupine quills; her wrap "a fine Makinaw blanket." Little Turtle and the other chiefs wore blue American cloth coats with gilt buttons, blue pantaloons, and waistcoats, while retaining their "leggings, moccasins, and large gold rings in their ears." To his Quaker hosts, "Little Turtle exceeded all his brother Chiefs in dignity of appearance—a dignity which resulted from the character of his mind." At dinner he and Wells "drew a comparison between savage and civilized life" in favor of the latter. "The visit ended very agreeably; the deputation shook hands with the Friends . . . and returned to their hotel."[49]

The next day Wells and the chiefs "examined all the objects of interest in the neighborhood." Little Turtle was impressed with the solid granite buildings of the town, its ironworks, and gristmill; he asked if the Quakers would construct one to benefit his village. Main Poche, however, underwent "no favorable change" in spite of having seen, as Wells intended, "so many evidences of the strength of the people he professed to despise." Instead, he continued "by no means reserved in his expression of hatred toward the whole [white] race." On the trip home, Wells found his conduct "insufferable. He exceeds everything I ever saw." In one of his drunken bouts he "even attempted to eat his wife." Wells and Little Turtle warned the surly Potawatomi rogue that if he ever tried that again they would have to kill him. Main Poche, in turn, threatened the life of anyone who tried to stop him from doing whatever he pleased. In Bedford the Beaver, a Delaware chief, met Black Hoof and decided to accompany the Shawnee to Washington. When he left the other chiefs in Cincinnati, Wells must have realized that his efforts to "tame" Main Poche and win his loyalty had failed and that his position as agent hung by a slender thread.[50]

WELLS, HARRISON,
AND THE FORT WAYNE TREATY OF 1809

In Washington the Beaver met with Dearborn and accused Wells of cheating the Delawares of their annuities. Black Hoof also expressed dissatisfaction. These criticisms were the last straw for Dearborn. The secretary of war selected the Fort Wayne factor John Johnston as agent and gave him a message notifying Wells of his dismissal. John Shaw, a Quaker who had worked on the farm at Dennis's Station, would be Johnston's assistant and Captain Hendrick would help the Delaware learn "Agriculture and Domestic arts." When Wells arrived at Louisville, he knew nothing of these developments. His brother Sam, a major general in the Kentucky Militia, lived in an eight-room brick house on 650 acres near the Ohio River. Wells hadn't seen his daughters in a year. They dressed as little ladies, went to school, and received religious instruction from his sister Elizabeth. Now that Kentucky was free of Indian attacks, the name William Wells had acquired a heroic aura. The former Miami warrior, U.S. scout, and Indian agent who had met with presidents Washington, Adams, and Jefferson had gained a romantic luster. Tales true and untrue were told of his exploits.[51]

After a brief courtship, Wells married Mary (Polly) Geiger on 7 March 1809. He was thirty-nine and she was eighteen, a difference in age quite common at the time. The bride's father, Frederick Geiger from Maryland, owned a saw and grist mill as well as a public ferry that crossed the Ohio to Jeffersonville. His home "Linden Hill" sat on two thousand acres in the present Butchertown district of Louisville. He and Sam were friends, as were his daughter and Sam's Rebekah, who probably encouraged Polly to set her cap for the famous frontiersman. Judging from a silhouette, Polly was attractive, while Wells, who had been rising in the world, wanted a respectable wife. To help her friend adjust to the hardships of life in the heart of Indian Territory, Rebekah accompanied the married couple to Fort Wayne.[52]

Unaware of his dismissal, or that William Eustis was Madison's secretary of war, Wells continued to send letters on frontier conditions. The good news was that "the Indians have abandoned the prophet" in large numbers and the Ohio legislature had passed a law prohibiting the sale of whiskey. Wells wrote to Harrison that the Chippewas, Ottawas, and Potawatomis had rejected the Prophet's proposal to "destroy all the white people at Vincennes and all those that live on the Wabash and Ohio." These Lake Indians might attack the Prophet "in consequence of so many of them dying" of disease at Tippecanoe. With less than one hundred warriors, the Prophet posed no threat to the white settlers: "At the same time I must say that it is and always has been my opinion that he only wanted power to make him dangerous." The host of hungry Indians begging for food "compels me to give them some provision. . . . I am convinced that the starved situation of the Indians in this agency fully justifies the quantity that has been issued." Wells offered to assist Harrison "purchase the land up the Wabash as high up as the Vermillion from the Miami and Wabash Indians. I think the time favourable."[53]

Harrison vacillated between seeing the Prophet as a harmless visionary or a dire threat. He decided that Wells's estimate of the Prophet's diminished strength was "erroneous" and concluded that the notion that the Lake Indians had turned against "the Prophet is a mere pretense suggested by the British to cover the real design . . . to fall upon our settlements." Therefore, he was preparing the militia for combat and ordering Wells to remind the Delawares, Miamis, and Potawatomis that they were bound by treaty to inform the United States of any "hostile intentions." Since "the Prophet is feared and hated by all the neighboring tribes, the Kickapoos excepted . . . it was only a dread of his supernatural powers" that kept him safe. Toussaint Dubois informed Harrison that the Prophet was plotting to attack first the settlements and then the friendly Indians. When Harrison learned that Johnston was the new agent, he told him to warn the Miamis that if the Prophet made war, they might get caught in "its Vortex" and suffer "the exemplary Justice which we shall inflict upon those Tribes who have the Temerity to attack us. . . . The war once begun . . . will be pursued to the utter extirpation of those who shall commence it." He also favored another treaty: "I have been for a long time extremely solicitous to make a purchase of the Miamis on this side of the Wabash as high up as the Vermillion River—Capt. Wells informs me that he thinks the Miamis would agree to sell it." Since the Weas owned the land in question, "their previous removal is necessary," which Harrison would effect through the assistance of the Miamis and Wells: "I know not the Cause of his dismission," he told Johnston, "but if it has not proceeded from the Commission of Some Crime & *you should yourself think it advisable,* he might with advantage be employed as an interpreter."[54]

Johnston was at the Black Hoof's village of Wapakoneta when Wells and his young wife arrived at Fort Wayne. On 12 April he returned and gave Wells the notification from Dearborn: "Your services as Indian Agent will be considered as terminating on the receipt of this letter." Because Wells suspected him of conspiring to gain his position, Johnston asked the War Department and the Friends in Baltimore to counter these rumors. Johnston *had* criticized Wells to Harrison, who passed the complaints on to Dearborn. Now the new Indian agent would try repeatedly to discredit Wells and drive him from Fort Wayne.[55]

Wells was devastated by his dismissal, which he received five weeks after his marriage to Polly. He wrote to Eustis that Dearborn's letter "was as unexpected as it was cruel and unjust and I may add contrary to the interest of the United States among the Indians of this country." The government had refused to honor the invoices he had submitted in the spring, before he knew he was no longer the agent. As a result "the heavy debt that is hanging over me . . . threatens my ruin." He enclosed vouchers for "upwards of 3000 dollars" that was owed to him, adding: "I always believed that the many important services I have rendered the United States in this country would certainly entitle me to be heard before I was condemned." Since he had been "a jealous advocate for the welfare of the Indians," the government should restore his job or appoint him "at the head of the civilization plan" for the Miamis. He had the support of "every Indian of importance in this country" and enclosed seven letters of recommendation.[56]

The Fort Wayne blacksmith, carpenter, and surgeon agreed that Wells was "the most proper person to have charge of Indian affairs in this country." The fort's commander Nathan Heald observed: "it has always appeared to me that . . . Wells acted with justice towards the Indians," noting his unsurpassed knowledge of and influence with them. Even Johnston said that the goods Wells purchased at his factory "I believe to have been applied to the use and benefit of the Indian Department and to no other purpose." Wells enclosed letters from Harrison, stating that the agent's knowledge of Indian languages and customs was "much greater than that of any other person in this country," and from Hamtramck, who praised the exceptional service of Wells and his spies during the Wayne campaign. Wells added a speech he had given to the Indians urging them to cooperate with Kirk. Unwilling to question his predecessor, Eustis filed Wells's packet with a notation that it contained "sundry testimonials corroborating his pretensions."[57]

To block the government from hiring Wells, Johnston charged that he was "an unprincipled bad man whom the government have very justly deprived of his office." In late May the Prophet told Johnston that he was for peace, blaming Wells and Little Turtle for "exciting the alarm" and causing Harrison to call out the militia. Several people at Fort Wayne knew of "some dishonest practice of the late agent," Johnston wrote, "yet . . . owing to his speaking the Indian language, there was scarcely any means of detecting" how he had "on many occasions defrauded" the tribes and the government, adding that "the removal of Wells has excited no displeasure among the Indians, on the contrary many of them are highly pleased with it."[58]

Wells and Little Turtle had not initiated the alarm about the Prophet's (or Tecumseh's) militant intentions; in fact, Wells had stated repeatedly he saw no immediate danger—Harrison thought he downplayed the real threat. As he had about a year of schooling to his credit, Wells's accounts would not have survived a rigorous audit. He did profit from selling liquor licenses and probably bartered whiskey with Five Medals and other friendly chiefs. How he handled the Indian annuities is a more complex matter. The charge the Beaver made to Dearborn that Wells had defrauded the Delawares proved to be unfounded. That Wells spoke several Indian languages was a great asset and a key to his unmatched expertise, but it also made him highly suspect to people like Johnston, who always had to rely on an interpreter. Wells favored Little Turtle, causing intense jealousy among the Miami factions, and the government was not wrong to question his actions and intentions, but Johnston had his own position to protect. A man of divided loyalties, Wells was neither completely "unprincipled" nor purely "bad."[59]

At Vincennes the Prophet failed to convince Harrison that he was a man of peace: "I must confess that my suspicions of his guilt have been rather strengthened than diminished in every interview I have had with him since his arrival. He acknowledges that he received an invitation to go to war against us, from the British, last fall." Harrison recommended strengthening the frontier's forts, but his eye was on the Weas. He was sure they could be persuaded "to cede the Country they now live on." The Wabash Indians, he told Eustis, had always been pro-French: "The happiness they enjoyed from their intercourse with the French is their perpetual theme—it is their golden age." One old chief asked him, "Why do you not make us as happy as our Fathers the French did? They never took from us our Lands."[60]

Harrison wished for peace with the Indians but wanted their land, especially the good prairie by the Wabash. After Eustis approved the treaty, Harrison, his interpreter Joseph Barron, and his secretary Peter Jones, who kept a journal, arrived at Fort Wayne on 15 September. In a move as shrewd as it was cynical, the Weas, whose homeland was in question, were excluded, as were the Kickapoos and Shawnees, while the Potawatomis came in force. Harrison met with "several of the most influential Chiefs" and, in the euphemistic words of Jones, "measures were taken . . . to explain the wishes of the Government . . . & to engage their cooperation." Harrison argued that the Weas would enjoy "great advantage" by joining their Miami and Eel River "brethren" to form a "respectable & formidable" nation. Wells had already suggested such a move, and "much mortified at being superseded," he had "very handsomely proffered his services & influence . . . in the capacity of interpreter" to help Harrison. He "reported to the Governor that . . . [the Miamis] had determined on no account ever to part from another foot of their land." On the 22nd Harrison gave a speech on "the vast benefit" the Indians received from annuities and their need to abandon hunting and the fur trade for farming. Their present poverty was owing to "their own improvidence & the advice of the British Traders."[61]

The Potawatomis "declared unequivocally in favor of the sale and were seconded by the Delaware." Little Turtle vowed to "exert himself to the utmost of his power to effect the proposed Treaty," but wanted fair compensation for the land. Two days later, when some Miami chiefs reiterated "their determination not to sell a foot of Land," the enraged Potawatomis denounced them "in the most bitter terms." Harrison was dismayed by this deadlock. Since the proposed treaty "would be beneficial to all. . . . Why then this disagreement amongst you? Is there some evil spirit amongst us that has set Brothers against Brothers & the Children against the Father?" With the Potawatomis in his pocket, Harrison focused on the Miamis: "My Children . . . what disconcerts you? . . . Bring your scattered members together & you will be strong." Denying the government's divide-and-conquer policy, Harrison asserted, "I love to see you all united. . . . Miamis I now tell you that nothing can be done without your consent." Little Turtle convinced several Miami and Eel River chiefs "to meet the Governor's wishes."[62]

The next day when the chiefs of the Mississinewa Miamis "declared that they would never consent to sell any more of their lands," the Potawatomis "poured upon them a torrent of abuse," threatening them "with the Tomahawk & setting up a shout of Defiance which was echoed by all the warriors." Harrison met with "the greater part of the Miami Chiefs at his lodgings" that evening, gaining a favorable answer from Pacanne once he was "a little mellowed with Wine." The Potawatomis apologized to the Miamis for their harsh words and "they shook hands and became friends again," but the crisis was not over. On the 29th the Owl, speaking for the Mississinewa Miamis, offered only some territory near Fort Recovery for two dollars an acre. As to "the land you want on the Wabash," its rightful owners "the Weas are not here." The Miamis wanted "to keep as far as possible from the White people. . . . We have nothing more to say."[63]

Harrison responded with a two-hour harangue, which must have left translator Wells with a scratchy throat and a bad taste in his mouth, depicting American Indian policy as superior to that of all "other civilized nations." He concluded that he would "submit to them the form of the Treaty which he wished them to sign and if they would not agree to it he would extinguish the council fire." Potawatomi chief Winamac gave his total support. "Your proposal is right and just," he told Harrison. "All that you have said is good, you have asked for land. We will give it to you." As soon as he "began to speak all the Mississinway Miamis left the Council House." In a final gambit, Harrison left Little Turtle and Wells behind and visited the chiefs who had walked out. He asked them to lay "open everything that oppressed their Hearts." Charley, son of the Soldier, now chief of the Eel River Miamis, and an old friend of Harrison and Wells, reminded the governor that he had promised the Miamis that they were sole owners of the Wabash region: "Why then are you about to purchase it from others?" Although he had deliberately used the Potawatomis to achieve his ends, Harrison asserted that they had come at the "particular request" of the Miamis, and that he had been surprised by their claim to "an equal right to the lands in question." If they insisted, the Miamis could receive all the compensation, thus offending the Potawatomis. Then he proposed stipulating that other nations receiving gifts were allies without any right to the land. Since intratribal rivalry was the issue, Harrison assured the Mississinewa chiefs that they "were the real Representatives of the Miami Nation."[64]

This last-minute intervention enabled Harrison to achieve his treaty—faced with a *fait accompli* the Weas consented to it at Vincennes in October. The Potawatomis, whose militancy intimidated the other nations, were "gratified with a considerable present in goods which they much wanted." Even so, there weren't enough gifts to go around and "some went off without a single article." Harrison spent $5,250 at Fort Wayne, plus an increase in annuities for each nation involved. Although the Indians drove a hard bargain, and "compensation" was higher than expected, the superb quality of the 2.9 million acres gained was worth it. Harrison wrote a letter to Eustis praising Wells: "in the capacity of Interpreter he has rendered most essential services—as well from his intimate knowledge of the Miami language as the great influence he possesses over some of the Chiefs." If Wells had not been dismissed for any serious crime, "I think from his former services (which I personally know were very great in the Indian war) he deserves a hearing, and if his removal has been occasioned by misrepresentations, & a vacancy should occur in the Indian Department the government would find their account in placing him in it."[65]

After the Fort Wayne Treaty of 1809, the most significant in the Northwest since Greenville in 1795, Wells renewed his pleas to Eustis to restore his job and pay him for past service. He had been hired as Indian agent on 2 March 1798, but never paid by the Adams administration, nor compensated as an interpreter at Fort Wayne. Given the frugality of the War Department, asking for money was not the best strategy, but Wells was short of cash. His firing was the fault of "private and concealed enemys and not . . . the government I have always been ready to serve with my life. . . . All I ask is justice." He had been told that the reason for his dismissal was "the large quantities of provisions" he had issued to the Indians. If that were true, Wells did deserve a hearing, since for the past two years starving Indians had overwhelmed his agency. As proof that "economy" and not "profusion" had guided his actions, he pointed out that he had spent far less on provisions at the Fort Wayne treaty of 1803 than had Harrison in 1809. The latter treaty was so unpopular that he and Little Turtle regretted their support and began to oppose it. The most vehement critic of all was Tecumseh. If the Indians wanted to save what was left of their land, he said, they must unite—and fight.[66]

WELLS, HARRISON, AND TECUMSEH'S CONFEDERACY

On 3 December 1809, Harrison wrote to Eustis summarizing his thoughts about Wells. His "enterprise & bravery were manifest throughout the [Wayne] Campaign & his knowledge of the Country & of the Indian Habits & Mode of Warfare were indispensable to the Success of our operations." At Fort Wayne, "his Services were highly useful uniting to his knowledge of the Indian Languages & Character great zeal & industry in the discharge of his duties." He also displayed "a disposition for intrigue & for the accumulation of property which perhaps was not always under the government of the most rigid rules of Justice." When he conspired against the Delaware Treaty of 1805, Wells would have lost his office had Harrison not intervened based on "his promises of future good Conduct." He was finally dismissed because Dearborn "became Convinced that his expenditure of the public Money was not always made for the public benefit." Wells and Little Turtle had "exerted themselves in favor of the Treaty [of 1809], but their Subsequent Conduct has been so highly improper as to do away all the favorable impressions which their zeal . . . had created." The question was what to do with Wells: "He is certainly capable of rendering very important Services & if he is not employed and remains where he is, every Measure of Government will be opposed & thwarted by himself & the Turtle." Both possessed "such talents for intrigue & are so well acquainted with the Indian Character as to be able to do a great deal of mischief." Wells should be given "a Subordinate Situation" that did not involve handling money—an appointment as "An Interpreter" would probably satisfy him. Eustis agreed, provided Harrison kept him "under your immediate control."[67]

In the spring of 1810, Harrison warned that the frontier militias were "radically defective," incapable of performing "the commonest evolutions," and unprepared to fight Tecumseh's confederation. Muster days were "generally devoted to riot and intemperance," and the officers were no "better informed than the men whom they attempt to teach." The sad truth was: "We have, indeed, no militia. That term is properly applied only to citizens who are disciplined, or trained for war." The problem was a foolish "belief that discipline is unnecessary, and that the untutored rifleman is the most formidable of all warriors." A better-armed and trained militia was essential, Harrison knew, if he were to attack Tecumseh at Tippecanoe.[68]

In the summer Johnston sent Harrison alarming information. The Fort Wayne interpreter Abraham Ash had a Potawatomi wife, whose brother confided that the British were telling the warriors "they must take up the tomahawk against the Americans. . . . The Indians has been secretly councilling respecting this business for three years past, and mostly go into the woods for fear of being discovered." The Miamis would attack Fort Wayne first, which "may be taken very easy," and Main Poche's men would capture "Chicago, or Fort Dearborn, [which] would be more difficult." The only Miami chief in on the plan was the Owl at the Mississinewa village. When Stephen Ruddle read a letter to Tecumseh from Harrison, the Shawnee "took it from his hand and threw it into the fire, declaring that if Governor Harrison was there, *he would* serve him so." Tecumseh vowed "that he never would be quiet until he effected his purpose, and that, if he was dead, *the cause* would not die with him." Unless the Shawnee brothers were "not put down soon," Johnston predicted, "some district of our country will receive a blow."[69]

Johnston blamed Wells and Little Turtle for stirring up opposition to Harrison's treaties. "The Turtle is contemptible, beyond description, in the eyes of the Indians. I shall not suffer him to go to the President [Madison], nor the Five Medals either. They have been there too often already." Instead, he would "cherish" the rival Mississinewa faction sympathetic to Tecumseh. He cautioned Harrison that Wells "is too unprincipled to be employed any where, except as an interpreter. . . . I could detail to you a thousand instances of his total disregard of every thing that is held sacred by honest and honorable men. . . . He has so long traveled in the crooked, miry paths of intrigue and deception, that he never could be made to retrace his steps, and pursue a straight, fair, and honorable course, such as might be creditable to himself and useful to his country." Johnston castigated Wells to get rid of him: "he is becoming a pest here, and will move off if he finds he cannot be reinstated."[70]

Wells went to Kentucky to gain the support of his brother Sam and his boyhood friend John Pope, a U.S. senator who could pressure

Eustis to return him to government service. Although Tecumseh led the resistance to the hated treaty of 1809, at the time his role was overshadowed by that of his brother: "the Prophet is organizing a most extensive combination against the United States," Harrison told Eustis, "his schemes are rapidly advancing to maturity." The Wyandots, keepers of "the belt which had formerly United all the Tribes as one," supported his confederacy. "The Indians of this Country are in fact Miserable," Harrison noted. "The greater part of each Tribe are half of the year in a state of Starvation. . . . Is it wonderful then that ignorant half starved Savages have been seduced by men who . . . understand the arts of deception?" Although the Miamis, Delawares, and most Potawatomis were "as inimical to the Prophet and his projects as they are friendly to the United States . . . I fear that the bold and popular eloquence of that artful Scoundrel" might induce the young men to take the warpath to reap "a rich harvest of blood and plunder."[71]

Michael Brouillette, a trader at Tippecanoe, reported that the Prophet rejected the salt annuity and left the barrels untouched on the bank of the river. When Tecumseh arrived from Detroit, he ordered the salt put back on board, and "Seized the [boat]master & several others by the hair and shook them violently asking whether they were Americans—they were all young Frenchmen." Nevertheless he called Brouillette "an American Dog." The friendly Potawatomi chief Winamac warned that the Prophet planned a strike against Vincennes and that he "has constant intercourse with some person or persons" in or near the town. The best way to block the Indians from considering "all their lands as common property" was to insist that "the Miami nation are the only rightful claimants of all the unpurchased lands." For this strategy to work, Harrison needed Little Turtle, and the key to the Miami chief was William Wells.[72]

Behind the scenes of Tecumseh's confederacy, Harrison saw the British pulling the strings. Matthew Elliott, whose "implacable enmity to his native country" dated to the Revolution, had instructed a Miami chief at Malden: "My son keep your eyes fixed on me—my tomahawk is now up—be you ready—but do not strike until I give the signal." In July Harrison sent Joseph Barron to tell the Prophet that he must choose between peace or war. The chain of friendship "may easily be repaired" while hostilities would only bring disaster: "Our blue coats are more numerous than you can count, and our hunting shirts are like the leaves of the forests." The Prophet threatened Barron: "Brouillette was here: he was a spy. Dubois was here: he was a spy. Now you have come. You, too, are a spy. There is your grave!— look on it." Tecumseh spoke frankly: "We can go no farther . . . [no more land] can be sold without the Consent of all." The chief said that he would convince Harrison at Vincennes that he had "listened to bad men" if he believed the confederacy "meditated war against the United States." Harrison now realized that Tecumseh was "really the efficient man—the *Moses* of the family . . . a bold, active, sensible man; daring in the extreme and capable of any undertaking."[73]

"The movements of the British agents amongst the Indians," Harrison told Eustis, were "a kind of political Thermometer" that registered "to a great degree of certainty" the danger of hostilities. He revealed that Jefferson's Indian policy had been covertly designed "to force them to change their mode of life and thereby to render them less warlike and entirely dependent upon us, or to remove to the West side of the Mississippi. This contemplated page of their future history has not, however, been so secretly kept as to escape their own or the sagacity of their British friends," hence the growing opposition to civilization programs or land cessions.[74]

Tecumseh with seventy-five of his warriors arrived at Vincennes on 12 August 1810 and was "constantly engaged" in discussions with Harrison, who found his orations "sufficiently insolent and his pretensions arrogant." Since he was "the great man of the party," however, his words were of crucial importance. A week later a crowd assembled to hear Tecumseh. He began by comparing the French, who gave many presents and only asked for "a small piece of the country," with the British, who had encouraged the Indians to go to war. The conduct of the United States was the worst of all. They had murdered ninety-five Delaware at Gnadenhütten, killed several peace chiefs, and broken many treaties. "How can we have confidence in the white people when Jesus Christ came upon the earth you kill'd him and nail'd him on a cross, you thought he was dead but you are mistaken." The Fort Wayne Treaty had been imposed by Potawatomi threats in Tecumseh's absence. To prevent the Americans from dividing the Indians, "we have endeavored to level all distinctions [and] to destroy village chiefs by whom all mischief is done." In two moons "a great council" would be held at Brownstown, where the warriors would decide how to stop further cessions and whether "to kill all the chiefs that sold you this land." The Indians did not want presents, Tecumseh said. They wanted justice.[75]

In his rebuttal Harrison was contrasting "the conduct of the United States towards their Indian neighbors, with the other civilized powers," when Tecumseh sprang to his feet and "with great vehemence and anger" called the governor a liar. He was seconded by his young men brandishing war clubs and tomahawks. General John Gibson, who spoke Shawnee, perceived an imminent danger and told Lt. Jesse Jennings to bring up an armed guard of a dozen men. Harrison drew his "small sword," Winamac "cocked his pistol," and a tense standoff ensued until the governor told Tecumseh that "he would put out the council fire & not set with him again."[76]

The next day Tecumseh apologized to Harrison, blaming his outburst on two persons "who are not true Americans." A "man of sense" had told him that "Harrison had purchased the lands without the consent of the government, and that one half of the people were also opposed to the purchase." Another said that at the Fort Wayne treaty the Indians had been given presents "with the intention to cheat them out of their lands." The governor was authorized to buy land if it was offered, "but not to use persuasions and threats to obtain it." Harrison had been "very smooth with the Indians," while boasting later of having deceived them. "I am alone the acknowledged head of all the Indians," Tecumseh stated. "I want the present boundary line to continue." A survey of the treaty cessions would be "productive of bad consequences."[77]

Later at the Indian camp, Tecumseh told Harrison that if the Americans would return the land ceded at Fort Wayne, and "agree never to make another treaty without the consent of all the tribes, he would be their faithfull ally." Harrison responded that all land cessions were by "fair purchase," and the Americans would defend them "by the sword," but he promised to send the chief's proposal to Madison. "I hope the Great Spirit will put sense enough into his head . . . to give up this land," Tecumseh replied. "It is true, he is so far off, he will not be injured by the war; he may still sit in his town and drink his wine, whilst you and I will have to fight it out."[78]

Harrison was certain that one of the men in touch with Tecumseh was William McIntosh, "a scotch tory who would not hesitate to adopt any measure that would be likely to do me an injury." The other was "beyond all doubt Wells!" Given their mutual hatred, that Wells and Tecumseh conspired together was unlikely. Yet Harrison believed "that Wells is in close correspondence with the [McIntosh] faction here" and had encouraged the Wea chief not to support the recent purchase of the Wabash lands. McIntosh was scheming to undercut his administration and "Wells was the instrument made use of to effect it."[79]

Harrison was more convinced than ever that only military might could deter Tecumseh's resistance movement. The key problem was not the inroads of American settlers, but rather a flaw in Indian character. Jefferson had committed "a political error" by encouraging "concord and friendship" among the nations of the Northwest. "The mind of a savage is so constructed that he cannot be at rest, he cannot be happy unless it is acted upon by some strong stimulus." The men hunt in the winter but "must go to war in the summer," thus "tranquility between the neighboring tribes will always be a sure indication of war against us." To intimidate the warriors at Tippecanoe, Harrison wanted "to establish a strong post & display a respectable force on the Wabash." Eustis agreed that force was "the only efficient language . . . the Prophet & his adherents" understood, but Madison decided not to build the fort that year.[80]

As the Indians gathered in October to collect their annuities at Fort Wayne, Johnston noted that the Mississinewa Miami showed a "great reluctance" to participate. After discussing Tecumseh's visit to Vincennes, "without naming Wells" Johnston accused them of agitating for Harrison's removal. "Whoever advised them to it was a wicked bad man, & was not their friend." Pacanne said that the Weas "were not satisfied with the treaty" and that the Miamis "were forced to agree to the sale of the Land [when] the Tomhawk was hung over their heads" by the Potawatomis. To demonstrate their opposition "the whole nation" had resolved not to accept "any part of the annuity due under the Treaty." In his response Johnston mocked them as "a band of the Prophet's followers." The agreement was "fair" and "they never would get a foot of the Land back again." If the Americans sent surveyors, Pacanne warned, they "must build a Bridge across it" for protection. Johnston replied heatedly that they "would build a bridge of warriors with rifles in their hands." At that the Mississinewa chiefs refused their annuities and left.[81]

Johnston had acted paternalistically. He was the stern, demanding father and the Indians wayward children in need of strict discipline. The Owl, who knew how much the agent hated his predecessor, implied that "all the mischief that is going on among them has sprung from Wells & the [Little] Turtle." Upon his return from Kentucky, Wells let it be known that Senator John Pope had promised to restore him to office. Johnston found this news "astonishing" and launched an assault on Wells's conduct. "The Agency was disgraced and contemptible in his hands and since his dismissal . . . he has done every thing that a bad man could do, to render the Indians disaffected to the public cause, and to destroy my influence among them." As a boy Wells had been guilty of "inveigling boats to shore and murdering and plundering the defenseless emigrants descending the river." During St. Clair's defeat, Wells had admitted that "he killed and scalped that day until he could not raise his arms to his head." His "highly useful" service as a spy for Wayne and as Indian agent had been amply rewarded, yet he had taken advantage of his position to amass a fortune "equal to $50,000." Even if Wells were an honest man, Johnston added, "he cannot keep accounts nor carry on the correspondence that is necessary . . . his ignorance of letters ought to be an insurmountable objection." Since only Little Turtle's faction of the Miamis had confidence in Wells, his reappointment would be "most unpopular" with the rest. "It would be a serious evil in any point of view to saddle the Indians again with such a rapacious unprincipled character as Wells."[82]

Johnston's hyperbolic indictment was based on partial truths. As we have seen, a few white captives did decoy flatboats along the Ohio, and Wells participated in St. Clair's defeat. Wells proved that some accusations concerning missing annuities were false, yet circumstantial evidence suggests that he might have profited dishonestly from his position at Fort Wayne. Johnston's figure of $50,000, however, appears highly inflated. Wells and Little Turtle did have a pattern of helping Harrison obtain treaties and then, due to second thoughts or guilty feelings, opposing what they had been complicit in accomplishing. For an unambiguously patriotic supporter of American policy like Johnston, such ambivalence was inconceivable. In his eyes Wells remained an unredeemed savage, lacking the proper education and moral sense of a gentleman. His expertise in Indian language and culture were unimportant, since the goal was to get the natives out of the way of American progress. Given his divided loyalties and mixed motives, the dismissal of Wells was inevitable. He had pledged to serve a government whose policies he questioned. Wells was no longer the young man eager to win approval; the passing years had sharpened his edges, fostering a contrary streak, a taste for intrigue, and a desire to thrive. He was averse to abiding by rules or being a link in a chain of command. Essentially a man of action, Wells was unsure of his footing in an emergent bureaucratic world. The middle ground he occupied between long-suffering Indians and land-hungry settlers was shrinking fast.[83]

Harrison also had made enemies. During his decade as governor he had used his powers for partisan purposes. His primary goals were to obtain enough land and settlers for Indiana to achieve statehood and to subvert the Northwest Ordinance's prohibition against slavery. Those favoring justice for the Indians and a ban on slavery resisted his administration. John Badollet found him "a moral chameleon," vulgar with "the lowest order" and polished with "the more refined" in order to impose his "despotic" will. Nathaniel Ewing complained of Harrison's "malice & injustice," the "tyrannical disposition of this man . . . [whose] government is by terror and corruption." He had "raised a dreadful alarm of Indians" to muster the militia, yet white visitors to Tippecanoe report that the Prophet's "people are peaceable and treats them well." While Harrison's enemies wanted him removed, his loyal minions sang his praises. The Vincennes *Western Sun* found the governor "in a superior degree capable of promoting the interest of our territory" because of his integrity, wisdom, and military talents.[84]

On 12 November 1810, Harrison opened his annual panegyric to the legislature on a discordant note. The "harmony and good understanding" with the Indians had been disrupted by "a combination formed under the auspices of a bold adventurer, who pretends to act under the immediate inspiration of the Deity." The Shawnees at Tippecanoe were excluded from the Fort Wayne treaty because "the Prophet is not a chief . . . but is an outcast, rejected and hated by the real chiefs." His "assertion that all the land upon the continent was the common property of all tribes . . . [was] extremely absurd." The Prophet was merely "a tool" of the British, who had formed the confederacy to "assist them in the defense of Canada." Without naming Wells and McIntosh, Harrison asked the legislature to punish the two white traitors who had encouraged Tecumseh "to oppose the execution of the late treaty."[85]

Although the 1809 treaty threatened to ignite the entire frontier, Harrison had the audacity to propose more cessions so as to speed up Indiana statehood. "Is one of the fairest portions of the globe to remain in a state of nature, the haunt of a few wretched savages, when it seems destined by the Creator to give support to a large population, and to be the seat of civilization, of science, and of true religion?" American land hunger had caused the affliction decimating the Indians, yet Harrison's antidote was to speed up the process. "In an era when surgeons bled patients to death," Robert Owens wryly observed, "perhaps this made sense."[86]

After Johnston's character assassination and the governor's legislative maneuvers to punish him as a traitor, the future of William Wells looked bleak. Yet Harrison thought he still might be of use. If the Miamis should agree that no tribal land could be sold without the consent of all, that would "shut the door against any further extinguishment." The best policy was to affirm that the Miamis were the sole owners of lands on the Wabash. Since the accusations against Wells as a catalyst of "the late disturbances amongst the Indians" had come exclusively from "his enemies" and were "not Supported by any positive proof," Harrison recommended that Eustis "give him an other trial by an appointment in the Indian Department if a Suitable Situation Could be found for him." In the meantime, Wells had been pushing hard for his reinstatement, informing Eustis that he already had the backing of Harrison and that Johnston had resigned. As a result, Harrison confessed to Eustis, "I was really never more embarrassed in my life than I am upon the subject of Wells." He certainly was a contentious person who made many enemies, yet he might "be the means of quieting the disturbances amongst the Indians." Furthermore, he had "a number of respectable connections in Kentucky whom I am anxious to oblige & Mr. [John] Pope and others . . . have also interested themselves in his favor." Harrison concluded "that more would be gained than lost by his reappointment." After a year in limbo and with this less than glowing endorsement, Wells could return to government service.[87]

THE PATH TO TIPPECANOE

When Johnston learned that Harrison favored employing Wells, he renewed his attack on both his rival and Little Turtle. Opposition to the Fort Wayne treaty had been "hatched" when the two "paid a secret visit" to the Miami village on the Mississinewa. Captain Hendrick informed Johnston that Wells was "in the practice of exhibiting the government of the United States to the Indians . . . in a very odious point of view." Why then would Harrison be "determined to put him into this Agency again" since no one knew "Wells' depravity" better than he did? Hadn't the governor termed him "the most dangerous unprincipled man in the Indian Country"? Whether Wells should be reinstated "was formally discussed" during the treaty of 1809, but only Little Turtle favored a petition to that effect. If Wells regained his job, Johnston predicted, his conduct would be "such as to render his dismissal necessary before three years." He also advised Eustis: "we need not be over solicitous in urging any extinguishments of Indian title, this country will all fall into our hands in the course of a few years" because "the game is disappearing fast." The civilization program was for "political effect only," he admitted, keeping "the Indians quiet and friendly with us" until they were compelled to "retire westward as they always have done."[88]

In the winter Wells "pressed for" his reappointment at Fort Wayne with the secretary of war, and was "very delicately seconded by the Hon. Mr. Pope." Eustis said he could not offer that office, since "objections had been made to his official conduct as Indian Agent." Wells produced a letter from Harrison, stating that he no longer objected to Wells being employed. Eustis passed the buck back to the governor, who was authorized to give Wells any position he "deemed expedient," with the exception of Indian agent at Fort Wayne. Eustis also put a damper on the governor's imperial ambitions. Madison had decided against another treaty to purchase land and "deferred" building a fort up the Wabash. The president wanted "to cultivate a good understanding with the neighboring tribes, and to prevent any causes of uneasiness."[89]

Harrison hired Wells as an interpreter at $365 a year and summoned him to testify in a slander trial at Vincennes. William McIntosh had accused the governor of using the Potawatomis at the Fort Wayne treaty to intimidate the Miamis to cede their lands, thus strengthening Tecumseh's confederacy. In 1804 Harrison's friend Benjamin Parke had challenged McIntosh to a duel. When he declined the honor, Thomas Randolph "attempted to cudgel [him] in the street . . . [and] received two or three stabs from a dirk" for his pains. That Parke served as one of three judges and Randolph as prosecuting attorney did not favor the defendant's chances in court.[90]

McIntosh's lawyer argued that his client had only spoken hypothetically. *If* the governor had defrauded the Indians by packing the council with Potawatomis, *then* it followed that this action had made many enemies and strengthened the Shawnee confederacy. Randolph termed this defense merely a *protestando*, an oblique, not a direct denial of the accusations, and thus nugatory, or, in Sir Edward Coke's phrase, "The exclusion of a conclusion." The judges agreed. Although McIntosh's charges were basically true, Wells testified that the treaty had been conducted properly. Harrison was vindicated and McIntosh was fined four thousand dollars in damages.[91]

As a further test of loyalty, Harrison sent Wells and John Connor to investigate recent depredations on the frontier committed by Potawatomi warriors. In July 1810 a renegade band raided a settlement and murdered Capt. William Cole and three other men. That winter they had camped near Tippecanoe and in the spring had stolen some horses. Harrison explained to Eustis that his vacillating depictions of Wells were due to "the contrary impressions" he produced. His "superior talents . . . might be used to advantage," but because he was potentially dangerous if dissatisfied, it might be best to "place him in the Interior of our Settlements, where he would never see and scarcely hear of an Indian." Harrison "sincerely believe[d] that he would *now* be faithful" and "his activity & talents need not be doubted," thus the best arrangement would be to appoint Wells as subagent for the Miamis and Weas.[92]

Because Tecumseh and the Prophet blamed him for arousing opposition to their movement and had even threatened his life, it took courage for Wells to ride into Tippecanoe for what could only be a confrontation. The brothers agreed to return four of the stolen horses but denied any involvement. The culprits had returned to their Potawatomi village on the Illinois. Wells "had much conversation with Tecumseh . . . [who] avowed his determination to resist the encroachments of the white people." When told that "he would never be able to accomplish his intentions, he declared that Wells would live to See the contrary." Wells's report reinforced Harrison's belief in "the rooted enmity of the Prophet to the U.S. and his determination to commence hostilities as soon as he thinks himself sufficiently strong." In June the Prophet had seized all the salt annuity intended for the Wabash tribes, stating that he needed to feed two thousand warriors because Tecumseh was "daily expected with a considerable reinforcement from the lakes." Harrison warned Eustis that "a crisis with this fellow is approaching."[93]

Harrison sent Walter Wilson with a message that accused the Shawnee brothers of plotting an attack: "the tribes on the Mississippi have sent me word that you intended to murder me, and then to commence a war upon our people," citing their seizure of the salt annuity as a deliberate insult and warning of dire consequences if combat began. Tecumseh was invited to Vincennes but should "bring only a few of your young men." Any land issues, however, must be negotiated with President Madison.[94]

Harrison requested presidential approval for a preemptive march against Tippecanoe. He was convinced that "the design of the Prophet . . . is to make some grand stroke as soon as he has collected a sufficient force." The recent murders in Illinois by renegade Potawatomis were a diversionary tactic in a larger plot to capture by surprise "his principal object," Vincennes. "Calamity might yet be avoided by marching a Considerable force up to our exterior boundary on the Wabash & requiring the immediate dispersion of the Banditti he has Collected."[95]

To Ninian Edwards, governor of Illinois Territory, Harrison expressed his frustration that he was not permitted to seize the initiative. He dismissed the Prophet as "a Contemptible fellow." His most formidable opponent was Tecumseh, who "has taken the Celebrated Pontiac as his model—He is determined to Commence his operations by attacking some Considerable place" and capturing "a Sufficiency of Arms & ammunition." His "great abilities" held the confederacy together and he "laughs to scorn the Chiefs who have refused to unite with him." Therefore, "We must Strike them at their Towns Capture their Women & Children & by destroying their Corn & eternally harassing them oblige them to Sue for peace."[96]

Like his predecessors, Eustis had never been west of the Appalachians and had to rely on information from others. On 17 July he granted Harrison leeway to respond: "in case circumstances shall occur which may render it necessary or expedient to attack the Prophet and his followers, the force should be such as to insure the most complete success." Madison wanted to impress upon Harrison that "every proper means may be adopted" to preserve the peace. While crimes must be punished and settlements protected, "the Banditti under the Prophet should not be attacked and vanquished . . . [unless] absolutely necessary." Because war with Great Britain was imminent, "hostilities . . . should be avoided." Despite these instructions, Harrison gloated to Edwards that Eustis had given him "a Carte blanche" to do as he saw fit: "By the Next Mail I Shall Communicate *my plan*."[97]

Tecumseh and 120 of his warriors arrived in Vincennes carrying knives, tomahawks, and war clubs. In his address Harrison "mentioned the great alarm which the late murders in the Illinois [Territory], and his appearance with so large a force had occasioned amongst our people." He reiterated that there would be "no negotiation . . . of the late purchase"; and complaints on that subject must be brought to Madison. Harrison also demanded to know why the salt annuity had been seized. Tecumseh wryly observed that the governor was "impossible to please"—last year he was angry because the annuity was refused and "this year equally so because it was taken." The next day Harrison stipulated that as a demonstration of good faith the two Potawatomis who killed Captain Cole must be surrendered. Tecumseh responded that "the murderers . . . were not in his Town" and, in light of all the unpunished killings on both sides, "they ought to be forgiven." Having united "all the northern Tribes," he would now unite those in the South. Because he spoke for all the nations, "nothing could be done" in his absence; "he wished every thing to remain in its present situation until his return." After his trip to the South, "he would then go and see the President and settle every thing with him."[98]

"The implicit obedience & respect, which the followers of Tecumseh pay to him is really astonishing," Harrison told Eustis, "& more than any other circumstance bespeaks him one of those uncommon geniuses, which spring up occasionally to produce revolutions & overturn the established order of things. . . . For four years he has been in constant motion" traveling all over the Old Northwest to form his confederacy. His grand design was obvious. Once the southern Indians joined his conspiracy he would attack. Ironically, the strong impression Tecumseh made on Harrison convinced the governor that "his absence affords a most favorable opportunity" for a preemptive strike. In comparison his brother, the Prophet, was "deficient in Judgment, talents & firmness." Harrison's "plan" was to pressure all the tribes to prove their loyalty. He demanded that the Miamis "disavow all connection with the Prophet" and order him from their land. The eviction of the Prophet and his followers at Tippecanoe would then be enforced by the "Militia of the Western Country . . . acting as mounted infantry."[99]

Harrison was playing a devious game. He repeatedly told Eustis, "I feel most forcibly the responsibility imposed upon me, by the president's directions 'to preserve peace if possible,'" while adding "we all agree in opinion as to the necessity of breaking up the prophet's establishment upon the Wabash." He had requested federal troops because "our demands & remonstrances must be supported by an exhibition of force." He asked Eustis to approve the plan and confirm that "the President intended that the principal direction of the Military should be with me." To Governor Edwards, however, he implied that his true purpose was not making peace but starting a war. To

Johnston he was more explicit. Friendly nations should protect themselves against "the exemplary vengeance which we shall inflict upon
those Tribes who have the temerity to attack us." Thus Harrison, supposedly in the name of peace, intended to march a large force to the
Wabash and demand that the Prophet's followers abandon him.[100]

Back at Fort Wayne, Wells investigated the killings in Illinois Territory and found that two unsuccessful war parties against the Osage,
so as to return home with a scalp, had murdered a few people. The
Prophet, Wells informed Eustis, "does not possess that influence over
the Indians of this country that it is supposed he does" and was not
responsible for the recent killings, but he was "gaining strength . . .
among part of the Miamies . . . owing to the improper management
of Indian affairs at this place." Over the past two years, Johnston had
spent most of his time in Piqua, Ohio, leaving the agency in the hands
of John Shaw. Whatever the truth about Indian affairs at Fort Wayne,
the information Wells sent to Eustis undercut Harrison's argument
that the time had come to attack Tippecanoe.[101]

Harrison requested additional troops for his "demonstration of
force on the Wabash" and sought a more aggressive mandate. Only
a large army would compel the Prophet to submit: "I do not think
him much of a warrior, but he is certainly daring, presumptuous
and rash." Furthermore, the frontier would welcome "an expedition into the Indian Country." Harrison sent a threatening message
to the friendly Wabash nations demanding that they either renounce
the Prophet or face the consequences. Several chiefs at Fort Wayne
expressed their indignation at this unwarranted ultimatum. "How
then does it happen that our father's heart is changed toward his red
children?" the Wea chief Lepoussier asked. "Our hearts is heavy as
the earth, and our minds are not easily irritated. We don't tell people
we are angry with them for light causes. . . . We are people of good
hearts." Little Turtle stated that the Miamis were "the same people
that we were at the Treaty of Greenville. . . . We pray you not to bloody
our ground if you can avoid it . . . let the Prophet be requested in mild
terms to comply with your wishes and if possible avoid the spilling
of blood. . . . My words are few but my meaning is great." In spite of
Little Turtle's wise advice to seek a peaceful resolution, Harrison was
determined to provoke a confrontation with the Prophet that in all
likelihood would end in bloodshed.[102]

THE DARKEST CORNER OF THE NIGHT

Since the crisis of 1807, the British had mended fences with the Indians, liberally distributing arms and supplies while reminding key chiefs that the Americans only wanted their land. In November 1810 Matthew Elliott, the veteran agent at Malden, reported that "the Indian Nations are now more ripe than ever for War. . . . I dread indeed that they will of themselves soon commence hostilities & our Government will be (indeed already is) blamed for encouraging them." After Tecumseh told him "we are now Men, and think ourselves capable of defending our Country," Elliott warned William Claus: "Our Neighbours are on the eve of an Indian War . . . the Confederacy is almost general." Both Maj. Gen. Isaac Brock and Sir James Craig expressed fears that Elliott had "imbibed their feelings and prejudices" and felt "too keenly the grievous wrongs . . . [the Indians] have suffered." While Harrison was planning to march on Tippecanoe, the British were striving to restrain Tecumseh's militancy and avoid an outbreak of combat on the frontier prior to a declaration of war—in which case Indian warriors would become crucial to the defense of Upper Canada.[103]

Harrison was right to suspect Tecumseh of plotting an attack once he had united the Indian nations and gained British support. Although the murders on the frontier, as Wells pointed out, had been committed by random Potawatomi war parties, nevertheless they provided the excuse Harrison needed to march up the Wabash and confront the Prophet while Tecumseh was in the South. The governor's supporters favored "prompt and decisive measures." John Badollet in Vincennes took a different view of Harrison: "All I fear is that such a madman will goad the Indians into some act of despair to make good all what he has got published of their pretended bloody views. . . . What therefore has begun by a farce may ultimately conclude by a Tragedy."[104]

Harrison left Vincennes on 27 September with "about one thousand Men." In mid-October, while the troops were constructing Fort Harrison near Terre Haute, a sentinel was shot in the thighs. Harrison blamed the Prophet: "He has not contented himself with throwing the Gauntlet but has absolutely commenced the War." Before leaving

Vincennes, Harrison had told his men that they "should have to fight the Indians." He would demand the stolen horses and any men who had committed murder and order the Prophet's followers to rejoin "their respective tribes." When the Indians failed to comply he would destroy their town.[105]

Harrison told Kentucky governor Charles Scott that he was "determined to disperse the prophet's banditti before I return, or give him the chance of acquiring as much fame as a Warrior, as he now has as a Saint." Fort Harrison was completed in late October, one hundred men stayed to defend it, and the rest of the troops then crossed into Indian Territory and headed toward Tippecanoe, eighty miles away. A few days later Sam Wells arrived with sixty mounted men, including a company led by Frederick Geiger, the father-in-law of William Wells. On 6 November the troops arrived at the outskirts of Tippecanoe.[106]

The army halted in a cornfield with the town in clear sight half a mile away. Harrison's men were in "a war pitch . . . eager to press forward and decide the contest." Several officers argued that now was the time to attack. "The Indians appeared much surprised and terrified" when they saw the troops, Adam Walker wrote. "We perceived them running in every direction . . . to regain . . . a breast work of logs which encircled the town from the bank of the Wabash." At that point chief White Horse rode forward to parley. Harrison would "have an interview with the Prophet & his chiefs" in the morning and until then a truce would be in effect. The Indians suggested Burnett's Creek as a suitable camping ground. Col. Marston Clarke and Waller Taylor approved the site, "a piece of dry Oak Land rising about ten feet above the level of a Marshy prairie in Front (towards the Indian Town) and nearly twice the height above a similar prairie in the rear." Taylor later testified that the ground "was the best that could be found any where near us." Harrison deployed his troops in "as near the form of a hollow-square as the nature of the ground would admit," and the men "built large fires in front of our tents, to dry our clothing, cook our provisions, etc." As was customary, the troops were ordered to sleep on their arms, prepared for a surprise attack. Because of a lack of axes, the camp was unfortified.[107]

Tecumseh had instructed the Prophet to avoid hostilities until his return, but Harrison's army presented an obvious danger. A black driver named Ben had been captured that day and threatened with death "if he did not inform them of the Governor's intention." Ben revealed that the plan was "to decoy them into servility, and . . . attack them the following day and burn their village." Based in part on this information, the Prophet decided to attack that night, intending to assassinate Harrison and then charge the camp. He prepared a magic potion and assured his fighters that they were invincible, while the soldiers would be blind and easy to kill. He then began to chant: "We shall conquer if we are brave." White Loon would lead the attack, while the Prophet would pray to the Great Spirit.[108]

Many years later, a veteran recalled that the first attack came "in the darkest corner of the night." George Peters, who led a front guard of forty-five militia, confirmed that "the night was one of the darkest I ever saw—the Wind blew it was cold and the Rain pour'd down in Torrents." Apparently a few Winnebagos precipitated the action before most of the warriors were ready. William Brigham said: "It was so very dark that no object could be discerned within three feet of me, and I could hear nothing except the rustling noise occasioned by the falling rain among the bushes." When an arrow smacked into the nearby brush, he and his companion ran for their lives, "the Indians close upon our heels." Another sentinel, Stephen Mars of Geiger's company, fired a warning shot that alerted the camp before he was killed by the advancing warriors.[109]

The attack began at half past four, shortly before three drum taps summoned the men "to rise and stand to their arms." Soldiers were already throwing fresh logs on the fires when the single shot, followed by "the horrid yells of the savages," awoke everyone. "The sentinels, closely pursed by the Indians, came to the line of encampment in haste and confusion." Captain Geiger's Kentucky volunteers and Capt. Robert Barton's regulars, at the rear left angle of the camp, were hit first. One man was cut down in front of his tent and an "Indian was killed in the back part of . . . [the] tent, while he was attempting to tomahawk the Captain." Ten of Geiger's company broke and ran, "which caused great injury to Barton's men." One regular wrote: "the men were in confusion, some in front and some in the rear of the tents firing—the Indians a rod in front of us. . . . Capt. Geiger's company of militia, stationed near us, were in great confusion—they could hardly be distinguished from the Indians." John Tipton recalled: "we could not tell the Indians and our men apart. They kept firing on three sides of us . . . our men fought Brave."[110]

Told that "Bartons Company had suffered severely and the left of Geigers entirely broken," Harrison sent two companies of regulars to reinforce them. Since neither his grey nor sorrel could be found, Harrison mounted a bay. His aide-de-camp Abraham Owen, on "a remarkably white horse," was promptly shot down by Indians who mistook him for the commander. "The manner the indians faught was desperate," Charles Larrabee stated; "thay would rush with horid yells in bodies upon the lines / being driven back, they would remain in perfect silence for a few seconds, then would whistle (on an instrument made for that purpose) and then commence the rush again, while others would creep up close to the lines on their hands and knees, and get behind trees for their support." Joseph Daveiss, U.S. district attorney for Kentucky, requested Harrison's permission "to dislodge those damned savages behind those logs." Unfortunately, "the Majors undaunted courage hurried him forward with too small a force," his "white blanket surtout" made him an easy target, and before reaching "his object he fell, shot between the right hip and ribs." He died later that day.[111]

"My great object was to keep the lines entire," Harrison said. Troops who had been driven from their posts were re-formed and fought well elsewhere. Repeated Indian assaults were repulsed. The high ground offered protection for the army, but campfires that had not been extinguished made the men easy targets. Sam Wells organized two companies of regulars along with his three Kentucky companies in a counterattack at the head of the camp: the Indians "were completely routed and the whole put to a precipitate flight." They "fled in every direction before the Bayonet of the regular Troops," while the dragoons drove them from "their lurking places" and into the nearby swamps where the horsemen could not follow. In this decisive action at the end of the battle, Sam Wells "maintained the fame which he had already acquired in almost every Campaign and in almost every battle which has been fought with the Indians since the settlement of Kentucky." Ironically, in the only major combat of the period in which William Wells did not participate, his father-in-law

Frederick Geiger's men fought off the first assault on the camp, and two hours later his brother Sam led a courageous charge that concluded the fighting.[112]

In the early morning light "the field of Battle presented a gloomy Spectacle," George Peters recalled: "48 of our men lay dead & 130 wounded." Charles Larrabee wrote that "their were dedd on both sides laying nigh the Battle round the whole extent of the camp." The victorious troops proceeded to bury their comrades and scalp the dead Indians. The next day was devoted to the sacking and burning of Tippecanoe as well as destroying five thousand bushels of corn. Two dozen wagons were loaded with the wounded for the agonizing trip back to Vincennes. Some twenty of them would die before the end of the year, bringing the death toll to sixty-eight. The Indians told the British that they had lost twenty-five warriors, but Harrison insisted many more had died.[113]

Harrison touted Tippecanoe as a great victory against at least seven hundred Indians that destroyed the Prophet's confederacy, but dissenting voices emerged. Elliott was informed that the Winnebagos and Kickapoos "had the Americans between two fires," but had to abandon the fight "for want of Arrows and Ammunition . . . not above one hundred Indians fired a shot, the greater number being engaged in" stealing horses and beef cattle. Winamac told Johnston: "The whole of the Prophet's force, at the time of the action, did not exceed 350 fighting men," mostly Kickapoos and Winnebagos, some Potawatomis, Shawnees, and Wyandots, but not one Miami or Delaware warrior. Harrison's second in command, Colonel John Boyd, wrote to Eustis that "the dastardly conduct of some whole militia companies led to exposure, and consequent loss of life." It was the brave regulars, "supported by the gallant Kentuckians," who saved the day. Harrison was criticized for letting the Indians select his campsite, failing to fortify it or send out patrols, and not leading effectively during the battle.[114]

His reputation at stake, Harrison launched a campaign to defend his conduct and impose his interpretation of the battle. Participants testified that the Indian force was large and well armed, and that his intrepid leadership had secured the victory. Although some militia ran for cover, most volunteers, supported by the regulars, fought hard. After the first assault, Harrison had managed to hold the lines of his encampment until the charge led by Sam Wells settled the issue. In truth, a few hundred warriors were involved. If their force had been as large as Harrison claimed and been led by Tecumseh, a disastrous American defeat might well have resulted. Victory was won, in part, by fortuitous events. Had Harrison mounted his own horse that morning, for example, he might have been shot at the start of the fight.[115]

After the battle, Johnston offered Eustis his services "to destroy" the Prophet's confederacy. Wells mocked the agent's failure to act and presented his own plan to raise a force of Wabash Indians "and march against the imposter." The rivalry between the two agents was as intense as ever. When Wells learned that Johnston adamantly opposed this risky scheme that mirrored his own proposal, he confronted him: "You have descended so low as to tell the Indians I was actuated by sinister views. You have attempted to prejudice the Indians against me." He even tried to provoke him into a duel: "Such base and cowardly conduct is unworthy of the meanest citizen of the United States." Wells never did lead his expedition against the Prophet, but he was reinstated at Fort Wayne as the subagent for the Miamis and Eel River Indians, while Johnston at Piqua would represent the Shawnees of Ohio.[116]

How much the events of 1811 had changed the situation in the Old Northwest remained to be seen. Tippecanoe lay in ashes and the Prophet's followers had scattered, at least temporarily, after accusing him of giving them a false sense of their invulnerability and American weakness. The Prophet explained that his wife had assisted in the preparation of his magic potion without telling him she was in her menstrual period, and that this had contaminated his powers. While many accepted this explanation, a few threatened him with death. Within weeks some of his followers returned to Tippecanoe. Whether the coalition he and his brother built up over the past several years had been irreparably damaged was the question. The answer depended on what would happen when Tecumseh returned from the South.[117]

CHAPTER TEN

DEATH AT FORT DEARBORN

At two o'clock in the morning of 16 December 1811, a great earthquake hit the heart of the country. The Mississippi rose and fell, swallowing its banks, swamping the land, and creating new lakes. On 23 January came another major shock, followed by the hardest of all on 7 February, which caused the Mississippi to flow backward. During the early months of 1812, the earth often trembled. The largest shocks rippled from Quebec to New Orleans—chimneys toppled in Cincinnati and church bells rang in Boston. New Madrid, Missouri, where ten died, was swept away. For many, these events presaged the end of the world. In 1812 alone, the Methodists gained fifteen thousand converts. "The Indians say the Shawnee Prophet has caused the earthquakes to destroy the whites," the *New York Herald* reported on 26 February. The Creeks said that Tecumseh had told Big Warrior that at Detroit, he would stomp his foot to show his power. Because the Creeks believed this story, as John Sugden has pointed out, it was a catalyst for the revolt of the Red Sticks in the South.[1]

Ten days after the first quake, Gen. Sam Wells hosted a dinner to commemorate the heroism of the Kentucky militia commanded by Col. Frederick Geiger at Tippecanoe. Several toasts captured the frontier attitudes that would soon result in war with Britain: "The Eagle of America, when summoned from her peaceful rock, may she hurl destruction on the British Lion (five cheers). . . . May the starry flag of 1812, soon triumphantly fly over the ramparts of Quebec (seventeen cheers)." At the same time that the Americans hungered for war, British officials in Canada sought to restrain their Indian allies: "The utmost caution should be used in our language to them," Sir George Prevost instructed British general Isaac Brock, "until hostilities are more certain . . . [then] we shall . . . expect the aid of our brothers."[2]

Following Tippecanoe some Indians professed peace, but many warriors wanted to avenge their dead and boasted of their prowess. The factor at Fort Dearborn reported: "They hold a very unfavorable idea of the Americans being able to stand a battle with them." Main Poche's men on the Kankakee told Thomas Forsyth that "not more than 80 or 90" were engaged, "they had no ammunition" to sustain the fight, and "only 24" were killed. Governor Edwards of Illinois Territory warned Eustis that the Potawatomis, Winnebagos, and Kickapoos would attack the frontiers to avenge Tippecanoe, and that there was "good cause to apprehend a formidable combination of Indians and a bloody war" in the spring.[3]

From Fort Wayne, Wells told Eustis that he considered it his "duty to inform you of such movements among the Indians as appears proper." The Winnebagos and Potawatomis at Tippecanoe had moved to the Kankakee branch of the Illinois, and the Kickapoos planned to leave the Prophet in the spring. Once war was declared, Main Poche, with 120 of his best warriors secretly stationed near the British at Malden, would "attack our settlements immediately." In the absence of acting Indian agent John Shaw, Wells had "lately given a few of the Indian chiefs a little provision." Even though he "was appointed agent to the Miamie and Eel river Tribes of Indians only," Wells promised to "keep a watchful Eye over all the Indians and keep you informed." He added that the warriors after the battle of Tippecanoe were "much raised in their own Estamation . . . [stating] that one Indian is sufficient to fight 4 white men."[4]

Convinced of his great victory, Harrison offered amnesty: "The Winnebagoes, Potawatomies, and . . . other tribes who joined . . . the Prophet, must return to their respective tribes—the President will forgive them, provided they remain at home and are peaceable." Madison, who suspected Harrison of provoking the attack at Tippecanoe, suggested that "the most influential chiefs," including Tecumseh and his brother, come to Washington to present their grievances.

Harrison, however, wanted the Potawatomis "to be made to suffer for their conduct" and requested permission to call up the militia and take aggressive action.[5]

THE RETURN OF TECUMSEH

Little Turtle informed Harrison in late January that most of the Prophet's followers, with the exception of some loyal Shawnees, had left him and that "Tecumseh has just joined him with eight men only. Our eyes will be constantly kept on them, and should they attempt to gather strength again we will do all in our power to prevent it." When he encountered his brother, Tecumseh was furious: "he blamed him much for not obeying his commands" and shook him violently by the hair, asserting that "if he had been there no battle would have taken place." He promptly began to restore his shattered confederacy. Edwards reported that he had "visited the tribes on our North Western frontier with considerable success." In addition, many of the Prophet's followers were returning to the fold. Wells warned Eustis that Tecumseh "has determined to raise all the Indians he can, immediately, with an intention, no doubt, to attack our frontiers." Seeking to replicate his derring-do exploits of the past, Wells suggested that the problem of the Prophet and his brother could be ended by having "150 or 200 mounted Riflemen . . . Dash at him instantly. . . . I would be glad to have charge of its Execution."[6]

As subagent for the Miamis, Wells resumed sending reports of Tecumseh's activities in the West. He was unaware that Johnston had gone to Washington intent on convincing Eustis to replace him. At the same time, Harrison, who was not involved in the decision, urged John Shaw to cooperate with Wells, even though he found him "personally objectionable," for the sake of the "Public business." On 7 March, Eustis told Harrison that he had appointed a new agent and Wells's position was no longer necessary: he "may therefore as was originally intended, be ordered either to Fort Harrison, or such other station as your Excellency may judge proper, and where his services may be useful." Harrison placed great value on the intelligence that Wells provided about Tecumseh and his brother, whom the governor believed were behind a series of lethal raids in April that had spread panic on the frontier. About thirty-five miles from Vincennes in Illinois Territory, Isaac Hutson's wife and four children as well as their hired man had been "most Cruelly Murdered." Shortly afterward, Hutson was killed. Harrison promised to remove Wells "as Soon as possible," but at present his services were essential; he was arranging a peace council at the Mississinewa village "under the Auspices of the Turtle and the Five Medals. As these two chiefs are particularly friendly to Wells and certainly and unequivocally *on our Side*, it would I imagine be bad policy to remove him at this moment."[7]

Fort Dearborn at Chicago was especially vulnerable. William Hull told Eustis in early March that unless an American army was sent "sufficient to oppose the British force, which may be collected at Amherstburg and its vicinity, Detroit, Michilmacanac, and Chicago, must fall." British possession of those forts "would be extremely calamitous to the United States." Thomas Forsyth agreed: "Chicago is the First place the Indians Contemplate to attack under the Expectation of Getting Arms & Ammunition—they appear to be Confident of Success against that post." The murder on 4 April of Liberty White and Jean Baptiste Cardin in a cabin three miles from Fort Dearborn was especially ominous. White "was mangled in a most horrible manner. The French man was only shot and scalped." A band of eleven Winnebagos were suspected, but the commander Nathan Heald could not be sure. Therefore, he ordered all Indians, friendly or otherwise, to avoid the fort. The few families in the area sought safety in "the Garrison and the Indian Agents House." If war came, warriors loyal to either Tecumseh or Main Poche were near, and support from Fort Wayne was far away.[8]

The Indians in Illinois presented a formidable threat. The Winnebagos, Potawatomis, and Kickapoos, a frontiersman noted, "retain the fierce, irritable, warlike and savage spirit of nature, unrestrained by much intercourse with, or benefits from, the Americans, and untaught by experience, in past years, in conflicts with us." Edwards told Eustis that many of the warriors "were not in the battle at Tippecanoe . . . [and] are therefore better prepared. Their force is superior to the Prophets," and they could assemble quickly and launch a major attack on Fort Dearborn or another settlement, "pouring down and sweeping away every white person. . . . They might, however, spare the French—but not one American." Main Poche was "waiting for the Signal, from Elliot the British Agent to commence hostilities on our frontier."[9]

For the first five months of 1812, every important official in the Northwest had sent repeated warnings to Eustis that the Winnebagos, Potawatomis, and Kickapoos were on the warpath. Two dozen people had already died in a series of isolated raids. If Great Britain should enter the conflict before proper defensive precautions were taken, the Indians would launch major assaults against forts Dearborn, Detroit, and Michilimackinac. In anticipation of this catastrophe, a large number of settlers were leaving. Yet Eustis and the Madison administration took no effective measures to prevent the coming disaster.

On 11 April 1812, the new agent Benjamin Franklin Stickney, a direct descendant of his famous namesake, arrived at Fort Wayne with a reinforcement of forty men. He told Eustis: "Wells is very friendly to me, and the views of Government. Although he does not speak in the most respectful manner of Gov. Harrison. He says publicly there certainly was not more than 350 Indians who attacked the Governor at Tippecanoe; and he does not believe any thing in the peace he has lately made." Stickney's intention was to pursue his usual "straight line of conduct in my official capacity" in order to secure good relations with Wells.[10]

Something of an eccentric (his sons were named One and Two, in order of succession), Stickney was a stickler for authority; he thought highly of his abilities and assumed that in Indian affairs he was answerable only to Eustis, for whom he had worked in the past, not Harrison. On 29 April a man named Henry Rush was shot and scalped near Greenville. The Miami county militia went in pursuit, "met with a party of Indians . . . killed two of them, wounded a third, and [had] taken two squaws and a boy prisoners." They were determined "to kill every Indian they meet with until they have further orders." On 7 May the brother of interpreter Abraham Ash's wife staggered into Fort Wayne, his wrist shattered, "naked . . . his flesh very much torn, and almost exhausted." He had been among a small "party of friendly and very inoffensive Indians" that had camped near Greenville hoping to buy some whiskey. The next morning "a number of white men armed with Rifles" shot them down in cold blood. The father of one dead man, "in strains of powerful eloquence," demanded justice. Stickney told him to "suspend his anger" while he investigated the case. "Why should I," the old man replied, "when I have evidence sufficient that he died an innocent man?" Wells advised Stickney to furnish them with "clothes, a Rifle, and a little whiskey, to enable the family to adopt another person."[11]

With Indian raids increasing and a war with Great Britain on the horizon, Wells made one more effort to regain his prestige by arranging a mid-May meeting on the Mississinewa, where a *métis* named Isadore Chaine would deliver a peace message from the Wyandots at Brownstown. Five Medals would head a delegation of Potawatomis, and Tecumseh had promised to come. At Fort Wayne, Five Medals blamed the crisis on the recent treaties, which had "alarmed our young men and Warriors. . . . They said their chiefs would sell all their land and ruin them. This destroyed the influence of the chiefs: since then, the young men have refused to obey us. It was now the young Shawanoe began to preach, and by this he gained his influence; and this has produced the mischief." Five Medals wanted Stickney "to communicate those sentiments as the voice of the Red people, to our Great Father . . . and . . . Gov. Harrison likewise: tell it on paper, and make it strong." Stickney scorned the chief's succinct assessment, treating him as an obstinate child: "To make bargains today and unmake them tomorrow, or even to talk about it—belongs to children and not to men. . . . We must take things as they are: not as we would have them." Stop complaining, he told him, selling the land "was your voluntary act."[12]

Six hundred men from twelve nations, each represented by "two leading Chiefs and two War Chiefs," gathered at a Miami village on the Mississinewa. Chaine assured them that it was "the determination of your elder brothers [the Wyandots], to put an entire stop to the effusion of blood." He presented a belt of white wampum, adding that "our fathers, the British . . . have advised all the red people to be quiet and not meddle in quarrels that may take place between the white people." Tecumseh asserted: "We have not brought these misfortunes on ourselves." Had he been at Tippecanoe, "there would have been no blood shed." He pointed to the Potawatomis, who had disobeyed his orders to avoid war, dismissing them as "a poor set of people . . . [whose] scuffle with the Big Knives I compare to a struggle between little children who only scratch each others faces." Since then that tribe had compounded the problem by killing twenty-seven people on the frontier. If because of this the Americans launched "an unprovoked attack on us at our village, we will die like men, but we will never strike the first blow." If necessary, the warriors of all the nations should "rise as one man" in the common defense.[13]

Five Medals said that the traditional chiefs were not to blame if "some of the foolish young men of our tribe . . . [who] followed the counsel of the Shawanoe, that pretended to be a prophet, have killed some of our white brothers this spring." Tecumseh responded angrily: "We defy a living creature to say we ever advised any one, directly or indirectly, to make war on our white brothers. . . . [The] pretended chiefs . . . that have been in the habit of selling land to the white people that did not belong to them" were at fault. A Delaware chief intervened to restore calm before Little Turtle added: "we all see that it would be our immediate ruin to go to war with the white people . . . [who] are entitled to satisfaction." The meeting ended with the twelve nations vowing to control their warriors and to work together for a lasting peace.[14]

Wells sent his "true translation" of the council to the Dayton *Ohio Centinel*, noting that the crimes on the frontier had been committed by twenty-five Potawatomis. "The chiefs of that tribe have assured me that they would bring these vagabonds to justice" and pledged their neutrality "should war take place between the United States and the British." Wells learned later that Elliott had sent Chaine to "preach peace in general, and tell the real views of the British government to a few." Not only did he carry a white belt of wampum but also a black one, calling for "all the Indians of this Western country . . . [to] be united as one nation" to attack the Americans at a given signal. William Claus told Brock that Tecumseh was upset by the Prophet's actions at Tippecanoe because "their plans were not sufficiently matured." Chaine's report to officials in Canada verified that he was a double agent: "the Indians knew the Americans too well, to believe that their intention was to attack only one nation, and if they struck a blow, it would be against the whole—That all the Nations are aware of the desire the Americans have of destroying the Red people and taking their Country from them."[15]

When the council chiefs told Stickney that "they had united 12 fires to be considered as one," he responded that the 17 fires of the United States believed in accountability and so should they. He would give them "one moon to give up their murderers." If they failed, the army would strike and destroy their villages. Stickney's ultimatum went beyond his mandate as agent, adding a new militancy to American Indian policy that put loyal chiefs like Winamac (Catfish) and White Pigeon in jeopardy. Wells also wanted the guilty punished, yet he knew that the agent's blunder might undermine the neutrality of the friendly Indians. Stickney told Eustis that he had "not yet had any difficulty with Wells. . . . But from the natural meddlesomeness of the man's disposition, I fear I shall necessarily offend him in doing my duty."[16]

On a visit to Louisville in early June, Harrison had learned from Frederick Geiger that Wells "intended shortly to resign his appointment and retire into Kentucky." Because "in the present critical state of Indian affairs . . . the public service would be benefited by his remaining some time longer at Fort Wayne," Harrison told Stickney to work with Wells. The agent bristled at this directive, asserting that he only received instructions from Eustis, "by the approbation of the President," and his orders were "to have nothing to do with Wells and that Wells is to have nothing to do with Indian affairs at Fort Wayne." Harrison informed Eustis that Stickney's actions were at odds with U.S. regulations and that his assertion of authority had "wounded the pride of Mr. Stickney, [whose] . . . construction . . . to his powers has already produced mischief." Keeping Wells at Fort Wayne was in "the public interests," since he was "able from his influence over a few chiefs of great ability to effect more than any other person particularly with regard to the *now* all important point of obtaining information." Because of "the wayward disposition of the man," however, Wells was to be under Stickney's direction "& through him only communicate with me."[17]

Harrison's letter to Stickney was not a model of tact. "That I am ignorant, inexperienced, and outrageously insolent," Stickney caustically replied, "I have paid particular attention to . . . and certainly I cannot dispute the point, when informed from so high authority." He had, after all, received contradictory instructions: Eustis, representing the president, wanted Wells dismissed, while Harrison, "the Superintendant of Indian affairs and Minister Plenipotentiary [who] was an officer of *vastly superior rank* to an agent of Indian affairs at Fort Wayne," wanted him reinstated. Once again Wells, whose desperately needed expertise was resented by Stickney, was at the center of controversy. Finally, Eustis confirmed that Stickney should indeed obey Harrison's orders.[18]

Without Harrison's intervention, by the time word of the War of 1812 reached Fort Wayne on 6 July, Wells and his family would have been in Kentucky. One reason for returning to Louisville might have been to work on a memoir. After the battle of Tippecanoe and before the Mississinewa council, Wells had written two short essays, "Indian History" and "Indian Manners and Customs," which appeared posthumously in *The Western Review* in 1820. An editor who reprinted the essays in 1883 noted that they had been "torn" from a manuscript the size of "a book." Perhaps Wells, who could "entertain a company for hours" with his stories, wrote an account of his life. If so it is a great misfortune for historians of the Old Northwest as well as students of captivity narratives that the complete manuscript has never been found.[19]

Little Turtle, his health failing, moved to the home of Wells near present Spy Run Avenue (named in his honor as was Wells Street four blocks away). The chief camped in the orchard, where Polly and his wives attended to him. In a conversation with the fort's surgeon, Abraham Edwards, Wells had said that Little Turtle "was the noblest man he ever knew." Certainly their twenty-two-year friendship, which remained strong even after the death of Sweet Breeze in 1805, was rare and remarkable—a testament to what was best in both men. On 14 July, Stickney reported, "Little Turtle breathed his last, at his camp near Fort Wayne. I had him buried on the 15th with the honors of War, and every other mark of distinction in my power. . . . He died with more firm composure of mind than any other person I have seen."[20]

According to Miami customs, Little Turtle was buried in his finest clothing, along with all the grave goods he would need to walk the spirit path. Captain Rhea was in charge of the military ceremony: "the muffled drums, the solemn march, the funeral salute, announced that a great soldier had fallen." His nephew Co-is-see spoke at his funeral. A typical oration, Wells wrote, lamented that the Great Spirit had called for a family member. "Our friend has only gone on the journey, a few days before us, which we shall all have to travel; we have therefore come to invite you to mourn no longer, and cover the body of our departed friend." The Cincinnati *Liberty Hall* stated: "Perhaps there is not left on this continent one of his color so distinguished in council and in war." Harrison noted his "very high order of talents": "He took great interest in everything that appertained to civilized life, and possessed a mind capable of understanding their advantages, in a degree superior to any other Indian." Little Turtle's abilities were indeed exceptional. He had won great victories against Harmar and St. Clair, confronted Wayne at the Treaty of Greenville, and then become a staunch advocate for peace. His lively mind and intellectual curiosity always stood out. "In his character he combined, in an eminent degree, the qualities of the military strategist, the wily diplomat, the orator, and the philosopher." Even Johnston praised him in retrospect: "Little Turtle—I consider him the superior of Tecumtha in all the essential qualities of a great man. . . . A distinguished orator, Councilor and Warrior, my acquaintance with him was long, intimate and gratifying. . . . Harrison often admitted his great tact and talent and the trouble which he gave him in the acquisition of the Indian lands." After his death, Wells added to his essay on Miami culture: "They generally celebrate the death of a distinguished chief or warrior by drinking, feasting, dancing, and singing."[21]

WAR IS DECLARED, FORT MACKINAC SURRENDERS

Madison had shared Jefferson's belief in the coercive power of the embargo, anticipating that it would reduce England to "poverty and despair." When Congress replaced the embargo with several Nonintercourse Acts, he thought that Great Britain would realize its dependence on American "necessaries," repeal its oppressive Orders in Council, and respect American free trade as a neutral nation. Both Madison and Jefferson refused to admit that England was in a war to the death with France. Impressments were essential to maintain the Royal Navy (25% of American seamen were British), and blockades were a crucial method to limit supplies to Bonaparte, whose armies controlled the continent. Restoring American maritime rights would only worsen Great Britain's dire situation. Madison began contemplating a declaration of war in the summer of 1811. An invasion of Canada might be the means to compel British concessions. What Canada meant to Madison, however, was not necessarily what it meant to the War Hawks, let alone to Federalists, who adamantly opposed the war. Henry Clay's supporters, who dominated key congressional committees, forced a vote. "The conquest of Canada is in your power," Clay told the legislators, and he demanded "nothing less than open and direct war." John Randolph complained: "Ever since the report of the Committee of Foreign Relations came into the House, we have heard but one word . . . Canada! Canada! Canada!" For many land-hungry Americans, the idea was to "conquer" Canada, not merely invade it. In their fervent view, God had ordained that "British power must be extinguished in America," so that the mighty Mississippi could be united with the Great Lakes and the St. Lawrence in one vast empire. "We are going to fight for the reestablishment of our national character," Andrew Jackson asserted, by means of "the conquest of all the British dominions upon the continent of North America."[22]

The Madison administration was eager to declare a war but reluctant to prepare for one. Like Jefferson, the president had an aversion to a standing army as well as a commitment to austerity. As a result, the armed forces were utterly unready. James Wilkinson, who should have been cashiered twenty years before, retained his command. A timid William Hull with a force of two thousand was belatedly sent to defend Detroit. Congress called for a regular army of twenty-five thousand men but failed to fund it. Over his head even in peacetime, Eustis was at a loss how to select officers and recruit troops, while providing arms, training, supplies, and logistics. Although the state militias were notoriously unreliable, the myth that they were the salvation of the nation was an article of faith among Republicans. Volunteers typically were ill-equipped and poorly led—"well regulated" was wishful thinking. Jefferson, as usual, was blithely optimistic:

"Upon the whole, I have known no war entered into under more favorable auspices." The capture of Canada "will be a mere matter of marching" and result in "the final expulsion of England from the American continent." If any Indians relapsed "into barbarism" and sided with the British, "we shall be obliged to drive them, with the beasts of the forests into the Stony Mountains." These bungled preparations and delusions of easy victory would have lethal consequences for many, including William Wells.[23]

Nothing put the lives of Wells and other westerners in greater jeopardy than the failure of the Madison administration to make preparations for their defense and to provide advance warning. When war was declared on 18 June, Hull's force of four hundred regulars and twelve hundred volunteers was still in Ohio, their progress slowed by the necessity to build a road. The first reports did not reach American posts until early July. The British in Upper Canada learned of the conflict earlier and gained a crucial advantage. In mid-June Tecumseh was in Fort Wayne, where he and Stickney "had lengthy conversations." Tecumseh told Wells that he "was on his way to Malden to receive from the British government 12 horse loads of ammunition for the use of his people at Tippecanoe." Stickney cautioned him it would be "an act of enmity" to go to Malden and that he would probably encounter General Hull's army at the rapids of the Maumee. Since Fort Wayne had received no word of war, he "did not think it prudent to stop him by force." Tecumseh listened to Stickney's veiled threats "very patiently, but he left . . . quite abruptly, without even the common formality of shaking hands." At Malden, he reported that Hull's army was on the march and "declared that he would join the British against the United States."[24]

Hull's orders were to take Fort Malden, and extend his "conquests as circumstances may justify." At the Maumee in early July, still unaware that war had been declared, he placed the officers' baggage, hospital supplies, and "his instructions from the war department" to Detroit in a sloop, which was captured near Malden. The British found the general's papers "of the first consequence. . . . [O]n examining them we got a complete insight into all his views." Most significantly, Hull was haunted by the prospect of hordes of Indians descending from the North and overwhelming his force. To intimidate the Canadian militia into going home, he issued a proclamation on 13 July, threatening that if the British let loose "the savages . . . to murder our Citizens and butcher our women and children, this war, will be a war of extermination. . . . *No white man found fighting by the Side of an Indian will be taken prisoner.* Instant destruction will be his lot." For the short term, this harsh proclamation was effective.[25]

Chicago and Mackinac were the most vulnerable American posts on the frontier. Robert Dickson, a fur trader and British agent whose influence among the Indians west of Lake Michigan was enormous, began gathering warriors. On 13 July 1812 his men were ready to attack Mackinac. Capt. Charles Roberts led the expedition, which included Canadian engagés, regular troops, and some seven hundred Indians, mostly Chippewas and Ottawas. On the 17th they surrounded the fort. Realizing that "it was impossible for the garrison to hold out against such a superior force," Lt. Porter Hanks surrendered. The arrival of the enemy was "the first intimation" he had received that war had been declared. "It was a fortunate circumstance that the Fort Capitulated without firing a Single Gun," John Askin, Jr., wrote, "for had they done so, I firmly believe not a Soul of them would have been Saved. . . . I never saw so determined a Set of people as the Chippewas & Ottawas were." This peaceful outcome was "without precedent," Roberts agreed, "and demands the greatest praise for all those who conducted the Indians." Wells would not be so fortunate.[26]

On 12 July 1812, two days before Little Turtle died and five before Fort Mackinac fell, the Prophet, accompanied by sixty Kickapoos, twenty Winnebagos, and twelve Shawnees, visited Fort Wayne. He told Stickney that he and his people had rejected the British offer "to take up the Tomahawk against the U.S." The Prophet promised to attend "the Grand Council at Piqua" and bring Tecumseh. He presented the agent "a large white belt of Wampum with a small spot of purple wampum in the center" and said his people were willing "to relinquish all claim to the Land" ceded by the Fort Wayne Treaty of 1809 and put themselves under the agent's protection. The Prophet noted that his "women and children were starving" and requested food as well as some powder and lead for hunting. Stickney did not consider it "prudent" to provide ammunition; instead he gave "powder & Lead to their Grandfathers the Delawares" to distribute as they pleased. The Prophet criticized Harrison, who "talked crooked, and very bad," and praised Stickney for talking "good things and straight." The agent knew he was being flattered, yet he accepted the Prophet at his word.[27]

The Prophet, an infuriated Wells told Harrison, has been "amusing . . . [Stickney] with professions of friendship and it is now evident that he has completely duped the agent . . . [who has] given him ammunition etc. to support his followers, until they can receive a supply from Tecumseh." Another witness supported this assessment: the Prophet had professed "his great and good intentions to maintain peace. Yet while he was lulling the agent into a belief of the rectitude of his heart, two Indians arrived from Tecumseh," who called for war. Kickapoo riders took "two horses from Captain Wells, the most valuable in the country," to carry the message to the West. When the Prophet told Stickney that "two of his *bad* men" had committed the theft, "the agent found no difficulty in swallowing the bait offered him and applauded the prophet for his honesty." Stickney told Harrison that Wells had confronted him "in a violent rage about the horses, and says the Prophet directed them to be stolen," and that the Indians intended "an attack upon Vincennes." Stickney dismissed this valid information: "You know Wells: and of course, know how much credit to attach to his representations."[28]

The Prophet left Fort Wayne on 22 July. If the western Indians failed to join him at Tippecanoe, Wells reported, then he would attempt "to save himself by professions of peace to the commissioners at Piqua." A week later Wells learned that Tecumseh had included a message to the Creek Indians, urging "all the Southern Indians . . . [to] attack the Southern States immediately." Since news of the fall of Mackinac had not yet reached Fort Wayne, Wells was optimistic that Hull, who was "now at Sandwich with his army," would face little resistance and that Malden might already have surrendered. When Harrison in Lexington received Wells's letter, however, he knew that the situation on the ground had changed: "I greatly fear that the Capture of Mackinac will give such éclat to the British and Indian Arms that the Northern Tribes will pour down in swarms upon Detroit, oblige Genl Hull to act entirely upon the defensive, & meet and perhaps overpower the

Convoys and reinforcements which may be sent him." Tecumseh's message to the Prophet had been sent "under the impression that Malden would shortly fall," but Hull's hesitation had "inspired them with other hopes, and given rise to other schemes." Wells warned Edwards that the Prophet planned to "strike a heavy blow in Indiana Territory." If he failed, then he would probably profess peace. "Tecumseh is the real officer & man of the prophets party," Edwards responded. "The Prophet will not be our friend while Tecumseh is our enemy. . . . It is hardly presumable that he will placidly abandon the measures which he has been so diligent & laborious in maturing."[29]

"The Capture of Michilimackinac may produce great changes to the Westward," Brock predicted. "The actual invasion of the Province justifies every act of hostility on the American territory." The fall of the fort fulfilled Hull's worst nightmare: "there is no doubt but a large body of hostile Indians may soon be expected here from the North." After Mackinac fell he abandoned the military initiative. In a series of skirmishes near Brownstown the British Forty-First Regiment and Tecumseh's warriors cut off American supply lines from Ohio, compelling the American army to recross the river and seek refuge in Detroit. Meanwhile, General Dearborn had agreed to a truce with the British, which enabled Brock to reinforce Malden. In a letter in early August to Sam Wells in Kentucky, Hull summarized his dilemma: "I hope you will lose no time in coming forward with a very respectable force: the fall of Michilmackinac; the tardy operations of our army at Niagara, and almost all the Indians having become hostile, having totally changed the prospect of this army." As the Detroit situation deteriorated, that of Fort Dearborn became untenable. The garrison should immediately retreat to Fort Wayne or Detroit. "Captn. Heald is a judicious officer" Hull noted, "and I shall confide much to his discretion." He told Matthew Irwin that he had "left it discretionary with Capt. Heald as to the propriety of evacuating Chicago." Yet his letter made no mention of the fall of Mackinac, implied that "the surrender of the British at Malden" was imminent, and explicitly ordered the evacuation of the fort and the destruction of "all arms and ammunition," suggesting that "the Friendly Indians" might escort the garrison to Fort Wayne. Thus Heald was given no leeway to rely on his own judgment.[30]

"THE MOST LAMENTABLE DAY I EVER SAW"

When Winamac returned to Fort Wayne after failing to punish the Potawatomi renegades for murders on the frontier, he reported that "the Indians west of Chicago [were] collected together in large bodies, and very much alarmed." Messengers from Tecumseh had circulated among them with a belt of black wampum and "carrots of Tobacco painted Red." Antoine LeClair confirmed that "all their talk is war with the Americans, and [they] were only waiting (and that with impatience) for the word from the British, and the first place they meant to attack was Chicago." Governor Edwards again warned Eustis that the Indians "certainly contemplate an attack upon Chicago and laugh at the idea of its holding out against the force with which they can attack it." The Potawatomis, Winnebagos, and Kickapoos wanted revenge for Tippecanoe and were in desperate need of food and powder. Some fifteen hundred men were gathered along the Illinois above Peoria, living on fish and with "canoes sufficient to carry the whole of them" quickly against exposed settlements. Heald's banning of all Indians from the vicinity of Fort Dearborn following the murders of White and Cardin in April had fueled the anger of the warriors. They had vowed to take possession of the fort and all its supplies.[31]

Since its founding in 1803, Fort Dearborn had been marked by competition among hostile factions vying to control the garrison trade. At the center of these disputes was John Kinzie, a veteran fur trader and silversmith born in Quebec in 1763, who came to Chicago in 1804. Wells had known him at Kekionga and on the Maumee, where Kinzie had moved after Harmar's Defeat in 1790. His wife Eleanor was the widow of Daniel McKillip, killed fighting against Wayne in 1794; her daughter Margaret McKillip had married Lt. Liani Helm in 1808. Kinzie and his half brother Thomas Forsyth at Peoria resisted any challenge to their successful trading operation. An overbearing and abrasive man, Kinzie was often embroiled in feuds. In 1811 the situation at Fort Dearborn worsened: the fort surgeon resigned, the Indian agent left, and a key lieutenant died. To resolve the crisis, Eustis rotated his commanding officers in the Northwest, sending John Whistler to Detroit, James Rhea to Fort Wayne, and Nathan Heald to

Fort Dearborn. Shortly after his arrival, Heald concluded that only a man with a family could be content to "live so remote from the civilized world" and requested a furlough. He returned with a young wife, Sam Wells's daughter Rebekah, who brought her slave girl Cicely. In May 1812 tragedy struck the couple: they had a son "born dead for want of a skilled midwife."[32]

The death of the Healds' first child came in the midst of renewed hostilities both within and outside the fort. When Jean Reheaum arrived in May with two Ottawas, Heald questioned him closely. The Frenchman admitted he was going to see Robert Dickson, but no incriminating documents were found. Before he left, a garrison private who doubted his story tried to shoot and stab him. In truth, Reheaum *was* a spy carrying a message to Dickson, concealed in an Ottawa's moccasins, to prepare the western nations for war. Meanwhile, Kinzie worked "daily to inflame the minds of the Subalterns against the Indians with probably interested motives. He openly opposes . . . [Heald's] pacific policy towards the Indians, yet *somehow or other* the Commanding Officer passes it over." Ens. George Ronan threatened the lives of interpreter Jean Lalime as well as other Frenchmen at Chicago. Lieutenant Helm vowed "to take the scalp" of the factor Matthew Irwin and told his men "he would rather be with the Kentucky Militia than at this Post, that he might murder Indians." The Kinzie faction plotted to stir up trouble among friendly Chippewas, Ottawas, and Sauks in the vicinity. Like many frontiersmen, Ronan and Helm hated Indians. What Kinzie's "interested motives" were is hard to determine. Irwin thought he wanted an Indian war to prevent an investigation into his conduct. Kinzie wasn't a British agent, but neither was he a patriot. Perhaps he thought that since war was inevitable, it should happen sooner rather than later. After it was over, regardless of the outcome, he would still thrive.[33]

The ban on trade with friendly Indians had cut the fort off from valuable information when it was most needed. Since Fort Dearborn at the time had no Indian agent, Heald was dependent on Kinzie's superior knowledge of the tribes and territory. The commander granted him a monopoly on the sutler's trade, which critics said only led to corruption and left Heald "a mere statue & instrument" of Kinzie's machinations. Surgeon's mate Isaac Van Voorhis called it a "partial, arbitrary, and . . . unjust system of oppression" carried

out by the "underhanded measures" of Kinzie, whose "sinister character" and "undue ascendancy . . . over Lt. Helm" meant that a few
officers benefited while the common soldiers were deprived "of their
hard-earned mites." The culmination of the internecine enmity tearing Fort Dearborn apart came on the evening of 17 June when Kinzie
killed Jean Lalime. Both Irwin and Van Voorhis witnessed the murder,
which the latter stated "was a perfect assassination and can be proven
to be such." The interpreter, a small, slightly built man semicrippled
from a broken leg, had that day defended "the pure motives & just
dealings" of Irwin against the "rash remarks" of Lieutenant Helm,
who with his father-in-law wanted "to undermine" the factor. Kinzie
family tradition maintained that the killing was in self-defense, citing
two *métis* women who related that Lalime had fired a pistol before
Kinzie stabbed the Frenchman to death. When Kinzie learned that
the crime had been witnessed, however, he stated that he was "a lost
man" and fled into the forest with the assistance of Lieutenant Helm,
who had ordered Lalime's body removed before an inquest could be
held. Although Kinzie was "lurking" near the fort, Heald's efforts
to apprehend him were ineffectual. After Lalime's murder, both Van
Voorhis and Irwin feared that their lives were in "imminent danger,"
while Kinzie told Forsyth he had "to leave Chicago for the present . . .
[because of] my unfortunate affair."[34]

Kinzie sought refuge in Milwaukee, where he learned that "all the
Indians on the Mississippi were inclined to be hostile to the Americans." Irwin left Chicago on 5 July "for the purpose of procuring an
Interpreter and to avoid certain intemperate persons . . . [who threatened his] personal safety." He arrived at Mackinac on the 16th, a day
before the fort capitulated: "The least resistance from the Fort would
have been attended with the destruction of all the prisoners who fell
into the hands of the British." By 6 August, he was in Detroit, where
Hull told him that the evacuation of Fort Dearborn had been left to
Heald's discretion. "Here, consequently, I must remain till I learn
what course this Captain will pursue." Irwin doubted that Kinzie
would be brought to justice, since there was not "any Civil authority
at Chicago."[35]

In late July and early August, Hull continued to send messages
to Eustis that revealed ambivalence about his mission. Although his
army was powerful enough "to take Malden by storm . . . it would

be attended, in my opinion, with too great a sacrifice under present circumstances." The governor-general of Canada, Sir George Prevost, fully aware that Malden was "a favorite object" of the Americans, drolly told General Brock, "I sincerely hope you will disappoint them." Experienced men in the Northwest saw the writing on the wall. "Genl. Hull has ordered Fort Dearborn at Chicago to be evacuated," Johnston told Eustis. "There is no calculating the friendship of the Indians after the loss of Michilmackinac and Chicago." On the same day Harrison wrote to Eustis that "the loss of Mackinac will be probably followed by the capture of fort Dearborn, and the suspension of offensive measures by Hull's army."[36]

Hull did indeed abandon his plans against Malden and withdrew to Detroit. On 16 August 1812 against the advice of his officers, he surrendered the town, the fort, and his army to Brock. A fear of Indian atrocities was at the heart of his decision, which he explained to Eustis a week later. The fall of Mackinac had "opened the northern hive of Indians, and they were swarming down in every direction. . . . The history of the barbarians of the north of Europe does not furnish examples of more greedy violence than these savages have exhibited. . . . I could not consent to the useless sacrifice of such brave men, when I knew it was impossible for me to sustain my situation." Thanks to Tecumseh's leadership and the presence of British troops, Brock was able to announce on the day of his triumph: "Two fortifications have already been captured from the enemy without a drop of blood being shed by the hands of the Indians; the instant the enemy submitted, his life became sacred."[37]

In the weeks that followed, warriors did commit "shameful depredations" in the area around Detroit. Tecumseh "behaved . . . remarkably well, he assisted us very much in trying to prevent the Indians from pillaging; but the Hurons [Wyandots] could not be prevented from taking what they wanted." Even so, Brock's assessment of the treatment of his prisoners was correct: the more than 2,300 people who surrendered at Detroit survived.[38]

What happened on 15 August 1812 at Chicago was a different story.

Upon learning that Mackinac had fallen, Wells feared that Dearborn had "met the same fate," yet when Hull's instructions arrived in early August at Fort Wayne, he volunteered to lead some thirty

Miami warriors to cover the garrison's retreat "through the woods to this place or Detroit." Wells knew that Hull had suffered setbacks in skirmishes with Tecumseh's warriors: "This will give strength to the enemy & weaken Genl. Hull's influence with the Indians—In a word it appears that our affairs in this quarter at present are rather gloomy." However flawed Wells's character might have been, no one questioned his courage. In this his last mission, his compassion also played a part: he was going of his own free will to rescue his beloved niece Rebekah and the beleaguered garrison, knowing that he might get there too late to avert a disaster and that his own fate hung in the balance.[39]

While Wells gathered his Miami escort along with several pack-horses to assist the evacuation, Winamac was sent ahead to convey Hull's orders to Heald. Unfortunately, Winamac had revealed that the Americans intended to abandon the fort as he passed through Potawatomi villages on his way to Chicago. Kinzie thought that Heald's delay was fatal, since more Indians arrived each day, increasing the danger. Since his combined force of regulars and militia numbered less than seventy men, several of whom were sick, Heald obviously placed great faith in the expertise of Wells to protect the retreat. Wells brought two pistols, a small gun, and a tomahawk, but also a peace pipe, which he hoped to smoke in council with the chiefs whose people surrounded the fort. Many warriors took offense at the Miami escort, which aroused their jealousy, and at Wells: "the Pottawatomies knew him, and regarded him as a base traitor," who, after growing up Miami, "afterwards joined his own race and fought against the Indians most desperately." As we have seen in the prologue, Heald felt honor-bound to obey his orders, while the presence of so many warriors made it imperative that the fort's arms and ammunition, as well as Kinzie's liquor supply, be destroyed first. Heald entrusted Wells to conduct the negotiations for the evacuation with the chiefs, and it was Wells who faced the brunt of their anger when they learned on 14 August that the powder their men desperately needed and the strong drink they craved would not be part of the settlement. At that point, Wells aggravated the situation by losing his temper and exchanging insults with Black Bird and Mad Sturgeon, leaders of the most hostile Potawatomis, who, when they learned that these highly desired items had been destroyed, considered "the agreement or capitulation as void."[40]

Wells understood that a display of utter fearlessness was something that every Indian admired. In a previous council with the Potawatomis in Fort Wayne, he had become aware that the warriors planned an act of treachery at "a grand dance and other performances" in a big tent prior to the negotiations. "A large and powerful chief . . . commenced his dance around the ring, and made many flourishes with his tomahawk. Then he came up to Wells . . . spoke in Indian, and made demonstrations with his axe that looked dangerous, then took his seat." Instantly, Wells gave an "unearthly war-whoop . . . and sprang up into the air . . . and picked up the jaw-bone of a horse or ox . . . [then danced] in a more vigorous and artistic Indian style than had been seen that evening . . . going up to the big Indian and flourishing his jaw-bone, and told him that he had killed more Indians than he had white men, and killed one that looked just like him, and he believed it was his brother, only a much better looking and better brave than he was." Wells later said that he had observed some Indians with blankets wrapped around their rifles and knew they posed a threat. "I had to meet bravado with bravado, and I think I beat," Wells explained. While this anecdote captures an impressive facet of Wells's character, bravery did not solve all problems. When the odds were ten to one against you, options were limited. Given the isolated and perilous situation at Fort Dearborn, there may have been no safe choice.[41]

On the evening of 14 August, the plight of the garrison became more desperate when a runner from Main Poche brought a "Belt of Wampum . . . all painted red with vermillion, acquainting the Indians that the British and their allies had had five pitched battles with the Americans, and that the British were always successful. . . . That the town & Fort of Detroit was taken by the British, that a Vessel would be sent out shortly to Chicago to furnish the Indians with arms, ammunition & clothing by their British Father, to immediately take up the tomahawk and strike the Americans." The arrival of this news from the dreaded Potawatomi war chief who had become Wells's nemesis, combined with the anger of the Indians over what they considered a broken American promise to turn over all the fort's supplies, determined the warriors "to attack the troops the next day after they were clear of the Garrison." That same evening He Who Sits Quietly (Topinbee) warned Kinzie to keep away from the marching column, and so he decided to send his family in a bateau via the lake. Although "Capt. Heald and Wells . . . used every exertion to persuade the Indians to let the troops depart in peace," by the morning of 15 August hundreds of warriors were primed for war.[42]

At nine o'clock, as a four-man fife and drum corps played a dead march, the south gate near present Michigan Avenue swung open and Fort Dearborn was evacuated. The officers led the way, followed by three oxen-drawn wagons loaded with baggage, women, children, and sick soldiers; next came a dozen militiamen and some fifty regular soldiers, with Wells and his Miami escort guarding the rear. Although "the bloodthirsty savages were killing and dressing their beeves" as the procession departed, Heald reported that the Indians had "conducted themselves with the strictest propriety till after I left the fort." Years later, his son confirmed this account: "The fort was evacuated quietly, not a cross word being passed between soldiers and Indians, and good-byes were exchanged. Not an officer objected to leaving. Nobody objected but Kinzie, who did so for personal reasons. . . . The Indians who took their share when the things were divided at the fort had no part in the massacre." Wells, his face blackened and dressed as an Indian, was mounted on a thoroughbred; Rebekah rode a beautiful bay mare. The soldiers and settlers numbered approximately ninety-five, including twenty-six women and children. Kinzie accompanied the group, while his family and a few others were offshore in a small boat. "The situation of the country," Heald noted, "rendered it necessary for us to take the beach, with the lake on our left, and a high sand bank on our right, at about 100 yards distance." Once the fort had been evacuated, Wells, with his Miami escort, rode to the front and scouted ahead.[43]

After they had marched about two miles along the beach, Wells spotted an ambush. At that point the Miamis, who wanted no part of this unfair fight, rode off into the prairie. Wells "pulled off his hat and swung it around his head once or twice," making a circle to signal: "We are surrounded by Indians." Several hundred Potawatomi and Winnebago warriors were spread out in a half-moon formation, blocking any advance in front and using a long line of sand dunes as cover to fire on the exposed caravan. Other Indians were "passing to the rear, to cut off their retreat to the fort." Rebekah Heald recalled seeing the heads of the Indians "sticking up and down again, here and there, like turtles out of the water." The troops responded promptly to the initial attack: "A kind of hollow square was immediately formed encompassing the women and children, and one round fired at the enemy." The American position on the beach, however, was exposed to a withering fire from Indians behind the dunes. If something wasn't done, they all would be shot down. Several sources say that Wells ordered the soldiers to advance: "Capt. Wells rode forward a little and found the Indians about 500 in number hid behind some sand banks and other places, he immediately returned to Capt. [Heald] and advised him to charge the Indians with his company, which was Done in a Gallant manner." Kinzie credited the commander: "Several men fell at the first shot, but Captain Heald formed his men with deliberation, and after firing one round, ordered a charge, and ascended the bank, after sustaining severe loss." The warriors retreated, but the triumph brought more trouble: "The Indians in front, fled to right and left, joining a deadly fire which was kept up from the flanks, and which it was in vain to resist." Some engaged the Americans in hand-to-hand combat: "They fought most desperately, on right and left, what old warriors called a rough-and-tumble fight." One Potawatomi raced up to Otho Hays "with a lifted tomahawk, but before the blow fell [the sergeant] ran his bayonet in the Indian's breast up to the socket, so that he could not pull it out; yet in this situation, the Indian tomahawked him, and they both fell dead together."[44]

By taking possession of the nearest sand bank, Heald had intended to remove the women and children from the line of fire. But the warriors continued their encircling movement and made an assault on the wagons, gaining "possession of all our horses, provisions, and baggage of every description." The militiamen defending the rear were all killed, as were two women and twelve children: "the brave, the innocent fair, and the helpless, fell prey to the savage crewilty of the tomahawk and scalping knife." Kinzie related that the Indians "had passed round the beach & got among the baggage where the women & children were & here perpetuated one of the most shocking scenes of Butchery perhaps ever witnessed—their shrieks of distress, their piteous appeals to father mother Brothers & Husbands for help & their prayers for mercy were there unheard & disavailing—the Tomahawk & knife performed their work without distinctions of age or condition." Rebekah's slave Cicely and her child were among the slain. Isabella Cooper, age nine, survived. She related that "a young Indian . . . grabbed her by the hair and pulled her out of the wagon, and she fought him the best she knew how, scraching and biting, until he finally threw her down and scalped her. She was so frightened she was not aware of it until the blood ran down her face. An old squaw intefered and prevented her from being tomhawked."[45]

Cowards die many times, the valiant but once. Wells was the exception—an indisputably brave man who in conflicting accounts died many deaths. Juliette Kinzie's popular version of the battle, first published in 1844 and loosely based on information she received from Margaret Helm, is perhaps the least reliable. The author depicts Wells's response to the slaughter of the women and children in the wagons:

> When Capt. Wells beheld it, he exclaimed, "Is that their game? Then I will kill too!" So saying, he turned his horse's head, and started for the Indian camp, near the fort, where had been left their squaws and children. Several Indians pursued him, firing at him as he galloped along. He laid himself flat, on the back of his horse, loading and firing in that position. At length, the balls of his pursuers took effect, killing his horse, and severely wounding himself. At this moment he was met by *Winnemeg* and *Wau-ban-see*, who endeavored to save him from the savages who had not overtaken him; but as they supported him along . . . he received his death-blow from one of the party, *Pee-so-tum*, who stabbed him in the back.

In this account the mayhem at the wagons, which the author attributes to "one young savage," takes place *after* the battle, and Wells, as yet unwounded, seeks vengeance at an Indian camp two miles away (while speaking words no one could have heard) before being stabbed in the back. None of the eyewitness sources support this unlikely set of events.[46]

Darius Heald's parents survived the battle and his mother Rebekah later wrote a memoir, which was lost during the Civil War. His version, repeated with variations, is highly romanticized but probably comes closer to the truth. He pictures Wells in the midst of the conflict firing two pistols and a small gun: "he generally had an extra bullet in his mouth which helped him to load fast when necessary. He could pour a little powder, wad it down, 'blow in' the bullet, prime and fire more quickly than one can tell the facts. The Indians broke and ran from him right and left." Shortly before the end of the battle,

> Mrs. Heald found herself in front, & near her uncle, who rode up beside her, saying, "My child, I'm mortally wounded"—the blood was oozing from his mouth & nose—shot through the lungs. She inquired if he might not possibly recover? "No—I cannot live more than an hour," and added—"my horse is also badly wounded, & I fear cannot carry me to where the wagons are—I must hasten." His horse fell, & caught one of the dying captain's legs under him; but Wells managed to disengage himself. Mrs. Heald now said to him, "See, there are Indians close by." He replied, "I care not—I can not last but a few minutes; I will sell my life as dearly as possible. . . ." He now fell to the ground, & shot as he lay, with his rifle & then with his pistol, thus dispatching two Indians; & while reloading several other Indians came up, & laying as if dead, he made a last effort, raised his rifle & killed another. . . . The advancing Indian host now came up, readily recognized him, though painted black & dressed like an Indian—& while some of them disingenuously, treacherously, spoke of saving him, one of their number pointed his gun at Wells' head, seeing which the dying man pointed his finger at his heart, & made a circular motion around the crown of his head, thus indicating where to shoot him, & take his scalp, in another instant he lay in death.

Although the dialogue is stilted, and the number of Indians killed exaggerated (Heald credits Wells with a total of ten!), other sources confirm that Rebekah was near Wells when he died and that he fell within sight of the wagons. John Kinzie related: "Mrs. Heald in her terror soon left me & fled to her Uncle Capt. Wells by whose side she received several shot wounds." Isabelle Cooper said "she saw Wells when he fell from his horse, and his face was painted." Wells probably did urge Rebekah to save herself and, as Heald added in another version, asked her to "tell my wife . . . I died at my post doing the best I could," or words to that effect.[47]

There is evidence that Wells, after being pinned beneath his fallen horse, exchanged words with a few Potawatomis before they killed him. Heald added that after Wells indicated where he wanted to be shot, he cried out, "Shoot away." John Johnston, as might be expected, gave a negative account: Wells "commenced using the most abusive and bitter invective toward them to provoke them to kill him, hoping doubtless in this way to avoid a slow & tortuous end—Finally one of the number could stand it no longer and shot Wells dead." In a more credible version a Potawatomi recalled that as Captain Wells lay dying, he was first approached by He Who Sits Quietly, who attempted to stop the warriors from further atrocities. "Father, I want to live," Wells told him, to which the chief replied, "'My son, you can live,' but others unrestrained and unrestrainable dispatched him in spite of the friendly efforts of To-pin-a-bee."[48]

Multiple sources state what happened to Wells after he was killed. Thomas Forsyth, who arrived in Chicago the day after the battle, wrote: "Poor Captain Wells is among the slain & was butchered in a horrid manner—his heart taken out and divided among the different bands." A Potawatomi named Benac later confirmed that "the Indians cut Wells' heart out and each Indian coming along took a bite of it." Kinzie stated that Wells "had his heart cut out, and other shocking barbarities commited upon his body, having rendered himself particularly obnoxious to the Indians, by his influence among those savage tribes, who remained friendly to the United States." The Heald family maintained another interpretation: "his heart was taken out cut up into small bits, distributed & eaten, that they might prove as brave as he was." Rebekah, wounded in six places, was captured at the same time: "an Indian cut off a piece, held it up to Mrs. Heald and insisted on her eating it. She shook her head. He then daubed her face with it. She shook her fist at him. They then called her "Epiconier! Epiconier!" this being their name for Captain Wells, and thus signifying that she was also a Wells—a person of pluck and bravery." The

Potawatomis ate the heart of William Wells to incorporate his brave spirit, yet no doubt sheer vengeance was also involved, since many bodies were mutilated.[49]

Walter Jordan, the soldier who accompanied Wells from Fort Wayne, later wrote letters about "the Most Limentable Day I Ever Saw," adding more gruesome details:

> I had to Surrender My Self to 4 Damd yellow indians tha Marche up to whar Wells Lay and one of them Spok English and Said Jordan I now [know] you[,] you gave me some tobacco at fort wain you Shant Be kild but See What I will doe with your Captain He then Cut of[f] his head and Stuck it on a pol while another tuck out his hart and divided it among tha Chieffs and tha[y] Eate it up raw.

Jordan was saved by White Raccoon, a chief that he had befriended at Fort Wayne. Shortly after his capture, he escaped and told his story. Sources confirm that Wells displayed great courage and was shot down as he rode to the defense of the women and children in the wagons. When he fell, he was pinned beneath his dead horse. Before he died, he was able to speak with Rebekah, also badly wounded, and a few Potawatomis, who then killed him and ate his heart. The "pol" that Jordan refers to was a ramrod of a gun. Wells *was* beheaded. Lieutenant Helm recalled looking down at the beach where the wagons were: "I was struck with horror at the sight of men, women and children lying naked with principally their heads off." After the battle, Black Partridge found "the body of Captain Wells . . . in one place, and his head in another; these remains were . . . buried in the sand where he fell."[50]

The death of William Wells occurred before Heald surrendered the remainder of his force. The Indians had quickly surrounded his position on the sand bank, killing and wounding most of his men. Once he realized that the Miami escort had deserted him, Heald reported: "I drew off the few men I had left, and took possession of a small elevation in the open prairies, out of shot of the bank or any other cover. The Indians did not follow me, but assembled in a body on the top of the bank, and, after some consultation among themselves, made signs for me to approach them." Heald was met by Black Bird and a *métis* interpreter named Pierre la Claire, who worked for Kinzie. "He advised the Capt. not to surrender until they should propose some terms—the Capt. accordingly refused to surrender unless they would give pledge for the lives of the prisoners—this they agreed to do with the exception of those who were mortally wounded & the remaining 28 men some of them badly wounded surrendered accordingly." Later that day "the Indians massacred five of our men that had not been wounded and two that were wounded." The next morning, as the captives "were leaving the fort the Indians killed two of our men who were wounded and appeared to have become exhausted." Heald stated that twenty-six soldiers, twelve militia, two women, and twelve children were killed, and thirty-eight people captured—eighteen were eventually released. The Indians lost seven men.[51]

Rebekah Heald had been struck by bullets in both arms—one of which was broken—as well as her breast and side, yet still she clung to her horse and used her whip to fend off an Indian woman who wanted her riding blanket. This show of courage, which confirmed her status as an "Ep-i-con-yare"—"that she was not only related to a brave man, but was the wife of a brave officer, and had proved herself a brave spirited woman"—won the approval of the Indians and saved her life. When an Indian raised a war club to kill her, she, "with extraordinary presence of mind . . . said, don't kill me, *I am a silversmith.*" Jean Baptist Chandonnis "purchased Mrs. Heald from her captor, for an old mule captured there, and a bottle of whiskey." She was then hidden in a birch canoe under some skins until reunited with her husband. Heald had been shot "in the hip by a one-ounce ball. That ball was never extracted, and caused his death twenty years afterward." Had they not been protected, both probably would have been killed because of their wounded condition. Kinzie and his family were also saved by friendly Indians. The Healds were taken to Mackinac, where Captain Roberts, a fellow Mason, paroled Heald; on 19 November he and Rebekah were reunited with Sam Wells in Louisville.[52]

Abraham Ash's brother-in-law, the same man Wells had aided after he had been shot near Greenville, brought the news of the disaster to Fort Wayne. It was he who first told Polly that her husband was dead. He presented her with the tomahawk that Wells had carried into battle and "disappeared; supposed to have returned to his people." Benac in 1817 gave Gen. Thomas Hunt "a pair of rifle-barrel pistols, taken from Wells after he was slain, and marked with his initials." The victorious warriors, for their part, "had a great war dance on their arrival at Malden." Milo Quaife, the foremost historian of the battle, concluded: "Wells was the real hero of the Chicago massacre, giving his life voluntarily to save his friends." He died as he had lived: a brave, conflicted man in the midst of the struggle for the Old Northwest. The War of 1812 had just begun. The remarkable career of William Wells now had ended.[53]

EPILOGUE

SAM WELLS AND THE WAR IN THE NORTHWEST

Had William Wells lived, he might have played an important role during the War of 1812 in the Old Northwest, possibly as a scout for Col. Sam Wells, whose Seventeenth U.S. Regiment, due to a lack of supplies, had not been able to reinforce General Hull at Detroit. Governor Shelby of Kentucky lamented that without such logistical delays "by forced marches the garrison at Chicago might have been saved." Colonel Wells was in Cincinnati when he learned of his brother's death at Fort Dearborn and that Fort Wayne was "in danger of immediate attack." Harrison, who had left his governorship of Indiana Territory to head the Kentucky militia, arrived shortly afterward. He and Wells then rushed their men forward, while William Oliver and three Shawnees—James Logan, Bright Horn, and Captain Johnny—made haste to inform the fort that relief was coming. Oliver found that the formerly friendly Potawatomi chiefs Five Medals and Winamac had added their warriors to the siege, which began in earnest on 5 September. The defenses of the fort had been neglected, and commander Capt. James Rhea "was as drunk as a fool" most of the time. When John Johnston's brother Stephen tried to go for help, he was murdered within sight of the garrison. Harrison's troops arrived in the afternoon of the 12th and were greeted with "great joy" by the survivors, including a pregnant Polly Wells and two-year-old Samuel.[1]

Although Fort Wayne suffered few casualties, the warriors slaughtered the livestock and ravaged the countryside. William Wells's "handsome farm in the forks of the river" fell victim to "the general devastation." To punish the Indians, Harrison directed Colonel Wells "to go against the potawatamie villages at Elk Hart," while General John Payne would "destroy the Miami towns at the forks of the Wabash" (Huntington). A few days later Wells's men returned "out of provisions, hungry, displeased, and considerably broke down, having destroyed the Five Medals' Town." Apparently Wells had quarreled with his militia officers and "a distinction . . . began to take place between the corps as volunteers and regulars." Harrison accompanied Payne. Finding the Miami villages abandoned, the troops cut up fifteen hundred bushels of corn and burned all the dwellings. Harrison then sent Col. James Simrall's dragoons to Little Turtle's Town on the Eel River. The village had about forty houses— some well-built cabins of hewn logs with "good plank floors above and below," plastered walls, and stone chimneys. "Finding no Indians, but a considerable quantity of plunder, we burnt and destroyed the whole, and cut up and picked about sixty acres of corn." Harrison knew that most of the Miamis had not been involved in the siege, but he wanted to deprive the hostile tribes of supplies in case they made "a second attempt upon Fort Wayne."[2]

At the same time warriors raided Pigeon Roost in southern Indiana, killing twenty-one settlers, while the Prophet's men from Tippecanoe attacked Fort Harrison (Terre Haute). They burned a blockhouse and, in the process, ignited "a quantity of whiskey" that sent flames to the roof. Capt. Zachary Taylor and most of his fifty men were sick; nonetheless they were able to defend the breach left by the fire, and the Indians retreated after driving off cattle and oxen. Taylor, whose stout defense made him a national hero, reported that the voice of the Wea chief Stone Eater was heard exhorting his warriors. In retaliation, Gen. Samuel Hopkins's troops destroyed the Prophet's Town as well as two nearby Winnebago and Kickapoo villages, some two hundred cabins in all. The next day an ambushed detachment lost eighteen men. On an expedition to White Pigeon's Potawatomi village on the St. Josephs, half of Col. Allen Trimble's militia refused to proceed, and he had to settle for destroying two smaller towns.[3]

When the war started the Miamis were deeply divided. Although the deaths of Little Turtle and William Wells had undercut the peace faction, most preferred neutrality; but the Potawatomis put great pressure on them to take up arms. A delegation of chiefs at Piqua in October asked for peace. Harrison saw this as a ruse "to palliate or deny the hostility of their tribe," and he accused them of supporting the attacks on Forts Harrison and Wayne and of encouraging the Delawares to fight. He ordered Col. John B. Campbell to destroy the Miami villages on the Mississinewa. On 17 December Campbell's six hundred men, "in the utmost confusion and disorder," attacked a town, whose dozen warriors "fled across the river without making any resistance." Eight were killed, including "one big negroe." The forty-two prisoners were mainly Munsees (a branch of the Delawares). Two other villages were burned that day before the men returned to the town. Before dawn the Miamis, led by Little Turtle's nephew, counterattacked "with great fury." The warriors took possession of one redoubt and "poured a tremendous fire" on the troops, who "stood firm." Because the attack was spread over a wide front, Campbell calculated that he faced a force of at least three hundred. The warriors "fought most bravely" for over an hour before withdrawing. Campbell buried nine of his men beneath a cabin before beginning the arduous trek home. By the time they reached Dayton, 303 were "so severely frostbitten as to be entirely unfit for duty." They had burned three villages, but Osage Town, a Miami stronghold near the mouth of the Mississinewa, was unharmed. During the war, however, it and most other villages in Indiana and Illinois would be destroyed, some several times. Although Harrison's stated objective was to protect his left flank, he also wanted to drive the Indians out of the territory.[4]

Colonel Wells served under Gen. James Winchester, who had yielded command of the northwestern army to Harrison. Near the Maumee the troops encountered British and Indian reinforcements belatedly headed for Fort Wayne. A few skirmishes ensued and several scouts were killed, among them James Logan, who had been captured as a boy during Benjamin Logan's raid on the Shawnee in 1786 and had taken his adoptive father's name. Logan, Bright Horn, and Captain Johnny had come upon Matthew Elliott's son Alexander

and five Potawatomis, including Winamac. Since they were outnumbered, the three implied that they had switched sides. As they rode
along, Winamac "boasted of his having caused William Well's death,
although he had gone with him as a friend to Chicago." When three
warriors "sauntered off on horse back in search of black haws," at
Logan's signal the Shawnee scouts opened fire. Elliott, Winamac, and
two other Potawatomis were killed in the ensuing fight. Logan was
mortally wounded and died back in camp after lingering "a few days
in excruciating pain."[5]

Because Colonel Wells and his men had rushed forward to rescue
Fort Wayne, their baggage had been left in Kentucky. Still dressed
for summer, with winter coming on and supplies low, many became
sick and some died. Harrison complained "that a fine body of regular
troops belonging to the 17th and 19th regiments under Col. Wells has
nearly been destroyed for the want of clothing." Col. John Allen's
regiment shared the same plight: "My heart aches for my poor, naked
men." Although Harrison was determined "never to make a detachment either to the front or rear which is not able to contend with" the
whole British and Indian force concentrated near Fort Malden, on
17 January Winchester, in response to a plea from the residents, and
against the advice of Wells, advanced his troops to the River Raisin,
scattered the defenders, and occupied Frenchtown (Monroe, Michigan). Two days later Colonel Wells and three hundred men arrived
and took up positions "on the right of the other troops about one hundred yards from them, in ground entirely open." On the 21st Wells
returned to the Rapids with Winchester's message that he would
hold his position, as well as a letter from Capt. Nathaniel Hart calling
for immediate reinforcements. Since Fort Malden was eighteen miles
away, the situation was precarious. To support this unauthorized
advance, Harrison assembled his army "as fast as possible," dread-
ing that "the enemy may overpower Genl. Winchester before I can
send him a sufficient reinforcement."[6]

Harrison's worst fears were realized when Gen. Henry Proctor
made a dawn attack and routed the Americans on the 22nd. Facing
heavy fire in the front from British regulars as well as Roundhead's
warriors on both flanks, the U.S. forces gave way and then broke into
a full retreat. Only the Kentucky troops protected by pickets were able

to hold their ground. When Winchester was captured by the Indians, Proctor demanded that he surrender his entire force. More than two hundred lay dead, and over five hundred were made captives and taken to Malden. In the absence of Colonel Wells, the "greater part" of his regiment had "been cut to pieces or taken prisoner." Some sixty to eighty wounded men were left behind at Frenchtown. Proctor promised to send sleds to bring them to Amherstburg. The next morning, however, fifty drunken Indians "commenced killing the wounded and set fire to the houses the wounded were in and consumed them." Those who tried to flee were slaughtered in the streets and left to scavenging hogs. Harrison sent Wells forward on the 24th to assess the situation. He returned that evening to report on the disastrous defeat, which had cost the lives of so many Kentuckians. It was then his sad duty to travel to Frankfort. On the evening of 2 February the people were celebrating Winchester's earlier victory at Frenchtown when Wells delivered his "distressing intelligence" of the shocking tragedy, which "filled the state with mourning" and made "Remember the Raisin!" a clarion call for retribution. Wells later learned that among those slain after being captured was his son Levi.[7]

Winchester's defeat spoiled Harrison's plan to recapture Detroit and placed his army on the defensive. Urgent efforts were made to strengthen Fort Meigs, located south of the Maumee across from Fallen Timbers and old Fort Miamis. Capt. Eleazer D. Wood supervised the digging of formidable earthworks, which became indispensable on 1 May when British batteries on the northern shore began shelling. Harrison's two thousand men hunkered down while hundreds of red-hot cannonballs hissed into the mud above their heads. As Tecumseh later said with disgust: "It is hard to fight people who live like ground hogs." On the 5th word arrived that fourteen hundred Kentuckians led by Brig. Gen. Green Clay were near. Harrison sent them orders to "take possession of the enemy's cannon, spike them, cut down the carriages, and return to their boats." Col. William Dudley's eight hundred men proceeded to drive off the defenders and disable the guns. "But that confidence which always attends Militia when successful proved their ruin." Instead of returning immediately to their boats, they were drawn into a skirmish, "whilst the British Troops and an immense body of Indians were brought up." The result was another disaster. Dudley and fifty of his men were killed and some five hundred were captured and brought to Fort Miamis. At the same time, Col. John Miller's 250 men, including the remnants of Colonel Wells's regiment, after some fierce fighting took out the British batteries on the south side of the river. The Indians "went off in high disgust" with the failure of Proctor to capture Fort Meigs, and Tecumseh intervened too late to prevent angry warriors from murdering some twenty Kentucky prisoners at Fort Miamis. After the siege was lifted, Harrison claimed victory, but the cost had been enormous.[8]

In July Harrison sent Colonel Wells to take charge of Fort Stephenson at Lower Sandusky (Freemont, Ohio). If the enemy approached in force, he was to destroy the fort and retire to Upper Sandusky. The next month the British and their Indian allies made a second attempt to take Fort Meigs. This time Tecumseh's strategy was to lure the garrison out in the open by staging a sham battle nearby. Since General Clay was not fooled, the British and Indians selected an easier target—Fort Stephenson. Harrison ordered Maj. George Croghan, who had replaced Wells, to burn the fort and bring his men to Seneca Town nine miles away. Since the enemy was near, the major replied, "We have determined to maintain this place, and by heavens we can." Harrison promptly sent Wells to "relieve" Croghan for disobeying orders. Once the major had explained himself to Harrison, however, he was allowed to resume his command, and on 3 August 1813 the Forty-First British Regiment attempted to storm the fort and were "repulsed with the loss of at least 100 killed wounded and prisoners." Croghan was celebrated for his intrepid defense while Harrison was widely criticized. In response, Wells and thirteen other field officers signed a letter reaffirming faith in their commander's merits.[9]

The 10 September triumph of Oliver Hazard Perry ("We have met the enemy and they are ours") over the British navy on Lake Erie enabled Harrison to take the offensive. Proctor's failure to demolish Forts Meigs and Stephenson, followed by Perry's victory, shattered his Indian alliance. Tecumseh had over three thousand warriors in the vicinity of Brownstown, but now the Miamis and other nations abandoned him when they learned that the British planned to burn Fort Malden instead of making a stand. Unlike Gen. Isaac Brock,

Proctor made inadequate use of his Indian allies. "I hate these savage barbarians," he confessed at the time. Tecumseh expressed his contempt: "We must compare our father's conduct to a fat animal, that carries its tail upon its back, but when affrighted, he drops it between his legs and runs off." He and his men vowed to fight the advancing Americans: "Our lives are in the hands of the Great Spirit. We are determined to defend our lands, and if it be his will we wish to leave our bones upon them."[10]

Robert McAfee, along with Colonel Wells, was part of Harrison's force of thirty-five hundred that on 27 September "came to the bones of 13 or 14 of our countrymen killed at the River Raisin . . . (they cry aloud for revenge)." Three days later the army liberated Detroit, where "the inhabitants received us with looks of pleasure & . . . every eye beamed with gratitude." Proctor had promised Tecumseh that he would fight once he found favorable ground. On 5 October he selected a spot by the Thames River near Moraviantown and positioned his British regulars and Canadian dragoons in two lines, with Tecumseh's warriors defending heavily wooded and swampy land on his flank. Harrison made the bold decision "to break the British lines at once by a charge of the Mounted Infantry. . . . I was fully convinced that it would succeed. The American woodsmen ride better in the woods than any other people." Harrison cried out, "Charge them my brave Kentuckians," and in a matter of minutes Proctor's men surrendered. Although outnumbered, Tecumseh's warriors presented a more difficult problem: "the Indians fired so hot that the companies had to dismount and fight from behind trees and logs in the Indian way & repeated charges and repulses took place on each side." The tide turned when Tecumseh was killed. "They gave the loudest yells I ever heard from human beings," one veteran stated, "and that ended the fight." After the battle, Anthony Shane identified the chief's body, which had been partially skinned for razor strops by the victorious Kentuckians. The death of Tecumseh marked the end of his pan-Indian alliance.[11]

A few days after the battle various Indian nations sought peace. Harrison declared that the Miamis and Potawatomis "deserve no mercy, they were the tribes most favored by us," yet he granted "an armistice in order to get them to their own grounds where they will

be perfectly in our power." While the Indians rebuilt their burned villages, he urged the secretary of war to send enough supplies "to relieve
their immediate and pressing wants." No land cessions should be
demanded, since once peace was established the United States would
be able to take whatever it wanted for "a consideration so trifling
that it ought not to be regarded." Harrison resigned his command
on 11 May 1814, and the following July conducted a grand council
at Greenville, which demanded that all the nations must side with
the United States against the British. Charley (Ketunga), son of the
Soldier and William Wells's boyhood companion at Snake-fish Town,
was the chief who most vigorously opposed Harrison, denouncing
the destruction of the Miami villages and insisting that his people
wanted to remain neutral. Nonetheless, he signed the agreement,
which "marked the end of Miami military power and influence on
the frontier." Harrison gloated over the downfall of this once mighty
nation: "The Miamies . . . are a poor, miserable, drunken set, diminishing every year . . . as soon as there is peace, or the British can no
longer intrigue, they will sell [their land]." Historians often note that
the Treaty of Ghent reestablished the status quo and resolved none
of the maritime issues that supposedly had caused the War of 1812,
but the Indian nations of the Old Northwest had suffered a devastating blow.[12]

THE FAMILY OF WILLIAM WELLS

In December 1812 the estate of William Wells, which would prove
to be both a blessing and a curse for his family, was appraised at
approximately nine thousand dollars, including five adult slaves and
their six children. Thanks to Harrison's policies, which were backed
by most French habitants and Kentucky settlers, the federal ban on
slavery in Indiana Territory was evaded. Two of Wells's slaves, for
example, were listed as indentured servants. He left behind $615 in
cash and was owed some $3,500 more from loans. His home "Wells-
ington," burned during the siege of Fort Wayne, was on a 320-acre
preemption known as "the Wells Reserve," and he owned an additional 1,200 acres near Piqua. He was a wealthy man for his time,

albeit not as rich as John Johnston had charged. His will of 17 January 1810 stated that his wife Polly and five of his children—Anne, Rebecca, William Wayne, Mary, and Samuel—should "share and share alike" the inheritance. Left out of the will were his daughter Jane by an unknown Miami and Yelverton Peyton, who would not be born until the fall of 1812. When Sam Wells came home from the war in 1814, he had lost not only his brother William and his son Levi, but also his wife Mary, who died 15 October 1812. In addition to his own six children, Sam helped educate those of Sweet Breeze and his brother. Rebecca attended a school in Lexington, where she was studying "the sciences . . . that our dear father wished for me to learn," while William Wayne prepared for West Point.[13]

In 1815 Anne married Dr. William Turner, who had come to Fort Wayne as a surgeon's mate five years earlier. Rebecca joined her sister at Wellsington and in 1817 married Capt. James Hackley, considered by her uncle Sam to be "one of my best young friends . . . a lovely man." That same year in Louisville, Polly Geiger Wells married Robert Turner, who became the stepfather of young Samuel and Yelverton. This match lasted many years but it put the Turner brothers at odds over control of Wells's estate. Dr. Turner's heavy drinking and extravagant living left Anne feeling "half deranged." He successfully conspired to replace Stickney as Indian agent, inflating his qualifications by claiming authorship of William Wells's essay on Miami culture. His tenure was brief, however; in 1820 he was fired for "unsatisfactory conduct" and died the following year. Because they profited by the Miami status of their wives, Turner and Hackley were called "Indians when interested and Whites when not." After Rebecca received land at the Treaty of St. Marys in 1818, Captain Hackley retired to farm his wife's grant. In 1826 during a dispute over the ownership of Wellsington, Hackley locked his wife in one room while he tried to murder Anne in another. That evening he hung himself. The widowed sisters were known in Fort Wayne as "ladies of refinement and intelligent piety" who held "a fine social position among our best people." They both died in 1834.[14]

In 1821 William Wayne graduated fourth in his class at West Point and served as a first lieutenant in the U.S. artillery. Due to a drinking problem and a "wayward disposition," in 1831 he resigned his commission and died in September of the following year. There are two versions of his death: one that he fell off a steamer crossing Lake Superior and drowned; the other that he succumbed to cholera at Erie, Pennsylvania. In March 1817 Mary Wells went with Sam, his new wife Elizabeth, and sixty other pioneers to Missouri. Four years later she married James Wolcott. When the Wells Reserve was sold in 1826, the couple used the proceeds to purchase land at Maumee, Ohio, where James became a judge. The Wolcott House is now a museum. Mary, who died in 1843, had seven children. In 1882 her son James wrote that the Wolcott family was "proud of our Little Turtle blood and of our Captain Wells blood. We try to keep up the customs of our ancestors." The family had preserved "the tomahawk . . . Wells had at the time of his death," a dress sword given by Harrison, and "a great many books . . . [which showed that Wells] was trying to improve himself. He did all he could to educate his children."[15]

When Anne learned that Jane was "in a state of want," she brought her half sister to live at Wellsington. Like William Wells's other Miami children, Jane received land at the treaties of 1818 and 1826. In 1830 she married John H. Griggs. They had six children and for fifty years resided near the mouth of the Mississinewa at Peru, where Jane was known as "a lady of refinement and position." In 1840 most Miamis were compelled to sell their land and move to Oklahoma, but several hundred remained behind. Today the headquarters of the Miami Nation of Indiana is located in Peru.[16]

Sam Wells had six children with his second wife. They lived in O'Fallon, Missouri, next to Rebeckah and Nathan Heald, on the former Zumwalt Plantation. When he died at the age of seventy-six in 1830, Sam owned more than two thousand acres of land and was considered one of the state's most prominent pioneers. His grave is in the Mount Zion Cemetery of O'Fallon near those of Nathan, who never fully recovered from his wounds and died in 1832, and Rebeckah, who died in 1857. She wrote a memoir about her life that included reminiscences of her uncle William Wells, but it was lost during the Civil War when troops from Illinois sacked her home. Of William's other siblings, two should be mentioned. Hayden went to Tennessee in 1779 and helped settle the Cumberland Valley. Elizabeth converted to Catholicism as a girl, became a nun, and in 1812 cofounded the

Sisters of Charity. "Sister Mary Rose," who later became a Dominican, died 25 June 1845 and is buried at St. Catherine, Kentucky.

THE SIGNIFICANCE OF WILLIAM WELLS

The Wells family migration across the Appalachians to Kentucky is
representative of the westward movement of Americans in the late
eighteenth and early nineteenth centuries. Sam Wells, who spent
thirty-five years fighting Indians, exemplified those restless, if not
relentless, pioneers. Yet the life of his younger brother William is of
greater significance, precisely because he was not a typical pioneer.
After a frontier boyhood on Beargrass Creek, Wells was captured and
became a Miami. Following his Vision Quest, "Blacksnake" went on
the warpath, raiding Kentucky and waylaying flatboats on the Ohio.
He fought for his victorious father-in-law Little Turtle in the battles
against Harmar and St. Clair. By the time he switched sides to work
for Rufus Putnam at the Treaty of Vincennes in 1792, Wells had lived
for eight years with the Miamis, an experience that left him with
divided loyalties for the rest of his life.

His status as a Miami enabled Wells to witness tribal councils on
the Maumee in 1792 and 1793; because of his unmatched knowledge
of the Indians, General Wayne relied on his elite scouting party for
invaluable intelligence while they protected the army from ambush.
Even after Wells was wounded, his advice proved crucial at Fallen
Timbers. The next year he stood as an interpreter between Little Turtle and Wayne during their heated debates at the all-important Treaty
of Greenville.

A man of strong resources and undaunted courage, Wells, like
many Americans, prided himself on his independence; yet, as are we
all, he was often shaped by forces beyond his control. The failed policies and faulty treaties of Britain and the United States, exacerbated
by the insatiable land hunger of the pioneers, brought continual conflict to the frontier. Albeit well intentioned, the decisions of Washington's Secretary of War Henry Knox led to Little Turtle's bloody
triumphs and then to Wayne's decisive victory. Jefferson's Indian
policy, despite its idealistic rhetoric, in practice was a duplicitous

program that Wells was expected to implement. Not surprisingly, both his ineffectual efforts to "civilize" the Indians and his able assistance at Harrison's treaties, which stripped the Wabash Indians of their homeland, call for censure. During this phase of his life, Wells was no hero, but his mixed motives and questionable actions still merit our attention. William Faulkner said that he wrote about "the human heart in conflict with itself." Better than any other American of his time, the divided heart and mind of William Wells epitomize the decline and fall of what Richard White has termed "the middle ground," which had flourished in the late seventeenth century when French fur traders and Indians of the *pays d'en haut* forged a new, intricate system of coexistence.[17]

In the last decade of his life Wells made many enemies, whose criticisms have encouraged a few historians to vilify him as, for example, "the most notorious and unscrupulous [American] agent" of his time. Because he warned that the Prophet's followers were "religiously mad" and that Tecumseh's confederacy posed a threat, he was hated by their supporters. Because he had second thoughts about treaties he helped achieve, and cautioned the Indians about their harmful effects, he was distrusted by Harrison and the government. The most vituperative attacks on Wells came from John Johnston, his Fort Wayne rival. To add perspective on this dispute, we must remember how common were character assassination as well as dueling at the time. John Adams's caustic remarks about Hamilton still have the power to shock, and one can only imagine what Hamilton said to infuriate Burr. After the death of Wells, the situation at Fort Wayne did not change for the better. One observer wrote that the Indians were "generally displeased" with Stickney, who was "not well qualified" for his position. Stickney, for his part, grew tired of the "fickle minded" Indians and even suggested a change in their diet to bring on diseases that "in 6 or 8 months [would cause] great mortality." Dr. Turner, while seeking Stickney's job, accused him of "extreme incapacity" and of giving "presents to two Indian women in return for their favors." Although these charges were "unfounded and untenable," Turner became the Indian agent, but "his habits were adverse to a proper execution of his duties." In addition Stickney suspected Johnston of "acting a double part notwithstanding his professions of friendship," while Johnston reported to the secretary of war: "I scarcely ever knew a man more truly unfortunate in conciliating the good will of the people around him than Mr. S." These backstabbing squabbles suggest that Johnston's harsh critiques of Wells should be taken with a grain of salt. Despite his shortcomings, Wells would never have welcomed, as did Stickney and Johnston, an Old Northwest without Indians.[18]

I have written this book to present a detailed and fully documented account of the remarkable life of William Wells, who deserves to be much better known, and to depict the story of the Ohio Valley frontier from both the Indian and American points of view. It is not for me alone to determine the final significance of William Wells, but I trust my analytical narrative makes his importance obvious and that it also will stimulate interest in a period and region that have too often been misinterpreted or ignored. The truth of history is to be found, I believe, not only in large perspectives but also in small particulars: understanding the origins of Jefferson's Indian policy is essential, but so is the fact that an Indian who captured Oliver Spencer ground his teeth as he smoked his pipe.

NOTES

ABBREVIATIONS

ASP,IA	*American State Papers, Indian Affairs*, vols. 1–2
ASP,MA	*American State Papers, Military Affairs*, vols. 1–2
BHC	Burton Historical Collection, Detroit Public Library
CHS	Chicago Historical Society
DM	Lymon C. Draper Collection, Wisconsin Historical Society
FCHQ	*Filson Club Historical Quarterly*
FHS	Filson Historical Society, Louisville, Kentucky
HP	*Papers of William Henry Harrison*, Douglas E. Clanin, ed. (microfilm)
HSP	Historical Society of Pennsylvania, Philadelphia
IHS	Indiana Historical Society, Indianapolis
JCB	John Carter Brown Library, Brown University, Provincetown, R.I.
JCC	*Journals of the Continental Congress*, National Archives
LC	Library of Congress, Washington, D.C.
MHS	Massachusetts Historical Society, Boston
MPHC	*Michigan Pioneer and Historical Collections*, 40 vols., Detroit Public Library
NA	National Archives, Washington, D.C.
NASW	National Archives, Secretary of War, Indian Affairs, Letters Sent and Received
OHS	Ohio Historical Society, Columbus
OHSQ	*Ohio Historical Society Quarterly*
RKHS	*Register of the Kentucky Historical Society*
WCL	William L. Clements Library, University of Michigan, Ann Arbor
WMQ	*William and Mary Quarterly*
WP	Anthony Wayne Papers, HSP and OHS (transcript: cited by volume *and* page)
WRLM	*Western Review and Literary Magazine*

PREFACE

1. Hutton, "William Wells," 183–222; Carter, *Life and Times of Little Turtle*; A. J. Youngson, *The Prince and the Pretender: A Study in the Writing of History* (New York: Routledge, Kegan & Paul, 1985), 23.

2. Gilbert, *God Gave Us This Country*, 228; White, *Middle Ground*, 500–501; Quaife, *Chicago*, 224.

3. See Carnes, Mark C., ed., *Novel History: Novelists and Historians Confront America's Past (and Each Other)* (New York: Simon & Schuster, 2001).

4. Heath, "Re-evaluating 'The Fort-Wayne Manuscript,'" 158–88.

5. Heath, "William Wells: From Miami Warrior to American Spy," 102–13.

6. For the past forty years Washington's biographers have failed to make adequate use of Wiley Sword's *President Washington's Indian War*, which is well researched and largely reliable on the key battles.

7. Wood, *Empire of Liberty*, 677.

8. For Ranke and history, see Robert Darnton, "Introduction," in *George Washington's Front Teeth* (W. W. Norton, 2003), xiii, 175n3; for paraphrasing and historical writing, see O'Brien, *Long Affair*, xi–xiv, 69–70.

PROLOGUE

For overviews of the battle of Fort Dearborn, see Quaife, *Chicago*, Keating, *Rising Up*, and Ferguson, *Illinois*.

1. Harrison to Eustis, 8 July 1812, Thornbrough, *Letter Book*, 151–52.

2. Cave, "Shawnee Prophet," argues that the battle did not significantly diminish the Prophet's importance. Jortner, *Gods of Prophetstown*, overstates the case; Sugden, *Tecumseh: A Life*, and Edmunds, *Shawnee Prophet*, suggest otherwise.

3. Edwards to Eustis, 10 February 1812; Jean Lalime to Benjamin Howard, 4 February 1812. Knopf, *Letters*, Part I: 42–43, 32.

4. Edwards to Eustis, 8 April 1812, Clanin, *HP*; Harrison to Eustis, 14 April 1812, Esarey, *Messages*, 2: 32–34; Edwards to Eustis, 12 May 1812; Nathan Heald to John Whistler, 15 April 1812, Knopf, *Letters*, Part I, 134, 196; Heald to Wells, 15 April 1812, in Quaife, *Chicago*, 213; Jacobs, *Beginnings of U.S. Army*, 383.

5. For a recent overview of the war, see Stagg, *The War of 1812*, 171–86, which has a useful essay on the standard scholarship.

6. Henry Clay, in Allen, *Indian Allies*, 118; Henry Adams, *History*, 2: 439. See Reginald Horsman, "Who Were the War Hawks," and Roger Brown, "The War Hawks of 1812: An Historical Myth," *IMH* 60 (1964): 121–36, 137–51.

7. Horsman, *Expansion*, 256–57; Hickey, *War of 1812*, 40–48; Hull to Eustis, 6 March 1812, Knopf, *Letters*, Part I, 78–80.

8. Askin to William Claus, 18 July 1812, in Cruikshank, *Documents*, 436; Harrison to Eustis, 6 August 1812, in Clanin, *HP*, 739–40.

9. Hull in McAfee, *History*, 89; Hull to Eustis, 29 July 1812, and to Heald, 29 July 1812, in Quaife, *Chicago*, 215–16.

10. Wells to Harrison, 3 August 1812, Clanin, *HP*, 735; Darius Heald interview, 25–26 May 1868, DM, 21S, 40–59.

11. Wells's daughters and his son William Wayne were by his Miami wife, Sweet Breeze. She died in 1805; Sammy was his first child with Polly, who gave birth to their second son, Yelverton Peyton, that fall.

12. Wilson, "Chicago," CHS; Quaife, *Chicago*, 164–65; Curry, *Story of Old Fort Dearborn*, 27; Matthew Irwin to John Mason, 12 October 1810, in Quaife, "Fort Dearborn Massacre," 567. Thomas Hamilton called it "one of the strongest wooden garrisons that I ever saw," to Lt. Col. Daniel Bissell, 24 August 1812, NA, LR, Adjutant General, reel 7, 107.

13. Wilson, "Chicago," 4; Van Voorhis to Eustis, 16 May 12; Irwin to Mason, 10 October 1812, in Quaife, "Fort Dearborn Massacre," 570. For Kinzie and the fur-trading community, see Keating, *Rising Up*, 21–32, and Ferguson, *Illinois*, 58–61.

14. There are at least twenty-five accounts of the battle either by participants or based on their stories. Mrs. John H. Kinzie's *Wau Bun* glorifies her husband's father, a man she never met. I have given priority to the accounts written by those closest to the event while taking into consideration the pro-Kinzie bias of some of them. Quaife, "James Corbin," 219–22; A. H. Edwards, in Wentworth, *Early Chicago*, 55; DM, 13YY, 55; "Darius Heald's Narrative," in Quaife, *Chicago*, 410; DM, 23S; Heald to Eustis, 23 October 1812, in Quaife, *Chicago*, 406; Williams, "Kinzie's Narrative," 347–52. Forts Wayne, Harrison, and Meigs withstood short sieges in the early part of the war. Fort Dearborn was 160 miles away from the next fort. Ferguson discusses the relative merits of the accounts, *Illinois*, 233–46.

15. Daniel Curtis to Jacob Kingsbury, 21 September 1812, Indiana Territory Collection, IHS, M 398; Peckham, "Recent Acquisitions," 409–18; Kinzie, in Williams, "Kinzie's Narrative," 351–52; Hunt, in DM, 21S, 46–47.

16. Helm, in Quaife, *Chicago*, 420; Heald, in Quaife, "Fort Dearborn Massacre," 116. Lieutenant Helm's account is suspect because it is so long, while Captain Heald's account is too brief—why doesn't he detail what led up to the tragedy? Helm's account places Heald in as bad a light as possible, while Darius Heald's account, based on what his parents told him, has the opposite purpose. Helm, for example, claims that the fort possessed six thousand pounds of powder, while another contemporary, Thomas Forsyth, gave a figure of 850 pounds. Quaife, *Chicago*, 246.

17. Williams, "Kinzie's Narrative," 351–52.

18. Joseph Bourassa's Potawatomi version in DM, 21S, 194; Pokagon, "Massacre," 652; Black Hawk, in Hurlbut, *Chicago Antiquities*, 181.

19. Helm, in Quaife, *Chicago*, 420. Helm's account states that Black Partridge returned his medal. See Alexander Robinson's Potawatomi version in DM, 21S, 286. Thomas Forsyth to Governor Howard, 7 September 1812, Carter, *Territorial Papers*, 16: 262; McAfee, *History*, 113–14; Williams, "Kinzie's Narrative," 352.

20. Johnston, DM, 11YY, 10; Hunt, DM, 21S, 47.

CHAPTER 1

On Kentucky during the Revolution: Hammon and Taylor, *Virginia's Western War*. The Filson Historical Society Archives (FHS) are essential for early Louisville, as are the Draper Manuscripts and Yates, *Two Hundred Years*.

1. In 1678 a John Wells received 363 acres on Doges Creek in Virginia's Northern Neck. His son Samuel inherited that land and then moved to Stafford. Beth Mitchell, *Beginning at the White Oak* (Berryville, Va.: Virginia Book Company, 1979), 85; *Prince William County, Deed Book Liber D, 1738–40* (1984), 5–9, 20; Fairfax Harrison, "The Country Called There Doages," in *Landmarks of Old Prince William* (Baltimore: Gateway, 1987), 41–55; George H. S. King, *Register of Overwharton Parish* (Fredericksburg, Va.: Southern Historical Press, 1961), 127. The birthdates of Samuel Wells's siblings are: Charles, 10 January 1740; John, 3 July 1742; Haydon, 9 September 1744; Eleanor, 19 April 1747; Benjamin, 22 August 1751; *Prince William Deed Book Q, 1763–8*, Part II, 18; *Order Book Abstracts of Prince William County, Virginia, 1753–7*. For the Farrows: Donald L. Wilson, "Hollywood out of Prince William," *Prince William Reliquary* 3, no. 1 (Jan. 2004), 29–30; Lee Lansing, *Dumfries Short Subjects* 23: 6, 12. For Farrow and Wells land on Quantico Creek: Bull Run Regional Library, Manassas, Virginia.

2. Fitzpatrick, *Writings*, 1: 773–76, 300–305, 470; Charles and Virginia Hamrick, *Colonial Supermarket: Daniel Payne's Ledger* (Athens, Ga.: New Papyrus, 2007), 15; *Prince William County Deed Book Q, 1763–8*, Part II, 18; Donald Wilson to K. L. Gould, 31 July 2001, Wells file, Bull Run Regional Library.

3. Griffin, *American Leviathan*, 60; Washington to Crawford, 21 September 1767, Butterfield, *Washington-Crawford Letters*, 3.

4. Thomas Gage to Lord Hillsborough, in Downes, *Council Fires*, 144; Map #22, Upper Tyrone Township, Uniontown, Pa., Public Library; see Hunt, *Wars of the Iroquois*; Samuel Murphy interview, 3 September 1846, DM, 3S, 1–67.

5. The children of Samuel and Anne Wells born in Virginia were Sam, 1754; Carty, 1757; Hayden, 1759; and Margaret, 1762 (approximate dates); in addition to William Wells's birth in 1770, Yelverton (possibly Charles) and Elizabeth Wells were born on Jacobs Creek; McClure, *Diary*, 62–63, 78, 96, 101, 105–109; Cresswell, *Journal*, 62–63, 97–100. Crawford's wife's sister Elizabeth Vance married Edward Doyle; if they had daughters, one might fit Cresswell's description.

6. Crumrine, *Virginia Court Records*, 46, 119, 127, 333.

7. Thwaites, *Dunmore's War*, 368–72; Downes, *Council Fires*, 163–64, 174–76; Murphy, DM, 3S, 7–8; Hoffman, *Simon Girty*, 57–58. See White, *Middle Ground*, 351–65.

8. Depositions of Thomas Young, John McIntire, Thomas Sweet, and Hayden Wells in the case of Alexander Marshall v. Thomas Young, DM, 6BB and 15C; Deposition of General Samuel Wells, 4 July 1805, DM, 6BB. The Wells Company of 1775 consisted of Samuel Wells, Hayden Wells, Thomas Tibbs, John Tibbs, Jonathan Higgs, William Triplett, John Rust, Thomas Young, and Richard Masterson.

9. In 1838 Joseph Shaw swore that he served in the Virginia Continental Line in the company of Capt. Samuel Wells in the regiment of Col. William Oldham, who did not

achieve high rank until 1791. NA, Old War Invalid File No. 14441. Hassler, *Old West-moreland*, 60–66; Murphy, DM, 3S, 22, 31; Carter, *Correspondence of General Gage*, 152.

10. John Brown to William Preston, in Van Every, *Company of Heroes*, 50.

11. Heald, DM, 23S, 58; McDowell Collection, FHS, Mss A, M 138a, 13: 219; William and Penelope Pope had eight children; Jane Pope Helm, at least three; Benjamin Pope had three sons; Van Every, *Ark of Empire*, 36.

12. Heald, DM, 23S, 58.

13. See R. E. Banta, *The Ohio* (New York: Rinehart, 1949).

14. Crogan, *Journal*, in Craig, *Olden Time*, 1: 406.

15. Jennings, Kathleen, *Louisville's First Families* (Louisville: Standard Printing, c. 1920), 70–71; Danke Dandridge, *George Michael Bedinger* (1909), 63.

16. Clark to Mason, in James, *Clark Papers*, 1: 138. The most recent biography is Nester, *George Rogers Clark*.

17. James, *George Rogers Clark*, 145; James, *Clark Papers*, 1: 272–78.

18. James, *Clark Papers*, 1: 243–44, 238.

19. Yates, *Two Hundred Years*, 2–10.

20. Dandridge, *Bedinger*, 54–73; Butler, *History of Kentucky*, 108–109; Simon Kenton, DM, 5BB, 115; James Patton, DM, 49J, 89; Talbert, *Benjamin Logan*, 74–81; Hammon and Taylor, *Virginia's Western War*, 106–107.

21. James, *Clark Papers*, 1: 150–51, 117; Hoffman, *Simon Girty*, 135–37; Collins, *Historical Sketches*, 172–73.

22. Todd to Preston, DM, 4B, 66.

23. See Trapp, "John Floyd," 1; Anna M. Carlidge, "Colonel John Floyd: Reluctant Adventurer," *RKHS* 66 (Oct. 1968): 336, 317–66; Trapp, "John Floyd," 1–24; Mrs. Laetita Preston Floyd, DM, 6J, 89–108.

24. Abernathy, *Western Land*, 191. Floyd's Station was on the west side of present Breckinridge Lane near the Jamestown Apartments. Hammon, "Beargrass Stations," 154–55; Yates, *Two Hundred Years*, 13–14.

25. Beckner, "Clickenbeard Interview," 112; Young, *Westward*, 74; Floyd, in Hammon, "dangerous situation," 219–20; Judge Moses Boone, DM, 12C, 28.

26. Fleming, "Journal," in Mereness, *Travels*, 622, 630, 636–37, 641; Durrett, *Centenary*, 66–67.

27. Hogan, "James Wade," *RKHS*, 30; General Frederick Haldimand to Lord George Germain, 23 October 1781, Haldimand Papers, *MPHC*, 10: 530.

28. Marshall, *History of Kentucky*, I: 104; Davis Gess, in James, *Clark Papers*, I: 398; Floyd, in Hammon, "dangerous situation," 220–21.

29. Carter, *Territorial Papers*, 7: cxxxv; Quaife, "Detroit Invaded Kentucky," 62–65. Young, *Westward*, 89. For McKee, see Nelson, *Man of Distinction*.

30. McKee, in Quaife, "Detroit Invaded Kentucky," 65.

31. Heald, DM, 23S, 58; Hammon and Taylor, *Virginia's Western War*, 145; Wilson, DM, 9J, 21; James, *Clark Papers*, I: 452–53, 482; Simon Kenton interview, DM, 5BB, 123; McAfee, "Life and Times" (Jan. 1927), 3; Beckner, "Clickenbeard Interview," 128; Hammon and Taylor, *Virginia's Western War*, 130; James, *Clark Papers*, 1: 483.

32. May to Beall, 22 August 1780, FCHS; James, *Clark Papers*, 1: 452–53; Talbert, "Kentucky Invades Ohio—1780," 298.

33. Vince Akers, "The Long Run Massacre," 26 January 1996, FHS, 19. Painted Stone was "on Clear Creek about midway . . . between the Eminence Road and the Burks Branch Pike," Akers, "Frontier Shelby County," July 1779, FHS, 976.884, A 315, 2. Murphy said he was "billeted at Wells' Station, some miles up Beargrass," DM, 3S, 37. Probably he meant Linn's Station, located west of present Hurstbourne Lane, Hammon, "Early Louisville and Beargrass Stations," 157.

34. John Floyd to Jefferson, 16 April 1781, James, *Clark Papers*, 1: 529–31.

35. George William Beattie and Helen Pruitt Beattie, "Colonel William Linn— Soldier Indian Fighter," *Pioneer Linns of Kentucky* (privately printed), FHS, 220–48.

36. Ronald R. Van Stockum, Sr., "Squire Boone," FHS, 18; Moses Boone, DM, 19C, 35.

37. James, *Clark Papers*, 1: 583; James Chamber's Statement, DM, 4S; Haldimand to Germain, 23 October 1781, *MPHC*, 10: 530; "Anderson's Journal," in James McBride, *Lives of the Early Settlers of Butler County, Ohio* (Cincinnati: Robert Clarke, 1869), 279.

38. James, *Clark Papers*, 1: 598, 602–603; Murphy, DM, 3C37; William Crawford's brother Valentine had a station on Jacobs Creek near the Wells family.

39. Thompson to De Peyster, 26 September 1781, McKee to De Peyster, 26 September 1781, *MPHC*, 10: 515–17.

40. G. T. Wilcox, "Floyd's Defeat," *Louisville Courier-Journal*, 28 July 1880. Wilcox was the son of Squire Boone's daughter Sarah and spoke with Isaiah Boone. His account says that "a man named Carris" accompanied Ballard, but other sources state that it was Sam Wells; Isaiah Boone, DM, 19C, 91; Akers, "Long Run Massacre," 9.

41. Isaiah Boone, DM, 19C, 97.

42. Isaiah Boone and Moses Boone, DM, 19C, 95–96, 36–37.

43. A historical marker on U.S. 60 near Long Run states: "Scene of massacre, undoubtedly the bloodiest one in early Kentucky, which took place in 1781. A Miami Indian party killed over 60 pioneers en route from Squire Boone's Painted Stone Station to safety at forts at Falls of Ohio." The actual number killed was probably nine to fifteen, not counting Samuel Wells and a dozen more killed the next day. The battle was originally called "Boone's Defeat."

44. Akers, "Long Run Massacre," 19; Murphy, DM, 3C, 40–41; Isaiah Boone, DM, 19C, 96; McKee to De Peyster, 26 September 1781, *MPHC*, 10: 517; Murphy, DM, 3C, 45; Collins, *Historical Sketches*, 173. Collins praised Sam Wells's act of selfless courage on two other occasions, 362, 519. Sam was 26 or 27 at the time of Floyd's Defeat.

45. Floyd to Clark, 14 September 1781, James, *Clark Papers*, I: 604. Samuel Murphy and four others were captured. Murphy, DM, 3C, 43. Murphy, Thomas Rosencroft, and Valentine King were taken to Detroit; all eventually returned. Hoffman, *Simon Girty*, 155; Murphy, DM, 3C, 44; McKee to De Peyster, 26 September 81, *MPHC*, 10: 518. At Detroit in October 1781, Miami warriors gave De Peyster seven scalps from the massacre.

46. Stockman, "Boone," FHS, 16–20.

47. Wells file, card catalogue, FHS.

48. Will of Samuel Wells, Wells file, FHS.

49. Sullivan's Station was near the Heritage House at 3411 Bardstown Road, Yates, *Two Hundred Years*, 15; Hammon, "Beargrass Stations," 158; Sullivan to Clark, James, *Clark Papers*, 1: 528; John May to Sam Beall, 14 July 1786, FHS.

50. See Drake, *Pioneer Life*, 3–30.

51. William Croghan to William Davies, 6 July 1782; William Irving to George Washington, 11 July 1782; John Hardin to William Davies, 28 July 1782, in James, *Clark Papers*, 2: 71, 76–77, 80. People in western Pennsylvania suspected the Indians at Gnadenhütten of aiding war parties against their settlements; in truth, the Moravian missionaries were supporting the American cause. Wallace, *Heckewelder*, 189–202. Americans made Crawford's torture a cautionary tale about the barbarity of their "savage" enemies, conveniently forgetting the massacre at Gnadenhütten, which caused it. The Indians did not forget. Tecumseh often mentioned it.

52. Steele to Benjamin Harrison, 26 August 1782, Daniel Boone to Harrison, 11 September 1782, in James, *Clark Papers*, 2: 97, 113.

53. James, *Clark Papers*, 2: 152.

54. Legras, 1 August 1782, James, *Clark Papers*, 2: 85; McKee to De Peyster, 28 August 1782, Canadian Archives, Ottawa, Colonial Office Records, Ser. 2, 20: 285–88; DM 52J, 28; Robert E. McDowell, "The Wilderness Road in Jefferson County," *Louisville Courier Journal & Times Magazine*, 20 June 1967, 20–22.

55. McDowell, "Wilderness Road," 12; a source says Sam Wells was there, DM, 13CC, 12; Hammon and Taylor, *Virginia's Western War*, 178; Tapp, "John Floyd," 222–23; Marshall, *History of Kentucky*, 1: 139; Isaac Hite to father, 26 April 1783, FHS.

56. Robert E. McDowell, "Bullitt's Lick: The Related Saltworks and Settlements," *FCHQ* 30 (1956), 241–69; Akers, "Frontier Shelby County," 25, 30. The station was east of the junction of Harrington Mill Pike and Scotts Station Road, "Taylor vs McCampbell" Bundle 157, Shelby County courthouse. Fresh water still flows from the spring.

57. Collins, *Historical Sketches*, 363; Durrett, *Centenary*, 71.

58. In Ira V. Birdwhistell, *Gathered at the River* (Louisville: Long Run Baptist Association, 1978), 4.

59. Heald, DM, 23S, 62–65; Butler, "Outline," 104; Hall, *Romance*, 113–19; Hammon and Taylor, *Virginia's Western War*, 252. The Waller-Williams Environmental School, 2415 Rockford Lane, is on the former site of Robert's Pond. My thanks to Judy Hill for this information.

CHAPTER 2

The best essay on the captivity experience is Axtell, "The White Indians," *Invasion Within*, 302–28, although he understates the negative side. Standard critical studies are Derounian-Stolda, *The Indian Captivity Narrative*; Ebersole, *Captured by Texts*; Namias, *White Captives*; and Sayre, *Les Sauvages Américains*. For the culture of the Miamis: Wells, "Manners and Customs"; Trowbridge, *Traditions*; and Rafert, *Miami Indians*. See Hutton, "William Wells," and Carter, *Life and Times of Little Turtle*.

1. Butler, "Outline," 104–105; Hall, *Romance,* 114–20. Butler had access to people who knew the story; Hall interviewed Dr. Lewis F. Linn, son of William Linn, in the 1830s. Most of the narratives cited in this chapter describe captivities from 1755 to 1795 in the Old Northwest. Although both Algonquian and Iroquoian cultures were involved, the treatment of captives among woodland Indians was similar. Ten concern boys ages 8–18. The three Miami narratives are about Thomas Morris, John Flinn, and Frances Slocum. Nelson, *Jonathan Alder,* 30. The Alder narrative is not exactly a "primary source." See Nelson's "Introduction" to the narrative, 1–25. Dunn, a scholar of the Miami language, interviewed Little Turtle's granddaughter Kilsokwa (The Setting Sun); she said that "the Miamis called William Wells A-pe-kon-it . . . the name of a plant called the 'wild potato' or Indian potato." Dunn added that a-pe-kon-it is known as the "ground-nut" or "wild bean" (*apios tuberosa*), *True Indian Stories,* 114–15, 254. Whether the name referred to the wild carrot, potato, or bean, Wells's hair color probably was the inspiration, although one Miami tradition claims it was because of the way the hungry boy devoured a bowl of wild carrot soup. Meginness, *Frances Slocum,* 28, 141–42; Beckner, "Benjamin Allen," 72, 74.

2. Hall, *Romance,* 114–15; Butler, "Outline," 104.

3. Johnston, "Narrative," 254–55; Spencer, *Captivity,* 46; Tanner, *Narrative,* 28; Axtell, *Invasion Within,* 309.

4. Tanner, *Narrative,* 24. Although many captives were eventually ransomed, and some were treated as slaves, adoption or death at the stake would have been foremost in Billy Wells's mind.

5. Johnston, "Narrative," 264, 261; Henry, *Travels,* 98; Benjamin Gilbert, "Captivity," Louden, *Outrages,* 2: 139; Beckner, "Benjamin Allen," 74.

6. Seaver, *Mary Jemison,* 30; Nelson, *Jonathan Alder,* 32.

7. Spencer, *Captivity,* 54–55; Johnson, "Narrative," 265, 279; Brickell, "Captivity," 44.

8. Ridout, "Captivity," 349–50; Seaver, *Mary Jemison,* 23; Spencer, *Captivity,* 66.

9. Nelson, *Jonathan Alder,* 36, 38; Brickell, "Captivity," 45.

10. Gilbert, "Captivity," Louden, *Outrages,* 2: 75; Henry, *Travels,* 112; M'Cullough, "Narrative," 257–58.

11. "The prisoners had to run the gauntlet, but seemed to merely go through a formality & did not try to hurt their children captives," Castleman Girls Captivity, DM, 19S, 231.

12. Smith, *Scoouwa,* 22. Smith was told the gauntlet "was only an old custom the Indians had, and it was like how do you do; after that he would be well used," 24; Bond, "Charles Stuart," 66; Brickell, "Captivity," 46; Gilbert, "Captivity," Louden, *Outrages,* 2: 135–36; Nelson, *Jonathan Alder,* 42–44.

13. Hall, *Romance,* 116; Moore, "A Captive," 289–90. The captive was Margaret Paulee.

14. Trowbridge, *Traditions,* 89. Lewis Cass wrote that the membership was confined to the Bear family and the name of the society was "Ons-e-won-sa," 88n9. Cass "suspected that the Wabeno meetings [were] a corruption of Medawin rites . . .

[and] sometimes used human victims," Anson, *Miami Indians*, 25; Morris, "Journal," Thwaites, *Travels*, 1: 312–16. Twenty years later Pechewa (Wild Cat), known as Chief John B. Richardville, rescued a prisoner to be burned at the stake at the urging of his mother, Tacumwah, sister of Little Turtle, to show his authority. See Meginness, *Francis Slocum*, 199–202; Wallace, *Heckewelder*, 271; Heckewelder reported the chief's name as Gawiahätte, a Delaware word that means Hedgehog; Dunn noted that there "must be some error" in Heckewelder's report and that the Miami word for hedgehog is ah-kah-wit. *True Indian Stories*, 114. Rufus Putnam spelled the chief's name Kaweahatta, *Memoirs*, 307, 323.

15. Godfroy, *Stories*, 100; Wells, "Manners and Customs," 184. My essay "Reevaluating 'The Fort Wayne Manuscript'" collates two articles Wells wrote about the Indians and published in 1820 with two later revised versions, one published anonymously as *The Fort Wayne Manuscript* (1883), the other falsely claimed to be the work of his son-in-law, William Turner. All quotes from Wells's two essays are cited from my essay. Rafert, *Miami Indians*, 138; Smith, *Scoouwa*, 29–30; M'Cullough, "Narrative," 260; Morris, "Journal," 315–16; Nelson, *Jonathan Alder*, 45; in Heard, *White Into Red*, 61.

16. Smith, *Scoouwa*, 30; Henry, *Travels*, 111–12.

17. Smith, *Scoouwa*, 31; M'Cullough, "Narrative," 259–60; Ridout, "Captivity," 348.

18. Frank Cushing, the most famous case of "going native" in the nineteenth century, became a member of a Zuni secret society. Sylvia Gronewold, "Did Frank Hamilton Cushing Go Native?" *Crossing Cultural Boundaries*, Solon T. Kimball and James B. Watson, eds. (San Francisco: Chandler, 1972), 33–50. Hunter, *Manners and Customs*, 22; Hunter, *Memoirs of a Captivity*, 214–15. Hunter's narrative is controversial; see Drinnon, *White Savage*; Calloway, "White Renegades," 43–66; Heard, *White Into Red*; Ackerknecht, "White Indians," 15–36; Hallowell, "American Indians," 519–31.

19. Crevecoeur, *Letters from an American Farmer* (1782; repr., New York: Albert & Charles Boni, 1925), 305–306; Alden T. Vaughan and Daniel K. Richter, "Crossing the Cultural Divide: Indians and New Englanders, 1605–1763," *Proceedings of the American Antiquarian Society* 90, Part I (1980): 23–99; Franklin, in Axtell, *Invasion Within*, 303; Todd, *Lost Sister*, 140–43. Todd wrote for "the child at home and at the Sabbath School." Still, the book contains a fairly authentic account of Frances Slocum's life on pages 131–55.

20. Ebersole, *Captured by Texts*, 7. See Sayre, *Les Sauvages Américains*, 289; Calloway, "White Renegades," 44. For what "the middle ground" meant, see Richard White, *Middle Ground*, and Taylor, *Divided Ground*.

21. Wells, "Manners and Customs," 187; Brickell, "Captivity," 46; Hunter, *Manners and Customs*, 27, 43; M'Cullough, "Narrative," 266; Spencer, *Captivity*, 77.

22. Moore, "A Captive," 288–91, 294–95.

23. Nelson, *Jonathan Alder*, 47–49, 127; M'Cullough, "Narrative," 270–71; Tanner, *Narrative*, 31–32, 212–14, 231–36, 270–75.

24. Nelson, *Jonathan Alder*, 80, 51, 79; Ridout, "Captivity," 355; Seaver, *Mary Jemison*, 426; Meginness, *Frances Slocum*, 120; Smith, *Scoouwa*, 66–68; Carver, *Travels*, 67,

136; Carver was adopted by the Sioux, and much of his information comes from other sources; Morris, "Journal," Thwaites, *Travels*, 1: 311.

25. Wells, "Manners and Customs," 186; Tanner, *Narrative*, 37; Spencer, *Captivity*, 117–18; Brickell, "Captivity," 47; Nelson, *Jonathan Alder*, 51–52; Ridout, "Captivity," 356–57. Two distinguishing marks of the Miamis were the white kernels of their corn and the diamond pattern on their moccasins.

26. Seaver, *Mary Jemison*, 46–48.

27. Nelson, *Jonathan Alder*, 49–52. Several captives, like Wells, learned multiple languages. John Flinn learned at least five. DM, 5U, 69; Spencer, *Captivity*, 120. "No man has ever seen an Indian in conversation, without being sensible, that the head, the hands, and the body, are all put in requisition to aid the tongue," Lewis Cass, "Indians of North America," *North American Review* 22 (Jan. 1826): 79.

28. Trowbridge, *Traditions*, 38–39; Hunter, *Manners and Customs*, 29.

29. Brickell, "Captivity," 47–48.

30. Smith, *Scoouwa*, 39, 43–44, 47, 58–59, 59–60, 80, 82, 55.

31. Wells, "Manners and Customs," 178.

32. Snake-fish Town was located between Adamsboro and Hoovers on the Eel River. Morris, "Journal," Thwaites, *Travels*, 1: 324; James Wilkinson, in *Indiana as Seen by Early Travelers*, Harlow Lindley, ed. (Indianapolis: IHS, 1916), 13–14; Voeglin-Wheeler et al., *Miami, Wea, and Eel-River*, 122; Winger, *Little Turtle*, 24–28; Dillon, *Indiana*, 268.

33. Alford, *Civilization*, 22–23; Wells, in Volney, *Soil and Climate*, 371. In this case the English edition translation (London: J. Johnson, 1804), 418, is more accurate. Volney's interview notes are lost: "L'absence de manuscripts relatifs aux œuvres s'expliquerait—selon les biographes—par le négligence de Mme de Volney, veuve et héritière, peu intéressée par des papiers dont elle ne connaissait pas la valeur. On ignore pourquoi le comte Daru a refusé le legs de Volney lui-même concernant ses archives et sa bibliothèque," Nicole Hafid-Martin, *Volney: Bibliographie des Ecrivains Français* (Paris: Editions Memini, 1999), 19; "John Leeth's Captivity," DM, 22S, 66–67; Hunter, *Memoirs of a Captivity*, 224–25; Daniel Boone, in John Filson, *The Adventures of Colonel Daniel Boon*, Alvin Salisbury, ed. (Xenia, Ohio: Old Chilicothe, 1968), 11; Trowbridge, *Traditions*, 130–36; Godfroy, *Stories*, 11–12, 61–62.

34. Nelson, *Jonathan Alder*, 55–56; Trowbridge, *Traditions*, 57; Smith, *Scoouwa*, 109; Hunter, *Manners and Customs*, 28; Henry, *Travels*, 99–101; Spencer, *Captivity*, 126–29.

35. Alford, *Civilization*, 62–63; Godfroy, *Stories*, 51–53; Trowbridge, *Traditions*, 75–77.

36. Alford, *Civilization*, 21–23.

37. Thompson, *Son of the Wilderness*, 38; Hunter, *Memoir of a Captivity*, 177; Volney, *Soil and Climate*, 365; Godfroy, *Stories*, 70, 41, 78.

38. Nelson, *Jonathan Alder*, 80. Wells never completely went native: "I myself . . . though taken away at thirteen . . . and adopted and well treated, could never forget the scenes and pleasures I had already tasted," Volney, *Soil and Climate*, 372; English edition: "the social pleasures I had already tasted," 419.

39. Wells, "Manners and Customs," 186–87. Wells: "A great warrior must do nothing but hunt and fight," *Soil and Climate* (London), 420; Perrot, *Memoir*, in Blair, *Indian Tribes*, I: 119–126. Kinietz, *Great Lakes*, 173–74.

40. Trowbridge, *Traditions*, 66–67. Wells in "Manners and Customs" does not mention hunting rituals. Martin, *Keepers of the Game*, 120–29, stresses the spiritual dimension of the hunt; I am not convinced that the Indians "went on a war of revenge" against animals they blamed for the spread of lethal diseases.

41. White, *Middle Ground*, 486–88.

42. Smith, *Scoouwa*, 100, 63; Nelson, *Jonathan Alder*, 133; Flinn, DM, 14C, 69, 4–5; Brickell, "Captivity," 47.

43. Perrot, *Memoir*, in Blair, *Indian Tribes*, 1: 87; Carver, *Travels*, 222; Hunter, *Memoirs of a Captivity*, 139; Smith, *Scoouwa*, 72; Henry, *Travels*, 125. See Sayre, *Les Sauvages Américains*, 218–47.

44. Smith, *Scoouwa*, 75; Henry, *Travels*, 125; Kinietz, *Great Lakes*, 23; Tanner, *Narrative*, 57, 60; Carver, *Travels*, 149.

45. Hallowell, "Bear Ceremonialism," 22–69; Hallowell finds bear ceremonialism in many parts of the world; Martin, *Keepers of the Game*, 118; Ben East, *Bears* (New York: Sedgewood, 1977), 14.

46. Smith, *Scoouwa*, 49–51; Tanner, *Narrative*, 131–32; Nelson, *Jonathan Alder*, 75–77; Godfroy, *Stories*, 5–6.

47. Henry, *Travels*, 135–39; Henry was in an "eat-all" feast: "There being . . . ten persons, upon whom it was incumbent to eat up the whole bear," 193–94; Volney stated that after a successful hunt the Indians "gorged to the throat," *Soil and Climate*, 369. Adrian Tanner, *Bringing Home Animals* (New York: St. Martin's, 1979), 158–69.

48. Heckewelder, *History*, 311, 256; Wallace, *Heckewelder*, 258–93. If a hunter came upon a Miami who had just killed a deer, it was customary to either divide it or give the entire prize to that person, Trowbridge, *Traditions*, 66.

49. Fleming, in Mereness, *Travels*, 631–32; Smith, *Scoouwa*, 51–52; Spencer, *Captivity*, 125–26; Henry, *Travels*, 70–71.

50. Wells, "Manners and Customs," 178–79; Trowbridge, *Traditions*, 67–68; Young, *Little Turtle*, 179. See Heath, *Blacksnake's Path*, 37–52.

CHAPTER 3

For the war in the West, see Calloway, *American Revolution*; Silver, *Savage Neighbors*; Cayton, *Frontier Indiana*; and Hammon and Taylor, *Virginia's Western War*. White's *Middle Ground* is indispensable for the entire period.

1. Schuyler, in Calloway, *American Revolution*, 278; Jones, *License for Empire*, 125–27.

2. Franklin, in Isaacson, *Franklin*, 417; Isaacson states that "as a master of the relationship between power and diplomacy, Franklin knew it would be impossible to win at the negotiating table what was unwinnable on the battlefield" (398), but that is indeed what was accomplished in Paris. Franklin, "Journal of the Negotiations for Peace with Great Britain," Van Doren, *Franklin's Autobiographical Writings*, 514–83.

3. Franklin, "Journal," 523; Isaacson, *Franklin*, 557; Carl Van Doren, *Benjamin Franklin* (New York: Viking, 1938), 671–72; Franklin, "Supplement to Boston Chronicle," Albert Henry Smyth, ed., *The Writings of Benjamin Franklin* (New York, 1907), 8: 437–42, 580, 633–34; Peter Silver has dubbed such blatant American propaganda "the anti-Indian sublime," *Savage Neighbors*, 83–86, 216–17, 246–51.

4. Colin Calloway, "Suspicion and Self-Interest," *The Historian* 48, no. 1 (Nov. 1985): 54.

5. Washington to the President of Congress, 17 June 1783, Fitzpatrick, *Writings*, 27: 16–18; Washington to James Duane, 7 September 1783, Fitzpatrick, *Writings*, 27: 133–40.

6. *MPHC*, 11: 370–72; 20: 119–30; Allen, *Indian Allies*, 55–56; Calloway, "Suspicion," 51–53; Colin G. Calloway, "The Continuing Revolution in Indian Country," Hoxie et al., *Native Americans*, 24.

7. Haldimand, in William L. Stone, ed. and tr., *Memoirs, and Letter and Journals of Major General Riedesel* (Albany: Joel Munsell, 1868), I, 168–69; Kelsay, *Joseph Brant*, 335–38, 341; Allen, *Indian Allies*, 55; Taylor, *Divided Ground*, 115.

8. Ephraim Douglass, in Nelson, *Man of Distinction*, 150; "Transactions with the Indians at Sandusky from 26 August to 8 September 1783," *MPHC* 20: 174–83; Taylor, *Divided Ground*, 110–18. Thomas Townshend (Lord Sydney) belatedly confirmed Halidman's policy; see Wright, *Britain and American Frontier*, 15–35.

9. "Treaty of Fort Stanwix, in 1784," Craig, *Olden Time*, 2: 404–32; Taylor, *Divided Ground*, 157–60; Horsman, "American Indian Policy," 38.

10. Richter, *Ordeal of Longhouse*; White, *Middle Ground*; Voegelin-Wheeler and Tanner, *Indians of Ohio*, 2: 249–319; Karl H. Schlesier, "Epidemics and Indian Middlemen . . . 1609–1653," *Ethnohistory* 23, no. 2 (Spring 1976): 129–45.

11. "Claims, reiterated by the British and also often voiced by the Six Nation Indians of New York, but denied by the French, that the Indians [of Ohio] represented conquered peoples, living on these lands by permission of the Six Nations of New York and under the overlordship of the latter lack, we conclude, any real validity . . . the Indian occupants of the Ohio Valley lands were . . . in actual control of these lands, and of their own destiny," Voegelin-Wheeler and Tanner, *Ohio Indians*, 318–19, 249–319; see Jones, *License for Empire*, 58–109.

12. *ASP,IA*, 1: 11; Voegelin-Wheeler and Tanner, *Ohio Indians*, 510d; "Letters of the Four Beatty Brothers," *Pennsylvania Magazine of History and Biography* 44 (1920): 253–54; Denny, *Journal*, 259; Harmar, in *Denny*, 415–16; Horsman, "American Indian Policy," 39; Buckongahelas, DM, 23U, 16–24. Captain Pipe and the Half King played prominent roles in routing Crawford's expedition. Pipe ordered Crawford's death as retribution for Gnadenhütten.

13. Capt. Doughty to Knox, 21 October 1785, Smith, *St. Clair Papers*, 2: 10; McKee to Johnson, 6 August 1785, DM, 23U, 26.

14. Armstrong, in Smith, *St. Clair Papers*, 2: 3–4; Butler, "Journal," 486.

15. Washington to Williamson, 15 March 1785, Fitzpatrick, *Writings*, 28: 168; Onuf, "Visions of the West," 179–213; Cayton, *Frontier Republic*, 3–36; Berkhofer, "Jefferson and the Ordinance," 231–62.

16. Putnam to Fisher Ames, 1790, Putnam, *Memoirs*, 246; see Cayton, *Frontier Republic*; Onuf, "Visions of the West"; Berkhofer, "Jefferson and the Ordinance"; Onuf, *Statehood and Union*. The first settlement in the Old Northwest was Clarksburg, Indiana, in 1784, as a part of Clark's Grant of bounty land for his frontier troops.

17. Montgomery, "Journal," 267–72; Alexander McCormick, in Doughty to Knox, 21 October 1785, Smith, *St. Clair Papers*, 2: 11; Butler, "Journal," 501, 512–15; Denny, *Journal*, 273–75.

18. Butler, "Journal," 519–31; Denny, *Journal*, 273–77. Butler and Denny differ on the details: Butler says that Kekewepelthy retracted his eloquent words in the afternoon; Denny that it was Moluntha; Butler claims that he "dashed" the wampum on the table; Denny, that Clark pushed it onto the floor with his cane and stepped on it.

19. Harmar to Knox, 16 July 1785, Smith, *St. Clair Papers*, 2: 418; "Message received from the Shawanese dated 29th April," *MPHC*, 24: 25–26. McKee urged the Shawnees not to cede land to the United States, though he claimed large tracts for himself from the Ottawas and Chippewas in Canada, *MPHC*, 24: 27–29.

20. Francisco Cruzat to Miró, 23 August 1784, Kinnaird, *Spain*, 2: 117; Bond, "Two Westward Journeys," 326–30.

21. Clarence Walworth Alvord, "Father Pierre Gibault and the Submission of Post Vincennes, 1778," *The American Historical Review* 14, no. 3 (April 1909): 552–56.

22. "Letter from Mr. [William] Park, 17 May 1786, *MPHC*, 24: 29–31.

23. Helderman, "Northwest Expedition," 324; Kinnaird, *Spain*, 2: 174; Helderman, "Danger," 458–59; Barnhart and Riker, *Indiana*, 256; Helderman, "Filson's Defeat," 187–91; William Park, in *MPHC*, 24: 30–31.

24. Le Gras to Clark, 22 July 1786, Kinnaird, *Spain*, 2 175–81; Helderman, "Filson's Defeat," 195; Cayton, *Frontier Indiana*, 95; Helderman, "Danger," 460. Filson states that Donnally was "expected to recover" and his wife killed and scalped the Indian; John Small said Donnally showed "no appearance of his recovery" and "the friends of the Wounded Man" killed the Indian. I believe Filson: why else would he mention the wife?

25. Kinnaird, *Spain*, 2: 175–78; Helderman, "Danger," 462–65.

26. Kinnaird, *Spain*, 2: 178–81; Helderman, "Danger," 462–65.

27. Kinnaird, *Spain*, 2: 179–81: Helderman, "Danger," 465–66; Helderman, "Filson's Defeat," 195–97.

28. Helderman, "Northwest Expedition," 323–27; Helderman, "Filson's Defeat," 195; Michael Ague to McKee, 19 September 1786, *MPHC*, 24: 33; John May, in Talbert, *Benjamin Logan*, 207.

29. Barnhart and Riker, *Indiana*, 258; Helderman, "Northwest Expedition," 324–28; Moses Boone, DM, 33J, 52–53; White, *Middle Ground*, 425–26; Kinnaird, *Spain*, 2: 190–91; Hamtramck to Harmar, 2 November 1790, Thornbrough, *Outpost*, 259–63. Helderman, "Norhwest Expedition," praises Clark's "bold thrust to the upper Wabash" that "saved" the Northwest, but Clark almost marched into the kind of disastrous ambush Arthur St. Clair's troops suffered on 4 November 1791.

30. Simon Girty to McKee, 11 October 1786, *MPHC*, 24: 34: Talbert, "Kentucky Invades Ohio," 290; Talbert, *Benjamin Logan*, 212–14; Lytle, "Personal Narrative,"

14–15; Joseph Jackson narrative, DM, 11CC, 62–63; Beckner, "Sarah Graham," 225–26. For murdering Moluthna, McGary was suspended from the militia for one year.

31. Lytle, "Personal Narrative," 15–17; DM, 8BB, 37–38; Talbert, *Benjamin Logan*, 212–14. Neither the primary sources nor historians agree on the number of Indian towns destroyed. These seven were the most likely targets: Wakatomica, two miles below Zanesfield; Mackachack, at the mouth of a creek by the same name near West Liberty; Blue Jacket's Town at Bellefontaine; McKee's Town, on a creek of the same name two and one-half miles southeast of Bellefontaine; Mingo Town, at Zanesfield; Pickaway Town, at West Liberty. Voegelin-Wheeler and Tanner, *Indians of Ohio*, 652–53.

32. Simon Kenton interview, DM, 5BB, 120–21; DM, 8BB, 37–38.

33. Harmar to Knox, 15 November 1786, Smith, *St. Clair Papers*, 2: 19; Denny, 13 November 1786, *Journal*, 297–98.

34. Kelsay, *Joseph Brant*, 391–402; Nelson, *Lord Dorchester*, 197–99: *MPHC*, 24: 39–40.

35. Kelsay, *Joseph Brant*, 398–403; "Speech of the United Indian Nations," 18 December 1786, *ASP,IA*, 2: 39–40: White stated that this council represented "the political peak of the confederation," *Middle Ground*, 443.

36. Kinnaird, *Spain*, 2: 190–91; Barnhart, *Indiana*, 259–61; *Calendar of Virginia State Papers*, 4: 202; Harmar to Knox, 14 May 1787, *St. Clair Papers*, 2: 20–22. Clark paints a different picture: "I . . . fortified myself in St. Vincens, and in the course of four weeks brought the whole of the Ouabache Indians to my own terms," Barnhart, 260.

37. Kelsay, *Joseph Brant*, 406; Harmar to Knox, 14 May 1787, Smith, *St. Clair Papers*, 2: 20–22; Allen, *Indian Allies*, 69.

38. Trowbridge, *Traditions*, 24; Hunter, *Memoirs of a Captivity*, 158.

39. Heard, *White Into Red*, 103, 120; Charles McKnight, *Our Western Border* (Philadelphia: J. C. McCurdey & Co., 1876), 602–603; Ruddell's Narrative, DM, 2YY, 120–30; Calloway, "White Renegades," 46, 65.

40. Nelson, *Jonathan Alder*, 80–81.

41. Wells, "Manners and Customs," 181; Eid, "Running Fight," 147–71. On occasion a woman led a war party, and men known as White Faces, who lived as women, participated in war parties, Trowbridge, *Traditions*, 26, 68.

42. Johnston, "Indian Tribes," 283; Barnhart, *Hamilton*, 122, 140; Wells, "Manners and Customs," 181; Morris, *Journal*; Thwaites, *Travels*, 1: 306; Hay, "Journal," 260; Delitte, in Kinietz, *Great Lakes*, 198–99.

43. Smith, *Scoouwa*, 118–19; Wells, "Manners and Customs," 182; Trowbridge, *Traditions*, 19–21; Tanner, *Narrative*, 122–23; White, *Middle Ground*, 18.

44. Smith, *Scoouwa*, 162–72; Eid, "Running Fight," 163; Voegelin-Wheeler and Tanner, *Indians of Ohio*, 2: 270.

45. Smith, *Scoouwa*, 169; Barnhart, *Hamilton*, 121–22, 137; Deliette in Kinietz, *Great Lakes*, 198.

46. Innes to Knox, in Clark, *Bradford's Notes*, 134–35; G. Glenn Clift, ed., "The District of Kentucky, 1783–1787," *RKHS* 54 (October 1956), 369–71; Van Every, *Ark of Empire*, 159.

47. Clift, "District of Kentucky," 371; Smith, "This Idea of Heaven," 82–83.

48. Silver, *Savage Neighbors*, 58; White, *Middle Ground*, 80; Burnett, *Notes*, 389; Beckner, Clinkenbeard, 104; Hogan, "James Wade," 19; see Smith, "This Idea of Heaven," 77–100.

49. Thornbrough, *Outpost*, 77, 108, 119, 166–67.

50. Wells, "Manners and Customs," 182; Johnston, "Narrative," 294; Carver, *Travels*, 158–59; Cadillac, in Kinietz, *Great Lakes*, 254; Eid, "Cardinal Principles," 246. See Van Every, *Ark of Empire*, 150–60.

51. Tanner, *Narrative*, 141; Bond, *Drake's Memoir*, 65; Pirtle, *James Chenoweth*, 38–40.

52. Denny, *Journal*, 330–31; Armstrong, in Thornbrough, *Outpost*, 174; Boone, 33J, 54–55; Beckner, "Sarah Graham," 233.

53. Silver, *Savage Neighbors*, 74, 85, 122, 294.

54. Nelson, *Jonathan Alder*, 80–91; Lytle, "Personal Narrative," 12.

55. Clark, *Bradford's Notes*, 107; Lytle, "Personal Narrative," 21–30; *ASP,IA*, 1: 84–85.

56. Young, *Little Turtle*, 157–58; McClung, *Western Adventure*, 206–11; Clark, *Bradford's Notes*, 107–109.

57. Johnston to Eustis, 6 November 1810, NASW.

58. Harmar to Knox, 8 December 1787, and 15 June 1788, Smith, *St. Clair Papers*, 2: 20, 38; also in Thornbrough, *Outpost*, 85–86; Wyllys to Harmar, 26 May 1788, Josiah Harmar Papers, DM, 409–11; St. Clair to Knox, 5 July 1788, Hamtramck to St. Clair, 19 April 1790, *St. Clair Papers*, 2: 48, 135; Kinnaird, *Spain*, 3: 112.

59. Beckner, "Benjamin Allen," 89; Wallace, *Heckewelder*, 267.

60. Johnston, "Narrative," 244–55; Collins, *Historical Sketches*, 435–37.

61. Johnston, "Narrative," 255–63, 290–94, 297–99; rape of female prisoners was rare, since warriors were under strict taboos to avoid sexual contact with women. Johnston noted that Peggy was wretched and melancholy. When he "endeavoured to ascertain the cause of this extraordinary change . . . she answered my inquiries only with her tears; leaving my mind to its own inferences." The duke de la Rochefoucault-Liancourt, who wrote another version of the Johnston captivity, stated that she did not speak "one single word" to Johnston when they met again, because "her present masters . . . used her more rudely than the former had done." *Travels* (London: R. Phillips, 1799), 209–10. *ASP,IA*, I, 86–88, 91. One decoy may have been Abraham Wiseman, 15U, 32.

62. DM, 8BB, 99–105.

63. Ridout, "Captivity," 344–48.

64. Ridout, "Captivity," 362–65, 371; Breckenridge, in Loudon, *Outrages*, 1: v; Voegelin-Wheeler and Tanner, *Indians of Ohio*, 2: 311; Beckner, "Sarah Graham," 233; Collins, *Historical Sketches*, 545–46; "Ridout Narrative," in Edgar, *Ten Years*, 317.

65. M'Clung, *Western Adventure*, 196–97.

66. "A Narrative of Capt. Wm. Hubbell," Drake, *Indian Captivities*, 342–48.

67. Quaife, "Introduction," Spencer, *Captivity*, xv; Slotkin, *Regeneration*, 312–15. In my novel, as a wink to the savvy reader, I take the authorial liberty of having Wells kill Filson and lift his scalp. Heath, *Blacksnake's Path*, 85–87.

68. Wells, "Manners and Customs," 182; Trowbridge, *Traditions*, 21–23; Kinietz, *Great Lakes*, 200.

69. Trowbridge, *Traditions*, 21–23; Wells, "Manners and Customs," 182.

70. Nelson, *Jonathan Alder*, 88; Heckewelder, *History, Manners, and Customs*, 210; Trowbridge, *Traditions*, 34–35; Godfroy, *Stories*, 110.

71. Trowbridge, *Traditions*, 82–90.

72. Trowbridge, *Traditions*, 21; Wells, "Manners and Customs," 180–81.

73. Smith, *Scoouwa*, 86–87; Nelson, *Jonathan Alder*, 101; Spencer, *Captivity*, 119–20; Moore, "A Captive," 293; Cresswell, *Journal*, 105–106. On Miami courtship, see Heath, *Blacksnake's Path*, 82–101.

74. Hunter, *Memoir of a Captivity*, 113; Henry, *Travels*, 190, 248; Biggs, in Beckwith, *Illinois and Indiana Indians*, 130–31; Alford, *Civilization*, 61. Alford is describing a Shawnee courtship dance.

75. Tanner, *Narrative*, 100–18; Cadillac, in Kinietz, *Great Lakes*, 272; Trowbridge, *Traditions*, 41; Carver, *Travels*, 188; Henry, *Travels*, 306.

76. Trowbridge, *Traditions*, 41–43; Carter, *Little Turtle*, 87; "Nancy" mentioned in Shirley S. McCord, ed., *Travel Accounts of Indiana, 1679–1961* (Indianapolis: Indiana Historical Bureau, 1970), 47.

77. Wells, "Manners and Customs," 180–81; Trowbridge, *Traditions*, 41–43.

78. Charles Callender, *Social Organization of the Central Algonkian Indians* (Milwaukee: Milwaukee Public Museum, 1962), 24–39; Heckewelder, *History, Manners, and Customs*, 162.

79. Wells, "Manners and Customs," 180.

CHAPTER 4

The standard biography is Carter, *Life and Times of Little Turtle*. Sugden, *Blue Jacket*, is a well-researched biography of the great Shawnee war chief. Basic studies are White, *Middle Ground*; Sword, *Washington's Indian War*; Cayton, *Frontier Indiana*; Nichols, *Indians, Federalists*. See Leroy Eid's essays for key battles. For St. Clair's Defeat, see Winkler, *Wabash 1791*. For British policy: Allen, *Indian Allies*; Horsman, *Matthew Elliott*; and Nelson, *Man of Distinction*.

1. "Complaints of the North Western Indians," March 1786, DM, 1W, 117–22.

2. DM, 1W, 377; Thornbrough, *Outpost*, 80.

3. Duncan to Harmar, 17 June 1787, DM, 1W, 299–302.

4. Tardiveau to Harmar, 6 July 1787, Thornbrough, *Outpost*, 26–33.

5. Harmar to Knox, 24 November 1787, Hamtramck to Harmar, 21 May 1788, 31 August 1788, and 28 November 1788, in Thornbrough, *Outpost*, 46–57, 77, 88, 139, 190–91.

6. Hamtramck to Harmar, 14 August 1789, Harmar to Knox, 24 November 1787, in Thornbrough, *Outpost*, 182–83, 57.

7. Smith, *St. Clair Papers*, 2: 48–49, 57–58, 88–90, 100. The Piankashaws at Terre Haute and the Weas at Ouiatanon were the other targets. For an overview of Federalist policy, see Nichols, *Indians, Federalists*.

8. Callahan, *Knox*, 287, 245–46, 268; Ward, *Department of War*, 76, 99. "Henry Knox," in Kaminski, *Founders*, 325–33.

9. Callahan, *Knox*, 260, 215; Knox to Washington, 29 December 1794, *ASP,IA*, 1: 544; Knox to Wayne, 5 January 1792, Knopf, *Anthony Wayne*, 165.

10. Knox to Washington, 7 July 1789, *ASP,IA*, 1: 52–54; Knox to Putnam, *Memoirs*, 235; Knox to Harmar, 12 May 1786, *Papers of the Continental Congress*, NA, Reel 164, 338–39; Knox to Harmar, 7 June 1790, DM, 2W, 268–73; "Report of Secretary at War on Indian Hostilities," 10 July 1787, *JCC*, 32: 327–29.

11. Knox to Harmar, 19 December 1789, Thornbrough, *Outpost*, 211; Knox to Washington, 15 June 1789, *ASP,IA*, 1: 13.

12. *JCC*, 33: 610–12, 711–12.

13. Hamtramck to Harmar, 31 August 1788, Thornbrough, *Outpost*, 119; St. Clair to Knox, 4 November 1788, Smith, *St. Clair Papers*, 2: 95–96. Given Miami militancy at this time, I assume it was Little Turtle who deliberately dropped the wampum.

14. Governor St. Clair to the Indians in Council, 13 July 1788, Carter, *Territorial Papers*, 2: 127–28; DM, 23U, 68–69, 93; St. Clair to Knox, 3 December 1788, Smith, *St. Clair Papers*, 2: 97–100; Denny, *Journal*, 330–31.

15. Timothy Pickering, Carter, *Territorial Papers*, 2: 180n76; Denny, *Journal*, 331; see DM, 23U, 60–154.

16. "Report," 9 August 1787, *JCC*, 33: 479–80; DM, 23U, 122, 133–34; Denny, *Journal*, 332–34; *ASP,IA*, 1: 5–7. Cornplanter complained that at Fort Stanwix in 1784 and subsequent treaties, "You have compelled us to do that which has made us ashamed." Washington refused to adjust the boundary, citing the Fort Harmar Treaty. *ASP,IA* 1: 13–14.

17. St. Clair to John Jay, 12 December 1788, to Knox, 18 January 1790, Smith, *St. Clair Papers*, 2: 101–103, 108–109; St. Clair to Washington, 2 May 1788, Carter, *Territorial Papers*, 2: 192–93; Knox to Washington, 15 June 1789, *ASP,IA*, 1: 13–14. For how the conference served to discredit "Iroquois claims of ascendancy," see White, *Middle Ground*, 445–47.

18. Knox to Washington, 4 January 1790, *ASP,IA*, 1: 60; Hamtramck to Harmar, 15 June 1789, St. Clair to Washington, 14 September 1789, Thornbrough, *Outpost*, 175–76, 183; Washington to St. Clair, 6 October 1789, Smith, *St. Clair Papers*, 2: 125; Knox to St. Clair, 19 December 1789, "Washington: Draft," December 1789, Carter, *Territorial Papers*, 2: 225, 227–28.

19. St. Clair to Knox, 26 January 1790, Smith, *St. Clair Papers*, 2: 132.

20. Hay, "Journal," 216–22; Tanner, "The Glaize," 15–39.

21. Hay, "Journal," 222, 255, 248–49. See Cayton, *Frontier Indiana*, 138–46, and White, *Middle Ground*, 448–53. Cayton specifies that Kekionga was Pacanne's village; White and other historians use the term to refer to Le Gris's village as well. For efforts of traders to save prisoners, see *MPHC*, 24: 168–69.

22. Hay, "Journal," 224, 220–21, 240–41, 225.

23. Ibid., 229–30, 246–47, 250, 255.

24. Ibid., 230–32, 234, 236–38, 242–43. Hay's journal provides rare references to the Porcupine, confirming that he was village peace chief and Blacksnake's adoptive father.

25. "Gamelin's Journal," Smith, *St. Clair Papers*, 2: 155–62. Gamelin stopped at Snake-fish Town twice, but the Porcupine "was absent," and the Soldier "is gone to war on the Americans."

26. St. Clair to Washington, 1 May 1790, Carter, *Territorial Papers*, 2: 245; St. Clair to Knox, 1 May 1790, Knox, "Summary Statement," 27 May 1790, *St. Clair Papers*, 2: 136, 146–47; Knox to Harmar, 7 June 1790, *ASP,IA*, 1: 97–99; Knox to St. Clair, 27 June 1790, *St. Clair Papers*, 2: 147–48; Denny, *Journal*, 343; Harmar to Hamtramck, 15 July 1790, 3 September 1790, Thornbrough, *Outpost*, 237, 255; St. Clair to Knox, 23 August 1790, *ASP,IA*, 1: 92; Knox to St. Clair, 23 August 1790, 14 September 1790, *St. Clair Papers*, 2: 163, 181–82.

27. Knox to St. Clair, 14 September 1790, Smith, *St. Clair Papers*, 2: 182–83; Knox to Harmar, 24 August 1790, *ASP,IA*, 1: 99; Washington to Knox, 13 August 1790, Carter, *Territorial Papers*, 2: 299; Washington to Congress, 8 December 1790, *ASP,IA*, 1: 83. At the time of his presentation, Washington had not yet received word of Harmar's defeat.

28. Beard, *Maclay*, 233.

29. St. Clair to Harmar, 1 October 1790, Harmar Papers, OHS; Denny, *Journal*, 344, 461; Denny to Butler, 16 September 1791, DM, 4U, 26; "Diary of Lieutenant Denny," in Meek, "Harmar's Expedition," 102–108; DM, 2W, 324.

30. Denny to Butler, DM, 4U, 28.

31. Irwin, "Harmar's Campaign," 393–94; "Thomas Irwin," McBride, *Pioneer Biography*, I, 115–45; David H. Morris, DM, 4JJ, 5–6; "Statement of Ensign Britt," Meek, 105; General Whiteman, "Harmar's Campaign," DM, 8BB, 20–35. Colonel Hardin said that part of the plan was the hope "that the enemy would fly to their fort" and Hardin's force would "keep them in their fort until General Harmar arrived with the artillery," "Court of Inquiry on General Harmar," *ASP,IA*, I, 34. Harmar released the Shawnee prisoner on 18 November 1790, Meek, 93.

32. "Letters from John Smith," *MPHC*, 24: 103; Todd, *Lost Sister*, 67; George Sharp to Alexander McKee, 17 October 1790, John Smith to Capt. Le Maistre, 20 October 1790, *MPHC*, 24: 105–106, 107–108.

33. Whiteman's accounts, DM, 8BB, 20–35, 9CC, 27–31; Clark, *Bradford's Notes*, 137; Morris, DM, 4JJ, 6; Irwin, "Harmar's Campaign," 394; DM, 2W, 328. Major Ziegler and Captain Doyle depositions, *ASP,MA*, 1: 26.

34. Harmar's diary, Capt. John Armstrong's journal, Furgeson's report, in Meek, "Harmar's Expedition," 91–92, 83, 99. Hardin deposition, *ASP,MA*, I, 34.

35. Denny, "Diary," Harmar, "Journal," in Meek, "Harmar's Expedition," 106, 92; Irwin, "Harmar's Campaign," 394; Morris, DM 4JJ, 7–9, 322; Clark, *Bradford's Notes*, 137; Armstrong deposition, *ASP,MA*, 1: 27.

36. Ferguson and Harmar, in Meek, "Harmar's Expedition," 99, 92; Denny, *Journal*, 350; Morris, DM, 4JJ, 8–9.

37. Denny, *Journal*, 349–50; Irwin, "Harmar's Campaign," 395–96; Clark, *Bradford's Notes*, 137–38; Van Cleve, "Memoirs," 18.

38. Winger, *Little Turtle*, 1–2; Carter, *Little Turtle*, 72–75; Cruzat to Galvey, 12 November 1780, Kinnaird, *Spain*, 2: 395–400.

39. Hugh Scott's narrative, DM, 4U; Clark, *Bradford's Notes*, 54; Armstrong, in Dillon, *Indiana*, 248; Irwin, "Harmar's Campaign," 395–96; Whiteman, 8BB, 20–35; Hartshorn and Armstrong depositions, *ASP,MA*, 1: 23, 27; Van Cleve, "Memoirs," 18. The battle took place near Old Hellers Corners, Indiana, in the southwest corner of Eel River Township, just west of U.S. Route 33 and about twelve miles northwest of Fort Wayne. Both Winger, *Little Turtle*, 5, and Carter, *Little Turtle*, 93, 98, are slightly confused about the site, which has never been studied.

40. Irwin, "Harmar's Campaign," 396; Elliott to McKee, 23 October 1790, *MPHC*, 24: 108–109; Denny to Butler, 19 September 1791, Denny, *Journal*, 349–50; Clark, *Bradford's Notes*, 137–38; Wells, "Customs and Manners," 174; Morris, DM, 4JJ, 10; Harmar, "Journal," in Meek, 92. Sugden assumes that Hardin was defeated by "a small force of Shawnees and Potawatomies" probably led by Blue Jacket but admits that "no one recorded whether Blue Jacket was personally at the head of his warriors," *Blue Jacket*, 102. See Hopkins, *Mission*, 63–64. Dillon stated that the Indians "were led by a distinguished Miami chief whose name was Mish-e-ken-o-quah, which signifies Little Turtle," *Indiana*, 267.

41. Ferguson, Ziegler, and Hardin testimonies, *ASP,MA*, 1: 22, 26, 35; Cist, *Miscellany*, 2: 197.

42. Morris, DM, 4JJ, 11; Hardin and Captain Asheton testimonies, *ASP,MA*, 1: 35, 28.

43. Morris, DM, 4JJ, 12; Irwin, in Cist, *Miscellany*, 1: 106; Whiteman, DM, 8BB, 20–35; Clark, *Bradford's Notes*, 138. Cist stated that "McMillan's force lost its way in the thickets," "Harmar's Campaign," 1: 183.

44. Jonathan Heart, in Guthman, *March to Massacre*, 193; Morris, DM, 4JJ, 13; Denny, *Journal*, 351–53; Burns Narrative, Cist, *Sketches*, 109–11; Whiteman, DM, 8BB, 20–35; Asheton, DM, 2U, 423–28.

45. Whiteman, DM, 9CC, 27–31; Hardin testimony, *ASP,MA*, 1: 35.

46. Eid, "Harmar's Two Defeats," 55; the first account of the battle stated that "but nine scalps were taken from the enemy, and perhaps not more than thirty slain," 62; Van Cleve, "Memoirs," 18; official list of casualties, *ASP,IA*, I, 106; Armstrong, testimony, *ASP,MI*, 1: 27; Whiteman, DM, 9CC, 27–31. Major Hall's battalion suffered the worst casualties among the militia; Whiteman recalled that only twenty of his seventy-six men returned alive. DM, 9CC, 27–31.

47. Harmar, in Meek, "Harmar's Expedition," 93; St. Clair to Knox, 29 October 1790, Smith, *St. Clair Papers*, 2: 188; Washington to Knox, 6 November 1790, Carter, *Territorial Papers*, 2: 310; Washington to Congress, 24 January 1791, *ASP,IA*, 1: 107. Senator Maclay noted in his journal that "the ill-fortune of the affair breaks through all the coloring that was given to it. 'Tis said one hundred Indians have been killed. But two hundred of our own people have certainly perished in the expedition," Beard, *Maclay*, 340.

48. Wells, "Manners and Customs," 174; Wells is supported by British reports of ten killed and fifteen wounded, *MPHC*, 24: 134, 141, 160; Wood, *Empire of Liberty*, 129; Lieutenant Kersey, testimony, *ASP,MA*, 1: 28; "Information of Blue Jacket," 1 November 1790, *MPHC*, 24: 134–35, also 132; lunar eclipse information courtesy of William

O'Toole, editor of the Hagerstown, Maryland, *Farmer's Almanac*. One British report suggests that "one of their principal men [had] a Dream," *MPHC*, 24: 160; Harmar claimed that the battle at Kekionga saved the army. On the 23rd, Harmar's troops were in fact strung out and vulnerable to attack, Sword, *Washington's Indian War*, 119.

49. Denny, *Journal*, 354; Morris, DM, 4JJ, 16–17; Hardin, testimony, *ASP,MA*, 1: 35; Armstrong, testimony, *ASP,MA*, 1: 27; Armstrong, Court of Inquiry, DM, 2U, 402; 2U, 448–49: Ferguson, 2U, 404–405. Custer made a similar mistake and suffered comparable casualties. That Harmar's Defeat is unknown illustrates the selective memory of Americans.

50. "Harmar's Expedition," by "G," stated that he was "told by Captain Wells" about the battle, 181; Butler, in his *History of Kentucky*, 191, cited Wells; Dunn, *True Indian Stories*, 116; Wells, "Manners and Customs," 174; Carter, *Little Turtle*, 85–86, 99; Hopkins, *Mission*, 63–64.

51. Hamtramck to Harmar, 2 November 1790, Thornbrough, *Outpost*, 255, 259–64.

52. DM, 2W, 342; *MPHC*, 24: 132, 134; Armstrong in Cist, *Miscellany*, 1: 106.

53. Heald interview [1868], *DM*, 23S, 62–64; Heald interview [1892], Kirkland, *Chicago Massacre*, 174; Hamtramck to Secretary of War, 1 November 1801, in Wells to Eustis, 25 June 1809, NASW; Wallace, *Heckewelder*, 271–72. Carty Wells traveled up the Wabash in January 1789, Thornbrough, *Outpost*, 145; other references to him 22, 40, 160. He lived at Coxe's Fort, near Bardstown. Wells told Heckwelder in 1792 that "he went first to Post-Vincent, where he found an opportunity to visit his brothers in the vicinity of Louisville." In the 1868 version the armed escort is "a dozen or more Indian friends"; by 1892 it has become seventy-five to one hundred warriors and Wells "picked a band of twenty-five." Given frontier hostilities, it is unlikely Sam would have visited Snake-fish Town or that warriors came to Louisville. What rings true is seeing his old home and the pond where he was captured. See Heath, *Blacksnake's Path*, 105–12.

54. *MPHC*, 24: 134–38; "Representatives to President Washington," [December 1790] Charles Scott Papers, Margaret I. King Library, University of Kentucky, Lexington; Todd and Johnson to Harmar, 20 November 1790, Wilkinson to Harmar, 24 November 1790, Harmar to Todd and Johnson, 29 November 1790, to Wilkinson, 29 November 1790, DM, 2W, 373–79, 352–60; Harmar, in Meek, "Harmar's Expedition," 96; Proctor, "Narrative," 598.

55. Knox to Washington, 10 December 1790, Carter, *Territorial Papers*, 2: 314; St. Clair to Knox, 26 November 1790, Hamtramck to St. Clair, 2 December 1790, Smith, *St. Clair Papers*, 2: 193–97, 197–98; Knox to Harmar, 31 January 1791, DM, 2W, 394–401.

56. Putnam to Washington, 8 January 1791, *ASP,IA*, 1: 121–22; Kingsbury to Harmar, 12 January 1791, DM, 2W, 365–67; Bond, "Drake's Memoir," 81–82; Van Cleve, "Memoirs," 19.

57. *MPHC*, 24: 220–23, 237–39; DM, 3BB, 18–19, 8BB, 94–98; *ASP,IA*, 1: 129; Sword, *Washington's Indian War*, 136–38.

58. Proctor, "Narrative," 566–621; Knox, "Instructions to . . . Proctor," "Message . . . to the Miami Indians," *ASP,IA*, 1: 146, 147; Brant to Reverend Samuel Kirkland,

8 March 1791, Cruikshank, *Simcoe*, 5: 2–4; *MPHC*, 24: 236–42, 249–50. Knox had ordered Proctor to report to Fort Washington by 5 May. Pickering Papers, MHS, vol. 60.

59. Denny to Harmar, 9 March 1791, DM, 2W, 400; Knox, "Instructions to Scott," 9 March 1791, *ASP,IA*, I, 129–30.

60. "Journal . . . at the Miamis," *MPHC*, 24: 221, 246–47, 251, 261; Scott to Knox, 28 June 1791, *ASP,IA*, 1: 131–32.

61. Scott to Knox, 28 June 1791, Wilkinson to Scott, 3 June 1791, *ASP,IA*, I: 132; Perkins, *Annals*, 569. Cayton, *Frontier Indiana*, 156–57.

62. Norton, *Journal*, 22–23; "Letter to McKee," 26 June 1791, McKee to Sir John Johnson, 20 June 1791, "Dorchester to Indians," *MPHC*, 24: 273, 262, 309–10; DM, 15U, 32, 49–50; *MPHC* 24: 248, 251, 261, 273–74; Bliss, *Diary of Zeisberger*, 199. "Eight men and two women were killed by the troops under general Scott," Wells, "Manners and Customs," 174.

63. Hamtramck to Harmar, 15 June 1791, Thornbrough, *Outpost*, 283–84; Maj. John Stagg, Jr., to Capt. Jacob Slough, 5 July 1791, McKee to Sir John Johnson, 20 June 1791, "Dorchester to the Indians," *MPHC*, 24: 282, 262, 309–10; "Brig. Gen. Chas. Scott to the Indians," *ASP,IA*, 1: 132–33, *MPHC*, 24: 244–46.

64. The most recent biography, Linklater, *Artist in Treason*, adds information on Wilkinson's relations with Spain but is unreliable about the Indians. See Jacobs, *Tarnished Warrior*, and Harrison, "James Wilkinson."

65. Marshall, *History of Kentucky*, 1: 244–45; anonymous, in Harrison, "James Wilkinson," 352; Linklater, *Artist in Treason*, 86–88; Kohn, "Wilkinson's Vendetta," 361.

66. "James Wilkinson's Relations with Spain, 1787–1816," *American Historical Review* 9, no. 4 (July 1904): 748–66; to "humor him," Miró paid Wilkinson seven thousand dollars, gave him money to bribe Kentucky "notables," and paid him a pension of two thousand dollars a year. See Linklater, *Artist in Treason*, 104; Harrison, "James Wilkinson," 349.

67. Wilkinson to St. Clair, 24 August 1791, Smith, *St. Clair Papers*, 2: 233–39; Perkins, *Annals*, 570; Cayton, *Frontier Indiana*, 158.

68. Wilkinson to St. Clair, 24 August 1791. Wells wrote that in the town "there were but a few women and children, ten old men, and three young ones who made no defense; four men and one woman was killed, the number of women and children taken is not recollected," Wells, "Manners and Customs," 174.

69. Wilkinson to St. Clair, 24 August 1791; Wilkinson to Scott, 16 August 1791, DM, 4BB, 46–47. Snake-fish Town, halfway between Ouiatanon and Kekionga, was probably Kilatika Miami, more often aligned with the Sandhill Crane Miamis at Kekionga than with the Weas. St. Clair refered to Snake-fish Town as Kikiah, Smith, *St. Clair Papers*, 2: 227, as did Bradford in Clark, *Bradford's Notes*, 151.

70. Notable exceptions are Sword, *Washington's Indian War*, Cayton, *Frontier Indiana*, and Nichols, *Indians, Federalists*. John Ferling, *A Leap in the Dark* (New York: Oxford, 2003), ignores the Indian wars entirely. Mark Puls, *Henry Knox* (New York: Palgrave, 2008), has one inaccurate sentence on Harmar's Defeat, 208, and omits St. Clair's Defeat. The list could go on.

71. "The Reply of the President," 29 December 1791; "Speech of Washington," 19 January 1791, *ASP,IA*, 1: 142–44; Knox report on "the frontiers of the United States," 15 January 1791, Knox, "A summary statement," 26 December 1791, *ASP,IA*, 1: 112–13, 140.

72. St. Clair, *Narrative*, v, 38, 20, 101, 111.

73. Symmes to Elias Boudinot, 12 January 1792, *OHSQ* 5: 95–96; Mr. Hinde, in Hildreth, *American Pioneer*, 137; Sargent, "Diary," 242; Van Cleve, "Memoirs," 21; Armstrong, in Heckaman, "Badly Clothed," 17; St. Clair, *Narrative*, 266, 14, 26–27, 196; Shakespeare, *Henry IV, Part I*, IV, 2, 64–67.

74. Ziegler, in St. Clair, *Narrative*, 206.

75. St. Clair, *Narrative*, 78, 94–95, 125–26; Symmes to Boudinot, 12 January 1792, *OHSQ* 5: 94.

76. St. Clair, *Narrative*, 207–208, 194, 219, 84, 88, 58, 63, 268, 11, 114–15, 13, 200–201; Sargent, "Diary," 242–45.

77. Sargent, "Diary," 240–41; St. Clair, *Narrative*, 72; Symmes to Boudinot, *OHSQ* 5: 100; Quaife, "Newman Journal," 64–71.

78. Denny, *Journal*, 355–57, 374.

79. St. Clair, *Narrative*, 102–104, 119, 5, 270, 106, 38. On soldiers killed and scalped by the Indians, Quaife, "Newman Journal," 63, Sargent, "Diary," 250; on being captured, Bunn, *Narrative*, 3–15; Darke, *MPHC*, 24: 333–34.

80. St. Clair, *Narrative*, 15–16, 31–36; Sargent, "Diary," 244–45.

81. Sargent, "Diary," 242, 250–51; Quaife, "Newman Journal," 72–73.

82. Smith, *St. Clair Papers*, 2: 250; St. Clair, "Diary," *The Debates of the Congress . . . October 24, 1791, to March 2, 1793* (Washington, D.C.: Gales and Seaton, 1849), 2: 1054–55; in his *Narrative*, St. Clair changed his orders to "twenty miles down the roads towards Fort Hamilton," and "towards Fort Hamilton, twenty miles only," 28, 265–66; Denny, *Journal*, 364–65; Darke, *MPHC*, 24: 332–33. On 31 October St. Clair's army was 22 miles north of Fort Jefferson, Van Cleve, "Memoirs," 24.

83. William Darke to Mrs. Sarah Darke, 1 November 1791, *MPHC*, 24: 332–33; Van Cleve, "Memoirs," 24; Sargent, "Diary," 251, 246; Quaife, "Newman Journal," 45–49.

84. Denny, *Journal*, 367–68; Sargent, "Diary," 252–53, 256; my thanks to Chris Keller and Nancy Knapke for helping me picture the deployment of St. Clair's troops on the evening of 3 November. See Winkler, *Wabash 1791*.

85. Bunn, *Narrative*, 8–13. Wells married Sweet Breeze between Harmar's Defeat and St. Clair's Defeat, possibly even before his wife Nancy and son were captured; it was not uncommon for a distinguished man to have more than one wife. Little Turtle's trust in him on 4 November would indicate they already had a close relationship.

86. Wells, in Hopkins, *Mission*, 65–66; Girty, in *MPHC*, 24: 329–30. Wells, "Manners and Customs," gives 1,133 as the number of Indians, 175; he told Hopkins it was 1,400. Girty is probably accurate when he states 1,040 left Kekionga; George Ash says they were joined later by 50 Kickapoos, Ash, "Story."

87. Norton, *Journal*, 177; Ash, "Story"; Wells, "Manners and Customs," 175; Joseph Brant to Joseph Chew, 30 December 1791, *MPHC*, 24: 358.

88. Account of Robert Branshaw in "St. Clair's Defeat," *Door County Advocate*, DM, 4U, 142–46.

89. Sargent, "Diary," 258–59; McDonough to McDonough, 10 November 1791, WCL; *Columbian Centinal*, 28 December 1791. The sun rose at 7:12 that morning, with first light appearing about a half hour before that; thus the battle began a little before 7 o'clock and lasted until about 9 o'clock. My thanks to William O'Toole for this information.

90. Denny, *Journal*, 369; Van Cleve, "Memoirs," 25; Symmes to Boudinot, 83; Sargent, "Diary," 259.

91. Sargent, "Diary," 271; St. Clair, *Narrative*, 130–31; St. Clair to Knox, 9 November 1791, Smith, *St. Clair Papers*, 2: 263; Spencer, *Captivity*, 24; "Anonymous letter," in Allen, *Indian Allies*, 74; Van Cleve, "Memoirs," 26; Johnston to Eustis, 6 November 1810, NASW. In 1846 Johnston repeated his account: "Wells, one of our interpreters, was there with and fought for the enemy. To use his own language, he tomahawked and scalped the wounded, dying and dead, until he was unable to raise his arm." Henry Whiting said that Wells "arranged his party behind logs and trees, immediately under the knoll on which the guns were, and thence, almost uninjured, picked off the artillerists, until, it is said, their bodies were heaped up almost to the height of their pieces." See "Mercer County" and "Lucas County," Howe, *Historical Collections*, 2: 231, 141; "Burns Narrative," Cist, *Sketches*, 113–14.

92. St. Clair, *Narrative*, 51, 222, 50; St. Clair to Knox, 9 November 1791, Smith, *St. Clair Papers*, 2: 263–64; Denny, *Journal*, 370; Van Cleve, "Memoirs," 26; Sargent, "Diary," 260; map, "Action between General St. Clair's Army & that of the American Indians," WCL.

93. Ash, "Story"; Norton, *Journal*, 178; Denny, *Journal*, 370; Branshaw, DM, 4U, 143.

94. Denny, *Journal*, 221–22; Sargent, "Diary," 266; Sword, *Washington's Indian War*, 185. For an account of how Edward rescued Thomas, see DM, 5W, 156; anon., in Allen, *Indian Allies*, 75; Norton, *Journal*, 178.

95. Denny, *Journal*, 370–71; Sword, *Washington's Indian War*, 187; St. Clair to Knox, 9 November 1791, Smith, *St. Clair Papers*, 2: 264; Van Cleve, "Memoirs," 26; Sargent, "Diary," 261, 254, 262; William Darke to George Washington, 9 November 1791, Knox Papers, MHS. "The battle always reminds me of one of those thunder-storms that comes quickly and rapidly," Thomas Irwin letter, 10 October 1844, McBride, *Pioneer Biography*, 1: 171–75.

96. St. Clair to Knox, 9 November 91, Smith, *St. Clair Papers*, 2: 264; Denny, *Journal*, 372; Sargent, "Diary," 261; Hopkins, *Mission*, 133–34.

97. Branshaw, DM, 4W, 143; Spencer, *Captivity*, 26; Denny, *Journal*, 221–22; Van Cleve, "Memoirs," 26–27; Collins, *History of Kentucky* (1847), 31–32; Sword, *Washington's Indian War*, 189–90; Martha E. Roher, *Historical Sketch of Fort Recovery* (Fort Recover, Ohio: Historical Society, 1991), 17–19.

98. Hinde, "Diary," McBride, *American Pioneer*, 2: 137–38; Sargent, "Diary," 254; St. Clair, *Narrative*, 48–49, 123.

99. Norton, *Journal*, 178; Spencer, *Captivity*, 27–28; Buntin, in Dillon, *Indiana*, 284; "Fowler's Story of the Battle," Howe, *Historical Collections*, 2: 227; Bradley, *Journal*, 117.

100. McKee to Sir John Johnson, 5 December 1791, *MPHC*, 24: 366; Wells, in Hopkins, *Mission*, 65; Howe, *Historical Collections*, 2: 231; Sargent, "Diary," 260; Denny, *Journal*, 375; St. Clair to Knox, 9 November 1791, *St. Clair Papers*, 2: 262. A number of "women and children" were adopted by the Indians, Bliss, *Zeisberger Diary*, 229–30. One nineteenth-century account stated that 250 women were present, 56 killed, most captured. Catharine V. R. Bonney, *A Legacy of Historical Gleanings*, I (Albany, N.Y.: Munsell, 1875), 12.

101. Wells, in Hopkins, *Mission*, 65; Wells, "Manners and Customs," 175; Sargent, "Diary," 272; Norton, *Journal*, 179; DM, 4U, 400; Sugden, *Blue Jacket*, 5–6, 120; Smith, *Scoouwa*, 161–62; Eid, "St. Clair's Defeat," 71–88. Blue Jacket was named as the leader by Ash and two other informants: Ash, "Story," Sargent, "Diary," 272; Wilkinson to Josiah Drake, 12 December 1791, DM, 4U, 166; other sources mention Little Turtle or a plural leadership of "the War Chiefs," Norton, *Journal*, 177, 178; anon., in Allen, *Indian Allies*, 74, and Spencer, *Captivity*, 28. On the rivalry between the two chiefs: "Blue Jacket, who, it is said had the Chief Command of the Indian Army on the 4th November 1791 against Gen'l St. Clair, The Little Turtle a Miami Chief who also claims that honor, & who is his rival for fame & power." Wayne to McHenry, 3 October 1796, Knopf, *Anthony Wayne*, 532.

102. Sugden, *Blue Jacket*, 6, 118; Spencer, *Captivity*, 90. Simon Girty told American spy William May: "The Shawanese did not behave well on the day of the action, and were called cowards by the Wyandots and Mingoes." He said that nine hundred Indians fought, with four hundred hunting or minding horses, *ASP,IA*, 1: 243.

103. Brickell, "Narrative," 50; anon., in Allen, *Indian Allies*, 75; McKee to Johnson, 5 December 1791, *MPHC*, 24: 337.

CHAPTER 5

For the Vincennes Treaty, see Putnam, *Memoirs*; Wallace, *Heckewelder*. For Indian councils of 1792 and 1793, see Edmunds, "Nothing Has Been Effected"; Hutton, "William Wells"; Smith, "William Wells"; Allen, *His Majesty's Indians Allies*; Nelson, *A Man of Distinction*; Sword, *Washington's Indian War*; White, *Middle Ground*.

1. DM, 21S, 57; Putnam, *Memoirs*, 297–98; Wallace, *Heckewelder*, 271–72; Hamtramck to Knox, 1 November 1801, in Wells to Eustis, 25 June 1809, NASW.

2. Wallace, *Heckewelder*, 272.

3. Volney, *Soil and Climate*, 371–74.

4. Wallace, *Heckewelder*, 269–70; Burnett, *Notes*, 33–35.

5. Wallace, *Heckewelder*, 272–73.

6. Richard Rush, *Washington in Domestic Life* (Philadelphia: J. P. Lippincott, 1857), 67–68; Washington "To the Senate and House," 12 December 1791, Fitzpatrick, *Writings*, 31: 442; Washington to Knox, 16 January 1792, Carter, *Territorial Papers*, 2: 359.

7. Knox, "The Causes of the Existing Hostilities," 22 January 1792, Carter, *Territorial Papers*, 2: 360–66.

8. Hawkins to Washington, 10 February 1792, Carter, *Territorial Papers*, 2: 367–69.

9. Washington, "Errors Towards the Indians" [Feb. 1792], Fitzpatrick, *Writings*, 31: 491–94.

10. Cayton, "Meaning of War," 373–89; "Brackendrige on the Indian Problem," in Clark, *Bradford's Notes*, 177–85.

11. Knox to Trueman, 3 April 1792, "Speech of James Wilkinson," 3 April 1792, "Speech of Knox," 4 April 1792, Wilkinson to Harden, 20 May 1792, "William May," 9 June 1792, *MPHC*, 24: 390–95, 413–15, 420. Freeman and Gerrard left for Kekionga in March; May deserted Fort Hamilton on 13 April; Trueman and Hardin left Fort Washington in mid-May.

12. Knox, "Instructions," 22 May 1792, Putnam, *Memoirs*, 257–67; Brant to McKee, 23 May 1792, *MPHC*, 24: 417–18.

13. Putnam to Knox, 5 July 1792, Putnam to Knox, 8 July 1792, 11 July 1792, Putnam, *Memoirs*, 274–76, 280–82, 292–93; Wallace, *Heckewelder*, 268; Hamtramck to Knox, 31 March 1792, Carter, *Territorial Papers*, 2: 380–81. The eleven prisoners were killed in a dispute over ownership, Doyle to Johnson, 23 July 1792, *MPCH*, 24: 428. For the deaths of Trueman, Hardin, and other messengers: Wayne to Knox, 6 August 1792, Putnam, *Memoirs*, 311–12; DM, 15U, 41–48, 5W, 1–15, 11YY, 11–13; *MPHC*, 24: 420, 427; Knox to Wayne, 22 June 1792, Knopf, *Anthony Wayne*, 22–23, also 53–60.

14. Putnam, "Speech," Putnam to Knox, 26 July 1792, Putnam to Knox, 16 August 1791, Putnam, *Memoirs*, 307–308, 311–12, 321–23.

15. Wallace, *Heckewelder*, 276–80; Heckewelder, *Manners and Customs*, 256, 311.

16. Wallace, *Heckewelder*, 280–82; Putnam, *Memoirs*, 379, 334–38.

17. Putnam, *Memoirs*, 341–49; see Putnam File, Marietta College Library, Marietta, Ohio.

18. Ibid., 351–58.

19. Ibid., 358–65; Wallace, *Heckewelder*, 283.

20. Wallace, *Heckewelder*, 283–84.

21. Putnam, *Memoirs*, 369–82.

22. Putnam to Wilkins, 28 November 1792, to Knox, 20 December 92, to Wayne, 21 December 1792, 21 January 1793 ibid., 371, 373, 375, 376–77.

23. Knox to Cornplanter, 7 January 1792, Washington to Five Nations, 23 March 1792, Pickering to Five Nations, 13 April 1792, *ASP,IA*, 1: 226, 233, 232; Kelsay, *Brant*, 464; Phillips, "Timothy Pickering," 163–93.

24. Kelsay, *Brant*, 462, 465, 471–73; Brant to Knox, 27 March 1792, *ASP,IA*, 1: 245; Brant to McKee, 23 May 1792, *MPHC*, 24: 417–18.

25. Knox to Wayne, 29 June 1792, Knox to Wayne, 7 August 1792, Knopf, *Anthony Wayne*, 25, 60; Brant to Knox, 26 July 1792, *ASP,IA*, 1: 245.

26. Knox, "Instructions to Aupaumut," 8 May 1792, *ASP,IA*, 1: 233; Aupaumut, "Embassy," 76–78, 89, 94–95, 97, 112. Taylor, "Captain Hendrick Aupaumut," 431–57, argues that he was no American dupe, but had his own agenda.

27. For a detailed description of the place, see Tanner, "The Glaize in 1792," 15–39.

28. Aupaumut, "Embassy," 97–114; McKee to England, 4 September 92, 6 September 1792, McKee to Chew, 11 September 1792, *MPHC*, 24: 476–77.

29. "Proceedings of a General Council of Indian Nations," *MPHC*, 24: 485–91; Aupaumut, "Embassy," 117–21; see "Questioning of Capt. Hendrick," 5 February 1793, Timothy Pickering Papers, MHS, Reel 59: 38–46.

30. "Proceedings," *MPHC*, 24: 491.

31. Ibid., 492–96; Aupaumut, "Narrative," 121; "Journal of William Johnson," *MPHC*, 24: 471.

32. Aupaumut, "Narrative," 118.

33. McKee to Simcoe, 30 January 1793, "From the Western Indians," Cruikshank, *Simcoe*, 1: 282–84.

34. Spencer, *Captivity*, 114. Spencer's narrative provides a lively picture of life at the Glaize in 1792.

35. Knox to Wayne, 8 May 1793, Knopf, *Anthony Wayne*, 233; Edmunds, "Nothing Has Been Effected," 23–35, argues that the 1792 treaty of Vincennes "reflects the bankruptcy of American Indian policy" since "the Indians who attended the negotiations were already friendly to the government" and afterward, Knox noted, "nothing has been effected." Yet at the time, Putnam's conduct and the terms of the treaty were a hopeful step forward, and not all the Weas and Eel River Indians were "already friendly" to the Americans; many of their warriors had waged war alongside the Miamis.

36. Spencer, *Captivity*, 115; Wilkinson to Knox, 6 November 1792, John Adair to Wilkinson, 6 November 1792, *ASP,IA*, 1: 335.

37. Hamtramck to Sargent, 6 February 1793, Winthrop Sargent Papers, MHS; Hamtramck to Secretary of War, 1 January 1801, enclosed in Wells to Eustis, 25 June 1809, NASW. Hamtramck to Wayne, 16 July 1793, Hamtramck Papers, BHC.

38. Cruikshank, *Simcoe*, 1: 257–58; *ASP,IA*, 1: 323–24. The Iroquois confederacy was known at the time as both the Five Nations, because the Oneida now sided with the Americans, and as the Six Nations.

39. Cornplanter and New Arrow to Wayne, 8 December 1792, *ASP,IA*, 1: 337; "Speech of H. Knox to the Indians," 12 December 1792, *MPHC*, 24: 518–19; to Wayne, 24 November 1792, 5 January 1793, Knopf, *Anthony Wayne*, 141, 171–72.

40. Simcoe to George Hammond, 21 January 1793, to McKee, 23 January 1793, to Gov. Alured Clarke, 27 January 1793, to Major General Clarke, 14 June 1793, *MPHC*, 24: 521, 523, 527, 549.

41. Western Indians to the Five Nations, 27 February 1793, Cruikshank, *Simcoe*, 1: 34–35.

42. Henry Knox, "Instructions to Lincoln . . . Randolph . . . Pickering . . ." 26 April 1793, *ASP,IA*, I, 340–42.

43. Knox to Wayne, 5 March 1793, 13 April 1793, 20 April 1793, Wayne to Knox, 27 April 1793, Knopf, *Anthony Wayne*, 198, 218–19, 221–24, 229–30.

44. Wayne to Knox, 2 July 1793, Knox to Wayne, 28 June 1793, Wayne to Knox, 10 July 1793, 8 August 1793, Knopf, *Anthony Wayne*, 251–54, 248, 256, 261–65.

45. Simcoe to Alured Clarke, 14 June 1793, to McKee and John Butler, 22 June 1793, Cruikshank, *Simcoe*, 1: 354–55, 365–66, *MPHC*, 24: 554–56.

46. "Brant's Journal of the Proceedings," Cruikshank, *Simcoe*, 2: 5–7.

47. Brant to Commissioners, 7 July 1793, Commissioners to Indian Delegation, 8 July 1793, Brant and Cat's Eyes to Commissioners, *ASP,IA*, I, 349–50; *MPHC*, 24: 561–66. See Pickering Papers, MHS, Reel 60: 145–85.

48. Smith, "William Wells," 217–26; Wallace, *Heckewelder*, 314–15.

49. Smith, "William Wells," 220; "Brant's Journal," Cruikshank, *Simcoe*, 2: 7–12.

50. Sa-wagh-da-wunk to Commissioners, 30 July 1793, Commissioners to Indian Delegation, 31 July 1793, *ASP,IA*, 1: 352–53.

51. Lindley, "Diary," 619–21; Carry-one-about to Commissioners, 1 August 1793, *ASP,IA*, 1: 354; Lincoln, "Journal," 150; see Wallace, *Heckewelder*, 318, and Savery, "Journal," 342.

52. "Brant's Journal," 12–17; Horsman, "Treaty of Lower Sandusky, 1793," 211–12; Smith, "William Wells," 222. Wells's account is based on direct observation. Subsequent accounts by participants state that McKee played a pivotal role in thwarting the treaty. Heckewelder's "Memorandum," Pickering Papers, MHS, Reel 59: 183–86.

53. Lincoln, "Journal," 154–56; Henderick to Pickering, 6 August 1793, Pickering Papers, MHS, Reel 59: 203–3A.

54. Savery, "Journal," 335, 339, 343–44; Lindley, "Diary," 588–89, 606, 625, 611–12, 591; Moore, "Journal," 315–16; Wallace, *Heckeweldeer*, 319.

55. Moore, "Journal," 329–31; Lindley, "Diary," 627–28; "Indians to the Commssioners," 16 June 1793, *ASP,IA*, 1: 356–57; Cruikshank, *Simcoe*, 2: 17–20.

56. *ASP,IA*, I, 357, 359; Lindley, "Diary," 627–28; Lincoln, "Journal," 138–41, 152–53; Wallace, *Heckewelder*, 319; Pickering to Henderick, 17 August 173, Pickering Papers, MHS, Reel 59: 209–9A.

57. Brant to Joseph Chew, 26 September 1793, McKee to Simcoe, 22 August 1793, Simcoe to George Hammond, 24 August 1793, *MPHC*, 24: 614, 595–96, 599–605; "Speech of the Chiefs of the Western Nations," Cruikshank, *Simcoe*, 2: 35–36.

58. Jefferson to Charles Pickney, 27 November 1793, Washington, *Writings of Jefferson*, 4: 85–86; Washington to the Secretaries of State, And Treasury, And the Attorney General, 17 February 1793, Fitzpatrick, *Writings*, 31: 348–49; Cruikshank, *Simcoe*, 3: 313. On 25 February the cabinet met at Washington's home and answered this question: "Have the Executive, or the Executive and Senate together authority to relinquish to the Indians the right of soil of any part of the lands North of the Ohio, which has been validly obtained by former treaties?" Only Secretary of State Jefferson voted that "they have no such authority to relinquish." In a letter to Henry Lee, Washington hinted at the more devious side of his strategy: "our hands are tied to defensive measures," although it might be "best for me to be silent on this head." The failure of the peace negotiations would "let the good people of these States see that the Executive has left nothing unessayed to accomplish" peace and it would "remove those suspicions which have been unjustly entertained that Peace is not" our goal; once the people see "the difficulties" of obtaining a peace, they will realize that "if the Sword is to decide, that the arm of government may be enabled to strike

home." Washington to Lee, 6 May 1793, Fitzpatrick, *Writings*, 31: 359–60n, 449. In instructions to Aupaumut on 4 June 1793, Pickering admitted that previous treaties had made "extravagant claims; but perhaps the present Commissioners may confine themselves to moderate limits & relinquish all the rest of the lands," but added that it would be "very difficult if not impossible now to give up" any settled lands north of the Ohio. Pickering Papers, MHS, Reel 60: 145.

59. Heald interview, DM, 23S, 64; Heald, in Kirkland, *Chicago Massacre*, 175.

CHAPTER 6

The most detailed account of the Wayne Campaign is Gaff, *Bayonets in the Wilderness*; Knopf, *Anthony Wayne*, contains key sources, as do his transcripts of the Wayne Papers at OHS and his editions of other primary accounts. See Sword, *Washington's Indian War*; Sugden, *Blue Jacket*; and Nelson, *Anthony Wayne*.

1. Hamtramck to Wayne, 11 September 1793, Hamtramck Papers, BHC; Wilkinson to Wayne, 14 September 1793, WP, HSP.

2. Wayne to Knox, 17 September 1793, Knopf, *Anthony Wayne*, 272–73.

3. Smith, "William Wells," 217–26; "Report of Mr. Rosencrantz," 23 September 1793, WP, HSP.

4. Wayne, Knopf, *Anthony Wayne*, 8; British officer and Wayne, in Tucker, *Mad Anthony Wayne*, 132, 14; for Wayne's Revolutionary career see Nelson, *Anthony Wayne*. Wayne deserves a better biography.

5. Nelson, *Wayne*, 129–30.

6. Jemy, Wayne, and Eaten, in Tucker, *Mad Anthony*, 12–13, 111, 229.

7. "Opinion of the General Officers," 9 March 1792, Fitzpatrick, *Writings*, 31: 509–15; Jefferson's Cabinet Notes, 9 March 1792, Franklin B. Sawvel, ed., *Complete* Anas *of Jefferson* (New York, 1903), 61–62; Wayne to Knox, 1 April 1792, Knox Papers, Morgan Library, New York City; George Hammond to Simcoe, 21 April 1792, Cruikshank, *Simcoe*, 1: 131–32.

8. Hobson's Choice, from an English innkeeper who rented one horse at a time, take it or leave it, meant no real choice at all. Gaff, *Bayonets*, 54, 18; Knopf, "Crime," 237; Wayne to Mary Wayne, 2 March 1782, WP, HSP, vol. 15. Historians exaggerate the superiority of Wayne's troops before they had been tested; for example, Gaff said of the Legion: "Superbly trained, officered, and equipped, Wayne's command bore little resemblance to the armies of Harmar and St. Clair that had preceded it into the wilderness," 157; yet when ambushed, Wayne's raw troops ran like most previous American recruits.

9. Wayne to Captain North, 11 December 1776, WP, HSP, vol. 2; Orderly Book, *MPHC*, 34: 476, 484–86, 470; Wayne to Sharp Delany, 14 November 1794, WP, OHS, 38: 88. Knopf noted that "the rules of justice which Anthony Wayne inherited . . . were almost *in toto* those which had governed the army during the Revolution. . . . One officer might be shot for desertion; another might receive only a week's extra duty for the same offense," Knopf, "Crime," 233–34.

10. Wayne to Knox, 5 October 1793, Knopf, *Anthony Wayne*, 276–77; Jonathan M. Scott, "Wayne's Expedition in 1793," Cist, *Miscellany*, 2: 55–56; Buell, *Diary*, 2; Orderly Book, *MPHC*, 34: 493–94. Fort St. Clair was between forts Hamilton and Jefferson near Eaton, Ohio, where Lowry and his fallen men are buried.

11. "Wayne," Cist, *Miscellany*, 2: 55; Bradley, *Journal*, 25; Underwood, *Journal*, 7–8; Hamtramck to Wayne, 19 October 1793, Wayne to John Edwards, 22 October 1793, WP, HSP; Wayne to Knox, 23 October 1793, Knopf, *Anthony Wayne*, 279. See deposition of Warren Murray, 24 July 1794, WP, OHS, 36: 239–42.

12. Flinn, WP, HSP, vol. 29; Wayne to Wells, 22 October 1793, WP, OHS, 30: 42.

13. Knopf, "Kentucky Volunteers," 254; McDonald, *Biographical Sketches*, 261–63.

14. Wayne to Scott, 2 November 1793, Robert Todd's record, DM, 16U; Wayne to Scott, 2 November 1793, Wayne to St. Clair, 7 November 1793, WP, OHS, 30: 95–97, 112–13; Knopf, "Kentucky Volunteers," 255–57; Burns Narrative, Cist, *Sketches*, 2: 116–17.

15. McDonald, *Biographical Sketches*, 190–91; see Hunt, DM, 21S, 44.

16. Bradley, *Journal*, 25–26; Simmons, *Forts*, 12–13; Wayne to Knox, 15 November 1793, Knopf, *Anthony Wayne*, 283. Wayne named the fort Greeneville and the treaty was sometimes spelled the same. The present town is Greenville.

17. "I want intelligence & scalps & therefore wish you success—& remember—a reward attends it." Wayne to Flinn, 14 November 1793, WP, OHS, 30: 149; Wayne to Knox, 4 December 1793, WP, HSP; Underwood, *Journal*, 9; "St. Clair's Defeat," Cist, *Miscellany*, 2: 30–31.

18. Wayne's orders to Burbeck, 22 December 1793, 28 December 1793, WP, OHS, 30: 171–72, 185; Simmons, *Forts*, 13–14; Underwood, *Journal*, 9–11; Buell, "Diary," 4; *Maryland Journal*, 19 February 1794. DM, JJ4, stated that the fort was named for the recovery of the cannon. Historians rarely credit Wells's role in finding the cannon.

19. "Robert McClellan," McBride, *Pioneer Biography*, 2: 30, 18, 38; McDonald, *Biographical Sketches*, 184; "Pay Roll of the Spies selected by William Wells," Muster Rolls of Volunteer Organizations: War With Northwest Indians, 1790–95, Record of the Adjutant General's Office, Record Group 94, NA. Dodson Tharp also appears in primary and secondary accounts as Dodson Thorp and Dodson Sharp. See Heath, "William Wells," 102–13.

20. WP, OHS, 32: 38–45; Cruckshank, *Simcoe*, 2: 132.

21. Wayne to Gibson, 17 January 1794, to Thomas Posey, 21 January 1794, WP, OHS, 32: 56, 76–79.

22. Wayne to Posey, 21 January 1794, WP, OHS, 32: 76–79; Harrison, *Aborigines of the Ohio Valley*, 50.

23. Wayne to Knox, 25 January 1794, Knopf, *Anthony Wayne*, 302–305; Wayne to Delawares, 26 January 1794, WP, OHS, 33: 136–38, 140; Buell, "Diary," 4. Rosencrantz later reported: "I do not find the least Difficulty with the Friends of the late Capt. Stiff Knee they Appear entirely Satisfied." Rosencrantz to Wayne, 19 June 1794, WP, OHS, 36: 30–31.

24. Buell, "Diary," 4–5; Bradley, *Journal*, 27.

25. Buell, "Diary," 8–9.

26. Wayne to Knox, 3 March 1794, Wayne to Knox, 10 March 1794, Knopf, *Anthony Wayne*, 306–10.

27. McDonald, *Biographical Sketches*, 184–87; Wayne to Wilkinson, 14 March 1794, WP, OHS, 33: 92; Underwood, *Journal*, 11–12. McDonald mistakenly stated that Henry Miller was with Wells and almost shot his brother Christopher.

28. "Statement of Christopher Miller," March 1794, WP, OHS, 39: 1–3; Underwood, *Journal*, 11–12; Wayne to Wilkinson, 14 March 1794, Wayne to Gibson, 19 March 1794, Gibson to Wayne, 11 May 1794, WP, OHS, 33: 92, 115, 194; *Kentucky Gazette*, 22 March 1794, DM, 33S, 220–21; Underwood wrote that "two were killed, and the third man ran and was taken."

29. Wayne to Gibson, 17 April 1794, Gibson to Wayne, 23 April 1794, 24 April 1794, 1 May 1794, WP, OHS, 33: 56–57, 85, 88, 128; Buell, "Diary," 6.

30. "Three Nations to Mckee," 6 May 1794, "Information from Sullivan," 2 June 1794, Cruikshank, *Simcoe*, 2: 230, 357–58.

31. "Lord Dorchester's reply to the Seven Villages of Lower Canada," Quebec, 10 February 1794, Hamtramck to Wayne, 13 May 1794, Jacob Slough to Wayne, 28 May 1794, Lieut. Strong to Wayne, 30 May 1794, WP, OHS, 33: 201–202; 34: 215; 35: 129–30, 143; Simcoe to McKee, 10 July 1794, Cruikshank, *Simcoe*, 5: 97; Buell, "Diary," 6.

32. Wayne to John Belli, 26 May 1794, to Gibson, 27 May 1794, Gibson to Wayne, 31 May 1794, Wilkinson to Wayne, 3 June 1794, Edward Butler to Wayne, 17 June 1794, Wayne to the Choctaws and Chickasaws, Gibson to Wayne, 24 June 1794, "Examination of two Shawanese Warriors," 22 June 1794, WP, OHS, 35: 117, 125, 151, 167–68, 235; 36: 18–19, 65, 77–79. "Examination of two Potawatomies," 7 June 1794, *ASP,IA*, 1: 489. On 14 June 1794 a British officer at the Glaize wrote: "Several Indians have been lately killed by the American scouts—a party was discovered a few days ago consisting of about twenty six men." "Diary of an Officer," Cruikshank, *Simcoe*, 5: 90.

33. Wayne to Gibson, 26 June 1794, Wayne orders, 28 June 1794, Wayne to Scott, 29 June 1794, WP, OHS, 36: 80–81, 82, 86–88; "Diary of an Officer," Cruikshank, *Simcoe*, 5: 93. The report that Wells killed five Indians may refer to an earlier skirmish in June. The key point is that Wells was seen as a formidable enemy.

34. "Diary of an Officer," Cruikshank, *Simcoe*, 5: 91–93; Norton, *Journal*, 181–82; Wells, "Manners and Customs," 176; Antoine Lasselle stated that "the Chippeways . . . insisted on attacking the fort," Smith, *From Greene Ville*, 312.

35. Buell, "Diary," 7; Gibson to Wayne, 30 June 1794, WP, OHS, 36: 94–96; "Isaac Paxton," McBride, *Pioneer Biography*, 2: 121–23; Underwood, *Journal*, 13; Hamtramck, "Letters," *American Pioneer* (1843), 301; Nelson, *Jonathan Alder*, 109. "There was a small block house . . . erected across the river in order to cover the watering place . . . defended by a corporal and six privates. . . . It is thought this small party destroyed more of the enemy than were killed from the fort," "Historical Anecdotes," *WRLM* (Lexington, Ky., 1820), 112–16.

36. Gibson to Wayne, 30 June 1794, Gibson to Wayne, 5 July 1794, WP, OHS, 36: 94–96, 149; "Diary of an Officer," Cruikshank, *Simcoe*, 5: 93; "Paxton," McBride, *Pioneer Biography*, 2: 121–22; *Kentucky Gazette*, 2 July 1794, DM, 33S, 235–36.

37. Nelson, *Jonathan Alder*, 109–13; Gibson to Wayne, 1 July 1794, WP, OHS, 36: 103–104; "Paxton," 121–22.

38. "Diary of an Officer," McKee to England, 5 July 1794, McKee to Simcoe, 5 July 1794, Duggan to Chew, 4 October 1794, "John Voris," 24 July 1794, McKee to Simcoe, 25 July 1794, Cruikshank, *Simcoe*, 5: 93–94, 96; 2: 306, 317, 341.

39. Wayne to O'Hara, 4 July 1794, Gibson to Wayne, 1 July 1794, 2 July 1794, 10 July 1794, "Examination of a Potawatime Warrior," 21 July 1794, WP, OHS, 36: 126–28, 103–104, 115–16, 173–74, 223–26; see Orderly Book, *MPHC*, 34: 526. James Neill and at least two other packhorsemen were taken prisoner; "he . . . saw about twenty dead [warriors] carried off"; he was later told "the Indians lost two to one that they did at St. Clair's defeat," *ASP,IA*, 1: 495; Wells, "Manners and Customs," 176. A Shawnee prisoner said "the Chippeways, Pattawatamie & Tawas made the attack;—the Delawares & Shawnese keeping back. . . . They had 20 killed in the attack and 20 men more had died of their wounds," Smith, *From Greene Ville*, 277. Many historians understate the Indians killed at Fort Recovery: "the Indian losses . . . were minor; indeed, it was the much heavier American losses that weakened the Indians, for the scalps and prisoners the Lake Indians had taken 'accomplished the call of their Belts,' and they went home," White, *Middle Ground*, 266.

40. Wayne to Gibson, 2 July 1794, Wayne to Capt. Thomas Pasteur, 9 July 1794, Gibson to Wayne, 5 July 1794, 10 July 1794, 16 July 1794, 22 July 1794, "Examination of a Potawatime Warrior," 23 July 1794, WP, OHS, 36: 118–19, 137–41, 149, 173–74, 196–97, 215, 223–26; Wayne to Knox, 7 July 1794, Knopf, *Anthony Wayne*, 347–49; *Kentucky Gazette*, 2 July 1794, DM, 33S, 235–36. See Sugden, *Blue Jacket*, 163, and Nelson, "Never Have They Done So Little," 43–55.

41. Hamtramck, 1 November 1801, in Wells to Eustis, 25 June 1809, NASW; McKee, in Sugden, *Blue Jacket*, 169.

42. Gibson to Wayne, 18 July 1794, "Examination of a Potawatime," 21 August 1794," Pasteur to Wayne, 4 August 1794, Vigo to Wayne, 6 August 1794, WP, OHS, 36: 196–97, 223–26, 263–66, 273–74; England to Simcoe, 22 July 1794, Cruikshank, *Simcoe*, 2: 333–34.

43. Smith, *From Greene Ville*, 249; Clark, "Journal," 419–20. Both Clark and the anonymous author of *From Greene Ville*, probably James Wilkinson himself, were hostile to Wayne, and their accounts emphasize the negative and overstate their valid criticisms. Wayne's rapid march did take a toll on horses and men.

44. Orderly Book, *MPHC*, 34: 532; Heckewelder, *Manners and Customs*, 192; Smith, *From Greene Ville*, 257.

45. Knopf, "Kentucky Volunteers," 261; Cooke, "Wayne's Campaign," 313; Smith, *From Greene Villes*, 262; Hart, DM, 5W; Wayne to Isaac Wayne, 10 September 1794, to Sharp Delany, 14 November 1794, WP, OHS, 37: 91–93; 38: 88–90.

46. Knopf, "The Fort Adams Incident," OHS, 37: 3; Gaff, *Bayonets*, 389n21; Wayne to Knox, 25 January 1795, WP, HSP; Bowyer, "Daily Journal," 316; Paul C. Cooper to Wayne, 15 August 1794, WP, OHS, 37: 18–19; Cooke, "Wayne's Campaign," 314–15; Clark, "Journal," 422; "Examination of a Shawnee prisoner taken by Capt. Wells," WP, OHS, 37: 9–10; "Confidential Intelligence by Abraham Williams," 10 November 1794, WP, OHS, 38: 81–83.

47. Hamtramck to Harmar, July 1793, DM, 5W; Quaife, "Wilkinson's Narrative," 82; Smith, *From Greene Ville*, 253, 255, 268–69; Clark, "Journal," 423; "Deposition of R. Newman, Green Ville," 1 December 1794, WP, OHS, 38: 150–57; Newman letter, Cruikshank, *Simcoe*, 3: 113–14. Newman later confessed "that he thought that general Wilkinson had received a Bribe from the British, or would receive one," Davison, "Jones," 167.

48. Wayne to Elliott and Williams, 8 December 1793, 10 September 1794, to Isaac Wayne, 10 September 1794, WP, OHS, 37: 94–96, 91–93; Wayne to Knox, 29 January 1795, Knopf, *Anthony Wayne*, 383. Linklater claims the affair was "contrived by Wayne to destroy JW's connections to the British in Canada," *Artist in Treason*, 351n142; see Gaff, *Bayonets*, 269–73.

49. Smith, *From Greene Ville*, 261–69; Clark, "Journal," 422; Knopf, "Precise Journal," 283.

50. Clark, "Journal," 422–23; Smith, *From Greene Ville*, 269–72.

51. Hart, DM, 5W; Knopf, "Kentucky Volunteers," 263; Bowyer, "Daily Journal," 316–17; Orderly Book, *MPHC*, 34: 542; see Sleeper-Smith, *Indian Women*, 73–95.

52. Clark, "Journal," 424; Cooke, "Wayne's Campaign," 314; Simmons, *Forts*, 15–16; James Truslow Adams, ed., *Dictionary of American History* (New York: Charles Scribner's Sons, 1940), 2: 127–28.

53. Smith, *Edward Miller*, 4; McDonald, *Biographical Sketches*, 194. McDonald stated that they rode back not to gather information, but to "give them a rally, in which each should kill his Indian," 193.

54. McDonald, *Biographical Sketches*, 193; Isaac and Enoch Boone, DM, 12C, 33S; Thomas Hunt, 21S, 42–44; DM, 8BB, 56, 64; Brickell, "Captivity," 52–53; Knopf, "Kentucky Volunteers," 263–64. Nicholas Miller was probably the sixth spy. William May might not have been involved. Thomas Hunt stated that Wells was not hit by a musket ball but rather a ramrod that a warrior in his haste forgot to remove, 21S, 44.

55. McDonald, *Biographical Sketches*, 194–95; Orderly Book, 13 August 1794, *MPHC*, 34: 14; "Examination of a Shawnee prisoner," 11 August 1794, WP, OHS, 37: 9–10; Smith, *From Greene Ville*, 276–77; DM, 8BB, 56; Smith, *Edward Miller*, 4; Cooke, "Wayne's Campaign," 315; McKee, 13 August 1794, Cruikshank, *Simcoe*, 2: 317.

56. Knopf, "Precise Journal," 286; Clark, "Journal," 425; Smith, *From Greene Ville*, 278; Cooke, "Journal," 315n1; Wayne's Peace Proposal, 13 August 1794, WP, OHS, 37: 11–12.

57. Clark, "Journal," 426; Knopf, "Precise Journal, 287–88; "Reply to Wayne's Peace Proposal," 15 August 1794, WP, OHS, 37: 14; Norton, *Journal*, 184; McKee to Richard England, 15 August 1794, *MPHC*, 25: 14.

58. Clark, "Journal," 427; Knopf, "Kentucky Volunteers," 265; Knopf, "Precise Journal," 288; Smith, *From Greene Ville*, 285–86.

59. Smith, *From Greene Ville*, 285–86; Bowyer, "Daily Journal," 318; Sword, *Washington's Indian War*, 296; Wilkinson to Wayne, 18 November 1792, WP, HSP; McKee to Joseph Chew, 27 August 1794, Cruikshank, *Simcoe*, 3: 8; "Paxton," McBride, *Pioneer Biography*, 2: 29; Brickell, "Captivity," 52–53. For May's past, see Gaff, *Bayonets*, 80–82. May learned that Trueman and Hardin had been killed; on his return he crossed St. Clair's battlefield, noting where some cannon were buried. Underwood and McBride assume that Wells was with May when he was captured.

60. Quaife, "Wilkinson Narrative," 84; Burns Narrative, Cist, *Sketches*, 118; Simmons, *Forts*, 18–19; Smith, *From Greene Ville*, 287; Sudduth, DM, 14U, 133; Clark, "Journal," 427; Norton, *Journal*, 184; McKee to Chew, 27 August 1794, Cruikshank, *Simcoe*, 3: 8.

61. DM, 5U, 124.

62. Norton, *Journal*, 184.

63. Nelson, *Jonathan Alder*, 114–15; Weld, *Travels* [1807], in Cruikshank, *Simcoe*, 3: 9.

64. "Clark's Journal," 427–28; Smith, *From Greene Ville*, 288–89; Sudduth, DM, 14U, 134–35. See Pratt, "Fallen Timbers," 4–34; Sword, *Washington's Indian War*, 287–311; Gaff, *Bayonets*, 290–340.

65. Bowyer, "Daily Journal," 318–19; Cooke, "Wayne's Campaign," 316; Sudduth, DM, 14U, 136.

66. McKee to Chew, 27 August 1794, Simcoe to George Hammond, 10 November 1794, Cruikshank, *Simcoe*, 3: 8, 179–80; Norton, *Journal*, 184–85; Clark, "Journal," 429.

67. Quaife, "Wilkinson Narrative," 84; Smith, *From Greene Ville*, 291–92.

68. Wayne to Knox, 28 August 1794, Knopf, *Anthony Wayne*, 352–53; Cleaves, *Old Tippecanoe*, 18–19; DM, 21S, 270–71; Knopf, "Kentucky Volunteers," 266; McKee to Chew, 27 August 1794, Cruikshank, *Simcoe*, 3: 8; Smith, *From Greene Ville*, 292–93.

69. Young, *Westward*, 141; Cooper, *The Last of the Mohicans*, Mohawk edition (New York: G. P. Putnam's Sons, 1890), 399; Sudduth, DM, 14U, 136; Norton, *Journal*, 185; Smith, *From Greene Ville*, 294–95.

70. Smith, *From Greene Ville*, 297; Quaife, "Wilkinson Narrative," 84–85; Clark, "Journal," 428–29; Knopf, "Kentucky Volunteers," 265–66; McKee to Chew, 27 August 1794, Cruikshank, *Simcoe*, 3: 8; Norton, *Journal*, 185; *ASP,IA*, 1: 491; Knopf, "Precise Journal," 299–300; Wells, "Manners and Customs," 176.

71. "They had fought with very inferior numbers, and in a disadvantageous position," Norton, *Journal*, 186; Wells, "Manners and Customs," 176. Most historians agree with Sugden: "Little Turtle opposed a stand but was overruled by the influence of Blue Jacket," *Blue Jacket*, 174–76, yet on 14 July 1794, Little Turtle said: "We will stop our Brother [Wayne] for ten days, we shall then have all our force collected and will go up and fight him," Gaff, *Bayonets*, 293.

72. Knopf, "Kentucky Volunteers," 266; Smith, *From Greene Ville*, 296, 320; Quaife, "Wilkinson's Narrative," 85–88; WP, OHS, 37: 30–33; Orderly Book, *MPHC*, 34: 546.

73. Quaife, "Wilkinson Narrative," 87; Wayne/Campbell letters, 21–22 August 1794, WP, OHS, 37: 40–47; Simcoe to the Duke of Portland, 20 December 1794, *MPHC*, 25: 67–74.

74. Wayne, 22 August 1794, WP, OHS, 37: 47; Clark, "Journal," 431; Knopf, "Kentucky Volunteers," 266; McKee to Chew, 27 August 1794, William Mayne diary, 1 October 1794, Cruikshank, *Simcoe*, 3: 8, 76; Norton, *Journal*, 186; Quaife, *Askin Papers*, 1: 373.

75. England to Simcoe, 30 August 1794, William Mayne diary, 26 September 1794, Cruikshank, *Simcoe*, 3: 20–21, 75; Campbell, 22 August 1794, Simcoe to the Duke of Portland, 20 December 1794, *MPHC*, 25: 20–21, 67–74.

76. "Clark's Journal," 432; "Isaac Paxton," McBride, *Pioneer Biography*, 2: 131; Smith, *From Greene Ville*, 302, 306, 318; Quaife, "Wilkinson Narrative," 88–89.

77. Bowyer, "Daily Journal," 433n; Smith, *From Greene Ville*, 306, 321–22.

78. Smith, *From Greene Ville*, 316, 309–10; Grand Glaize, 6 September 1794, Wayne at Grand Glaize to Sachems & Warriors, Wayne to Hunt, 13 September 1794, WP, OHS, 37: 83, 102–104, 106–107; see Cruikshank, *Simcoe*, 3: 79–80.

79. Knopf, "Kentucky Volunteers," 271; Bradley, *Journal*, 32; Bowyer, "Daily Journal," 353; Clark, "Journal," 438; Woehrmann, *Headwaters*, 46–47; Knopf, "Precise Journal," 297; Cooke, "Wayne's Campaign," 341; Wayne to Knox, 17 October 1794, Knopf, *Anthony Wayne*, 368; Simmons, *Forts*, 19–20.

80. Cooke, "Wayne's Campaign," 342–43; Smith, *Edward Miller*, 16–17, Knopf, "Precise Journal," 296.

81. Isaac Williams to the Chiefs and Warriors of Sandusky, 25 September 1794, WP, OHS, 37: 134–35; Council at Brown's Town, 13 October 1794, Dorchester to the Lord of Portland, 1 January 1795, *MPHC*, 25: 45–46, 83–84; Smith to McKee, 23 October 1794, Richard England, Information of Antoine Lasselle, 1 November 1794, Cruikshank, *Simcoe*, 3: 117, 166.

CHAPTER 7

Biographers of Washington and Adams rarely discuss negotiations with the Indians; nor do biographers of Henry Knox and James McHenry, who served as secretary of war during this period. See Nicholas, *Indians, Federalists*; White, *Middle Ground*; Cayton, "Noble Actors." For interpreters, see Merrell, *Into the American Woods*.

1. *ASP,IA*, 1: 567; Carter, *Little Turtle*, 145–47.

2. WP, OHS, 37: 134–39; 38: 28–29; 39: 105–107; *ASP,IA*, 1: 549–50, 528.

3. *ASP,IA*, 1: 548–49, 526; Simcoe's Reply to the Indians, Smith to McKee, 25 October 1794, Cruikshank, *Simcoe*, 3: 121–25, 119; Information from Tarhe, WP, OHS, 38: 180–83.

4. Knox to Wayne, 2 December 1794, 5 December 1794, Knopf, *Anthony Wayne*, 366–68; Simcoe to Duke of Portland, 20 December 1794, 22 December 1794, *MPHC*, 25: 67–77; Wayne to Hardy, 22 December 1794, to Delany, 14 November 1794, WP, OHS, 38: 235–37, 88–90.

5. Portland to Simcoe, 8 January 1795, *MPHC*, 25: 85; England to Simcoe, 4 February 1795, Antoine Lasselle to Jacques Lasselle, 31 January 1795, Cruikshank, *Simcoe*, 3: 286, 281; Hamtramck to Wayne, 29 December 1794, *MPHC*, 34: 734; Buell, "Diary," 15; Speech by Wayne to the Sachems, 19 January 1795, WP, OHS, 39: 16–22.

6. Speech of Richerville, 22 January 1795, Speech of Bad Bird, 19 January 1795, WP, OHS, 39: 28–29, 22–25; Buell, "Diary," 16.

7. Lasselle to Lasselle, 31 January 1795, Cruikshank, *Simcoe*, 3: 281; Blue Jacket's Speech, 8 February 1795, Telebockiaha's Speech, WP, OHS, 39: 47–51; Wayne to Knox, 24 January 1795, 12 February 1795, 29 January 1795, to Pickering, 8 March 1795, Knopf, *Anthony Wayne*, 379–81, 384–85, 383.

8. Council of the Six Nations, 25 October 1793, Simcoe to Duke of Portland, 22 December 1794, Dorchester to Portland, 1 January 1795, *MPHC*, 25: 47–61, 75–77, 83–84; Pickering to Wayne, 8 April 1795, Knopf, *Anthony Wayne*, 394–96.

9. Pickering to Wayne, 8 April 1795, Knopf, *Anthony Wayne*, 396–403.

10. Pickering to Wayne, 8 April 1795, 15 April 1795, Knopf, *Anthony Wayne*, 399, 405–406.

11. Wayne to Wells, 9 March 1795, DM, 16U; Wayne's speech to the Wabash Indians, 19 March 1795, WP, OHS, 39: 83; Hamtramck to Wayne, 27 March 1795, *MPHC*, 34: 735–36.

12. Council at Fort Knox, 19–21 April 1795, WP, OHS, 40: 35–49.

13. Robert Hunter to Wayne, 5 May 1795, DM, 16U, 92.

14. Heath, "Rhys Diary," 154, 156–57.

15. Merrell, *American Woods*, 28–32. When Nicholas Gevelot carved West's painting above the north door of the Rotunda in the 1820s, he added an interpreter, "perhaps because he was himself a foreigner in the early republic," 334–35n25. Another version of Christy's painting is in the Garst Museum in Greenville, Ohio. See Kawashima, "Forest Diplomats," 1–14, and Hagerdorn, "A Friend," 60–80.

16. Merrell, *American Woods*, 20–22, 153–54; Hagerdorn, "A Friend," 61–63.

17. Hagerdorn, "A Friend," 61; Merrell, *American Woods*, 55–56.

18. Hagerdorn, "A Friend," 61, 64–65; Merrell, *American Woods*, 187–88, 202, 212–17; Hamtramck to Wilkinson, 28 March 1796, *MPHC*, 34: 738.

19. Kawashima, "Forest Diplomats," 8; Hagerdorn, "A Friend," 61–65; Merrell, *American Woods*, 56, 213–15.

20. Knopf, *Surgeon's Mate*, 39; Carter, *Little Turtle*, 103.

21. Cayton, "Noble Actors," 235–69; *ASP,IA*, 1: 565–67.

22. Heath, "Rhys Diary," 157–59.

23. Ibid., 159–62; Treaty of Greenville, *ASP,IA*, I: 564–65; Orderly Book, *MPHC*, 34: 620.

24. Orderly Book, *MPHC*, 34: 590, 614–15, 621, 626–28, 640; Rhees, *Altar of Peace*, NWOH 80, no. 2 (Spring 2013): 168–71; Davison, "Jones," 139.

25. *ASP,IA*, 1: 567–68. Voegelin-Wheeler and Tanner, *Indians of Ohio*, 2: 377–427. The other interpreters were: Jacques Lasselle, M. Morris, Baptiste Sans Crainte, Christopher Miller, Robert Wilson, Abraham Williams, and Isaac Zane.

26. *ASP,IA*, 1: 568–69. "Little Turtle . . . by reason of his superior intelligence towered above all the chiefs," Carter, *Little Turtle*, 149; "More than any other Indian leader, he [Blue Jacket] delivered the peace," Sugden, *Blue Jacket*, 200. Blue Jacket urged the various nations to attend; Little Turtle was the most forceful speaker at the council.

27. *ASP,IA*, 1: 569–70; Davison, "Jones," 139–40.

28. *ASP,IA*, 1: 570–71; Askin to England, 19 August 1795, Cruikshank, *Simcoe*, 4: 70; Knopf, *Surgeon's Mate*, 60–61. After the treaty, David Zeisberger wrote: "they were not forced, but as they found themselves too weak and helpless to continue the war with the States, they have chosen to make peace," Bliss, *Diary*, 418.

29. *ASP,IA*, 1: 571–72.

30. Ibid., 573–74.

31. Ibid., 574–75.

32. Ibid., 575–76. Tarhe presented a speech written by Isaac Williams.

33. Ibid., 576–78; Davison, "Jones," 140; Pickering to Wayne, 29 June 1795, Knopf, *Anthony Wayne*, 430–34; "He [Wayne] has obtained more land than was expected," Pickering to Washington, 28 September 1795, Carter, *Territorial Papers*, 2: 537.

34. Davison, "Jones," 140; *ASP,IA*, 1: 578–82. For a description of the medals, see Wilson, *Council Fire*, 67–68.

35. Robert Steele to R. G. England, 20 August 1795, Cruikshank, *Simcoe*, 4: 72; *ASP,IA*, 1: 582–83.

36. Linklater, *Artist in Treason*, 159–60; Wayne to McHenry, 10 August 1796, Knopf, *Anthony Wayne*, 509.

37. Wayne to McHenry, 28 August 1796, Knopf, *Anthony Wayne*, 515; Weld, *Travels*, 2: 187; Bald, *Detroit's First Decade*, 63.

38. Wayne to McHenry, 20 September 1796, Knopf, *Anthony Wayne*, 526–27; Denny, *Journal*, 271–72; Bald, *Detroit*, 17–27; Weld, *Travels*, 187; Heath, *Blacksnake's Path*, 226–27. Detroit did burn to the ground in 1805.

39. Wayne to McHenry, 30 September 1796, Knopf, *Anthony Wayne*, 530–31.

40. Wayne to McHenry, 3 October 1796, Knopf, *Anthony Wayne*, 532–33. Wells's injury was to the wrist, not the arm.

41. Janson, *Stranger*, 183, 185–87; Niemcewicz, *Vine and Fig Tree*, 36–38; Bailey, *Life and Adventures*, 146.

42. Jeremy, *Henry Wansey*, 122–23; Griswold, *Republican Court*, 324–25, 439; Robert Baldrick, ed., *The Memoirs of Chateaubriand* (New York: Knopf, 1961), 135; Weld, *Travels*, 2: 22; Roberts and Roberts, *American Journey*, 280–84; Janson, *Stranger*, 25.

43. Weld, *Travels*, 2: 261–67; Smith,*"Lower Sort,"* 16–19; Roberts and Roberts, *American Journey*, 291, 302–303, 309.

44. McHenry to Washington, 28 November 1796, George Washington Papers, LC; "Letters to [the] President [of] the United States," John Adams Papers, NA, Reel 384, 40–70; see James McHenry Papers, WCL.

45. McHenry to Washington, 28 November 1796, Washington Papers, LC; Elkins and McKitrick, *Age of Federalism*, 629–30; Griswold, *Republican Court*, 242, 325–26; Beard, *Maclay*, 135, 201.

46. Abigail Adams to Mary Cranch, 5 January 1790, John Adams to Benjamin Rush, 11 November 1807, Gouverneur Morris to John Marshall, 26 June 1807, in Kaminski, *The Founders*, 504, 516, 513; Weld, *Travels*, 2: 105.

47. John Adams to Benjamin Rush, 21 June 1811, Daniel Webster to James Hervey Bingham, 5 February 1800, Kaminski, *The Founders*, 517, 512; Heath, *Blacksnake's Path*, 231–32.

48. Washington to The Secretary of State, 1 July 1796, Fitzpatrick, *Writings*, 35: 112; Ellis, *American Creation*, 130. Ellis, in chapter four, "The Treaty," asserts that the Washington and Knox peace initiative to the Creeks represented "a wholesale reversal of American Indian policy" and a transformation of the president's philosophy, but this is overly optimistic, as a closer look at the Old Northwest would have made clear.

49. To the Chiefs and Warriors, 28 November 1796, Fitzpatrick, *Writings*, 35: 299–302.

50. Kelsay, *Brant*, 418–22; Speech of Red Pole, 30 November 1796, Talk of the Secretary of War to the Chiefs . . . 8 December 1796, John Adams Papers, NA, Reel 384, 40–70.

51. Talk to the Cherokee Nation, 29 November 1796, Fitzpatrick, *Writings*, 35: 193–98.

52. Brigham, *Public Culture*, 17–22, 44, 61–62; see Sellers, *Peale's Museum*, 20–90.

53. Sellers, "Good Chiefs," 10–18; Sellers, *Peale's Museum*, 91; *The Selected Papers of Charles Willson Peale* (New Haven, Conn.: Yale University Press, 1988), 2: 160–64.

54. McHenry Papers, 1 December 1796, WCL; Adams Papers, NA, Reel 384; Sellers, "Good Chiefs," 10.

55. "Farewell Address," 19 September 1796, Fitzpatrick, *Writings*, 35: 214–38. Washington to General William Heath of Roxbury: "The conduct of France towards the United States is . . . outrageous beyond conception . . . we should do justice to *all* but have no political connexions with *any* of the European powers." 35: 448–50.

56. "Eighth Annual Address to Congress," 7 December 1796, Fitzpatrick, *Writings*, 35: 214–38; McHenry to Washington, 10 December 1796, McHenry Papers, WCL; McHenry to Little Turtle, 10 December 1796, James Wilkinson Papers, CHS. The statement Wells signed on 9 December 1796 is reproduced in Woehrmann, *Headwaters*, following page 157.

57. Maj. Isaac Craig to McHenry, 3 February 1797, *Hazard's Register of Pennsylvania* (1833), 12: 63; Sellers, "Good Chiefs," 14. Red Pole's body and marker now reside in the chancel of Trinity Cathedral in Pittsburgh.

58. Steiner, *James McHenry*, 208–25, 259–66; Wilkinson to McHenry, 15 May 1797, McHenry Papers, WCL.

59. Wilkinson, *Memoirs*, 2: Appendix 46; Baron Carondelet's Instructions, 26 May 1797, appendix 54.

60. Adams to Wilkinson, 2 February 1798, Adams, *Works*, 8: 563–64; General Wilkinson's Appeal to President Adams, 26 December 1797, *Memoirs*, 2: appendix 38; Linklater, *Artist in Treason*, 172–75.

61. John Adams, in Hawke, *Benjamin Rush*, 132; Nathan G. Goodman, *Benjamin Rush* (Philadelphia: University of Pennsylvania Press, 1934), 193, 290, 240–41; J. H. Powell, *Bring Out Your Dead* (Philadelphia: University of Pennsylvania Press, 1949), 136; Corner, *Autobiography*, 80, 240–41.

62. Corner, *Autobiography*, 240–41.

63. Speech of the Little Turtle to Adams . . . , 7 February 1797, JCB: Misc. Mss., http://wardepartmentpapers.org.

64. Volney, *Soil and Climate*, v–vi, 354–55, 377.

65. Ibid., 356–63.

66. Ibid., 263–70, 385.

67. Ibid., 270–79.

68. Ibid., 375–79; English translation, 426–27.

69. Volney, *Soil and Climate*, v–vi. American novelist Charles Brocken Brown, his translator, noted: "Volney is an enthusiast against the savages, and is as zealous to depreciate, as Rousseau was to exalt their character." Volney makes the intriguing claim that Rousseau intended his essay to favor civilization, but Diderot goaded him to make a more controversial defense of primitive man instead. See note, 386–37.

70. Niemcewicz, *Vine and Fig Tree*, 47; Charles Merrill Mount, *Gilbert Stuart* (New York: W. W. Norton, 1964), 220; Mantle Fielding, *Gilbert Stuart's Portraits of Washington* (Philadelphia: printed for subscribers, 1923), 70; Kelley, *Colonial Philadelphia*, 132–34; Young, *Little Turtle*, 147. Young follows Moses Dawson's stilted version of what Little Turtle probably said.

71. Niemcewicz, *Vine and Fig Tree*, 45; Roberts and Roberts, *American Journey*, 247–48; L. H. Butterfield, ed., *Letters of Benjamin Rush* (Princeton, N.J.: Princeton University Press, 1951), 2: 788–89; Young, *Little Turtle*, 147.

72. Ferling, *John Adams*, 336; Beard, *Maclay*, 84; Freeman, *Affairs of Honor*, 105; Kaminski, *The Founders*, 37, 46, 53; Wood, *Empire of Liberty*, 209.

73. McCullough, *John Adams*, 489; Freeman, *Affairs of Honor*, 174; Wood, *Empire of Liberty*, 229. See Wood's chapter 5, "The French Revolution in America," and Howe, "Republican Thought," 147–65.

74. McHenry to Little Turtle, 20 February 1798, JCB, wardepartmentpapers.org.

75. Niemcewicz, *Vine and Fig Tree*, 33–34; Claude G. Bowers, *Jefferson and Hamilton* (Boston: Houghton Mifflin, 1925), 260; see Alberts, *Golden Voyage*; for a dinner at the Binghams', see Heath, *Blacksnake's Path*, 247–54.

76. Alberts, *Golden Voyage*, 333–35; Wood, *Empire of Liberty*, 241–47, 260–68; Elkins and McKitrick, *Age of Federalism*, 585–88.

77. McHenry to Wilkinson, 6 March 1798, Donald G. Mitchell to McHenry, 25 March 1798, JCL, wardeparmentpapers.org; Jacobs, *Tarnished Warrior*, 166, 171.

CHAPTER 8

For Jefferson's Indian policy, see Wallace, *Jefferson and Indians*, and Sheehan, *Seeds of Extinction*. For Jefferson's foreign policy: Tucker and Henderson, *Empire of Liberty*, and O'Brien, *Long Affair*. For Indiana and Harrison: Cayton, *Frontier Indiana*, and Owens, *Jefferson's Hammer*.

1. Jefferson to General Chastellux, 7 June 1785, Peterson, *Writings*, 801; Jefferson to John Adams, 11 June 1811, Bergh, *Writings of Jefferson*, 13: 160; Wallace, *Jefferson and Indians*, 48–49; Jefferson to Madison, 30 January 1787, Peterson, *Writings*, 882. Fliegelman suggested that Outacite's departure speech "served Jefferson as a way of addressing, mourning, and ennobling the death of his father," *Declaring Independence*, 99.

2. Adams, "Autobiography" [1802], Kaminski, *Founders*, 687–88; Wills, *Inventing America*, 78; Jefferson to Daniel Webster, 4 December 1790, Boyd, *Papers*, 18: 132.

3. Adams, *History*, 1: 188, 641; Charles Francis Adams, in Ellis, *American Sphinx*, 124; John Adams to Abigail Adams, 26 December 1793, John Adams to Benjamin Rush, September 1807, Kaminski, *The Founders*, 300, 314. For slavery metaphor, see Bailyn, *Ideological Origins*, and Dorsey, *Common Bondage*.

4. Ellis, *American Sphinx*, xii, 10, 122–23; Jefferson to Maria Conway, 12 November 1786, Peterson, *Writings*, 870; Wallace, *Jefferson and Indians*, 14–16; Jefferson to Edward Rutledge, 30 November 1795, Ellis, *American Sphinx*, 134. See Dumas Malone, *Jefferson and His Time* (Boston: Little, Brown, 1948–77); Peterson, *Jefferson & the New Nation*; Onuf, "Scholars' Jefferson," 671–99; and Shuffelton, *Cambridge Companion*. Jefferson's most recent biographer Jon Meacham skims over his two-term presidency in less than one hundred pages, giving a single paragraph to the Indians of the Old Northwest, 392; the Prologue alludes vaguely to "battles by proxy with . . . British allies among the Indians," *Art of Power*, xxvii.

5. See Sheehan, *Seeds of Extinction*, 66–87. Jefferson began the *Notes* when he was governor of Virginia during the Revolution and revised it in Paris, where it was published in 1785. Jefferson considered the 1787 English edition closer to his intentions. His additional notes and revisions are included in the Peden edition.

6. Jefferson, *Notes*, 58–59.

7. Ibid., 59–64, 227–57; Wallace, *Jefferson and Indians*, 2–13.

8. Wallace, *Jefferson and Indians*, 96–102. Jefferson's excavation of the Indian mound was crude, his collection of Indian vocabularies was stolen and destroyed, and his speculations about his findings unreliable, yet his pioneering investigations were a step toward more thorough and reliable research. The construction "we have suffered" Indian tribes "to extinguish" obscures exactly who was doing the suffering —victims or victimizers?

9. Jefferson, *Notes*, 200–202, 93, 83–85. Jefferson's findings were supported by Charles Thomson's expert commentaries, included as an appendix to the *Notes*.

10. Jefferson, in Wallace, *Jefferson and Indians*, 138; Jefferson, *Notes*, 138; Jefferson to the Marquis de Chastellux, 7 June 1785, Peterson, *Writings*, 800. See Miller, *Wolf by the Ears*, and Jordan, *White Over Black*.

11. Jefferson, *Notes*, 138–63; Jefferson, *Autobiography*, Peterson, *Writings*, 44.

12. Jefferson to John Page, 5 August 1776, Boyd, *Papers*, 1: 485–86; Jefferson to Edmund Pendleton, 13 August 1776, Peterson, *Writings*, 754; Padover, *Complete Jefferson*, 449–52.

13. Onuf, *Statehood and Union*, 63; Benjamin Hawkins, 13 August 1786, Boyd, *Papers*, 10: 240. Wills noted that the antislavery provision in the ordinance owed more to Timothy Pickering than Jefferson, *"Negro President,"* 23.

14. Jefferson to Charles Carroll, 15 April 1791, Peterson, *Writings*, 977; Hammond to Jefferson, Bergh, *Writings of Jefferson*, 27: 328–29.

15. Speeches of Indian Chiefs, 1 February 1793, Padover, *Complete Jefferson*, 453–58.

16. Jefferson was the "head of the party in Congress who had opposed every measure deemed necessary by the federalists," George Baer to Richard H. Bayard, 18 April 1830, Davis, *Memoirs*, 2: 116–17; Hamilton to James McHenry, 6 June 1800, Adams to Benjamin Rush, 25 January 1806, Adams to Abigail Adams, 31 December 1796, 9 January 1797, Hamilton to John Jay, 7 May 1800, Kaminski, *The Founders*, 52, 208, 200, 303. See Elkins and McKitrick, *Age of Federalism*, 692–753.

17. *Washington Federalist*, 6 February 1801, Isenberg, *Fallen Founder*, 211; deposition of James A. Bayard, 3 April 1806, Davis, *Memoirs*, 2: 124–31; see Wills, *"Negro President,"* 49–86; Elkins and McKitrick, *Age of Federalism*, 739–50. In the case of a first-place tie, the Constitution stated that the House "shall immediately choose, by ballot, one of them for president; and if no person have a majority [of the electoral vote], then from the five highest on the list." See Bruce Ackerman and David Fontana, "How Jefferson Counted Himself In," *The Atlantic Monthly* (March 2004), 84–95.

18. Hamilton to James A. Bayard, 6 August 1800, to Gouverneur Morris, 24 December 1800, Theodore Sedgwick to Hamilton, 10 January 1801, Hamilton to James A. Bayard, 16 January 1801, Kaminski, *The Founders*, 86, 87–88, 90–11, 91–93; James A. Bayard to Hamilton, 7 January 1801, Davis, *Memoirs*, 2: 113–14; Burr in Elkins and McKitrick, *Age of Federalism*, 746. Bayard and other Federalists wanted Jefferson to give "assurances . . . [that he would] support the system of public credit and financing the debt . . . not dismantle the navy and thus weaken commerce, and . . . not remove federalist officials 'on political grounds only.'" Samuel Smith told Bayard "that Mr. Jefferson would conduct, as to those points, agreeably to the opinions I had stated to him." George Baer to Richard H. Bayard, 18 April 1830, and depositions of James A. Bayard, 3 April 1806 and Samuel Smith, 15 April 1806, Davis, *Memoirs*, 2: 116–18, 124–36.

19. First Inaugural Address, 4 March 1801, Padover, *Complete Jefferson*, 384–87; "conciliation" and "mollifying" in Elkins and McKitrick, *Age of Federalism*, 752–53; "magnanimity," Henry Knox to Thomas Jefferson, 16 March 1801, Oberg, *Papers of Jefferson*, 33: 313; Jefferson to James Madison, 15 March 1789, to John Taylor, 4 June 1797, to P. S. Dupont de Nemours, 18 January 1802, Peterson, *Writings*, 944–45, 1049–51, 1100–1101; Jefferson to Thomas McKean, 24 July 1801, in Adams, *History*, 1: 217; Ellis, *American Sphinx*, 182–83; Jefferson to Levi Lincoln, 25 October 1802, Ford, *Writings of Jefferson*, 8: 175–76.

20. Jefferson to Elbridge Gerry, 29 March 1801, Peterson, *Writings*, 1088–89; Carl E. Prince, "The Passing of the Aristocracy," *The Journal of American History* 57, no. 3 (Dec. 1970), 563–75; Wills, *"Negro President,"* 91–93. For a defense of Jefferson: Malone, *Jefferson and His Time* (1970), 4: 487–93.

21. Wood, *Empire of Liberty*, 294–301.

22. Wells to Meriwether Lewis, 10 May 1801, in Oberg, *Papers of Jefferson*, 36: 274–76; Martha E. Tyson, "Appendix," in Hopkins, *Mission*, 159–69. Little Turtle's nephew the Toad died two years later.

23. Hopkins, *Mission*, 169–75; Jackson, *Civilization*, 101.

24. Bordewich, *Washington*, 60, 30, 9.

25. Gallatin, in David Lean Chandler, *The Jefferson Conspiracies* (New York: William Morrow, 1994), 121–22; Royall, *Sketches*, 130; contemporary observers quoted in Young, *Washington Community*, 98–102, 26; Janson, *Stranger*, 215; Benjamin Henry Latrobe, *The Journal of Latrobe* (New York: D. Appleton, 1905), 133; Heath, *Blacksnake's Path*, 262–64.

26. Young, *Washington Community*, 41; Bordewich, *Washington*, 73; Harris, "Washington's Gamble," 529.

27. Janson, *Stranger*, 213; "Mitchell's Letters," 743; Kaminski, *Founders*, 305, 297–98, 313–14.

28. "Mitchell's Letters," 743; Malone, *Jefferson and His Time* (1970), 4: 106–109; "Presentation of the 'Mammoth Cheese,'" Oberg, *Papers of Jefferson*, 36: 246–52; Pasley, *Beyond the Founders*, 31–56; Cutler, *Life*, 2: 54–55.

29. First Annual Message to Congress, 8 December 1801, Padover, *Complete Jefferson*, 388; Address of Little Turtle, Oberg, *Papers of Jefferson*, 36: 280–86. See editorial note, Conference with Little Turtle, Oberg, 274–79.

30. Erney, *Henry Dearborn*, 333, vi–vii, 122; Jacobs, *U.S. Army*, 245–56; Oberg, *Papers of Jefferson*, 36: 285. Dearborn appointed Wells as "Assistant Agent for Indian Affairs in the Indiana Territory" on 1 January 1801. NASW, vol. B, 144. After Napoleon's triumphs, Dearborn admitted that "this country" should abandon the "idea of depending on Militia for prosecuting war." Kohn, *Eagle and Sword*, 301; Harrison to Dearborn, 1 September 1801, Clanin, *HP*, 172.

31. Jefferson Reply, Henry Dearborn Reply, Response of Little Turtle, Society of Friends Memorial, 7 January 1801, Jefferson, To the Senate and House of Representatives, 27 January 1801, Oberg, *Papers of Jefferson*, 36: 286–90, 278–79, 440–43; Wells in Tyson, appendix, Hopkins, *Mission*, 175–79.

32. Jefferson to David Redick, 19 June 1802, Dearborn to Wells, 11 January 1802, Oberg, *Papers of Jefferson*, 36: 627, 279; Dearborn to Harrison, 23 February 1802, Clanin, *HP*, 265–67.

33. Harrison to Dearborn, 15 June 1801, Esarey, *Messages*, 1: 25–30.

34. The earliest biography is Moses Dawson, *Narrative*; see Cleaves, *Old Tippecanoe*, Owens, *Jefferson's Hammer*, and Jortner, *Gods of Prophetstown*. For Indiana territory under Harrison, see Cayton, *Frontier Indiana*. On duties of agents, Dearborn to Harrison, 23 February 1802, Esarey, *Messages*, 1: 39–40. Wells's essay on the Miamis probably originated with these instructions. See Heath, "Re-evaluating 'The Fort Wayne Manuscript,'" 158–88.

35. Symmes, 2 March 1796, Bond, *Intimate Letters*, 82. Harrison lowered the amount of land to 320 acres and terms of payment were made easier. Dearborn to Harrison, 23 January 1802, Clanin, *HP*, 193–95.

36. Harrison to Madison, 19 January 1802, to Albert Gallatin, 5 February 1802, Dearborn to Harrison, 23 April 1802, 17 June 1802, Clanin, *HP*, 241–42, 255–56, 292, 320–22. Charles C. Royce, *Indian Land Cessions: Eighteenth Annual Report* (Washington, D.C.: U.S. Government, 1899), part 2, tract 26.

37. Dawson, *Narrative*, 25–27; Notes of Speeches at an Indian Council, 15 September 1802, Clanin, *HP*, 387–97; Minutes of Indian Conference, 17 September 1802, Esarey, *Messages*, 1: 56–57.

38. Jefferson and the French Revolution: Jefferson to Madison, 28 October 1885, to George Wythe, 3 August 1786, to Abigail Adams, 22 February 1787, to Comte Buffon, 1 October 1787, to Madison, 6 September 1789, to Diodate, 3 August 1789, to Lafayette, 16 June 1792, to William Short, 3 January 1793, Peterson, *Writings*, 841–42, 859, 889–90, 911, 950, 959–60, 957, 1003–1006; see O'Brien, *The Long Affair*, 1–112.

39. O'Brien, *The Long Affair*, 137, 197–201, 220; Jefferson to Trench Coxe, 1 May 1794, Peterson, *Writings*, 1013–15; Jefferson to Démeunier, 29 April 1795, in O'Brien, *The Long Affair*, 219.

40. Gen. Claude Perrin Victor's expedition was canceled in May 1802. Kukla, *Wilderness*, 216–34; Carl Ludwig Lokke, "Jefferson and the Leclerc Expedition," *The American Historical Review* 33, no. 2 (Jan. 1928): 322–28; Carl Ludwig Lokke, "The Leclerc Instructions," *The Journal of Negro History* 10, no. 1 (Jan. 1925): 80–98. On 22 July 1801 Pichon wrote to Talleyrand without specifying when he had met with Jefferson. Saint Domingue is Haiti, Santo Domingo is the Dominican Republic. Jefferson and other Americans at the time used the term Santo Domingo.

41. Charles Pickney to Jefferson, 6 October 1801, Fulwar Shipwith to Jefferson, 30 October 1801, Oberg, *Papers of Jefferson*, 35: 395–98, 526–41; Rufus King to Madison, 31 October 1801, Brugger, *Papers of Madison*, 2: 214.

42. Leclerc to Decreés, 9 August 1802, to Bonaparte, 7 October 1802, Adams, *History*, 1: 264–69, 280–81; Leclerc to Bonaparte, 6 August 1802, and 9 August 1802, Kukla, *Wilderness*, 223–25.

43. Zuckerman, *Almost Chosen*, 175–218, stresses Jefferson's racist motivations; O'Brien, *Long Affair*, 292–93, assesses the pros and cons; Tucker and Henderson, *Empire of Liberty*, provides an analysis of the events leading up to the Louisiana Purchase, 87–171, 281–316; on Jefferson's lack of military preparedness, Adams, *History*, I: 274; on Jefferson's policy of bluffing a "deal" with France and Talleyrand's offer, Tucker, *Empire of Liberty*, 109–122, 300–301n83; "Damn sugar," Willis, "*Negro President*," 114. Napoleon said Santo Domingo was one of his "greatest follies," Kukla, *Wilderness*, 216. "The deeper truth was that Louisiana was a providential gift from the insurgent slaves and the malaria-carrying mosquitoes of Santo Domingo," Ellis, *American Sphinx*, 207.

44. See "Hamilton on the Louisiana Purchase," *WMQ*, Third Series, 12, no. 2 (April 1955), 268–81; Tucker and Henderson, *Empire of Liberty*, 157–71, aruges that empire was at least as important to Jefferson as liberty, 159–62. The preceding two chapters describe Jefferson's efforts to obtain the Floridas. Adams captures the absurdity, *History*, 1: 467–69.

45. See Gordon-Reed, *The Hemingses*; for dissenting views, Robert F. Turner, ed., *The Jefferson-Hemings Controversy* (Durham, N.C.: Carolina Academic Press, 2011). For Callender's life and death, see Durey, *Callender*. To my knowledge no historian has investigated the possibility that Jefferson's "people" may have murdered Callender. The Jefferson administration did consider assassinating the Shawnee Prophet.

46. Jefferson to Dearborn, 29 December 1802, Wallace, *Jefferson and Indians*, 221; Jefferson to Benjamin Hawkins, 18 February 1803, Peterson, *Writings*, 1113–16.

47. Jefferson to Harrison, 26 February 1803, Peterson, *Writings*, 1117–20.

48. Ibid.; Jefferson to Andrew Jackson, 16 February 1803, Wallace, *Jefferson and Indians*, 220–21.

49. Confidential Message Recommending a Western Exploring Expedition, 18 January 1803, Padover, *Complete Jefferson*, 398–99; Wills, *"Negro President,"* 115–16.

50. To the Miamis and Delawares, 8 January 1803, Padover, *Complete Jefferson*, 462–64. Tetepachsit, Buckongahelas, and other Delaware chiefs were a part of this delegation.

51. Harrison to Dearborn, 3 March 1803, Esarey, *Messages*, 1: 76–84. In November 1802 at the constitutional convention for Ohio in Chillicothe, Wells testified "that Lake Michigan would be found to be much farther south than was supposed," thus making Toledo part of Ohio, Hezekiah Lord Hosmer, *Early History of the Maumee Valley* (repr., Ann Arbor: University of Michigan Library, 2005), 59–60. My thanks to Charles Coutellier for this reference.

52. Address of Black Hoof, 5 February 1802, Oberg, *Papers of Jefferson*, 36: 517–19; Dearborn to Wells, 7 March 1803, 16 March 1803, 10 May 1803, Dearborn to Johnston, 11 May 1803, NASW.

53. Dawson, *Narrative*, 47–50; Journal of the Treaty Negotiations, 2–7 June 1803, Clanin, *HP*, 578–89.

54. Treaty with the Eel Rivers et al., 7 August 1803, Treaty with the Kaskaskias, 13 August 1803, Clanin, *HP*, 600–34; Dawson, *Narrative*, 50–51; Harrison to Dearborn, Esarey, *Messages*, 1: 115; Jefferson, Third Annual Message, 17 October 1803, Padover, *Complete Jefferson*, 401–405.

55. Wells File, CHS; Dearborn to Wells, 19 January 1804, to Wells, 18 May 1803, NASW; Carter, *Territorial Papers*, 7: 168; William Burnett to Harrison, 10 September 1803, Clanin, *HP*, 600–66; Dawson, *Narrative*, 53.

56. Harrison to Jefferson, 12 May 1804, Treaty with Delawares, 18 August 1804, Treaty with the Piankashaws, 27 August 1804, Clanin, *HP*, 798–99, 856–60, 881–84; Jefferson, Annual Message, 8 November 1804, Padover, *Complete Jefferson*, 406–409.

57. Wells to Wilkinson, 6 October 1804, NASW.

58. Dearborn to Wells, 20 October 1804, 24 December 1804, NASW.

59. Delaware Indians to Wells, 30 March 1805, Patterson to Wells, 5 April 1805, Harrison to Dearborn, 26 April 1805, Jefferson to Harrison, 28 April 1805, Esarey, *Messages*, 1: 117–18, 121–23, 125–26, 128. The Moravian missionaries on the White River confirmed that Tetepachsit, Buckongahelas, and Hackinkpomska had sent

Billy Patterson to Wells with "a complaint that they had been tricked at the treaty," Gibson, *Moravian Mission*, 329.

60. Dearborn to Harrison, 24 May 1805, Harrison to Dearborn, 27 May 1805, Indian Council, Fort Wayne, 21 June 1805, Wells to Gibson, 22 June 1805, Esarey, *Messages*, 1: 130, 132–34, 137–39, 139–40.

61. Gibson and Vigo to Harrison, 6 July 1805, Esarey, *Messages*, 1: 141–46. Johnston did not criticize "the conduct of Mr. Wells . . . and [said] nothing to impreach his character," but he did think Wells got Little Turtle to protest the treaty, Johnston to Harrison, 28 February 1806, Carter, *Territorial Papers*, 7: 343–45.

62. Harrison to Dearborn, 10 July 1805, Esarey, *Messages*, 1: 147–51; Owens, *Jefferson's Hammer*, 101.

63. Dawson, *Narrative*, 67–68; Horn, "The Treaty of Grouseland," 203–34; Harrison to Dearborn, 26 August 1805, Esarey, *Messages*, 1: 161–64; Wallace, *Jefferson and Indians*, 228–33.

64. Harrison to Dearborn, 10 August 1805, Dearborn to Harrison, 11 October 1805, Harrison to Dearborn, 26 August 1805, Esarey, *Messages*, 1: 161, 169–70, 161–64; Fifth Annual Message, 3 December 1805, Padover, *Complete Jefferson*, 416–20.

65. Jackson, *Civilization*, 102; Hopkins, *Mission*, 4–6.

66. Hopkins, *Mission*, 46–49, 52–61; Carter, *Little Turtle*, 103.

67. Hopkins, *Mission*, 59–78.

68. Ibid., 85–91; Winger, "A Pioneer Experiment in Teaching Agriculture," 1–15 in *Little Turtle*.

69. Tyson, appendix, Hopkins, *Mission*, 182; Dennis to Baltimore Friends, 26 June 1804, 26 August 1804; Wells to Baltimore Friends, 30 June 1806, Baltimore Yearly Meeting, 15 October 1804; Jackson, *Civilization*, 107–109.

70. Jackson, *Civilization*, 108. Wells did spend treaty annuities to implement the civilization program. By 7 March 1805 workmen "had already made 14,000 rails in the Indian towns. . . . After the enclosures have been made, the work shall be inspected by a commission . . . and then Mr. Connor is to receive payment for his labors," Gibson, *Moravian Mission*, 338–39. A flood washed the fences away.

71. Jackson, *Civilization*, 108–109; Woehrmann, *Headwaters*, 117.

72. Dearborn to Wells, 28 February 1806, 1 May 1806, 26 August 1806, Dearborn to Johnston and Whipple, 1 May 1806, NASW.

73. Hill, *John Johnston*, 9–13, 139–42; Orderly Book, *MPHC*, 34: 644; Conover, *Forefathers*, 26–39, 89–91. Johnston said he left the West in 1794, but actually he was in Kentucky in 1795, DM, 11YY.

74. Woehrmann, *Headwaters*, 91–103; Johnston to Dearborn in 1805, to Captain N. J. Vischer, 18 September 1805, Hill, *John Johnston*, 22–23.

75. Kluge and Luckenbach, in Parsons, "Civilizing the Indians," 208–209; Wells to Dearborn, 20 August 1807, Carter, *Territorial Papers*, 7: 469–71; Dearborn to Wells, 3 November 1806, Wells to Dearborn, 1 March 1807, NASW.

76. Kirk to Dearborn, 28 May 1807, NASW.

77. Ibid. Johnston did not blame Wells for Kirk's failure, Johnston to Draper, DM, 11YY.

78. Edmunds, "'Evil Men,'" 8–9; Wells to Kirk, 18 June 1807, NASW; Wells to Harrison, June 1807, Dawson, *Narrative*, 91–92; Smith to Wells, 9 July 1807, NASW. "Although hard evidence to implicate William Wells in these activities is limited, the circumstantial evidence is overwhelming," Edmunds, 9. In an earlier essay Edmunds took a harsher view of Wells's conduct: "Redefining Red Patriotism," 13–24.

79. Wells to Dearborn, 28 August 1807, Carter, *Territorial Papers*, 7: 469–71; Indians to President, 23 August 1807, NASW.

80. Dearborn to Wells, 5 August 1807, Carter, *Territorial Papers*, 7: 467.

81. Sheehan, *Seeds of Extinction*, 277.

82. White, *Roots of Dependency*, 21–22; Jackson, *Civilization*, 35–50. See Sleeper-Smith, *Indian Women*, 73–95.

83. Hawkins, Sheehan, *Seeds of Extinction*, 165–66; Wells to Dearborn, 31 December 1807, Carter, *Territorial Papers*, 5: 510–11.

CHAPTER 9

The best biography is Sugden, *Tecumseh: A Life*. See Edmunds, *Shawnee Prophet*; Gilbert, *God Gave Us This Country*; Dowd, *Spirited Resistance*; Gilpin, *War of 1812*; Cayton, *Frontier Indiana*; and White, *Middle Ground*. Jortner's *Gods of Prophetstown* is provocative but unbalanced and overstates the powers and influence of the Prophet.

1. Jackson, *Civilization*, 42–43; Wallace, *Death and Rebirth*, 245, 259, 303; "the Old Way of Handsome Lake" still has adherents among the Senecas, 239–302.

2. Gibson, *Moravian Mission*, 96, 194–95, 262, 337–40, 354, 358, 382–83, 402–403, 531.

3. Andrews, "Shaker Mission," 122; Nelson, *Jonathan Alder*, 147; Anthony Shane, DM, 2YY, 55. See Drake, *Life of Tecumseh*; Sugden corrects factual errors found in previous biographies. See *Tecumseh: A Life*, 113–26.

4. Andrews, "Shaker Mission," 122–25.

5. Andrews, "Shaker Mission," 113–28; Gibson, *Moravian Mission*, 392; Tanner, *Narrative*, 155–57. Wells to Harrison, 12 April 1806, Esarey, *Messages*, 1: 518–19; see Cave, "Tippecanoe," 641–45.

6. "Report from Champaign County," 16 February 1806, DM, 8BB; James Vance to Benjamin Drake, DM, 2YY, 108; J. R. McBeth, DM, 5BB, 75; Moore's Report, 18 February 1806, DM, 7BB, 28–29: Tiffin's message, 19 February 1806, DM, 7BB, 30; Shawnee to Tiffin, 20 March 1806, DM, 7BB, 31–33. Moore was accompanied by Simon Kenton, James McPhearson, and a Mr. McGlavin. Tecumseh, Round Head, or The Prophet could have spoken; see Sugden, *Tecumseh: A Life*, 134.

7. Gibson, *Moravian Mission*, 401–402, 411–21, 433, 559–62, 618–22. Cave, "Witch-Hunt," presents a more balanced picture of what transpired than Miller, "1806 Purge," or Jortner, chapter 8, in *Gods of Prophetstown*, both of whom argue that the victims, in effect, got what they deserved, at least according to Delaware belief.

8. Wells to Harrison, Harrison, "Message to the Delawares," *Indiana Gazette*, 12 April 1806, Clanin, *HP*, 518–19, 520–21; Dawson, *Narrative*, 83–84.

9. Drake, *Life of Tecumseh*, 91; Edwards, *Shawnee Prophet*, 48–49. Jortner, *Gods of Prophetstown*, 3–14, implies that the eclipse was a genuine miracle performed by the

Prophet; he apparently assumes that whatever true believers believe is real, including tinkering with the solar system. He correctly notes that Tucker's account in his *Tecumseh*, 99–101, is unreliable.

10. Wells to Dearborn, 31 December 1806, 31 March 1807, NASW, M221, 14; Andrews, "Shaker Mission," 115–28.

11. Andrews, "Shaker Mission," 115–28; J. P. MacLean, "Shaker Mission to the Shawnee," *OAHP* 11 (1903): 227–29.

12. Wells to Dearborn, 31 March 1807, 19 April 1807 NASW, M221.

13. Anthony Shane interview with Benjamin Drake, 1821, DM, 12YY, 47–54; Wells to Shawnee at Greenville, 22 April 1806, SW, NASW, M221. See Drake, *Life of Tecumseh*, 92–93; DM, 2YY, 27–28.

14. Wells to Dearborn, 19 April 1807, NASW, M221; Dearborn to Wells, 15 May 1807, NASW; Wells to Harrison, June 1807, Dawson, *Narrative*, 91; Wells to Dearborn, 14 July 1807, Carter, *Territorial Papers*, 7: 465; Petition to Wells from Staunton, Ohio, 8 July 1807, NASW, M221; "the Founders viewed religious enthusiasm as a kind of madness, the conceit 'of a warmed or overweening brain,'" Wood, *Empire of Liberty*, 577. Cane Ridge, Ky., revivals began in 1802.

15. James Vance to Benjamin Drake, DM, 2YY, 110–16; J. R. McBeth, DM, 5BB, 83–84.

16. Malone, *Jefferson and His Time* (1974), 5: 415–38; Adams, *History*, 1: 931–45; Allen, *Indian Allies*, 88–122. One of the men taken, Jenkin Ratford, had deserted from HMS *Halifax* and was subsequently hanged.

17. Harrison Message to the Legislature, 17 August 1807, Harrison to Dearborn, 29 August 1807, Esarey, *Messages*, 1: 229–36, 243–44; Wells to John Gerrard, 22 August 1807, DM, 7BB. The Prophet's beliefs were expressed in a speech by the Trout, an Ottawa chief and disciple, 4 May 1807, *MPHC*, 40: 127. Fisher served the British as an interpreter and informant, Horsman, *Matthew Elliott*, 139, 146, 168–69, 185; John Johnston information, DM, 2YY and 11YY.

18. Harrison to Dearborn, 5 September 1807, Message to the Prophet, Esarey, *Messages*, 1: 247–51; Letter to Governor Kirker, 5 September 1807, DM, 7BB, 40–60; "An Indian Talk!" *Chillicothe Freedonian*, 25 September 1807.

19. Thomas Worthington and Duncan McArthur to Governor Kirker, 22 September 1807, DM, 7BB, 40–60.

20. Ibid.

21. *Fredonian*, 25 September 1807; John A. Fulton, in Drake, *Life of Tecumseh*, 97; Thomas Hinde Papers, DM, 16Y, 45–51; John McDonald, "The Tragical Death of Wawilloma," *The Western Christian Advocate*, 22 April 1836, 205; Thomas Kirker to Jefferson, 8 October 1807, Jefferson to Dearborn, 12 August 1807, Daniel Parker Papers, MS, 466, HSP; Jefferson to Adams, 20 April 1812, in Klinck, *Tecumseh*, 53. See Sugden, *Tecumseh: A Life*, 3–8, *Blue Jacket*, 251–52.

22. Wells's letter, 1 October 1807, printed in the Vincennes *Western Star* and then the Chillicothe *Fredonian*, 20 October 1807.

23. Sugden, *Tecumseh: A Life*, 148–49. For an astute assessment of Sugden's biography, see Richard White, "Complexity in Arms," *The New Republic*, 31 August 1998, 41–45.

24. Wells to Dearborn, 14 August 1807, NASW; Wells to Dearborn, 20 August 1807, Carter, *Territorial Papers*, 7: 469.

25. Wells to Harrison, 20 August 1807, Esarey, *Messages*, 1: 239–43; Wells to Dearborn, 30 September 1807, 21 December 1807, NASW, M221; Wells to Dearborn, 5 December 1807, Carter, *Territorial Papers*, 7: 499; William Claus to Lt. Prideau Selby, 3 May 1808, Claus to Lt. Gov. Francis Gore, 27 February 1808, Esarey, *Messages*, 1: 285–86, 290.

26. Wells to Dearborn, 31 December 1807, Carter, *Territorial Papers*, 7: 510; Johnston to Dearborn, 31 December 1807, NASW.

27. Harrison to Dearborn, 18 February 1808, Dearborn to Harrison, 20 February 1808, Esarey, *Messages*, 1: 283–85; Wells to Dearborn, 7 January 1808, NASW, M221.

28. "The 'Main Pogue,'" Thomas Forsyth, DM, 8YY, 57–59; Edmunds, "Main Poc," 259–72. In French, Main Poche roughly means hand-in-pocket; the name is also spelled Main Poc or Main Pogue; Wells called him Marpock.

29. Wells to Dearborn, 31 January 1808, Dearborn to Wells, Dearborn to Johnston, 10 March 1808, NASW.

30. Wells to Dearborn, 6 March 1808, Carter, *Territorial Papers*, 7: 531–33; Carter, *Little Turtle*, 203; Wells to Dearborn, 30 June 1808, NASW, M221, roll 33.

31. Wells to Dearborn, 2 April 1808, 20 April 1808, Carter, *Territorial Papers*, 7: 540–42, 555.

32. Wells to Dearborn, 20 April 1808, Carter, *Territorial Papers*, 7: 555–60. Wells reported that Little Turtle's delegation spoke to the Prophet, Harrison said it was Tecumseh; Harrison to Dearborn, 19 May 1808, Esarey, *Messages*, 1: 290–91.

33. Claus to Gore, 27 February 1808, Claus to Lt. Prideau Selby, 3 May 1808, Esarey, *Messages*, 1: 286–87, 290; Wells to Dearborn, 26 May 1808, 5 June 1808, NASW, M221. Main Poche at Fort Wayne 1 October 1807 to 26 May 1808.

34. Wells to Dearborn, 30 June 1808, Connor to Dearborn, 18 June 1808, NASW, M222.

35. Prophet to Harrison, Harrison to Prophet, 24 June 1808, to Dearborn, 12 July 1808, Esarey, *Messages*, 1: 291–96.

36. Prophet to Harrison, 1 August 1808, Harrison to Dearborn, 1 September 1808, Esarey, *Messages*, 1: 299–300, 302; Dawson, *Narrative*, 107.

37. Harrison to Dearborn, 1 September 1808, Harrison, Annual Message, 27 September 1808, Esarey, *Messages*, 1: 302, 304–10.

38. Jefferson received Wells's request of 5 June 1808, writing in the margin on 12 July 1808: "I think the invitation posed by Wells is advisable." War Department to Wells, 2 August 1808, NASW, 389; Wells to Dearborn, 30 September 1808, Wells to Dearborn, 19 November 1808, Kirk to Dearborn, 10 December 1808, Duchouquet to Kirk, 4 December 1808, enclosed, NASW, M221, roll 33.

39. Levy, *Civil Liberties*, 70–90, 105–24; Malone, *Jefferson and His Time* (1974), 5: 606, 583; Wood, *Empire of Liberty*, 647.

40. Tucker and Henderson, *Empire of Liberty*, 190–95; Wood, *Empire of Liberty*, 742–43, 650; Levy, *Civil Liberties*, 136–38.

41. Janson, *Stranger*, 213–14; Malone, *Jefferson and His Time* (1974), 5: 530–35; Jefferson to Madison, 28 January 1808, Jefferson to Dupont de Nemours, 2 March 1809, Peterson, *Writings*, 1199–200, 1203; Josiah Quincy, in Adams, *History*, 1: 1172.

42. Kinard, "Sir Augustus J. Foster," 192–205; Janson, *Stranger*, 230–35.

43. Jefferson to the Chickasaws, 7 March 1805, Jefferson to the Fox, Sac, and Potawatomis, January 1805, Jefferson to the Osage et al., 4 January 1806, Jefferson to Ottawas, 22 April 1808, Padover, *Complete Jefferson*, 471, 469, 476–77, 493–94.

44. Jefferson to the Miamis, Potawatomis, Delawares, and Chippewas, 21 December 1808, ibid., 496–97.

45. Jefferson to Main Poche, ibid., 499–500.

46. Jefferson to Captain Hendrick, December 1808, ibid., 502–504.

47. Jefferson, "Deposition," 21 December 1808, Thornbrough, *Letter Book*, 53–54; Dearborn to Kirk, 22 December 1808, NASW.

48. Wells to Dearborn, 24 December 1808, 29 December 1808, NASW, M221.

49. Tyson, appendix, Hopkins, *Mission*, 185–90. The chief called "the Raven" is probably Black Bird.

50. Hopkins, *Mission*, 185–93; Wells to Dearborn, 16 January 1809, NASW.

51. Dearborn to Captain Hendrick, 27 January 1809, NASW, *Letter Book B*, 428–30; Thornbrough, *Letter Book*, 54–55; Meuter, *Long Rifle*, 21. My thanks to Judy Hill for sending photos of the Wells home in Glenview.

52. "Jefferson County, Va.–Ky. Early Marriage Book I, 1781–July 1826," typescript, FCHS, 70. The Geiger House was at the corner of Frankfort and Story avenues. Polly Geiger's silhouette is at the Chicago Museum of History.

53. Wells to Dearborn, 31 March 1809, NASW; Wells to Harrison, 8 April 1809, Esarey, *Messages*, 1: 337–39.

54. Harrison to Eustis, 18 April 1809, 26 April 1809, Carter, *Territorial Papers*, 7: 340–43, Harrison to Eustis, 3 May 1809, Harrison to Johnston, 4 May 1809, Clanin, *HP*, 409–18.

55. Dearborn to Wells, 27 January 1809, NASW; Johnston to Eustis, 16 April 1809, Johnston to P. E. Thomas, 15 April 1809, Johnston to John Smith, 15 April 1809, John Smith to Johnston, 24 May 1809, Thornbrough, *Letter Books*, 36–43, 52; Friends to Johnston, 30 May 1809, Hopkins, *Mission*, 104–106.

56. Wells to Eustis, 25 June 1809, NASW.

57. Ibid.

58. Johnston to Eustis, 1 July 1809, NASW, M221, roll 24.

59. Conover, *Forefathers*, 89.

60. Harrison to Eustis, 5 July 1809, Clanin, *HP*, 446–56.

61. "Journal of the Treaty Negotiations," Clanin, *HP*, 487–500; Harrison to Eustis, 3 October 1809, Wells File, CHS.

62. "Journal of the Treaty Negotiations," Clanin, *HP*, 501–508.

63. Ibid., 509–22.

64. Ibid., 523–29.

65. "Journal of the Treaty Negotiations with the Wea," Harrison to Eustis, 1 October 1809, Harrison to Eustis, 3 October 1809, Clanin, *HP*, 597–600, 564–65, 567–71.

66. Wells to Eustis, 10 October 1809, Wells to Eustis, 5 December 1809, NASW.

67. Harrison to Eustis, 3 December 1809, Eustis to Harrison, 10 January 1810, Clanin, *HP*, 668–73, 719.

68. Harrison to Charles Scott, 10 March 1810, 17 April 1810, Clanin, *HP*, 758–70, 807–24.

69. Johnston to Harrison, 24 June 1810, Esarey, *Messages*, 1: 430–32; Johnston to Harrison, 24 June 1810, "John Shaw's Translation of a Report from [Mrs. Abraham Ash]," 24 June 1810, Clanin, *HP*, 58–66.

70. Johnston to Harrison, 24 June 1810, Esarey, *Messages*, 1: 430–32; on 4 September 1810, Eustis's response was: "Mr. Johnston . . . represents the conduct of Mr. Wells as highly represensible in fomenting disconent among the Indians and by other nefarious practices, therefore hopes he will never again be employed in government service, etc. etc. etc."

71. Harrison to Eustis, 14–19 June 1810, Clanin, *HP*, 38–49.

72. Harrison to Eustis, 14 June 1810, 4 July 1810, Deposition of Michael Brouillet, 30 June 1810, Clanin, *HP*, 38–49, 78–86; Harrison to Eustis, 26 June 1810, Brouillette to Harrison, 30 June 1810, Esarey, *Messages*, I, 433–40.

73. Harrison to Eustis, 26 June 1810, 18 July 1810, Harrison to Prophet, 19 July 1810, Esarey, *Messages*, 1: 434, 447–50; Harrison to Eustis, 6 August 1810, Clanin, *HP*, 126–27.

74. Harrison to Eustis, 25 July 1810, 1 August 1810, Esarey, *Messages*, 1: 449–53; Clanin, *HP*, 113–20.

75. Tecumseh's Speech to Governor Harrison, 20 August 1809, Esarey, *Messages*, 1: 463–67, Clanin, *HP*, 156–62. Harrison later stated that the 1809 treaty at Fort Wayne was the "rock upon which the popularity of Tecumseh was founded and that upon which the influence of *Little Turtle* was wrecked," Wayne to Armstrong, 20 March 1804, Carter, *Territorial Papers*, 10: 2.

76. "Negotiations at an Indian Council," "Speeches of Tecumseh," 12 August–21 August 1810, Clanin, *HP*, 144–50, 156–57; "Tecumseh's Speech," 20 August 1810, Esarey, *Messages*, 1: 467–68; Dawson, *Narrative*, 156–57.

77. "Tecumseh's Speech," 21 August 1810, Esarey, *Messages*, 1: 468–69; "Negotiations," "Speeches of Tecumseh," Clanin, *HP*, 146–50, 162–67.

78. Dawson, *Narrative*, 158–59.

79. Harrison to Eustis, 22 August 1810, 28 August 1810, 24 October 1810, 26 October 1810, 7 November 1810, Esarey, *Messages*, 1: 461–62, 470–71, 481–84.

80. Harrison to Eustis, 28 August 1810, Eustis to Harrison, 26 October 1810, Esarey, *Messages*, 1: 470–71, 482–83.

81. Johnston to Eustis, 14 October 1810, Clanin, *HP*, 231–38.

82. Johnston to Eustis, 6 November 1810, NASW, M221, roll 38.

83. On 18 November 1809 the Vincennes *Western Sun*, a mouthpiece for Harrison, explained Little Turtle's opposition: "After the [Fort Wayne] treaty he made an attempt to procure from the Indians a recommendation of a friend [i.e., Wells] which failed altogether; this disgusted him so much that it is not impossible that he *may with some encouragement* endeavour to make the Indians dissatisfied with the treaty. But his opposition is of no consequence,—his influence is gone forever," in Owens, *Jefferson's Hammer*, 204.

84. Badollet to Gallatin, 13 November 1809, Thornbrough, *Correspondence*, 116–17; Ewing to Gallatin, 26 June 1810, Carter, *Territorial Papers*, 8: 25–28; Citizens of the Indiana Territory to James Madison, 11 November 1810, Esarey, *Messages*, 1: 485–87; *Western Sun*, 4 November 1810, Dawson, *Narrative*, 162–64.

85. Harrison, "Annual Message," 12 November 1810, Esarey, *Messages*, 1: 487–96.

86. Harrison, "Annual Message," 12 November 1810, Esarey, *Messages*, 1: 487–96; Owens, *Jefferson's Hammer*, 206.

87. Harrison to Eustis, 24 December 1810, 15 January 1811, 21 January 1811, Clanin, *HP*, 291–98, 322–23, 326–28.

88. Johnston to Eustis, 8 February 1811, NASW, M221, roll 38.

89. Eustis to Harrison, 12 February 1811, Carter, *Territorial Papers*, 8: 106–108; Eustis to Harrison, 7 March 1811, Clanin, *HP*, 413.

90. "William McIntosh," William Wesley Woollen, *Biographical and Historical Sketches of Early Indiana* (Hammond, Ind., 1883), 378–83; Vincennes *Indiana Gazette*, 2 September 1804; Badollet to Gallatin, 13 November 1809, Thornbrough, *Correspondence*, 120.

91. WHH vs. William McIntosh, Harrison to Eustis, 23 April 1811, Clanin, *HP*, 197–212, 290–510, 489; Dawson, *Narrative*, 175–76; Dawson's account is biased in Harrison's favor.

92. Harrison to Eustis, 24 April 1811, Clanin, *HP*, 484–93.

93. Harrison to Eustis, 6 June 1811, 19 June 1811, Esarey, *Messages*, 1: 512–17, 519–21; Harrison to Eustis, 19 June 1811, Clanin, *HP*, 574–77.

94. Message to the Shawnee Prophet and Tecumseh, 24 June 1811, Message from Tecumseh, 4 July 1811, Clanin, *HP*, 581–84, 623–24.

95. Harrison to Eustis, 25 June 1811, 2 July 1811, 10 July 1811, Clanin, *HP*, 586–90, 604–609, 629–37.

96. Harrison to Ninian Edwards, 4 July 1811, Clanin, *HP*, 613–22. Illinois became a separate territory in January 1809.

97. Eustis to Harrison, 17 July 1811, 20 July 1811, Harrison to Edwards, 7 August 1811, Clanin, *HP*, 651–52, 655–56, 682–83.

98. Harrison to Eustis, 24 July 1811, 6 August 1811, Clanin, *HP*, 657–59, 671–79.

99. Council, Vincennes *Western Sun*, 3 August 1811, Harrison to Eustis, 7 August 1811, Clanin, *HP*, 663–66, 684–88.

100. Harrison to Eustis, 13 August 1811, Harrison to Edwards, 10 August 1811, Harrison to Johnston, 23 August 1811, Clanin, *HP*, 713–17, 702–704, 737–40.

101. Wells to Eustis, 27 August 1811 [two letters], Shaw to Johnston, 18 August 1811, Johnston to Eustis, 29 August 1811, NASW.

102. Harrison to Eustis, 2 September 1811, Waller Taylor to Harrison, 15 September 1811, Benjamin Parke to Harrison, 13 September 1811, Clanin, *HP*, 752–55, 776–81; Harrison to Eustis, 17 September 1811, Harrison to the Miamis, Eel Rivers, and Weas, Speeches . . . at Fort Wayne, Esarey, *Messages*, 1: 576–82, 570–75.

103. Horsman, "Prelude to War," *Matthew Elliott*, 177–90.

104. Resolutions of Vincennes Citizens and Petition to President Madison, Esarey, 1: 538–43; Thornbrough, *Correspondence*, 195–97. For the campaign: Cleaves, *Old Tippecanoe*, 82–111.

105. Harrison to Eustis, 25 September 1811, 13 October 1811, 26 November 1811, Eustis to Harrison, 3 October 1811, Clanin, *HP*, 816–19, 837, 855–57, Reel 6, 82–88; Tipton, "Journal," 176.

106. Harrison to Sam Wells, 13 October 1811, to Charles Scott, 25 October 1811, to Eustis, 2 November 1811, Clanin, *HP*, 868, 877–80, Reel 6, 23–24.

107. Watts, "Larabee's Account," 243–46; Adam Walker, "A Journal of Two Campaigns," Esarey, *Messages*, 1: 700–701; Harrison to Eustis, 18 November 1811, Clanin, *HP*, 47–50; Dawson celebrates Harrison's conduct: *Narrative*, 196–250.

108. Elliott to Brock, 18 January 1812, Funk's Narrative, Esarey, *Messages*, 1: 616–17, 720; Thornbrough, *Correspondence*, 205–206; Shabonee and Judge Isaac Naylor in McCollough, *Tippecanoe*, 8–9, 13; C. C. Trowbridge, *Shawnese Traditions*, Vernon Kinietz and Ermine W. Voegelin, eds. (Ann Arbor: University of Michigan Press, 1939), 18; "the Prophet . . . preached up his followers, before the battle, that the Great Spirit would render the arms of the Americans unavailing! That their bullets could make no impression on the Indians; that it would be total darkness among the Americans, that they could not see the enemy, and light with the Indians," Johnston in Cincinnati, *Liberty Hall*, 30 November 1811.

109. David Turpie, *Sketches of My Own Times* (Indianapolis: Bobbs-Merrill, 1903), 66–67; J. R. Peters to James Whitelaw, 17 January 1812, Vermont Historical Society; Statement of William Brigham, Esarey, *Messages*, 1: 703; Gilpin, *War of 1812*, 17.

110. Brigham, "Statement," Walker, "Journal," Harrison to Eustis, 28 December 1811, Statement of Sergeant Orr, Harrison to Eustis, 18 November 1811, Esarey, *Messages*, 1: 703–704, 701, 686–88, 702, 618–32; Tipton, "Journal," 9. For an alternative scenario, see Cave, "Tippecanoe," 652–59.

111. Harrison to John M. Scott, Brigham, "Statement," Funk, "Narrative," Esarey, *Messages*, 1: 608–13, 704, 721–22; Peters to Whitelaw, VHS, 41–42; Watts, "Larrabee's Account," 235–46.

112. Harrison to Eustis, 18 Novembr 1811, Walker, "Journal," Funk, "Narrative," Esarey, *Messages*, 1: 618–32, 701–702, 722; Peters to Whitelaw, VHS, 41–42.

113. Peters to Whitelaw, VHS, 41–42; Watts, "Larrabee's Account," 235–36; Naylor, "Account," in McCollough, *Tippecanoe*, 11–12; Elliott to Brock, 12 January 1812, Brigham, "Statement," Funk, "Narrative," Esarey, *Messages*, 1: 616–17, 705, 722–23; Johnston to Eustis, 28 November 1811, Clanin, *HP*, 213–14.

114. Elliott to Brock, 12 January 1812, Esarey, *Messages*, 1: 616–17; Johnston to Eustis, 28 November 1811, Clanin, *HP*, 2131–4; Johnston, letter in Cincinnati, *Liberty Hall*, 30 November 1811; Boyd & Prescott, in *Western Sun*, 8 February 1812.

115. Harrison to Eustis, 26 November 1811, Harrison to Scott, 13 December 1811, Esarey, *Messages*, 1: 649–52, 666–72.

116. Johnston to Eustis, 28 November 1811, Clanin, *HP*, 314–15; Wells to Johnston, 13 December 1811, NASW, M221. For Tecumseh in the South, see Sugden, *Tecumseh: A Life*, 237–51.

117. Josiah Snelling to Harrison, 20 November 1811, Esarey, *Messages*, 1: 643–46.

CHAPTER 10

For the War of 1812, see Skaggs, *Harrison*; Stagg, *War of 1812*; Gilpin, *War of 1812*; and Latimer, *1812*. For the Fort Dearborn battle, see Quaife, *Chicago and the Old Northwest*, and Keating, *Rising Up*. For Wells, see Hutton, "William Wells," and Carter, *Little Turtle*.

1. Carolyn V. Platt, "Nightmare on the Mississippi," *Timeline*, Sept.–Oct. 1993, 18–31; Van Every, *Final Challenge*, 104–10; Tucker, *Tecumseh*, 211; Sugden, *Tecumseh: A Life*, 250–51. This was the strongest set of earthquakes in American history; at least five registered 8.0 or more on the Richter scale.

2. Report on the dinner at Samuel Wells's home, 27 December 1811, Vincennes, *Western Sun*, 4 January 1812; Prevost to Brock, 24 December 1812, Allen, *Indian Allies*, 119–20.

3. Stone Eater's speech, Frankfort *Argus*, 25 December 1811; Jean Baptist Lalime to Benjamin Howard, 4 February 1812, Forsyth to Howard, 18 February 1812, Edwards to Eustis, 3 March 1812, Knopf, *Letters*, Part 2, 32, 57, 68–69; Irwin to Eustis, 10 March 12, Carter, *Territorial Papers*, 16: 195.

4. Wells to Eustis, 10 February 1812, Knopf, *Letters*, Part 2, 44–45.

5. Harrison to Eustis, 17 January 1812, 19 January 1812, 19 February 1812, Harrison to Meigs, 26 February 1812, Clanin, *HP*, 284–85, 308–309, 378–79, 401–403.

6. Little Turtle to Harrison, 25 January 1812, Esarey, *Messages*, 2: 18–19; Anthony Shane interview, DM, 12YY, 47, 57–58; Harrison to Eustis, 4 March 1812, Clanin, *HP*, 412–14; Edwards to Eustis, 3 March 1812, Wells to Eustis, 1 March 1812, Knopf, *Letters*, Part 2, 67–69. On the Prophet's "continued prominence," see Cave, "Tippecanoe," 665–67.

7. Johnston to Eustis, 4 March 1812, Harrison to Shaw, 6 March 1812, Knopf, *Letters*, Part 2, 70, 76–77; Eustis to Harrison, 7 March 1812, Harrison to Eustis, 14 April 1812, Clanin, *HP*, 424–25, 487–90.

8. Hull to Eustis, 6 March 1812, Forsyth to Rhea, 10 March 1812, Knopf, *Letters*, Part 2, 78–80, 83; Stickney to Eustis, 28 April 1812, Thornbrough, *Letter Book*, 112–13.

9. Stanley Griswold to Eustis, 5 March 1812, Edwards to Eustis, 12 May 1812, Shaw to Eustis, 10 March 1812, Knopf, *Letters*, Part 2, 73–75, 197–99, 89.

10. Stickney to Harrison, 18 April 1812, Stickney to Indians and Charley's response, 18 April 1812, Stickney to Eustis, 21 April 1812, Thornbrough, *Letter Book*, 102–107, 108–10, 111–12.

11. Stickney to Eustis, 28 April 1812, to Heald, 29 April 1812, to Eustis, 8 May 1812, to Harrison, 8 May 1812, to Eustis, 15 May 1812, to Meigs, 15 May 1812, Thornbrough, *Letter Book*, 112–15, 118–20, 123–25; Dayton *Ohio Centinel*, 4 June 1812.

12. Stickney to Hull, 25 May 1812, Speech of Five Medals and Stickney's reply, 12 May 1812, Thornbrough, *Letter Book*, 127–28, 120–22.

13. Col. William Claus to Brock, 16 June 1812, Speech of the Indians, Cruikshank, *Documents*, 310–14; Speeches of Indians at Massassinway, 15 May 1812, Esarey, *Messages*, 2: 50–53. I have drawn on two different versions of Tecumseh's speech, one by Wells, whose transcript was in the Vincennes *Western Sun*, Dayton *Ohio Centinel*, 4 June 1812, and Cincinnati *Liberty Hall*, 16 June 1812.

14. Speeches at Massassinway, Esarey, *Messages*, 2: 50–53. The council was held under Little Turtle's auspices; he was suffering from the gout and may not have been the Miami speaker.

15. Dayton *Ohio Centinel*, 4 June 1812; Stickney to Hull, 25 May 1812, to Johnston, 22 June 1812, Thornbrough, *Letter Book*, 127–28, 144–45; Claus to Brock, 16 June 1812, Cruikshank, *Documents*, 310–11.

16. Stickney to Hull, 25 May 1812, to Harrison, 29 May 1812, to Meigs, 8 June 1812, to Eustis, 7 June 1812, Thornbrough, *Letter Book*, 127–29, 131–32, 137–41; Wells in Dayton *Ohio Centinel*, 4 June 1812; Thomas Forsyth to Edwards, Carter, *Territorial Papers*, 16: 250–53.

17. Harrison to Eustis, 8 July 1812, Esarey, *Messages*, 2: 67–70; Stickney to Harrison, 30 June 1812, Thornbrough, *Letter Book*, 149–51.

18. Stickney to Harrison, 24 July 1812, Thornbrough, *Letter Book*, 169–72.

19. Heath, "Re-evaluating 'The Fort-Wayne Manuscript,'" 158–88; Hiram W. Beckwith, ed., *The Fort-Wayne Manuscript*, printed in Harrison, *Aborigines of the Ohio Valley*, 64; Richard Wright, ed., *The John Hunt Memoirs . . . 1812–1835* (Maumee, Ohio: Maumee Valley Historical Society, 1979): 38.

20. Griswold, *Pictorial History*, 177, 183, 190, 192–94; Edwards, 8 September 1884, DM, 10YY; Stickney to Eustis, 19 July 1812, to Johnston, 20 July 1812, to Harrison, 21 July 1812, Thornbrough, *Letter Book*, 161, 165, 167.

21. On Miami burial customs, see Wells, "Manners and Customs," 184–85, 188; a witness to Little Turtle's funeral, in Brice, *Fort Wayne*, 201; obituary, Cincinnati *Liberty Hall*, 21 July 1812; Beckwith, *Fort-Wayne Manuscript*, 71n; Johnston in Hill, *John Johnston*, 59, 161–62. Little Turtle's burial site was found at 634 Lawton Place in July 1912; the grave included silver armlets, anklets, medals, crosses, two bead necklaces, four brooches, and a pair of large ear hoops, as well as a pocketknife, a clasp knife, three skinning knives, a drinking cup, a spoon, a pair of scissors, a hammer, a gun, a bullet mold, a pistol, a flintlock, an axe, a tomahawk, a pair of steel spurs, a copper kettle, a flask, and a bottle of vermillion paint, Carter, *Little Turtle*, 228–92; Griswold, *Pictorial History*, 177, 190.

22. Stagg, *Mr. Madison's War*, "James Madison," 3–34; Horsman, "On to Canada," 1–24; Egan, "Origins," 72–75; Latimer, *1812*, 31–33; Jackson, Division Order, 12 March 1812, in John Spencer Basset, ed., *The Correspondence of Andrew Jackson* (Washington, D.C.: Carnegie Institute, 1926), 1: 221–22.

23. Jefferson to Kosciusko, 28 June 1812, to Adams, 11 June 1812, Peterson, *Writings*, 1263–67; Jefferson to Colonel Duane, Bergh, *Writings of Jefferson*, 13: 180–82.

24. Stickney to Hull, 20 June 1812, to Johnston, 22 June 1812, Thornbrough, *Letter Book*, 141–43, 144–46; Wells to Harrison, 22 July 1812, Esarey, *Messages*, 2: 76–78.

25. Hull to Eustis, 18 June 1812, 24 June 1812, 26 June 1812, 7 July 1812, 9 July 1812, 19 July 1812, Anonymous, 7 July 12, Knopf, *Letters*, Part 2, 48–49, 55, 60, 81–82, 85, 88, 110; Eustis to Hull, 18 June 1812, 24 June 1812, Captain Dixon to Lt.-Col. R. H. Bruyeres, 8 July 1812, Hull's Proclamation, 13 July 1812, Cruikshank, *Documents*, 35, 37, 48–49, 58–60.

26. Capt. A. Gray to Sir George Prevost, 13 January 1812, Robert Dickson to Brock, 13 July 1812, Articles of Capitulation, 17 July 1812, Captain Roberts to Colonel Baynes, 17 July 1812, Roberts to Brock, 17 July 1812, John Askin, Jr., to William Claus, 18 July 1812, Lt. Porter Hanks to Hull, 4 August 1812, Cruikshank, *Documents*, 9–11, 56, 63–69.

27. Stickney to Eustis, 18 July 1812, to Johnston, 20 July 1812, to Harrison, 21 July 1812, 24 July 1812, Thornbrough, *Letter Book*, 161–72.

28. Wells to Harrison, 22 July 1812, Esarey, *Messages*, 2: 76–78; Letter to Maj. William Ruffin, 27 July 1812, Cruikshank, *Documents*, 77–78; Stickney to Harrison, 21 July 1812, Thornbrough, *Letter Book*, 168.

29. Wells to Harrison, 22 July 1812, Esarey, *Messages*, 2: 76–78; Wells to Harrison, 30 July 1812, NASW; Harrison to Eustis, 12 August 1812, Edwards to Eustis, 8 August 1812, Knopf, *Letters*, Part 3, 25–28, 14.

30. Brock to Prevost, 29 July 1812, Hull to Eustis, 29 July 1812, Irwin to Eustis, 6 August 1812, Knopf, *Letters*, Part 3, 103–104, 139, 10–11; Hull to Sam Wells, no date, NASW.

31. Stickney to Johnston, Thornbrough, *Letter Book*, 154–55; Harrison to Eustis, 7 July 1812, Clanin, *HP*, 662–65; Forsyth to Eustis, 13 July 1812, Howard to Eustis, 18 July 1812, Edwards to Eustis, 21 July 1812, Knopf, *Letters*, Part 3, 93–95, 109, 119–21; LeClair report, 14 July 1812, Carter, *Territorial Papers*, 16: 253–55.

32. For John Kinzie: Quaife, *Chicago*, 145–52, 176–77, and Keating, *Rising Up*, 21–33, 66–77.

33. Heald to Irwin, 12 April 1812, Irwin to Eustis, 16 April 1812, 28 April 1812, 15 May 1812, Isaac Van Voorhis to Eustis, 16 May 1812, Knopf, *Letters*, Part 1, 129, 137, 164, 211, 213–14, 220–21. See Haydon, "John Kinzie," 183–99.

34. Van Voorhis to Eustis, 30 June 1812, Irwin to Eustis, July 1812, Kinzie to Forsyth, 7 July 1812, Knopf, *Letters*, Part 2, 67–68, 69–71, 86–87. See Keating, *Rising Up*, 112–23, and Kirkland, *Chicago Massacre*, 185–95.

35. Kinzie to Forsyth, 7 July 1812, Irwin to Eustis, 6 August 1812, Knopf, *Letters*, Part 2, 86–87, Part 3, 10–11.

36. Hull to Eustis, 22 July 1812, Knopf, *Letters*, Part 2, 125; letter from Cook, 28 July 1812, Prevost to Brock, 31 July 1812, Brock to Baynes, 29 July 1812, Cruikshank, *Documents*, 105, 113–14, 107–108; Hull to Eustis, 8 August 1812, Johnston to Eustis, 6 August 1812, Knopf, *Letters*, Part 3, 16, 13; Harrison to Eustis, 6 August 1812, Cruikshank, *Documents*, 123.

37. Hull to Eustis, 26 August 1812, Brock, General Order, 16 August 1812, Cruikshank, *Documents*, 184–90, 149–50.

38. Lieutenant Dewar to Henry Proctor, 28 October 1812, Journal of Charles Askin, Cruikshank, *Documents*, 173–74, 244–45.

39. Wells to Harrison, 3 August 1812, William Wells File, CHS.

40. Kinzie, in Schoolcraft, *Narrative*, 256–57; John Wentworth, DM, 5YY; Pokagon, "Massacre," 652; Irwin to John Mason, 12 October 1812, in Quaife, "Fort Dearborn Massacre," 567. Apparently a delegation of chiefs left Chicago for the treaty at Piqua, met Winamac on the way, and returned to Fort Dearborn to wait for Wells to escort the garrison to Fort Wayne. Haydon, "John Kinzie," 185; Forsyth to Howard, 7 September 1812, Knopf, *Letters*, Part 3, 117–18.

41. A. N. Edwards to Wentworth, 10 June 1881, in Wentworth, *Fort Dearborn*, 56–57.

42. Forsyth to the Governor of Louisiana Territory, 7 September 1812, Carter, *Territorial Papers*, 16: 261, Knopf, *Letters*, Part 3, 117–18; Kirkland, *Chicago Massacre*, 64–66; Daniel Curtis to Kingsbury, 21 September 1812, Indiana Territory Collection, IHS, M398. See Curtis to Friend Cullen, 4 October 1812, in Slocum, *Maumee*, 1: 275–79.

43. Kirkland, *Chicago Massacre*, 64; Mrs. John H. Kinzie, *Narrative*, 20–21; Curtis to Kingsbury, 21 September 1812, HIS, 1–3; Kinzie, in Schoolcraft, *Narrative*, 256–57; Captain Heald, in Quaife, *Chicago*, 406–408; Heald, in Kirkland, "Chicago Massacre," 116–17. Quaife's *Chicago* reprints key primary sources. Keating's *Rising Up* is good on depicting the multicultural community of Chicago but gives scant attention to the battle and the death of Wells. Crimmins's historical novel, *Fort Dearborn*, discusses the battle in detail. For an evaluation of sources, see Ferguson, *Illinois*, 55–78, 233–46.

44. Heald, in Kirkland, "Chicago Massacre," 116–17; Heald, DM, 23S, 45–46; McAfee, *History*, 114–15; Curtis to Kingsbury, 21 September 1812, 1–3; Charles Askin, "Diary," 22 September 1812," in Quaife, "Fort Dearborn Massacre," 563–64; Kinzie, in Schoolcraft, *Narrative*, 256–57; Pokagon, "Massacre," 652; Capt. David Bates Douglass in Williams, "Kinzie's Narrative," 349–50. Both Quaife and Williams reprint valuable primary sources and provide analysis. Most accounts estimate the number of warriors involved as four hundred to five hundred. Thomas Hamilton wrote they were "attacked by 200 Indians," Hamilton to Lt. Col. Daniel Bissell, 24 August 1812, NA, Letters Received, Adjutant General, reel 7, 107.

45. Captain Heald's Official Report, 23 October 1812, in Quaife, *Chicago*, 406–408; Curtis, 21 September 1812, 1–3; Douglass, in Williams, "Kinzie's Narrative," 349–50; Isabella Cooper, in Wentworth, *Fort Dearborn*, 54, 56. The battle probably took place at about 12th Street and South Michigan; see Musham, "Battle of Chicago," 21–40.

46. Mrs. John H. Kinzie, *Narrative*, 23–25; see also Mrs. Kinzie's *Wau Bun*, 179–80.

47. Heald, DM, 23S, 48–53; Heald, in Kirkland, "Chicago Massacre," 118–19; Douglass, in Williams, "Kinzie's Narrative," 349–50; Isabelle Cooper, in Wentworth, *Fort Dearborn*, 54, 56; Heald, "Particulars."

48. Heald, in Kirkland, "Chicago Massacre," 118–19, Johnston, DM, 11YY, 9–15; Potawatomi, DM, 23S, 194–95.

49. Forsyth to Howard, 7 September 1812, Knopf, *Letters*, Part 3, 117–18; General Hunt, DM, 21S, 46–47; Douglass, in Williams, "Kinzie's Narrative," 349–50; Heald, DM, 23S, 48–53; Heald, in Kirkland, "Chicago Massacre," 118–19. James Van Horne saw other bodies with their hearts removed, *Narrative*, 6, 8.

50. Barnhart, "New Letter," 187–99; Quaife, *Chicago*, 224–25, 419.

51. Heald, in Quaife, *Chicago*, 406–408; Douglass, in Williams, "Kinzie's Narrative," 349–50; Quaife, "James Corbin," 222–23; Helm maintained that he was the one who insisited on a pledge to protect the prisoners while Heald surrendered his sword without consulting the men, Quaife, "Fort Dearborn Massacre," 572–73; on casualties, Heald, DM, 17U, 33–36, and Forsyth to Howard, 7 September 1812, Knopf, *Letters*, Part 3, 117–18; for accounts of the captives: Quaife, *Chicago*, 232–61, and Keating, *Rising Up*, 162–72. Van Horne names six men who were killed after the battle, mentions two others killed on the first march, and describes his captivity, *Narrative*, 5–6, 9, 5–18.

52. Heald, DM, 23S, 48–53; Heald, "Particulars"; Heald, in Kirkland, "Fort Dearborn Massacre," 118–19; Captain Heald, DM, 17U, 33–36.

53. James Rhea to Johnston, 19 August 1812, DM, 11YY; James Wolcott to John Wentworth, in Kirkland, "Chicago Massacre," 177–78; Taylor to Eustis, 8 September 1812, in Knopf, *Letters*, Part 3, 124–25, Quaife, *Chicago*, 228; DM, 21S, 47.

EPILOGUE

1. Shelby to Eustis, 5 September 1812, Esarey, *Messages*, 2: 113; Woehrmann, *Headwaters*, 226–33; Daniel Curtis, in Peckham, "Recent Acquistions," 414–18; William Oliver to Mr. Gallagher and "Oliver's Expedition," *Ladies Repository* [Cincinnati, March 1861], DM, 7U.

2. McAfee, *History*, 144; Harrison to Shelby, 18 September 1812, to Eustis, 21 September 1812, Esarey, *Messages*, 2: 127–28, 143–45; Col. John Allen to George M. Bibb & Henry Clay, 1 December 1812, DM, 7U, 1–2; Col. J. Simmale letter [no date], DM, 7U.

3. Taylor to Harrison, 10 September 1812, Esarey, *Messages*, 2: 125–28; Dawson, *Narrative*, 319–20; Curtis, in Peckham, "Recent Acquistions," 249–50.

4. Harrison to Eustis, 13 October 1812, 15 November 1812, to Campbell, 25 November 1812, Campbell to Harrison, 18 December 1812, "Mississineway Expedition," Pittsburgh *Gazette*, 22 January 1813, Esarey, *Messages*, 2: 175–76, 211, 229–31, 248–61, 270–73; William B. Northcutt, "War of 1912 Diary," *RKHS* 56 (1958): 257. The Miami force was less than three hundred; see Godroy, *Stories*, 94. A memorial to the Mississinewa battle is in downtown Marion, Indiana. See Holliday, *Mississinewa*, 7–28.

5. Allen to Bibb and Clay, 2 December 1812, DM, 7U, 18–21; Oliver to Gallagher, DM, 7U; Dunn, *Stories*, 164–80. For the leadership dispute between Harrison and Winchester, see Skaggs, *Harrison*, 79–95.

6. Harrison to Monroe, 4 January 1813, Esarey, *Messages*, 2: 296–97; Allen to Bibb and Clay, 2 December 1812, DM, 7U, 22; McClanahan to Harrison, 26 January 1813, Harrison to Monroe, 20 January 1813, Winchester to Monroe, 23 January 1813, Esarey, *Messages*, 2: 338–39, 316–17, 327–29; Skaggs, *Harrison*, 142–45; McAfee, *History*, 230–31.

7. McClanahan to Harrison, 26 January 1813, Winchester to Monroe, 23 January 1813, Labbadi to Harrison, 11 February 1813, Harrison to Monroe, 24 January 1813, Shelby to Harrison, 9 February 1813, Baker to Winchester, 25 February 1813, Esarey, *Messages*, 2: 340–41, 327–28, 362, 332–33, 353, 371–75; Harrison to Shelby, 2 February 1813, Meuter, *Long Rifle*, 135; see Atherton, *Narrative*, 26–68, McAfee, *History*, 220–53, and Skaggs, *Harrison*, 154–72.

8. Harrison to Gen. Green Clay, 5 May 1813, Harrison to Armstrong, 5 May 1813, Speech of Tecumseh, 18 September 13, Harrison, General Orders, 9 May 1813, Harrison to Armstrong, 13 May 1813, Esarey, *Messages*, 2: 440–41, 431–33, 541–43, 437, 443–44; McAfee, *History*, 284–93. A British private who tried to prevent the massacre at Fort Miamis was shot by the Indians. During the siege, 135 Americans were killed, 188 wounded, and over 630 taken prisoners. The British lost 14 dead, 27 wounded, and 41 prisoners. See Latimer, *1812*, 137–39.

9. Harrison to Armstrong, 24 June 1813, 23 July 1813, 24 July 1813, Green Clay to Harrison, 26 July 1813, Harrison to Croghan, 29 July 1813, Croghan to Harrison, 30 July 1813, Harrison to Croghan, 30 July 1813, Croghan to Harrison, 3 August 1813, Harrison to Armstrong, 4 August 1813, Croghan to Harrison, 5 August 1813, Field Officers to Harrison, 29 August 1813, Esarey, *Messages*, 2: 478, 494, 496, 499–500, 502, 503, 506, 509, 511–13, 515, 530–31.

10. Perry to Harrison, 10 September 1813, Speech of Tecumseh, 18 September 1813, Esarey, *Messages*, 2: 539, 541–43; Proctor, 26 September 1813, in Cleaves, *Old Tippecanoe*, 189. After the fall of Detroit, Proctor replaced Brock, who died at the Battle of Queenstown Heights, 13 October 1812. A hypothetical question of the war is whether Brock and Tecumseh, working together, might have captured Fort Meigs and prevented Perry from building his ships. If these things had happened, Harrison could not have advanced when he did and Michigan might have become a part of Canada in the Treaty of Ghent.

11. McAfee, "Life," *RKHS*, 28: 120–28; Harrison to Armstrong, 9 October 1812, Esarey, *Messages*, 2: 561–65; Sugden, *Tecumseh: A Life*, 378–79. See Latimer, *1812*, 185–91; McAfee, *History*, 393–431; and Skaggs, *Harrison*, 183–215.

12. Harrison to Armstrong, 10 October 1813, 21 December 1813, 22 March 1814, Esarey, *Messages*, 2: 573–74, 610–11, 637–41; Anson, *Miami*, 174–75; Owens, *Jefferson's Hammer*, 236–38. Harrison's letter of 22 March 1814 is especially revealing in terms of the Wabash nations and his treaty negotiations with them.

13. Carter, *Little Turtle*, 248–49; Probate hearing, 14 December 1812, William Wells File, Indiana State Library; Wendler, *Kentucky Frontiersman*, 38–39. Three other siblings died in Kentucky at this time: Anne, 1810, Carty, 1812, and Margaret, 1814.

14. Wendler, *Kentucky Frontiersman*, 42–55; Heath, "Re-evaluating," 168–69; McBride, *Pioneer Biography*, 2: 100–101.

15. Col. Thomas Hunt interview, DM, 21S, 45; Judge James Wolcott, DM, 21S, 90–93; John Johnston interview, DM, 11YY, 89; Wendler, *Kentucky Frontiersman*, 57–62; Wentworth, *Fort Dearborn*, 46. The Wolcott House and Museum is at 1031 River Road. Sam's new wife Elizabeth Adrian Hoffman was the widow of the post doctor in Detroit. Her son James Adrian married Sam's daughter Mary; they also lived in Missouri, as did Sam's brother Charles, whose son William Wells died at the Alamo.

16. Wendler, *Kentucky Frontiersman*, 40; Wells File, CHS; Wolcott interview, DM, 21S, 91. For the Miamis after 1815, see books by Anson and Rafert; for the descendants of Wells and Little Turtle, Carter, *Little Turtle*, 240–54. I am grateful to Marilyn Peterson and Judy Smalley Hill for Wells family information.

17. White, *Middle Ground*, xi–xxxii.

18. Jortner, *Gods of Prophetstown*, 159; McArthur to Monroe, 15 March 1815, Stickney to Harrison, 18 July 1813, to Crawford, 1 October 1815, Stickney quoted in Cass to Crawford, 27 August 1816, Crawford to Cass, 23 January 1817, Judge Larned, 25 June 1817, Stickney to Cass, 27 July 1816, Johnston to Cass, 9 November 1817, Thornbrough, *Letter Book*, 219, 196–97, 240–41, 245–49. In their later years, both Stickney and Johnston mellowed considerably.

SELECTED BIBLIOGRAPHY

ABBREVIATIONS

AAS	American Antiquarian Society
APS	American Philosophical Society
CHS	Chicago Historical Society
FCHQ	*Filson Club Historical Quarterly*
HSPM	*Historical Society of Pennsylvania Memoirs*
IHS	Indiana Historical Society
IMH	*Indiana Magazine of History*
JISHS	*Journal of the Ilinois State Historical Society*
MPHC	*Michigan Pioneer and Historical Collections*
MVHR	*Mississippi Valley Historical Review*
MWH	*Magazine of Western History*
NWOH	*Northwest Ohio History* (formerly *Northwest Ohio Quarterly*)
OAHQ	*Ohio State Archaeological and Historical Quarterly*
OAHS	*Ohio Archaeological and Historical Publications*
OHSQ	*Ohio Historical Society Quarterly*
OPHS	*Ohio Philosophical and Historical Society Quarterly*
PMHB	*Pennsylvania Magazine of History and Biography*
RKHS	*Register of Kentucky State Historical Society*
WCL	William L. Clements Library, University of Michigan, Ann Arbor
WMQ	*William and Mary Quarterly*
WPHM	*Western Pennsylvania History Magazine*

ARCHIVAL SOURCES

Glenn A. Black Laboratory of Archaeology, Ohio Valley-Great Lakes, Indiana University, Bloomington

The Shawnee, Miami, and Delaware Files contain transcripts in chronological order of correspondence between William Wells and the War Department.

John Carter Brown Library, Brown University, Providence, R.I.
   John Adams Papers
   Secretary of War Papers: http://wardepartmentpapers.org. Contains copies of
      correspondence between William Wells and the War Department.
Chicago Historical Society
   Wilson, Grant James, ed. Dr. John Cooper. "Chicago from 1803–1812."
   Ninian Edwards Papers
   Henry Dearborn Papers
   William Wells file
   James Wilkinson Papers
Cincinnati Historical Society
   John Cleves Symmes Papers
William L. Clements Library, University of Michigan, Ann Arbor
   Josiah Harmar Papers
   James McHenry Papers
   Northwest Territory Collections
Bull Run Regional Library
   Genealogy Room, Manassas, Virginia. Records of Land Ownership in the North-
      ern Neck of Virginia
Detroit Public Library
   Michigan Pioneer and Historical Collections. 40 vols.
   Burton Historical Collections
   Askin Papers
   Haldiman Papers
   Hamtramck Papers
Filson Historical Society Files, Louisville, Ky.
   Vincent J. Akers Papers
   Neal O. Hammon Papers
   Robert E. McDowell Papers
   Pope Family Papers
   William Wells File
Historical Society of Pennsylvania, Philadelphia
   Anthony Wayne Papers
   Daniel Parker Papers
Indiana Territory Collection, Indiana Historical Society, Indianapolis
   John Armstrong Papers
   William Henry Harrison Collection
   Indiana Territory Collection
   Jacob Kingsbury Papers
Library of Congress, Washington, D.C.
   George Washington Papers,
      http.//memory.loc.gov/amen/gwhtml/gwhome.html.
Marietta College, Marietta, Ohio
   Rufus Putnam Papers

Massachusetts Historical Society, Boston
   Henry Knox Papers
   Timothy Pickering Papers
   Wintrop Sargent Papers
Morgan Library, New York
   Henry Knox Papers
National Archives, Washington, D.C. www.archives.gov.
   American State Papers: Indian Affairs. 2 vols.
   American State Papers: Military Affairs. Vols. 1–2
   John Adams Papers
   Journals of the Continental Congress
   Records of the Secretary of War: Indian Affairs. Letters Sent and Received
      Record Group 107: Registered Series, M 211, Rolls 9–15. Unregistered Series,
      M 222. Record Group 75: M 271, M 15.
      http://wardepartment.org. (Glenn A. Black Laboratory and John Carter
      Brown Library also have copies of Wells's correspondence.)
Newberry Library, Chicago
   Edward E. Ayer Collection
   Ayer Manuscript 589: William Turner, "A Description of . . . the N. Western
      Indians"
   Ninian Edwards Papers
Ohio Historical Society, Columbus
   Draper Papers (manuscript copy)
   Harmar Papers
   John Johnston Papers
   St. Clair Papers
   Anthony Wayne Papers: transcripts by Richard C. Knopf
Virginia Historical Society, Richmond
   Calendar of Virginia State Papers. 11 vols.
Wisconsin Historical Society, Madison
   Lyman C. Draper Collection 480 vols. For use of this extensive collection, see Jose-
      phine L. Harper, *Guide to the Draper Manuscripts.* Madison: Historical Society
      of Wisconsin, 1983.
   Series C: Daniel Boone Papers; Series J: George Rogers Clark Papers; Series S:
      Draper Notes; Series U: Frontier Wars; Series W: Josiah Harmar Papers; Series
      X: William H. Harrison Papers; Series BB: Simon Kenton Papers; Series CC:
      Kentucky Papers; Series YY: Tecumseh Papers.

PUBLISHED PRIMARY SOURCES

Adams, Charles Francis, ed. *The Works of John Adams.* Boston: Little, Brown, 1853.
Alford, Thomas Wildcat. *Civilization.* Norman: University of Oklahoma Press, 1979.
Ash, George. "Story of George Ash." *Cincinnati Chronicle and Literary Gazette*
   (7 November 1829).

Atherton, William. *Narrative of the Suffering & Defeat of the North-Western Army under General Winchester.* 1842; repr., New Delhi: Isha Books, 2013.

Aupaumut, Hendrick. "An Embassy to the Western Indians," edited by B. H. Coates. *Pennsylvania Archives* 2, no. 1 (1827).

———. "A Short Narrative of My Last Journey to the Western Country." *HSPM* 2 (1827): 61–131.

Bailey, Robert. *Life and Adventures of Robert Bailey.* Berkeley Springs, W.Va.: Walsworth Publishing Co., 1978.

Barnhart, John D. *Henry Hamilton and George Rogers Clark.* Crawfordsville, Ind.: R. E. Banta, 1951.

———. "A New Letter About the Massacre at Fort Dearborn." *IMH* 61 (1945): 187–99.

Beard, Charles A., ed. *The Journal of William Maclay.* New York: Albert & Charles Boni, 1927.

Beckner, Lucien, ed. "Shane's Interview with Benjamin Allen." *FCHQ* 5, no. 2 (April 1931): 63–98.

———. "Shane's Interview with Mrs. Sarah Graham of Bath County," *FCHQ* 9 (1935): 222–41.

———. "Shane's Interview with William Clinckenbeard." *FCHQ* 2, no. 3 (April 1928): 95–128.

Bergh, Albert E., ed. *Writings of Thomas Jefferson.* Washington, D.C.: Jefferson Memorial Association, 1907.

Blair, Emma Helen., ed. *The Indian Tribes of the Upper Mississippi Valley and Region of the Great Lakes.* 2 vols. Cleveland: Arthur H. Clark, 1911.

Bliss, Eugene F., ed. and trans. *Diary of David Zeisberger.* 2 vols. Cincinnati: Robert Clarke, 1885.

Bond, Beverley W., ed. "The Captivity of Charles Stuart, 1755–1757." *MVHR* 13, no. 1 (June 1926): 58–81.

———. *The Correspondence of John Cleves Symmes.* New York: Macmillan, 1926.

———. "Dr. Daniel Drake's Memoir of the Miami Country, 1779–1794." *OAHO* 18, no. 2–3 (April–Sept. 1923): 39–117.

———. *The Intimate Letters of John Cleves Symmes and His Family.* Columbus: HPSO, 1956.

———. "Two Westward Journeys of John Filson." *MVHR* 9, no. 4 (March 1923): 320–30.

Bowyer, John. "Daily Journal of Wayne's Campaign." *American Pioneer* 1 (September 1842): 315–22, 351–57.

Boyd, Julian, et al., eds. *The Papers of Thomas Jefferson.* 20 vols. Princeton, N.J.: Princeton University Press, 1950.

Bradley, Daniel. *The Journal of Daniel Bradley.* Edited by Frazer E. Wilson. Greenville, Ohio: Garst Museum, 1935.

Breckenridge, Hugh Henry. *Modern Chivalry.* New Haven, Conn.: College and University Press, 1965.

Brickell, John. "John Brickell's Captivity Among the Delaware Indians." *American Pioneer* I (1842): 43–56.

Brown, Clarence, ed. "General Wayne's Orderly Book." *MPHC* 34: 341–740.

Brugger, Robert J., et al., eds. *Papers of James Madison*. Charlottesville: University Press of Virginia, 1986.

Buell, John. *The Diary of John Hutchinson Buell*. Edited by Richard C. Knopf. Columbus: OHS, 1957.

Bunn, Matthew. *Narrative of the Life . . . of Matthew Bunn*. 1827; repr., New York: Garland, 1977.

Burnett, Jacob. *Notes on the Early Settlement of the North-West Territory*. 1847; repr., New York: Arno, 1975.

Burton, Clarence, ed. *Michigan Pioneer and Historical Collections*. 40 vols. Lansing, Mich., 1877–1929.

Butler, Mann. "An Outline of the Origin and Settlement of Louisville," *The Louisville Directory for the Year 1832*. Louisville: Richard W. Otis, 1832: 104–105.

Butler, Richard. "Journal of General Butler." In Craig, *The Olden Time*. 2: 433–64, 481–531.

Butterfield, L. H., ed. *Letters of Benjamin Rush*. Princeton, N.J.: Princeton University Press, 1951.

Butterfield, Colonel Wilshire, ed. *Washington-Crawford Letters*. Cincinnati, 1871.

Carlson, Richard G., ed. "George P. Peters' Version of the Battle of Tippeanoe." *Vermont History* 45, no. 1 (Winter 1977): 38–44.

Carmay, Donald F. "Spencer Records' Memoir of the . . . Frontier, 1766–1795." *IMH* 55 (Dec. 1959): 323–77.

Carter, Clarence E., ed. *Correspondence of General Thomas Gage*. New Haven, Conn.: Yale University Press, 1931.

———, ed. *Territorial Papers of the United States*. Vols. 2–3 (1934): *The Territory Northwest of the Ohio River, 1787–1803*. Vols. 7–8 (1936, 1939): *Indiana Territory, 1800–1810*. Vol. 16 (1948): *Illinois Territory, 1809–1814*. Washington, D.C.: U.S. Government Printing Office, 1934–62.

Carver, Jonathan. *Jonathan Carver's Travels Through America, 1766–1769*. Edited by Norman Gelb. New York: John Wiley & Sons, 1993.

Cist, Charles, ed. *The Cincinnati Miscellany*. 2 vols. Cincinnati, 1845–46.

———. "Garrett Burns Narrative." In Charles Cist, *Sketches of Cincinnati in 1859*. Cincinnati, 1859.

Clanin, Douglas E., ed. *The Papers of William Henry Harrison, 1800–1815*. Indianapolis: IHS, 1999, microfilm.

Clark, Thomas D., ed. *Voice of the Frontier: John Bradford's Notes on Kentucky*. Lexington: University Press of Kentucky, 1993.

Clark, William. "William Clark's Journal of General Wayne's Campaign." *MVHR* I (1914–15): 418–44.

Collins, Lewis. *Historical Sketches of Kentucky*. 1848; repr., New York: Arno, 1971.

Cooke, John. "General Wayne's Campaign in 1794 & 1795." *American Historical Record* 2 (1973): 311–16, 339–45.

Corner, George W., ed. *The Autobiography of Benjamin Rush*. New York: Greenwood, 1970.

Craig, Neville G., ed. *The Olden Time.* 2 vols. 1846; repr., Lewisburg, Pa.: Wennawoods, 2003.

Cresswell, Nicholas. *The Journal of Nicholas Cresswell, 1774–1777.* Port Washington, N.Y.: Kennikat, 1968.

Cruikshank, E. A., ed. *The Correspondence of . . . John Graves Simcoe.* 5 vols. Toronto: Ontario Historical Society, 1923–31.

———. "Diary of an Officer in the Indian Country, 1794." *MWH* 2 (1885): 387–96.

———. *Documents Relating to the Invasion of Canada and the Surrender of Detroit, 1812.* 1912; repr., New York: Arno, 1971.

Crumrine, Boyd, ed. *Virginia Court Records in Southwestern Pennsylvania, 1775–1780.* Baltimore: Geneaological Publishing, 1995.

Cutler, William Parker, and Julia Perkins Cutler, eds. *Life, Journals and Correspondence of Rev. Manasseh Cutler.* 2 vols. Athens: Ohio University Press, 1987.

Davis, Matthew L. *Memoirs of Aaron Burr.* 2 vols. New York: Harper & Brothers, 1837.

Dawson, Moses. *A Historical Narrative of the Civil and Military Services of William H. Harrison.* Cincinnati, 1824.

Denny, Ebenezer. *Military Journal of Major Ebenezer Denny.* 1859; repr., New York: Arno, 1971.

Denny, William., ed. "Military Journal of Ebenezer Denny." *HSPM* 7 (1859): 205–409.

Drake, Benjamin. *Life of Tecumseh and His Brother the Prophet.* Cincinnati, 1855.

Drake, Daniel. *Pioneer Life in Kentucky, 1785–1800.* New York: Henry Schuman, 1948.

Drake, Samuel G., ed. *Indian Captivities or Life in the Wigwam.* 1851; repr., Bowie, Md.: Heritage Books, 1995.

Esarey, Logan, ed. *Messages of William Henry Harrison, 1800–1816.* 2 vols. 1922; repr., New York: Arno, 1975.

Fitzpatrick, John C., ed. *The Writings of George Washington.* 39 vols. Washington, D.C.: U.S. Government Printing Office, 1931–44.

Ford, Paul L., ed. *The Writings of Thomas Jefferson.* New York: G. P. Putnam's Sons, 1892–99.

G. "Harmar's Expedition." *Western Review and Miscellaneous Magazine* 2 (1820): 179–82.

Gibson, Lawrence Harvey, ed. *The Moravian Indian Mission on the White River.* Indianapolis: IHS, 1938.

Gilbert, Benjamin. "Benjamin Gilbert's Captivity." In Loudon, *Outrages*, 2: 69–159.

Godfroy, Chief Clarence. *Miami Indian Stories.* Winona Lake, Ind.: Light and Life Press, 1961.

Gordon, Nelly Kinzie, ed. *The Fort Dearborn Massacre.* Chicago: Rand McNally, 1912.

Hammon, Neal, and James Russell Harris, eds. "'In a Dangerous Situation': Letters of Col. John Floyd, 1774–1783." *RKHS* 83, no. 1 (Winter 1985).

Harrison, William Henry. *Aborigines of the Ohio Valley.* Chicago: Fergus Historical Series 26 (1883).

Hay, Henry. "Henry Hay's Journal from Detroit to the Mississippi River." In Milo M. Quaife, ed. *Proceedings of the State Historical Society of Wisconsin* 63 (1915): 208–61.

Heald, Nathan, and Rebekah Heald. "Particulars of the Surrender." *The Crawford Weekly Messenger*, Meadville, Pa., 21 October 1812. Reprinted in *The Reporter*, Lexington, Ky., 18 November 1812.

Heath, William. "Re-evaluating 'The Fort Wayne Manuscript': William Wells and the Manners and Customs of the Miami Nation." *IMH* 106, no. 2 (June 2010): 158–88.

Heath, William, ed. "The Morgan Rhys Diary and the Treaty of Greenville." *NWOH* 80, no. 2 (2013): 148–64.

Heckewelder, John. *History, Manners, and Customs of the Indian Nations*. 1876; repr., New York: Arno, 1971.

Helderman, Leonard C., ed. "Danger on the Wabash: Vincennes Letters of 1786." *MVHR* 34 (1938): 455–67.

———. "The Narrative of John Filson's Defeat on the Wabash." *FCHQ* 21, no. 4 (1938): 187–99.

Henry, Alexander. *Travels and Adventures in Canada and the Indian Territories, 1760–1776*. Edited by James Bain. Edmonton: M. G. Hurtig, Ltd., 1969.

Hodge, Frederick W., ed. *The Narrative of Alvar Nunez Cabeza de Vaca*. New York: Barnes & Noble, 1959.

Hogan, Rosanne, ed. "Buffaloes in the Corn: James Wade's Account of Pioneer Kentucky," *RKHS* 69, no. 1 (Winter 1991): 1–31.

Hopkins, Gerald T. *A Mission to the Indians* . . . Philadelphia: T. Ellwood Zell, 1862.

Hunter, John D. *Manners and Customs of Several Indian Tribes Located West of the Mississippi*. 1823; repr., New York: Garland, 1975.

———. *Memoirs of a Captivity Among the Indians of North America*. Edited by Richard Drinnon. New York: Schocken, 1972.

Irwin, Thomas. "Harmar's Campaign." *OAHP* 19 (1910): 393–96.

Jackson, Halliday. *Civilization of the Indian Natives*. Philadelphia: Marcus T. C. Gould, 1830.

James, Alton James, ed. *George Rogers Clark Papers, 1771–1789*. 2 vols. Springfield: Illinois Historical Society, 1912–26.

Janson, Charles William. *The Stranger in America, 1793–1806*. 1807; repr., New York: Press of the Pioneers, 1935.

Jefferson, Thomas. *Notes on the State of Virginia*. Edited by William Peden. Chapel Hill: University of North Carolina Press, 1955.

Jeremy, David John, ed. *Henry Wansey and His American Journal*. Philadelphia: APS, 1970.

Johnston, Charles. "A Narrative of the Capture of Charles Johnston." In Richard VanDerBeets, ed. *Held Captive By the Indians*, 243–318. Knoxville: University of Tennessee Press, 1994.

Johnston, John. "Account of the Present State of the Indian Tribes Inhabiting Ohio." Worchester, Mass.: AAS, 1820.

Kaminski, John P., ed. *The Founders on the Founders*. Charlottesville: University of Virginia Press, 2008.

Kellogg, Louise Phelps, ed. *Early Narratives of the Northwest, 1634–1699*. New York: Scribners, 1917.

Kinard, Margaret, ed. "Sir Augustus J. Foster and 'The Wild Indians of the Woods,' 1805–1807." *WMQ* 9 (1952): 192–205.

Kinniard, Lawrence, ed. *Spain in the Mississippi Valley, 1765–1794.* 4 vols. Washington, D.C.: Government Printing Office, 1949.

Kinzie, Mrs. John H. *Narrative of the Massacre at Chicago . . .* Chicago: Ellis & Fergus, 1884.

Klinck, Carl F., ed. *Tecumseh: Fact and Fiction in Early Records.* Englewood Cliffs, N.J.: Prentice-Hall, 1961.

Knopf, Richard C., ed. *Anthony Wayne: A Name in Arms.* Pittsburgh: University of Pittsburgh Press, 1960.

———. *Documentary Transcriptions of the War of 1812 in the Northwest.* 10 vols. Columbus, Ohio: Anthony Wayne Parkway Board and Ohio State Historical Society, 1957–1962.

———. *Letters to the Secretary of War, 1812.* Vol. 6, Parts 1–3. Columbus: OHS, 1959.

———. "A Precise Journal of General Wayne's Campaign . . ." *AAS* (1955): 273–302.

———. *A Surgeon's Mate At Fort Defiance.* Columbus: OHS, 1957.

———, ed. "Two Journals of the Kentucky Volunteers 1793 and 1794." *FCHQ* 27 (July 1953): 247–81.

Lacey, John. "Journal of a Mission to the Indians of Ohio by Friends from Pennsylvania." *Historical Magazine and Notes and Queries* 7, 2nd Series (1870): 103–107.

Lincoln, Benjamin. "General Lincoln's Journal." *Collections of the Massachusetts Historical Society* 5, Third Series (1836): 109–76.

Lindley, Jacob. "Diary." *Friends Miscellany* 2 (1836): 49–156, 566–632.

Loudon, Archibald, ed. *A Selection of Some of the Most Interesting Narratives of Outrages Committed by the Indians.* 1801; repr., New York: Arno, 1971.

Lytle, William. "Personal Narrative of William Lytle." *OPHQ* 1 (1906): 3–30.

McAfee, Robert. *History of the Late War in the Western Country.* Lexington, Ky., 1816.

———. "The Life and Times of Robert B. McAfee." *RKHS* 25: 5–37, 111–43, 77–94. *RKHS* 26 (1928): 4–23, 108–36, 230–48.

McClure, David. *Diary of David McClure, Doctor of Divinity, 1748–1820.* New York: Knickerbocker, 1899.

McCollough, Alameda, ed. *The Battle of Tippecanoe: Conflict of Cultures.* Lafayette, Ind.: Tippecanoe County Historical Association, 1973.

M'Cullough, John. "A Narrative of the Captivity." In Loudon, *Outrages,* I: 252–301.

Meek, Basil. "General Harmar's Expedition." *OAHS* 20 (1911): 74–108.

Meginness, John F. *Biography of Francis Slocum.* 1891; repr., Jersey Shore, Pa.: Zebrowski, 1991.

Mereness, Newton D., ed. *Travels in the American Colonies.* New York: Macmillan, 1916.

Mitchell, Samuel L. "Doctor Mitchell's Letters from Washington, 1800–1813." *Harper's,* April 1, 1879, 740–55.

Montgomery, Samuel. "A Journal Through the Indian Country Beyond the Ohio, 1785." Edited by David I. Bushnell, Jr. *MVHR* 2 (1915), 267–72.

Moore, John H., ed. "A Captive of the Shawnees." *West Virginia History* 23, no. 4 (July 1962): 287–96.

Moore, Joseph. "Joseph Moore's Journal." *Friends' Miscellany* 6, no. 7 (February 1835): 289–343.

Nelson, Larry L., ed. *A History of Jonathan Alder: His Captivity and Life with the Indians.* Akron, Ohio: University of Akron Press, 2002.

Niemcewicz, Julian Ursyn. *Under the Vine and Fig Tree.* Edited and translated by Metchie J. Budka. Elizabeth, N.J.: Grassman Publishing Co., 1965.

Northcutt, William B. "Mississinewa . . . Diary." In G. Glenn Clift, ed. *The Battle of the Mississinewa 1812,* vol. 2. Marion, Ind.: Grant County Historicial Society, 1969.

Norton, John, *The Journal of Major John Norton, 1816.* Edited by Carl F. Klinck and James T. Talmen Toronto: The Champlain Society, 1970.

Oberg, Barbara B., et al., eds. *The Papers of Thomas Jefferson.* Vols. 31–39. Princeton, N.J.: Princeton University Press, 2004–12.

Padover, Saul K., ed. *The Complete Jefferson.* New York: Duell, Sloan & Pearce, 1943.

Peckham, Howard H. "Recent . . . Acquisitions to the Indiana Historical Society . . ." *IMH* 44 (1948): 409–18.

Peterson, Merrill, ed. *Thomas Jefferson: Writings.* New York: Library of America, 1984.

Pokagon, Simon. "The Massacre at Fort Dearborn." *Harper's Magazine* 98 (March 1899): 649–56.

Proctor, Thomas. "Narrative of the Journey of Col. Thomas Proctor . . . 1791." *Pennsylvania Archives* 41, 2nd Series (1896): 551–622.

Putnam, Rufus. *The Memoirs of Rufus Putnam.* Edited by Rowena Buell. Boston: Houghton Mifflin, 1903.

Quaife, Milo. *Chicago and the Old Northwest.* 1913; repr., Urbana: University of Illinois Press, 2001.

Quaife, Milo, ed. "Gen. James Wilkinson's Narrative of the Fallen Timbers Campaign." *MVHR* 16 (June 1929): 81–90.

———. *The John Askin Papers.* Burton Historical Collection, 1928.

———. "The Journal of Captain Samuel Newman." *Wisconsin Magazine of History* 2 (1918–19): 40–73.

———. "The Story of James Corbin: A Soldier at Fort Dearborn." *MVHR* 3, no. 2 (1916): 217–28.

———. *The Western Country in the 17th Century.* Chicago: Lakeside Press, 1947.

———. "When Detroit Invaded Kentucky." *FCHQ* 1 (1927): 53–57.

Records, Spencer. "Pioneer Experiences. . . ." *IMH* 15 (1919): 201–32.

Ridout, Thomas. "My Account of My Capture by the Shawnee. . . ." *WPHM* 223 (1928): 289–314.

———. "Narrative of the Captivity of Thomas Ridout." In Matilda Edgar, *Ten Years in Upper Canada in Peace and War.* Toronto: William Briggs, 1890.

Roberts, Kenneth, and Ann Roberts, eds. and trans. *Moreau de St. Mercy's American Journey, 1793–1798.* Garden City, N.Y.: Doubleday, 1947.

Royall, Anne. *Sketches of History, Life, and Manners in the United States.* New Haven, Conn., 1821.

St. Clair, Arthur. *A Narrative of . . . the Campaign Against the Indians.* 1812; repr., Salem, N.H.: Ayer, 1991.

Sargent, Charles, ed. "Winthrop Sargent's Diary." *OAHSQ* 33 (1924): 237–73.

Savery, William. "The Journal of William Savery." *Friends Library* 1 (1837): 327–69.

Schoolcraft, Henry R. *Narrative Journal of Travels from Detroit. . . .* Albany, N.Y., 1821.

Seaver, James Everett. *A Narrative of the Life of Mary Jemison, the White Woman of the Genesee.* New York: American Scenic and Preservation Society, 1932.

Smith, Dwight L., ed. *From Greene Ville to Fallen Timbers: A Journal of the Wayne Campaign,* 239–333. Indianapolis: IHS, 1952.

———. *With Captain Edward Miller in the Wayne Campaign of 1794.* Ann Arbor, Mich.: Clements Library, 1965.

Smith, James. *Scoouwa: James Smith's Captivity Narrative* (1799), with illustrative notes by William M. Darlington and additional annotation by John J. Barsotti. Columbus: OHS, 1978.

Smith, William Henry, ed. *The St. Clair Papers: The Life and Public Services of Arthur St. Clair.* 2 vols. Cincinnati: Robert Clarke, 1882.

Spencer, O. M. *The Indian Captivity of Oliver Spencer.* Edited by Milo M. Quaife. New York: Citadel, 1968.

Tanner, John. *A Narrative of the Captivity and Adventures of John Tanner.* Edited by Edwin James. 1830; repr., New York: Garland, 1975.

Thornbrough, Gayle, ed. *The Correspondence of John Badollet and Albert Gallatin, 1804–1836.* Indianapolis: IHS, 1963.

———, ed. *Letter Book of the Indian Agency at Fort Wayne.* Indianapols: IHS, 1961.

———, ed. *Outpost on the Wabash, 1787–1791.* Indianapolis: IHS, 1957.

Trowbridge, C. C. *Meearmeear Traditions.* Edited by Vernon Kientz. Ann Arbor: University of Michigan Press, 1938.

Thwaites, Reuben G., ed. *Early Western Travels, 1748–1846.* 32 vols. Cleveland: Arthur H. Clark, 1904–1907.

Thwaites, Reuben G., and Louis P. Kellog, eds. *Documentary History of Lord Dunmore's War, 1774.* Madison: University of Wisconsin Press, 1905.

Tipton, John. "John Tipton's Journal." *IMH* 2 (1906): 170–84.

Underwood, Thomas. *Journal of Thomas Taylor Underwood.* Cincinnati: Society of Colonial Wars, 1945.

Van Cleve, Benjamin. "Memoirs of Benjamin Van Cleve." *HPSO* 16 (Jan.–March 1922): 1–71.

VanDerBeets, Richard, ed. *Held Captive By the Indians.* Knoxville: University of Tennessee Press, 1994.

Van Doren, Carl, ed. *Benjamin Franklin's Autobiographical Writings.* New York: Viking, 1952.

Van Horne, James. *Narrative of the Captivity & Sufferings of. . . .* 1817; repr., Middleboro, Mass.: Weathercock House, 1966.

Volney, C. F. *A View of the Soil and Climate of the United States*. 1804; repr., New York: Hafner, 1968.

Wallace, Paul A. W., ed. *Thirty Thousand Miles with John Heckewelder*. Pittsburgh: University of Pittsburgh Press, 1958.

Washington, H. A., ed. *The Writings of Thomas Jefferson*. New York, 1984.

Watts, Florence G., ed. "Lt. Charles Larabee's Account of the Battle of Tippecanoe, 1811." *IMH* 57 (1961): 225–47.

Weld, Isaac. *Travels Through . . . Upper Canada . . . During the Years 1795, 1796, and 1797*. London: John Stockdale, 1807.

Wells, William. "Indian History." *The Western Review and Miscellaneous Magazine* 2 (1820): 201–204. In "Re-evaluating 'The Fort Wayne Manuscript': William Wells and the Manners and Customs of the Miami Nation." Edited by William Heath. *IMH* 106, no. 2 (June 2010): 158–88.

———. "Indian Manners and Customs." *The Western Review and Miscellaneous Magazine* 2 (1820): 1–12. In "Re-evaluating 'The Fort Wayne Manuscript.'" *IMH* 106, no. 2 (June 2010): 158–88.

Wilkinson, James. *Memoirs of My Own Times*. 4 vols. Philadelphia: Abraham Small, 1816.

Williams, Mentor L., ed. "John Kinzie's Narrative of the Fort Dearborn Massacre." *Journal of Illinois State History* 46 (1953): 347–52.

Young, Chester Raymond, ed. *Westward Into Kentucky: The Narrative of Daniel Trabue*. Lexington: University of Kentucky Press, 1981.

SELECTED SECONDARY SOURCES

Aaron, Stephen. *How the West Was Lost*. Baltimore: Johns Hopkins University Press, 1996.

Abernathy, Thomas Perkins, *Western Land and the American Revolution*. New York: D. Appleton-Century, 1937.

Ackerknecht, Erwin H. "'White Indians': Psychological and Physiological Peculiarities of White Children Abducted and Reared by North American Indians." *Bulletin of the History of Medicine* 15 (1944): 15–36.

Adams, Henry. *History of the United States*. Vol 1: Jefferson Administration; vol. 2: Madison Administration. New York: New American Library, 1986.

Alberts, Robert C. *The Golden Voyage: The Life and Times of William Bingham*. Boston: Houghton Mifflin, 1925.

Alford, Clarence. *The Illinois Country, 1673–1818*. 1920; repr., Urbana: University of Illinois Press, 1987.

Allen, Robert S. *His Majesty's Indian Allies: British Indian Policy in the Defense of Canada, 1771–1815*. Toronto: Dundurn, 1992.

Andrews, Edward Deming. "The Shaker Mission to the Shawnee Indians." *Winterhur Portfolio* 7 (1972): 115–28.

Anson, Bert. *The Miami Indians*. Norman: University of Oklahoma Press, 1970.

Axtell, James. *The Invasion Within: The Contest of Cultures in Colonial North America.* New York: Oxford University Press, 1985.

Bald, Clever F. *Detroit's First Decade.* Ann Arbor: University of Michigan Press, 1948.

Bailyn, Bernard. *The Ideological Origins of the American Revolution.* Cambridge, Mass.: Harvard University Press, 1967.

Barnhart, John D., and Dorothy L. Riker. *Indiana to 1816: The Colonial Period.* Indianapolis: IHS, 1971.

Barr, Daniel P., ed. *The Boundaries Between Us: Natives and Newcomers along the Frontiers of the Old Northwest Territory, 1750–1850.* Kent, Ohio: Kent State University Press, 2006.

Beckwith, Hiram. *The Illinois and Indiana Indians.* 1884; repr., New York: Arno, 1975.

Belue, Ted Franklin. *The Hunters of Kentucky.* Mechanicsburg, Pa.: Stackpole, 2003.

Berkhofer, Robert K., Jr. "Jefferson and the Ordinance of 1784, and the Origins of the American Territorial System." *WMQ,* Third Series, 29, no. 2 (April 1972): 231–62.

Blair, Emma Helen, ed. *The Indian Tribes of the Upper Mississippi Valley and Region of the Great Lakes.* 2 vols. Cleveland: Arthur H. Clark, 1911.

Booraem, Headrick. *A Child of the Revolution: William Henry Harrison and His World, 1773–1798.* Kent, Ohio: Kent State University Press, 2012.

Bordewich, Fergus M. *Washington: The Making of the American Capital.* New York: HarperCollins, 2008.

Bowlus, Bruce. "A 'Signal Victory': The Battle of Fort Stephenson, August 1–2, 1813." *NWOH* 63 (Summer/Autumn 1991): 43–57.

Brice, Wallace A. *History of Fort Wayne.* Fort Wayne, Ind.: D. W. James & Sons, 1868.

Brigham, David R. *Public Culture in the Early Republic: Peale's Museum and Its Audience.* Washington, D.C.: Smithsonian Institution Press, 1995.

Burstein, Andrew, and Nancy Isenberg. *Madison & Jefferson.* New York: Random House, 2010.

Butler, Mann. *History of Kentucky.* Louisville, Ky.: Wilcox, Dickerman, 1834.

Callahan, North. *Henry Knox: General Washington's General.* New York: Rinehart, 1958.

Calloway, Colin G. *The American Revolution in Indian Country.* Cambridge: Cambridge University Press, 1995.

———. "Beyond the Vortex of Violence: Indian-White Relations in the Ohio Country, 1783–1815." *NWOH* 64, no. 1 (Winter 1992): 16–26.

———. "Neither White Nor Red: White Renegades on the American Indian Frontier." *The Western Historical Quarterly* (January 1986): 43–66.

———. "Simon Girty: Interpreter and Intermediary." In James A. Clifton, ed. *Being and Becoming Indian: Biographical Sketches of North American Frontiers,* 38–59. Chicago: Dorsey, 1989.

Carter, Harvey Lewis. *The Life and Times of Little Turtle.* Urbana: University of Illinois Press, 1987.

Cave, Alfred A. "The Failure of the Shawnee Prophet's Witch-Hunt." *Ethnohistory* 42 (Summer 1995): 445–75.

————. "The Shawnee Prophet, Tecumseh, and Tippecanoe: A Case Study of Historical Myth-Making." *Journal of the Early Republic* 22, no. 4 (Winter 2002): 637–73.

Cayton, Andrew R. L. *Frontier Indiana*. Bloomington: Indiana University Press, 1996.

————. *The Frontier Republic: Ideology and Politics in the Ohio Country, 1780–1812*. Kent,
Ohio: Kent State University Press, 1986.

————. "The Meaning of the War for the Great Lakes." In Skaggs, *Sixty Years' War*,
373–89.

———— "'Noble Actors' upon 'the Theatre of Honour': Power and Civility in the
Treaty of Greenville." In Cayton and Frederica J. Teute, eds. *Contact Points:
American Frontiers from the Mohawk Valley to the Mississippi, 1750–1830*, 235–69.
Chapel Hill: University of North Carolina Press, 1998.

Cleaves, Freeman. *Old Tippecanoe: William Henry Harrison and His Times*. New York:
Scribners, 1939.

Coles, Harry L. *The War of 1812*. Chicago: University of Chicago Press, 1965.

Collins, Lewis. *Historical Sketches of Kentucky*. Maysville, Ky., 1848.

Conover, Charlotte Reeve. *Concerning the Forefathers*. Dayton, Ohio: National Cash
Register Co., 1902.

Crimmins, Jerry. *Fort Dearborn*. Evanston, Ill.: Northwestern University Press, 2006.

Curry, Seymour J. *The Story of Old Fort Dearborn*. Chicago: A. C. McClurg, 1912.

Davison, James A. "Reverend David Jones." *The Chronicle* 4 (1941): 157–67.

Deloria, Philip J. *Playing Indian*. New Haven, Conn.: Yale University Press, 1998.

Derounian-Stodola, Kathryn Zabelle, and James Arthur Levernier. *The Indian Captivity Narrative, 1550–1900*. New York: Twayne, 1993.

Dillon, John B. *A History of Indiana*. Indianapolis: Bingham & Doughty, 1859.

Dorsey, Peter. *Common Bondage: Slavery as Metaphor in Revolutionary America*. Knoxville: University of Tennessee Press, 2009.

Dowd, Gregory Evans. *A Spirited Resistance: The North American Indian Struggle for
Unity, 1745–1815*. Baltimore: Johns Hopkins University Press, 1992.

Downes, Randolph C. *Council Fires on the Upper Ohio*. Pittsburgh: University of Pittsburgh Press, 1940.

Drinnon, Richard. *White Savage: The Case of John Dunn Hunter*. New York: Schocken,
1972.

Dunn, Jacob Piatt. *True Indian Stories*. Indianapolis: Sentinel Printing Company, 1909.

Durey, Michael. *"With the Hammer of Truth": James Thomson Callender and America's
Early National Heroes*. Charlottesville: University Press of Virginia, 1990.

Durrett, Reuben D. *The Centenary of Louisville*. Louisville, Ky.: Filson Club, 1893.

Ebersole, Gary L. *Captured by Texts: Puritan to Postmodern Images of Indian Captivity*.
Charlottesville: University Press of Virginia, 1995.

Edmunds, R. David. "'Evil Men Who Add to Our Difficulties': Shawnees, Quakers,
and William Wells, 1807–1808." *American Indian Culture and Research Journal* 14,
no. 4 (1990): 1–14.

————. "Main Poc: Potawatomi Wabeno." *American Indian Quarterly* 9, no. 3 (Summer 1985): 259–72.

———. "'Nothing Has Been Effected': The Vincennes Treaty of 1792." *IMH* 4 (1978): 23–35.

———. *The Potawatomis: Keeper of the Fire.* Norman: University of Oklahoma Press, 1978.

———."Redefining Red Patriotism: Five Medals and the Potawatomies." *Red River Valley Historical Review* (Spring 1980): 13–24.

———. *The Shawnee Prophet.* Lincoln: University of Nebraska Press, 1983.

———. *Tecumseh, and the Quest for Indian Leadership.* Boston: Little, Brown, 1984.

Egan, Clifford L. "The Origins of the War of 1812: Three Decades of Historical Writing." *Military Affairs* 38 (April 1974): 72–75.

Eid, Leroy V. "American Indian Military Leadership: St. Clair's Defeat." *The Journal of Military History* 57 (Jan. 1993): 71–88.

———. "The Cardinal Principles of Northeast Woodland Indian War." In William Cowan, ed. *Papers of the Thirteenth Algonquian Conference*, 243–50. Ottawa: Carleton University, 1982.

———. "'A Kind of Running Fight': Indian Battlefield Tactics in the Late Eighteenth Century." *WPHM* 71, no. 2 (April 1988): 147–71.

———. "National War among Indians of Northwestern North America." *Canadian Review of American Studies* 16 (1985): 125–54.

———. "'The Slaughter was Reciprocal': Josiah Harmar's Two Defeats, 1790." *NWOH* 65, no. 2 (Spring 1993): 51–67.

Elkins, Stanley, and Eric McKitrick. *The Age of Federalism.* New York: Oxford, 1993.

Ellis, Joseph J. *American Creation: The Triumphs and Tragedies at the Founding of the Republic.* New York: Knopf, 2007.

———. *American Sphinx: The Character of Thomas Jefferson.* New York: Knopf, 1997.

Erney, Richard Alton. *The Public Life of Henry Dearborn.* New York: Arno, 1979.

Faragher, John Mack. *Daniel Boone: The Life and Legend of an American Pioneer.* New York: Henry Holt, 1992.

Ferguson, Gillum. *Illinois in the War of 1812.* Urbana: University of Illinois Press, 2012.

Ferling, John. *John Adams: A Life.* New York: Henry Holt, 1992.

Fliegelman, Jay. *Declaring Independence: Jefferson, Natural Language, and the Culture of Performance.* Stanford, Calif.: Stanford University Press, 1993.

Flexner, James Thomas. *George Washington and the New Nation, 1783–1793.* Boston: Little, Brown, 1969.

Freeman, Joanne B. *Affairs of Honor.* New Haven, Conn.: Yale University Press, 2001.

Friend, Craig Thompson, ed. *The Buzzel About Kentucky: Settling the Promised Land.* Lexington: University Press of Kentucky, 1999.

Furstenberg, François. "The Significance of the Trans-Appalachian Frontier in Atlantic History." *American Historical Review* 113 (2008): 647–77.

Gaff, Alan D. *Bayonets in the Wilderness: Anthony Wayne's Legion in the Old Northwest.* Norman: University of Oklahoma Press, 2004.

Gaff, Donald H. "Three Men from Three Rivers." In Barr, ed., *Boundaries*, 143–60.

Gilbert, Bil. *God Gave Us This Country: Tekamthi and the First American Civil War.* New York: Atheneum, 1989.

Gilpin, Alec R. *The War of 1812 in the Old Northwest.* Lansing: Michigan State University Press, 1958.

Gordon-Reed, Annette. *The Hemingses of Monticello.* New York: W. W. Norton, 2008.

Griffin, Patrick. *American Leviathan: Empire, Nation, and Revolutionary Frontier.* New York: Hill and Wang, 2007.

Griswold, B. J. *The Pictorial History of Fort Wayne.* Chicago: Robert O. Law, Co., 1917.

Griswold, Rufus. *The Republican Court.* New York: D. Appleton, 1867.

Guthman, William H. *March to Massacre: The First Seven Years of the United States Army, 1784–1791.* New York: McGraw-Hill, 1975.

Hagerdorn, Nancy L. "'A Friend to go between them': The Interpreter as Cultural Broker duing Anglo-Iroquois Councils, 1740–70." *Ethnohistory* 35, no. 1 (Winter 1988): 60–80.

Hall, James. *The Romance of Western History.* Cincinnati: Robert Clarke, 1885.

Hallowell, Irving A. "American Indians, White and Black: The Phenomenon of Transculturalization." *Current Anthropology* 4, no. 5 (Dec. 1963): 519–31.

———. "Bear Ceremonialism in the Northern Hemisphere." *American Anthropologist* 28, no. 1 (Jan.–March 1926): 1–175.

Hammon, Neal O. "Early Louisville and the Beargrass Stations." *FCHQ* 52, no. 2 (April 1978): 147–64.

Hammon, Neal O., and Richard Taylor. *Virginia's Western War, 1775–1786.* Mechanicsburg, Pa.: Stackpole, 2002.

Harper, Rob. "Looking the Other Way: The Gnadenhütten Massacre and the Contextual Interpretation of Violence." *WMQ* 64, no. 3 (July 2007): 621–44.

Harris, C. M. "Washington's Gamble, L'Enfant's Dream: Politics, Design, and the Founding of the National Capital." *WMQ* 56 (July 1999): 527–64.

Harrison, Lowell H. "James Wilkinson: A Leader for Kentucky." *FCHQ* 66, no. 3 (July 1992): 334–68.

Hassler, Edgar W. *Old Westmoreland.* 1900; repr., Westminster, Md.: Heritage, 1998.

Hawke, David Freeman. *Benjamin Rush: Revolutionary Gadfly.* New York.: Bobbs-Merrill, 1971.

Haydon, James Ryan. "John Kinzie's Place in History." *Transactions of the Illinois State Historical Society* 39 (1932): 183–99.

Heard, Norman. *White Into Red.* Metuchen, N.J.: Scarecrow, 1973.

Heath, William. *Blacksnake's Path: The True Adventures of William Wells.* Westminster, Md.: Heritage, 2008.

———. "William Wells: From Miami Warrior to American Spy." *NWOH* 78, no. 2 (Spring 2011): 102–13.

Heckaman, David T., "'Badly Clothed, Badly Paid and Badly Fed," *St. Clair's Defeat 1791.* Fort Wayne, Ind.: Fort Wayne Public Library, 1954.

Helderman, L. C. "The Northwest Expedition of George Rogers Clark, 1786–1787." *MVHR* 25, no. 3 (Dec. 1, 1938): 317–34.

Hickey, Donald R. *The War of 1812.* Urbana: University of Illinois Press, 1989.

Hill, Leonard Uzal. *John Johnston and the Indians in the Land of the Three Miamis*, with *Recollections of Sixty Years.* Piqua, Ohio: Stoneman, 1957.

Hoffman, Philip W. *Simon Girty: Turncoat Hero.* Franklin, Tenn.: Flying Camp, 2008.

Holliday, Murray. *The Battle of the Mississinewa 1812.* Marion, Ind.: Grant County Historical Society, 1964.

Horn, David Agee. "The Treaty of Grouseland of August 21, 1805." *American Indian Ethnohistory* (Garland Series): 203–34.

Horsman, Reginald. "American Indian Policy in the Old Northwest, 1783–1812." *WMQ* 18, no. 1 (Jan. 1961): 35–53.

———. "The British Indian Department and the Abortive Treaty of Lower Sandusky, 1793." *OHQ* 70, no. 3 (July 1961): 189–213.

———. *Expansion and American Indian Policy.* Lansing: Michigan State University Press, 1967.

———. *Matthew Elliott.* Detroit: Wayne State University Press, 1964.

———. "On to Canada: Manifest Destiny and the United States Strategy in the War of 1812." *Michigan Historical Review* 13, no. 2 (Fall 1987): 1–24.

Howe, Henry, ed. *Historical Collections of Ohio.* 2 vols. Cincinnati: C. J. Krehbiel & Co., 1902.

Howe, John. "Republican Thought and the Political Violence of the 1790s." *American Quarterly* 19, no. 2 (Summer 1967): 147–65.

Hoxie, Frederick E., Ronald Hoffman, and Peter J. Alberts, eds. *Native Americans and the Early Republic.* Charlottesville: University Press of Virginia, 1991.

Hunt, George T. *The Wars of the Iroquois.* Madison: University of Wisconsin Press, 1940.

Hurlbut, Henry H. *Chicago Antiquities.* Chicago: printed by author, 1881.

Hutton, Paul. "William Wells: Frontier Scout and Indian Agent." *IMH* 74 (1978): 183–222.

Isaacson, Walter. *Benjamin Franklin: An American Life.* New York: Simon & Schuster, 2002.

Isenberg, Nancy. *Fallen Founder: The Life of Aaron Burr.* New York: Viking, 2007.

Jacobs, James Ripley. *The Beginnings of the U.S. Army, 1783–1812.* Princeton, N.J.: Princeton University Press, 1947.

———. *Tarnished Warrior: Major-General James Wilkinson.* New York: Macmillan, 1938.

James, Alton James. *The Life of George Rogers Clark.* Chicago: University of Chicago Press, 1929.

James, Peter D. "The British Indian Department in the Ohio Country, 1789–1795." *NWOH* (Summer 1992): 78–95.

Jones, Dorothy V. *License for Empire: Colonials by Treaty in Early America.* Chicago: University of Chicago Press, 1982.

Jones, Landon Y. *William Clark and the Shaping of the West.* New York: Hill and Wang, 2004.

Jordan, Winthrop. *White Over Black: American Attitudes toward the Negro, 1550–1812.* New York: W. W. Norton, 1968.

Jortner, Adam. *The Gods of Prophetstown: The Battle of Tippecanoe and the Holy War for the American Frontier.* New York: Oxford University Press, 2012.

Kawashima, Yasuhide. "Forest Diplomats: The Role of Interpreters in Indian-White Relations on the Early American Frontier." *American Indian Quarterly* (Winter 1989): 1–14.

Keating, Ann Durkin. *Rising Up from Indian Country: The Battle of Fort Dearborn and the Birth of Chicago.* Chicago: University of Chicago Press, 2012.

Kelley, Joseph J., Jr. *Life and Times in Colonial Philadelphia.* Stackpole, 1973.

Kelsay, Isabel Thompson. *Joseph Brant, 1743–1807: Man of Two Worlds.* Syracuse, N.Y.: Syracuse University Press, 1984.

Kinietz, Vernon W. *The Indians of the Western Great Lakes, 1615–1760.* Ann Arbor: University of Michigan Press, 1965.

Kinzie, Mrs. John H. *Wau Bun, the "Early Days" in the Northwest.* 1856; repr., Menasha, Wisc.: National Society of Colonial Dames in Wisconsin, 1948.

Kirkland, Joseph. "The Chicago Massacre in 1812." *Magazine of American History* 28, no. 2 (August 1892), 111–20.

———. *The Chicago Massacre of 1812.* Chicago: Dibble, 1893.

———. *The Story of Chicago.* Chicago: Dibble, 1892.

Knopf, Richard C. "Crime and Punishment in the Legion, 1792–1793," *OHPS* 14: 230–40.

Kohn, Richard. *Eagle and Sword: The Beginning of the Military Establishment in America.* New York: Free Press, 1975.

———. "General Wilkinson's Vendetta with General Wayne." *FCHQ* 45, no. 4 (October 1971): 361–72.

Kukla, Jon. *A Wilderness So Immense: The Louisiana Purchase and the Destiny of America.* New York: Knopf, 2003.

Latimer, Jon. *1812: War with America.* Cambridge, Mass.: Harvard University Press, 2007.

Levy, Leonard W. *Jefferson and Civil Liberties: The Darker Side.* Cambridge, Mass.: Harvard University Press, 1963.

Linklater, Andro. *An Artist in Treason: The Extraordinary Life of General James Wilkinson.* New York: Walking, 2009.

Lunkford, George E. "Losing the Past: Draper and the Ruddell Indian Captivity." *The Arkansas Historical Quarterly* 49 (1990): 214–39.

Malone, Dumas. *Jefferson and His Time.* 6 vols. Boston: Little, Brown, 1948–77.

Marshall, Humphrey. *The History of Kentucky.* Vol. 1. Frankfort, Ky.: Geo. S. Robinson, 1824.

Martin, Calvin. *Keepers of the Game.* Berkeley: University of California Press, 1978.

McBride, James. *Pioneer Biography.* Cincinnati: Robert Clarke, 1871.

McClung, John A. *Sketches of Western Adventure.* 1832; repr., New York: Arno, 1969.

McCullough, David. *John Adams.* New York: Simon & Schuster, 2001.

McDonald, John. *Biographical Sketches of General Nathaniel Massie, General Duncan McArthur, Captain William Wells, and General Simon Kenton.* Cincinnati: E. Morgan and Son, 1838.

Meacham, Jon. *Thomas Jefferson: The Art of Power.* New York: Random House, 2012.

Merrell, James H. *Into the American Woods: Negotiations on the Pennsylvania Frontier.* New York: W. W. Norton, 1999.

———. "Some Thoughts on Colonial Historians and American Indians." *WMQ* 46 (1989): 94–119.

Meuter, Maria Kitty. *The Long Rifle, the Bow & the Calumet.* Louisville, Ky.: Wells Books, 2000.

Miller, Jay. "The 1806 Purge among the Delaware: Sorcery, Gender, Boundaries, and Legitimacy." *Ethnohistory* 41, no. 2 (Spring 1994): 145–66.

Miller, John Chester. *The Wolf by the Ears: Thomas Jefferson and Slavery.* New York: Free Press, 1977.

Musham, H. A. "Where Did the Battle of Chicago Take Place?" *JISHS* 36 (March 1943): 21–40.

Namias, June. *White Captives.* Chapel Hill: University of North Carolina Press, 1993.

Nelson, Larry L. "Dudley's Defeat and the Relief of Fort Meigs during the War of 1812." *RKHS* 104 (2006): 5–42.

———. *"A Man of Distinction Among Them": Alexander McKee and British-Indian Affairs along the Ohio Country Frontier, 1754–1799.* Kent, Ohio: Kent State University Press, 1999.

———. "'Never Have They Done So Little': The Battle of Fort Recovery and the Collapse of the Miami Confederacy." *NWOH* 64, no. 2 (Spring 1992): 43–55.

Nelson, Paul David. *Anthony Wayne: Soldier of the Early Republic.* Bloomington: Indiana University Press, 1985.

———. *General Sir Guy Carleton, Lord Dorchester.* Madison, N.J.: Farleigh Dickinson University Press, 2009.

———. "Mad Anthony Wayne and the Kentuckians of the 1790s." *RKHS* 84 (Winter 1986): 1–17.

Nester, William R. *George Rogers Clark: "I Glory in War."* Norman: University of Oklahoma Press, 2012.

Nichols, David Andrew. *Indians, Federalists, and the Search for Order on the American Frontier.* Charlottesville: University of Virginia Press, 2008.

O'Brien, Conor Cruise. *The Long Affair: Thomas Jefferson and the French Revolution, 1785–1800.* Chicago: University of Chicago Press, 1996.

Odum, William O. "'Destined for Defeat': . . . the St. Clair Expedition of 1791." *NWOH* (Spring 1993): 68–93.

Onuf, Peter S., ed. *Jeffersonian Legacies.* Charlottesville: University Press of Virginia, 1993.

———. "Liberty, Development, and Union: Visions of the West in the 1780s." *WMQ* Third Series 43, no. 2 (April 1986): 179–213.

———. "The Scholars' Jefferson." *WMQ* Third Series 50, no. 4 (Oct. 1993): 671–99.

———. *Statehood and Union: A History of the Northwest Ordinance.* Bloomington: Indiana University Press, 1992.

Owens, Robert M. *Mr. Jefferson's Hammer: William Henry Harrison and the Origins of American Indian Policy.* Norman: University of Oklahoma Press, 2007.

Parsons, Joseph A., Jr. "Civilizing the Indians of the Old Northwest, 1800–1810." *IMH* 56, no. 3 (Sept. 1960): 195–216.

Pasley, Jeffrey L., et al., eds. *Beyond the Founders: New Approaches to the Political History of the Early American Republic.* Chapel Hill: University of North Carolina Press, 2004.

Peckham, Howard H. "Josiah Harmar and His Indian Expedition." *OAHQ* 50, no. 3 (1946): 227–41.

Perkins, Elizabeth A. *Border Life: Experiences and Memory in the Revolutionary Ohio Valley.* Chapel Hill: University of North Carolina Press, 1998.

Perkins, James. *Annals of the West.* Pittsburgh: James R. Albach, 1857.

Peterson, Merrill. *Jefferson & the New Nation.* New York: Oxford, 1970.

Phillips, Edward Hoke. "Timothy Pickering At His Best: Indian Commissioner, 1790–94." *Essex Institute Historical Collections* 102, no. 3 (July 1966): 163–93.

Pratt, Michael G. "The Battle of Fallen Timbers." *NWOH* 67 (1995): 4–34.

Prucha, Francis Paul. *American Indian Policy in the Formative Years.* Cambridge, Mass.: Harvard University Press, 1962.

Quaife, Milo M. *Checagou, 1673–1835.* Chicago: University of Chicago Press, 1933.

———. *Chicago and the Old Northwest, 1673–1835.* 1913; repr., Urbana: University of Illinois Press, 2001, with introduction by Perry R. Duis.

———. "The Fort Dearborn Massacre." *MVHR* 1, no. 4 (March 1915): 112–37.

Rafert, Stewart. *The Miami Indians of Indiana: A Persistent People, 1654–1994.* Indianapolis: IHS, 1996.

Richter, Daniel K. *The Ordeal of the Longhouse: The Peoples of the Iroquois League in the Era of European Colonization.* Chapel Hill: University of North Carolina Press, 1992.

Roberts, Bessie Keeran. "William Wells: A Legend in the Councils of Two Nations." *Old Fort News* 17 (1954).

Sayre, Gordon. *Les Sauvages Américains: Representations of Native Americans in French and English Colonial Literature.* Chapel Hill: University of North Carolina Press, 1997.

Sellers, Charles Coleman. "'Good Chiefs and Wise Men': Indians as Symbols of Peace in the Art of Charles Willson Peale." *The American Journal of Art* 7 (1975): 10–18.

———. *Mr. Peale's Museum.* New York: W. W. Norton, 1980.

Sheehan, Bernard W. "The Famous Hair Buyer General: Henry Hamilton, George Rogers Clark and the American Indian." *IMH* 79 (1983): 1–28.

———. *Seeds of Extinction: Jeffersonian Philanthropy and the American Indian.* Chapel Hill: University of North Carolina Press, 1993.

Shuffelton, Frank, ed. *Jefferson.* Cambridge: Cambridge University Press, 2009.

Silver, Peter. *Our Savage Neighbors: How Indian War Transformed Early America.* New York: W. W. Norton, 2008.

Simmons, David A. *The Forts of Anthony Wayne.* Fort Wayne, Ind.: Lincoln Printing, 1977.

Skaggs, David Curtis, and Larry L. Nelson, eds. *The Sixty Years' War for the Great Lakes, 1754–1814.* East Lansing: Michigan State University Press, 2001.

———. *William Henry Harrison and the Conquest of the Ohio Country: Frontier Fighting in the War of 1812.* Baltimore: Johns Hopkins University Press, 2014.

Sleeper-Smith, Susan. *Indian Women and French Men: Rethinking Cultural Encounters in the Western Great Lakes.* Amherst: University of Massachusetts Press, 2001.

Slocum, Charles Elihu. *History of the Maumee.* Defiance, Ohio: printed by author, 1905.

Slotkin, Richard. *Regeneration Through Violence: The Mythology of the American Frontier, 1600–1900.* Middletown, Conn.: Wesleyan University Press, 1973.

Smelser, Martin. "Tecumseh, Harrison, and the War of 1812." *IMH* 65 (March 1969): 25–44.

Smith, Billy G. *The "Lower Sort": Philadelphia's Laboring Poor.* Ithaca, N.Y.: Cornell University Press, 1990.

Smith, Daniel Blake. "'This Idea of Heaven': Image and Reality on the Kentucky Frontier." In Friend, *Buzzel About Kentucky,* 77–100.

Smith, Dwight L. "Wayne's Peace with the Indians of the Old Northwest, 1795." *OAHQ* 59 (1950): 239–55.

———. "William Wells and the Indian Council of 1793." *IMH* 56 (1960): 217–26.

Stagg, J. C. A. "James Madison and the Coercion of Great Britain: Canada, the West Indies, and the War of 1812." *WMQ,* 3rd Series, vol. 38, no. 1 (Jan. 1981): 3–34.

———. *Mr. Madison's War.* Princeton, N.J.: Princeton University Press, 1983.

———. *The War of 1812: Conflict for a Continent.* Cambridge: Cambridge University Press, 2012.

Steiner, Bernard C. *The Life and Correspondence of James McHenry.* Cleveland: Burrows Brothers, 1907.

Steinle, John. "Unlucky Soldier: Josiah Harmar's Frontier Struggle." *Timeline* (April–May 1991): 3–17.

Sugden, John. *Blue Jacket: Warrior of the Shawnees.* Lincoln: University of Nebraska Press, 2000.

———. *Tecumseh: A Life.* New York: Henry Holt, 1997.

Sword, Wiley. *President Washington's Indian War: The Struggle for the Old Northwest, 1790–1795.* Norman: University of Oklahoma Press, 1985.

Talbert, Charles G. *Benjamin Logan: Kentucky Frontiersman.* Lexington: University of Kentucky Press, 1962.

———. "Kentucky Invades Ohio—1780." *RKHS* 52 (October 1954): 291–300.

Tanner, Helen Hornbeck. "The Glaize in 1792: A Composite Indian Community." *Ethnohistory* 25, no. 1 (Winter 1978): 15–39.

Taylor, Alan. "Captain Hendrick Aupaumut: The Dilemmas of an Intercultural Broker." *Ethnohistory* 43, no. 3 (Summer 1966): 431–57.

———. *The Civil War of 1812: American Citizens, British Subjects, Irish Rebels, & Indian Allies.* New York: Knopf, 2010.

———. *The Divided Ground: Indians, Settlers, and the Northwest Borderland of the American Revolution.* New York: Knopf, 2006.

Thompson, Charles N. *Son of the Wilderness: John and William Conner.* Indianapolis: IHS, 1937.

Todd, Rev. John. *The Lost Sister of Wyoming: An Authentic Narrative.* Northampton, Mass.: J. H. Butler, 1842.

Trapp, Hambleton. "Colonel John Floyd, Kentucky Pioneer." *FCHQ* 15, no. 1 (Jan. 1941): 1–24.

Tucker, Glenn. *Mad Anthony Wayne and the New Nation.* Harrisburg, Pa.: Stackpole Books, 1973.

———. *Tecumseh: Vision of Glory.* Indianapolis: Bobbs-Merrill, 1956.

Tucker, Robert W., and David C. Henderson. *Empire of Liberty: The Statecraft of Thomas Jefferson.* New York: Oxford, 1990.

Van Every, Dale. *The Ark of Empire: The American Frontier, 1784–1803.* New York: William Morrow, 1963.

———. *A Company of Heroes: The American Frontier, 1775–1783.* New York: William Morrow, 1962.

———. *The Final Challenge.* New York: William Morrow, 1964.

Vidal, Gore. *Burr.* New York: Random House, 1973.

Voegelin-Wheeler, Erminie, and Helen Tanner. *Indians of Ohio and Indiana Prior to 1795.* 2 vols. New York: Garland, 1974.

Voegelin-Wheeler, Erminie, et al. *Miami, Wea, and Eel-River Indians of Eastern Indiana.* New York: Garland, 1974.

Wallace, Anthony F. C. *The Death and Rebirth of the Seneca.* New York: Knopf, 1973.

———. *Jefferson and the Indians: The Tragic Fate of the First Americans.* Cambridge, Mass.: Harvard University Press, 1999.

Ward, Harry M. *The Department of War, 1781–1795.* Pittsburgh: University of Pittsburgh Press, 1962.

Warner, Michael S. "General Josiah Harmar's Campaign Reconsidered: How the Americans Lost the Battle of Kekionga." *IMH* 83 (March 1987): 42–64.

Wendler, Marilyn V. *The Kentucky Frontiersman, The Connecticut Yankee, and Little Turtle's Granddaughter: A Blending of Cultures.* Maumee, Ohio: Maumee Valley Historical Society, 1997.

Wentworth, John. *Early Chicago.* Chicago: Fergus Printing, 1881.

———. *Fort Dearborn: An Address . . .* Chicago: Fergus Publishing, 1881.

Wentworth, W. A. "Tippecanoe and Kentucky Too." *RKHS* 40 (1962): 36–44.

Weslager, C. A. *The Delaware Indians.* New Brunswick, N.J.: Rutgers University Press, 1972.

White, Richard. *The Middle Ground: Indians, Empires, and Republics in the Great Lakes Region, 1650–1815.* 20th anniversary edition. Cambridge: Cambridge University Press, 2011.

———. *The Roots of Dependency.* Lincoln: University of Nebraska Press, 1983.

Willig, Timothy. *Restoring the Chain of Friendship: British Policy and the Indians of the Great Lakes, 1783–1815.* Lincoln: University of Nebraska Press, 2008.

Wills, Garry. *Inventing America: Jefferson's Declaration of Independence.* Garden City, N.Y.: Doubleday, 1978.

———. *"Negro President": Jefferson and the Slave Power.* Boston: Houghton Mifflin, 2003.

Wilson, Frazer E. *Around the Council Fire*. Mt. Vernon, Ind.: Windmill, 1975.

Winger, Otho. *Little Turtle, The Last of the Miamis*. North Manchester, Ind.: printed by author, 1961.

Winkler, John F. *Wabash 1791: St. Clair's Defeat*. Oxford, Ohio: Osprey, 2011.

Wise, S. F. "The Indian Diplomacy of John Graves Simcoe." *Canadian Historical Association* (1953): 36–44.

Woehrmann, Paul. *At the Headwaters of the Maumee: History of the Forts of Fort Wayne*. Indianapolis: IHS, 1971.

Wood, Gordon S. *Empire of Liberty: A History of the Early Republic, 1789–1815*. New York: Oxford, 2009.

———. *The Radicalism of the American Revolution*. New York: Knopf, 1992.

Wright, J. Leitch. *Britain and the American Frontier, 1783–1815*. Athens: University of Georgia Press, 1975.

Yates, George H. *Two Hundred Years at the Falls of the Ohio*. Louisville, Ky.: Heritage, 1979.

Young, Calvin. *Little Turtle*. 1917; repr., Mt. Vernon, Ind.: Windmill, 1990.

Young, James Sterling. *The Washington Community, 1800–1828*. New York: Columbia University Press, 1966.

Zuckerman, Michael. *Almost Chosen People: Oblique Biographies in the American Grain*. Berkeley: University of California Press, 1993.

INDEX